I TATTI STUDIES IN
ITALIAN RENAISSANCE HISTORY

Published in collaboration with I Tatti
The Harvard University Center for Italian Renaissance Studies
Florence, Italy

GENERAL EDITOR
Kate Lowe

# TUSCANY IN THE AGE OF EMPIRE

## BRIAN BREGE

Harvard University Press

Cambridge, Massachusetts

London, England

2021

First printing

Library of Congress Cataloging-in-Publication Data

Names: Brege, Brian, 1985– author.
Title: Tuscany in the age of empire / Brian Brege.
Other titles: I Tatti studies in Italian Renaissance history.
Description: Cambridge, Massachusetts : Harvard University Press, 2021. |
    Series: I Tatti studies in Italian Renaissance history | Includes
    bibliographical references and index.
Identifiers: LCCN 2020044805 | ISBN 9780674251342 (cloth)
Subjects: LCSH: Tuscany (Italy)–Politics and government–1434–1737. |
    Tuscany (Italy)–Economic conditions–1434–1737. | Tuscany
    (Italy)–Foreign relations.
Classification: LCC DG737.3 .B74 2021 | DDC 945/.506–dc23
LC record available at https://lccn.loc.gov/2020044805

*For M.A.C.*

# CONTENTS

# Introduction

$\mathcal{I}$n the heart of Florence, deep inside Palazzo Vecchio, is a room that encompasses the world. Cabinets originally designed to hold exotic wonders line every wall. Encircled by fifty-three maps of the world, the Guardaroba Medicea is both immersive and expansive, encouraging careful perusal of distant coasts and cities.[1] Sparking the imagination and challenging the viewer's knowledge, this fragment of the Late Renaissance illustrates Florence's global outlook as it reinvented itself as a regional monarchy's capital. From the 1560s until the early years of Grand Duke Cosimo II's reign (r. 1609–1621), Florence sought to carve out a place for itself, not merely as a curious observer but as an active participant in the First Global Age.

This study considers the global Florence that emerged in the half century symbolically bracketed by the lavish funeral for Michelangelo Buonarroti (1475–1564) that marked a Medici claim to Renaissance Florence's artistic glory and Galileo Galilei's (1564–1642) return to Florence in 1610 to serve as a glittering star of Cosimo II's court.[2] By the final decade of Cosimo I's (r.1537–1574) reign, the Medici had established a firm grip on Tuscany.[3] As Spanish imperial dominance at once protected Tuscany and prevented it from further expansion in Italy, the Medici sought opportunities further afield under Grand Dukes Francesco I (r. 1574–1587) and Ferdinando I (r.1587–1609). These Tuscan projects were manifold. Some involved research and collecting that brought seeds, animals, exotic luxuries, and a trove of information to Tuscany from places like Japan, China, India, and the Americas. Economic projects were similarly wide-ranging. Through the development of the free port of Livorno (Leghorn), creative deployment of financial capital, cooperation with the Dutch and English, and diplomatic maneuvering, the Medici sought to reap the riches of global trade. They bid for Portuguese pepper contracts, pursued the resources of Brazil, and explored joining the Dutch United East India Company (VOC: Verenigde Oostindische Compagnie). Finally, through espionage, naval raiding, and diplomatic deals with figures like a rebel pasha in Syria and Shah 'Abbas I (r. 1588–1629) in Iran, Tuscany tried to shatter the Ottoman Empire into a series of friendly successor states with which Tuscany could work.

## Late Renaissance Tuscany in the World

This study explores the manifold ways in which the Grand Duchy of Tuscany as a state interacted with the wider world. Nearly all the components of this framing are subject to interpretative complications, and so some definitions are in order. First, although the Grand Duchy of Tuscany officially came into being in 1569, Cosimo I de' Medici's regime had *de facto* control of almost all its territory by 1557. The major territorial, political, and international developments in Cosimo's long reign make any sharp institutional and temporal definitions fraught, for shared personnel and political practices spanned the reign. The stabilization of Tuscany's domestic frontiers in the 1550s opened space for international action, and the shifting military position of the major powers and return of sustained conflict to the Italian peninsula would close it. Thus, while some examples are drawn from early in Cosimo I's reign, the focus is on the period from the fall of Siena (1555) to the immediate aftermath of Ferdinando I's death and the winding up of his policies in the 1610s.

In seeking to consider a segment of the seamless cloth of history, the pieces left aside for the time being by the historian's choices must be frankly acknowledged. Most important are the private Florentines, often scions of patrician families, who operated at long-distance.[4] This study considers the activities of private individuals only in so far as they interacted with its principal subjects, the Tuscan state and the ruling Medici dynasty. Private Florentines' overseas activities sometimes overlapped with those of the state, but they also diverged in important ways, shaped principally by the lower political barriers to access and greater freedom of action private actors enjoyed. As a result, the state depended on their example and contacts to act at a distance far more than such individuals relied on Medici support; indeed, Florentine patricians' overseas operations are such a large topic that I will consider them in a separate monograph.

While drawing an analytical distinction between the state and private actors reflects the political restrictions that constrained the former more than the latter, important caveats bear consideration. The Tuscan state and the Medici dynasty were two internally diverse components of a new political order. In this arrangement, the Medici sought to concentrate de facto power in an inner group dependent on the prince, intentionally conflating state and private interests. By the 1560s, the arrangement sustained a solid monarchical polity on the ruins of ancient and querulous republics that had spent the better part of three centuries in recurring armed conflict. As the ancient tradition of plotting and staging armed interventions by exiles waned, Tuscany and its Medici princes assumed a more stable and prominent place on the international stage. Domestically, although the Medici ruled cities that had been famously politically precocious, from Cosimo I onward, Medici princes exercised legislative and executive control through a new administrative layer placed over existing structures of government and law. This system allowed Medici princes and their close associates to exercise great personal power when they elected to do so but also preserved a legally and politically variegated polity that crystallized much of the legal and administrative legacy of the Florentine and Sienese republics.[5] Such was Cosimo I's success in developing the Tuscan state into an absolute monarchy, that his regime appeared in Marchamont Needham's 1656 account of polities—from imperial Rome to the Ottomans and the king of France—whose princes had used salaried troops to assert absolute power.[6] The actual process of co-opting the

Florentine patriciate into the state's burgeoning bureaucracy was viti-
ated by corruption and the persistence of politics within the nominally
absolutist structures.[7] As with many polities, then, Tuscany appeared
more clearly to outsiders as a centralized state than it did internally.
Although the Tuscan state was exiguous by modern standards and its
absolutist pretensions only partially realized, there is value in using
the historical actor's category. Indeed, Florentines played a prominent
part in developing the intellectual framework that would see the state
as a distinct impersonal entity whose preservation and security were
preeminent goals. Other thinkers, especially Italian and French ones,
would develop the concept into the reason of state tradition.[8]

Having established a working sense of the Tuscan state, the definition of "wider world" with which it interacted remains to be settled.
As an analytical category, I take the wider world to be defined as the
negative space demarcated by a pair of interlinked ideas that had considerable currency in the period: Latin Christendom and Europe. If neither referred to entirely stable geographic entities, core areas fit by all
definitions. Even so, both conceptions of space blurred at the boundaries, changed over time, and were not entirely coextensive even in the
Renaissance. Of course, the idea of Europe and its appropriate boundaries remains sharply contested. Conventionally, major developments
of the fifteenth and sixteenth centuries—the Renaissance, printing,
the Reformation, exploration, empire building, and intensive bouts of
interstate warfare—collectively contributed to the idea of Europe dis-
placing that of Latin Christendom. As with nearly any metageographic
paradigm, there are nearly insoluble boundary-crossing cases, like the
Ottoman Empire or Venice, whose constituent pieces fell on either side
of dividing lines that depend on the political, geographic, ethnic, religious, linguistic, or other criteria used. Then as now, multiple para-
digms operated simultaneously in unresolved tension, as for instance
between the perceived unities and divisions within and between Europe
and the Mediterranean.[9] For the purposes of this study, a working definition of the wider world is needed. For Tuscany in this period, such a
definition can be provided by the boundaries of violence. Tuscany and
the Tuscan-based and Medici-sponsored Order of Santo Stefano were
actually or potentially in open-ended conflict with nearly the entire
southern and eastern Mediterranean, usually on explicitly religious

grounds. Therefore, in this study, the category of "wider world" is taken as the southern and eastern shores of the Mediterranean and places accessed through ocean travel outside Europe.

Though definitionally challenging, the category of the wider world is a composite of political realities. In Latin Europe, the Spanish and Portuguese crowns claimed monopoly rights to all travel and commerce beyond Europe and the Mediterranean. The Ottoman Empire's contemporaneous and similarly dramatic expansion gave it the power to control all traditional routes linking the Mediterranean and the Indian Ocean. Although the Dutch and English challenged monopoly claims and developed a route through Muscovy and the Safavid Empire, this did not mark a substantial liberalization of commerce because rights of participation were still strongly politically mediated. Iberian monopoly claims, a geostrategic and religious inability to ally openly with Protestant challengers, and the sixteenth century militarization of the Mediterranean frontier meant that any Tuscan state action in the wider world was presumptively subject to political resistance escalating to concerted violence by more powerful states.[10] To put the matter plainly, in legal and political terms, the Tuscan state ought not to have had anything to do with the wider world. And yet it did. This, then, is the central puzzle. How did Tuscany act at a distance and why did it elect to do so in the face of such resistance?

This study explores Tuscany's long-distance action analytically according to its modes of engagement. Tuscany briefly experimented with direct commerce and independent colonization, but its ventures amount to a counterpoint to Tuscany's three primary approaches. I have organized these approaches analytically according to their type, but it should be recalled that the types do not represent chronologically distinct phases. Part 1 considers the Tuscan state's efforts to develop a symbiotic partnership with Europe's transoceanic powers starting first and foremost with the Spanish Habsburgs.[11] From 1580 to 1640, the Portuguese and Spanish realms shared a Spanish Habsburg monarch in the Iberian Union, even as they were largely administered separately; I refer to these collectively as the Iberian empires. Building on strong dynastic, military, financial, religious, and strategic ties, the Medici persistently sought to embed the Tuscan state in the Iberian overseas empires through investments in monopoly commercial rights, direct

trade, and subimperial colonial possessions under the aegis of Spanish
Habsburg authority. For example, Tuscany pursued the monopoly contract for the distribution of Portugal's spices in Europe and both the
right to trade directly with and acquire a donatary captaincy in Brazil.
What to Tuscans seemed like generous offers of deep symbiotic alliance could seem to the Iberians like an effort to parasitize their empires, depriving Iberians of their exclusive privileges and leaving them
with the costs of empire. Stymied in their efforts to partner with the
Iberians, Tuscans explored independent alternatives with Spain's English and Dutch rivals. Tuscany considered a partnership with the VOC
and Dutch proposals for trade with Brazil. Even Tuscany's most direct
challenge to monopoly claims—its expedition to the Amazon—relied on
a form of partnership, in this case with the large community of English mariners in Tuscany's primary port of Livorno. The unique character of the Amazon expedition points to the geopolitical structures
that constrained Tuscany. In practice, then, the Grand Duchy of Tuscany's participation in transoceanic ventures depended on negotiated
partnership.

If the efforts of the Tuscan state to act at long distance through
formal partnerships and direct trade foundered on the rocks of political intransigence, its pursuit of the fruits of the wider world through
other means met with success, if not with smooth sailing. Part 2 follows
Tuscan agents, merchants, and diplomats as they wended their way
through a thicket of administrative, legal, and political barriers. Such
barriers proliferated in the sixteenth and seventeenth centuries even as
technical and logistical constraints eased. Restrictions were a global
phenomenon, not only protecting the nationals of the Atlantic empires,
but also constraining European access to China, Japan, and Korea and
to rights of transit trade across Muscovy.[12] The problem of access to
trade with and information, *naturalia,* and luxury imports from the
wider world was, then, fundamentally a political one dependent on a
combination of negotiated relationships and subterfuge.[13] Whereas
Tuscany largely failed in its quest to secure a formal political partnership with the great empires of its day, it was notably successful in
achieving access to many of the fruits of those empires.

So extensive and effective was the network of agents, affiliates,
and diplomats that the Medici court overflowed with global goods

and information. They supplied Medici dynastic collections well on the way to becoming famous museums and collecting institutions like libraries, menageries, villas, botanical gardens, and the Guardaroba. In parallel with the collections, Medici Tuscany saw a rapid growth in bodies devoted to processing objects, exotica, *naturalia,* and information.[14] Beyond the University of Pisa and proliferating academies, they notably included the Galleria dei Lavori in Pietre Dure, the Fonderie of the Casino di San Marco, the botanical gardens, and the Tipografia Medicea Orientale. This abundance enabled Medici Tuscany to play an unusually central role both as a diplomatic hub for the exchange of global goods and as a critical center of intellectual and cultural engagement with the vastly expanded world to which Europeans now had regular maritime access.

As a tool of analysis, I characterize Florence as acting as a shadow capital to the Iberian empires, although only in a few narrowly defined ways. Caveats are essential and bear noting at the outset. Tuscan troops and ships fought long and hard in support of the Spanish Habsburgs, but politically Florence was at best a secondary ally constrained to follow Madrid's lead and limited in its ability to affect policy. Similarly, Tuscan financiers played an important role at crucial moments in keeping the Spanish imperial system operating, but Genoa was undoubtedly a much more important offshore financial center for Spain.[15] The idea of the shadow capital, then, applies only to the efflorescence of institutional developments that left Florence with a hypertrophic infrastructure for collecting, refining, and redistributing global goods and information and an outsized diplomatic role.[16]

Whereas Tuscany's transoceanic access depended in the final analysis on political arrangements with the Atlantic powers, in the Mediterranean, Tuscany possessed significant scope for independent military action. Not only did Tuscany's Spanish alliance give it a mighty protector, but the grand duchy developed a formidable system of modern fortifications and a powerful amphibious assault force protected by a modern and effective navy. Part 3 explores how Tuscany sought to combine its independent hard power and diplomatic heft to reshape the politics of North Africa and the eastern Mediterranean by being the tail that wagged imperial Spain into military adventures. For all their apparent incongruity, Tuscany's ventures were neither quixotic nor ill-informed,

even if they were ultimately unsuccessful. Indeed, Tuscany's explicit disavowal of territorial gains in favor of commercial, diplomatic, and religious objectives enabled Tuscany to engage in creative coalition building
involving partnerships with political actors of widely varying power and
legitimacy from Morocco, Cyprus, and Lebanon to Syria and Iran. These
relationships were explicitly structured as pacts of mutual aid, which
advanced the Grand Duchy of Tuscany's commercial, religious, and
strategic interests by mobilizing Tuscany's resources and alliances to ag-
grandize friendly powers. Lacking either conquistadors or colonists, the
grand duke carefully regulated the use of force and the distribution of
diplomatic favors to carve out a distinct role.

Tacitly, Tuscany's strategy appears to have been nearly opposite
that of Venice, and so the latter's approach bears brief consideration
here. As a legacy of half a millennium and more of maritime enterprise,
Venice retained scattered overseas possessions, known as the Stato da
Màr, until the end of the republic. They were governed by a rotating
group of Venetian patricians, sometimes in collaboration with local
elites, with the goal of serving the capital's interests and protecting the
Catholic hierarchy even in predominantly Orthodox lands. For all Venice's naval might, its maritime empire slowly contracted under periodic
Ottoman assaults. Fleeting victories notwithstanding, Venice could
not sustain the struggle with a much larger foe that was also Venice's
major overseas market. Even so, Venice tenaciously defended its traditional model, using its naval power and heavily fortified overseas possessions to direct trade to its privileged capital and to protect its merchant marine, which was preferably engaged in intensive peaceful trade
with the Ottoman Empire. Likewise, trade in the capital remained subject to an explicit regime of preferential access to Venetian citizens and
a whole battery of rules carefully regulating both commerce and the
diverse groups who came to Venice in pursuit of it. Venetian historiography stresses that, amid its gradual relative decline, Venice glorified
itself in myth, architecture, and pageant. It engaged in occasional bouts
of reforming zeal before settling into a watchful neutrality sustained by
a superb diplomatic and intelligence apparatus.[17]

Tuscany's late and comparatively brief engagement with Venice's
traditional domains differed markedly. The newly rebuilt free port of
Livorno, with its comparatively liberal regime of religious toleration,

open trade, and low taxes, stood in sharp contrast to Venice.[18] Lacking
an established domestic merchant marine or a port that required politically directed traffic, Tuscany had no need to incur the expense of es-
corting its merchant fleet or of acquiring and defending overseas ports.
Free from the threat of retaliation, Tuscany could unleash its fleet for
offensive operations. Likewise, unconstrained by deeply entrenched
commercial ties, Tuscany could negotiate both with the Ottomans and
with their many enemies for advantageous terms. Uninterested in territory, Tuscany could build trust with local actors suspicious of European motivations. Free from the need to defend an unpopular Catholic
hierarchy ruling over a majority non-Catholic population, Tuscany
could proclaim itself as both a protector of Catholics and a defender
of anti-Ottoman interests be they Maronite, Druze, Shia, Sunni, or
Orthodox. That is, Tuscany could be both more ostentatiously and
aggressively Catholic than Venice, yet also more credible with rebels
suspicious of Venice's territorial interests and commercial ties to the
Ottomans. As with Tuscany's other projects for overseas engagement,
this was both an unusually innovative approach and not wholly successful. Unlike with Tuscany's other projects, Tuscany's problem lay less
with the intransigence of Tuscany's would-be collaborators than with
the military defeat of Tuscany's ally in a major, multiday battle with the
Ottoman imperial army.

## On Empire

As with other essential terms, the "age of empire" in the title requires
some explanation. Although some early modern states were regularly
called empires at the time—the Tuscans referred to the Ottoman Empire by that title, for instance—my use of the term is a conventional analytical choice.[19] In political terms, I take empire to be a relatively territo-
rially extensive and powerful polity that frequently privileges a central
territory or group, which often rules over diverse subjects.[20] Linguistic,
religious, and ethnic difference are fragile bases for definition, however,
not least since empires often generate a measure of unity among previously diverse peoples. Similar problems obtain with the issue of scale.
Venice is conventionally regarded as an empire, yet its domains, however geographically dispersed and ethnically and religiously diverse,

were never especially populous nor did their aggregate land area consti-tute an impressive total.[21] A much larger state, like Renaissance France, is rarely regarded as an empire, but the contemporary Holy Roman Em-pire is, albeit of a peculiar kind.[22]

The slipperiness of political empire does not end with issues of scale, structure, and identity, for questions of boundaries are not easily resolved. Empires often exert influence beyond their frontiers, yet their claims to control within their nominal borders also frequently stretch beyond their effective grasp. Self-definition is no more reliable. It is a commonplace that Americans usually do not see themselves as be-longing to an empire, a view regularly contested elsewhere. In contrast, for legal, religious, and political reasons, Henry VIII's parliament in-sisted in the Act in Restraint of Appeals that England was an empire long before it met modern historians' definition of one.[23] Although one could easily multiply exceptions and objections, the idea of empire re-mains a powerful analytical tool. Indeed, so potent is the idea that it has been readily extended from its original political significance to cover many other instances that combine the ideas of power, extensiveness, and a central organizing point. One need only think of the world of money where banking, business, commercial, economic, financial, and property empires have widely understood, albeit imprecise, meanings.

If empire is a slippery, but useful term as both an actors' and ana-lytical category, the notion of an age of empires is equally fraught. Em-pires are an exceptionally old and widespread form of political organ-ization, so there have been many ages of empires, from deep antiquity to the early twentieth century.[24] The sixteenth and early seventeenth centuries, however, have a particularly strong claim to be an age of em-pires. The case is perhaps historiographically clearest in Eurasia, where it is conventional to see the five large early modern states—Ming China, Mughal India, Safavid Iran, the Ottoman Empire, and Muscovy—as suc-cessors, if sometimes indirectly and with complications, of the Mongol and Timurid Empires and their devolved components.[25] Within this group, there is a strong historiographic tradition of seeing the Mughals, Safavids, and Ottomans as early modern Islamic Empires, though the religious framing can obscure the fact that all three ruled over large numbers of non-Muslim subjects.[26] While it has recently been argued that Ming China should be seen as a Great State, it remains historiographically conventional to speak of Imperial China; and early modern China's vast scope, system of rule, and sense of its centrality certainly fit the imperial model neatly enough.[27] As to Russia, during the sixteenth and seventeenth century, Muscovy became an exceptionally extensive state, one that kept growing as Imperial Russia through to the twentieth century; from 1613, under the Romanovs, the empire grew at an average of fifty-five square miles per day.[28]

Turning to Europe, "the Empire" and "the Emperor" traditionally referred to the Holy Roman Empire and its ruler.[29] The historiographic convention has been to treat the Atlantic European overseas possessions as empires even at the risk of eliding important differences in scale and political structure. Whether or not this is wholly satisfactory, it is thus customary to see the Spanish and Portuguese empires as paving the way for the Dutch, English (later British), and French ones.[30] The case of Spain is clearest, for even if King Philip II's disparate possessions in Europe were merely a very extensive composite monarchy, his possessions in the Americas included lands conquered from the Triple Alliance in Mesoamerica and the Inka Tawantinsuyu in Peru; it has long been customary to refer to these polities as the Aztec / Mexica and Inka empires, respectively.[31]

Iberian empire could interact in complex ways with existing empires. The defeat of the Portuguese and the death of their King Sebastian I at the Battle of Alcácer Quibir (Al-Ksar al-Kabir) in Morocco in 1578 set off a succession crisis in Portugal that culminated in the Iberian Union (1580) in which Philip II of Spain became Philip I of Portugal.[32] Ahmad al-Mansur's greatly strengthened Moroccan regime struck south across the Sahara in 1591 and toppled the Songhai Empire.[33] Morocco's expansion at the expense of older empires was paralleled by the crippling blow dealt to the Vijayanagara Empire by the Deccan Sultanates of Ahmadnagar, Bijapur, Golconda, and Bidar at the Battle of Talikota (1565).[34] The Ethiopian Empire likewise faced military threats from expanding Muslim polities but successfully navigated the challenges, helped by timely Portuguese assistance to victory in 1543.[35]

As Tuscany turned to the wider world, it confronted a political environment filled with both rising and falling empires. That it did so while nominally within the frontiers of the Holy Roman Empire while in fact confronting a profusion of smaller polities in northern and central Italy both within and beyond the boundaries of the Empire—the Republics of Lucca, Genoa, and Venice; the Papal States; the Spanish-ruled Duchy of Milan; and the Duchies of Savoy, Urbino, Ferrara (to 1597; then Modena and Reggio), Mantua, and Parma; and a multitude of micropolities— serves as a reminder that this age of empire was also an era of regional states.[36] This study takes empire's ambiguity and multiple valences as an opportunity for productively exploring the functions, purposes, and boundaries of the geographically extensive polities that mushroomed in the early modern period. Tuscany's position as a creative small power renders it a particularly compelling vantage point for examining the complex and reciprocal relationships between a state that was not an empire and those that were. In light of the centrality to this story of the Tuscan state and its rulers, servants, and subjects, a brief account of the dramatic changes that swept Tuscany in the sixteenth century is in order.

## A Medici Monarchy in Tuscany

The existence of a principality ruled by the Medici dynasty in Tuscany was a byproduct of the sometimes fraught relationship between the Spanish and the papacy in the tumultuous years of the Italian Wars (1494–1530 or 1559). Expelled in 1494 and 1527, the Medici had required massive Spanish military intervention to emerge as Florentine princes. Two Medici popes, Leo X (r. 1513–1521) and Clement VII (r. 1523–1534), used the considerable powers of their office to secure their house's position in Florence over the objections of powerful republican opposition. The final suppression of the republicans in the devastating siege of 1529–1530, conducted by Holy Roman Emperor Charles V's (1500–1558) forces, bound the Medici and Spanish Habsburgs by ties of mutual dependence. In the early years, this dependence was largely that of a satellite regime on its mighty protector to ensure its survival against a conquered people. The Medici regime and Florentine independence seemed precarious, as underlined by Charles V's acquisition of Milan in 1535. Florence teetered on the brink of a Spanish annexation with the assassination of Alessandro de' Medici (1510–1537) in 1537 before the tenuous installation of the scion of a cadet line of the Medici, the seventeen-year-old Cosimo de' Medici.[37]

The fall of the Florentine republic in 1530 famously marked the collapse of an illustrious republican tradition. On its ashes rose a stable Medici monarchy, a transition traditionally regarded as the end of Florence's golden age by dismayed Anglophone historians. The dark portrait has undoubted merits. Regional consolidation had been costly. A series of wars, revolutions, and revolts saw Prato sacked and Pisa, Florence, and Siena successfully besieged and captured between 1509 and 1555. From this violence, a centralized autocratic state emerged, snuffing out centuries of republicanism. Seen from the perspective of Florence's economy, international standing, and internal peace, however, the replacement of an unstable republic in hostile rivalry with Siena and exercising lordly dominion over sometimes seething subject cities—such as Arezzo, Volterra, or Pisa—with a remarkably stable regional monarchy offered significant advantages. The advantages could only be secured, however, if Tuscans could bear the costs and maintain their independence. For decades, this seemed a doubtful prospect.

Cosimo I's critical insight, however, was to appreciate that the mutuality of Spanish-Medici dependence could be turned to his advantage. The extensive bloodshed that resulted from installing the Medici and the reliance on Imperial garrisons gave the Spanish Habsburgs few friends in Tuscany. Short of direct annexation—a policy that, for reasons of legitimacy, public image, and expense, was ultimately unattractive—the Medici offered the best prospects of a stable regime that could make a net contribution to the Imperial cause. Domestically, Cosimo I created a space between the poles of Francophile republicanism and Spanish rule that proved acceptable to the bulk of the politically active populace. To a country scarred by war and social and political turmoil, he offered stability, the eventual withdrawal of foreign troops, and an independent regime that could turn patricians into aristocratic courtiers while excluding Savonarolan *piagnoni* and die-hard republicans. Mixing threat and incentive, Cosimo could portray all this as the best that could be achieved against an Imperial party suspicious of republicanism and itching for a more repressive, autocratic option. To the Imperial party, Cosimo could act as a bulwark of stability against religious and political radicalism and Francophile republicanism. More than this, Cosimo I could offer an ever-more impecunious Emperor the option of replacing an expensive military occupation with net contributions by an ever-faithful ally bound by dynastic marriage ties. Through patient state-building and occasional boldness in pushing the boundaries of acceptable action, Cosimo I transformed the Spanish satellite Duchy of Florence into the Spanish ally Grand Duchy of Tuscany. With the strong support of his powerful Spanish-Imperial allies, Cosimo I's regime defeated exile armies in 1537 and 1554 and acquired most of the territory of Siena (1554–1557) after a brutal siege of the city (1554–1555).[38]

With the conquest of Siena, the Medici both completed their substantive expansion in Tuscany and secured an unassailable position as Florence's hereditary princes. Buoyed by Florence's robust recovery and a peace dividend, the Medici could afford to turn outward in a way that no regime in Florence had been able to do for generations. Flush with the success of unifying most of Tuscany as an absolutist, bureaucratic, and centralized polity at peace with its immediate neighbors, the Medici could devote considerable resources to foreign adventures. The heavy fortification of Tuscany—it has been likened to Sébastien Le Prestre de Vauban's (1633–1707) later defenses of France—Medici alliance with the Spanish Habsburgs, and the stability of the regime's political position meant that force could be used overseas with relative impunity.[39]

A few words on names may be in order. As the foregoing sketch indicates, Florence and the other polities of Tuscany underwent repeated political changes in the sixteenth century. At the beginning of the century, four republics and a small lordship ruled the ancient historic region of Tuscany. The largest among them was the Florentine Republic, then in the midst of a bitter war with the rebel Republic of Pisa, which it would finally conquer in 1509. The Republics of Siena and Lucca and the much smaller Lordship of Piombino all retained their independence, ever wary of Florence's ambitions. By 1557, the Medici had long since effectively transformed the old Republic of Florence into a hereditary duchy. To this, they had added control of the Republic of Siena, except for key coastal territories, mostly from the old Republic of Siena, which the Spanish retained as the Presidial (from *presidio* or fortress) States.[40] In 1569, Pope Pius V granted Cosimo I the novel title of Grand Duke of Tuscany, thereby transforming the remnants of these rival republics into the new Grand Duchy of Tuscany.[41]

At no point, however, did the Medici realize their ambition to control all of Tuscany, for the Republic of Lucca successfully defended its independence against all comers until 1799. Thus, when I use "Tuscany" and "Tuscans" throughout this book, I generally deploy these words in a political sense, as shorthand for the Medici monarchy that became the Grand Duchy of Tuscany and that state's subjects and representatives. The intrinsically ambiguous relationship between these political terms and the larger historic cultural region of Tuscany is productive, however, in that it points to how early modern Tuscans used history for political ends. Although the Medici never made good their political claim to all of Tuscany, in good Renaissance fashion they unabashedly appropriated the heritage of Etruria and the Etruscans as the truly ancient historical basis for their new state.[42] As untroubled by a need for a singular, consistent basis for their rule as most Renaissance princes, the Medici also merrily appropriated Roman, medieval, Renaissance, religious, and mythic bases for legitimacy when it suited them.[43] Above all, however, the Grand Duchy of Tuscany grew out of the old Florentine Republic. The grand dukes promoted other cities in Tuscany, including, notably, Pisa and Livorno, but Florence retained a clear primacy. As a result, it remained fairly common to refer to Florence, Florentines, and the duke of Florence as if the Grand Duchy of Tuscany had not supplanted its more famous republican predecessor. In some settings, there were power dynamics and claims to status and legitimacy associated with the use of one term or the other, but equally the choice could be a matter of casual usage. Generally, I have sought to limit the usage of Florence and Florentines to the specific case of the city and its citizens and to use Tuscany and Tuscans for the state and its citizens, but I have also followed the sources in their usage of the terms. In any event, ambiguity on this score dates to the late sixteenth century itself, reflecting unresolved questions about the relationship between Tuscany, its dominant city, and the legacy of the old republic.

## Florence's Historians and the Grand Duchy of Tuscany

Crossing the boundaries of numerous specialties, this study covers a period of Tuscan history that had once been neglected but is now flourishing. For nearly half a century from the end of the Second World War,

Renaissance Florence constituted a major locus of Anglophone scholarship.[44] This was overwhelmingly the Florence of the republic, especially that of the fourteenth and fifteenth centuries. Animated by a belief in Florence as the torchbearer of civic republicanism, capitalism, and the cultural efflorescence that emerged from the flourishing of competitive individualism, Anglophone scholars working in the context of the Cold War characterized Florence from Dante Alighieri (1265–1321) to Niccolò Machiavelli (1469–1527) as experiencing a Golden Age critical for the advancement of Western Civilization. Inspired by Jacob Burckhardt's notions of both the state and the individual as works of art and Hans Baron's thesis about the relationship between Florence's beginning of the fifteenth century military crisis and civic humanism , to the postwar generation of Anglophone historians, Florence's role as the birthplace of the Renaissance and as restorer of classical republican political traditions seemed naturally convergent.[45] Several acknowledged tensions lay at the heart of this story, however, for scholars also appreciated the failings of Florence's republic. Above all, they had to wrestle with the role of Florence's most famous family, the Medici, who worked diligently to subvert republican institutions even as they lavishly patronized the Renaissance.[46]

Mounting evidence of the practical functioning of the Florentine state and an emerging left politics in the 1970s and 1980s that focused on class conflict presented an altogether less sunny image. In this story, Florence's social history meshed with its political history to cast Florence as a society beset by struggle, culminating in the tragic victory of the Medici.[47] The end of the Cold War and its ideological battles and the broadening of the narrative of the Renaissance beyond Florence opened historiographic space for new questions but also reduced the automatic centrality of Florence. Comparing Florence with other polities and seeing it in a longer time horizon showed the complex dynamism of other states in Tuscany, Florence's relationship to the broader story of the rise and fall of the communes, and the key role of the lordships of central and northern Italy in the Renaissance.[48]

Even as the story of the Renaissance has broadened, Florence has retained its claim to a special role on several grounds. Most of them—for instance, those pertaining to art history—are beyond the scope of this study, but a few bear mentioning here. For one, Florence has retained a very large number of public and private records. Exceptionally, Florentines generated both extraordinary family records, especially the *ricordanze* and accounts books of the patriciate, and detailed, albeit problematic, tax records from the first *catasto* of 1427 onward. These have enabled the writing of very detailed family, neighborhood, and social histories that have few parallels elsewhere.[49] In light of Florentine families' critical role in the history of banking, finance, and the rise of capitalism, there has been a confluence of family and business studies, which often sit at the base of larger studies of Florence's economy.[50] Likewise, the torrent of writing about the tortuous and ultimately unsuccessful politics of the Florentine republic has given Florence an enduring place in the history of political thought, culminating in Machiavelli and Francesco Guicciardini (1483–1540). As a result, an understanding of the precise details of late republican Florentine politics is essential and has fueled continual inquiry.[51] These studies share a tacit endpoint with the fall of the last republic in 1530 or the rise of the Grand Duchy, as, for instance, in John Najemy's now standard *A History of Florence: 1200–1575*.[52]

Even as the traditional fields of Florentine history have seen a relative decline in recent decades, Medici Tuscany in the reigns of Cosimo I, Francesco I, and Ferdinando I has been the subject of increasingly intensive scholarship. Of course, new interest among Anglophone scholars has not marked the beginning of grand ducal historiography—far from it. An illustrious Italian tradition of writing on this period stretches from the work of Jacopo Riguccio Galluzzi (1739–1801) through Luciano Berti's study of Francesco I to the three-volume history of the Grand Duchy by Furio Diaz.[53] Even so, Anglophone interest has been helped by early ducal Tuscany's dynamism, the abundance and accessibility of sources held at the Archivio di Stato di Firenze, and the relative neglect of the period by previous generations, which had prompted Eric Cochrane to write his seminal *Florence in the Forgotten Centuries, 1527–1800*.[54]

This book is written in that broader historiographic framework, situating Tuscany's global actions in the context of an abundance of recent research on the Grand Duchy, particularly the period known in the Archivio di Stato di Firenze as the Mediceo del Principato (1537–1743).[55] The contours of scholarship on the grand ducal Medici differ markedly from the more familiar works on the fifteenth and early sixteenth centuries. Politically, interest has concentrated on the Medici project of successfully co-opting both the previously rival cities of Tuscany and the Florentine political elite into an autocratic political system. This developed into a prototypical absolutist, bureaucratic, and centralized state epitomized by the construction of the Uffizi (offices, in Tuscan dialect).[56] In a region traditionally contested by rival republics riven by internal strife, such a new monarchy required an accompanying cultural and religious framework of legitimation, as has been explored in several recent studies.[57]

Autocratic centralization not only transformed Tuscany's political history but also gave scope for new, large-scale development projects that challenged the traditional urban hierarchy and political economy of Tuscany. The Medici attempted this most successfully in the newly redeveloped city of Livorno, which grew spectacularly as a result of the development of the physical and especially legal infrastructure that turned it into a pioneering free port. Recent studies by Francesca Trivellato, on communitarian cosmopolitanism, and Corey Tazzara, on the development of the free port, have shown how the conjuncture of economic growth and relative religious tolerance transformed Livorno into a dynamic cosmopolitan center and hub of the Sephardic diaspora.[58] Even as Livorno grew into a major nexus of peaceful trade, the centralized regime that built it also developed it as the operational base both of the Tuscan navy and of the separate naval military order of the Knights of Santo Stefano. Throughout the period considered in this book, the Medici grand dukes strained to transform Tuscany into a remarkably active naval power. To this end, the Medici regime hosted northern Europeans in Livorno, facilitating their epochal commercial and piratical entry into the Mediterranean as a whole.[59] In so doing, the grand dukes sought to move beyond the fifteenth-century galley system of the Florentine republic to tap the deeper legacy of Pisa as one of the great medieval maritime republics and to play an active role in Spanish-led naval coalitions in both the Mediterranean and the Atlantic.[60]

In light of the tremendous scale of the surviving documentation, range of Medici actions, and depth of the historiography, this study seeks not to be comprehensive but rather to play the role of a puzzle piece crafted to slot together with exciting work occurring on many fronts, especially among a new generation of Italian scholars. For instance,

Giorgio-Giòrs Tosco's recent dissertation undertakes a thorough and systematic comparison of Tuscan and Genoese efforts to enter world trade, primarily focused on the seventeenth century.[61] New dissertation projects ongoing at the University of Padua and the Scuola Normale Superiore of Pisa consider Tuscany's sugar trade and Ferdinando I's ventures in Morocco.[62] The role of fifteenth- and early-sixteenth-century Florentine merchants in early Iberian trade and exploration, with particular attention to the Florentine community in Lisbon, has been the subject of a series of studies, many displaying remarkable archival virtuosity.[63] In keeping with a broader historiographical interest in reassessing early modern projects for intellectual engagement with the Islamic world—principally the Ottoman and Safavid Empires—the last decade has seen research on the Tuscan-Papal Medici Oriental Press and the work of Giovanni Battista Raimondi (1536–1614).[64] Likewise, exhibitions on Tuscany's ties to Russia and on the operation of the Medici Oriental Press have produced important companion volumes, which have proved invaluable.[65] I draw on these studies without seeking to reproduce them. Similarly, I briefly summarize the findings of Hair and Davies on Tuscany in Sierra Leone and of Kaled El Bibas on Tuscany's relationship with the Lebanese emir Fakhr ad-Dīn; I have also benefited from the latter's work on Tuscany's interaction with Morocco.[66] The present study seeks to embed these discrete episodes in a broader framework that captures the range of Tuscan activity and the political logic that bound its multifarious enterprises together.

In parallel with the transformation in historians' approach to the period, art historians have directed our attention to a broader vision of material culture and new conceptions of collecting, influence, and imagination that engage with Renaissance Italy's long-distance connections.[67] To their careful reconstructions and analyses both of the Grand Duchy's collections and of the products of the Medici workshops, the present study adds the broader political framework through which objects and information could move to and from Tuscany.[68] It explores the general patterns of action that gave the Medici access to objects from around the world, specific instances when Medici agents sent items to Florence, and times when the Medici dispatched luxury goods as diplomatic gifts.

Central to Grand Ducal Tuscany's historiographic rehabilitation has been a deepening appreciation of its pioneering role in the history of science, not only as patron of Galileo, but also as a center of botanical inquiry. The network of Medici agents, affiliates, and diplomats who sent samples to Tuscany's new botanical gardens, there to be depicted by talented artists, also brought the rare and exotic items that filled Medici collections and supplied Grand Ducal workshops. This book seeks to elucidate some of the social, political, and diplomatic structures that enabled exotic flora and fauna, luxury goods, and information to come to Tuscany. The institutions that were developed to house and analyze them, from the botanical gardens and villas to the collections of the Guardaroba, are considered primarily in so far as they pertain to Tuscany's long-distance activities and their diplomatic and political dimensions.[69]

Just as the need to constrain the scope of this study thematically requires the imposition of artificial subject boundaries, so also this book wrestles with the same logistical challenges that face any individual's attempt to write global history. Research for this volume rests primarily on Italian, Spanish, Portuguese, and English manuscripts, with small amounts of German, French, and Latin in other sources. The Medici, however, had to contend with a much wider variety of languages in their global projects. Even in the Medici archives, I have relied on the accompanying early modern translations of diplomatic documents in languages like Arabic and Russian. The Medici addressed this same problem of language by commissioning their polyglot dragoman-diplomat, Michelangelo Corai, to negotiate on their behalf in Cyprus, Lebanon, Syria, and Iran and by patronizing the Tipografia Medicea Orientale (Medici Oriental Press). Language and logistical constraints—Tuscany's most important rebel ally was based in Aleppo, which has been shattered by rebellion and defeat again so recently—mean that this is a project told largely from the point of view of the Tuscan state and its archives, with all that that entails. Fortunately, at least, the Tuscan side of this story has become vastly more accessible thanks to the Medici Archive Project and its BIA database, which renders visible much that would otherwise be obscured by the vast scale of the Medici archives.[70]

## On Global History

Globalization comes in waves. Late-nineteenth- and early-twentieth-century globalization went hand in glove with expanding European,

North American, and Japanese empires, both formal and informal. The current period of globalization, by contrast, gathered momentum amid a wave of decolonization and took off dramatically in an era of political fragmentation and the apparent dominance of the private economy and information networks.[71] Historians' accounts of subjects that would now be classified as global history have thus far mirrored broader trends and can be expected to continue to do so. From the stories of colonization and decolonization, through Marxist-infused economic analyses, to a dawning awareness of environmental change, global histories have now been extended to cover nearly every subject that historians investigate.[72] After apparently sweeping all before it, global history has, however, faced a new wave of critiques.[73] Amid all this historiographic energy, a few major trends in early modern global historiography bear particular mention here: nationalism and multiculturalism; collecting; commodities, trade patterns, and the groups involved; seas and the diasporas that span them; and comparative and connective history.

In telling the story of Tuscany's engagement with the wider world, this study does not seek to contribute to tacitly nationalist narratives that tally the exploits of famous Italian travelers; indeed, it is meant to challenge implicitly national frameworks.[74] In this, it leans against an old tradition in Italian scholarship that sees two accomplished Florentine travelers who play an important role in this book, Filippo Sassetti (1540–1588) and Francesco Carletti (1573 / 1574–1636), as exemplars of Italian travel in a line stretching back through Amerigo Vespucci to Marco Polo.[75] The story of a third equally important Medici affiliate offers a useful corrective. Michelangelo Corai—a renegade Syrian dragoman, Mantuan knight, Tuscan diplomat, Persian mining commissioner, and spy—plays a central role in part 3 herein and certainly cannot be easily fit into any national narrative.[76] While the case of Corai challenges nationalist narratives, it is also not an especially close fit for the last generation's reveling in ambiguous, multiple, and unresolved identities as precursors of modern multiculturalism.[77] Corai crossed more frontiers and negotiated more difficult circumstances, sometimes at excruciating personal cost, than most anyone, but he was nothing if not committed to his mission; embracing a more flexible identity would have saved him a great deal of suffering, but like Carletti, he did so only briefly and instrumentally. As we shall see, truly ambiguous agents, like Anthony Sherley, came to grief. In a religiously militant age punctuated by many long, bloody wars, sloughing off identities was costly, especially if done more than once.

The Grand Duchy of Tuscany participated enthusiastically in efforts to collect rare and exotic items from around the world. Standing at the intersection of text and object, collecting fits well with existing structures of knowledge and methods of research in multiple disciplines and has been the subject of intensive inquiry. Recent studies have considered things in motion and the various shades of meaning they assumed as they were swept around the world, generally taking the object or the specific courtly or institutional collection as their point of analysis.[78] For the Medici, the meanings attached to these objects were profoundly inflected both by expert opinion and considerations of their political utility in display and gift giving. Although the Medici certainly held onto some items tenaciously, much of their collection of exotica was, at least in potential, constantly available for circulation to other courts. Thus, collecting is both an essential framework for analysis and also a static snapshot of an ever-changing body of materials embedded in mobile networks of exchange.

With the rise of an increasingly integrated global economy and the decline of empire, the economic side of global history has moved to center stage. Commodities, prominent high-value trades—especially in spices, stimulant foods, dyes, and textiles—and the relative power of various groups in Indian Ocean and Asian trade have all received a great deal of attention of late.[79] This study draws on this valuable research but also points to its limitations. Focusing on long-term structures and patterns, economic approaches sometimes downplay the importance of politics and the specific moment. Something similar might be said for the important wave of studies of seas and the diasporas that span them, which have productively challenged national histories but sometimes understated the still important role of the state and nationality in constraining access.[80] By considering a polity whose interests flitted across all the major trades and oceans, this study brings together the many objects of global history with attention to the political basis for their acquisition, use, and trade. In that way, this book is closer to studies of specific cities and their relationship to commerce and the wider world.[81]

In parallel with the economic arguments, historians have sought to trace the origins of the political and military divergences that yawned so widely in the nineteenth century by undertaking large-scale comparative investigations. These have, of necessity, sought to advance structuralist or technological explanations based on a mechanism of action, like competitive state systems or the role of the steppe frontier or engagement with gunpowder weaponry, to explain the rise of European states and their formidable militaries.[82] This book makes no claim to a grand theory of history, but it does offer evidence to challenge simple binary comparisons—northwest Europe and China are favorites—and the putatively dominant role of economic institutions or particular geographical features in explaining how the early modern world developed.[83]

While I draw on the grand syntheses, this book builds on connected histories, which have sought to trace the movement of individuals and ideas across the early modern world.[84] Whereas comparative history has flourished in studies of Europe and China, connected history has concentrated on the longer, deeper, and more fragmentary relationship between Europe and India in the early modern period. The richness of the ties has permitted subtle studies both of India itself and the various iterations of the idea of India for Europeans.[85] Prominent and articulate Tuscan travelers like Sassetti and Carletti regularly appear in cameo roles in these larger accounts of early modern Europe's intellectual engagement with the wider world.[86] Since the Medici and their affiliates played an important role in European botany and medicine's early efforts to come to terms with the massive wave of information generated by the first global age, this study benefits from the tremendous growth of research in the early modern global history of science.[87] Even so, this study focuses on the role of the Tuscan state in fostering research, collecting samples, commissioning related work, and moving materials through diplomatic networks, rather than on the content of scientific inquiries.

Medici affiliates interacted with a remarkably wide array of places, frequently commenting on and occasionally participating in local politics along the way. To make sense of this, for places like Muscovy, Japan, and Southeast Asia, where Tuscany's interactions were relatively few, I depend on a small set of standard scholarly surveys for reference.[88]

Though I draw on a broader array of specialist studies, particularly related to the Jesuits, mapping, and the patterns of global trade, in the consideration of Tuscan activities in Colonial Latin America, China, and India, here too I rely on recent synthetic scholarly volumes.[89] This creates an immediate imbalance in perspective between a precise historiographic consideration of early modern Europe in general and Renaissance Italy in particular and the much broader brushstrokes of my engagement with Ming China or Mughal India. To stretch a metaphor, it is a historiographic contrast between pointillist precision and an impressionist's rapid painting. This reflects the limitations of my own knowledge rather than the underlying historiography.

Between these poles, I have delved somewhat more deeply into the historiography of the Ottoman and Safavid Empires in recognition of the depth and scale of Tuscan involvement in seeking to ally with the latter to destroy the former. Within the broad expanses of Ottoman historiography, I have concentrated on the Ottomans in the Mediterranean and Indian Ocean, the classical empire's structure, and the imperial crises that beset and transformed the empire at the beginning of the seventeenth century. Tuscany certainly contributed to exacerbating these latter, stretching its military and diplomatic resources in support of Ottoman rebels and the Safavids in the hopes of shattering the Ottoman Empire. The Tuscans did not, of course, succeed, but the Ottoman Empire did structurally transform in ways that are consistent with Tuscany's perception that local notables with regional power bases would drain de facto power from the center.[90]

The Tuscans were similarly perceptive in appreciating that Shah 'Abbas I's reformist dynamism, force of personality, and strategic acumen unlocked possibilities unavailable to his predecessors (or successors, for that matter). Tuscan optimism that 'Abbas might break through to the Mediterranean, through his alliance with Ottoman rebels along a crescent running from Iraq to Lebanon, was not ill-founded. As we shall see, only the result of a three-day battle between the Ottoman rebels in Syria and the main Ottoman imperial army under the personal command of the grand vizier prevented Tuscany's desired outcome. Safavid historiography has wrestled with the seriousness of 'Abbas's European allies, the complications associated with his diplomatic practices, and the structural factors motivating and constraining European engagement.

The present study suggests that the Tuscans were actually quite well-informed about the Safavids, that they were in deadly earnest about their alliance, and that the plans for a Tuscan-Ottoman rebel-Safavid alliance were well considered and nearly successful. The alliance rested less on the commercial interests of the silk trade that ran from Iran through Aleppo to Europe, as has been traditionally stressed, than on a confluence of strategic and religious interests in expelling the Ottoman imperial administration from the Levant.[91]

## Engaging with the Atlantic Empires

Tuscany's most important relationship, however, always remained that with the Spanish Habsburgs. Under Philip II (1527–1598) and Philip III (1578–1621), the Spanish Habsburgs not only dominated the Italian peninsula but also retained a huge lead over other European powers in long-distance trade and empire, even as their monopoly position eroded under Philip III. As a result, Tuscany's prospects for participating in overseas trade and empire depended to a large degree on the Spanish Habsburgs. Spanish imperial historiography is traditionally quite introspective, telling a national story of rise and fall. Political historical debates have concentrated on issues of frontiers, resistance to a unified Castilian-dominated empire, the hardening of boundaries and attitudes to Islam and Judaism, the extent of Spanish domination in Italy, and the reasons for Spain's slow defeat in the Eighty Years' War in Flanders.[92] Attention has concentrated on the person of Philip II and whether the set of choices he made led to Spanish decline, especially with respect to northwest Europe.[93] Perhaps naturally, Anglophone comparative political scholarship has also focused on northwest Europe, especially England and, to a lesser extent, the Dutch Republic and France.[94] Global Spanish imperial historiography has lately also considered connections with Asia, principally through the Philippines and the Manila Galleon.[95]

Though traditionally marginal in Spanish imperial historiography, Tuscans both contributed to and experienced shifts in Iberian policy quite forcefully. The connections extended from tangible Tuscan contributions to Spanish coffers and fleets and private trade on the Manila Galleon to the establishment of a large Sephardic community in

Livorno and the arrival of the Florentine Codex, to say nothing of the direct Spanish role in installing the Medici. Fortunately, a vein of historiography on the Iberian empires has turned to considering the role of non-Iberians. Building on arguments advanced in a debate over the decline of Spain in *Past and Present* a quarter century before,[96] Henry Kamen has offered a significant reinterpretation of Spanish imperial history in *Empire: How Spain Became a World Power, 1492–1763*.[97] Separating the story of imperial rise and fall from that of the underlying society and economy, Kamen argued that what grew and fell was the Spanish imperial system and that this system depended essentially on people from outside the Iberian peninsula, especially Italians.[98]

The Grand Duchy of Tuscany's experience within the Spanish imperial system was complex and evolved with shifting political circumstances and power dynamics. In the reign of Francesco I, Tuscany sought to leverage its naval alliance and robust financial support for the Spanish Habsburgs into a partnership. Though the relationship would cool under Ferdinando I, especially in the 1590s with the turn to France, Tuscany continued to return to the idea of joining the Iberian imperial project. Its efforts deepened with the Spanish Habsburg acquisition of the Portuguese Empire in 1580, which had been supported by Tuscan financing for the invasion. The Portuguese system of administration—with its auctions of monopoly contracts and its relative openness to foreign investment in imperial rights—and Tuscany's close relationship with the Spanish Habsburgs seemed to offer tantalizing possibilities, yet the political barriers to Tuscan state participation could not ultimately be surmounted.[99]

Stymied by Iberian intransigence over their monopoly position, the Tuscans explored working closely with the Dutch and English as partners in their projects of global trade and empire. Although the final results were modest, the implications of Tuscany's early engagement with these protagonists of the seventeenth century story are not. Tuscany's intimate knowledge of Dutch and English maritime affairs, its close collaboration with communities of Dutch and English mariners, its large stock of investment capital, and its deep wells of financial and commercial expertise made such collaboration not only feasible but mutually attractive. Contrary to standard assumptions about the role of information, institutions, initiative, or other endogenous explanations for northern European success, Tuscany's ultimate inability to fully capitalize on the possibilities of global trade and empire rested on political considerations. These included not only Tuscany's unwillingness to undertake a course of action that would lead to war with the Spanish, but also less-well-known Dutch efforts to block Tuscany's global trade ambitions from disrupting Dutch monopoly pretensions. The successful violence of mercantilist empires seeking monopoly, even those possessing some modernizing capitalist characteristics like the Dutch and English East India companies, more than the superiority of commercial institutions or technology, is sufficient to account for the differential outcome.[100]

## On Protagonists and Heroes

The Grand Duchy of Tuscany justified its bellicosity by frequent recourse to a discourse that denounced Ottoman tyranny. The Tuscans certainly seemed to have believed the Ottomans to be tyrannical, thereby participating in a long-standing interpretative framework.[101] The Medici claim to resist tyranny, however, sat awkwardly with their pioneering absolutist monarchy, let alone Tuscany's alliance with the Spanish Empire, then in the process of acquiring the reputation that became the Black Legend, and the papacy, then overseeing various inquisitions and the Index of Prohibited Books. Medici Tuscany was, after all, a model autocratic state built on the ashes of Renaissance Tuscany's famous republics. As Robert Dallington put it in his assessment of Tuscany in 1596, there were more than three hundred ruinous and obsolete old fortifications, "By which number may very probably bee coniectured their many and divers States in this small circuite in former times: for as it appeareth by Historie, not onely *Florence, Siena,* and *Pisa* (which of late yeares were reduced into one Government) but also *Pistoia, Arezzo, Volterra,* and almost all the Cities now under the great duke, had every one their severall and distinct State. Whereupon it was necessarie, each State should have her Castles and Fortes to affront those that confined upon them."[102] This new Medici state had inherited and extended the Republic of Florence's project of absorbing Tuscany's other polities. With centuries of rivalry leaving a rich legacy of victories, defeats, betrayals, and triumphs, holding this state together presented serious problems. Although the Medici were ultimately quite successful with co-optation and other noncoercive tactics, Tuscany at the outset was held in military subjection reinforced by Medici citadels in Tuscany's major cities. Dallington vividly described the purposes of the guns in the citadels "as to keepe in awful termes the Cities themselves"; the grand duke's cannons were there to fire on rebels in the city.[103] So intimidating were they that they contributed to Tuscany's transformation from one of Europe's most politically volatile regions to one of its most placid. They did so not by shelling Tuscany's rebel republicans into submission, but instead by deterring organized resistance to Tuscany's sociopolitical transformation into a hierarchical hereditary monarchy.

Even within the framework of a society that accepted monarchy, the grand duke's claims to resist tyranny conflicted with the enthusiastic Medici embrace of Mediterranean galley slavery. As we shall see, the grand duke of Tuscany actively promoted his leading role in captive-taking as an indication of the potency of his military forces and the success of his campaign to harm the Ottoman Empire. Likewise, even Francesco Carletti's ringing denunciation of slavery and manumission of his own slaves came after he had participated in the Atlantic slave trade.[104] Although some of the figures who appear here, including especially Carletti, displayed remarkable qualities that excite admiration, and others reveled in sweeping whole communities of innocent civilians into slavery, this study steps away from the classical and Renaissance historiographic tradition of seeing history as a branch of moral philosophy. The Medici regime and its affiliates are the protagonists of this story, not the heroes or the villains. As will be clear by the end of this study, any moral calculus about Tuscany is a complicated one. For instance, Tuscany's failure to acquire a sugar colony saved it from direct responsibility for the chattel slavery used to run a sugar economy, but this did not prevent other Europeans from doing just the same thing in the same place. Rather than pursue these questions, which so easily slip into anachronistic counterfactuals, this study remains an analytical political history that seeks to explain what happened and why, leaving judgment to the reader.

# Part I

# Parasitism and Symbiosis

# 1

# Finance and the Spanish Alliance

*I*ntertwined alliances with the Spanish Habsburgs and the papacy and more complex relations with France showed the Medici as valuable allies whose net financial, political, and military contributions gave them influence at the centers of power. The Medici state used its diplomats, active navy, and deep purse to secure influence among the mighty in pursuit of security, family honor, the advancement of Catholicism, commercial advantage, and access to distant lands. Such alliances underpinned Tuscany's global ambitions.

## Tuscany's International Position

Medici obligations to Spain for extensive military support, which had restored them to power in 1512 and 1530 and assisted in the conquest of Siena (1554–1557), constituted a central pillar of the new foreign policy developed in the wake of the republic's fall. Insular, dependent on commerce, and fixated on the defense and expansion of Florence's domains in central Italy, under the republic Florentine diplomacy had been defensive and prone to shifting alliances. Militarily, Florence focused on maintaining an effective army of mercenaries and militia. In this context, the republic had reflexively looked to France and Milan for support against the ambitions of the Emperor, the pope, Aragon (and the Aragonese kings of Naples), and rival Italian powers.

After the conquest of Siena, the Medici monarchy pursued a diametrically opposed policy. This new Tuscany was aggressive, outward-looking, willing to compromise commerce in pursuit of religious and political goals, and grounded in a fixed alliance with Spain, the papacy, and Spain's other allies in Italy (for example, Genoa). Military activity therefore concentrated on the navy, the Order of Santo Stefano, expeditionary forces, and fortifications. Equally, the conduct of diplomacy and its personnel, methods, and objectives all changed with the creation of a real court. This transformation in Tuscany's international position enabled the Medici to slot into a stable, mutually beneficial role in the Spanish alliance structure.

The Grand Duchy of Tuscany's strategic position made securing influence by providing military assistance and money an attractive proposition. Tuscany was protected by an extensive and growing network of fortifications, a small professional military supplemented by quite a substantial trained militia, and powerful allies, especially the Spanish Habsburgs. Although no part of Italy was impervious to attack, Tuscany was exceptionally well situated, being at the far end of the range of Ottoman and North African naval power, yet also distant from the main scenes of contention in northern Italy: the Venetian-Austrian-Ottoman frontier zone in the northeast and the French-Savoyard-Spanish Milan zone in the northwest. This relative security was newly won, potentially reversible, and, above all, dependent on the Spanish relationship. Although other powers did seek to displace Spain from its dominant position on the Italian peninsula, in the late sixteenth and early seventeenth centuries Spain's control was quite secure. The grand dukes could engage in distant expeditions and send troops and ships to help allies, but Tuscany could not engage in any conflicts on the Italian peninsula aside from those undertaken in the defense of the status quo.

The Medici could have taken the opportunity to use Spanish protection to economize on military and diplomatic spending, which would have freed up vast resources with which to enjoy the fruits of peace and prosperity; modern states confronted with analogous situations have tended to do so. In the sixteenth century, however, such a policy was not a particularly attractive option to a new monarchy in general and to the Medici in particular. The Medici may have had undisputed military control of Tuscany, but they were a new princely family whose background was financial, patrician, and ecclesiastical, not royal or even aristocratic. In a world profoundly attentive to issues of hierarchy, status, legitimacy, and recognition, the Medici were constrained to prove that they were in fact real princes who should be treated as such.[1] In particular, the dynasty needed to secure recognition of its claimed titles and arrange prestigious marriage connections not only as ends in and of themselves but also as a means of ensuring its security from questions about legitimacy both domestically and internationally. By the reign of Grand Duke Francesco I, the Medici dynasty had ruled as princes in name and in domestic political reality for more than forty years, but the Grand Duchy as then constituted was only a few years old. It needed validation.

The need for validation was coupled with a desire for access. Physical access to large sections of the world, let alone economic opportunity, was, quite unlike the modern system of relatively open trade and movement, deeply constrained by rules meant to favor certain groups. Protectionism, favoritism, privileges, and arbitrary and discriminatory restrictions were the norm, especially for those polities that saw more advantage in exploiting their own assets than in accessing those of others. In the last decades of the sixteenth century, some of the foremost practitioners of these restrictive policies were the Iberian empires of Castile and Portugal with their expansive global claims. If their monopolies could be maintained, riches seemed assured. Reserving the profits of global commerce and empire to privileged nationals thus appealed strongly to Spanish and Portuguese domestic political constituencies. Securing access, then, involved convincing the Iberian monarchies to pay a political price to help the Florentines.

Finally, the Medici cared deeply about the shape of the international order, in particular the state of Catholicism and the political situation in France. On the religious front, the Medici wanted to see, at minimum, the current Catholic territories held against both Protestants and the Ottomans. They would almost certainly have preferred an extension of the Catholic domains, although their preoccupation in this period was largely with the threat from the Ottomans and the opportunities for rolling back the Ottoman tide. That the Medici should take such a position in the Catholic cause is quite unsurprising in light of the family's deep historic connections to the papacy and its more recent alliance with the papacy to secure the grand ducal title. Intertwined with, but not quite identical to, Tuscany's support for Catholicism was its enthusiastic involvement in French politics. Tuscan goals in France were, broadly, a Catholic dynasty with ties to the Medici ruling over a stable state; France would then serve as a protector, thus strengthening Tuscany's position and freedom of maneuver in its relationship with Spain.[2]

In sum, the Medici sought legitimation, dynastic advancement, commercial access, Catholic victory, and an improvement in the French political order. Medici military action could help with some of these goals; Medici money could help with all of them. Both Medici contributions helped secure Medici access and influence. Such were the absolutist politics of Tuscany in this period that the Medici agenda advanced with this influence was also, by definition, Tuscany's agenda.

## The Orsini, the Medici, and Spain

With Tuscany bordered by the Papal States on the east and south and bisected by the Via Francigena linking Rome with France, and with numerous expatriate Tuscans continuing a centuries-old tradition of maintaining extensive religious and financial ties, papal Rome was essential to all Renaissance Florentine governments. This was doubly so for the Medici, whose position in Florence depended on their ties to Rome, especially during the reigns of the Medici Popes Leo X (r. 1513–1521) and Clement VII (r. 1523–1534). With the conquest of Siena, Florentine ambitions for influence extended across the border into northern Lazio and the Patrimony of St. Peter. In this context, the Medici developed an intimate, sometimes fraught, relationship with the powerful Orsini family and Florentine bankers in Rome. This they did with a characteristic mixture of financial entanglements, kinship and marriage ties, the position of the Medici cardinal, and political power. Out of this tangled skein emerged robust Medici relationships with major families with one foot in central Italy and another in the Iberian Empires.[3]

Leaders of one of the great Roman baronial factions, the Orsini had long battled for dominance in Rome with the Colonna. With their extensive lands, numerous retainers, strategically valuable strongholds, and ramifying connections across central Italy, the Orsini could be important allies to cultivate. Never quite princes in their own right, they epitomized the overmighty vassal. Vulnerable to the bureaucratic centralization of Renaissance states, such vassals were famously brought to heel by monarchs and their new artillery trains throughout Europe. In central Italy, however, minor polities and major aristocrats had an alternative. There, they could offer a bridling influence on ambitious centralizing states to a foreign power in exchange for protection. Especially after the Peace of Bologna (1530), Emperor Charles V cemented his position on the Italian peninsula by developing mutually beneficial relationships of protection and service not just with new regimes, like that of the Medici, but also with minor polities like Piombino and Lucca.[4]

The Orsini, who lacked truly sovereign territory but were more than mere subject aristocrats, charted a path between the nobles of Spanish-ruled territories like Naples and that of the independent princes. In recognition of their position and a record of past, and perhaps prospective, service and loyalty to Spain, both Emperor Charles V and his son and successor King Philip II granted the Orsini the remarkably elevated official status of grandees of Spain of the first rank.[5] Such favors were important. For instance, when the Orsini duke of Bracciano received the Order of the Golden Fleece, a Tuscan diplomat at the Spanish court reported the news to Francesco I.[6] Likewise, the Medici archives retain a "Relation to His Majesty of the Duke of Bracciano and of the Cardinal Orsino his Brother in Rome on 10 December, 1620," which traces Orsini service to Spain back four hundred years before offering a more detailed account of principally military service in the previous century. Stressing the value of the Orsini to the king of Spain, the relation notes that "one must consider also that the Dukes of Bracciano and their successors can be effective instruments for helping Your Majesty on whatsoever occasion of revolution in Italy, and for securing the Kingdom of Naples" before listing the specific fortresses that would be of value and estimating that the duke of Bracciano could raise a thousand well-armed horsemen from his vassals. Finally, in a slightly discordant note, the relation makes a virtue of Cardinal Orsini's renunciation of his status as Cardinal Protector of France and offer of service to Spain.[7] All understood that the Orsini were potentially valuable friends to have.

Medici-Orsini marriage ties were at the heart of the emerging Medici dynasty. Lorenzo the Magnificent (1449–1492) and Clarice Orsini (1452–1488) married by proxy in 1468 and in person in 1469 and had seven children who survived infancy, including Giovanni, the future Pope Leo X.[8] Clarice and Lorenzo's son Piero de' Medici (1472–1503), whose poor leadership during the French invasion of 1494 led to the expulsion of the Medici, married Alfonsina Orsini; Piero and Alfonsina's son Lorenzo would be the duke of Urbino.[9] Alfonsina Orsini de Medici and Lorenzo, duke of Urbino, participated in the proxy marriage of Francesca Orsini, Marchesa di Paduli, with Lorenzo di Ceri dell'Anguillara in 1516.[10] There were, therefore, substantial precedents for ties between the Medici and Orsini when Duke Cosimo I, head of a different branch of the Medici, consented to the marriage of his daughter Isabella de' Medici (1542–1576) to Paolo Giordano Orsini (1541–1585), duke of Bracciano. The engagement was agreed in 1553 and they wed in 1556.[11] The youth of the couple indicates the political character of the marriage. Shortly after his accession to the Duchy of Bracciano in 1560, at the beginning of 1561, Paolo Giordano settled the usufruct of the Duchy of Bracciano and Vicovaro on his wife, Isabella Medici, and his sister Felice Orsini.[12] Paolo Giordano continued to live in Florence at the request of Cosimo I, who provided the couple with the villa of Poggio Imperiale in 1565.[13]

By the early 1560s, then, Cosimo I had secured effective dominance over the Orsini position on the northern approaches to Rome, on the shores of the lake that still provides Rome with the bulk of its water. Indeed, using the mixture of financial muscle, political savvy, and family connections that underpinned Medici policy, Cosimo I further entangled Tuscany with the Duchy of Bracciano by renting the duchy from Paolo Giordano Orsini in 1563 for 30,000 gold *scudi* to help Orsini satisfy his creditors.[14] That Paolo Giordano should have contracted such substantial debts while still a child led to a lengthy and complex dispute waged between 1564 and 1571. In brief, it appears that the debts taken on behalf of Paolo Giordano Orsini to secure control of a castle while still an eight-year-old child in 1549 had involved the estate of Paolo Giordano in costly debts with the Cavalcanti-Giraldi bank in Rome. The Cavalcanti and Giraldi were both important Florentine families. Paolo Giordano's complaint alleged lies, deceptions, and sharp financial practices. Although this particular occasion involved a legal dispute between ancient families with ties to Rome and Florence, all the actors in it would retain close connections with the Medici. In particular, both the Giraldi and Cavalcanti families would play important roles in Medici contacts with early colonial Brazil, as will be explored in Chapter 2. The notarized account of the dispute, dated April 28, 1571, opens with references to Pope Pius V (r. 1566–1572) and Grand Duke Cosimo I.[15] Pius V and Cosimo I had quite a close relationship, with the pope granting Cosimo I his title as Etrurie Magno Duce (Grand Duke of Tuscany) in 1569 and crowning him in Rome on March 5, 1570.[16] The admiration was long-standing, as Pius V had praised Cosimo I, in a letter of April 20, 1567, to Paolo Giordano Orsini, writing "because we, holding the lord Duke of Florence as one of the wisest heads of Italy, will always praise all of those deliberations that you undertake with the most prudent advice and will of his Excellency."[17]

The deepening Medici involvement with their Orsini relatives, who were simultaneously Roman magnates and Spanish grandees, continued both before and after the death of Isabella de' Medici.[18] It was far from smooth sailing, however. Cosimo I again bailed out Paolo Giordano Orsini in 1570 and specified a vast bequest of 124,000 *scudi* for Paolo Giordano to discharge his debts, but at his accession in 1574, Francesco I declined to uphold this part of the will and cut off Paolo Giordano financially.[19] The relations between brothers-in-law collapsed further after the death of Isabella, after which Francesco had Paolo Giordano's property in Florence taken and auctioned to discharge Paolo Giordano's debts.[20] The bitterness seems not to have outlived Paolo Giordano, however, with Cardinal Ferdinando de' Medici taking the lead in protecting Paolo Giordano's son Virginio Orsini (1572–1615) even after the conflicts over Paolo Giordano's late marriage to Vittoria Accoramboni (1557–1585).[21] Cardinal Ferdinando, as Virginio Orsini's uncle, ordered the inventory of Paolo Giordano Orsini's goods on December 13, 1585.[22] In 1594, Ferdinando, now Grand Duke of Tuscany, was named along with Cardinal Montalto as one of the two guardians of Virginio Orsini's wife, Flavia Peretti, and heir in Virginio Orsini's will; a copy of a codicil is dated from Livorno on April 6, 1599, and witnessed by Lorenzo Usimbardi (1547–1636), a leading Medici diplomat and official.[23] Ferdinando played the role of benevolent uncle on a grand scale, lending Virginio Orsini the astonishing sum of 100,000 *scudi,* apparently interest-free, on July 1, 1599; Virginio repaid a first installment on July 3, 1600.[24] Not incidentally, vast indebtedness also kept this strategically placed branch of the Orsini firmly in the Medici orbit, a reality perhaps acknowledged in the names of some of Virginio and Flavia's children: Cosimo, Ferdinando, Alessandro, and Isabella.[25]

Medici strategy required intensive engagement with the papacy and influence in Counter-Reformation Rome.[26] Confronted with the structural uncertainty of an elective monarchy in Rome, the Medici sought multiple Orsini allies. Although the dukes of Bracciano seem to have been the senior branch, the Medici simultaneously pursued ties with the Orsini counts of Pitigliano. The effort began badly. Cosimo I was accused of conspiring with Alessandro Orsini and Angelo Franschini of Siena to kill Niccolò Orsini, count of Pitigliano, and invade his small state on the border between Siena and the Papal States. Cosimo denied the accusation, saying that he did not wish the death of the count.[27] Even so, the Medici state hounded the count of Pitigliano, pushing an ultimately unsuccessful prosecution for heresy, misrule, and assistance to the French.[28] The unpromising start notwithstanding, Pitigliano was eventually swept into the Florentine orbit, first through marriage to the Capponi family, then through Medici patronage of the depredations of the Orsini of Pitigliano, and finally with the sale and annexation of Pitigliano by Count Giovanni Antonio Orsini to settle his debts in 1604.[29] The case of Pitigliano shows how the Medici wished expansion to work: marriage into a politically reliable Florentine house, financial stringency resulting in dependence on Florentine patronage, and finally sale and annexation.

The southward thrust of the Medici state into the strategically valuable hill fastnesses separating Siena and Rome using a combination of money and family ties shows a potent mechanism of action. It offered a way into the Papal States, but also much further afield. The Orsini, as Spanish grandees of the first rank, offered a second access point into the upper echelons of the Spanish nobility to match Duchess Eleonora's Toledo kinsmen. As important, all three of the elite Florentine commercial and banking families who play a major role in the Orsini story—the Giraldi, the Cavalcanti, and the Capponi—extended their reach deep into the Iberian possessions in the Americas, from early colonial Brazil to New Spain. Tuscany's projects for entering into cooperative partnerships with the Iberian empires rested on following their example. To do so, the Medici needed to present themselves as the most faithful of allies. In this, they achieved early success. The Emperor Charles V, in his 1548 *Political Testament* for his son Philip, wrote of Cosimo I that "he has been very solicitous for me and my affairs; and I think he will befriend you too, since he has received so many favours" and that Cosimo "has a good brain and good judgement, and keeps his territories well-ordered."[30] Cosimo I would fully vindicate the wily old Emperor's assessment of him.

## The Spanish Alliance

The relationship between the Spanish Habsburgs and the Medici grand dukes was certainly punctuated by periods of tension and marked by occasional Tuscan experiments with securing other allies. Even so, the Habsburgs and Medici can be seen as more or less continuously allied from the restoration of the Medici in 1530 through the early years of the Thirty Years' War (1618–1648). In this, Tuscany's experience was typical of the states of the Italian peninsula, with the notable exception of Venice.[31] Indeed, the Genoese and Tuscans referred to Spain as "our side," and Spain's truce offer with the Ottomans in the 1570s was negotiated on behalf not only of its territories of Milan, the Presidial States, Sardinia, Sicily, and the Kingdom of Naples, but also of a roll call of Italian states: Ferrara, Florence, Genoa, Lucca, Mantua, Parma, Piombino, the Papal States, Urbino, and Savoy, along with the nearby Knights of St. John on Malta.[32] The Medici sought primacy among Spain's Italian allies as the most devoted and faithful realm, which therefore deserved the greatest respect and favor. Symbolically, Grand Duke Ferdinando I, whose relationship with Philip II's Spain was anything but consistently smooth, conveyed his allegiance to Spain with obsequies for Philip II's death that were intended to be the most elaborate in Italy. The closing of Vincenzo Pitti's richly illustrated and immediately published (1598) account of the affair, concluded, after praising the grandeur of the funeral components, by stating,

> but above all the Magnificence of the Grand Duke was exalted, who, without sparing any expense, wanted to have such magnificent obsequies, this honor, which well demonstrated the true Spirit of the Prince, as no less grateful than

Magnificent and great. Therefore, as he is greater than the other Princes of Italy for the abundance of expert men, he was able, with greater facility, to exercise such things with similar greatness. Thus, he wanted with his whole force to demonstrate to such a Glorious King, the greatest of them all, as he [Philip II] was always not less the Protector and favorer than the Emperor Charles the Fifth, his Father, exalter of the Most Serene House of Medici, so it was quite worthy that, with the greatest magnificence and greatness possible, he [Philip II] was by him [Grand Duke Ferdinando I] recognized and honored.[33]

This event expressed the Medici sense of preeminence among the Italian princes and of the obligation to honor the Spanish Habsburgs. Tuscany's claim to such eminence among the Italian princes rested as much on the scale and consistency of its contributions to Spanish Habsburg power as it did on the size of Tuscany or the history of Spanish support for the Medici house. Above all, Tuscany regularly supplied ships and money to Spain's many wars even though Tuscany's relative security would have permitted it to adopt a less costly policy of isolation.

The medieval Republic of Pisa had been a formidable naval power before its decisive defeat by Genoa at the Battle of Meloria (1284), but Florence, as an inland city situated on an unreliable river, had had a very modest naval tradition dependent on its control of Pisa.[34] Cosimo I set out to change this from 1547, buying and building galleys, establishing a base at Portoferraio, and recruiting foreign sailors, only to see Tuscany's fleet of seven galleys utterly shattered in a series of operations at Djerba, Cyprus, and Corsica around 1560.[35] At the same time, from 1557 to 1562, the grand duke established the naval crusading Order of Santo Stefano, based on the model of the Knights of St. John at Malta. Though often intertwined with the operations of the Tuscan navy, the Order of Santo Stefano's fleet was a separate entity.[36] Committed to rebuilding the Tuscan navy, Cosimo restored its numbers to seven galleys in 1566, rented twelve galleys of a then larger fleet to the pope for the Lepanto campaign of 1571, and saw Tuscan naval forces reach eleven galleys, a pair each of galleons and galleasses, and a half-dozen frigates with the help of Spanish subsidies. With the removal of the subsidies,

the Tuscan fleet shrank to four galleys in 1574, revealing Tuscany's dependence on the Spanish alliance system.[37]

Even at is greatest size, the Tuscan fleet could not fight any substantial naval power. Fortunately, it was never intended to do so. Though
the Tuscan navy could muster an amphibious expeditionary force and
contest the seas with North African corsairs, in the 1560s and 1570s
it primarily existed to serve in allied squadrons led by Spain. Spain's
Mediterranean fleet consisted of numerous small contributions, mostly
from its Italian territories and those of its Italian allies and contractors.[38] Although Tuscany's ships seem never to have been much more
than 10 percent of the total, the seven galleys of Tuscany's 1566 fleet
still comfortably represented more than two thousand men.[39] Tuscany
hardly needed to mobilize fully to support seven galleys, but neither
was it a trivial task year in year out.

Fortunately for Tuscany, the Tuscan galleys did not serve for free.
While on service to Philip II, the Tuscans were theoretically paid 250
ducats per galley per month.[40] Early modern galleys, with their simple
construction, light armament, and heavy manpower needs, functioned
very differently from the immensely costly galleons, carracks, and ships
of the line, with their multiple decks, elaborate sail arrangements,
heavy artillery complement, and modest crews. Though the oarsmen's
benches were increasingly filled with convicts and slaves suffering
brutal conditions, manpower was still so costly that the expenses were
roughly the same, about 6,000 ducats, to operate a galley for a year as
to build a new one.[41] In light of this cost structure, Tuscany's naval contribution to the Spanish fleet rested more on the organizational and
financial element of gathering, equipping, supplying, and paying the
crews than it did on the contribution of galleys. With Tuscany's later
acquisition of heavily gunned sailing warships at the beginning of the
seventeenth century, the dynamics would change.

Philip II's government was notorious for undertaking military
commitments vastly in excess of its resources, recurrently dragging the
Spanish Habsburg system into bankruptcy.[42] It is no surprise, then,
that the Spanish fell behind on their subsidy payments and the Tuscans complained about the default. A 1565 letter from Francesco de'
Medici—who had by then taken over some of the reins of government
from his father—to his ambassador points out that in future the Medici

government would be unable to put its galleys in the service of Philip II if payment was not made.[43] The statement was not, of course, strictly true. A state as large and prosperous as Tuscany could certainly have managed seven galleys. Indeed, Tuscany would operate considerably larger fleets on its own account later, as shall be explored in Chapter 8. Francesco's complaints, however, illustrate the contractual nature of the Medici relationship with the Spanish Habsburgs and the limits that the Medici sought to impose on the assistance provided.

Tuscany's reaction to losses in battle likewise underline the hybrid contractor-ally character of its position. For instance, when Tuscan ships joined Spanish operations in North Africa, they were exposed to losses in battle. The Tuscan fleet participated in the Spanish-led siege of Tripoli in 1559, the Tuscan galleys going by way of Naples. Sieges can be dangerous for a ship, yet Tuscan diplomacy sought to shift some of the consequent costs to Spain. In 1560, Duke Cosimo I wrote to the Spanish viceroy of Sicily to endorse the compensation claim of Florentine merchants who had suffered losses when the ship *Santo Stefano*, damaged by Tripolitan artillery, was sunk in the siege of Tripoli.[44] Eight years later, the Tuscan ambassador in Spain was still asking about compensation for the munitions expended in the siege.[45]

For all Tuscany's complaints about failure of payment, their enthusiasm for participation in the Spanish fleet did not diminish. Indeed, a memorial, probably from 1567, concerning the new contract *(asiento)* for the galleys manages to complain about "the great damage because of the small salary assigned to them" while still suggesting that the Tuscans would be willing to raise the number of galleys assigned to the Spanish fleet from ten to fifteen.[46] They sought this expanded role because it brought political influence. The Medici ambassador wrote as the opening line of his letter on the subject, "I have always been of the opinion that it is much to the reputation and greatness of Your Illustrious Excellency to have a good number of galleys, and not of small utility as well, every time that this Majesty [Philip II] wants to pay for them."[47] Ambassador Nobili continued later on the page, observing, "which causes much understanding, and confidence with him [His Majesty, Philip II]: because it will always be of no small account that [there will always be] many naval forces hastening with the promptness of the Tuscan people in all of his needs."[48] Convinced of the galleys' reputational importance, Nobili advocated raising the number of Tuscan galleys to twenty.[49] Twenty galleys went beyond Spain's needs or ability to pay, so the eventual *asiento* agreed was for ten galleys.[50] Nobili's plan for the Medici to make a dramatic gesture, however, would have contributed to Tuscany's reputation as an ever-faithful ally, the limitation of its service determined by Spain's needs, not Tuscany's willingness serve. The Medici did not achieve all their goals with the galleys, but they did secure two critical points: a substantial Tuscan fleet served with the Spanish fleet and Tuscany received payment for it. Late and partial payment it may have been, but chests of silver coins were still dispatched from Spain.[51] As Medici enthusiasm for increasing the number of ships in Spanish service indicates, it was a negotiated alliance with which Tuscany was fundamentally content. Spain secured inexpensive galleys whose payment could be deferred for years, while Tuscany received subsidies for its fleet and influence at the imperial center.

Even after the effective demobilization of the Spanish Mediterranean fleet, with the Spanish-Ottoman truce of 1581, ended the annual need for the Tuscan galleys, Tuscany stood ready to provide naval assistance.[52] Indeed, Tuscany and the papacy often worked hand in glove to draw the Spanish Habsburgs into ambitious ventures, a pattern that would recur into the seventeenth century. Most famously, Francesco I played a central role in initiating the Spanish Armada, offering a cost estimate as early as February 1585 in the instructions to Luigi Dovara (1535–1596).[53] Both Pope Gregory XIII (r. 1572–1585) and Pope Sixtus V (r. 1585–1590) sought to work through Dovara—a knight of the Order of Santo Stefano, frequent Tuscan ambassador, commander of the Tuscan light cavalry, and Medici courtier—to persuade Philip II to undertake the invasion of England, offering the financial assistance of the papacy and Tuscany.[54] After Sir Francis Drake's (1540–1596) raid on the towns of Bayona and Vigo in Galicia in the autumn of 1585, Philip II agreed to the invasion of England with the provisions that it be delayed until 1587 and that the pope and the grand duke of Tuscany supply between half and two-thirds of the costs.[55]

In November 1586, the grand duke of Tuscany's galleon, then in Spain, was chartered to carry munitions to Havana, transporting merchandise on the return run.[56] This galleon—Tuscany only had one at the time, the *San Francesco*—joined the Marquis of Santa Cruz's expedition against English piracy in the Viceroyalty of Peru in 1587.[57] Fatefully,

Tuscany's galleon then carried on a decades-old tradition and joined the Invincible Armada. The *San Francisco de Florencia* (sometimes just the *Florencia* or the *San Giovanni*), had been built in Tuscany, perhaps in the 1570s. At 961 tons with 89 sailors and 294 soldiers while at Corunna, it was by no means the heaviest or most extensively manned ship, but its complement of 52 guns was the largest of any ship in either the Spanish or the English fleet.[58] Such was its power that it served as Gaspar de Sousa's flagship in the Squadron of Portugal.[59] For all Tuscany's role in encouraging, financing, and contributing to the operation, in February 1588 Tuscany's representative remained uncertain about the fleet's target, whether England, Ireland, or Zeeland and Holland. The Tuscan government archives also hold an *avviso* from May 28, 1588, detailing the fleet composition.[60] This would tend to suggest that the Tuscans were not being regularly and efficiently informed by the Spanish Habsburg court about the allied fleet's composition and goals. The Medici desperately wanted the operation to succeed and even received, enclosed in a letter of August 21, 1588, from the legation secretary Camillo Guidi (1555–1623) in Madrid, a spectacularly inaccurate *avviso* about the Armada's success; Guidi correctly doubted its accuracy but sent it anyway.[61] The ultimate defeat of the Armada left Tuscany with particularly bitter cause to lament, since the *Florencia* met a fiery doom on the expedition.[62]

## The King of Coin

With the advent of a settled peace in Tuscany in the late 1550s after more than sixty years of intermittent war and violent political turmoil, the revenues of the centralizing Medici state and the returns on the Medici patrimony began to enrich the dynasty.[63] While Tuscany regularly contributed to Spain's military ventures, it avoided the truly crippling expense of the age: large-scale warfare. Domestic peace, a modest peacetime army, and high taxes combined to generate fiscal surpluses.[64] Indeed, Ferdinando I's advice to his successor, Cosimo II, stressed the importance of the princely wealth these taxes enabled, but he also stressed the need to avoid new taxes except as a short-term expedient in a war of defense.[65] In this, Ferdinando I had continued where his brother had successfully left off. Francesco I had accumulated a fortune reputed to amount to 7,000,000 *scudi*.[66] There is reason to believe the figure is plausible, at least as an order of magnitude. An undated, but apparently contemporary, description of Tuscany lists the components of annual grand ducal revenue and gives an estimate of overall expenditure (see Tables 1 and 2). The figures suggest that the public budget was regularly in surplus to the tune of 345,000 ducats, relying solely on public revenues. The Medici also derived considerable private income from their extensive personal patrimony.[67] In this context, heavy Medici lending to France, Spain, and Portugal looks demanding, but manageable.

Medici wealth and fiscal surpluses were the sine qua non of a foreign policy in which large loans and other financial transfers underpinned influence. For the Medici to reap the full diplomatic and political rewards of this position, though, they needed a matching reputation. This they achieved even in England. Robert Dallington's (1561–1637) "suruey

*Table 1.1* The grand duke of Tuscany's estimated annual tax revenues. The estimate appears to date from 1596, in Ferdinando I's reign. Text in brackets refers to the amounts in Dallington's printed estimate, which correctly add up to the summary total of 1,095,000 ducats given in Table 1.2; the manuscript version is short 80,000 ducats. Source: National Archives at Kew, State Papers (SP) 9/204, 277r–277v and Dallington, "A suruey of the great dukes state of Tuscany," 47 (28). In Dallington's account, the figures are given in "Duckets" (ducats).[1]

| Tax | Revenue (Ducats) | City | Revenue |
| --- | --- | --- | --- |
| Gate Tax | 100,000 | Pisa and Livorno | 70,000 |
| Customs Revenues from Florence | 100,000 | Pistoia | 60,000 |
| Salt Tax | 120,000 | Arezzo | 20,000 |
| Flour Tax | 120,000 | Volterra | 15,000 |
| Meat Tax on Butchers and Slaughterhouses | 20,000 [80,000] | Montepulciano | 10,000 |
| Dowry and Contracts Tax | 70,000 | Fiesole, desolate city | 2,000 |
| Fines from Malefactors | 65,000 | Colle, new city | 3,000 |
| [Cortona] | [20,000] | The City of Siena renders annually | 240,000 |

1. The two lists mostly match, and so the figures probably derive from the same source and pertain to Ferdinando I's reign. In the manuscript at Kew, there is a vague "55000" below a line under Colle and above a line over the total for Siena. National Archives at Kew, State Papers (SP) 9/204, 277r–277v.

Table 1.2    Summary of the grand duke of Tuscany's estimated income and
expenses, ca. 1596. The figures derive from the manuscript, which
gives the same summary total as Dallington, even though the manuscript's line items do not add up to 1,095,000. Source: National
Archives at Kew, State Papers (SP) 9/204 277r–277v, and Dallington,
"A suruey of the great dukes state of Tuscany," 47 (28).

| Income and Expenses | Amount (in ducats) |
| --- | --- |
| Sum [of incomes] | 1,095,000 |
| Ordinary expenses | 530,000 |
| Extraordinary expenses, ordinarily | 220,000 |
| [Sum of expenses] | 750,000 |
| Remains annually | 345,000 |

of the great dukes state of Tuscany In the yeare of our Lord 1596,"
printed in London in 1605, offers this extraordinary description of Ferdinando I: "But the thing which most argueth his Riches, and whereof
hee and other Princes haue their daily vses, and whereby they bee valued,
is ready Money and Coine; which the world (and no doubt vpon good
reason) iudgeth to be very great: insomuch as the *Neapolitan* calleth him
the King of coin: for in their play at *Primero* (their foure sutes of cardes
being *Denari, Coppe, Spad, Picche, Coyne, Cuppes, Swords, Pikes*) when (as the
manner is) ye aske him for what Carde he pulleth, if he pull for a *Denaro*,
hee answereth; I pull for the great Duke of *Tuscany*."[68] In the heart of
Spanish Italy, in the viceregal capital of Naples, the Medici had become
synonymous with money. Dallington continued, arguing that there
were four major states in Italy—tellingly ignoring Milan—each of which,
"exceed[s] one another. The Pope greatest in authority, the Kingdome
of Naples greatest in land-forces; the *Venetians* mightiest at Sea; and
this great Duke mightiest in purse."[69] Having established his financial
primacy among princes, which applied only if one ignored the greater
wealth wielded by the Genoese financiers, Ferdinando then made good
use of mystery. Speculation about the vast extent of his fortune raged
such that "Of whose present money some let not to say that hee hath
thirty millions of Duckets, others talke of fiue and twenty, none vnder
twenty; but how truly, must be left to euery mans pleasure to iudge, as
a thing vtterly vnknowne, except wee may guide our coniectures by this
inference which may thus be collected."[70] Inference and estimation were
essential for judging Medici power, since it so clearly rested on money.

The ancient Roman aphorism, *pecunia nervus belli* (money is the sinew of war), was a touchstone of Renaissance politics and had been a locus of debate between the Florentines Niccolò Machiavelli (1469–1527) and Francesco Guicciardini (1483–1540). Machiavelli had asserted categorically that "the common opinion that the sinews of war are money could not be more false" and that "Quintus Curtius affirms that the sinews of war are money. This maxim is cited every day and followed by princes who are not sufficiently wise," all in his aptly titled chapter "The Sinews of War Are Not Money, as Common Opinion Would Have It." Instead he insisted that "all the above-named men were beaten by those who deem good soldiers to be the sinews of war, not money"; "war is waged with steel, not gold"; and "so again I repeat that not gold but good soldiers are the sinews of war."[71] His fame and fervor, however, availed him little. Instead, the general consensus of the era most definitely fell on the side of Guicciardini and those who insisted on the centrality of money to power.[72] This applied above all to the Venetians, whose prime mythmaker and ideologue, Gasparo Contarini (1483–1542), had characterized the public treasury of Venice as (in the Elizabethan translation) the "very fountayne whence the other parts of the commonwealth receiue their nouriture and sustenance" and offered a spirited defense of the use of mercenaries.[73] In this context, it is not at all surprising to find that Dallington's analysis of grand ducal wealth rested on the report of the Venetian ambassador. Dallington wrote, "Duke *Francisco* in the yeere 1576. reported to the *Venetian* Embassador, that his father *Cosimo* dying, left him in debt eight hundred thousand Duckets: for the payment whereof he was forced to take vp great summes of the *Genoeses,* at vnreasonable interest. Notwithstanding it appeareth by the relation of the said Embassador, that within ten yeeres after he was cleared of that debt, & had imbursed into his coffers fiue Millions. It may then be probably argued, that if in ten yeeres there were six millions increase, in twenty yeers more, there be at least twelue more added."[74] Dallington continued in this speculative vein, arguing that those that cite the expenses of a treasonable plot must consider that free-spending Francesco I still managed to accumulate substantial surpluses and that Ferdinando I was quite a frugal prince.[75] Dallington continued, "It is likewise knowne, hee hath great summes of money in banke, which must needs bring their yeerely gaine, besides three-score thousands duckets entrat, which he yerely detaineth from his brother *Don Piero,* who liueth in *Spaine,* & the gaine of Wheat before remembred; all which with his yeerely reuenue may make one strongly perswaded, that his ready mony is little lesse then that which is iudged of them, which rate it at the highest."[76] Dallington's calculation from the Venetian ambassador's report would have put Ferdinando I's wealth in 1596 at some 17,000,000 ducats, while the highest estimates, which Dallington thought credible, put it at some 30,000,000. These are extraordinary and quite unlikely figures on a public income of just over 1,095,000 ducats and a regular surplus of 345,000 even accepting large returns from the Medici patrimony. The speculations about Ferdinando I's wealth do show, though, the facility with which the public might reason from a few anecdotes. It suggests, in turn, that the occasional comment and a bit of display might produce great effects in crystalizing a reputation that, if well handled, might be useful to Ferdinando as he pursued ambitious projects that required the approval of a chronically fiscally stretched Spain. In short, for Ferdinando I, avoidance of major war produced the financial reserves that could serve as the sinews of someone else's war; they were, therefore, diplomatically precious.

## Princely Financiers

The Medici had long understood the relationship between finance and political power, both domestically and in concert with essential allies. The combination had been central to their rise to power in Florence and the trajectory of the original Medici bank, closed with the expulsion of the family in 1494, but already in serious difficulties at the death of Lorenzo the Magnificent in 1492.[77] Cosimo I came from a cadet branch of the family and was born a quarter century after the closure of the Medici bank, and so the direct connection to the banking heritage was limited. Instead, the Medici participated in a Florentine patrician culture in which family banks and engagement with high finance remained normative even for increasingly aristocratic families. As Florence retained its ancient role as a financial center, Florentines continued to have widely dispersed investments, playing an especially important role in France and Spain.[78] For all the antiquity of Florence's role and the preeminence of certain Florentine banks in the fourteenth and fifteenth centuries, in the sixteenth century Genoa comprehensively overshadowed Florence, which now took on a secondary position within the front rank of European high finance.[79]

The Genoese operated on a larger scale than the Florentines, but both drew on stocks of capital, connections, and knowledge that made them, by general consensus, simply better at finance than many of their otherwise commercially sophisticated peers. This can be seen most clearly with the great merchant republic of Venice, which seems to have been colonized by Florentine and Genoese bankers who brought new techniques in the last quarter of the sixteenth century.[80] At least, such was the Venetian perception, with the *Cinque Savi alla Mercanzia* stressing the breadth and sophistication of the Florentine network in 1606.[81] The Florentines and the Genoese, the *Cinque Savi alla Mercanzia* also reported, tapped Venetian funds to speculate on the exchanges of Besançon.[82] Indeed, the interdependence of the Genoese, Venetians, and Florentines in matters financial had been made plain a decade earlier when the Spanish default of 1596 had shaken the Florentine and Venetian money markets, which disrupted Ambrogio Spinola (1569–1630) and Giovanni Giacomo Grimaldi's efforts to send funds for Philip II to the Low Countries.[83] Financial interdependence and sophistication extended right to the top in Florence. Another Venetian complained, around 1603, about the grand duke's profitable sale of 200,000 crowns to the Venetian mint *(Zecca)*.[84] Dealing in currency and securities was hardly a grand ducal monopoly. The ubiquitous Capponi did so as well, selling 500,000 ducats to the Venetian mint on contract in 1584.[85] Just five years later, Luigi Capponi was part of the Doria-Velluti-Amatto consortium for the Antwerp *asiento* market in 1589.[86] From currency and debt speculation to, as we shall see, the acquisition of Portuguese donatary captaincies, the exceptional element of the Medici lay precisely in their insistence on behaving just like other prominent Florentine patricians.[87] Even as they proclaimed themselves a princely dynasty fit to supply queens of France, sent out fleets and armies, and wielded absolute political and judicial authority, the Medici regularly used their network of agents like a Florentine banking house.

## The Price of Influence

For all the importance of Tuscany's ships, Medici Tuscany was a much more significant financial than a military power. As Tuscany's major ally, the Spanish Habsburgs received the largest Tuscan contributions. The Medici were, however, eager to cultivate a wide range of allies and so offered military and financial assistance to other powers. Ever ready to make war on the Ottomans, for instance, three decades after Lepanto, the Medici offered to send the Austrian Habsburg Holy Roman Emperor an army.[88] Generally, though, the powers that Tuscany sought to support were not lacking in forces, but rather in the means to pay the forces they already had. Indeed, to have sent more troops and ships might merely have compounded the problem.

In light of the shortage of funds among the leading powers, Medici willingness to make large risky loans constituted a major source of influence. As with the development of the fleet, so also Tuscan sovereign lending took off only after the conquest of Siena solidified the Medici political and fiscal position. To finance this costly war, Cosimo I had borrowed at least 2.5 million *scudi*, principally abroad.[89] As ever, war led to dramatical reversals. In 1552, Cosimo I had lent Charles V 200,000 ducats, but Cosimo I had to borrow 100,000 *scudi* from Philip II in 1555.[90] As postwar prosperity set in, however, the lending seems to have become entirely one way: out from Tuscany.[91] Although the grand duke provided 200,000 *scudi* to Emperor Maximilian II (1527-1576) in 1565, lending concentrated on the increasingly overstretched Philip II.[92] Tuscany offered Philip II 200,000 *scudi* in 1572, but the duke of Alba's direct request to the grand duke for funds in 1572, to support his struggles with the deteriorating situation in Flanders, was later disavowed by Madrid as a result of suspicion about Tuscan activity in France.[93] Suspicions of Medici intrigue were often well founded. In 1569, Cosimo I lent 180,000 *scudi* to France's King Charles IX (1550-1574).[94] The Florentines negotiated against the Spanish with the young king as the dispute over Cosimo I's new grand ducal title left him temporarily estranged from the Habsburgs, but the Queen Mother, Catherine de' Medici (1519-1589), demurred from outright confrontation.[95] In this, as in other moments of estrangement, Tuscany retained its fundamental orientation to Spain. That the grand duke was willing to provide timely financial assistance to help Spain out of a difficult spot in 1572—even when in disfavor at the Spanish court—and that the duke of Alba thought of the grand duke in his distress indicates the role that Tuscany typically played. Tuscany's period of disfavor was, in any event, brief. The accession of Francesco I and the death of Charles IX in 1574, as well as the Spanish default on short-term debt in 1575, changed the political situation.[96] Tuscany had returned to Philip II's good graces by 1576.[97]

In 1579, Philip II borrowed 400,000 crowns from the grand duke of Tuscany as part of his campaign of rearmament in preparation for the invasion of Portugal.[98] In this, the Tuscans showed considerable political agility, for they had loaned the Portuguese 200,000 crowns for the disastrous invasion of Morocco, which sparked the succession crisis in the first place.[99] With such large financial commitments and strategic implications for Tuscany, Tuscan diplomats followed events in Portugal in extraordinary detail.[100] Indeed, the Spanish invasion of Portugal in 1580 seems to have been the apogee of Tuscan support for Spain, with the invoices for the recruitment and transportation of thousands of troops and the acquisition of thousands of small arms going straight to the grand duke. Francesco I also covered the cost of five of the Doria galleys used for transport and paid some wage arrears to unpaid *tercios*.[101] Tuscan military financing continued with a Spanish request for a loan of 400,000 ducats for Flanders in 1582.[102] Over the whole period of 1579–1583, the Medici and the Averona and Caccia, Carnesecchi, and Strozzi banks of Tuscany advanced Philip II a total of 1,414,667 *scudi*.[103] These were quite vast demands for a small state. The return of the Genoese and south German lenders reduced the Prudent King's pressure on Tuscany, but Philip II still borrowed 600,000 crowns from the Florentines in 1589.[104] These loans came with obvious and significant investment risks, but the risks, returns, and associated political benefits of sovereign lending had been familiar in Florence since at least the early fourteenth century.[105] Spain continued to default, as in 1596 and 1607. While this would eventually be costly for Tuscany, in the late sixteenth century the example of the Genoese seemed to show that lending to Philip II could be profitable.[106]

The Tuscan government may have had to write off at least part of the value of its loans, but it did not have to continue to make them if an alternative ally and protector emerged.[107] For a decade from the late 1580s, it seemed that Henry IV of France (r. 1589–1610) might play this role. Ferdinando I proceeded to marry Christine of Lorraine (1565–1637), a distant relative, the granddaughter of Queen Catherine de' Medici, who had been at her baptism in 1565.[108] Catherine de' Medici's marriage at the behest of her guardian, the Medici pope Clement VII, to the future King Henry II (r. 1547-1559) had demonstrated how a glittering French marriage could keep political options open for the Medici amid their dependence on the Spanish Habsburgs.[109] Cosimo I's cadet branch of the Medici adopted the same policy, tying Ferdinando I immediately to the House of Lorraine and pursuing an even more ambitious match for Francesco I's orphaned daughter Maria (1573-1642).[110] Marriage negotiations with Henry IV involved rumors of a 1,000,000 *scudi* dowry in 1592.[111] Seven years later, negotiations resumed with French hopes that the grand duke would cancel the debt of more than 1,000,000 *scudi del sole (écus au soleil)* that had accumulated over the years and for which the grand duke held the Château d'If and the Îles Pomègues as pledges.[112] So extensive was Tuscan financial involvement in France in these years that even the rebel regime in Marseilles asked for support in 1594, though that support was refused.[113] The dowry of 600,000 florins eventually agreed for Marie de' Medici by her uncle, Ferdinando I, and signed on April 25, 1600, consisted of 350,000 *scudi* in cash and 250,000 *scudi* in debt relief; this was the largest dowry of any queen of France to that date.[114] Medici Tuscany's extensive program of sovereign lending made it a strategically valuable ally and opened possibilities to which it would not otherwise have had access. With extensive holdings of Spanish and French debt and marriage ties not only to the French, Spanish, and Roman aristocracies but even with the French monarchy, Medici Tuscany's international recognition and influence were assured.

As in 1569, the turn to France in the 1590s did not provide Tuscany with complete independence from the Spanish monarchy, nor was it really intended to, for Tuscany remained tightly structurally intertwined with Spain. Disappointing levels of French support certainly played a role in foreclosing alternatives.[115] More substantively, Tuscany's geostrategic position and deep financial, military, religious, and familial entanglements with the Spanish Habsburgs and their alliance system in Italy meant that the French connection was never likely to bring complete independence. Deeper French political involvement would have required major military effort and made Tuscany a French instead of a Spanish client. Indeed, turning to France ultimately worked poorly for Duke Odoardo Farnese (1612–1646) and Duke Charles Gonzaga de Nevers (1580–1637) in the next generation, when France was much stronger and Spain much weaker.[116] Rather, the astute Ferdinando I appreciated that a French connection would help him to reject Spanish demands for infrequently honored loans and force the Spanish to abandon claims to overlordship over Siena. In this, Ferdinando succeeded.[117] Even so, as the obsequies to Philip II and Tuscany's continuing deep entanglements with the Habsburgs indicate, the changes in the alliance Ferdinando secured marked a renegotiation, not a rupture. Whether tilting toward Spain, as Tuscany did for most of the latter half of the sixteenth century and the first decades of the seventeenth century, or toward France, Tuscan access and influence was purchased at the price of large financial transfers and loans.

## Money and Tuscan Diplomats in Spain

The loans of ships and money that underpinned Tuscan foreign policy placed exacting demands on Tuscan diplomats. As we have seen, the service of Tuscan ships in the Spanish fleet was governed by complex, routinely renegotiated agreements. The regular movement of thousands of Tuscan subjects and valuable Tuscan military equipment very much into harm's way created numerous opportunities for friction even when the allies were in full agreement and funds forthcoming. To these challenges and the usual tensions in relations between powers that, after all, shared a border in Tuscany and concerned themselves with their respective relationships with third parties, were added a host of matters large and small. The present section considers the Tuscan diplomatic network's structure, practices, and costs as it sought to secure information and payment for Tuscany's extensive interests in Spain.

Ostensibly, the Medici ruled as absolute princes and nowhere more so than in foreign affairs. The development of a bureaucracy, co-optation of truculent Florentine elites and of non-Florentine Tuscans, and the use of new men to exert the prince's will, form the core of the political story of the new Medici state both at home and abroad in its first decades.[118] Alessandra Contini has argued that the Medici used diplomacy as a primary site to exercise autocratic power.[119] In practice, the men who ran the diplomatic network mattered greatly because they could carve out considerable scope for independent action. Ambassadors at major courts played important representational and social roles that dramatically constrained the possible choices, leading Cosimo I to generally select from the traditional patriciate.[120] For instance, Tuscany's ambassador in Madrid in 1580, Bernardo di Lorenzo Canigiani (1524–1604), a literary figure who had already had a distinguished career of diplomatic service to the Medici in Ferrara and at the Imperial court, appears to have been an efficient and regular correspondent, but he struggled with the language and employed a translator.[121] To exercise a measure of control over these patrician ambassadors and add to the embassy's capacity, ambassadors were accompanied by legation secretaries—often new men—who maintained an independent and close relationship with the grand duke.[122] Indeed, legation secretaries could maintain elements of a Medici mission even after the formal withdrawal of the ambassador.[123]

Well aware of the perquisites and honors of ambassadorships, the Medici exploited the private resources of their wealthy and prestigious subjects, forcing them to bear a substantial portion of the expenses.[124] For instance, Ambassador Leonardo di Antonio de' Nobili (1526–1574)—Tuscan ambassador to Philip II's court in 1565—sought more funds by providing a detailed account of his expenses incurred going to Spain and setting up his household.[125] His accounts indicate that he received 500 *scudi*, but that his expenses had amounted to more than double that: a further 685 *scudi*.[126] He appealed the next month to the first secretary of the prince of Florence, noting "the scarcity of the country, the expense of this court, and conforming to his greatness, he would want me to have reputation."[127] In a subsequent letter, the ambassador returned to his point about the connection between spending and reputation.[128] This reliance on the private funds of ambassadors was a two-way exercise of power. The prince's coercive authority and ability to grant honors gave him access to private resources.[129] On the other hand, the dependence on private resources constrained the choice of personnel. Although the cost savings of underpaying ambassadors were not insignificant, diplomatic personnel choices were also driven by considerations of political power, skill, loyalty, and symbolism.

The Tuscan diplomatic team in Spain typically consisted of an underpaid Florentine patrician ambassador, a highly qualified legation secretary with a direct relationship with the grand duke, the ambassador's household, and a wide assortment of agents at various levels often engaged in securing and transferring various objects for the Medici. As we have already seen with the case of Luigi Dovara and the Armada, agents might serve two lords openly when there was a confluence of interests. The service consisted above all in the transfer of information. Ambassadors wrote very regularly and extensively, as did their legation secretaries, filling volume after volume of the state archives in Florence with news, gossip, actions taken, information received, commentary and analysis, updates on ongoing matters, and more, usually taking care to assign each topic its own paragraph.[130] At the court of Europe's most powerful prince, many people, from ambassadors and agents to courtiers, servants, and visitors, had an interest in acquiring and exchanging information. In this context, Tuscan ambassadors took every opportunity to make use of temporary advantages, sharing dispatches that had traveled through Florence from the Levant with Philip II in 1565, for instance.[131] Generally, though, the Florentines sought secret information by paying bribes to the subordinates of the great officials.[132] More ambitiously, Cosimo I spent lavishly on his relationship with Charles V's leading minister, Nicolas Perrenot de Granvelle (1486–1550).[133] Tuscany richly deserved its reputation for corruption and espionage.

In subsequent chapters, we shall meet one of Tuscany's most accomplished secret ambassadors and follow the story of his high-stakes espionage and intrigue through war, torture, and an arduous journey by caravan over snowcapped mountains. Generally, though, diplomacy was not like that. The prosaic reality of most Tuscan diplomatic correspondence is that the vast majority of letters were sent in the clear and contained information that circulated reasonably openly. Its openness did not make the information unimportant, however, as the careful cataloging and retention of news over the centuries testify. Among the most important items for Tuscany was the arrival of bullion in Spain, which directly affected Spain's schedule of repayments to large creditors like Tuscany. For instance, a letter from Fabrizio Ferrari in Milan on August 6, 1561, reported the arrival of a fleet from the Indies and the expectation of another fleet coming from Peru; ships from the Viceroyalty of Peru can be reasonably assumed to have been carrying silver bullion.[134] On July 4, 1564, Garçes in Madrid reported the arrival of eleven ships from the Indies, apparently carrying bullion, and others from the island of San Domingo carrying sugar and hides.[135] Likewise, on November 17, 1567, in a typically omnibus letter, Ambassador de' Nobili reported on the arrival of five million from the Indies.[136] Indeed, diplomatic correspondence from the Iberian peninsula regularly contained notes on the arrival of bullion and other high-value goods destined both for the king and for other recipients.[137] Tuscan diplomats in Spain not only kept track of arrivals, but also of departures, as they did with 19 Spanish galleons that set out from Cádiz to fetch Peruvian silver in 1586.[138] Though Tuscan agents were careful to send this information, it also circulated publicly, as a 1569 *avviso* from Venice on the arrival of money from the Americas attests.[139] The Medici tracked this flow of funds so closely not only because of its direct impact on international power balances, but also and indeed perhaps primarily because they expected to receive this bullion in Tuscany. To this end, they retained a *relazione* from 1607 detailing the arrival of goods in Spain from Mexico, their value, and the sums due to a list of illustrious creditors.[140] The Tuscans could be quite explicit in drawing the connections. On July 17, 1609, a letter was sent to King Philip III of Spain in Spanish on behalf of the Tuscan ambassador requesting payment of Maria Magdalena von Habsburg's 300,000 *escudo* dowry as part of her marriage to Cosimo II; the funds were to come from American silver arriving in 1608–1610.[141]

For all the delays, frustrations, and shortfalls, large amounts of Spanish bullion did make its way to Italy, helping to power Genoese high finance and repay Spanish debts to Tuscany.[142] Florence, as a financial center, served as a vital link in transactions involving the movement of silver from Spain to its final destinations, which were often well beyond Tuscany.[143] Vast sums, sometimes millions at a time, moved out of Spain aboard the galleys to Italian and German recipients; it is not surprising that destined recipients included the grand duke of Tuscany.[144] In addition to these official shipments, bullion leaked out of Spain to Tuscany, especially to the port of Livorno, in small shipments, both licit and otherwise.[145] These transfers of silver required diligent attention and the watchful management of a state apparatus committed to the recovery of lent money.

The dangers of loans and the need to retain Medici wealth would be carefully passed on as instructions to the succeeding prince. A letter retained in the Österreichisches Staatsarchiv (Austrian States Archives) summarizes Cosimo II's secret testament as enjoining "And about the Treasure, with many prohibitions and serious penalties, he ordered that it should not be touched in any way, except in certain cases of necessity, which he declared, regarding the need and interest of the House. He expressly prohibited that either from the Guardians, or with the authority of the Council, during the minority of the Prince, could loans be made to any Prince, Republic, or Potentate, or other person, nor could it be allowed that similar Personages borrow from the Monte di Pietà of the City of Florence even if they offered security and a pledge in the states of His Highness, nor the could the same Guardians offer security, with many considerations and precepts."[146] Tuscany's international position was a fragile one, based on the prudent husbanding of resources and the careful management of relations. Beyond the usual fears about regencies looting the state, the Medici had particular cause for concern that Tuscany not be swept too deeply into the expanding maw of the just beginning Thirty Years' War. As it happened, Tuscany did manage the transition, and Ferdinando II (r. 1621–1670) carefully and, in Niccolò Capponi's analysis of his reign, rather successfully, managed Tuscany's difficult position.[147]

## Influence and Access

The ambitious Medici projects to involve themselves and their people in the expanding possibilities of the first global age explored in the following chapters were predicated on Tuscany's relationship with the major powers, above all the Spanish Habsburg monarchy. Neither Philip II and Philip III nor Henry IV would ultimately prove as accommodating to Medici ambitions as the Medici had hoped they would be. Even so, Tuscany achieved an impressive degree of access and influence for a small state run by the cadet branch of an upstart banking family. This chapter has shown how the Medici used their robust financial position and newly constructed naval forces to secure their relationship with the Spanish Habsburgs. Vast loans, some effectively grants, and prestigious marriages then built an alternative connection to France that allowed Tuscany to successfully renegotiate its alliance with Spain, an alliance to which its geostrategic situation had effectively committed it. Tuscany's position depended not only on its commitment of resources to the Spanish alliance, but also on its reputation for immense wealth, a potentially bountiful supplier of an empire in need. Whatever the reality of Medici wealth, Florentine diplomats actively worked to ensure that it was not unduly compromised by its commitments to Spain, negotiating hard-nosed naval contracts, pursuing compensation claims, and tracking bullion shipments. The relationship they negotiated laid the groundwork for the Tuscan state's efforts to follow the successful example of private Florentines and to develop a partnership with the Iberian overseas empires, as Chapter 2 explores.

## 2

# Cooperative Empire

*A*s the Medici dynasty became increasingly tightly bound to Iberian financial and military systems and Florentine patrician families pursued their fortunes in the Iberian Empires, a persistent idea emerged in several guises. Perhaps the Medici could make an arrangement with Portugal or Spain that would allow the Medici to buy into their overseas empires? This idea had the potential to transform the Iberian empires into open platforms for trade and investment that friendly individuals and states could join. Various versions of the idea of integrating Tuscany into a cooperative empire captured projectors' imaginations sufficiently to be proposed repeatedly. All failed. The failure of the proposals, however, is revealing, indicating both the importance of the choices made by princes and their councils and the structures that made those choices so consistently seem the right ones. The governing assumptions that underlay the eventual decision to exclude Tuscany pushed the Iberian empires off the path of accommodating others' ambitions within the capacious bounds of their monopoly claims—which they had experimented with repeatedly in the sixteenth century—and into the seventeenth-century world of competing mercantilist empires.

This monopolistic Iberian decision drove states either to withdraw from the contest for empire or to build their own, competing walled gardens. Many chose the latter course, which left the Iberian empires to fight a long, lonely, and increasingly unsuccessful defense of their old preeminence.[1]

Three types of proposals for bringing Tuscany into the Iberian empires became politically significant: (1) investment in an existing contract, (2) direct trade, (3) and shared colonial empire. Most persistent and least disruptive to Iberian structures was Tuscan investment in existing monopoly contracts. There were repeated proposals throughout the 1570s and 1580s for the Medici to acquire some or all of the distribution rights in Europe for the Portuguese pepper trade. This would have transformed Florence or, more probably, Pisa or Livorno into a Western European center of spice distribution in direct competition with Venice's lingering eastern Mediterranean trade. The Portuguese Crown also auctioned the contract for the import of spices from India to Portugal, both while independent and when held by the Spanish Habsburgs in the Iberian Union. The requirement that spices pass through Lisbon at a fixed price made the contract a financial speculation and a commercial organizational project with few ancillary economic development benefits.[2] The Medici were certainly not averse to financial speculation, but they typically preferred positive spillovers, whether political or economic, for Tuscany. Such spillovers were much more likely to occur from the contract to distribute spices in Europe. Tuscany would, counterintuitively, be more deeply transformed by imperial commerce if it focused on the European rather than Indian side of the trade.

Direct trade offered yet greater possibilities for economic development in Tuscany than the monopoly contracts. In the 1590s, the Medici repeatedly explored the introduction of a sugar refining industry to Livorno based on the direct importation of Brazilian sugar. Commercially, the venture was a plausible and much less state-dependent proposition that offered a viable path to maritime industrial development. Livorno's growth might have been even more dramatic than it already was had it become a direct participant in the burgeoning Atlantic economy. Technically, participation was not difficult to achieve, and, with the Cavalcanti, the Medici eventually secured a friend among the Brazilian sugar magnates. The matter hinged on making the politics work.

Finally, the Medici explored a much more explicitly political pair of projects in the first decade of the seventeenth century. These centered on the use of vast Medici wealth to create an appanage for a Medici prince. Rather than do so from Tuscany's distinctly modest territorial base at home, the Medici sought to emulate the success of expatriate Florentine patricians and acquire a Portuguese donatary captaincy. In this, they were geographically flexible and considered both Sierra Leone and Brazil. Should subinfeudation prove a political bridge too far, the Medici were also willing to consider the possibilities of licensed direct colonial trade.

Nearly four decades of detailed negotiations and analyses left the Medici with minimal state-sanctioned contacts with the colonial economies of the Iberian empires. As we shall see in subsequent chapters, the Medici would explore alternative paths oriented to collecting and intellectual engagement within the framework of Iberian empire. They would also dabble in much more aggressive and violent measures in defiance of Iberian restrictions. This chapter, by contrast, shows how the Medici sought to build on private Tuscan experience to craft a mutually beneficial partnership between the Tuscan state and the Iberian empires and why so many projects to do so ultimately failed.

## Private Florentines and Medici Ambitions

How did the Medici monarchy, effectively reestablished under Cosimo I, transform Florentine patterns of travel and trade? War, political revolution, and republican exile, especially in the decade 1527–1537, led major Florentine commercial families based abroad to follow time-honored tradition and reorient their interests to their host societies. For a time, many of these exited the Florentine political story. Yet the failure of the *fuorusciti* (exiles), the stabilization of the Medici regime, and Florence's dramatic demographic and economic recovery rendered the aftermath of the final defeat and Spanish Habsburg grant of Siena and most of its territories in 1557 a turning point.[3] No longer particularly troubled by threats to the regime's longevity, the Medici state willingly cooperated with existing Florentine commercial networks in the pursuit of global opportunities. For Florentines abroad, rising Medici political influence, especially in Habsburg Spain, but also in Portugal, France, the Holy Roman Empire, and the papacy, offered potentially invaluable assistance in a world of politically mediated commerce where large arbitrage and monopoly profits awaited the well connected. As important, Medici private wealth and large Tuscan fiscal surpluses combined with the lure of an increasingly opulent ducal, then grand ducal, court to attract Florentine merchants to the possibilities for wealth and preferment.

The Medici sought to weave together private Florentine webs of family, financial ties, and political influence with their own connections to secure access to the possibilities of Iberian empire. Family ties and Medici patronage allowed some Florentines to burrow through the barriers of national exclusion, but only if the politics could be managed. The Medici proved effective in supporting Florentine commercial families with their political influence, but such families' efforts to reciprocate and allow the Medici in through the back door faced political resistance. Nowhere was this more clearly apparent than in the Portuguese Empire.

Political turmoil in Florence and burgeoning economic opportunity in the Portuguese Empire in the early decades of the sixteenth century led Florentines first to Lisbon, where they had long been established as a prosperous merchant and banking community, and then to Portuguese overseas possessions. These footholds positioned them especially well to capitalize on and participate in the explosive growth of Portuguese commerce.[4] Even as some long-time resident Florentines acculturated and became increasingly Portuguese, relatively shorter-term resident Florentines, like Filippo Sassetti, also thought highly of Lisbon. Indeed, Sassetti wrote of it as one of the finest cities in Europe, praising its climate and its harbor filled with hundreds of ships coming with a rich and diverse array of goods from around Europe and the coasts of Brazil, Africa, and India.[5] Attracted by the opportunities so evident in the world's commerce riding at anchor in Lisbon, Florentines boarded the Carreira da Índia and set sail for the widely dispersed outposts of the Portuguese Estado da Índia.[6] These Florentine travelers to Asia included members of patrician houses whose surnames punctuate the story of Florence's golden fifteenth century. Lorenzo Strozzi, for instance, lived in Goa and served as banker to Filippo Sassetti, handling

Sassetti's money transfer to Goa.[7] Medici power in Florence depended on co-opting as many of these patricians as possible and excising the irreconcilables.[8] Even families of exiles usually made their eventual peace with the Medici.

The house of Giraldi traced this Florentine patrician trajectory in spectacular fashion. Luca Giraldi (1493–1565) first appears in Lisbon in 1515 and would decisively transfer his base there with his brother Niccolò in 1527.[9] As committed Florentine republicans, they opted for exile but retained commercial connections with Florence and especially other Florentine families. Luca's career illustrates the remarkable opportunities of what has been called "a world on the move," ranging from entering into the sugar business in Madeira to captaining a ship to India (1540) and becoming a Portuguese noble (1550s).[10] The intersection of their continuing Florentine ties and their new Portuguese status placed the Giraldi in a strong position to serve Portuguese elites in their financial transactions with Rome.[11]

As seems often to have been the case with Florentine patricians, intermarriage created a web of connections that underpinned far-flung commercial and financial ties across generations. The Giraldi, for instance, built robust connections with two other ancient and famous Florentine houses, the Capponi and Cavalcanti. Luca Giraldi's younger brother Giovanni married Argentina di Jacopo di Piero Guicciardini. Their daughters, Costanza and Caterina, married Giovan Battista di Tommaso Cavalcanti and Gio di Arcangelo Cavalcanti, and their son Vincenzo married Luisa Capponi. Luca Giraldi was the son of Niccolò di Giovanni Giraldi and Margherita di Luca di Agostino Capponi and retained financial ties in the Roman bank with his niece's husband Giovan Battista Cavalcanti. That is, the Giraldi, Cavalcanti, and Capponi who played such a prominent role in the early Portuguese Empire were a repeatedly intermarried set of families.[12] We have met the Giraldi-Cavalcanti already on the other side of a dispute with the Orsini, yet neither this conflict nor republican principles nor their pursuit of Portuguese interests left them isolated from Florence and the Medici. First, however, both the Giraldi and the Cavalcanti vigorously pursued burgeoning opportunities in early colonial Brazil.

The distinctive Portuguese approach to colonization on the coast of Brazil gave expatriate Florentine patricians the chance to play a prominent role. Enthralled by the vast commercial and strategic prospects opening from Mozambique to Malacca, Portuguese interest in Brazil in the early sixteenth century was confined to the trade in brazilwood through coastal *feitorias*. Only with the emergence of a serious French interloping threat did the Portuguese Crown seek to exert tangible control, dispatching a royal expedition (1530–1534) under Martim Afonso de Sousa to expel the French and create a settlement near Santos. Cognizant that Portuguese royal resources were insufficient to fund Brazil's rapid colonization, the Crown drew on Portugal's experience with Atlantic island colonization as a model for mobilizing private resources. In 1532–1533, Afonso de Sousa divided the coast claimed by the Portuguese into fifty-league captaincies; the pattern was later extended north to the Amazon in 1534–1536. The Crown ultimately granted fifteen donations (*doação*—hence donatary) of hereditary and ostensibly inalienable captaincies to twelve recipients. Serving as political and military leaders vested with judicial and fiscal rights, the donatary captains were to stand between the king and the subgrantees *(sesmeiros)* who were charged with developing the land. Ten captaincies were quickly established, two of which, Pernambuco and São Vicente, prospered immediately. As anticipated, developing ports, sugar mills, and shipping and fighting wars with (justifiably) aggrieved Amerindians whose lands were being expropriated cost a fortune.[13]

The captains' consequent financial distress opened the way to Florentine bankers like Luca Giraldi. In 1547, Giraldi invested in colonization rights in the captaincy of São Jorge dos Ilhéus, where he held one of the four *sesmarias*. He had a mill built and invested alongside the other *sesmeiros* in sugar production, bringing both slaves from Guinea and agricultural animals, tools, and people from Lisbon. War with the Tupinkin wrought considerable damage, leading Jerónimo de Alarção de Figueiredo, son and heir to the original captain, to sell the captaincy of Ilhéus to Giraldi in 1561 for 4,825 *cruzados*.[14] The same Giraldi political position that facilitated Luca's acquisition of Ilhéus underpinned his legitimized son Francesco's illustrious career in royal service, as Portuguese ambassador to France and England and royal governor of Bahia.[15] Francesco also inherited his father's Brazilian captaincy with royal approval on February 23, 1566.[16]

Becoming Portuguese had been a great success, but the Giraldi did not abandon their Florentine roots. Indeed, Francesco Giraldi and his cousin Vincenzo were in Florence in 1560. When Francesco was Portuguese ambassador in England in the 1570s, he corresponded with Vincenzo in Florence.[17] At some point, Francesco Giraldi also developed links with the Medici. After he was appointed Portuguese royal governor of Bahia, he wrote to Francesco I on November 1, 1586, to offer his service to the grand duke.[18] In late December 1586, Francesco I wrote to Francesco Giraldi to ask that "when some curiosity or seeds come to your hands, which are not here" in Tuscany that he send them.[19] Giraldi seems to have replied with relative alacrity, since the Medici ambassador to Spain, Vincenzo di Andrea Alamanni (1537–1591), wrote to Ferdinando I from Madrid on April 30, 1588, that he was sending a case he had received from *cavaliere* Francesco Giraldi.[20] Exotic plants were important to the Medici, but the correspondence extended to other subjects; Governor Giraldi also reported that the Crown of Portugal was severely afflicted by English raids.[21] For Giraldi, loyalty to Portugal and to Florence could coexist. For the Medici, the Giraldi family offered access to exotica, information, and the highest levels of Luso-Brazilian society.

The Giraldi with interests in Brazil and those partnered in the Giraldi-Cavalcanti bank of Rome both developed connections—from loans and gift exchange to the sharing of political information—to the Medici and their extended network. The ties seem to have been discontinuous and occasionally acrimonious, but they indicate that the house of Giraldi remained linked to Florence. The relationship was consistent with Florentine commercial traditions based on geographically extensive development of family networks. Florentine patrician families had long developed and maintained investments in family clusters of firms or in dynastic firms in a variety of partnership structures that, while not always confined to a single family, tended to involve a fairly limited set of partners.[22] In this context, some members of a lineage were nearly always away from Florence—often for a long, but frequently ultimately temporary, stay—even as the family maintained its status at home.[23] As political influence and commercial opportunity traveled along chains of friendship and affinity, cultivating open-ended connections might offer the prudent house support, protection, or opportunity in the future.

The Giraldi's partners in Rome, the Cavalcanti, likewise both set down deep roots in Brazil and maintained connections to the Medici.

The principle source for their family history, Scipione Ammirato (1531–1601), expressed the underlying attitude to the importance of the lineage in his manuscript *History of the Cavalcanti Family* and his posthumously published *Of the Noble Florentine Families* (1615).[24] As Luca Giraldi had done earlier in the century, Filippo Cavalcanti set out from Florence for Lisbon around 1550. From there, he crossed the Atlantic to Olinda, center of the dynamic sugar region of Pernambuco, in northeastern Brazil. There he married Donna Caterina, daughter of Lord Girolamo Albuquerque, whose noble Portuguese family provided him with equipment for sugar refining. Turning himself into a wealthy sugar magnate, Filippo Cavalcanti and Caterina Cavalcanti (née Albuquerque)'s children became part of the emergent Luso-Brazilian colonial elite. The Portuguese practice of primogeniture made Antonio Cavalcanti, born in 1560, Filippo's main heir. Antonio's long service to the Spanish Habsburgs and marriage to Lady Isabella di Vasconsalos secured the position of their large family—eleven of twenty children were alive at the time of Ammirato's writing—and of his principal heir Girolamo, who was also wealthy and in Spanish service.[25]

As a Brazilian sugar magnate with a record of Spanish Habsburg service, Antonio Cavalcanti occupied a position similar to Francesco Giraldi's. The intersection of their residual Florentine status and their effective integration into the Portuguese elite made them attractive allies for a globally ambitious Medici monarchy. It was in this context that the Medici decided to help Antonio Cavalcanti with a problem. Writing to Ferdinando I from Madrid on April 16, 1607, Tuscan ambassador Sallustio Tarugi explained that Antonio Cavalcanti had requested Medici support in proving that, far from being Florentine, Antonio was authentically Luso-Brazilian. Tarugi wrote, "Antonio Cavalcanti, who lives in Brazil, has showed me a letter of the Grand Duke our Lord in which His Highness says that, having ordered Signor Roderigo Alidosi his Ambassador in that time with the name, authority and favor of His Highness to help and favor certain pretensions of the said Cavalcanti, by virtue of the same letter and order, he would now like me to speak to these Lords of the Council of Portugal and where it would be necessary for the good dispatch of his pretensions, which must be, as far as I understand, to be declared natural to these Kingdoms and eligible for all the favors and privileges that are customarily enjoyed by naturals and noblemen."[26]

Not knowing Cavalcanti's identity, Ambassador Tarugi was understandably perplexed.[27] Alidosi had been ambassador in Spain in 1602 and was the Medici envoy to Poland by 1605, so Cavalcanti's letter from the grand duke probably dates to 1602–1604.[28] The situation was certainly fraught with irony, but it also points to the mechanisms of influence and favor exchange that lay at the heart of Florentine penetration of the Iberian empires. Medici influence could offer Cavalcanti a way out of a Portuguese legal dead end that stood in the way of his hopes. Perhaps Cavalcanti influence in the world of Brazilian sugar might also have been most useful to the Medici had their ambitions come to fruition. An explicit *quid pro quo* was unlikely, but the doing and receiving of favors was the essence of power, and Florentine patricians abroad suited Medici power projection of this sort quite well.

## Florentine Patricians and the Portuguese Spice Trade

The spice trade, like many early modern commodity trades, rested on a fairly clear dynamic. Efficient production was concentrated at points geographically distant from the centers of demand. The cost of production was a very small percentage of the market price at which large quantities could be sold in far-off markets across Eurasia. The business was, then, superficially a straightforward arbitrage in which transportation, security, and taxation costs and political and military limits on competition determined profits. In fact, markets mechanisms interacted with politics and violence in complex ways in a trade that involved arbitrage in multiple directions. Bullion and coined money were also commodities, and payment took place not only in coinage metals but also in various commodities that served as money. The trade worked as regularly as it did because coinage metals, especially silver, were much more valuable in Asia than in Europe. As a result, the shipment of bullion was also subject to arbitrage dynamics. Trade could be a three-way transaction because payment at points of production in what is now Indonesia was often in Indian cloth, which Europeans acquired in India with silver, which in turn typically came from mines in the viceroyalty of Peru or, later, New Spain. Though often caricatured as having nothing substantive to offer but violence—an impression reinforced by the periods when the Portuguese and Dutch sought to shoot their way into monopolies and by the violence of later European empires—most European business in Asia did not take place at gunpoint. The reason was, in part, of course, that Asian states had rather more guns on the ground than Europeans did into the eighteenth century. It was also because, starting with the Portuguese, Europeans regularly settled into mutually beneficial commercial relationships with Asian merchants. Europeans offered a reliable transportation service that resulted from a combination of new and old routes, which provided Asian producers with access to a much larger array of markets. The Europeans did so in often violent competition with traditional intermediaries and port cities, but the infrastructure they established and the access to bullion and weapons it provided proved popular with many Asian merchants.[29]

Just as there was more to Europe's position in Asia than cannon mounted amidships, so also the focus on the high-value spice trade itself can be misleading. Certainly, European naval power remained essential to their position, and the quest for spice monopoly profits led both the Portuguese and the Dutch east. But the reality of running the Portuguese Estado da Índia—the Portuguese empire of ports and forts in Asia, the Middle East, and East Africa governed from Goa—differed markedly from this simple model. Intra-Asian trade, what would come to be called the country trade, and, from the 1550s, the Portuguese Crown's sale of rights to royal monopoly voyages in the areas under the Estado da Índia's jurisdiction, provided a dramatic boost to the prosperity of the *Estado*, though not necessarily to the royal treasury.[30] Even on the Cape Route, the great artery of the spice trade, the records of the ships' manifests tell a different story from that which we have come to expect. James Boyajian has shown that the truly valuable part of the *Carreira da Índia*—the annual voyage linking Lisbon and India—under the Habsburgs was private trade, which in 1580–1599 constituted only 40 percent of the weight, but 91 percent of the value, of the *Carreira*.[31] Still more striking, his analysis of surviving complete manifests of *Carreira* cargo from 1580 to 1640 indicates that 62 percent of the value was in textiles, 14 percent was in diamonds and other gems, and 22 percent in the broad category of *drogas*.[32] The pepper trade was central to the king's finances, but not the basis for the Estado da Índia.[33]

Although the pepper trade no longer constituted the core of the *Carreira da Índia*, it remained a very large business. The typical annual gross state revenues of the Carreira da Índia amounted to some 390,000 *scudi* in 1580–1588 out of the total Portuguese state revenue of about 1,664,000 *scudi*.[34] The revenues from the Carreira da Índia could be imagined in purely financial terms for the same reason that Tuscan participation was possible, because the Crown treated the rights to participation in various elements of the trade as financial instruments. From the 1560s, the Portuguese had been moving away from their old system of direct royal exploitation of the pepper monopoly on the Cape of Good Hope route to a contract model in which royal rights were sold for a five-year period.[35]

After Philip II's conquest of Portugal—financed with Tuscan money, as we have seen—he quickly sought to restore his finances by selling contracts for royal rights to the Cape of Good Hope trade route. By 1586, even the right to collect customs duties in Lisbon on arriving cargoes from Asia had been sold.[36] Investors could bid for contracts for the customs; for carracks for the voyage, typically five per year at a fixed price of 50,000 *cruzados* each; for the contract to import pepper to royal warehouses in Lisbon; and for the contract to buy that pepper at double the import price for distribution throughout Europe.[37] Since the *Carreira* was within the royal prerogative, the Habsburgs could and did assign its revenues to their creditors to finance warfare.[38] From the Spanish Habsburg perspective, the result was to extract revenues from the Portuguese portion of the empire for general use. For the Medici, who were among the Crown's major creditors, it would not have been a long step to go from receiving payments funded by spice contracts revenues to assuming the contracts directly.

As with so many Medici ventures, a Florentine patrician family both showed the way into the spice business and offered a cautionary tale. We have met Luca Giraldi as the Florentine who transformed himself into a Portuguese noble and financier, a commander of ships to India, and a donatary captain of Portuguese Brazil. His story is inextricably intertwined with those of the intermarried Italian merchant families of Lisbon and Antwerp, with their many ties to Florence and Rome, who played a prominent role in financing the Portuguese spice trade. Luca Giraldi enters this story first through the Affaitati family, originally of Cremona but based in Antwerp, who assumed a major role in the Portuguese sugar and spice trades. Relatively early in his career,

in 1529, Luca Giraldi served as procurator for Giovanni Francesco Affaitati (d. 1529), who, shortly before his death, had arranged to be the
monopoly importer of sugar from Madeira.[39]

Luca Giraldi's close relationship with the Affaitati would ultimately offer him a remarkable opportunity to enter the spice trade. In
1532, Giovanni Carlo Affaitati (1500–1555) and Diogo Mendes secured
a monopoly on Portuguese spices from King John III (r. 1521–1557).[40]
They then created a consortium to bear the vast costs associated with
this privilege. The arrangement rapidly fell into crisis with Diogo
Mendes's arrest by the Inquisition on suspicion of heresy and assisting
New Christian—typically the descendants of forcibly converted Iberian
Jews—emigration to the Levant. Even after Portuguese royal intercession secured his release, shipping goods under the Mendes name was
dangerous, and so Giovanni Carlo Affaitati brought Luca Giraldi and
a group of New Christians resident in Lisbon, but well known in Antwerp, into the business.[41] As Nunziatella Alessandrini has persuasively
argued, the privilege granted on August 6, 1533, to Luca Giraldi to trade
in any type of nonprohibited merchandise from India, including spices,
was probably closely related to his new position in the spice syndicate.[42]

The Mendes-Affaitati partnership continued to operate on an extraordinarily large scale, dealing in the 1540s in 40,000 quintals of
spices valued at 1–2 million *cruzados* and making King John III such
large loans that he owed 2,169,252 *cruzados* by 1543. By 1554, the king
could not sustain his debts. He renegotiated them, removed spice mar-
keting from the Affaitati in Antwerp, and brought the sale of spices to
Lisbon.[43] In the meantime, Luca Giraldi had considerably deepened
his involvement with the Portuguese Estado da Índia, serving as the
captain of the ship *Urca* on its voyage to India in 1540 and likewise on
the *Bom Jesus* in 1551. A wealthy man, Luca Giraldi was the shipowner
together with Álvaro Barradas of the ship *Espirito Santo* in 1544. Together with his younger brother Niccolò Giraldi, Luca Giraldi was also
the shipowner of the *Nossa Senhora do Loreto* in 1553. That same year, he
seems to have shrugged off an Inquisition denunciation for a decade
of illicit trade in Morocco.[44] Even as Luca Giraldi successfully integrated his family into the Portuguese elite, his son reinforced the ties
with the Affaitati that had helped to make the family fortune. Luca retained strong business links, and his son Francesco eventually married

Lucrezia de Lafetá, daughter of Giovanni Carlo Affaitati and Lucrezia Affaitati and niece of Count Affaitati.[45]

For all their immense wealth, the extended family network of elite Italian financiers in Antwerp and Lisbon that the Giraldi had joined struggled to handle their interests in the spice business in the decades after the withdrawal of the Affaitati contract. In 1560, Luca Giraldi and Jacome de' Bardi joined with Diogo de Castro and Diogo Martins in a four-year contract with the Portuguese Crown. The contract stipulated that they should annually send 100,000 *cruzados* for pepper purchases and dispatch five ships to India. Fulfilling the contract proved beyond their resources and they asked to be excused a year early.[46] In 1570, Luca Giraldi—this was probably Niccolò Giraldi and D. Caterina de Sousa's eldest son who became a *moço fidalgo* (first class, third rank fidalgo) on June 4, 1556, since the elder Luca Giraldi had died in 1565[47]—received from the young King Sebastian (1554–1578; r. 1557–1578) a five-year contract to send ships to India; Giraldi's venture ultimately failed and the contract was taken up by António Calvo.[48] Major Florentine patrician families had thus already been involved in the challenging business of spice contracting for decades when, in the 1570s, the Medici sought to enter the spice trade.

## The Medici and the Spice Trade

The repeated failure of spice contracts in the 1560s and 1570s opened the way to new entrants able to operate on a grand scale and willing to bid for the contracts on the basis of broader economic and political interests. Though not yet the King of Coin, the Medici grand duke of Tuscany certainly had the financial resources to consider a bid. As important, patrician Florentine banking families' decades of activity in the Portuguese spice business and involvement with the Portuguese Carreira da Índia meant that the Grand Duke might reasonably expect to be able to secure precise and reliable information. Early in his reign, Francesco I took the plunge.

In 1575, the grand duke joined in the creation of a Tuscan pepper import company focused on bringing pepper from Lisbon. Francesco I acted as the lead investor, putting in 100,000 ducats. Though anchored by this major investment, the company's prospects also relied on the concerted efforts of a familiar group of families formed into a consortium: the Cavalcanti and Giraldi and the Bardi and Giraldi of Lisbon and the Bardi and Affaitati of Madrid. The Bardi and Giraldi of Lisbon were to take the lead in importing pepper, and the company's administration included Jacome de' Bardes (Jacopo de' Bardi). The plan was to have the company bring pepper from Lisbon and use the proceeds to buy Tuscan goods, primarily grain. These goods would be shipped in the galleys of the grand duchy and the proceeds from the transaction invested in uncut diamonds.[49]

The same year, 1575, Francesco I sent an ambassador to Portugal to negotiate for the so-called contract of Europe, the monopoly right to distribute Portuguese spices in Europe.[50] Tuscany's ambassador was unsuccessful, losing out to a consortium that included a familiar Florentine family, the Bardi. In 1576, the contracts of Asia and of Europe instead went to a German-Portuguese-Italian consortium led by Conrad Rott that included Jacome de' Bardes, Diego de Castro, Giovan Battista Rovellasca, and the Welsers.[51] Tuscany's failure to acquire the pepper monopolies of 1575 ultimately proved to be a boon in disguise when King Sebastian suspended the consortium's rights in 1577–1578, a suspension that was not lifted until the king's death in battle brought a new monarch.[52]

The repeated failures and suspensions of contracts bespeak a persistent structural problem in the political economy of the Portuguese spice trade. The prize might be glittering, but only if the terms were shrewdly negotiated and the contract honored. For a regime as financially savvy as that of the Medici to consider taking on such a risk required a commensurately attractive reward, though not necessarily a direct financial one. As we have seen, the Medici made a policy of undertaking major financial commitments in the pursuit of primarily political advantages even as they hoped to avoid losing money on their loans. In the case of the pepper trade, the ancillary benefits of the pepper contract attracted them. A letter sent on December 26, 1576, from Madrid to Antonio Serguidi, secretary to Francesco I, clearly articulates the rationale for investing.[53] In it, the legation secretary to the Tuscan embassy in Spain, Oliverotto Guidotti, relates the substance of a suggestion made by the Portuguese ambassador.[54] In Guidotti's telling, the Portuguese ambassador laid out a broad vision of why Tuscany ought to acquire the distribution rights to

Portugal's spices. It is striking that detailed discussion of the direct profitability of the spice sales had nowhere near the central role one might expect. Instead, the benefits of Tuscany's assumption of the spice contract would include a return to reputation and greatness, low-cost access to armed ships, advantages in distributing Florence's textiles, primacy in Italy, and the chance to improve the Florentines' position relative to the Genoese in Spain. Whether the argument was an accurate assessment of the Portuguese ambassador's suggestion or a disguised memorandum from Guidotti advocating a policy position that was evidently congenial to him, the rationale laid out for Tuscan involvement is strongly oriented to political and secondary economic benefits, not the profitability of spice sales.[55]

The Medici did not receive the contract, but Fernand Braudel suggests a link between a loan of 200,000 crowns made by the Medici and Florentine merchants to King Sebastian at this time and a large shipment of pepper to Livorno.[56] A letter sent from Antonio Vecchietti in Lisbon on September 27, 1576, likewise reports a large shipment of pepper due to arrive in Livorno from Marseille.[57] Hard on the heels of the Venetian-Ottoman War (1570–1573) that had resulted in the Venetian loss of Cyprus (1571) and the Holy League's victory at Lepanto (also 1571), this Florentine interest in the pepper trade alarmed the Venetians. As late as 1570, the Medici had ordered spices from Venice.[58] Indeed, while the glory days of the fifteenth-century spice profits were long past, Venice continued to play a major role in the spice trade. Venice could continue to compete by taking advantage of difficulties in Portuguese Atlantic shipping, the Portuguese shift to licensed trade in the Indian Ocean, and Portugal's failure to achieve absolute mastery of the Indian Ocean, the Red Sea, and the Persian Gulf. Together, these Portuguese difficulties allowed spice supplies onto the Levantine caravan routes and undermined the economics of the Atlantic trade. Even as the Venetians suffered at the hands of the Ottomans on Cyprus, they had had cause to appreciate the Ottoman ability and willingness to contest Portuguese control of the Indian Ocean.[59] In this context, Florentine ambitions could provoke alarm in Venice. Braudel cites a report from Venice to Philip II in which the Venetians, pointing to the grand duke's negotiations with the Ottomans, are said to have alleged that the grand duke's "aim was nothing less than the world monopoly of pepper."[60]

This was closer to Venice's remembered fifteenth-century prosperity than to Tuscany's contemporary conditions and wildly overstated Tuscany's ability to secure peaceful, let alone profitable, relations with the Ottoman Empire, but it registers Venice's fears about the grand duke's ambitions.

In the late 1570s, the Venetians were certainly right that the Tuscans were becoming deeply involved in the spice business. Tuscany imported some 3,157 sacks of pepper from 1577 to 1579, an enterprise that Marica Milanesi has suggested may have involved Filippo Sassetti.[61] Be that as it may, Filippo Sassetti eventually took up the chief pepper purchasing post in India for Giovan Battista Rovellasca, one of the principals of the Rott-Rovellasca-led consortium that held the first pepper contract (1580–1585) after the Iberian Union (1580–1640).[62] With Filippo Sassetti in such a prominent role in the pepper business, Francesco I, Cardinal Ferdinando de' Medici, and the network of Florentine elites to whom Sassetti was attached all gained access to a formidable source of information both on the spice trade and the broader regional context.

Filippo Sassetti's role as a provider of a wide range of information on the Indian Ocean world in general and the Estado da Índia in particular will be considered later, but a few of his key insights pertain so directly to the spice trade that they belong here. First and foremost, Sassetti was a formidable critic of the Carreira da Índia. The failure of his first voyage to India and a miserable second voyage certainly did not improve his opinion.[63] Still, his criticism ran deeper than the complaints of a traveler and pointed to structural problems that may well have given the Medici pause. Noting the losses of sailors overboard and the miserable conditions for the soldiery, Sassetti wrote to Francesco I from Cochin on January 22, 1584, "If you consider the manner of treatment of these poor people in a voyage that is quite troublesome, it will be a greater miracle that four or six percent live than if all of them died, because, if the king spends as much as would be necessary to send his soldiers comfortably, all come to be robbed by the captain, dispensers, clerks, guards, and others above, these set up shop on the hardship and hunger of the poor people with nobody listening to their resentments, waiting for the thieves and everything else that the officials of the land feel like on their part, leading the dissolution to the point of selling the water set aside for munitions."[64] The diagnosis was clear: corruption and mismanagement plagued the ships on which the spice trade depended. Sassetti, watching the terrible havoc that scurvy wreaked on this poorly provided crew, described the illness's progression to death and lamented at the end that "the dispenser shares out their advances with the other officials, and they return home rich and well provided."[65] Corruption and death haunted the *Carreira da Índia*.

Modern scholarship tends to agree with the judgment that something was terribly amiss. James Boyajian has pointed to three types of problem: the structure of the contracts for the shipping, which encouraged corner cutting; naval conservatism, a focus on troop transportation, and the liberties granted to officers and crew, which led to the use of overlarge ships with a hazardous design; and late sailing caused by the monarchy's underinvestment.[66] For Sassetti, however, the problem was not so much structural as a result of corruption and neglect that might easily be remedied by the correction of personal misconduct through supervision. He wrote to Francesco I, "because I am treating of the transport of soldiers, Your Highness knows in what manner they are led whence you will know consequently with what great ease, notwithstanding the length of the voyage, that it would be possible to transport the same people if they were honestly provided and if the officials that led them had to render accounts, which they do not have to do in Portugal, of the things that were given and laden for the sustenance of the soldiers."[67] Since the grand duke was unlikely to send soldiers of his own to India, this analysis would have been primarily useful in aiding the grand duke's approach to the pepper contract. The problems facing the Carreira da Índia were serious and in need of remedy before the Medici invested, but competent and efficient administration could solve them. Whether the Medici could have provided that is uncertain, but their heavy investment in Tuscany's centralized bureaucracy suggests that they may well have been confident of their state's administrative prowess.

Sassetti's letters constituted a bounteous source of information for the Medici on many aspects of the Estado da Índia, but perhaps none would have been more immediately useful than his report on the contest for control of the spice trade. The value of the Portuguese spice contracts in Lisbon fundamentally depended on how effective the Portuguese were in interdicting alternative sources of supply across the Middle East and on to Venice.[68] In a letter sent to Francesco I from Cochin on February 11, 1585, Sassetti wrote, "Of the cloves, nutmeg, and mace that the same Javanese carry from the Moluccas and the cinnamon, which from Ceylon is carried by the Moors, they load the ships for Mecca in December and entering the channels of the islands of the Maldives, they emerge and take the route of the coast of Arabia and they enter the Red Sea where sometimes a Portuguese fleet goes."[69] Characteristically, Sassetti then attributed Portuguese efforts to close the Red Sea to a corrupt personal motivation. Still, he noted that there was some prospect of taking Aden and building a fortress to block the arrival of spices in Alexandria.[70] Sassetti concisely sketched the dynamics of a contest stretching from what is now eastern Indonesia to Egypt. In this struggle, Portuguese actions at the Bab el Mandeb, separating Yemen from what is now Djibouti, would influence the spice market of Alexandria that supplied the Venetians. Sassetti's letter thus gave the grand duke a framework for understanding how strategic developments in the Indian Ocean would affect prices in Italy.

The vast geographic scope of the spice trade called for equally grand and wide-ranging undertakings to secure anything approximating control. In his 1585 letter to Francesco I, Sassetti offered a concise account of the projects of the Estado da Índia as they ranged from southeast Africa to southeast Asia:

> In these parts, there are planned three undertakings of great importance. One is the discovery of a silver mine, that they say the mineral keeps the *** of Plata [silver] in a river called Cuamo near Sofala and Mozambique, where there remains a band of Portuguese who went to discover it. The second undertaking is the conquest of the island of Ceylon. That island is possessed by a pagan prince called *Ragiù* who is a very great enemy of the Portuguese. Faced with almost continuous travail, they have maintained a fortress called Colombo, located on the western part of Ceylon. Each year, they spend a great deal of money on it for both maintenance and defense. The third undertaking is the conquest of a port on the island of Sumatra that they call Dacem. Today,

it is controlled by Moors, although the island itself is controlled by diverse pagan kings. But these dogs [the Moors]
enter through dissimulation and are honored by the pa-
gans. In this port, they load three quarters of the ships that
carry spices to Mecca and Suez, because from that place
they ship pepper that we call *gauro*, which comes from the
island of Java and from a place they call Sunda.[71]

All three projects would have had a direct impact on the spice trade. The
conquest of Ceylon (now Sri Lanka) would have given the Portuguese
control of cinnamon production.[72] Sassetti made plain the role the seizure of Dacem (probably Pacem, the Portuguese rendering of the important spice trading port of Pasai) on Sumatra would have had in disrupting the competing Muslim spice trade.[73] The confluence of religious
fervor and fierce commercial competition may account for Sassetti's po-
lemically anti-Muslim language in discussing this venture. Finally, the
African silver mine might well have been nearly as consequential as interdicting the Islamic spice trade. The Portuguese spice trade depended
on the importation of Atlantic silver. A source of supply along the preferred Portuguese route to India, at a resupply point no less, would have
been quite a boon to the balance of payments.

In his next annual letter to Francesco I of February 10, 1586, from
Cochin, Sassetti returned to an account of the wide scope of Portuguese actions. He recounted Portuguese preparation of a fleet that was
gathering to head first to the Red Sea and then to the Persian Gulf,
there to support the Safavid Shah.[74] Fittingly for an agent of the spice
monopoly, Sassetti thought that a move by the Portuguese fleet against
Dacen (probably Dacem) in Sumatra "would be the best thing in the
world."[75] Sassetti provided the Medici with a sharp critical analysis of
the Carreira da Índia and the state of Portuguese efforts to secure the
Indian Ocean spice trade. The information would have been of considerable use in making judgments about the prudence of entering the
spice trade through the Portuguese spice contracts. If the Cape of Good
Hope fleets were unreliable and the Indian Ocean fleets were insuffi-
ciently effective in choking off Red Sea supplies, then the Portuguese
claim to monopoly would have been hollow and the high prices that
that might command unsupportable.

Philip II's ultimate dissatisfaction with the Rott-Rovellasca consortium Sassetti had served led the Prudent King to seek other Italian partners. He offered the Venetians the contract as early as 1581 and discussions of that continued unsuccessfully until 1584; a second offer was made in 1585.[76] Certainly some Venetians thought they should accept, in part for fear that the contract would be offered to Tuscany instead, as indeed it was. As it happened, neither the Florentines nor the Venetians found the terms Philip II offered sufficiently congenial and declined to take up the contract.[77] Whatever the real level of Venetian interest in buying Portuguese pepper, the Tuscans certainly kept tabs on such discussions, for a letter, perhaps from 1587, held in the archives of the Medici in Florence contains a report on Venetian-Spanish negotiations on the pepper trade.[78]

Tuscany's concern for Venetian interest in the pepper trade stemmed not only from strategic competition but also from a serious investigation of the possibilities of Tuscany accepting Philip II's 1587 proposal. To this end, Francesco I wrote to one of Tuscany's deeply experienced diplomats, the ambassador in Madrid, Vincenzo di Andrea Alamanni.[79] The grand duke began, "We have been persuaded and invited to take the contract offered by His Catholic Majesty [Philip II] for all of the pepper from India taken to Portugal and to make the contract in our name and then in accordance with usual we will be able to distribute the pepper where we judge there to be space and give part of the said contract to our vassals and also in accordance with what will be our pleasure and convenience."[80] This was to be the traditional contract of Europe with the grand duke taking the lead role, behaving just as other Italian patrician financiers did. We can readily imagine the list of Tuscan families who might have been among "our vassals," having seen the Bardi, Cavalcanti, and Giraldi involved in spice trading above. Francesco I followed this opening with an easy assurance, perhaps derived from experience with heavy lending to Philip II and cooperation in the preparation of the Armada, set to sail the next year. He wrote, "And because we love to treat with his Highness our association with him will make it easy to agree on honest and reasonable things, but because we have not been fully informed in what state are the negotiations we desire, ahead of a government resolution, to know the things and appreciate their important points."[81] The grand duke followed this hopeful prelude with a series of probing questions about exact prices, the volume of pepper on offer—"Look to learn the precise sum, or thereabouts of the pepper that his Catholic Majesty wants to give to the Contractor"—and the terms and conditions.[82] These last included an inquiry about the details of the consignment schedule and the timing of payment to be made in Lisbon.[83] The grand duke then returned to a precise insistence on a maximum price and an injunction to Ambassador Alamanni to "Get more certain information if you can what amount of pepper now remains in Lisbon in the hands of the *Casa della Contrattione*, how much in the hands of particular others."[84] As a prudent investor ought, Francesco I then asked Alamanni to investigate "which are the merchants usually interested in the contracts" and specifically to ask for "information from Girolamo Duarte Jimenez and from Andrea Jimenez, [both] Portuguese from Lisbon."[85] The goal generally was to "understand what past practice is."[86] These searching questions and the instructions to seek expert advice underline the seriousness of Medici due diligence and their keen understanding that a key to successful bidding on government contracts is careful attention to the details.

Having established the basic matters of price, volume, payments, and exclusivity and having asked about the usual practices from those traditionally involved in the trade, Alamanni would have been in a strong position to advise on the investment. A further instruction, however, points to the connection with previous Medici ventures. Specifically, Francesco asked whether "after the Contractors have received the pepper they will be able to take it from Lisbon or from the Kingdom to whichever place they wish by sea or by land, [and] what cost there will be from fees or duties or other."[87] This last would have been critical for fulfilling the vision of spillover benefits for Tuscany laid out by the Portuguese ambassador and recounted by Oliverotto Guidotti in late 1576, as we saw earlier. Price and volume clearly mattered to the grand duke as part of the commercial proposition, but the terms and conditions would have mattered as much if the pepper trade was to energize Tuscan commerce. The extent of the due diligence makes clear that the project to secure the pepper monopoly was not simply a speculative idea floated among Tuscan officials but an explicit policy that the grand duke pursued in the way one would expect of an investor about to commit spectacular amounts of money to an investment. Prudent and serious, the grand duke's personal interest in the pepper trade brought him close to securing the contract, but not close enough.[88] In the end, the contract went to a Rovellasca-Fugger-

Welser-Ximenes consortium; the terms of the six-year contract were far less favorable than those of 1580.[89] In any event, Francesco I would not have had time to see his negotiations come to fruition, for he died on October 20, 1587, just over three months after writing to Alamanni.[90]

Tuscany's exploration of pepper opportunities had been a project throughout Francesco I's reign. The efforts reflected Francesco I's deep entanglement of Tuscany in Iberian affairs and his consistent financial and military commitment to Philip II's imperial projects. As we have seen, Francesco I's successor, Ferdinando I, did not break with Spain, but he did successfully secure a renegotiation of the relationship on terms more favorable, albeit also more distant, than had prevailed under Francesco I. In this context, Tuscany's final engagement with the pepper project was reimagined as a way to reduce, not deepen, Tuscany's financial support for Philip II's heavily indebted government. After the defeat of the Armada and the loss of Tuscany's flagship the previous year, on April 13, 1589, Ambassador Alamanni wrote to Ferdinando with a proposal from Giraldo Paris. Paris suggested that Philip II could redeem his debts to Ferdinando I by granting him the contract of Europe for four years. Because the suggestion antedated the *livornine* and the rise of Livorno as Tuscany's major port, Paris envisioned the prospect as being particularly beneficial to the trade of Pisa.[91] It is not surprising that Philip II preferred to retain his debts to Ferdinando I and secure cash revenues from auctioning the contract. Florence might still play a role as a regional distribution center for pepper, supplying German merchants in Italy, for instance.[92] Yet the vision of Florence as the new Antwerp or Venice, acting as Europe's main distribution center for pepper and other spices, was not to be. But notwithstanding all the tensions in Florence's relationship with Spain over Medici entanglements in France in the 1590s, Tuscan efforts to secure a niche in Philip II's empires did not come to a neat end at this point—far from it. Hard on the heels of the last pepper project came a new and perhaps more creative and ambitious idea for bringing the profits of empire to Tuscany.

## Brazilian Sugar in Livorno

After the effective abandonment of efforts to join the pepper trade, the Medici ambassador to Philip II's court had the opportunity to negotiate for a new valuable colonial commodity brought from the Portuguese Empire: sugar. The Portuguese, like the Spanish, had an elaborate system of restrictions that directed their imperial trade to ports in the mother country. The prize for such a bulky commodity as sugar was not in mediated trade, with its expensive middlemen and logistical costs, but instead in direct trade in competitively priced sugar. The Tuscans planned to use such imported sugar not as a raw commodity to be consumed and reexported, like pepper, but instead as feedstock for an industrial complex to be built in Livorno. For this to work, direct trade could not be subject to the erratic supplies and evasions of smuggling. The Dutch, with their vast merchant marine, could make interloping on Iberian trade the basis for their business, but Tuscany's relationship with the Iberians could not bear the tensions it would cause.

Tuscany's ambitious new port of Livorno needed two qualities to serve as the center of a sugar-processing industry: the ability to receive large oceangoing ships and permission to trade directly in colonial sugar. Mediated access to Spain and Portugal presented no technical difficulties—Mediterranean sailors had, of course, been making the journey to Iberian Atlantic ports for millennia—nor were there substantive administrative barriers to the reexport of many Iberian colonial goods. Even when Livorno was still a very small port, Tuscan records show the regular arrival of colonial goods from Portugal and Spain.[93] Certainly, there was no technological barrier to long-distance navigation to and from Livorno. The exploits of Tuscany's powerful galleon in the New World and with the Armada shows this clearly in a military capacity. The same, as is no surprise, held true with commercial shipping. For instance, a ship laden with brazilwood arrived in Livorno directly from Brazil in November 1581.[94] Indeed, much longer journeys were possible. Two ships, probably Portuguese, arrived from Goa and the East Indies in 1610 carrying large cargoes of pepper, demonstrating the political, rather than technical, limits on Tuscan trade.[95]

Livorno's possible role as a sugar port moved beyond the theoretical with the arrival of a consignment of six hundred chests of sugar from Brazil in 1590.[96] Such a modest trade would have been helped by the relatively liberal trading regime between Portugal and Brazil that permitted fairly small ships from small Portuguese ports to trade in Brazilian sugar.[97] Unlike the case of the large carracks plying the route between Lisbon and India and the elaborate monopoly procedures enforced on the spice trade, extending the Brazilian sugar trade to Livorno with these smaller ships would have been fairly straightforward. The Tuscans quickly saw the opportunity and sought a new legal framework to enable the expansion of the trade. On December 15, 1591, Ambassador Girolamo Lenzoni (1541–1594) wrote from Madrid about a proposal to send ten foreign ships from Brazil to Livorno. He explained that it was impossible because of Portuguese law.[98] The negotiation did not end there, however, for Lenzoni wrote again from Madrid on March 1, 1592, indicating the ongoing efforts he had made, requesting more information, and lamenting the king's probable slowness in the matter.[99] The plan was clearly viable logistically. Rising Brazilian sugar production—from six to ten thousand metric tons between 1580 and 1610—would have permitted some to be diverted to Tuscany without unduly disrupting Portuguese ports. Sugar's modest contribution to royal finances and the promise to pay taxes addressed the Crown's financial interests.[100] On the face of it, the plan seemed eminently reasonable to the Tuscans. Portuguese law and the political economy of privilege that sustained it, however, stood resolutely opposed. To override this would have required Philip II to pay a political price with metropolitan Portuguese to please the Florentines and Luso-Brazilian sugar producers. Philip II and Philip III, however, were willing to enforce blockages between the Spanish and Portuguese empires, even though they were kings of both, to honor entrenched privileges. In this context, the politics of granting the Tuscans exemptions were so challenging that Lenzoni's pessimism was well founded.

Nothing daunted, one of the leading Medici diplomats and state secretaries, Belisario di Francesco Vinta (1542–1613) wrote to the new Tuscan ambassador to Spain, Francesco di Agnolo Guicciardini (d. 1602) concerning a new project.[101] Vinta wrote,

> Our merchants would like to make here a sugar refinery, the which would be of great use to them and of great commodity to our states and where now it is done in Venice with all the profit in the hand of the Infidels it would be directed here with utility for Christians, on condition that this same Majesty would be content and would give grace that eight

ships, at minimum, and up to ten, at the most, loaded with sugar would be able to come from Brazil by a direct route through the strait of Gibraltar and from there to Livorno, fleeing the long route and the peril of going to Lisbon and having then to go from there to come to Livorno. And, for the rights and taxes of this Majesty, they would oblige themselves and they would give security to pay them and would pay them to His Majesty not otherwise then if they had passed through Lisbon with all the greater surety that the Ministers of the said Majesty would require, and because until the time of Ambassador Lenzoni who, however, never put his hand to this business if it was written of there, I send, in the name of the merchants, the memorials.[102]

In sum, the proposal was to allow eight to ten ships to sail directly from Brazil to supply a sugar refinery in Livorno and pay taxes to the Portuguese crown as if the ships had stopped in Lisbon. Rhetorically, Vinta assigned the blame for the project's failure to Guicciardini's predecessor's inattention to the matter. Tacitly, however, Vinta recognized the difficulty of securing acquiescence in the proposal by specifying that "a good and honorable tip" of 1,000 *scudi* might be given secretly to the Imperial ambassador for his help with the project.[103] Bribing a fellow ambassador—and a bribe it certainly was, for the merchants undertook to "do it without making any report or appearance thereof"—and somehow doing so such "that with dexterity without nominating us you will try in whatever good way if the Ambassador might accept this business" does not bespeak much confidence about Philip II's government's receptiveness.[104]

From Tuscany's perspective, the direct Brazilian-Tuscan trade was a mutually beneficial arrangement wherein danger and expense might be avoided at no cost to Philip II's treasury. What with the extent of Philip II's debts to the Medici and Florentine merchants, however, the transaction may not have been quite as clearly financially neutral as the Tuscans presented it. Of probably greater consequence, the measure would have set a precedent for authorizing direct trade with the American colonies. Political resistance from the existing privileged constituencies and demands for equal privileges from other ports within Philip

II's many domains might well have been expected. More generally still, nearly all the reasons the trade might attract the Tuscans could equally be marshaled to support its continuation in Portugal. If sugar importation was to drive development in Livorno, why should it not do so in Portugal's ports? Finally, the Spanish Habsburgs were keenly aware of the way that commercial connections can become political interests. It would have taken a creative political approach to see the proposal not as a threat to a jealously guarded treasure, but instead as an asset in binding together an alliance network. As we shall see in Chapter 3, the exclusion of Tuscany worked in exactly the opposite way it was intended, driving the Florentines to negotiate with the Dutch for Brazilian sugar well before the Dutch became a mortal threat to Portuguese Brazil.

## Subinfeudation and Cooperative Empire

Under Ferdinando I, the Grand Duchy of Tuscany explored the possibilities of cooperation with the French in the 1590s and with the Dutch and English in the opening decade of the seventeenth century. For all this, the Medici remained profoundly tied into the Spanish Habsburg system. As a result, the Medici continued to experiment with ways to restructure the relationship to better suit Tuscan interests. They did so by pursuing projects for deepening Tuscany's integration with the Spanish Habsburgs' empires. Of the two, the Portuguese empire seemed the more attractive prospect to Tuscany. As we have seen, Florentine patrician ties to Lisbon, the world of Portuguese commerce, and Portuguese Brazil were robust and multifarious. The Cavalcanti showed a way into the Portuguese elite in the heartland of Brazilian sugar production. The Giraldi went one better. Francesco Giraldi was at various points Portuguese ambassador, royal governor in Brazil, and Brazilian donatary captain. Structurally, too, the Portuguese Empire was more open to Tuscan investment because it had developed around ways of making its constituent pieces suitable sites of investment. As we have seen in the cases of the pepper contracts and the donatary captaincies, the Portuguese turned to the private resources of investors and *fidalgos* alike.

Once imperial possessions became a species of private property, a tension could emerge over the imperatives of personal finances and those of political allegiance. Over time, the financial fortunes of individual families might be expected to rise and fall and for their interests to shift. Should one prominent Portuguese noble sell to another, no great disturbance might be expected. Financial entanglements with foreign princes were a different matter. The example of Medici relations with Roman nobles is instructive. As we have seen in the case of the Orsini, arrangements could involve the rental of a duchy, as at Bracciano, or the sale of a county, as at Pitigliano. Both cases presented worrisome precedents. Bracciano was firmly inside the Papal State and strategically located close to Rome, and so its rental had clear political implications. The case of Pitigliano was sharper still, for it became part of Tuscany with its sale in 1604. The transaction casts a different light on the activities of a sovereign investor like the grand duke of Tuscany. The ambiguous status of donatary captaincies within the Portuguese Empire both attracted the Grand Duchy and made Philip III's government wary. If the grand duke purchased a subimperial territory, where did its allegiance ultimately lie? Had that territory exited the empire? What would happen in the case of war with a third party or conflicting views about law?

In 1608 Ferdinando I explored acquiring the donatary captaincy of Espírito Santo in Brazil for his second or third son.[105] Espírito Santo had been a troubled captaincy in its early years, its fledgling sugar economy crushed by an Amerindian revolt against the appropriation and radical transformation of their land. Vasco Fernandes Coutinho eventually renounced his captaincy to the royal governor in the late 1550s, but it was then granted to his nephew, Francisco de Aguiar Coutinho in 1560.[106] As we have seen, Luca Giraldi acquired the troubled captaincy of Ilhéus in 1561 and his son Francesco inherited it in 1566. There was, then, a clear precedent for private Florentines, albeit ones closely integrated into elite Portuguese society, to hold a captaincy. But Ferdinando I's proposal took matters a step further, by proposing a Medici prince as captain.

On November 9, 1608, Ferdinando I wrote to Sallustio Tarugi, his ambassador at the Spanish Habsburg court, to express his desire to acquire "some place in New Spain or on the Coast of Brazil" under "obedience to His Catholic Majesty." The openness to a site in New Spain dovetailed with Tuscany's intellectual engagement and private Florentines', especially the Capponi family's, commercial interests in the region, ties that will be explored in Chapter 4. Ferdinando I, however, directed his attention primarily to Brazil and in particular to a single captaincy, that of Espírito Santo, "under the Crown of Portugal" and "held in perpetual fief by certain Portuguese."[107] The grand duke expected little sugar, nor did he expect to find mines, but he considered its wood supplies to be valuable.[108] Keenly aware of possible political obstacles, Ferdinando offered to send one of his sons as an attraction to Philip III, but he then conceded to Tarugi that "it would suffice therefore to have license to be able to send two vessels every year for as many years as it should seem to His Majesty, the which vessels would be able to go and come freely, paying to His Majesty his rights as is required."[109] The proposal managed to be both the most ambitious Tuscan offer and, alternatively, a quite modest modified version of the 1590s sugar-trade plans. Ferdinando I's knowledge of the opportunity presented by Espírito Santo suggests that he was quite well informed, drawing on Florentine émigrés in Brazil, Medici diplomats in Spain, and occasional letters from Brazil that reached Florence.[110] The Medici bid was perceptive and plausible. Philip III's government nonetheless rejected it.[111]

The Tuscans and some Portuguese, however, continued to see merit in the idea of Tuscan participation in Portuguese Empire. As late as the closing months of Ferdinando I's reign, the grand duke explored buying the rights to (as yet unconquered) Sierra Leone from Pedro Álvares Pereira, a Portuguese noble who had been granted, by Philip III in 1606, a captaincy on condition of settlement.[112] Structurally, the arrangement was would have been quite similar to the proposal for Espírito Santo, a connection made by Paul Hair and Jonathan Davies in their study of the Sierra Leone venture.[113] As with the donatary captains in Brazil, an outside investor became involved after a negative change in circumstances for the original captain. Pereira had tried to settle Sierra Leone in 1607–1608 but fell from favor at the court of Philip III in 1608; only then did Francisco Pereira, a senior Augustinian and half-brother of Pedro Álvares Pereira, secretly contact Ferdinando I.[114] The grand duke was certainly interested, for, on December 29, 1608, the day after receiving the terms for Tuscany's involvement in Sierra Leone, Ferdinando I wrote to Cardinal del Monte in Rome, "I would be greatly desirous of procuring the most minute *relazione* that may be possible." He knew that the Jesuits had been there and hoped "that perhaps there is today in Rome one of the said Fathers that was there."[115] As it happened, there was little time for the Grand Duke's engagement to blossom.

Pereira's improving circumstances and Ferdinando I's death in February 1609 stopped the plan, but it would have faced serious challenges in any event,[116] mainly the same political issues of restrictions on settlement and trade, to the Portuguese and to Lisbon respectively, issues about appointments, and concerns about political allegiance.[117] In a document probably attributable to Francisco Pereira at the end of 1608, quite extravagant claims are made about Sierra Leone as "this is a site that puts in hand the Key to the East Indies and the West and all the navigation, and that the King will come to be deeply engaged with whoever will be the Patron, and somewhat dependent, in such a way that the King will want to be cautious about it."[118] No place could lay claim to the kind of importance attributed to Sierra Leone and certainly not a small unconquered colony in West Africa that might expect to face quite stiff resistance from its current inhabitants. The analysis of Philip III's probable political concerns, however, struck at the heart of the matter both in West Africa and Brazil.

As Ferdinando I's reign drew to a close, so too did the possibilities for negotiated partnership with the Iberian empires. Florentine patrician families had successfully presented at least some branches as being sufficiently reliable to be entrusted with pieces of the Portuguese Empire and its commerce. The Medici grand dukes of Tuscany had been reliable allies, providing massive financial subventions and military support to the Spanish Habsburgs. Indeed, Philip II had had the funds to become king of Portugal in part because Francesco I had lent them. As we shall see, even in the final years of his reign, Ferdinando I treated the Spanish Habsburgs as close allies and sought to rally the old alliance in support of his plans for a new order in the eastern Mediterranean. Tuscany, however, remained an expansionist foreign state that trysted with the Dutch and English and sought to build an alliance with France. It could be trusted while surrounded by Spanish territories in Italy; beyond Italy, Tuscan money was welcome, but neither changes in trade rules nor political control could be accepted. There was, however, an alternative. Under Ferdinando I, the Tuscans experimented with forming cooperative partnerships with the Dutch and the English to access the wider world; Chapter 3 tells that story.

# 3

# The Northern European Alternative

$\mathcal{W}$ith the arrival of an exhausted peace in Tuscany after the war that ended Sienese independence, the Medici regime turned outward, pursuing a program of investment and diplomatic engagement that sought to bring the benefits of expanding global commerce to Tuscany.[1] We have seen how the Medici tried, unsuccessfully, to leverage their political connections on the Iberian peninsula to enter the Portuguese spice trade, secure permission to import Brazilian sugar directly to Livorno, and buy a Brazilian donatary captaincy. This chapter shows how, from the 1590s, stymied by Iberian protectionist policies and political suspicions, the Medici began to explore alternative options for long-distance trade and colonization by developing new relationships with the Dutch, English, and other merchants in northern Europe. From trade with Russia and partnership with the Dutch East India Company to an expedition to the Amazon, for two decades, Tuscany pursued an ambitious array of projects. The successes and more numerous failures reveal the hard geopolitical constraints on Tuscan activities, which ultimately presented the grand dukes with an unpalatable set of choices. Far from being uninterested in or somehow technically constrained from entering global commerce, Tuscany's ultimately modest returns on its vast ambitions reflect the ineluctable result of being bound to the Spanish Habsburg system. This political problem ultimately kept Tuscany from accepting the offered partnership with the Dutch and English to join in making the companies and overseas empires that transformed seventeenth-century commerce.

Tuscany's long coastline on the Tyrrhenian Sea might seem to have offered it numerous maritime opportunities along a key artery of Mediterranean trade. A combination of geography, politics, and environmental change, however, actually confined Medici Tuscany to a small handful of usable ports. Politically, the Grand Duchy of Tuscany controlled relatively little of the usable coast. This reflected a Spanish policy of retaining control of the Sienese coastal territories of Talamone, Monte Argentario, Orbetello, and San Stefano as the Presidial States and protecting the independence of the micropolity of Piombino. Of the significant ports, Tuscany retained Portoferraio on Elba and Porto Pisano and Livorno (Leghorn) on the mainland.[2] Until the 1540s, the latter functioned simply as the seaside docks for Pisa, for the silting of the Arno undermined Pisa's direct maritime access.[3] Throughout the sixteenth century from Cosimo I's initial engagement with Livorno, the city underwent a transformation from a small functional outpost into one of Italy's premier ports. The development was driven by major infrastructural investments, innovative policy, substantial immigration, and respect for a body of commercial customs that developed beyond the strict boundaries of original Medici policy. Livorno famously became the original free port and a relatively tolerant outpost in which separate communities could engage in commerce and trust each other while retaining their autonomy.[4]

Beginning by briefly recounting Livorno's core story, this chapter then turns to how Livorno's dual roles as a true *entrepôt* and as a nest of corsairs enabled Tuscany's engagement with long-distance commerce and conflict. Chapter 6 will consider Livorno as a naval base and center of operations for the Order of Santo Stefano in the context of Tuscan commercial interests, diplomatic maneuvers, and military operations in North Africa. This chapter, by contrast, focuses on how Livorno's rapid growth as a relatively religiously tolerant free port with excellent port facilities attracted a resident community of northern European merchants, pirates, and religious exiles. This community offered Tuscany access to technical skills, resources, and commercial opportunities that differed markedly from the Iberian connections explored in Chapters 1 and 2. Thus, after a brief introduction to the city, focused on its demography, legal and physical infrastructure, and English views of it, the chapter turns first to the projects of the Dutch and then to those of the English, concentrating in particular on projects to link Livorno directly with the major circuits of colonial trade.

## A Free Port

Livorno had been purchased from Genoa in 1421, but its real emergence would have to wait for a century. Cosimo I invested heavily in fortifications, port infrastructure, a harbor, and a canal to the Arno, this last completed in 1574, the year of his death; on the legal front, he provided the city with unique autonomy and fiscal advantages in 1545. Francesco I carried the physical building forward by commissioning Bernardo Buontalenti (1531–1608) to design the city in 1576 at a time when its population was a mere 500.[5] For all Cosimo and Francesco's efforts to foster the port and lay the foundations for its future growth, it remained a remarkably small place until the reign of Ferdinando I. Livorno's population ranged from perhaps 530 to 700 in 1591 and perhaps as much as 1,140 in 1592 to somewhere between 5,000 and 8,663 in the first decade of the seventeenth century. It experienced substantial growth in the seventeenth century, such that the population in the eighteenth century was regularly between 30,000 and 44,000.[6] This growth was fueled not so much by Livorno's physical as by its legal architecture, including low customs duties and a welcoming attitude to religious minorities and foreigners.[7]

Although Cosimo had sought to bring New Christians—in this context, converted (typically forcibly) Iberian Jews and their descendants—to Tuscany from 1545, Levantine Jews in 1549, and Armenians, Greeks, and Muslims from the Ottoman realm from 1551–1563, grand ducal Tuscany was not universally kind to Jews and engaged in discriminatory practices against local Italian Jews in the 1570s. Indeed, there was a move away from welcoming New Christians as Christians in Florentine society, where they had been accepted between 1545 and 1591, to bringing people self-identifying as Jews to Livorno and Pisa after 1591. The goal was not toleration per se, but the recruitment of economically useful groups.[8] That is, the grand duchy's leadership saw the offer of refuge to merchants, especially those of Iberian Jewish descent often targeted by the Inquisition, as a means of promoting the growth of its upstart port. Faced with a grain crisis and seeing Livorno's central role in resolving it, Ferdinando I redoubled his commitment to Livorno. Pursuing the logic of religious toleration as a means of attracting merchants, Ferdinando I issued the *Livornine* of 1591 and 1593, which welcomed a wide range of people "merchants of all nations, Levantine and Ponentine, Spanish and Portuguese, Greeks, Germans and Italians, Jews, Turks and Moors, Armenians, Persians and others."[9] There seems to be a general consensus in the historiography that in practice the *Livornine* were directed primarily to attracting Jews with, as Corey Tazzara notes, forty-one of forty-four provisions addressing the position of the new Jewish community.[10] The efforts took some time to bear fruit; there were only 134 Jews in Livorno in 1601. Still, by 1622, the Jewish community had swelled to 711.[11] The small population at this point did not prevent Livorno from emerging as a center of trade by the end of the sixteenth century.[12]

This growth certainly impressed the northwest Europeans, principally the Dutch and English, who were the major new participants in Mediterranean trade in the late sixteenth century. They contributed centrally to transforming Livorno into both an entrepôt and a center of their Mediterranean operations.[13] Originally, they came to address an agricultural emergency. Tuscany's growing population had faced a bad harvest in 1590,[14] which led Ferdinando I to dispatch Neri Giraldi and Riccardo Riccardi to acquire Baltic grain, which they did on a large scale, traveling to Danzig and organizing shipment to Tuscany on Dutch, English, and Hanseatic ships.[15] Grain shipments could be politically sensitive. For that reason, Ferdinando I supported his agents' activities with diplomatic efforts to provide security along the transit route. The grand duke wrote to Queen Elizabeth I (r. 1558–1603) to request that she permit the movement of grain being sent by Florentine merchants to Livorno to serve the grand duke's states, in which there was a shortage; Ferdinando tactfully noted the presence of English ships in his domains.[16] The tacit threat to profitable English trade perhaps helped Queen Elizabeth and her subjects look past Tuscany's leading role in the Armada, no doubt helped by its utter defeat. Thirty grain ships reached Tuscany between December 1590 and April 1591 and grain imports saw nearly a ninefold increase from a decade earlier, as Livorno became a grain port for both Tuscan and regional distribution.[17] The practice of religious leniency in Livorno, the issuance of the *Livornine*, and the exactly contemporary import of Baltic grain contributed to the creation of economic ties with distant places signified by the arrival of a half-dozen consuls of non-Italian polities by 1597.[18] In short, Livorno became a major base of operations for northern European merchants operating in the Mediterranean.

## A Militarized Livorno

Livorno's pioneering role as a free port and site of religious tolerance has been justly celebrated in the historiography. For this early period, however, a focus on the roots of the city's later successes can obscure its original character. A pair of early English accounts of Livorno offer a useful corrective, conveying the port's Janus-faced quality as both a bustling center of commerce and the base for Tuscan-sponsored maritime violence. The first account appears in Sir Thomas Sherley (II)'s (1564–1633 / 1634) idiosyncratic manuscript travel account, the "Discours of the Turkes," which dates to 1606–1607.[19] Sir Thomas Sherley (II), one of the sons of Sir Thomas Sherley (I) (c. 1542–1612), is the first of three Sherley brothers we shall meet in the following chapters. He is primarily distinguished in Tuscan history for his brief anti-Turkish exploits; he served the grand duke in 1602.[20] In this period, gentlemen regularly traveled abroad to gain experience at court and in the practice of arms, actions that, if well considered, might enhance their position upon their return home. Unfortunately, matters went poorly for Sherley, who attacked an island in the Cyclades in January 1603 and was captured by the Turks.[21] Imprisoned first in Negroponte and then in Istanbul, he was ransomed and then released on December 5, 1605. After his release, he toured Istanbul before returning to England via Italy and Germany in the course of the next year.[22] His description of Livorno is brief, but instructive (modernized orthography):

Livorno is a fair harbor, but exceeding open to all the western points of the compass. The town is not yet finished, but it will be the finest small town of Italy, all built at the Duke his own charges.

The fortification is one of the best that ever I saw, for there wanteth no manner of thing to it that the wit of a soldier can devise, it is so excellently well flanked with bulwarks of rare form & strength, the ditch deep & broad. To these there is added a citadel within the rampart, if the town should be taken. There is a moat within the walls for the safe keeping of the galleys, but it is too shallow for ships. They have ground enough within the town to make a new fortification if this should be lost.

There are 1,200 foot in garrison in it, but no ordinance yet mounted, save only in the old castle, which serveth to no purpose but to command the harbor.

This place was once subject to the Genoese, & it hath in harbor such a lantern as that of Genoa.[23]

Sherley was, of course, a military man, which accounts for some of his attention to Livorno's fortifications. Even so, his military focus is not without significance, for his thumbnail description of the fortified city of Florence entirely ignores military matters, "Florence is one of the finest towns in Italy for the exact building, comeliness of the streets, & neatness; & it is great, though inferior to many for bigness; the river of Arno runneth through the middle of it."[24] This sympathetic account of the city was matched by his positive take on Ferdinando I and Ferdinadno's relations with the English. Discussing the English position in Tuscany—the king in the following is James I—Sherley wrote, "The Duke of Florence is one of the most politique & prudentest prince in the world, & justest in his government; not given over to too many passions, yet a man; & (in my opinion) I find no prince in any court where I have been so true a friend to the king as he, for he seemeth to love his person, his honor, & his realm, & he is bound to this loving respect but only in affection to his royal person; for he hath not such causes of state to move him to this profession as other princes have, for the king can less offend him (if he were at enmity with him) then he can do most other princes, his territory being altogether in terra firma & far remote from England; & the English trade in Tuscany is of least profit to him & his country of any other."[25] Sherley's glowing portrayal of Ferdinando I strikingly concentrates on how Tuscany's strategic situation, limited English trade, and relative invulnerability to English coercion rendered Ferdinando's friendship credible. Later in the century, Tuscany's relative position would deteriorate, but at this juncture the image is of a militarily secure partner who offered friendship to the English from a position of strength.

We can be fairly confident that the author of our second account, William Davies, did not share Sherley's sentiments. The London barber-surgeon, originally of Hereford, published an account of his Tuscan travails in 1614.[26] This drew on his earlier unhappy experience with Livorno, which had overlapped with Sherley's time in Tuscany. Davies left London on January 28, 1597, on an English ship "being laden with Fish, and Herrings, and such like commodities," on a commercial voyage to Civitavecchia, the main Tyrrhenian Sea port of the Papal State. He made Civitavecchia without incident.[27] Only later in his ship's Mediterranean itinerary did disaster strike. Leaving Tunis for the Aegean carrying Turks and Turkish goods on the ship "Francis of Saltash, being bound to Syo within the Arches of Archipelago," the English were "most fiercely set upon by five of the Duke of Florence his Gallies, (who being in continuall warre with the Turke, tooke us as a Turkish prize) which spit fire like divels."[28] After a costly fight, the English were defeated, their ship ruined by Tuscan cannon fire. At that point, "thus were we taken, and stript every man starke naked, and then were we distributed, some into one Gallie, and some into another, where we had as many Irons knocked upon us, and more, than then we were able to beare."[29] The English ship was repaired and brought back immediately to Livorno. In contrast, the Tuscans kept the English prisoners on the galleys for a month, where they "were all shaven both head and beard, and every man had given him a red coate, and a red cap, telling of us that the Duke had made us all Slaves, to our great woe and griefe: where I continued eight yeeres and ten moneths in this slaverie."[30] Davies's slavery rested on his ship's trade with the Muslim Turks, yet, as we shall see, Tuscany conducted a lively commerce and had regular diplomatic relations with North Africa, including both Tunis and Ottoman Alexandria. Furthermore, Latin Christians were not supposed to enslave each other. In any event, the use of galley slavery as a form of summary extraterritorial punishment for smuggling sat awkwardly with Tuscany's burgeoning relationship with England.

In Davies's description of his slavery, he lived as a slave who pulled a cart of materials around for three years and as a galley slave for five.[31] Davies seems to have been a committed Protestant himself and certainly noted the kindness of English Protestants to the galley slaves and absence of such kindness by English Catholics. Recounting his extraordinary miseries, he explained that he did not commit suicide, as others did, because he believed it would lead to worse miseries in the afterlife.[32] The English tread a fine line in Livorno. English slaves, with their red coats and caps, coexisted very visibly with English merchants in what was still a small town. English merchants arriving were welcomed and honored, but those trading with Tuscany's enemies—that is, half the Mediterranean—were subject to extreme coercion.

Davies's long enforced residence in Livorno contrasted sharply with the aristocratic Sherley's short visit. Even so, Livorno's coercive apparatus stood at the heart of both their accounts. Davies wrote,

> Ligorne is a Cittie of the Duke of Florence, and lyeth in low ground, having many towers without it standing in the Sea, also to this Towne doth belong a wilde road, and two very faire moulds for the safetie of the Dukes Gallies. In the entrance of these moulds is a very strong Castle with great store of Ordnance planted: also the Towne is very strongly fortified, for it is the chiefe garrison of the great Dukes, where is continually great store of Souldiers in pay. Which Souldiers are always imployed in his shipping or Gallies, wherewith he doth more offend the Turke then all Christendome, for they doe take Gallies and Carmizals and Briganteens, and Townes of the Turkes and Mores: possessing of Men, Women, and Children, selling them in Markets like to Horses, Cowes, or Sheepe, reserving the strongest for his owne slavery; In this place I lived eight yeeres, and ten moneths."[33]

As an oppressed cog in the Tuscan military machine, Davies saw especially clearly Livorno's role as a center of naval warfare, raiding, and slavery.

Fernand Braudel has argued that this darker side of early Livorno meant that, in the wake of the great naval conflicts of midcentury and the relative rise of corsairs and raiding, Livorno became one of the "capitals of warfare" and that "Malta and Leghorn were Christendom's Algiers, they too had their bagnios, their slave-markets and their sordid transactions."[34] Indeed, as a heavily fortified garrison town filled with slaves, soldiers, and pirates dealing in ransoms and stolen goods, Livorno was, Braudel argued, essential to the Barbary ports' economy of theft.[35] Livorno's infrastructure of organized violence likewise enabled northern European interlopers who might live on both sides of the law and not care to have too many questions asked about the provenance of their goods.[36] For the English, Livorno was also a haunt of exiles and expatriates, reflecting intense religious repression in late-sixteenth-century England. Whatever their reasons for coming, many of the Dutch and English followed Thomas Sherley's piratical raiding model. The grand dukes offered them the necessary protection to reap economic rewards, to amplify the effects of Tuscany's own wide-ranging raiding, and to give Tuscany access to ships, men, and technology. Livorno proved so attractive that, by 1610, there were a dozen English corsairs operating out of the port, contributing to its becoming, in Gregory Hanlon's characterization, "Italy's largest corsair base."[37]

A nest of corsairs and a naval base, a grain port and an emergent free port, a center of slavery predicated on religious warfare and a place of relative religious tolerance, Livorno had many facets. Above all, these roles were new, the result of the confluence of Medici policy and the actions of those who thought that this protean city might be made to serve their interests.[38] For such a place, it was possible to imagine still other possibilities, above all as a center of sugar refining, a colonial port, and a hub in long-distance networks of commerce. For the Dutch and English, both of whom were at war with Philip II and Philip III's Spanish and Portuguese Empires in the 1590s and cognizant that even a victorious peace was unlikely to result in relaxation of official monopoly policies, Tuscany's new port of Livorno offered a welcome haven and its grand duke a potential ally and investor in their risky long-distance enterprises.

## The Dutch and Their Projects

The success of the grain trade to Tuscany offered the Dutch a steady business opportunity linking the grain surpluses of the Baltic with the deficits of the Mediterranean. Once Livorno's viability as a center for Dutch business and a haven for Sephardic Jews had been demonstrated by experience, wider prospects opened for Tuscany. Some of them were familiar, like liaising with the Dutch to access economic opportunities in the areas previously dominated by the Portuguese. Perhaps it is unsurprising that proposals concentrated on two areas that the Tuscans had already explored at length, Brazilian sugar and trade with the East Indies. At the same time, however, Tuscany made initial headway on a wholly new plan to enter the Russian trade, opening diplomatic and tentative commercial links with Muscovy. This section will begin with sugar and then continue to the curiously entwined stories of Tuscany's efforts to enter the Muscovy and East India trades.

Whatever specific business logic convinced early modern investors, the idea of bringing Brazilian sugar to Livorno for refining continued to recur. As we have seen, Tuscany sought to negotiate such an arrangement with the Habsburg administration of the Portuguese Empire in the first half of the 1590s, apparently without success. In 1602–1603, the Tuscans turned to a variant of the idea. On January 10, 1603, Don Giovanni de' Medici (1567–1621)—the grand duke's illegitimate half-brother and a major military and diplomatic figure in Tuscany—wrote to Ferdinando I from Antwerp.[39] Aware that Ferdinando had long wanted to introduce sugar refining into Livorno, he had spoken with some merchants who assured him that introducing it would be easy and that Flemish (apparently Dutch) ships regularly brought sugar from Brazil to Zeeland without stopping in Lisbon; they offered to open up a route to Livorno.[40] Stuart Schwartz has shown, using the records of a New Christian merchant in Bahia and Pernambuco between 1595 and 1601, that ships from numerous northern European ports, and even Ragusa on the Adriatic, were used for shipping sugar from Brazil, ostensibly under Portuguese license.[41] At just this time, Amsterdam and the Dutch Republic assumed an essential role in colonial trade, helped by large numbers of Antwerp merchants relocating there in 1600. These merchants provided the Brazilian sugar industry with essential goods and services and, by 1621, dominated Brazilian export carrying, sugar refining, and sales.[42] They were thus particularly well positioned to incorporate Livorno into their new sugar business. A flurry of letters that winter discussed the project. Though the merchants were credible, the politics of the plan were not. Specifically, the Flemish merchants wanted a letter of protection from Queen Elizabeth I that would permit their ships to stop in ports subject to the Spanish Crown without being attacked by English ships.[43] Tuscany could not secure this protection from a dying Elizabeth I while England and Spain were at war.

Another improbable political precondition underlay a similar project to introduce sugar refining to Livorno by establishing direct trade with Brazil.[44] Outlined in a Tuscan memorandum on direct trade between Livorno and the Indies in 1608, this project involved securing permission for two or three Flemish ships (again apparently Dutch) to load sugar in Brazil for Livorno.[45] The commercial dimensions of the project, involving both sugar and brazilwood, reasonable scale, and a multisided trade, seem to have been sound.[46] As Giuseppe Gino Guarnieri has pointed out, however, there was little chance that Philip III would grant permission; no substantial sugar refining seems to have been set up in Livorno at that time.[47] Livorno's qualities and Tuscany's marginal status as a problematically independent Spanish ally made these proposals possible. Iberian distrust, protectionism, and, perhaps, a failure of imagination, however, made Philip III's government unwilling to concede direct trade privileges to Tuscany. Politics shaped economic development and it was not until the very different political circumstances of the 1620s that sugar refining would come to Livorno. As Eddy Stols has shown, sugar refining was eventually established in Livorno by a Dutchman from Hoorn, Bernard Jansz Van Ens, who, with Theodor Reiniers, received a ten-year monopoly from the grand duke in 1624. Van Ens's death in 1626 led the business to be picked up by the Flemings Daniel Bevers and Paris Gautier with financing from the Amsterdam merchant Nicolas Du Gardin; the business started to decline from 1630.[48]

Even as the Medici negotiated with Dutch merchants about bringing Brazilian sugar to Tuscany in 1603, a different Medici connection to Amsterdam briefly opened the prospects of a wholly new trade route. Never hesitant to enter a politically uncertain situation, the Medici opened negotiations with Tsar Boris Godunov (r. 1585 (regent) / 1598 (tsar)–1605).[49] In the relative peace of 1602–1603, the Medici supported the missions of Avraham Lussio (Lus), which were to establish reciprocal trade ties; political turmoil in Russia from 1605 marked the effective end of the opening.[50] The tsar's letter to Grand Duke Ferdi-nando makes quite the visual impact, written in Cyrillic with a shim-mering golden fringe, as it was doubtless intended to do; the grand duke, however, relied on a functional translation into Tuscan. In any event, the contents would have been most welcome. The tsar's letter, ap-parently of 1602, not only embraced friendship with the grand duke, but conceded to the father Sione, and his sons Abramo, Isaach, and Matia, rights to trade through the Castle of Archangel and to have se-cure and free traffic to Moscow.[51]

This trade route had been pioneered by the accidental arrival of an English expedition seeking a northern maritime route to China in 1553 and regularized with the tsar's grant of trading privileges to the Muscovy Company in 1555. To facilitate this commerce, Archangel (Arkhangelsk) on the Northern Dvina by the White Sea was established in 1583.[52] Its importance was enhanced by two developments. In the same year as Archangel's founding, Muscovy accepted defeat in its war with Poland-Lithuania and Sweden and the loss of its Baltic coast. In the south and east, by contrast, Muscovy went from strength to strength, taking the Khanates of Kazan (1552), Astrakhan (1556), and Sibir (1582–1598). The conquests of Kazan and Astrakhan in particular provided a secure route down the Volga to the Caspian Sea and on to Safavid Iran.[53] Thus, Archangel and Astrakhan, separated by the full breadth of European Russia, were linked by the network of rivers and portages running from the Northern Dvina in the north to the Volga in the south. The route was long and arduous, but it opened an alternative means of access to Safavid Iran's silk trade and anti-Ottoman diplo-matic initiatives.

The Medici regime was not slow to grasp the range of commercial possibilities that trade concessions from the tsar offered. A heavily marked-up draft response from the grand duke of May 12, 1603, thanked the tsar for the privilege and asked that it be amplified and extended to all his subjects.[54] A further draft letter to the grand chancellor of Mus-covy of the same date asked for the continuation of the favor granted to the Lussio (Lus) family and its extension "in granting them the right to be able to send one of their men to get the caviar, and the murex in As-trakhan, and to extract it from there for Italy, and in particular for Tus-cany."[55] The new trade route from Livorno to Archangel, Moscow, and

Astrakhan offered bright prospects, especially if it could be extended to all Tuscan subjects. So much seemed possible in the spring of 1603.

Ferdinando I had sought amicable commercial relations with Muscovy, received a favorable response, and then sought to extend that commercial relationship. His initiative was promising, but the timing could not have been worse. Particularly cold weather, especially frost in the late summers of 1601 and 1602, devastated Russian agriculture, resulting in severe famine. The crisis led to massive population losses and contributed to serious outbreaks of brigandage, a situation that Tsar Boris Godunov, in declining health, struggled to control. Political conditions swiftly deteriorated. Grigory Otrepev ("False Dmitry," d. 1606) invaded in October 1604, culminating in a civil war that had not been resolved by Tsar Boris Godunov's death in April 1605.[56] As with political news more generally, the Medici were aware of developments in Russia. They received a report from the city of Archangel on July 7, 1605, about the tsar's ostensible defeat in the war with the False Dmitry and suicide by poisoning on April 13, 1605.[57] Whatever the accuracy of this report, the tsar had indeed died. With Muscovy's descent into civil war and foreign invasion, which would devastate the country until the end of the Time of Troubles in 1613, any trade concessions granted would have been a dead letter.[58]

Tuscany's Russian project quickly came to naught, but Ferdinando I's relationship with the Lus family continued. This is not surprising, since the only tangible outcome of the negotiations with Muscovy was a special trade concession for the family. When Ferdinando I launched an ambitious venture to start a direct spice trade with the East Indies using his own galleon, the ship was seized by the Dutch government, the States General of the United Provinces. With great difficulty, the ship's release was secured and it came into the possession of Jan van der Neesen as he reported to Abraham Lus in Livorno on September 12, 1606.[59] Early in 1607, the Medici received separate assurances from Jacques Lores in Amsterdam that Sion Lus and his son Abraham Lus had not induced the seizure of the grand duke's "grand galleon."[60] Tuscany's long-distance projects nearly always relied on experts like the Lus, on whose probity and ability to navigate local politics the Medici depended.

In a matter as important as the galleon, the Tuscans had planned to draw on the services of their best-traveled expert, the relatively recently

returned Florentine circumnavigator, Francesco Carletti. A letter from
Don Giovanni de' Medici in Paris to Ferdinando I in Florence of November
10, 1606, recounts a conversation Don Giovanni had had with Henry IV
of France. Don Giovanni reported to Ferdinando that he had suggested
that the States General had detained a Florentine ship because some
merchants there wanted to send it to India from Livorno with Carletti.
Henry IV had laughed at this and told Don Giovanni that he had been
poorly informed. The king instead pointed to Dutch annoyance with
Tuscan loans to Spain.[61] Whatever the exact composition of the group of
Tuscans involved with the galleon and the specific political basis for its
detention, the Dutch were determined to defend their monopoly claims.

While the Medici were disappointed by Dutch intransigence, they
also knew the limits of Tuscan freedom of maneuver, as they were well
aware both of Dutch naval power and of their militarized monopoly
company, the Dutch East India Company (Vereenigde Oost-Indische
Compagnie, VOC). Aggrieved as Carletti was with the Dutch over the
seizure of his goods—a story to which we shall return in Chapter 4—
he nonetheless reported in glowing terms of the superiority of Dutch
shipping over its Portuguese competitors because of its better management.[62] By then, Carletti had sailed on Genoese, Spanish, Japanese, and
Portuguese ships from Tuscany to Saint Helena before his unexpected
return voyage on a Dutch ship, and so he was in an exceptionally advantageous position to make a comparison. Although Carletti regarded
the Dutch in the East as more thieves than merchants and complained
continuously about his treatment, he nonetheless continued to recognize both the scale and nature of Dutch naval power.[63] For instance,
he mentioned in passing that as a petitioner to the States General he
sailed among a fleet of 2,800 ships attacking Sluis.[64] Even allowing for
exaggeration and small average ship size, it was maritime power of a
wholly different order of magnitude than Tuscany's. Carletti addressed
the Dutch maritime orientation quite directly, recounting the vast scale
of shipping in Amsterdam before insisting that "the interest of which
depends entirely on the sea and for that it is no marvel that they have
looked for new trades and new navigations in new worlds."[65] Accounts
like Carletti's helped Medici Tuscany internalize quite early the extraordinary maritime potential of the Dutch and English and the vulnerability of the Portuguese.

Well informed as they were, the shift in Medici interests from the Portuguese pepper trade in the 1580s to deals with the Dutch in the 1600s closely matched the changing power dynamics of overseas trade. Similarly, the Tuscans possessed a clear understanding of the structural organization of Dutch commerce. Carletti described the VOC's structure in his account of his journey, but the brevity of his comments on the VOC and joint stock companies suggests that he thought that the Medici already knew all about them.[66] This is confirmed by two documents. The Medici archives contain a 1602 report—the year of the VOC's foundation—that provides substantial detail on the Dutch East India trade, including, for instance, ship numbers and spice volumes from the 1599 expedition.[67] Likewise, the Medici had been apprised in some detail both of the pre-VOC Dutch spice trade and of how matters stood under the new dispensation. For instance, a 1603 report dispatched to Ferdinando I considers the activities of "this new company," the VOC, as part of its overall discussion of the Dutch Republic.[68]

Well informed about the VOC and stymied in their efforts to challenge its monopoly, the Medici faced a familiar situation. For all its innovative corporate structure and efficient shipping, the VOC was as insistent on its monopoly rights as the Portuguese Estado da Índia had long been. Just as the Medici had explored projects both to break Portuguese trade restrictions and to invest in Portuguese-issued monopoly contracts, so also the Medici explored projects to challenge the VOC monopoly and to join it. For instance, a pair of unsigned memoranda, probably of 1608, concern the development of two new lines of direct trade between Livorno and the Indies.[69] The second of these, on opening a business in Livorno refining sugar shipped directly from Brazil, we encountered above. The first proposal, however, was vastly more ambitious and innovative. Indeed, although I have found no indication that it was acted on, it represents such an extraordinary opportunity that it bears close examination.[70] Addressing the grand duke, the text opens, "If Your Most Serene Highness wants to do business by the route of the sea of Holland in the East Indies, which until now has been a business of great utility and to start the said trade, one must build or purchase, four good ships, the one larger than the other together of a burden of about six thousand or a little less, which ought to be able to depart in the month of December or at the latest in January, the which is the true time, well provided with wines, oils, and other supplies artillery and ammunition enough for a like voyage, of about two years, with two hundred mariners at a *soldo* a month," before continuing to specify that three payments should be given before departure and the type of trade goods, like certain types of Spanish cloth, coral, and compasses, that would serve.[71] The memorandum provides quite specific cost estimates and justifies them on the grounds that "those of the Dutch company sent to India cost this."[72] The memorandum continues with detailed estimates of the returns of a recent Dutch fleet, listing volumes and prices fetched by the pepper, mace, and cloves and deducting for costs like artillery and ammunition. The trade was certainly profitable. Indeed, the memorandum suggests that a *scudo* invested would quadruple. Even with what sounds like insurance, the returns were excellent, "and when Your Serene Highness wants to make assurance of all one makes for the going 18 percent and as when one wants to return you will find that it makes from 20 to 22 percent."[73]

Tuscany's activities were predicated on a close relationship with the Dutch in part to avoid such unpleasantness as had occurred with Tuscany's seized galleon. The memorandum advocates, therefore, an arrangement whereby Tuscany would acquire Dutch ships operating on behalf of the VOC. "To advance you would need to buy or have made the ships in Holland and to dispatch from there all and to send it and dispatch that was from there straight to the said East Indies, with most full order and provision, which then would be able to come on the return directly to Livorno with their full load of pepper and other drugs and spices, truly to not cause a glut, you could send two ships to Holland directly from the Indies, but all would be of the Company as far as the Highness of Spain [was concerned], that He would be able to separate the one from the other."[74] This amounts to a clever legal workaround whereby Livorno would serve as a distribution hub and source of capital for a fundamentally Dutch company. The reference to the king of Spain, however, indicates the difficult politics. Tuscany, as a traditional Spanish ally, had a more secure flag than the rebel Dutch. Even so, Tuscan-financed ships were to fly a Dutch flag. Even anticipating the impending Twelve Years' Truce (1609–1621), heavily burdened Dutch East Indiamen passing by the Iberian peninsula on the way to Livorno might have been attractive targets, but the Dutch seem to have been confident in their naval prowess. Dutch willingness to bear this risk would have solved part of Ferdinando's political problem. The Tuscans could not launch some of the largest ships of the age under the Tuscan flag without drawing unwanted attention, but they might receive Dutch spice shipments at Livorno in its capacity as a free port regularly visited by northern European ships.

As with the Portuguese pepper proposal made decades earlier, the attraction of this project for Tuscany lay as much in the opportunities for economic development in Livorno as in the returns on invested capital. To finish and prepare for a further voyage from Holland, the ships that had unloaded at least part of their cargo at Livorno would need to be loaded with new, Italian goods. The memorandum then envisages the ships closing the loop by setting out "for Holland[,] London or Halle de grace, with alums or for Holland with salt [,] rice and oil and other merchandise, and then returned there in the said places to make the preparation to send it newly for the said Indies" before noting the much lower cost of outfitting further expeditions there.[75] The writer of the memorandum seems to have been particularly well informed about commercial conditions on the East Indies route, stressing that "here if only you would buy all the round, polished coral that you could find to send in the said Indies, it would sell there with a very large advantage and result."[76] In time, Mediterranean coral processed in Livorno would eventually became an important export to India.[77] Indeed, in 1593, the grand duke issued a five-year monopoly contract on the production of coral in Livorno to a group of merchants from Florence, Genoa, Marseilles, and Pisa.[78]

Among the many projects for driving Livorno's economic development through colonial trade, this memorandum was as much distinguished for the caliber of its apparent sponsors as for its detail. The final paragraph makes clear that the offer is from a close affiliate of the VOC to the grand duke and an extraordinary one at that. Addressing Ferdinando I, the text continues,

> And Your Serene Highness resolving to make this business, we pray that our work be worthy[,] promising to serve Your Serene Highness with every affection and fidelity and in case Your Serene Highness should find it good to send in the

said Holland one or two of your faithful ministers to take
care of everything and administer the said in our Company,
you could do it and to the end that everything remained secret and so that the design of Your Serene Highness be not
discovered he can stay in our house under the name of foreign merchants recommended by me, or as a passenger, even
though it is not usual to accommodate anyone in our
houses ----- And for greater secrecy if that is what will please
Your Serene Highness the things that will come to Livorno
could be consigned to me, and our proposed business would
keep much secrecy and be administered with every sincerity
and advantage—In case that Your Serene Highness does not
want to begin the said business with a very large capital you
can only for the first time begin with two large ships and a
little ship that with everything sent by sail, including the
merchandise will come to cost about one hundred thousand *scudi*, and with the approval of Your Serene Highness
we are content to have one quarter, ---------[79]

This was a proposal to secretly cut the grand duke into the VOC. Not
only would the grand duke participate as an investor, but his primary
port of Livorno would be integrated into the major northwest European centers of trade. The implications of the counterfactual are
breathtaking. The VOC was quite simply the most important investment opportunity of the seventeenth century. The success that Livorno
might have had as a terminus of an East India route would have been
extraordinary, with ramifying implications for Tuscany's economy and
politics.

One can continue in this vein, imagining a much happier future
for Tuscany than it experienced. It did not happen, though. Why? The
need for secrecy points to a key problem. The VOC was, in effect, at permanent war with the Spanish Habsburgs and their possessions beyond
the lines. The wily old Ferdinando I, long accustomed to intrigue and
pushing the boundaries of acceptable behavior, might have sustained
the deception. Had he done so effectively it might then have continued
after his death. Perhaps, as we shall see in the case of the Amazon expedition, Ferdinando was contemplating a new willingness to directly

challenge Philip III's monopolistic pretensions overseas. But the evidence of Tuscany's activities in this period is not, on balance, in favor of an outright Tuscan break with the Spanish Habsburgs. Although a secret investment might have been sustained for a while, such a break would have been required once the secret eventually leaked, as surely it would have. Tuscany was not willing to make this choice, moving instead to increasing neutrality over the course of the seventeenth century.[80]

## The English Option and the Amazon

After the failure of the Spanish Armada in 1588 and the development of Livorno in the 1590s, a small community of English expatriates, exiles, and émigrés began to develop in Tuscany. Although Tuscany would eventually become a fixture of the Grand Tour, in the first decade of the seventeenth century the attractions were largely the social, cultural, and economic opportunities offered by the wealthy Medici court and the maritime possibilities of Livorno. The free port offered enterprising English captains a congenial place to operate as merchants, smugglers, pirates, and explorers for hire. It was this community that the Grand Duchy of Tuscany tapped for its most ambitious maritime enterprise, an expedition to the Amazon.

Today, the Amazon is inextricably linked with Brazil, yet for a century the Portuguese largely bypassed it. In fact, from 1621, shortly after the Portuguese arrived in force, the Amazon region was governed administratively separately from Brazil as the *Estado do Maranhão*.[81] The limits of this early Portuguese presence left a space for other Europeans. Indeed, the legacy of five of their empires can be still felt in the region between Trinidad and Belém: Venezuela (Spain), Guyana (British), Suriname (Dutch), French Guiana (France), and the Brazilian states of Amapá and Pará (Portugal).

In the century from 1550 to 1650, the Dutch, English, Irish, French, Portuguese, and Tuscans sought to explore, trade, or settle in the lower Amazon.[82] Joyce Lorimer has persuasively divided this into periods of exploration (1596–1611) and settlement (1612–onward).[83] The tempo of lower Amazon ventures—English expeditions in 1596, 1598, 1609–1612, and 1611; a Tuscan expedition led by an Englishman in 1608; and a Dutch one in 1598—presaged intensive competition. As has happened so often in colonial history, in northern Brazil the initial premise was to find and extract precious metals. Already in 1536, a nine-hundred-man Portuguese expedition in search of gold and silver had been shipwrecked on the coast of nearby Maranhão.[84] Eventually, the Portuguese found gold in great abundance elsewhere in Brazil, but initial hopes were disappointed in the Amazon. Instead, Amazonian forest products, extracted with indigenous knowledge, and tobacco formed the basis of the stable economy developed in the period of European settlement. From 1612, northern European and Portuguese outposts were built with remarkable speed. Ultimately, the Portuguese responded forcefully to competition, evicting the French (1615) and other northern Europeans (1623 and 1625).[85]

Tuscany's expedition took place near the end of the reconnaissance period and its preoccupation with gold. The Florentine navigator and self-publicist Amerigo Vespucci had famously journeyed there more than a century before, but Tuscany's expedition drew primarily on expatriate English expertise.[86] As we have seen, the English adventurer Thomas Sherley thought Ferdinando I to be both friendly to James I and relatively immune to English coercion. This independence allowed Tuscany to host figures like Sir Robert Dudley (1574–1649), the illegitimate son of Robert Dudley, earl of Leicester.[87] Wealthy, well educated, and a figure at Elizabeth's court, Dudley not only was fascinated with navigation and scientific instruments, but had also been to the region of Tuscan interest; in November 1594, he took three ships to Trinidad, the mouth of the Orinoco, and Puerto Rico, returning in 1595.[88]

In 1605–1606, after losing his suit seeking recognition as his father's legitimate heir, Dudley and Elizabeth Southwell went to France, married, and converted to Catholicism.[89] Although Dudley's subsequent transfer to Florence in 1606–1607 was controversial, Tuscany could ignore English complaints if it wished. Whether doing so was worthwhile, however, depended on the credibility of Dudley's promises. Not all expatriate Englishmen with plans were credible, after all. For instance, a certain Captain Richard Gifford's proposal to raid Turkish shipping in the Red Sea appeared in an October 1, 1604, letter that Belisario Vinta wrote to Sallustio Tarugi in Valladolid.[90] Gifford's very long-range expedition seems not to have come to anything. Indeed, Gifford appears to have fallen afoul of both the English and the Tuscan authorities at various points in the following years before being pardoned in England no later than 1610.[91] Tuscany wished to avoid such an outcome with the much higher profile Dudley case. Dudley's assurances required tangible proofs. Happily, these Dudley proved capable of providing, starting with a book. A January 8, 1607, letter from Belisario Vinta to Dudley explains that Captain Robert Eliot had presented Dudley's book to Vinta and that Vinta was impressed. Having succeeded with his book, Dudley then delivered on his major promise. By March 1608, Dudley's galleon *San Giovanni Battista* (Saint John the Baptist, Florence's patron saint) had been launched. As a noble Catholic convert with demonstrated expertise in matters maritime, Dudley was precisely the type of figure that Counter-Reformation Tuscany sought to attract. Under Medici protection, Dudley ultimately settled permanently in Florence; he and his wife had a dozen or so children starting in 1609.[92]

Dudley's position in Tuscany came to be part of a broader set of diplomatic tensions. We can see these tensions at play in a series of letters from the Tuscan envoy in Venice, Asdrubale Barbolani di Montauto, sent in the spring and summer of 1607. Montauto's sparring partner was the English ambassador in Venice, Sir Henry Wotton. In May, Montauto wrote from Venice to Vinta in Florence discussing several important points of conflict in the rocky Tuscan-English relationship. Montauto seems to have forced Wotton to admit that Wotton had in fact sent an Englishman—who had been arrested in Livorno—to carry a letter from James I to Dudley. We might imagine that James I was not thrilled with Dudley's conversion and departure to serve as an adviser and naval architect for a foreign prince and that the letter was not one of congratulation on Dudley's exile in Florence. Having been caught sending an agent into Tuscany—not surprising in light of Tuscany's repressive internal structure and long practice of espionage—Wotton's response appears to have been that the best defense is a good offense. Thus, Wotton in turn complained about Count Montecuccoli's seizure of an English merchantman and about three Livorno-specific problems: the use of Englishman who had been Turkish slaves as chained galley slaves, the sale of English ships' artillery, and English Jesuits accused of sedition.[93] These were old problems, as William Davies's long unhappy servitude in Livorno attests.

Discussions with Wotton continued at least into August as a pair of letters from Montauto to Ferdinando I indicate. Wotton was at pains to point out the wickedness of a certain Robert, probably Robert Dudley, and discussed English prisoners with Montauto. Tuscany ultimately ignored English diplomatic concerns, as Thomas Sherley's characterization of Tuscany's independent position suggested it was fully capable of doing. Dudley repaid Tuscan confidence in him not only as a skilled naval expert, but also as a leader of the English maritime community. As a former commander of an expedition, a designer of ships, and, perhaps most important, possessing illustrious parentage, Dudley was well positioned to play this role. In any event, the Tuscan government found him a convenient interlocutor. On July 4, 1610, for instance, Belisario Vinta wrote to Dudley, whom the Tuscans knew as the Count of Warwick, about the prospects of English ship captains cooperating with the Tuscans against the Turks.[94]

As resident naval expert and Medici conduit to the English community in Livorno, with relevant expertise in navigation around Trinidad and the mouth of the Orinoco to boot, Dudley naturally played a central role in organizing the Medici Amazon expedition. Indeed, Dudley wrote the instructions for Robert Thornton, the expedition's leader, outlining the goals of the Tuscan-backed voyage. The expedition was to search for gold and other mining and commercial opportunities.[95] Thornton seems to have been typical of Livorno's English captains. He was the owner of the *Mercante Reale (Royal Merchant)* during an August 30, 1601, voyage to Genoa. Four years later, he commanded the vessel *Il Leon Rosso (The Red Lion)*, as part of an expedition with Count Montecuccoli against the Turks; he also acquired a house and vineyard in Livorno at this point.[96] As we have seen, Count Montecuccoli became a source of tension with the English government.

Our best source for the Amazon expedition, however, is William Davies, for his participation freed him from captivity and was therefore central to his autobiographical account. He explained that "The great Duke fitted a ship, a Tartane and a Frigot, being very well appointed and victualed dispesing of them into the West Indies, and chiefly for the River of the Amazons, appointing Captaine Robert Thornton, an Englishman to be chiefe Commander of the Ship, the Tartane and the Frigot."[97] Thornton, in need of need an experienced ship's surgeon, secured Davies's freedom on condition that he serve.[98] As a slave hauling dirt and stones, however, Davies was hardly in a position to provide the required financial surety that he would take the voyage. Solidarity within the English community sufficed for this, for Davies received a surety of 500 crowns from "Master William Mellyn of Bristow."[99] Having provided this surety, Davies then claimed to have had an audience with the grand duke in which he conversed in Italian with Ferdinando I, who offered Davies whatever he needed on the grounds that "the great Duke of Florence wants no money." After a courtly interchange, the grand duke gave Davies one "hundred Crownes to spend to strengthen himselfe, and bring himselfe to courage."[100]

Freeing an English slave would have been diplomatically convenient, addressing one of Ambassador Wotton's complaints. Davies would, however, ultimately be a rhetorical liability for Tuscany because he highlighted the miseries of his captivity and the instrumental quality of his release. Of the expedition, Davies related in brief that "By this time all things were prepared and made readie for the performance of our pretended Voyage, now being bound to serve in the good Ship called the Santa Lucia, with a Frigot, and a Tartane, well victualed, and well manned, and chiefly bound to the River of Amazones, with other severall Rivers, the which the Duke would have inhabited, hoping for great store of gaine of Gold, but the Countries did afford no such thing, as hereafter shall be spoken of. Upon this Voyage we were fourteene moneths, making little gaine, or benefit for the Duke, for there was nothing to be gained."[101] Closing his account of the expedition, Davies mentioned an English pirate's unsuccessful night attack.[102] In the end, the expedition was still clearly Tuscan enough to be vulnerable to English piracy.

Davies was at extraordinary pains to confirm the veracity of his account, prefacing it with a long list of witnesses, including "Robert Thornton. Master of the good ship called the *Royall Marchant* of London."[103] Davies's account of the greater Amazon region, where he claimed to have been for ten weeks, included comments on the river's impact on the sea, the frequency of rainstorms, ubiquitous mosquitoes, anthropological details, and more, which tend to confirm his participation.[104] Giuseppe Gino Guarnieri has separately estimated that the *Santa Lucia Buonaventura* spent forty-two days at the Amazon and made stops of twelve days in Guiana, ten at the Orinoco, and fifteen at Trinidad.[105] Although conspiracy marred the expedition, the *Santa Lucia Buonaventura* had returned by July 10, 1609, with forty-seven men. The ship also brought six indigenous South Americans, five of whom died of smallpox; the sixth served at the court of the Cardinal de' Medici and learned Italian.[106]

Stepping back to consider the overall picture, the expedition seems to have been a qualified success. Many ventures ended in shipwreck or horrifying losses to disease, supply failure, or conflict. The brief run-in with the pirate and some turmoil among the crew notwithstanding, the expedition seems to have gone fairly smoothly. Two distinctive aspects, however, would prove to be important. The Tuscan expedition seems to have left behind no permanent fort and the voyage was not repeated. This was ultimately, then, a voyage dedicated to the exploration of commercial possibilities more than a colonial venture. With the change of ruler and limited immediate commercial opportunity, nothing further was done. This was probably a sound business decision, but it also ensured that there would be no official Tuscan outpost in South America.

## Conclusion

Geopolitics ultimately imposed hard constraints on Tuscany's options. The overwhelming need to maintain peaceful relations with the Habsburgs kept independent ventures like the Amazon expedition as isolated experiments. Hemmed in by the powerful Spanish navy and Spanish garrisons in Milan, Naples, and the coast of Tuscany, actively supporting the heavily armed commerce of the East India Company or the VOC would have been a remarkably risky choice. In light of the devastation that Odoardo Farnese, Duke of Parma, would bring to his subjects and himself by breaking with Spain in the following generation, Tuscany's decision to avoid risking outright conflict was probably prudent, if also one that foreclosed many possibilities.[107] Instead of pursuing the risky independent path charted by the Amazon expedition, the Tuscans took a different, more pacific course, concentrating increasingly on peaceful commerce and the profitable business of hosting foreigners.

# Part II

# A Global Tuscany

# 4

# The Uses of Access

*N*o Tuscan colony rose on the shores of the Atlantic, nor did Tuscany capture the Brazilian sugar trade or a dominant position in the pepper market. Florentine patricians might successfully acculturate and rise to the top echelons of Portuguese society, but the grand duke could not follow, try as he might. Did this make Tuscany's deep financial and military commitments to its Iberian friends a failure? As a matter of quid pro quo, of Florentine loans and investment for colonial assets and contracts, it is hard to argue otherwise. The alliance in Europe certainly provided Tuscany with security, advanced the frontiers of the Counter-Reformation church militant, and allowed private Florentine commercial interests to prosper, but it can be doubted that Florentine financing for the invasion of Portugal was necessary to achieve any of this. Superficially, the story is clear. The Grand Duchy of Tuscany's projects to join the Spanish and Portuguese overseas empires as a true partner failed after decades of negotiations. Outward appearances can deceive, however. From a different angle, Tuscany did quite well out of its partnership with the Iberian empires and the access to the wider world they provided.

For a first indication of the deeper game, let us return to the players. Some private Florentines slid around imperial restrictions to travel, trade, and settle throughout the Iberian empires, helped occasionally by Medici intervention. More essential than slipperiness, Florentines benefited from a sophisticated understanding of how power, money, family ties, the Church, and patronage could make the people who actually ran the Iberian empires and their constituent institutions reimagine exactly where their interests lay. At various points, Spanish and Portuguese governors, a Spanish captain, Portuguese nobles, Italian merchants, the Jesuits, and the pope aided Florentines in their quest for access. Active loyalty and the pursuit of Florentine patronage might induce individuals to volunteer their support, but others required persuasion, whether honeyed words, a favor granted, or a well-placed gift. Beyond these instrumental relationships, the Medici and the Florentine patrician elite with which they were closely aligned maintained widespread networks based on friendship, affinity, or shared interest. This last could be narrowly financial but quite often involved cultural, intellectual, and religious commitments. Such ties casually and routinely ignored the political boundaries on which the Spanish Habsburgs had so firmly insisted in their rejection of Tuscan partnership in their empire.

Even as the status of the Medici as sovereign princes impeded the project of cooperative empire, so it also opened possibilities by giving them the right to post diplomatic missions to foreign states. By the late sixteenth century, the practice of posting resident ambassadors, developed on the Italian peninsula in the late fifteenth and early sixteenth centuries, had spread throughout Europe such that it was conventional.[1] Two points command our attention here. First, relative to Tuscany's modest size, it maintained a very substantial diplomatic network, one that benefited from unusually systematic recordkeeping and a cadre of loyal Medici servants. Although they were by no means members of a coherent diplomatic service in the modern sense, long careers involving repeated postings seem to have been common. Second and critical for the patterns of engagement explored in this chapter, Medici diplomats and the broader penumbra of agents with whom they interfaced provided an arterial and capillary infrastructure for Tuscan access to the goods, information, plants, animals, and people pouring in from around the world.

How did the Medici reap some of the benefits of an empire they did not possess? This chapter begins by considering the stories of Tuscany's two most famous and best-recorded travelers, Filippo Sassetti and Francesco Carletti. Not only were both Medici clients who secured rare and exotic goods for their patrons, but both directed lengthy documents replete with their observations and analyses to the Medici. From these rich sources, this chapter selects certain themes, starting with the logistics of travel and information and the essential role of Medici patronage and protection. The chapter then offers a brief account of the kinds of political and strategic information that distant informants could provide. Turning from words to objects, it then considers the ways Tuscan diplomats and agents secured luxury items—diamonds, pearls, ebony, elite Asian goods, and semiprecious stones—and had them sent to Tuscany. Finally, the chapter closes with an account of how the Medici network worked both to transport botanical naturalia to Tuscany and to secure the information to make those plants meaningful.

## Filippo Sassetti

As we have seen, members of prominent Florentine patrician families, like the Giraldi and Cavalcanti, built immensely successful careers by launching from Lisbon to Brazil. Others, however, kept their operations based in the Portuguese capital. Prominent among them were the Capponi. Their social and political standing in Florence and extensive interests in the Iberian empires meant that their influence extended into several facets of global commerce and intersected repeatedly with the activities of Medici affiliates.[2] Among their various interests, the Capponi had a firm with a branch in Lisbon from 1577 till 1581.[3] It was at this company that Filippo Sassetti developed his high regard for Lisbon and learned the pepper business.[4]

Sassetti, as it happens, was quite an unusual employee with a remarkable career ahead of him. The Sassetti were an ancient house with a palazzo near the heart of Florence and a close family relationship with the Medici. Francesco Sassetti (1421–1490) had been the director general of the Medici bank (1463–1490) during both its apogee and its decline, a patron of the humanists with an excellent library, and the sponsor of the Sassetti chapel in Santa Trinita, famously frescoed by Domenico Ghirlandaio (1482–1485).[5] For all his great-grandfather's fame, Filippo Sassetti was born in considerably reduced circumstances, which required him to work as a merchant until his family's improved financial position enabled him to leave the merchant's life at twenty-four years of age.[6] Following the fashion of his social milieu, Sassetti turned to literary and botanical pursuits, studying at the University of Pisa under the guidance of Pietro Vettori, joining the Accademia Fiorentina and the Accademia degli Alterati, and writing on Aristotle, Dante, and Ariosto.[7] Having moved among Florence's literary elite, his independent financial position then collapsed with the onset of his brother's financial difficulties, constraining Sassetti to return to gainful employment.[8] He did so in characteristic fashion, by combining his literary skills with his commercial expertise in the treatise *On Commerce between Tuscany and the Levantine Nations* (1577). This he dedicated to Bongianni Gianfigliazzi (1549–1616), a knight of Malta, gentleman of the Medici court, and shortly to be Medici ambassador to the Sublime Porte (1578), a post for which Gianfigliazzi's long captivity in the city (1571–1577) suited him well.[9] Sassetti had, then, dedicated his work to the right person at the right time.

Having established his intellectual, social, and political standing among the Florentine elite, Sassetti secured a position with the Capponi firm, heading first to Madrid and Seville and then to Lisbon in the autumn of 1578.[10] It was quite a remarkable time to be in Portugal, for the childless king Sebastian I had just been killed and much of the Portuguese nobility captured at the Battle of Alcácer Quibir (Al-Ksar al-Kabir) in Morocco on August 4, 1578.[11] As we have seen, the Medici had close financial ties to King Sebastian I and, in association with a consortium of Florentine banking houses, underwrote Philip II's government and its invasion of Portugal in 1580. Sassetti's role in the affair is murky, though it has been argued that he served as a front for the financial dealings of Francesco I.[12] Certainly, Sassetti's movements and the actions of the Capponi firm synchronize closely with political events. The duke of Alba invaded Portugal to vindicate Philip II's claim to the Portuguese throne, an operation whose swift success was assured by the decisive victory at the Battle of Alcântara on August 25, 1580. Philip entered Portugal in December 1580 and in April 1581 was acclaimed king of

Portugal at Tomar rather than Lisbon to avoid the virulent influenza epidemic in the capital.[13]

Sassetti left Lisbon in January 1581 for Madrid, Medina del Campo, and Seville dealing in pepper arriving from the east.[14] At this point, he left the Capponi and took up a more senior position with one of the pepper contractors, Giovan Battista Rovellasca, as chief purchasing agent in India.[15] While in Madrid, Sassetti became a source of valuable information for the Medici ambassador, Bernardo Canigiani, who mentioned him without further explanation in a letter to the grand duke from Madrid on June 26, 1581.[16] In a letter from Canigiani on July 10, 1581, Sassetti appeared as an informant, with news of the progress of the plague in Seville.[17] As late as October 16, 1581, Sassetti appeared in a letter from Canigiani to the grand duke as a resource for the location of places in Lisbon; Canigiani described Sassetti as "most expert about Lisbon."[18] Before leaving Europe, then, Sassetti was familiar to the Medici court and regarded as a reliable witness.

Sassetti first attempted to depart for India from Lisbon in April 1582 with his Tuscan companions Orazio Neretti and Giovanni Buondelmonti.[19] Canigiani, writing on August 6, 1582 about the arriving fleet, mentioned Sassetti in passing noting, "The ship *Caragial* of the fleet of India of Portugal, where Sassetti went, arrived safely at Cape St. Vincent."[20] Unfortunately, Sassetti had not in fact gone to India. On September 17, 1582, Canigiani related further news of the arriving fleet including that the *Caragial* was carrying "the first yet conducted to Lisbon an elephant calf of those of *Zilan* [Ceylon], that they say is a nice thing" before reporting that

> the *S. Filippa* that left for there on the 5th of April, on the 5th of September in the River Tagus at Cascais was reported our Sassetti, where also he had to throw the things in the sea and the ship was about to sink; but it escaped by the prayer and miracle of Our Lady, after 5 months and about 2500 leagues of perilous voyage and fearful of being devoured now by the Anthropophagi now by the Sharks or by the whirlpools of the waves, notwithstanding the discomfort and fears suffered and the bad sign of Fortune that has loosed a most rare and unusual bolt, he is preparing to pass

> to Cochin with the same company at the end of next March
> having, he says, learned by the experience something more
> that he had not known and seen many stars of the other
> Pole, having been there by the equator on the coast of Brazil
> about the River St. Agostino, in the shorter days that are
> there, more than 13 days.[21]

Characteristically curious, Sassetti remained undaunted by his fruitless voyage. Indeed, Canigiani reported to the grand duke from Madrid on November 22, 1582, about "his virtuous and good servant Filippo Sassetti, who is well resolved, not to say obstinate to return to India at the end of March."[22] Sassetti and his companions eventually made it to Goa on the second try in 1583.[23] Once in India, Sassetti's work for the pepper consortium involved sailing his small ship up and down the Malabar Coast, purchasing pepper from the small producers and the minor kings.[24] Simultaneously with this work, Sassetti acted as a correspondent and agent of the Medici. In this capacity, he interpreted his duties as including the supply of commercial and strategic information, rare and exotic goods, and botanical samples and analysis.[25]

As a correspondent, Sassetti perforce relied on the mediation of Tuscans on the Iberian peninsula to transmit the letters and items he remitted to Tuscany. The most important link in this chain was provided by none other than Bongianni Gianfigliazzi, the dedicatee of Sassetti's commercial treatise and now the Medici ambassador in Spain (1583–1587).[26] Gianfigliazzi wrote to the grand duke very regularly, as was expected of ambassadors, and so his correspondence offers an index of communication speed. Sassetti reached the Malabar coast on September 8, 1583.[27] The ambassador wrote from Madrid on July 9, 1584, noting Sassetti's arrival in India.[28] On the 28th, Gianfigliazzi wrote to Francesco I that Sassetti's letters had been received.[29] In parallel, on that same day Giulio Battaglini (1548–1600) also wrote from Madrid to Pietro Usimbardi (1539–1612) in Rome explaining that Sassetti's letters had arrived in Lisbon; Battaglini would later serve as a Medici agent in Naples, while Usimbardi would become secretary of state for Ferdinando I.[30] By September 6, 1584, Francesco I had written to his ambassador in response to Gianfigliazzi's letters of July 19 and 28 and August 10 noting that he had heard from Sassetti.[31] That is, it was almost exactly a year between Sassetti's arrival in India and Francesco I's letter about Sassetti.

A Medici client with a major commercial position and a prominent intellectual with a wide correspondence, Sassetti acted as an organizing point for Tuscan affiliates east of the Cape of Good Hope, starting with his traveling companions. Giovanni Buondelmonti was born in 1540, just a few months before Sassetti, to another patrician Florentine house and had the shortest stay in India, taking ship in January 1585.[32] He returned carrying seeds from Sassetti for Francesco I.[33] The next year, Sassetti wrote from Goa about Giovanni Battista Britti, one of a pair of travelers commissioned to work on behalf of the Tipografia Medicea Orientale (Medici Oriental Press). Britti had encountered trouble with pirates on the way from Hormuz and had ended up in Goa.[34] Sassetti kept the Medici apprised of their affiliates' fortunes, describing Britti as "a servant of the lord Cardinal"—presumably Ferdinando de' Medici— in a letter to Francesco I from Cochin on February 10, 1586.[35]

In 1588, Giovanni Battista Vecchietti, the other of the pair of travelers for the Medici Oriental Press, also appeared in India. He stayed there with Sassetti in Goa and Cochin. Sassetti's untimely death that year led Vecchietti to give a funeral oration for him in Florence.[36] Clearly well liked and respected, Sassetti also received obsequies from his friend and traveling companion, Orazio Neretti. Neretti served as Sassetti's executor and wrote this Latin epitaph for him, which was inscribed at his grave in the Church of the Company of Mercy,[37]

> Filippo Sassetti Florentine citizen
> Overseer of office for spice exports
> Distinguished in the study of nature and mathematics
> Renowned for eloquence in Greek Latin and Etruscan
> To study new things
> Rather than for gain
> Traversed the empty African Ocean
> Stayed in Goa in India
> Nearly all of Europe
> Was enriched by his most excellent observations
> Of the treasures of India
> Orazio Neretti Florentine

> Perpetual dear companion
> With many tears set down
> His dear life and yet still abroad at 46 years
> died in Goa in the year 1588[38]

Sassetti had died in Goa in what he had believed to be an early stage of his journey. His journey was cut short, but his vision for global travel continued as a model and a memory.

In his last surviving letter to the Medici, to Cardinal Ferdinando in 1586, Sassetti had proposed to continue in Medici service. His plan was to circumnavigate the globe, taking seven or eight years to travel to Malacca, the Moluccas, China (presumably Macao), Manila, on the Manila Galleon to Acapulco, two years throughout the Americas, and finally to return to Tuscany.[39] Circumnavigation on a single ship was rare but had been done. Sassetti's proposal was different. His ambitious journey involved no great feats of individual navigation. Instead, he saw the possibilities inherent in the recent expansion of Iberian power and in the just-created Iberian Union. The first key component of Sassetti's plan had slotted into place with the development of the small Portuguese outpost in Macao in 1557.[40] The critical link, however, came into being fourteen years later, with the establishment of the Spanish outpost of Manila in 1571.[41] With the development of a triangular trade among Nagasaki, Macao, and Manila, European trade routes now spanned the world, but they were fragile and narrow at their extremities.[42]

Politics, however, remained a different matter, as Sassetti had clearly understood. In his letter soliciting the support of Cardinal Medici for his plans, Sassetti pointed out that imperial officials were quite hostile to the presence of foreigners within their domains, being suspicious of the information they might gain. Indeed, the Castilians prohibited travel by foreigners through the Indies without a license.[43] Sassetti was entirely correct to stress the importance of the legal privileges that carefully guarded access to specific pieces of Iberian overseas empire. In 1563, for instance, António Galvão published a treatise on the discoveries to 1550. In it, Galvão explained that at the death of Queen Isabella (1504), the subjects of the Crown of Aragon (Aragonese, Catalans, and Valencians) were to be excluded and the discoveries confined to Isabella's former subjects. Only with Ferdinand's accession as regent of Castile in 1506 was access to the Castilian share of the Indies granted to all residents of Iberia, except for the Portuguese.[44] The exclusion of the Portuguese specifically took on an added significance with Philip II's accession to the Portuguese throne. Far from dissolving his possessions into a unified, centralized empire, Philip solemnly promised to govern Portugal and its overseas possessions separately.[45] Strictly speaking, this meant that the regular commercial routes of Philip II's domains annually circled the world but circumnavigation using these possessions was illegal, especially after Philip II's explicit prohibition on trade between the Portuguese and Spanish outposts in Asia in 1587.[46] Sassetti, ever the official figure, politely solicited permission in advance for his proposed itinerary. There was, however, another way. Enter, the smugglers.

## Francesco Carletti

On May 20, 1591, at the age of eighteen, Francesco Carletti set out from Florence.[47] Departing from Livorno on the ship of the Genoese Pietro Paolo Vassallo, he arrived at Alicante and transferred from there to Seville, where the young man worked for the Florentine merchant Niccolò Parenti. Two years later, Antonio Carletti, Francesco's father, came to Seville. There, Antonio came to a secret agreement with another resident Tuscan, Cesare Baroncini of Pisa, who was married to a Spanish woman who Francesco does not name in his account. This marriage provided the legal fig leaf for Carletti's journey. Carletti ostensibly traveled as Baroncini's wife's proxy, while a second document set out the real state of affairs. Somehow raising no suspicions, the young Carletti then hired a little four-hundred-*salme* ship, cleared inspections, and set sail in January 1594 with Antonio Carletti onboard entirely illicitly.[48] Using and abusing the malleability of identity and family ties, a group of substantial Tuscan merchants easily subverted Spanish rules. This type of activity is, of course, typically invisible, recorded either as Spanish commerce or not at all. Yet it has been argued that, for some parts of the Spanish imperial economy, this shadow commerce overshadowed the official economy.[49]

The initial plan seems to have been a simple slaving voyage, buying slaves from the Portuguese on the Cape Verde Islands and selling them to the Spanish in Cartagena de Indias in South America.[50] In a situation fraught with ironies, Francesco Carletti was arrested in Cartagena, not for either of his actual smuggling offenses—his father Antonio successfully landed secretly in Cartagena—but instead for a purported shortage of slaving licenses, invented, in Francesco Carletti's telling, as a way to corruptly extract bribes. He also seems to have been cleared more through Medici influence than the merits of the case. His imprisonment lasted but three days before letters arrived on a Spanish fleet from Don Pietro Medici to Don Pedro Bravo de Acuña, a knight of St. John of Malta and the Spanish governor of the city.[51] Prince Pietro di Cosimo I de' Medici (1554-1604), son of Cosimo I and Eleonora of Toledo, former general of the Tuscan galleys, general of the Italian infantry in Spain, and lieutenant of the Italian infantry in the invasion of Portugal, was quite the ally for the Carletti to have.[52] The letters prompted an immediate change in attitude. Francesco Carletti was released from his tropical prison cell and the two Carlettis were granted permission to travel and trade in the Spanish Americas as if they had been granted a license by Philip II. Francesco Carletti's status as a proxy held and the governor generously offered Antonio Carletti permission to travel for the modest sum of 500 reales, and so the Carletti were free to depart, which they did on August 12, 1594.[53]

Having crossed the Isthmus of Panama between Nombre de Dios and Panamá City, the Carlettis arrived in Lima in January 1595. There they encountered further layers of Spanish bureaucracy, as they had to secure, with some trouble and expense, a license that confirmed, in effect, that they had no outstanding legal, tax, commercial, religious, or marital obligations in Peru before heading to the Viceroyalty of New Spain.[54] This license sufficed for their journey to Mexico City, where they stayed from June 1595 to March 1596.

Having used Medici influence to access the Spanish Americas, the Carlettis could easily have returned to Spain, completing a two-and-a-half-year journey. Doing so would have been safe and legal. Smugglers that they were, however, the Carlettis saw possibilities for vast arbitrage profits in Asia and took the opposite tack. Francesco explained that legal access to the Manila Galleon was restricted to those licensed by the viceroy, which was granted only to those seeking to emigrate or to those serving aboard ship.[55] Nothing daunted, the Carlettis made a deal with the captain of one of the two ships. Antonio was registered as artillery constable and his son as ship's guardian; the captain kept their salaries and provided two actual sailors to perform the duties.[56] The Carlettis confronted another, similar licensing problem shipping their goods, apparently principally silver, since only 500,000 *scudi* could be legally transported annually.[57] As ship's officers, however, the Carletti secured a license and, paying the captain 2 percent, transported their goods safely. The Carlettis were experiencing, in fact, how the vast majority of goods traveled, to the tune of a million gold *scudi*. That is, the Carlettis' experience with licensing restrictions is significant precisely for how common it was.[58]

Having made it to Manila in May 1597, the Carlettis found that the obstacles, legal and commercial, to returning quickly to New Spain were formidable. Particularly significant was the temporary scarcity of Japanese and Chinese goods after a large fire in the *parian* outside Manila.[59] Here, the Carlettis made their most creative move. If Japanese and Chinese goods were unavailable in Manila, why not go to the source, skip the bottleneck of Manila, and return by continuing west? The simple answer, as Francesco Carletti recognized, was that doing so was entirely illegal. It required a license from the governor of Manila to avert the prohibition on travel between the Portuguese and Spanish possessions in the East. Francesco Carletti frankly acknowledged that such a license was never granted and that the penalties for violations included confiscation of goods, imprisonment, and shipment in chains to Lisbon.[60] Carletti was well informed about the rules, which was just as well, for they had recently been reiterated.

In March 1594 King Philip II wrote to his viceroy in Goa reaffirming his prohibition on commerce between the Portuguese East Indies and Castilian West Indies. Specifically, he commanded "that no one from those parts that are under the government and administration of the Castilians will go to that of the Portuguese, nor any others without my special license given by provision signed by me, and not by my Viceroys, or Governors, because they are not fit to be able to give them such licenses!"[61] The king then addressed the obvious inconvenience to the global activities of the Catholic Church by insisting specifically that religious traveling from the Philippines to Macao, Malacca, or India— that is, to the principal Portuguese posts—required "my express license passed by the ministers of the said Crown of Portugal to be able to go to the said parts."[62] To be certain these rules were respected, the royal command was "to be published in the public places of Goa, Cochin, Malacca, and Macao."[63] As the example of Governor Acuña in Cartagena showed, Spanish governors were in the habit of issuing precisely the sort of license that Philip II expressly prohibited. The Carlettis' timing was unfortunate, however, for an order only issued in 1594 had probably been received no earlier than 1595 or even 1596; in this context, it might well have been obeyed with some alacrity in Manila in 1596–1597.

To the Carlettis, legal barriers were a surmountable inconvenience when set against the glorious possibility of circumnavigation, which Francesco Carletti exalted as being possible to complete in under four years using the Iberian empires.[64] Confronted with a blanket prohibition and unwilling to remain stuck in Manila, the Carlettis devised a legal workaround that they believed ought to have been satisfactory. Making an arrangement with a Japanese ship, which was trading in flour to Manila from Nagasaki, the Carletti loaded their wealth in silver bars and secretly slipped on board at night, without so much as seeking permission to leave Manila.[65] The Carlettis seem not to have considered that secretly smuggling silver on a Japanese ship might not be considered consistent with the law upon arrival in Macao. For the time being, however, the plan worked smoothly, and the Carlettis landed safely with their goods in Japan in June 1597.[66]

Some hint of the difficulties they would face, however, came with a consequence of the infrequency of contacts between Manila and Macao: calendar time. Meeting the Portuguese coming from Macao in Nagasaki, Carletti found that they could not agree on the date, each having adjusted the time in the opposite way in their journeys from Lisbon and Seville. A de facto dateline had emerged. Carletti, ever the believer in unfettered travel, immediately appreciated the most vulnerable point for the Iberian prohibition. Citing occasional, perhaps imagined, single-day journeys between Nagasaki, which operated on Portuguese time, and Manila, Carletti pointed out the absurdity of possible double-celebrations of the same holiday or of celebrating two different holidays on the same day. This was a canny point, for Carletti focused on Easter and Christmas; the uniform celebration of the former had long been a Catholic priority.[67]

Resident in Nagasaki, the Carlettis were in a legally tenuous situation. They could not return to Manila without reckoning with their illicit departure. Having had no official contact with the Estado da Índia, they had no legitimate path to entering Portuguese territory. Their best hope lay in three features of the Portuguese position east of Melaka (Malacca). The first and foremost was the exiguousness of the Portuguese state,[68] which opened the way for other actors with other priorities to play a proportionally larger role. So scarce was Portuguese manpower that they relied heavily on the Japanese to help make it work at all, with the Japanese providing both shipping of their own and manpower for mixed-ethnicity Portuguese vessels.[69] Finally, the Portuguese both supported and relied on the activities of the religious orders, above all the Jesuits, whose religious mission played a disproportionately large role in East Asia.[70] Confronted with this situation, the Carlettis sought the aid of both the Jesuits and the Japanese. The normal Portuguese ship having failed to arrive, the Carlettis chose to embark on a Japanese ship heading for Cochin China (Vietnam) under the command of a half-Japanese, half-Portuguese captain; the ship left Nagasaki on March 3, 1598.[71] Well aware that they faced the confiscation of their goods for traveling without a license, the Carlettis befriended the Jesuits aboard ship. Using their well-honed nocturnal skills, they landed their goods at midnight and brought them to the Jesuits for protection.[72] As expected, the Carlettis were then arrested and imprisoned in Macao.[73]

The Carlettis' plan seems to have relied on using the legal loophole provided by their itinerary and nationality and the influence of the Jesuits to make a deal that would launder their illicitly imported goods. The Jesuits had good reasons of their own to support these Medici-affiliated Florentines. As a universal order reporting directly to the papacy, their mission stood in structural tension with the *Padroado Real*, which granted the Portuguese Crown extensive rights of patronage and control over the Church in the Portuguese Empire.[74] Policies of national exclusion that explicitly prohibited the free movement of religious personnel and wreaked havoc on the uniform practice of Catholicism would have been particularly uncongenial to the Jesuits. The earliest Jesuits in Macao would have had particular cause to disdain policies of national exclusion, since so many were Italian. Carletti derived his information on the expenses of the missions to China and Japan from the Visitor who gave the orders, Alessandro Valignano (1539–1606), and three early Jesuits in China were Matteo Ricci (Macerata, 1552–Beijing, 1610), Michele Ruggieri (Spinazzola, 1543–Salerno, 1607), and Francesco Pasio (1554–1612).[75] Because Ferdinando I had been Cardinal Medici and still exerted considerable influence in Rome, the Carlettis' status as Medici clients would also have stood in favor of the Jesuits' offering support.

Their goods might be safe with the Jesuits, but the Carlettis still faced the matter of their imprisonment by the Portuguese imperial authorities, who asked whether the Carlettis were not aware of the prohibition. To this "we replied that we had come to the Philippine Islands, and from those to Japan and then in this of Amacao from where it was our thought and desire to pass to the East India for our wonderment and curiosity and not for any other interest or anything else that contravened or transgressed the Royal orders of the one or the other Crown, moreover that we were of the Italian nation, and that we had come from a free Country, as was Japan, at no point subject to the one or the other Spanish nation and that going through the world was a thing that is permitted to all the nations."[76] This failed to impress the Portuguese authorities. They fined them 2,000 *scudi* but also released them from jail after three days with the injunction that they go to the viceroy in Goa at the first opportunity. Presumably, the Carlettis' reliance on the Jesuits succeeded in protecting their goods, since Francesco Carletti subsequently bought high-quality porcelain with Jesuit assistance.[77]

The Portuguese authorities were both protecting traditional Portuguese privileges and responding to royal directives. This policy of royal firmness would continue unabated. On March 19, 1609, Philip III wrote to viceroy Ruy Lourenço de Tavora "about the prohibition of the commerce from the West Indies with the East" specifying "that in no way the said commerce be permitted for one or other part." He nonetheless conceded that the military needs of the Philippines could be most conveniently addressed from Macao and authorized the transfer of munitions.[78] The Carletti claim to freedom of navigation was never likely to succeed in a political environment focused overwhelmingly on restrictions, privileges, and security. In the intimate world of Portuguese Macao, however, the full rigor of the law was strongly susceptible to modification in light of personal circumstances. We have seen this operate elsewhere in the form of personal influence. It could also operate on the basis of sympathy. Antonio Carletti died in Macao on July 20, 1598, and his son had him buried in the cathedral with an appropriate inscription. Francesco Carletti, perhaps just twenty-five years old, was then quietly excused his punishment and allowed to proceed freely.[79]

Left adrift in Macao, Francesco Carletti might have been in a difficult position. Fortuitously, less than a fortnight later, succor arrived in the form of a veteran traveler who knew the pain of composing an epitaph for a lost companion in Asia: Sassetti's friend Orazio Neretti.[80] Carletti and Neretti became close friends and neighbors in the seventeen months that they stayed together in Macao.[81] The meeting was extraordinarily fortunate for Carletti, for Neretti was an old Asia hand, having spent the last decade and a half there. This, as it happened, was not the half of it, for Neretti would eventually write to Grand Duke Cosimo II from Macao on January 8, 1617, sending two bamboo screens and recounting his personal history.[82] He wrote, "It pleased God that, the youthful ardor of seeing new countries and people that I had never seen before, it is already thirty-eight years since I left Tuscany, of which I spent some in the East Indies in the service of the King of Spain, others I spent in this last part of the world, in China and Japan, and finally, laden with years, and with a leg rendered useless by an arquebus ball fighting at sea with the Moors of Malabar, I remained as citizen in this city of Macao, port of China, with house, wife, and children."[83] Neretti had been wounded in valorous maritime conflict in 1593, which left him sick for the next four years and crippled thereafter.[84] His reference to royal service may be to his later diplomatic work but probably refers to military service, which would date to between 1588, the year of Sassetti's death, and 1593. As the Giraldi and Cavalcanti found, ties to Florence and to the Medici lingered for decades and across thousands of miles. They could also be affirmed by return to Florence, a trip that Carletti slowly began in December 1599.

Staying briefly in Malacca, Carletti arrived in Cochin in March 1600 and a few days later landed in Goa. There he would stay until Christmas 1601. Boarding the *Saint James*, a ship of the Carreira da Índia, Carletti then set out for Lisbon. He never made it, for his ship was defeated and captured in battle by the Dutch off Saint Helena on March 14–16,

1602.[85] Carletti's Portuguese companions were left, stripped of their possessions, on the island of Fernando de Noronha. Had Carletti fully embraced Portuguese identity, he too would have been left penniless on a remote island with nothing but a boat to secure help from Brazil.[86] Carletti, however, shed his Portuguese affiliation, just as before he had shed his Spanish identity, and identified himself as Tuscan. After the Portuguese defeat in naval battle, when it looked as if the damaged Portuguese carrack might not survive the night (though it did), Carletti used his Italian to arrange a deal with an Italian-speaking mate aboard the Dutch ship; this allowed Carletti to transfer to the Dutch ship. Language and nationality were critical, although so also was class, for this deal was predicated on Carletti's wealth, including in jewels, musk, and "the little structure in which the bed was, with other curious things that I was bringing to Your Serene Highness," Ferdinando I.[87]

Carletti had escaped the miserable marooning of the Portuguese by returning to his Tuscan identity and boarding the Dutch ship. Indeed, Carletti not only returned with the Dutch to Zeeland, but was treated with courtesy, given his clothes back, and invited to sleep near the captain and to dine with him in a friendly manner. Carletti understood these gestures as resulting from a calculation. Carletti had "fortified my reasons to induce them to do me this service by telling them to remember the courteous treatment and cherishing that Your Serene Highness continually gives them when they come to your port of Livorno, the which thing many remembering, they favored me and arranged to please me."[88] Carletti's positive language politely masks that he was saved by threatening the Dutch with retribution, a threat that he, bearing a silk canopy from China embroidered with the Medici arms, could credibly make.[89] In 1602, the Dutch were interlopers in the Mediterranean and still needed Livorno.

Awareness of this power dynamic propelled Carletti not to content himself with return to Europe.[90] Rather, he did something that defied the logic of religiously tinged high seas warfare. He sued the Dutch. Leaving aside the irony of such an accomplished smuggler posing as a law-abiding citizen, this was a remarkable move that threatened to create quite unpleasant precedents. Fascinating as they are, the details of Carletti's multiyear legal struggle—they constitute the final tenth of his account—need not concern us here because, as so often in Carletti's life, the law was not what settled his case. Power did. To secure access to this power, Carletti needed to reopen direct ties with the Medici. As it happened, there was then a Florentine, Paolo Franceschi, in Middleburg. He apprised Carletti, who had been out of Europe since 1594, of the situation, including that of the grand duke.[91] Carletti wrote immediately to Giovanni Macinghi in Florence seeking Ferdinando I's intercession on his behalf. The grand duke honored Carletti's request for letters of support directed to the *Stadtholder* Maurice of Nassau (1567–1625), but Carletti had misunderstood the Dutch political system. Carletti reported that he was graciously received at the siege of Grave (July 18–September 20, 1602) by Maurice of Nassau, but that Nassau reported that he did not have jurisdiction over such matters.[92] Even so, Carletti's early success in mobilizing Medici support boded well for his case.

Here the distinction between the Medici and Tuscany matters, for Carletti's most powerful protector, if not his most effective, was Marie de' Medici, Queen of France. Carletti noted gratefully that he had received letters of support from both the grand duke and the queen of France. They reacted differently, however, to the matter of Medici property. The Dutch sent the bed "and the other curiosities, which I was carrying for Your Serene Highness" to Marie de' Medici because the grand duke had refused them, not wanting to prejudice Carletti's cause by accepting them.[93] The original offer to Ferdinando I was a natural enough attempt to settle the case, addressing the seizure of a sovereign prince's property while leaving Carletti's personal misfortune out of it. Ferdinando I certainly could have accepted this distinction between Carletti as a carrier of Medici property and Carletti as a private merchant who took the same risks as did other Portuguese merchants. This seems to have been what Marie de' Medici did, presumably because the precedent for Florentine merchants mattered less to her than to Ferdinando.[94]

Ferdinando I, however, rejected the distinction between Medici agent and Florentine merchant, extending his protection to Carletti and, tacitly, to Florentine property generally. His action is not surprising on three levels. First, Ferdinando's prestige was involved in the protection of his client. As the ruler of a commercial society, the grand duke also had strong political reasons to assert his protection over the

numerous Tuscan merchants operating outside Tuscany. Failure to protect them would have been politicly unpopular. Although Medici rule
was sustained by dynastic right and naked force, it was also founded
on the idea that a strong and stable state would defend the interests of
elite Florentines. These were still generally merchants and bankers, as,
indeed, were the Medici after a fashion. The decision to refuse relatively
unimportant luxury goods to avoid setting the precedent thus made
good economic and political sense. Finally, Ferdinando I was interested
in promoting Tuscan trade and activity outside its traditional circuits,
which would have been helped by securing protection for Tuscans from
the Dutch.

The Carletti affair was a particularly good test case for Ferdinando.
That Carletti was a Medici client made it difficult for the Dutch to
ride roughshod over his rights. The optics and the power dynamics
also worked in his favor. The Dutch were, of course, heretics from the
Tuscan perspective. As Carletti wrote of the sailors from Zeeland in the
course of his Korean servant's trick to secure rescue from the stricken
Portuguese vessel, "these as being Calvinist heretics for the most part
did not want to see pictures of saints nor of the selfsame God cruci-
fied."[95] Carletti knew of what he spoke with regard to Dutch beliefs, for
his legal troubles kept him in the Dutch Republic from July 7, 1602 to
December 1605.[96] Standing up to what the Florentines would have seen
as heretical pirates was certainly good politics in Counter-Reformation
Tuscany.

The power politics also worked in the grand duke's favor. This
proved decisive. The States General ultimately settled with Carletti
because Ferdinando I escalated the case, threatening the Dutch quite
directly. Referring to the States General, Carletti explained "when Your
Serene Highness wrote that letter that if they did not render me my
goods and curiosities that I was carrying for Your Highness you would
be forced to retaliate for it against their ships, merchandise, and people,
who might come and trade in these your ports. About that the Province of Holland recovered its senses and made a solemn Protest to that
of Zealand, that they needed to render me mine."[97] The very prepon-
derance of Dutch shipping and the persistent weakness of the Tuscan
merchant marine—a very old situation—meant that a tit-for-tat game
of confiscations would go poorly for the Dutch.[98] There was simply

less in the way of vulnerable Tuscan property to seize. A further escalation would also have been quite undesirable for the Dutch because Tuscany always had the option of being more helpful to its traditional ally, Spain, in its struggle with the Dutch Republic. Tuscany would have been a small addition to the big problems the Dutch faced, but the case highlights the fact that the relative harmony, indeed warmth, of Dutch-Tuscan relations in commercial and maritime matters was anomalous and subject to reciprocal goodwill. The Dutch recognized this as well. In the bare-knuckles arena of seventeenth-century trade, piracy, and naval warfare, the Grand Duchy, its institutions, and the new port of Livorno were showing their utility. Unlike their position under the Republic, the Medici now had a tool to respond to arbitrary confiscations of Tuscan commercial property. The tool worked.

Sensing the power of his position, Carletti was ultimately dissatisfied with the final settlement; it was, nonetheless, extraordinary. The 1605 retrial was to be settled amicably between him and the "Administrators of the company of Merchants who do business with the East Indies" (the VOC), with Carletti receiving the remarkable sum of 13,000 florins. Both sides agreed to accept that they made the settlement "not because they mistrusted the justice of their goods reasons, but to please the said States General, and for respect of the favor of the letters of the Queen of France, and of those of the Grand Duke of Tuscany." This reference to the political rationale for the settlement and the unwillingness to concede on de jure grounds dovetailed with a firm insistence that Carletti's case set no precedent either for actions against "that Company or other that do similarly to others for a certain consequence and obligation, but only for the aforesaid considerations."[99] With hindsight we can see how extraordinary it was for Carletti to take on the VOC and win.[100] The VOC's charter dates to 1602, the year Carletti arrived on a Zeeland ship demanding redress and posing a serious threat to the VOC's originally predatory model.[101] The settlement may not have set a precedent protecting all Florentine merchants, but it did free Carletti to leave with a large sum, protected the VOC's model, and relieved the grand duke from acting on his threats,[102] which ultimately preserved Tuscan-Dutch relations.

Carletti faced a conundrum after his partial success with the Dutch. What to do next? He was clearly a well-informed, accomplished merchant with capital on hand. Carletti reported that his original plan was to return to Spain via England in spite of entreaties from Dutch merchants that he work on their behalf.[103] One can see why the Dutch might have been interested because of Carletti's long experience—especially his intimate inside knowledge of the Iberian overseas empires—and indefatigable resilience. Similarly, it is not hard to see why Carletti would have been disinclined to assist the Dutch not only because of his experiences with the VOC but also because of his conventional Catholicism. The choice was ultimately an easy one, however, for the Dutch were not the only ones interested in Carletti's knowledge.

No less a figure than the king of France wrote to Carletti asking him to come to his court. Henry IV of France did not, of course, do so unprompted, for Carletti had met beforehand with the French ambassador to the States General. Carletti's excitement about the invitation to come to Paris to discuss the possibility of working for Henri IV was palpable. He memorized Henry IV's brief personal invitation and offered to recite it to the grand duke. Carletti's decision to include the letter in his account marks the extent to which it validated his status as a global expert. For Ferdinando I, it must have been gratifying that the king of France was also interested in Carletti's services. In any event, Carletti traveled to Paris and met with the king. Flattering Ferdinando I, Carletti's account of his meeting with the Henry IV likened his royal complex to that of Florence, comparing a passage from the Louvre to the Tuileries to the passage linking Palazzo Vecchio and Palazzo Pitti. Ultimately, Carletti was not employed by Henry IV—a result of internal court politics in Carletti's account—but he was paid for his trouble and took the opportunity to pay his respects to his supporter in his travails with the Dutch, Queen Marie de' Medici, before returning to Florence on July 12, 1606.[104]

The Medici role as protectors of Tuscans abroad dovetailed with the way that Tuscan identity, while hardly exclusive, remained quite enduring. Francesco Carletti could become Spanish, Antonio Cavalcanti insist on his Luso-Brazilian status, Orazio Neretti settle as a citizen in Macao, and Filippo Sassetti live in Spain, Portugal, and Goa while dreaming of world travel, and yet all were ineluctably tied to both Florence and the Medici. Others, like Francesco Giraldi, might respond with courtesy to Medici requests, tacitly recognizing an old tie. Not all the affiliations were positive: Luca Giraldi stayed away from Florence with the Medici destruction of the republic, the Cavalcanti-Giraldi bank was on the opposite side of a quarrel with the Medici-backed Paolo Giordano Orsini, and both Paolo Giordano and the Orsini of Pitigliano sometimes had openly conflictual relations with the Medici. The Medici were, of course, also not synonymous with Florence nor were they always unified, as Ferdinando's sometimes fractious relationship with Don Pietro Medici shows. For all that, whether in the small hill towns of southern Tuscany or a remote Portuguese outpost on the coast of China, the Medici and the interleaved network of Florentine patrician families that had made their peace with the regime exerted a powerful pull.

Private Tuscans affiliated with the Medici squeezed their way through the half-opened doors of the Iberian empires. Relying on family, friends, and patrons; malleable identities; the universal institution of the Catholic Church; and a bit of subterfuge, they entered prohibited spaces and carved out influential and profitable positions. These private Florentines offered ways for family ties, money, and patronage both to insert the Medici into places where they could not go in their official capacity and to bring items and information back to them.

## Thinking Strategically about Asia

In a political environment in which news increasingly proliferated in the form of letters, *avvisi, relazioni,* books, pamphlets, and personal accounts, access to essential information about Europe and the Mediterranean could be secured by a wide variety of actors, official and private. The Medici certainly benefited from the services of a comparatively efficient and well-organized bureaucracy, a large and effective diplomatic network, and a broad range of agents and correspondents who sent, received, collated, and analyzed recent information. For the immediate needs of the Grand Duchy of Tuscany and the Medici, this information served quite well. On a much smaller scale, the Medici and a restricted set of Florentine patricians were also privy to manuscript and private information from much further afield, which allowed them to think globally about politics and society. Some of this information might have facilitated judgment about investment opportunities in Asia or the prospects of empires and trading companies. Intellectual curiosity, commitment to the global project of spreading Catholicism, and a general interest in the organization of society for politics and warfare also made Florentine travelers' reports treasured items, retained in the Medici collections and later published and republished.

Foremost among these were the letters of Filippo Sassetti and Francesco Carletti's *Ragionamenti* describing his circumnavigation.[105] Between them, Sassetti and Carletti offered the Medici brief, compelling analyses of the principal relevant polities in maritime Asia. Carletti also wrote extensively about Spanish America, but the present section will concentrate on Asia. Sassetti sketched the strategic position of the Estado da Índia, the structure of the polities of South India, the power of the Mughal Empire, the dynamics of the Muslim spice route, and the violent Iberian actions in Maluku (the Spice Islands). To this portrait, Carletti added perceptive analyses of Japan, China, and the fragile position of the Spanish and Portuguese in East and Southeast Asia. Here I sketch their principal themes and conclusions to show that, by the early seventeenth century, the Medici possessed a remarkably clear sense of Asian politics and society.

### Portuguese Fortresses

Filippo Sassetti's striking breadth of vision about the spice trade and the stinging critiques he leveled at key elements of the Portuguese system—particularly the role of corruption, mismanagement, and self-seeking in undermining such core activities as the Carreira da Índia and the interdiction of Muslim spice trading—have already featured in my discussion of Tuscany's interest in acquiring the pepper contract. Here, I turn to Sassetti's strategic judgment about the Portuguese Empire. Resident at the heart of the Estado da Índia, Sassetti understood that it was held together by fortified points.[106] This matches the modern historiographic stress on the centrality of fortified naval bases to the long defense of Portugal's extraordinarily stretched Estado da Índia, beset as it was by numerous and powerful foes.[107] Portugal's network of fortifications fit a very old pattern for maritime powers, one pursued by thalassocracies from ancient Athens through medieval Venice and Genoa. It involved ringing the edges of a commercially critical sea with fortified bases and holding island outposts to control trade routes, maintain secure anchorages, and dominate critical export centers. When it worked, such a model allowed a small state to secure a wildly disproportionate share of the revenues from commerce, bringing prosperity to the imperial power and its affiliates while avoiding the expense and difficulty of landed domains. The approach, however, had intrinsic structural weaknesses. At sea, the expensive network of fleets and fortifications leads a maritime empire to pursue monopoly, squeezing out competitors and free riders on maritime security. To do so required an aggressive and explicitly selfish policy directed against peaceful commerce, one that nearly guaranteed resentment and opposition. On land, the maritime power was, almost by definition, locally outnumbered by inland polities who saw the profits of their commerce skimmed by a foreign monopolist. For some major continental powers, such an arrangement offered certain political and commercial attractions, like access to markets, weapons, and technology provided by a power that, while difficult to dislodge, was controllable and seemed to pose no strategic threat. In the case of Portugal's empire in the east, the Estado da Índia, the fortresses might overawe minor principalities, but they could not resist a major empire. Even so, for technical reasons related to the power of newly improved European naval gunnery and artillery fortifications, Asian powers typically found European fortresses to be difficult to take and at this early period rarely did so without assistance from other European powers. The major fortresses that fell to Asian states, like Hormuz and Malacca, only fell in East India Company (English)-Persian and VOC (Dutch)-Johor allied operations; more minor fortresses were rather more vulnerable.[108]

The Medici, ensconced in their own heavily fortified state, might well have been receptive to a strategic analysis of political power that placed fortresses at the center. Well attuned to the Medici court's interests and perceptive in his analysis of Portuguese strengths and weaknesses, less than three months after his arrival in India, Sassetti wrote to Francesco I about the Portuguese fortresses on the Malabar (southwestern) coast of India, "The Portuguese retain many places on this seacoast, where they have certain fortresses made anciently and with many of these there is a population; where their people live, not without great danger of falling prey to the natives at their every desire, being all poorly provisioned and badly cared for; and what is worse, they often give them many reasons" for offense.[109] Fortress design having undergone a revolution centered on the Italian peninsula in the first few decades of the sixteenth century, the reference to the age of the fortresses was probably intended to convey that they were not the state-of-the-art angle-bastioned artillery fortresses but of a more vulnerable older type.[110] Sassetti was an informed outsider, not a military professional, and so he was generally unconcerned with technical details. He noted numbers, types, and quality, but not much else. This was more than sufficient to underpin Sassetti's view of the Estado da Índia as decrepit and vulnerable, though not terminally so. In his letter of February 11, 1585, to Francesco I, Sassetti explained that Philip II had dispatched a Milanese engineer, probably to be identified as Filippo Magrera, to review the fortifications and perhaps to reform the militia and justice as well. Sassetti lamented that "for one thing and the other it is reduced to a state of compassion and to expect all the bad results" a pessimism relieved only by his equal disregard for the local Indian population's ability to resist.[111] The fortresses were not sufficient, however, for the Indian Muslims—"these Moors of Malabar"—used what Sassetti regarded as piratical tactics to raid in small, heavily manned boats to such effect "that they are those that have destroyed in a certain way this state and brought much shame to the Portuguese fleet."[112]

The next year, on February 10, Sassetti wrote to the grand duke from Cochin about a Portuguese effort to build a fortress at Panane (now Ponnani) on the Malabar coast about 70 kilometers south of Calicut (now Kozhikode),: "now there is, at the point, a fleet of seven galleys and seventy galliots [a small, fast galley], with two thousand five hundred soldiers, to go and build the city and fortress that the Zamorin consented for them to make in his port, called Panane, sixteen leagues from Cochin, where there is a river, a very secure post for the vessels, and it is where the Moors used to dispatch a large part of their ships that they used to send to Mecca."[113] The Portuguese had concentrated a large part of their forces in the Estado da Índia to build a diplomatically sanctioned fortress directed at protecting their fleets and policing the Muslim spice trade. The fortress hardly evinced trust, however, for "this fortress is esteemed for keeping this prince in check."[114] For all Sassetti's critique of decrepitude, then, the Estado da Índia was still expanding.

Sassetti's report on the Portuguese project of extending their fortification network fit in with a broader pattern of Medici information gathering. Sassetti's description was particularly timely and directed individually to the grand duke, but the Medici also tapped other sources for news about military developments in the Estado da Índia. A decade before Sassetti's arrival in Goa, the Medici had received a letter from Goa that discussed political and military developments in India and the Middle East and the spice trade from Maluku to Aleppo.[115] Two years after Sassetti's report, Camillo di Francesco Guidi (1555-1623), then a Medici diplomat in Spain, sent an *avviso* describing an apparently successful Portuguese military action near Malacca (now Melaka).[116] In the first decade of the seventeenth century, the Medici were still receiving reports on military actions in the Estado da Índia, in this case on the military contest between the Dutch and Portuguese over Ternate, whence the cloves came.[117] The Medici were well positioned to contextualize this news from Ternate, for Sassetti had written to them about the drama in the Spice Islands.

The troubled history of Ternate and its neighbors among the Spice Islands in the years after the opening of European seaborne contact constitute an intricate and ultimately tragic narrative. The pursuit of riches on beautiful tropical isles mixed with remarkable violence and religious fervor brought successively the Portuguese, Spanish, English, and Dutch. These last eventually imposed a coercive monopoly from the 1630s.[118] In a February 10, 1586 letter to the grand duke, Sassetti relayed news delivered by a Chinese junk that had arrived in India from Malacca. A force of six hundred Castilian infantry had set forth on frigates from "Manila to conquer the island of Ternate, the king of which was a rebel of this state."[119] Sassetti briefly sketched the causes of the quarrel, explaining that "the father of this modern king was a great friend of the Portuguese" who had wanted to send his son to be schooled in Christian doctrine. Sassetti then explained that there was, by an old agreement, a fortress with a garrison of two hundred Portuguese soldiers.[120] The captain of the Portuguese fortress then murdered the king of Ternate in the gateway of the fortress "in cold blood." Naturally the act provoked rebellion and the Portuguese were forced to flee to neighboring Tidore, where they set up a fortress.[121] The Portuguese fortresses, then, symbolized their presence and facilitated their actions, but they did not grant impunity. Ominously for their future, the Portuguese position in this valuable corner of the spice trade was underpinned by a Castilian military intervention made possible by the Iberian Union even as that same union sought to prohibit commercial ties between the Philippines and the Estado da Índia.

Indian Politics

Despite the astonishingly broad scope of Portuguese activity and the very large role that the Estado da Índia and its corresponding informal empire played in long-distance international commerce, the Portuguese were minor political players in both Asia and Africa. Portugal's outposts stood at the edge of a world of much larger polities, from Iran to Japan. In South Asia, the challenge consisted of two parts. In the north, the rapidly expanding Mughal Empire loomed, a threat that culminated in the near total conquest of the subcontinent briefly achieved at the end of the seventeenth century. Sassetti's assessment of Mughal prospects was judicious and prescient. He carefully reported Mughal conquests and assessed their chances.[122] Consistent with his good strategic judgment, Sassetti feared the Mughals as a threat of a much higher order of magnitude than the rulers of Cochin, Calicut, or Ceylon. Already by 1586, in a letter to the grand duke, Sassetti issued quite a clear warning about the Mogor (Mughal Emperor Akbar [r. 1556–1605]): "however, as the ambition is without end, he will come to conquer all of India without anyone being able to oppose him."[123] Akbar's sweeping conquests did not quite amount to all of India, a project that would absorb his successors and eventually exhaust the empire, but Sassetti was fully justified in fearing the scale of military power the Mughals had at their disposal and the scope of their ambition. Because a relatively minor Indian monarch had besieged Goa but ten years before, only to be foiled by betrayal among his captains, Sassetti had plenty of cause to fear a much more substantial sovereign.[124]

Closer to the center of Portuguese activity, the south was intensely politically fragmented after the 1565 sack, by a coalition of its neighbors, of Hindu Vijayanagara, capital of the greatest South Indian empire, which started its long collapse. When the Portuguese built their fortresses on the coasts of peninsular India, they faced a series of small coastal states, the waning power of the Vijayanagara Empire, and the expansionist Deccan sultanates.[125] Sassetti engaged in several deep investigations into the multifarious elements of the local political situation in peninsular India, probably because natural curiosity about his new residence and his need for information as agent of the pepper monopoly aligned with the concerns of the Medici. In his first letter to Francesco I, of January 22, 1584, Sassetti described Cochin, giving the size of the city, the details of the port, including what tonnage of ships could dock and which had to stand off the coast, and where the locals lived. Prefacing his comments on the ruler of Cochin's military, Sassetti wrote that "this king, a modern man of thirty-eight years or so, is of good aspect and serious, of a mulatto color, a very good friend of the Christians."[126] Having provided this thumbnail sketch of the ruler, Sassetti's analysis turned to Cochin's forces. Perhaps drawing on his humanist training and the vogue for Tacitus then sweeping the Accademia degli Alterati, of which Sassetti was a member, Sassetti presented an account of Cochin's forces well within the genre established by classical historians.[127] Sassetti wrote,

> His force consists in a manner of soldiers they call *amocchi* who are obliged to die at the wish of their king, and all of those soldiers in a war in which their king or their general is lost retain this obligation, in which the soldiers serve the king or then in urgent cases, sending some to die fighting now in a swarm now another way, in conformity with the necessity. The militia of these people in appearance is terrible because they go naked, the color black, their hair torn and with many extravagant gestures, accompanied by good arms they make themselves considerable; a part of them carries swords and small circular shields, others lances, others bows and arrows and others finally arquebuses; their militia is all on foot, because the land does not give horses and the few that are here come from Arabia and Persia; and for this service of war, they are not useful, living on apple flour and with many delicacies such that in the war they cannot be put to work. The king rides an elephant when he goes out to the country, everyone else is on foot.[128]

Concisely and clearly, Sassetti had described Cochin's and, by implication, the other minor kingdoms' militaries in a way that fit neatly into classicizing tropes. Furious assaults, extravagant gestures, and un-clothed warriors were consistent with classical images of the barbarian warrior, who often ended up being less militarily formidable than he appeared. Likewise, the absence of cavalry and the lack of substantial armor would have been clear indications of limited military strength, though the presence of firearms cautioned against complacency.

Sassetti's analysis of Indian politics stressed the relationship of loyalty, military forces, and political power. For Sassetti, military treachery constituted a structural problem for local regimes. As we have seen, Sassetti characterized the siege of Goa as having ended with be-trayal. He returned to this theme in his account of the Great Mughal's ambition to conquer the *Zamalucco*.[129] Sassetti reached back into history to describe how the *Zamalucco* and three other captains, two Muslims and a "Gentile," had acquired their states by carving up the realm of the king of Narsinga (Vijayanagara) into four new states.[130] The father of the deposed king "had conquered that State in the same way, betraying his king," as the captains had betrayed the son. In short, "these mu-tations follow and always followed in these parts," because by giving captains control of 10,000, 12,000, 15,000, or 20,000 cavalry, the king in effect ruled over lords free to do as they wished. Sassetti's analysis was structural more than specific, presenting the grand duke with his general sense of the dynamics of Indian politics.[131]

Just as Sassetti's explanation of the actions of the cavalry-based states used the model of betrayal and political fragmentation as its pri-mary organizing device, so his treatment of the distinctively South and Southeast Asian pattern of *amocchi*—warriors that run amok—focused on structural matters.[132] Sassetti tied together the rules of war in South India, and implicitly parts of Southeast Asia, and local religious beliefs to explain the nature of local military forces and conflicts. Explaining the war between the two most relevant rulers for the strategic situation in Malabar, Sassetti wrote that "The hatred between the two princes has been newly inflamed by the wounding of the person of the Zamorin against the ordinances and capitulations of their war." Sassetti explained that these sought to prohibit conflict near the monarch, whose position was marked by "an eminent baldachin above his tent, which distin-guishes it from all of the soldiers, to the end that no one sends arms into those parts."[133] This reverence due to the person of the monarch related directly to a key institution of political order that militated against the betrayals seen elsewhere. As Sassetti explained,

> The cause of this respect is not that goodwill they give or that they had taken care of conservation of the one or the other person but for the public good they learned that, following the death of a king in battle, all of his men-at-arms that are found to have been with him are obligated to die at the will of his successor. And they do not have this death of soldiers simply and without *vendetta*, on the contrary they have it with much slaughter in the land of the enemy; but at the commandment of having to go to die at the will of the successor, armed with all of their arms, they are moved with the impetus that moves a desperate man, and in the manner of fire not sparing anything living, placing all in the line of sword, fire, and blood. . . . They call such a militia, which is obligated to die at the wish of their king, the *amocchi*, and that prince that has the most of these is reputed to be the most powerful.[134]

Sassetti was clearly very impressed both with the military capabilities of the *amocchi* and with the strong incentive it gave soldiers for loyalty and protection of their monarch. The contrast with the serial betrayals of the cavalry kingdoms, run mostly by Muslims in Sassetti's description, could not have been greater. Sassetti's well-established rhetorical hostility to Muslim polities—which aligned with his commercial interests in the spice trade, the strategic priorities of the Estado da Índia, and the preferences of the militantly Catholic grand duke—probably affected his sharply drawn contrast. Certainly, Sassetti was attentive to the role of religion in warfare, noting that the king of Cochin, as a Brahmin, had a larger force of *amocchi*, some 30,000, than the *zamorino*, who was of a lower caste.[135]

Sassetti's structural analysis of the positions of the Portuguese, the South Indian monarchs, the Deccan sultanates, and the Mughal Empire provided the Medici with an imperfect but valuable sense of the balance of power in South Asia. His accounts gave the Medici a satisfying combination of the useful and the fascinatingly exotic, as Sassetti the literary figure surely appreciated. At the same time, Sassetti worked this strategic information into a series of coherent narratives about the major regional actors the Portuguese faced in the spice trade. Though Sassetti acknowledged sites of Portuguese action, the pessimism of his account, with its focus on Portuguese corruption, decrepitude, and weakness, would not have encouraged confidence in the Portuguese administration. Perhaps Sassetti's assessment weighed in the final Medici decision not to offer the sort of terms required to secure the contract of Europe. In any event, his reports on the situation in the Indian Ocean world bespeak a high level of Medici interest.

### Travelers' Narratives and Strategic Information

Sassetti's firsthand account of the position of the far-flung Estado da Índia and political developments on the Indian subcontinent gave the Medici the information and analytical categories to think strategically, shadowing the habitual practices of their Spanish Habsburg allies. In light of the regular Iberian administrative apparatus stretching from Mozambique to Manila, however, Tuscan information would always be comparatively scarce and out of date. Perhaps partially for this reason, Sassetti concentrated more on patterns and structures and less on the specific details except in so far as they revealed patterns. As the travel times lengthened and the Iberian network thinned, however, a Tuscan traveler's structural social analysis could constitute something close to the most current information. With the return of Francesco Carletti to Tuscany, the Medici secured such a portrait of three remote Iberian outposts—Manila, Macao, and Malacca—and two powerful states, Japan and China.

   Sassetti's and Carletti's analyses of the Iberian positions in Asia and Asian polities both appeared as private communications with the Medici court. The genre of their accounts differed, however, with Sassetti's dispersed across a series of annual letters and Carletti's concentrated in a book-length manuscript. The latter ostensibly records the contents of a series of twelve daily presentations delivered in person to the grand duke after Carletti's return to Florence in 1606.[136] Sassetti's epistolary audience was ostensibly Grand Duke Francesco I and his brother Ferdinando, the cardinal and future grand duke, but Medici archival practice and Tuscan social norms in fact opened the letters to an elite Tuscan public and preserved them for future generations. Sassetti understood this, rarely repeating information in his letters, which he expected to circulate. For instance, a copy of one of Sassetti's letters to Piero Vettori (1499–1585), held in a miscellaneous collection of documents on Tuscany compiled in the 1590s, suggests that at least his letters to private correspondents circulated immediately.[137] Those to the Medici, with their military intelligence and details of purchases, may have circulated along more restricted tracks, but they were certainly carefully retained in the Medici archives.[138]

In an era of scarcity, scraps of information were regularly collated to form a general image of the state of affairs. This was true even in traveler's otherwise firsthand narratives. For instance, Francesco Carletti cited the contents of a letter received from a Jesuit in India to describe how in 1608—two years after Carletti's return to Florence and more than six years after Carletti's departure from Goa—"the Grand Mughal Monarch of the best and the largest part of all that India" had transferred from Lahore to Agra with "more than 200,000 men, and 200,000 horses, six thousand elephants," and "more than 40,000 camels and oxen."[139] The description pertained to a new emperor, Jahangir (r. 1605–1627), who had come to power while Carletti was in the Dutch Republic.[140] Indeed, Carletti seems never to have entered Mughal territory. Still, the figures were too useful to omit. We should imagine Carletti's manuscript, Sassetti's letters, and other sources, ranging from Jesuit letters and traveler's accounts to the *relazione* and *avvisi* forwarded by Medici diplomats, as having been used as tesserae in a mosaic of slowly updated information about the world.

Carletti's expectations for how the information he collected would be used help to explain the way he went about constructing his account. Following closely in the rhetorical footsteps of Marco Polo, the personal elements of Carletti's narrative relate overwhelmingly to the logistics of travel—from the mode and route of transport to the ways prohibitions were circumvented—punctuated by occasional anecdotes intended to reveal how Carletti knew things. Carletti affirmed the accuracy of his account of penis studs in the Philippines, for instance, by noting that he had paid to see one to confirm the report he had heard.[141] Likewise, he engaged with the penis rattles of Southeast Asia by comparing his observations with those Niccolò dei Conti had made in 1444, suggesting that things had changed over time.[142] Carletti continues to be cited in modern historiography as a reliable witness on these matters, and so the strategies of verification he pursued have remained effective.[143] For all his spectacular empiricism when confronted with what, from a Tuscan perspective, were quite exotic sexual practices, Carletti could not uphold this standard for most of the strategic information he related. For this, Carletti relied, like Sassetti, on the reports that he could secure in port cities: Manila, Nagasaki, Macao, Malacca, and Goa; he gave scant indication that he ever went beyond these metropolises. The loss of Carletti's notes amid the travails of his journey compounded this limitation, forcing him back on memory.[144] For all the caveats about Carletti's observations, they constituted a precious resource for the Medici—such was the rarity of travels such as his.

Carletti's most unusual experience related to his time in four cities. The Iberian triad of Manila, Macao, and Malacca collectively facilitated Spanish and Portuguese trade with China, while Nagasaki was then commercially linked to both Macao and Manila. Carletti, as Sassetti had done, wrote at length about local social customs, food, plants, animals, urban structure, commerce, and more. Following Marco Polo, Carletti also offered thumbnail portraits of these cities, stressing their core socioeconomic and political dynamics. He began with Manila, which he reached via the Manila Galleon. Likening its layout to Mexico City, he stressed the power of its fortifications, needed to defend against the many enemies that threatened the Philippines, the most feared of which were the Japanese. Carletti continued, "that city of Manila is inhabited by Spaniards, who conquered it, and they remain there easily and with many means, absolute lords of the land, and of the men, and of the women also, all of which pay tribute and many have under them five-hundred, and a thousand, who pay at least eight *giulii* each year."[145] This stood in contrast to the *parian*, a wooden district for Japanese and Chinese commerce, which had burned before Carletti's arrival.[146] In short, a small Spanish elite, supported by a large group of tributary Filipinos, presided over a trading outpost sustained by Japanese and Chinese commerce based on the exchange of their manufactures and wheat for the silver of the New World.[147] Structurally, the situation of the Portuguese in Malacca (Melaka) matched that of the Spanish in Manila. Just as in Manila the Spanish relied on Japanese and Chinese merchants to conduct commerce outside the walls under the watchful gaze of a potent fortress, so also in

Malacca the Portuguese rigorously excluded the Javanese merchants who sustained the spice trade from entering the walled city and fortress.[148]

By contrast with Manila and Malacca, the tiny Portuguese commercial position in Nagasaki and the small autonomous city of Macao were barely tolerated outposts on the fringes of much more powerful states. Carletti wrote about his time in Japan, in 1597–1598, "I was in the said city of Nagasaki all peopled by Japanese Christians with a few small houses of Portuguese merchants, that lived there under the government of that King," Toyotomi Hideyoshi (1536–1598).[149] The years surrounding Carletti's arrival in Japan marked the peak of Japanese military aggression and violence as the country was reunified and rallied to invade Korea. Carletti was aware of this, recounting in brief the story of Toyotomi Hideyoshi, including his rise to supreme power on the death of Oda Nobunaga (1534–1582).[150] When Carletti first introduced the islands of Japan as a threat to Manila—"and those of Japan, which are to be feared more than the others as much for being close, as for their being those bellicose people devoted to always warring among themselves and with the neighbors"—he may have had recent Japanese history in mind.[151] In any event, Carletti described the Japanese war with Korea in some detail, providing information on the large size of the Japanese army, the types of Japanese weaponry, the provinces of Korea, and even the domestic political advantages that Toyotomi Hideyoshi reaped from sending the lords to fight in Korea.[152] Coupled with Carletti's gruesome account of the persecution of Christians—including their crucifixion—the frequency of capital punishment, the practice of testing katana sharpness on the bodies of the executed, and the Japanese street security system, the image was of a powerful, bellicose society. In Carletti's account, Japan was a power to be reckoned with. It was not much of a leap to conclude that the Iberian position in East Asia was permitted at Japanese sufferance because it was more convenient to trade and ally with the Portuguese and Spanish than to fight them. In this vein, Carletti mentioned a Japanese army that was regularly of 300,000 men armed not only with traditional bows, swords, and lances, but also with arquebuses.[153] The description was of a vast force, but the estimate was perhaps not too far off.[154]

In short, the grand duke would have had plenty of information about the scale of military power in East Asia and the structural difference between the Iberian position there and in the Americas. It would be 250 years before the Europeans had the military forces to impose terms. Beyond the issue of the balance of power in East Asia, Carletti's account of the situation of Christians in Japan would have been of interest to Ferdinando I as a former cardinal. It also seems to reflect at least some of Carletti's personal interests, for while we cannot read much into his conventional piety, we have seen that he had a strong relationship with the Jesuits in Macao.

The vast military power that Carletti described in Japan was matched by his sense of the overwhelming scale of Ming China (1368–1644). As in Japan, this he experienced perched at the edge of the realm in a Portuguese enclave. Carletti stressed that Macao, the city of Nome de Deus, hosted a small, unfortified Portuguese settlement administered by a royally appointed Portuguese captain.[155] Carletti was particularly astounded by the scale of the country, from the physical geography and population to the income of the emperor (the Wanli emperor (r. 1572–1620) and the number of boats on the Yangtze.[156] Though the view from Macao was at best partial, Carletti managed to glean a great deal. Matching his sense of extraordinary scale was a clear recognition of the antiquity and creativity of Chinese civilization. Carletti not only acknowledged that printing, gunpowder, and artillery all came from China but also attributed to China even greater importance than it in fact had.[157] Carletti explained in wonder that

> these inventions are so ancient in China that thousands of years have passed and one can without any doubt believe that everything comes from them, and I would concur in saying that not only this but every other invention good or bad, beautiful or ugly had come from that country or at least I can affirm that they have the knowledge of everything of their own and not from us nor from the Greeks or other nations, which have taught us, but from native authors in that so large country and so ancient as they say, the which surpasses by thousands of years the creation of the world described by Moses; a thing of theirs no less proud than false, if well believed by them, who abound in everything, and every mechanical art, and politics, and they pro-

fess moral philosophy, mathematics, astrology, medicine,
and other sciences, in which they keep the first men in the
world, and they do not think that there is knowledge outside of their nation, holding all others for barbarous
people."[158]

Carletti placed this profile of China's illustrious tradition in the context of Chinese intellectual self-confidence and the extraordinarily erudite character of Chinese elite life. This related directly to the political
structure of society, for Carletti correctly perceived that public office
and honors depended on intellectual achievements and that this
strongly shaped life patterns.[159] Protestations about reliance on
memory notwithstanding, he continued his discussion of the role,
status, and wealth of officials; imperial concubinage and marriage
practices; and the general organization of political order.[160] Carletti's
purpose in providing these details was in part to convey a vision of Chinese society radically at odds with that presented of Japan, stressing the
civilian, demilitarized character of Chinese domestic society and the
relatively low esteem in which the Chinese held the military, arguments,
and violence.[161] Continuing in this vein, he drew the connection to China's civil method of government.[162]

Carletti's long residence in Nagasaki and Macao, from June 1597
to December 1599, allowed him to look past the apparent similarities
of material culture to understand the radical dissimilarity of Japanese
and Chinese governance.[163] In this, he matched Sassetti's recognition
that the polities of South India structurally functioned quite differently
from the cavalry-based states further north. In both instances, Sassetti
and Carletti offered the Medici a compelling portrait not merely of the
size and armaments of the Asian states with which the Portuguese interacted, but also a sense of the internal social, military, and political
dynamics driving their actions. Careful observers free of the imperialist
bombast of later centuries, both Florentines were frankly impressed
with what they saw among the Asian states and openly critical of the
Iberian empires.

Let us imagine what those living by the banks of the Arno might
have made of all this. Reading Sassetti's letters and Carletti's manuscript at a desk in the Uffizi, a Florentine official might, in the space of a

day, develop a relatively clear picture of the Portuguese Estado da Índia, Spanish Manila, the spice trade from the Red Sea and Persian Gulf to Malacca and Ternate, and the political situation in India, China, and Japan. Tuscany's agents allowed the Medici, the patriciate, and those involved in Tuscan government to think globally, a project immeasurably enriched by their success in shipping material culture from all over the early modern world.

## All the World's Luxuries

Florence's justly famous artistic legacy and vast artistic collections rightly continue to serve as a locus of intensive art historical scholarship. It is beyond the purpose of this section to summarize that, even as art history's turn to the global matches this book's core premise.[164] By considering a few examples of the movement of luxury goods over long distances, the present section shows how Medici agents and affiliates used the Tuscan diplomatic network and access to the Iberian empires to secure a global selection of luxuries and exotica.

In the present era, with its integrated global economy served by fast and reliable communication and transportation networks, the primary limit on acquiring most items is price. By contrast, although European markets in the sixteenth century were stocked with an incomparably richer array of goods than they had been a century before, many items were still best acquired through special orders. Access to the people who could fulfill such orders and to the legal privileges to move these pieces was not solely a matter of money. The opulent display and vast collections for which the Medici were so famous, then, expressed not only their wealth but also their political and social position. Typical of the interpenetration of family and state interests, the Tuscan diplomatic network simultaneously discharged what are now considered public functions—representation, negotiation, information gathering, consular services, and the rest—and served to assist Medici collecting and consumption in myriad ways.

Consider the case of diamonds. A string of letters documents their shipment to Florence from Lisbon. Antonio Vecchietti's letter to Francesco I of September 27, 1576, for instance, sheds light both on the complexities of shipping and on the new roles assumed by the scions of Florence's elite houses. Responding to Francesco I's request for diamonds, Vecchietti explained that Jacopo de' Bardi had sourced the stones and that they would be sent to Madrid, to the Medici ambassador, Bartolomeo Orlandini (1520–1598).[165] The same financier from an ancient Florentine patrician house who was part of the investment group that had won the pepper contract in 1576 found the grand duke his diamonds. The Tuscan diplomatic network then swung into action, moving them across international frontiers swiftly. By October 10, Ambassador Orlandini wrote to Francesco I that the diamonds had arrived. He informed the grand duke that Vecchietti had instructed him to send the diamonds "by whichever route seemed best to me, and one at a time to divide the risk."[166] Three further letters from Orlandini explained his delay in sending the diamonds (October 15), his decision to send the diamonds to Florence with Filippo Lenzi (October 27)—"it seeming to me the most secure way"—and that Lenzi would be taking to Francesco I two packets of diamonds from Lisbon (December 6).[167] This use of the official diplomatic network for diamond forwarding from Lisbon to Florence would recur. On October 29, 1590, the Medici legation secretary, Camillo Guidi, noted that Carlo Velluti had sent from Lisbon a packet containing eighty-two diamonds in Ferdinando I's name and asked whether they were to be forwarded to Florence.[168] Likewise, on October 30, 1592, Ferdinando I wrote to his ambassador in Madrid, Francesco di Girolamo Lenzoni, about a packet of seventy-four diamonds sent by Carlo Velluti to Leone Ricasoli.[169] This was the same Ambassador Lenzoni who had worked on the project to secure permission to send Brazilian sugar directly to Livorno.

Small, precious items like diamonds fit neatly into the diplomatic network's patterns of intensive letter writing. The same held true for pearls. For instance, on April 23, 1588, Niccolò Bartoli in Lisbon wrote to Ferdinando I that he had "sent the pearls in a little bundle of letters by that Captain Nasachi, Ragusan, to the ambassador" Vincenzo Alamanni in Madrid.[170] Bartoli explained to the grand duke that Alamanni was to "deliver them on the order of Your Highness to Bataglino with one of my letters with an order that follows the will of Your Highness, as you ordered me awhile ago."[171] We met have met both Battaglini and Alamanni before. Battaglini had written from Madrid in 1584 on the arrival of Sassetti's letters, and Ambassador Alamanni sent a case he had received from Francesco Giraldi a week after Bartoli's letter. In this same letter, Alamanni confirmed that he had received the pearls Niccolò Bartoli had sent from Lisbon.[172] The pearls moved quickly. Reports of their dispatch and arrival were separated by a week, though Lisbon and Madrid are more than six hundred kilometers apart, probably because the pearls moved with the packets of letters.

The case of an ebony shipment is structurally quite similar. Not a month after Ambassador Alamanni's letter on the pearl shipment, on May 28, 1588, Alamanni wrote to Ferdinando I another letter filled with news and a discussion of securing ebony from Portugal, saying, "I wrote to Lisbon to a Giulio Nesi and recommended this service to him very warmly."[173] Two months later, on July 28, 1588, Alamanni wrote again discussing news items, told of a jeweled feather that had been seized by customs officials but was now recovered, and reported that Giulio Nesi had written to him about buying "the very beautiful ebony, and by his last tells me that he will send it to Livorno."[174] Evidently there were some unexpected delays, for an October 15, 1588 letter from Alamanni to Ferdinando explained, "Your Highness's ebony, about which Giulio Nesi of Lisbon writes to me, is loaded for Livorno aboard a pinnace [a small, fast ship] of Ponzetto Martinez of San Torpè, with the bill of lading directed to Napoleon Cambi depositary, so that he may receive it. Nesi estimates the cost for the Depositary to be 59.2.1 gold *scudi*."[175] Addressing the package to Napoleone di Girolamo Cambi (1521–1603), Florentine senator and depositary general under Francesco I and Ferdinando I, was both natural and an expression of the official quality of a transaction organized by the ambassador.[176] Unlike the diamonds and pearls, this shipment did not go with the official diplomatic correspondence, but the address to an official recipient may well have smoothed the ebony's passage. The shipment's ambiguously official status reflects the interpenetration of public and private that went with the Medici habit of behaving, in some respects, as simply the greatest of the Florentine patrician houses.[177]

The Medici diplomatic network functioned, then, as a regular system for moving rare and expensive items from the Iberian peninsula—above all, Lisbon—to Florence. In the late sixteenth century, Lisbon had truly become, as Annemarie Jordan Gschwend and Kate Lowe call it, "the global city."[178] Goods, people, and cultural influences flowed in on the great carracks of the Carreira da Índia that rounded

the Cape of Good Hope linking Goa, and through it the widely scattered Portuguese posts from Mozambique to Macao, with Lisbon.
They also came on the ships that visited the *feitorias*, settlements, and
outposts strung along the African shore from Morocco to Angola and
on the rising tide of ships carrying Brazilian sugar and the wonders of
South America. Measured by the diversity of goods, Lisbon may have
been the world's greatest market. Even so, the Medici wanted more. Not
content with buying in Lisbon, they used it as a base from which agents
departed and through which they remitted their acquisitions.

Filippo Sassetti left Lisbon in 1583 entrusted with 800 ducats from
the Medici, 500 from Francesco I and 300 from Cardinal Ferdinando.
As Sassetti wrote to Francesco I from Lisbon on February 7, 1583, he
had been instructed to acquire "those things that I will judge that may
be able to, for their gentility and novelty, give satisfaction."[179] This was
a substantial, but not extravagant, shopping budget, requiring Sassetti
to use his knowledge, discretion, and privileged access while in India
to secure exotica for the Medici collections.[180] This he proceeded to do
expeditiously. In his first letter to the grand duke from India, Sassetti
closed with a list of items purchased with the money entrusted to him,
"A cape of Bengal embroidered with hunting scenes as described, with
pearls and certain rubies cost... 100 *serafini*. [ / ] Two capes of iridescent
silk from China embroidered with hunting scenes with gold and silk
... 100 *serafini*. [ / ] A little porcupine stone ... 40 *serafini*. [ / ] A piece of
Maldive coconut marrow (two ounces) ... 20 *serafini*. [ / ] The total cost
of these ... 200 *serafini* [ / ]. It remains to me to spend on Your Highness's account 736 *serafini*, 2 *tanghe* and 16 *basalucchi*."[181] Sassetti served
his prince in Goa and Cochin much as Medici agents in Madrid and
Lisbon did, securing both local goods and items from much further
afield. The great distances involved required Sassetti to act with independent discretion and added an intermediary layer of agents on the
Iberian peninsula.

In the middle of February 1585, Sassetti sent three letters in quick
succession to the Medici. In his letter of February 10 to Cardinal Ferdinando, Sassetti mentioned that he had remitted items to Andrea Migliorati in Lisbon the previous year, explained that he would be sending
the textiles and coins the same way this year and excused himself for
failing to send seeds. Sassetti used the same transmission mechanism

for the two swords from Malabar sent to Francesco I, as he explained at the end of his letter to the grand duke of the following day. A week later, in what appears to be an addendum to his previous letter, Sassetti explained that a ship from Malacca and three from China had arrived and that he expected to find something for the grand duke.[182] In his letter of the following year, dated February 10, 1586, Sassetti offers some insight into the way he dealt with the intrinsic fragility of communications. Nearly three pages (in the standard modern edition) before the end of his letter, he wrote, "That which was written up to here is the copy of my letter that I wrote to Your Highness with the ship *San Francesco*."[183] The practice of writing multiple copies of the same letter to be sent on different ships permitted Sassetti to add new material, but doing so raised the risk of confusion, which his note sought to obviate. In this new section of the letter, Sassetti continued in revealing detail with a discussion of his shipping practices:

> I have then loaded this ship the *Sant'Albero* with the box in which goes the bed canopy and its furnishings, purchased for Your Highness. It goes indirectly together with the gilded wood to Migliorati of Lisbon, because I send everything for Your Highness there. In the same load goes a little chest filled with seeds and medicines assembled this year in Goa, and in the same little chest is the invoice of the little pouches and with this that declaration that I could get out of it. In the ship *San Lorenzo* another similar small chest will go to the lord Cardinal. If it [the ship] winters at Mozambique, which leaving a little late it could be, the lord Cardinal will be able to take action concerning half of these, about which, in any case, I will give thanks to do part. To the depositary I send the reckoning of Your Highness's account, on which for the rest of it I have drawn three hundred and seventy-six ducats: of which he will give particular account to Your Highness, with license of which he will complete the transfer. The jasper stones will come aboard the ship *San Lorenzo*, as I will advise.[184]

Sassetti shipped items aboard three ships, exchanging complexity for security. This did not end with their arrival in Europe. Indeed, Sassetti's cousin, Carlo Velluti, and Ferdinando I were still corresponding in May 1588, the year Sassetti died, about the transportation from Lisbon to Florence of items Sassetti had remitted.[185]

Transportation of luxury goods posed substantial risks. The bed Sassetti sent in 1586 was, in fact, the second he sought for the Medici. The first, a bed ordered from Canton (Guangzhou), had sunk along with the junk (Chinese sailing ship) on which it was traveling. The second bed was also Chinese but acquired in far southwestern India, in Cochin.[186] As so often, Francesco Carletti followed directly in Sassetti's footsteps, ordering a bed embroidered with Ferdinando I's coat of arms from Canton (Guangzhou) during his long stay in Macao (1598–1599). Fittingly in light of Medici interests in nature, the design for the bed, "the which was of diverse and fantastic animals and birds and flowers, of which this country abounds, esteemed more for their sight than their smell . . ." was also accompanied by "foliage and all very natural." This bed too met with mishap. As we have seen, the Dutch captured the bed and gave it to Marie de' Medici.[187]

Carletti's collection of Ming vases followed a similar trajectory. Sold as captured booty at Middleburg in Zeeland, two of the large vases were purchased by a merchant who then sent them to Ferdinando I. Perhaps seeking to rhetorically recover some of the value of the gift, Carletti explained that he had purchased five such vases and filled them with ginger of the highest quality along with the medicinal herb china root of good quality. Characteristically, however, Carletti focused on his core interest in describing the world of trade. In a short, dense passage on porcelain, Carletti explained the local bimetallic currency system, its conversion to Spanish silver coinage, the role of the Jesuits in acquiring items for Carletti, and his preference for blue and white porcelain. Accurately, but perhaps not ideally when claiming credit as a gift giver, Carletti stressed how very inexpensive porcelain was in China.[188]

Carletti's account, written after he had returned to Florence and lost most of his possessions, tends to address items he had acquired and the logistics of transporting them as part of broader narratives. The story of a golden chain illustrates the point. In an account of being searched by soldiers for jewels during the shipboard passage to the attack on Sluis, Carletti mentioned "a gold chain of forty *scudi* that Your Serene Highness wanted made in China, on which hung two Reliquaries also of gold" that he was ultimately allowed to keep.[189] The phrasing tends to suggest that Carletti had received a commission from the Medici, and it is hard to see why Carletti would recount retaining such an item and then fail to transfer it to the grand duke, but he does not say explicitly that he did so. Likewise, in his account of his stay in Goa, Carletti mentions in passing that he had personally shown the grand duke the remarkable fineness of a shirt of Bengal cotton that could "fit into a hand."[190] More important than the specific items he transferred, by transforming himself from a prosperous merchant into a Medici informant, Carletti repaid Ferdinando I's protection in a uniquely valuable way. Carletti was, quite simply, as prolific a source of current information about the early modern world as anyone Ferdinando I was ever likely to meet.[191]

Although Carletti's journey was extraordinarily unusual, perhaps unprecedented, his role at court was not. Indeed, nearly a half-century before, Bernardo Nasi, a formerly wealthy man who had lost his fortune aboard a Portuguese ship, had offered to serve Cosimo I. Ambassador de' Nobili's letter describing the offer contains a glowing recommendation of Nasi as extremely knowledgeable of maritime affairs. According to de Nobili, Nasi was already very rich when, returning from the Indies, a ship sank with all his goods. The ambassador explained that, now that he had suffered these losses, Nasi offered to serve the Medici in maritime affairs.[192] Dangerous and unpredictable as the world of early modern trade was, there was always a steady supply both of real merchants and of charlatans in an analogous position, offering expertise in exchange for favor and an income. Nasi, like Carletti, however, benefited from a good Florentine name. In Nasi's case, his namesake was a Florentine prior and ambassador of the late fifteenth century.[193] Indeed, Ambassador de' Nobili described Bernardo Nasi in his recommendation as "Bernardo Nasi brother of Messer Francesco Nasi who is in Florence."[194] The prospect seems to have worked out for him in the end, for a Bernardo Nasi was a sea consul in Pisa and captain of a great galleass (a larger, heavily armed galley) in 1572.[195]

### *Pietre Dure* and the Cappella dei Principi

Although the Medici court, with its capacious demand for luxuries and regular regifting, constituted a consistent center of demand, Medici interests extended beyond the court to specific projects. Perhaps the most opulent of these was the Cappella dei Principi (Prince's Chapel) at San Lorenzo in Florence. Still dazzling to behold, it is above all distinguished by the materials of its construction and the quality of the workmanship. An expanse of marble and inlaid semiprecious stones (pietre dure) greets the viewer, not merely on the floor, but also wall to wall, creating an immersive, overwhelming effect.

Both the space and the materials reflect the princely grandeur of Ferdinando I's reign. Among the most successful of the grand ducal initiatives, the Galleria dei Lavori in Pietre Dure (Gallery of Works in Semiprecious Stones), founded by Ferdinando I in 1588, achieved an international reputation and remains in operation under its nineteenth-century name, the Opificio delle Pietre Dure (literally, Hard Stone Factory). The design (1602) and construction (1604) of the Prince's Chapel, the foremost showcase of pietre dure, also began in Ferdinando I's reign.[196] Tuscany famously abounds in high-quality marble, but semiprecious stones often had to be imported, Ferdinando I's proclamation restricting the usage, damage, or export of such stones as were present in Tuscany notwithstanding.[197] The demands of an art form that depended so heavily on the specific colors and patterns of the underlying stones and that so dramatically displayed their quality left quite limited scope for substitution. Florence's access to jasper supplies depended on Spanish Sicily and Genoese Corsica, and Ferdinando sought agate and translucent chalcedony imported to the Iberian peninsula from Goa.[198] In light of the fame of the new Medici chapel, suppliers also came to Medici agents. On December 10, 1604, Cosimo Baroncelli wrote from Antwerp to Belisario Vinta in Florence relating that "a principal Portuguese merchant came to find me and says he has a most beautiful piece of oriental jasper beyond compare."[199]

When possible, the Medici sought to cut out such intermediaries and go straight to the source. A 1608 memorandum on acquiring stones for the Medici Chapel explains both the licenses that would be required for three or four men to go to Cambaia, India, and laid out the need to secure space with the senior crew aboard ship. All this was fairly standard advice. The remarkable element of the document is the paragraph that begins "from the Hague in Holland," which expressed the need to secure a safe conduct for the grand duke's men traveling from Lisbon to India in the event that their ships should be taken by the Dutch.[200] It has been argued that this document should be attributed to Francesco Carletti.[201] Certainly, Carletti had experience of just such an eventuality and the memorandum incorporates the lessons of his travails. The era of Iberian dominance was drawing to a close.

As ever, the necessary permission from the Spanish Habsburg administration of Portugal proved difficult to secure. On December 16, 1608, Belisario Vinta wrote to the Medici ambassador in Madrid, Bishop Sallustio Tarugi, about the four young Florentines then waiting for permission to travel. Vinta expressed the grand duke's frustration. He instructed the ambassador that "His Highness wants every effort to be made to give impulse to them, because truly they go to look for balas [rubies] in stone for the chapel of His Highness and not for anything else. And they go to Cambaia and it should not be in the dominions of this Majesty, and the license has to serve them only for the passage."[202] The request struck at the fundamental issue. For the Florentines, the Portuguese Empire was a gateway to parts beyond, and restrictions on travel were unwarranted. For the Portuguese, control of access to non-Portuguese territory provided by the scattered outposts of the Estado da Índia was the essence of their monopoly. Occasional politically important exceptions might be made, but the principle was not one the Spanish Habsburg administration or any Portuguese regime would have been apt to concede. This remained true not only of Tuscan commercial ventures with private parties, but also of diplomatic ventures with a commercial aspect. For instance, in 1610, the Tuscan ambassador in Madrid, Orso Pannocchieschi d'Elci (1569–1636), was asked to secure permission from the Spanish Habsburgs for the Tuscans to trade balas rubies for diamonds with the Mughal emperor Jahangir.[203]

Medici diplomats worked diligently to penetrate the various barriers to commerce and diplomacy presented by the persistent Iberian efforts to maintain a world monopoly on long-distance maritime trade with Europe. Simultaneously, widely dispersed Florentine merchants, financiers, and nobles elected to align themselves with the Medici, serving in agency relationships that bored holes in the wall of restrictions.[204] The merchants, purchasing agents, botanical collectors, and ambassadors used their expertise, social position, personal networks, and physical location to act on their patrons' behalf. The agents' status and expertise often also allowed them to act in ways their patrons could not have even if they had been present.[205] The Medici acted through these agents to secure supplies for domestic institutions that required them, most demandingly for the botanical gardens. For them, the Medici needed the best samples accompanied by reliable information. This presented a much more substantial logistical task than moving precious stones around the world. Florentine diplomats and botanical collectors rose to the challenge.

### Botanical Agents

After the establishment of one of the first botanical gardens in Europe at Pisa, the Medici made a project of acquiring seeds from around the world. Under Francesco I, grand ducal Tuscany relied on a network of prosperous merchants, intellectuals, and diplomats to provide seeds and samples from their travels. As we shall see in Chapter 5, the seeds and samples were shared both with the Medici court and the linked networks of correspondents and institutions engaged in the botanical enterprise in Tuscany and neighboring parts of central Italy. Although Medici suppliers generally operated as part-time botanical collectors, their engagement with the project could be substantial.[206] Likewise, the Medici diplomatic network regularly added to the packets they sent to Tuscany botanical materials remitted by such agents.

Tuscan diplomats not only dispatched seeds, plants, and botanical information from the Iberian peninsula, but they also kept track of the Spanish imperial botanical institutions. For instance, on December 6, 1582, Medici ambassador Bernardo Canigiani wrote from Madrid to Antonio Serguidi, a knight of the Order of Santo Stefano and secretary to Francesco de' Medici, about his visits to the royal gardens of Aranjuez, the hunting lodge turned palace of the Pardo, the massive complex at the Escorial, and more. The ambassador wrote about Tuscany's own collection of sites—Castello, the Boboli Gardens, Pratolino, the Casino di San Marco—and sent seeds of Indian jasmine along with information about its flowering and care.[207]

We have already met Canigiani's successor as Medici ambassador, Bongianni Gianfigliazzi, as the dedicatee of Sassetti's treatise who later reported on Sassetti's arrival in India. Although Gianfigliazzi's role as a link between Sassetti, a prolific botanical supplier, and the Medici court was important, so was his coordination of separate botanical shipments for the Medici.[208] A flurry of letters between the grand duke and his ambassador from May to August of 1584, for instance, address the project to secure a Moglis tree. On May 28, Gianfigliazzi reported to Francesco I that he had written to Sebastián Santoyo about the Moglis tree. Santoyo had responded that the size of the tree made transporting it impractical, but that he would send seeds.[209] Santoyo was himself a politically connected figure, lord of the Villas of Carabaña, Valdelecha, and Orusco and secretary of the Chamber (Cámara) to Philip II, and so the use of Gianfigliazzi for the affair reflected the Medici ambassador's dual logistical and political roles.[210] On June 9, Gianfigliazzi reported to Francesco I that Santoyo had sent him the Moglis seeds; Gianfigliazzi actually dispatched the seeds on June 14.[211] In a letter of July 19, 1584, Francesco I acknowledged receipt of the Moglis seeds, "the which we will have sown in many ways to test if it will be possible to make them grow," and asked Gianfigliazzi to thank Santoyo.[212] A month later, on August 25, Gianfigliazzi wrote to Francesco I saying that he had given Santoyo the grand duke's letter thanking him. A new cycle then began, as Gianfigliazzi reported that the papal nuncio in Madrid "told me that he wants to write to Your Highness to beg for the grace of the oil against poison and that for the stomach, the water for petechiae, and the elixir."[213] This last played into a Medici tradition. As Cristina Bellorini has recently shown, the Medici not only rhetorically played on their name (medici = doctors) but also demonstrated a significant commitment to producing medicines and distributing them in much-coveted boxes filled with specially made medicines.[214] As for Santoyo, the Medici relationship with him was so extensive that the Medici archives hold a voluminous inventory of items sent from Santoyo in Spain, which included both luxury goods from China, India, and Spain and natural items like bezoar stones from both the Portuguese East Indies and "the Indies of Castile," ambergris, horns, and a Maldive coconut mounted in silver.[215]

Just as Francesco I continued his father Cosimo I's passion for botany, so also did Francesco's brother Ferdinando I pursue botanical collecting along much the same lines. For instance, on September 8, 1588, Ferdinando wrote to Ambassador Vincenzo Alamanni in Madrid instructing him that "from Portugal we would like a plant of the tree

that makes the blood of the dragon that one finds there." The grand
duke continued, "and with that will come to us also seeds, bulbs, and
plants of every sort of the most notable sent from the India of Portugal
and that of Spain" with assurances that the expenses would be reimbursed immediately.[216] As ever, the ambassador set to work finding a
supplier and securing the item. On February 4, 1589, Alamanni replied to the grand duke that "Giulio Nesi has sent me those seeds of
the tree that makes the blood of the dragon in certain pods that will
be with this, the which, not being certain if they will grow, he says he
will procure two plants from Terzera and send them at the first convenience." The dragon blood trees were to come, then, from Terceira in
the Azores.[217] The timing was closely run, for the English under George
Clifford (1558–1605), third earl of Cumberland, raided the islands that
year.[218] We shall return to the trees that produce dragon's blood at the
end of the chapter, but now we turn to the agents in the field.

Filippo Sassetti played a leading role among the Medici botanical
agents both by virtue of the extent of his travels and, especially, his
education. This latter allowed him to remit samples accompanied by
extensive analysis. His letters from India touch on an array of natural
historical subjects, but they concentrate on three areas: general comments on local plants and animals, collecting and transporting plants
and seeds, and an extended discussion of cinnamon. In one of his letters to Cardinal Ferdinando de' Medici, for instance, Sassetti described
the use of elephants to load and unload boats, commenting in particular on their strength.[219] He went on to discuss a variety of animals,
from beasts of burden and birds to tigers and crocodiles.[220] Sassetti explained to the cardinal that "On land all new things present themselves
in view, plants, animals, and people. The plants are all different from
ours" before apologizing that the lateness of his arrival in India precluded him from remitting seeds and samples immediately.[221] Indeed,
collecting and transporting plants and seeds was fraught with hazards
and difficulties. In one letter, for instance, Sassetti not only explained
betel chewing, but also the failure of previous efforts to transport betel
to Lisbon without its losing its taste.[222]

The same handful of ships that carried objects and letters back
from India also brought other Tuscans, some of whom would see the
grand duke in person. The audiences started with Sassetti's inner circle,

his friend Giovanni Buondelmonti, who had traveled to Goa with him and whose return to Florence helped Sassetti complete a commission.[223] In a 1585 letter to the grand duke, Sassetti recalled that he had been commissioned to collect seeds for the Medici. Primarily engaged in the pepper business, Sassetti could not devote his whole time to the pursuit of seeds and employed a "pagan physician"—that is, probably, a Hindu—to tend to it when he left Goa for Cochin. Even so, Sassetti wrote to explain that "Of the diverse domestic fruit of the land, Giovanni Buondelmonti, who returns there with this armada, brings nuts and seeds. Conducting himself safely, he will kiss the hand of Your Highness and, if they [the samples] are conserved on the road, he will give them to you. That which I can assemble, I will send for the coming year."[224] Buondelmonti had been Sassetti's companion since their departure from Portugal, traveling "to see this land and because in this voyage his company was desired as a true gentleman" and was to return on the *Buon Giesù*; it is hard to imagine Buondelmonti's audience as not involving an extensive report.[225] Oral transmission of information may well have enriched the value of the remitted seeds. Certainly, the personal delivery of seeds from an expert in India to the grand duke would have differentiated Sassetti's seeds from those acquired in the markets of Lisbon.

In 1586, the year after Buondelmonti's departure, Sassetti wrote to Baccio Valori (1535–1606), a jurist, grand ducal official, and brother of another merchant with literary interests, Sassetti's old university friend Francesco Valori, "I put one of these pagan physicians in the mind to recognize and breed simples. I went this year and saw a few plants and medicines, of which I send seeds to His Highness, with what little that, in little time, I could find out [about them]. I have purchased to this effect a garden in Goa, where I plan to put up to a hundred of the most identified plants in these parts, those that are spoken of as marvelous."[226] This was to be Sassetti's personal botanical garden, optimally designed to serve as a supplier for collectors and their botanical gardens in Italy. Sassetti had a fraught relationship, however, with the local experts on whom he depended. A letter Sassetti wrote to the grand duke illustrates the shape of the problem as he saw it: "The Portuguese and mestizo apothecaries do not have in these parts any curiosity about simples; and to deal with them on this is to give them material to laugh.

The Gentile physicians, the science of which is completely empirical, know it well enough, but, most avariciously, do not want to show almost anything."[227] Access to the secrets of Indian nature was socially mediated. Sassetti, as an outsider, was particularly well motivated to acquire and diffuse knowledge, or at least that was the role in which he cast himself.[228]

Sassetti approached his new botanical task with the tools of his university training. He was certainly familiar with contemporary botanical writing, referring in his 1586 letter to Bernardo Davanzati (1529–1606) to the works of the Sienese doctor Pietro Andrea Mattioli (1500 / 1501–1577 / 1578), Garcia de Orta (1501–1568), and Cristóbal de Acosta (1515–1594). Even so, as an accomplished literary figure, Sassetti's interest and expertise seem to have been strongly oriented to classical texts.[229] In particular, Sassetti had internalized the ethos of humanist scholarship. Thus, while Sassetti drew on the corpus of Western classical and authoritative medieval Islamic authors, he also studied Sanskrit as the local classical language.[230] His letters from India, then, not only commented on anthropological, botanical, and geographic subjects but also paid close attention to language, noting a connection between Sanskrit and Greek and Latin.[231] Similarly, he offered a traditional humanist critique when he suggested that Indian knowledge of Aristotle, Galen, and Avicenna had been rendered confused by the problems of double translation and poor translation quality from Arabic.[232] He seems, however, to have been more interested in the Indian classical heritage, considering it directly analogous to the European classical tradition. Sassetti wrote that "these Gentiles have here their own Dioscorides, Hippocrates, and all the other Doctors, the science of which is very pointed" before delving into their mode of proceeding.[233] In another letter, Sassetti returned to the connection between the Indian and European traditions, writing, "The aforementioned Proprietor is a most ancient Gentile doctor, who wrote in these parts [on] the subject of simples and is called Niganto. He discussed more than three thousand plants quite briefly, as was translated. And all of this work is in verses. And his sayings about this subject and those of the other physicians that are studied by them are collected as common maxims; among them they have authority without contradiction. And many of these one sees drawn from Hippocrates, or those of Hippocrates drawn from these people, since it is presumed, based on most ancient records, that in all times they knew more than now."[234] Sassetti's willingness to recognize the potentially superior antiquity of Indian knowledge and the possibility that part of the Western classical corpus might actually derive from India is striking, but perhaps ultimately unsurprising, for it was this same kind of thinking that underlay Sassetti's insights about the commonalities between Sanskrit, Greek, and Latin.

For all the centrality of understanding the textual corpus to Sassetti, his fundamental project for the Medici involved the collection, study, and transmission of botanical samples. Doing so required a confrontation with an empirical reality at variance with the European classical texts he knew so well. In considering cinnamon, Sassetti eventually wrote "one sees manifestly that the ancients were poorly informed about this and many other things."[235] How did he arrive at this conclusion? Sassetti deployed his textual skills on the samples provided by local suppliers. This can be seen most clearly in his more extended effort to understand cinnamon. In his "Discourse on Cinnamon," included in a letter sent to Baccio Valori in Florence from Cochin in January 1587, Sassetti laid out the views of various authors on the correspondence between the ancient *cinnamomo* and modern plants.[236] Sassetti wrote,

> Taking myself to India, I saw this *cannella* plant many times in the land of Malabar, Canara, and Goa. They call it *di mattos*, emphasizing the making and the quality of all the root, as above the green earth how it is cut and dried. By observing the white sprigs, the black, and the various [colors of the plant], I judged that it cannot be other [than] *cinnamomo*. This is the same plant found on the island of Ceylon. There, they remove the husk for the *canella*, cut from its shrub with all its parts, and carried to our country. For two years, I continually paid people who went to that island to bring me *cannella* plants of that land in order to test my theory. The second time I did so, they brought me two large bundles of trees or roots of the said plant, with all the branches, leaves, bark, and other parts, just as they had grown in nature. After analyzing these, I assured myself that the *cinnamomo* of the ancients was no other than the

stalk of the *cannella* plucked from its bush just as nature created it. It matched up with all the qualities that the ancients
attributed to it.[237]

Sassetti's description and analysis continue, but the essentials are here.
He relied on agents to gather samples from the point of origin and used
the evidence of those samples to evaluate and explain the opinions of
the ancients.

The Medici network might be extended as far as Ceylon (Sri Lanka),
but only through long chains of mediation. In India, this involved Sassetti's reliance on a set of unnamed agents. Once Sassetti had processed
the samples they gathered for him, the cinnamon had to travel several
further steps. In his enclosing letter for the "Discourse on Cinnamon,"
Sassetti wrote to Valori, "Last year, I was working on understanding
what the *cinnamomo* of the ancients actually was. I wrote to Your Lordship that I would send what I believed it to be. I wrote, I do not know
what I wrote, and I sent a plant of my *cinnamomo* in a case, which goes
to Lisbon to my cousin, Carlo Velluti, and he will send it to Pisa."[238] Botanical collecting, then, involved a combination of textual analysis and
sample gathering. Both the samples and the accompanying text had to
move through networks of mediation, not an official postal system. As
was typical for Florentine patricians, Sassetti relied on his relative in
Lisbon to connect Cochin and Pisa. Had the sample made it to Pisa, it
would then have been connected to the Medici through Baccio Valori's
position and Sassetti's status as a Medici agent. In this way, the tendrils
of Medici influence could extend across the world. Fragile as they were,
they could also break without warning. This happened with the case,
which seems to have met with ill fortune, as Sassetti explained in a follow-up letter sent to Baccio Valori in 1588:

> Last year, I sent to Your Lordship my concept of *cinnamomo*,
> such as it was. Alas, the case it was in was sent on a ship that
> capsized. Since the island of Ceylon is now at war, I do not
> know when I will return there to acquire another specimen.
> It would have been better, perhaps, if my writing had never
> come to your hands (if this could have been, saving the
> other things), because it is necessary to correct some faults
> about the fruit. That can be subject to the amount of faith

one can give those who report on the state of things in
India. I have been left deceived, despite having observed the
specimen with my own eyes. Having left Cochin, when I returned to Goa the year before, they were asked to make me a
large vase of this fruit to conserve. I aimed to give it to whoever might wish to view it, because the flavor is aromatic and
good and drawn from the resin of pistachio. However, I
ought not to have believed these simpletons diligent enough
to be trusted with this task. It turned out to be an idiocy,
and they did not serve at all. They tried my patience, asking
me questions like "what good was that seed?" That is the
reason that these people give to the things that are not to
their humor. I have not had occasion to converse with men
of science where I might have been able to portray something worthy of coming to your knowledge.[239]

Sassetti regretted his letter's survival because it had become an artifact
of failures of communication and understanding in India. The sample,
though, would have been accurate, yet Sassetti's observation of it in
India had been insufficient to protect him from error.

Sassetti's experience with cinnamon and his broader botanical
project point to several features of Tuscan botanical enterprise in the
context of the Iberian empires. As the lost case of samples and the confusions of correspondence show, breakdowns in the fragile network of
communication could undermine the interrelationship between text
and object that distinguished Tuscan activity in the field from market
transactions. That Sassetti sought to settle major disputes about cinnamon by relying primarily on observation, almost ninety years after
the Portuguese had arrived in India, is telling. The Iberian policies of exclusion and obfuscation meant to protect their imperial predominance
were at least partially successful when it came to the diffusion of information about economically valuable commodities from the Indies.[240]
This was helped by the high level of expertise and intellectual sophistication required to understand fully the impact of the new discoveries on
the edifice of European knowledge. Qualified people willing to brave the
extreme perils of long-distance travel were few and far between. The new
information could not simply be bolted onto the classical inheritance,

but instead constituted a challenge to its authority and veracity; as is well known, the challenge did profound damage to epistemologies based on the authority of revered pasts and the texts such pasts generated. Sassetti's interest in and ability to reconcile empirical and classical claims, then, allowed him to play quite a rare, if by no means unique, role.

Filippo Sassetti's private botanical garden and extensive correspondence set a high standard for Tuscan botanical agents. For all that, he was not alone in his efforts. As we have seen, Sassetti's exact contemporary and considerable social superior, Francesco Giraldi, sent the Medici seeds from Portuguese Brazil in response to a grand ducal request. Such a request seems to have been a standing one among Medici affiliates. Giovanni Battista Britti and Giovanni Battista Vecchietti, who we met as agents of the Medici Oriental Press, carried a similar commission to collect seeds, this time from Cardinal Ferdinando.[241] Not all collectors worked part time. The naturalist ("semplicista") and head of the Pisa botanical gardens, Giuseppe Casabona (ca. 1535–1595), who served both Francesco I and Ferdinando I, was dispatched to collect botanical samples in Crete by Ferdinando I in 1591.[242]

Even so, it was the part-time collectors and informants who operated on a truly global scale and who provided the Medici with first-rate information. Among these, Filippo Sassetti seems to have led in the provision of samples and learned discourses. He was not, however, the best traveled. This honor clearly fell to Francesco Carletti, who likewise sent seeds from furthest away. After describing two types of edible Japanese citrus fruit, Francesco Carletti explained that he and his father had written from Japan to Tuscany and had sent the grand duke seeds. Writing years after the event, Carletti related the result of the transfer, recording that only Francesco Capponi's plant had grown. This had been the source of seeds for other plants, but none had fruited, which Carletti explained had been due to the absence of grafting from wild citrus.[243] The role of Francesco Capponi in Carletti's story indicates the way that botanical samples, like information and commercial contacts, regularly and easily circulated among Florentine patricians. Similarly, impressed by the Chinese lychee and the aesthetic quality of the fruit on the trees, Carletti also made substantial purchases of lychee with the plan of planting it in Tuscany.[244] That Carletti made no further mention of the lychee suggests that they did not successfully make the journey. Even so, Carletti's inclination to remit useful and attractive flora to Tuscany casts a new light on Carletti's numerous comments about the plants encountered during his travels. This chapter will close, then, with a brief survey of the range of Carletti's botanical observations followed by a look at a few notable examples from the Americas.

Setting out into the Atlantic, relatively few plants struck Carletti's eye, which focused more on the fauna, especially of the sea.[245] Even so, he noted a few of the tropical staples, like coconuts and plantains on Cape Verde and cassava brought to Cartagena from Santo Domingo.[246] Crossing over to Peru, Carletti retained his focus on key agricultural staples, discussing potatoes, cucha (a maize drink), and coca, along with the llamas.[247] It was in New Spain, however that Carletti truly warmed to his subject. His lengthy and glowing description of chocolate, which accompanies his account of his voyage from Peru to Mexico, covers the value of the cacao crop and its sites of production, the raising and harvesting of cacao beans, their use as commodity money, the preparation of chocolate, the consumption of chocolate by Spaniards and indigenous peoples, the method of drinking chocolate, and the extraordinary pleasures of consuming it.[248] Carletti repeated quite fantastic claims about his daily chocolate consumption, chocolate's nourishing qualities, and the social importance of chocolate as a gift.[249] An early modern chocolate aficionado, Carletti's early adoption of chocolate matched the contemporary diffusion of chocolate from the New World first to Spain—where it became established between 1590 and 1610—and then, through elite aristocratic and clerical circles, to other Spanish-influenced regions in Europe.[250]

While Carletti's passion for chocolate seems to have been personal and profound, many of his comments on Mesoamerican plants instead reflect his perception of Medici interest. Carletti focused his attention on those that gave him delight or that he thought would be of use in Tuscany. Of the agave, on whose usage as a source of alcoholic beverages Carletti concentrated, Carletti compared it to aloe growing in Ferdinando I's "Giardino delle Stalle."[251] Similarly, Carletti seems to have been attuned to Medici interest in dragon blood, writing at length about a tree in Acapulco with white bark that, when cut, produced a red liquid useful for toothpaste. He took the dragon feature a step further suggesting that "the seed of this tree is enclosed in a leaf in the shape of a Dragon with all its parts masterfully designed by nature, a thing of admiration and worthy to be seen"; he noted that he had attempted to bring the leaves back to Tuscany, but that these had been among the things that he had lost.[252]

Carletti's dual roles as an active merchant and Medici client made him particularly attentive to economically important crops that might be useful to Tuscany. One such was cochineal, a valuable red dye made from the bodies of tiny red insects killed with either hot water or quicklime.[253] Like silk production on mulberry trees, cochineal involved raising insects on their favored plant, the nopal cactus.[254] Carletti recounted the elaborate official bureaucracy surrounding the transfer of such a valuable dye to Spain, "aboard the Galleons that carry the gold and the silver, it not being of a lesser price and value than the one or the other metal," valuing the exports to Spain at 600,000 *scudi*.[255] This extraordinary economic value explains Carletti's claim that it was a "plant truly deserving to be commended by others than in my simple discourses."[256] He recommended that "nonetheless, there is no plant that I believe would be more gratefully seen in these countries, if this could be conducted here," that is, to Tuscany.[257] Introducing the nopal cactus was, then, about creating a cochineal industry. Pursuing import substitution, this would have saved on imports and given Tuscan textile manufacturers an edge.[258] The project's failure can probably be attributed to the certainty of Spanish resistance and the technical challenges of transferring such an agricultural system.

Tuscans did, however, pursue information about and power in the cochineal market. It is hardly surprising, then, that the Tuscan government kept track of cochineal news. Letters in the Medici archives from 1586 and around 1598, for instance, discuss the movement of cochineal to Spain, and a 1605 *avviso* from Antwerp mentioned the arrival of cochineal among other goods in Holland.[259] The Tuscan government also collected reports on the arrival of cochineal in Tuscany, as a letter from 1571 and a bill of lading from 1577, both from Livorno, show.[260] Tuscans put market information to dramatically effective use. A politically connected Florentine firm owned by a family we have met often, the Capponi, had controlled the contract for cochineal from the Americas imported to Seville.[261] In 1585, the Capponi joined the Maluenda of Burgos in taking advantage of low supplies to successfully corner the market, reaping windfall profits through high prices until 1586.[262] Information had been the key to power and profit. Carletti's account of the nopal cactus and its utility, then, would have met an already well-informed and receptive audience, likely to agree that its cultivation in Tuscany would be commercially beneficial.

Carletti's remaining descriptions of plants do not concentrate as explicitly on their transfer to Tuscany. Even so, his focus on agricultural products and optimism about the transferability of plants reflects the enthusiasm of the early centuries of the Columbian Exchange when the world's agricultural systems were transformed and enriched, at no small cost, by the global spread of favored plants.[263] The Medici and their agents were among those most excited about doing the exchanging. A brief list of Carletti's remaining discussions of plants reveals the pattern. In Mesoamerica, Carletti added descriptions of tobacco, maize, and pepper to nopal cacti, cacao, and agave.[264] Arriving in Asia, he recounted bananas, types of breadfruit, palm alcohols, and a combination of betel and areca palm in the Philippines.[265] Carletti's comparatively limited discussion of items from Japan—tea, rice wine, Japanese citrus and melons, *misol* sauce—and China—Chinese oranges, mangoes, and lychee—reflected both the shared elements of temperate Eurasian agriculture and especially Carletti's position in cities at the very edge of these vast countries.[266] By contrast, his comparatively brief visit to Southeast Asia, principally Malacca, on the way to India elicited discussions of durians, pineapples, rose apples, mangosteen, pepper, cloves, nutmeg, and mace.[267] Carletti rounded out his discussion with cinnamon, coconuts, and a distinctive type of flower in Goa.[268] The lists are dominated by staples, culturally important stimulants and drugs, and export items, especially the prized spices, Maldive coconuts, and cochineal.

In closing this chapter, let us turn to one of the wondrous tropical fruits that caught Medici botanical collectors' and observers' eyes. Consider the pineapple. In a 1584 letter to Piero Spina, a knight of Malta, Filippo Sassetti provided a fairly extensive description of the pineapple written as if Spina had never seen such a thing.[269] That same year, Sassetti wrote to Francesco I that "pineapples seem to me to be the tastiest fruit that there is" and gave a shorter, but similar, description to the one given to Spina.[270] This does not necessarily mean that the pineapple had not arrived, but it suggests that it was uncommon. It was becoming less so, though, for Jacopo Ligozzi (1547–1627) made an extraordinary drawing of the pineapple. Lucia Tongiorgi Tomasi suggests that it is among the first such drawings known and that the browning of parts of the pineapple in the image reflects the rarity of the preserved sample from which Ligozzi worked.[271] By the time Francesco Carletti returned to Florence, the pineapple was a known item. He still included a description of pineapples in his account—he had, after all, seen them in a much fresher state—but he noted that he had seen pineapple preserves in the grand ducal pantry.[272]

The case of the pineapple points to the body of samples, drawings, and descriptions accumulating in the institutions of grand ducal Tuscany. These objects and pieces of information arrived from all over the world through the combined efforts of Tuscan diplomats, Medici affiliates operating often as part-time agents, and—usually at a socially higher level—participants in networks of gift exchange. Primarily through the relationship with the Iberian empires, Florentines enjoyed privileged access not just to the Iberians' extensive domains, but also to the wider world, especially in Asia. Medici Tuscany rapidly developed a remarkable network of institutions to house, analyze, and engage with the objects, living organisms, information, and people that poured into Tuscany.

5

# The Shadow Capital

*W*hat makes an imperial capital? In a political sense, the criteria seem clear. The capital city functions normatively as the administrative and symbolic center of a polity. What happens to such a city, however, when the empire is lost or the state much reduced? Of course, a capital may be sacked, abandoned, or fall into decay, but sometimes, as in modern London, Paris, and Vienna, it retains a hypertrophic grandeur out of all proportion to its current political role. This is clearest in Vienna, whose late imperial institutions, above all its cultural and intellectual ones, are so monumentally aligned along the Ringstraße. They are much larger than anything to be found in Austria's similarly sized and even richer alpine neighbor, Switzerland, for instance. For all their grand scale, at the centenary of the empire's demise, the intellectual and cultural institutions of Vienna's imperial era remain vibrant and extensively used. The political and intellectual challenge of empire and its resources may have contributed to their foundation, but they do not depend on its continuous existence. If the imperial intellectual and cultural institutions can operate without the empire, then, is an empire strictly necessary for their creation in the first place, or is a lively interest in understanding the world sufficient?

This chapter argues that Florence and the surrounding network of Medici villas operated as a shadow cultural and intellectual capital for the Spanish empire. At the outset, it is critical to delineate the boundaries of its role. For all the precocious bureaucratic development of the Uffizi, the failure of Medici colonial and military projects meant that Florence was not a political capital of anything more than Tuscany. Likewise, whereas linked networks of patrician banking families and the Tuscan state turned Florence into an important financial center, it was Genoa, not Florence, that was the financial capital of the Spanish Empire.[1] Although the Medici failed to parlay their financial and military contributions into an imperial partnership, they did secure unusual access to the Iberian empires. The Medici used the access to good effect, building an extensive set of sites and institutions in and around Florence that served as fledgling centers of calculation, in Bruno Latour's framework, albeit ones more concerned with collection than analysis. It is in this cultural and intellectual sense that this chapter treats Florence as a shadow capital.[2]

Let us now consider the sites and institutions wherein Tuscans housed, observed, and analyzed the objects and information, the flora and fauna dispatched by the agents considered in the last chapter. Plants went either to the botanical gardens in Pisa or Florence, one of the Medici villas, the Boboli Gardens of Palazzo Pitti, or the gardens of one of the various closely linked patrician families. Rare and exotic animals were also housed at the villas, in the Boboli Gardens, at Palazzo Vecchio, at Piazza San Marco, or in the grand ducal menagerie; this last also hosted the many birds brought to Florence from distant lands. The wondrous and luxurious objects dispatched by Medici agents found their way to the Guardaroba, decorated with a set of maps that collectively covered much of the world, and were brought out for various court occasions in the Medici palaces. Medici art collecting and the central role of the Uffizi in the history of the museum are, of course, well known, but they enter our story only insofar as the Medici collected objets d'art from around the world. In the spirit of the Kunst- und Wunderkammer (cabinet of art and curiosities), the Uffizi, Guardaroba, and Medici palaces—not then sharply institutionally separate, but simply parts of the Medici court apparatus—housed artistic, archaeological, anthropological, and natural historical collections of outstanding range and quality.[3] The presence of the Florentine Codex at the Biblioteca Medicea Laurenziana is emblematic of the equally impressive collection of books, manuscripts, and archival records that the Medici accumulated and successfully preserved.[4]

The collecting institutions were matched by those for production and, to a lesser extent, analysis. The Medici Fonderie and the Galleria dei Lavori in Pietre Dure of the Casino di San Marco, the former celebrated in Stradano's fresco in the Casino di San Marco, relied on imported materials and models. We have seen the use of Indian semiprecious stones in the creation of a suitably grand mausoleum for the dynasty, but Medici ambitions extended much further. The Casino di San Marco also saw experiments in porcelain production in Florence that produced items still housed in the world's major museums. Meanwhile, an artist of the caliber of Jacopo Ligozzi was employed to depict the plants of the botanical gardens. The many objects, flora, and fauna collected from around the world, their depictions in naturalistic drawings, and their transformations into elaborate pieces of art or complex medicinal boxes—all entered socially mediated networks of gift exchange.[5] Reflecting their grand ducal status, much of the Medici participation in the overlapping aristocratic and intellectual networks then coalescing into the Republic of Letters was mediated by the same group of secretaries and diplomats who facilitated Medici engagement with the wider world.

The botanical gardens, the reinvigorated University of Pisa, the villas, the menagerie, the Uffizi, the Guardaroba, the Fonderie, the Studiolo, the Galleria dei Lavori in Pietre Dure, and the Biblioteca Medicea Laurenziana complemented a lively intellectual environment in Florence and Pisa centered on academies and the court. Mixing in various measures curiosity, serious intellectual engagement, patrician sociability, club formalism, play within established genres, and occasional passionate commitment, the academies included not only those like Sassetti's Alterati, but also such enduring bodies as the Accademia della Crusca, dedicated to the study of the Italian language. Ranging in formality and official status, these social bodies complemented official Medici institutions yet were neither isolated nor exclusively Florentine. Instead, scholars, learned patricians, merchants, and clerics circulated regularly among Florence, Bologna, and Rome in intensive overlapping networks of patronage, sociability, and intellectual exchange. Even as botanical samples, learned letters, Medici and papal subventions, and innumerable gifts bound together the elites of these cities, so also some major figures and institutions bridged multiple cities and patrons. This famously occurred at an elite level, as the Bolognese naturalist Ulisse Aldrovandi (1522–1605) corresponded with Francesco I, and Florence's Galileo Galilei (1564–1642) served from 1610 as the mathematician and philosopher to the grand duke while maintaining close ties to Rome.[6] It equally held for the Roman-Florentine Tipografia Medicea Orientale (Medici Oriental Press) and the networks of religious orders like the Jesuits, who tied central Italy to the far-flung outposts of a resurgent Counter-Reformation Church.[7]

A full account of these many institutions and individuals is well beyond the scope of this this book. Instead, this chapter engages with some of the ways that the animals and plants, books and information, treasured objects, and people who made their way to and from Tuscany interacted with these institutions and entwined them with long-distance networks. The myriad linkages that brought the world to Florence in a literal as well as imaginative sense contributed to Florence's development of such an extensive cultural and intellectual apparatus.[8] Picking up where the last chapter left off, this chapter begins with an analysis of the institutions of botanical enterprise in Tuscany before turning from flora to fauna. The animals that traveled to and from Tuscany came and went along commercial and especially diplomatic routes, earning the Medici social and political capital. From the botanical gardens, villas, and menagerie, the chapter then turns to the pleasures of thinking globally, considering both people and institutions. The section touches on the non-Florentines who came and went to Tuscany from the most distant lands—from the Amazon and Japan to Lebanon and Muscovy—the grand ducal workshops that were dedicated to reworking natural materials, and the palaces, libraries, and academies where geography, human diversity, and language were discussed, studied, and recorded.

## The Botanical Gardens and Villas

Botanical enterprise developed early and rapidly in Tuscany, helped by the generous patronage and assiduous personal interest of Cosimo I. The enterprise began with the key institution, the botanical gardens in Pisa, founded by Luca Ghini (1490-1556) with Cosimo I's support in 1543-1544. Ghini also led the creation of a botanical garden in Florence in late 1545, named the Giardino delle Stalle after its proximity to the ducal stables.[9] We have already seen Carletti mention that he had seen aloe growing there. Cosimo I's personal interest in and knowledge of botany is well attested, including acts of patronage and collecting, a 1543 request for the classification of a plant, and his marginal comments on the *Commentaries (Commentarii / Discorsi)* of Pietro Andrea Mattioli (1501-1577).[10] Reading this last would have been congenial, with its compliment on Cosimo I's construction, at Ghini's behest, of the botanical gardens at Pisa.[11]

Cosimo I's enthusiasm for botany dovetailed neatly with a family tradition of creating gardens and villas, revived under Duke Cosimo I and Duchess Eleonora of Toledo (1522-1562).[12] Perhaps Cosimo's childhood spent at Villa Castello contributed to his commitment to the villas.[13] Eleonora also played a central role in developing the Medici commitment to gardens, palaces, and villas. She acquired the Pitti Palace and began the process of renovating it as the primary ducal palace. Work on the accompanying Boboli Gardens started under Niccolò il Tribolo (1497-1550) and was continued by Bartolomeo Ammannati (1511-1592) and Bernardo Buontalenti (1531-1608) after Tribolo's death.[14] Although the Boboli Gardens were the grandest in the city, the Medici were not done. Francesco I set up a garden for rare plants on the roof of the Loggia dei Lanzi in 1582.[15] This new garden, the Boboli, and the Giardino delle Stalle already constituted a substantial investment in a dense stone city, yet they were just the tip of a much larger network. Many of the Medici villas, both inherited and newly created, clustered so closely around Florence that most could easily be reached in a morning's ride, though a few villas oriented to hunting or inherited from the fifteenth century were located slightly further from the city (see Table 5.1). Nearly all were depicted in seventeen lunettes by Justus Utens created at Villa Artimino from 1599 to 1602.[16]

The villas played a central role for the Medici, so much so that Cosimo I began work on remodeling the garden at Castello shortly after his accession in 1537 and apparently liked it so much that he retired there in 1564.[17] Even as Cosimo stayed at Castello, Francesco began the development of his famous villa Pratolino (1569), which became strongly associated with him.[18] His brother and successor Ferdinando I

Table 5.1  Grand ducal Medici villas during the reigns of Francesco I and Ferdinando I[1]

| Villa Name | Distance (km) from Boboli Gardens | Medici Acquisition | Renovation (before 1630) | Justus Utens Lunette? (Y/N)[2] |
|---|---|---|---|---|
| Ambrogiana | 23.3 | 1574 | 1574; 1587 | Y |
| Artimino | 21.9 | Built 1596–1600 | Justus Utens lunettes painted 1599–1602 | N |
| Cafaggiolo | 28.9 | Mid-fourteenth century | 1430s; enlarged with a hunting reserve under Cosimo I | Y |
| Careggi | 6.5 | 1417 | First half of the fifteenth century; burned in 1529; repaired 1535–1536 (grotto from 1609) | N |
| Castello | 7.9 | 1477 | 1538 (gardens); 1588–1595 (villa) | Y |
| Cerreto Guidi | 36.6 | 1555 | 1566–after 1575 | N |
| Collesalvetti | 77 | Cosimo the Elder's time (mid-fifteenth century) | Property enlarged in the second half of the sixteenth century | Y |
| Fiesole | 7.4 | Mid- fifteenth century | | N |
| Lappeggi | 11.5 | 1569 | Acquired for then Prince Francesco; Ferdinando I gave it to Don Antonio de' Medici | Y |
| La Magia | 28.5 | 1583 | 1585–1586; Ferdinando I gave it Don Antonio de' Medici | Y |
| Marignolle | 3.2 | 1559 | Renovated for Francesco I; given to Don Antonio de' Medici in 1587; further revision in 1621 to Girolamo di Gino Capponi | Y |

*Table 5.1*  (continued)

| Villa Name | Distance (km) from Boboli Gardens | Medici Acquisition | Renovation (before 1630) | Justus Utens Lunette? (Y/N)[2] |
|---|---|---|---|---|
| Montevettolini | 42.4 | Before 1595 | After 1595 | Y |
| La Petraia | 8 | 1544 | 1566 (false start); 1588–1598 | Y |
| Boboli Gardens (Pitti Palace) | N/A | 1549 | 1549–1593 | Y |
| Poggio a Caiano | 18.5 | 1474–1477 | 1485–1492 (partial building); 1512/13–1521 (continued work); under Cosimo I (garden and stables); 1568 (inherited by Francesco I); 1578–1582 | Y |
| Poggio Imperiale | 2.0 | 1565 | Cosimo gave it to Isabella de' Medici; Virginio Orsini inherited it on her death in 1576; inherited by Maria Maddalena of Austria; restructured 1622–1625 | N |
| Pratolino (now part of Villa Demidoff) | 13.6 | 1569 | Completed in 1575 | Y |
| Seravezza | 107 | 1513 | 1555 | Y |
| Stabbia | 43.1 | Republic had it from the early fifteenth century | 1548–1568; given to then Cardinal Ferdinando and Don Pietro de' Medici by Cosimo; inherited by Don Lorenzo de' Medici in 1606 | N |

| La Toppia | 9.0 | Mid-sixteenth century | Use granted to Scipione Ammirato and Benedetto Varchi; extensively renovated with a focus on the garden under Cosimo III | N |
| Trebbio | 26.2 | Late fourteenth century | 1428; enlarged under Ferdinando I | Y |

1. These distances are based on Google Maps walking directions from the relevant sections of Isabella Lapi Ballerini, *The Medici Villas: Complete Guide*, trans. Michael Sullivan and Eleonor Daunt, rev. ed. (Florence: Giunti, 2010). Among the villas that Lapi Ballerini profiles, but which are omitted from the table, are Villa di Agnano (1486–1492; sold 1494), 83; Villa di Spedaletto (1486–1491; sold 1494), 84–85; Villa di Camugliano (under Alessandro de' Medici and Cosimo I; granted to Giuliano Gondi by Cosimo I; returned to the Medici under Cosimo II by Matteo Botti, who had purchased it from Gondi; upon Botti's elevation to marquis of Campiglia d'Orcia in 1615; transferred to Filippo Niccolini in 1637), 86–89; and Villa di Coltano, 107–109 (acquired in 1558 and granted to the Order of Santo Stefano in 1562. The villa was used as a Medici hunting lodge but is omitted for its agricultural focus and ties to the Order). This roughly tallies with the thirteen Medici villas and gardens in Tuscany—Careggi, Castello, Petraia, Boboli Gardens, Poggio Imperiale, Cafaggiolo, Trebbio, Fiesole, Cerreto Guidi, Pratolino, Poggio a Caiano, Artimino a Carmignano, Palazzo di Seravezza, and La Magia that were added to the UNESCO list of World Heritage sites in 2013: http://www.beniculturali.it/mibac/export/MiBAC/sito-MiBAC/Contenuti/MibacUnif/Comunicati/visualizza_asset.html_1344485679.html. On the villas, see also Cristina Bellorini, *The World of Plants in Renaissance Tuscany: Medicine and Botany* (Burlington, VT: Ashgate, 2016), 40–49. For a detailed account of the Boboli Gardens, see "Appendix IIB, Chronology of the Boboli Garden in the Sixteenth Century," in Claudia Lazzaro, *The Italian Renaissance Garden: From the Conventions of Planting, Design, and Ornament to the Grand Gardens of Sixteenth-Century Italy* (New Haven, CT: Yale University Press, 1990). See also Helena Attlee, *Italian Gardens: A Cultural History* (London: Frances Lincoln, 2006).

2. Three of the lunettes are unknown; one of the missing ones is likely to have been of Artimino, Lapi Ballerini, *Medici Villas*, 116.

built two other villas, Artimino and Ambrogiana, both slightly further out, presumably in part because the Medici already had five villas close to the city.[19] Although the Medici remained tightly focused on Florence and the valley of the Arno, they carried their commitment to villas to Rome, where Ferdinando's villa Medici on the Pincio had a carefully arranged garden.[20] Not all the Medici villas focused on gardens. Some of the Medici villas were more strongly oriented to hunting, fishing, or the administration of nearby estates.[21] Even so, they collectively constituted a formidable array of sites well suited to hosting the many plants and animals that came to Tuscany.

In a deeply hierarchical society made more so by the creation of the Grand Duchy, the Medici court set the tone for an increasingly aristocratic patrician elite. That the Medici seem to have largely governed surrounded by their gardens in elaborately decorated villas set a pattern for Tuscany as a whole. It was not difficult to do, for Florentines were already famous for investing their wealth in palaces in the countryside, a habit that the Venetian ambassador to Florence in 1527, Marco Foscari, noted in his *relazione* as a source of vulnerability.[22] With the establishment of profound peace and security in the center of Tuscany, the military vulnerability that had long limited Florentine building dissipated and Tuscany's famous gardens could bloom with plants sent from all over the world. Although the following will concentrate on the Medici, recall that Francesco Capponi had grown Carletti's Japanese citrus. Carletti does not say where, but the villa in Arcetri acquired by the Capponi in 1572 and now known as Villa Capponi is a reasonable supposition.[23] Though Carletti does not mention it, as a Medici client he might also have sent the citrus to join the Garden of the Citrus Fruits at Villa Castello, which dates to the late sixteenth century; Castello now has some five hundred potted citrus specimens.[24]

Beautiful, well preserved, and artistically rich, Florence's villas have a rich historiography.[25] The central point here is that the villas and botanical gardens constituted a dense, closely monitored, and abundantly resourced constellation of sites capable of raising and transferring the plants Medici agents so diligently secured for Florence. In this context, it is not surprising to find that Cosimo I had a banyan tree at Castello or that banyan trees could be found at a later date at Villa Petraia and the Salviati and Rucellai gardens.[26] None of them was officially a botanical garden, yet they had fine botanical specimens. The project of using the villas for introducing new plants and animals began quite early. A letter of May 5, 1548, from Cristiano Pagni, secretary to Cosimo I, to Pier Francesco Riccio (1501–1564), Medici treasurer and *maggior-domo maggiore*, noted that Indian grain (perhaps maize; *"grano d'India"*) had been sown at Castello, a box of plants had arrived in Pisa from Padua in good health, and nine of the fifteen herons that had been sent had survived the journey.[27] At botanical gardens and villas in Tuscany, plants from places that had been unknown or impossibly distant in the era of Lorenzo il Magnifico (1449–1492) now grew regularly.

The botanical gardens of the university cities of Pisa and Padua were founded nearly contemporaneously, in 1543–1545.[28] New plants seem regularly to have come in rapid succession to both, as happened with the American agave that appeared in Padua in 1561 and then in Pisa and Florence.[29] The botanical gardens remained important under Francesco I, who had them expanded, and his successor. Beyond Casabona's Cretan venture discussed in Chapter 4, Ferdinando I sponsored a collecting and acquisition trip to Genoa in 1599 by University of Pisa botanist Francesco Malocchi.[30] Earlier, Casabona had played his part in distributing new plants, sending rare plants to Cardinal Ferdinando at the Villa Medici in Rome.[31] As in Florence, so also in Rome, Cardinal Ferdinando benefited from Medici connections on the Iberian peninsula. In late 1584 and early 1585, Augusto Tizio corresponded with Pietro di Francesco Usimbardi, promising to send and then sending an array of items to Rome, including an antidote from New Spain (Mexico) and seeds from India for Cardinal Ferdinando.[32] Indeed, Usimbardi's requests could stretch the Medici botanical infrastructure. In a March 9, 1585, letter from Niccolò Gaddi in Florence to Usimbardi in Rome, Gaddi spoke of undertaking to draw on Medici gardens in Florence and Pisa and his own to forward plants and seeds, "but in the sheet sent to me, there are many plants that not only do we not have here, but which I do not think have been seen in Italy, yet I will diligently do all that I can do."[33] Eventually, a whole panoply of tropical fruit and consumable plants made their way to Tuscany, which included tobacco and Carletti's favorite, cacao.[34]

With such a visible level of commitment to the villas and botanical gardens over more than a half a century, Medici princes stood at the center of Italian botanical networks. They not only participated in courtly gift exchange, but also entered into intellectual disagreements that show a high level of engagement. In the spring of 1586, Francesco I and Ulisse Aldrovandi exchanged seeds, and Francesco disagreed with Aldrovandi about the Guanabano they had been discussing, asserting that it was not the Baba of India.[35] Aldrovandi was one of the great scholars of late Renaissance natural science, but Francesco had unusual access to botanical information from India, not least that provided at exactly this time by Filippo Sassetti. The interchange, then, was not merely one of seeds and resources, but a genuine exchange of expertise. The exchange continued at an intense pace, as Francesco wrote gratefully to Aldrovandi a month later, "I received the seeds with the notes and information that came with them and you can believe that they are very dear to me as much for their rarity and quality as that they come to me from you, who I love so much."[36]

Medici commitment to serious botanical inquiry operated simultaneously with full participation in aristocratic networks of gift exchange. Then, as now, products from personal gardens were popular gifts, reflecting an intimate and special connection outside the shared marketplace. The Medici gave three categories of such gifts: plants from the Indies, food from their gardens, and medicines from their laboratories. In 1583, for instance, the grand duke gave seeds from the East Indies to the duke of Urbino with instructions that they were to be planted in the duke's garden, not regifted.[37] The Medici might also send food from their own gardens as a gift along with things from Portugal and India, as they did in March 1586 to Guglielmo I Gonzaga, duke of Mantua and Montferrat (1538–1587).[38] Most elaborately, the Medici gave gifts of medicine from their own laboratory, some produced with their own hands.[39] This was a systematic element of diplomatic practice. An inventory of the Medici embassy in Madrid from 1600 includes "two ebony boxes of medicines" among the items in preparation for distribution as gifts.[40] Refining the plants of empire with Tuscan knowledge transformed them into prestigious medicines in a high-value box, suitable to be given as diplomatic gifts at the center of Iberian empire. Even ebony itself, as we have seen, the Medici imported from Iberia.

## Animals: Medici Collecting and Diplomacy[41]

Though perhaps all regions of Europe can lay claim to some distinctive animal, Tuscany would not appear near the top of any Renaissance list.

With its thousands of years of urban development, intensively farmed and mined countryside, and the absence of a royal or aristocratic structure to create and preserve large forest lands for hunting, its fauna was probably more heavily tilted to the domesticated variety than most. It is striking, then, that under the Medici grand dukes, Tuscany assumed a central role in the acquisition and distribution of animals, not just in Italy but to the Holy Roman Emperor, the duke of Bavaria, the king of Spain, and the king of France. How did this happen? Although the institutions developed for botanical enterprise and the Medici diplomatic network on the Iberian peninsula certainly contributed substantially, the case of the animals shows the Medici extending their commercial and especially diplomatic reach in a much broader and less mediated way. Independent Medici relationships with distant lands meant that the Medici built a well-deserved reputation for having a fabulous collection of rare and exotic animals, a reputation whose diplomatic utility they exploited to the full. As with plants, the Medici used their exotic animals to make a spectacular impression.

The linked notions that rulers' courts should include exotic animals and that they are suitably princely gifts are, of course, ancient ones. In Renaissance Italy, however, it received a fresh impetus with Portuguese and Spanish efforts to impress the pope. In the early decades of European exploration and conquest, gifts to the pope served the double purpose of currying favor and displaying command of the rare and exotic. King Manuel I of Portugal (r. 1495–1521), who oversaw the creation of the Estado da Índia, had mastered this art, famously giving Pope Leo X (r. 1513–1521) Hanno the Elephant.[42] The rhinoceros the Portuguese also attempted to send never did make it to Rome, lost in a storm near La Spezia in 1516, but Albrecht Dürer's woodcut of it based on reports he received has become an iconic image.[43] In any event, the precedent was set. Rare and exotic animals from distant lands carried a strong symbolic charge, underlining who had an empire filled with such creatures and who did not.

Had Tuscany succeeded in one of its efforts to acquire a donatary captaincy or establish direct trade with Brazil, Tuscany might have been able to follow Portugal directly. Instead, the Medici had to rely on their diplomatic network. Their network proved more than up to the challenge. The following section will consider how this worked, starting with birds, horses, and dogs. These animals will be examined briefly because of their ubiquity, focusing particularly on the birds that came from the Indies and Africa and on those cases that illustrate features of the Medici network that moved them to and from Tuscany. The remaining animals will be addressed by geographic section, starting with Africa, followed by those that went through the Iberian peninsula, and ending with Europe, whose less densely settled regions provided the Medici with a formidable array of beasts. In so doing, we shall also consider where the animals lived in and around Florence, which possessed an animal infrastructure to match its botanical one. Finally, the section will close with an account of the exotic animal products that the Medici collected.[44]

### Aristocratic Exchange—Birds, Horses, and Dogs

Animals of the hunt—birds, horses, and dogs—served as emblems of an aristocratic ethos that the Medici and the Florentine patriciate cultivated in their extended and not wholly successful effort at passing as nobles. That these animals shaded easily into those treasured for their beauty, racing skill, and companionship helped, for it allowed them to fit neatly into more traditional patterns of urban patrician sociability centered on Florentine *palazzi* and suburban villas. The relative role of Florence's animals can be seen in the impression left on the author of the French essayist Michel de Montaigne's (1533–1592) travel journal as he passed through Florence in the autumn of 1580. After arriving in Florence, Montaigne's party, "saw the grand duke's stable, very large, vaulted, in which there were not many valuable horses; indeed, he was not there that day. There we saw a sheep of a very strange shape; also a camel, some lions, some bears, and an animal the size of a very big mastiff and the shape of a cat, all marked in black and white, which they call a tiger."[45] The grand duke was short on the classic equestrian stock on which the duke of Mantua or the nobles of the Kingdom of Naples so prided themselves.[46] Generally negative on Florence, though impressed by the Duomo, the gardens of the villa at Castello, and the villa of Pratolino, the brief account of the city closes with "also there is no worth-while practice either of arms, or of horsemanship, or of letters."[47] Catherine de Medici (1519–1589) may still have been prominent in France, but her Florentine relations were not succeeding as French-style aristocrats. By contrast, the grand duke was long on animals so rare and wondrous that Montaigne's party struggled to describe them.

Whatever the critiques of traveling French aristocrats, the Medici certainly did participate in aristocratic networks of animal acquisition and gift exchange centered on the hunt. This especially pertained to the perhaps more easily given and received category of falcons. For instance, Cosimo I gave falcons to Marchese Fernández Manrique de Lara (1539).[48] Cosimo I likewise received a falcon from someone else in 1557.[49] It bears stressing that much of the falconry was local, although the Medici did receive ten gyrfalcons and a goshawk in 1572, and in 1591 Ferdinando I received an Icelandic gyrfalcon from Marco Pio III (1568–1599) of Savoy, lord of Sassuolo, then in Brussels.[50] The falcons were not merely kept at the villas, but used for hunting, as Cosimo I appears to have been preparing to do when he ordered the transfer of a half dozen falcons between the villas at Trebbio and Poggio a Caiano in late July of 1547.[51] It is not surprising that numerous administrative documents track the payment, clothing, and other needs of the falconers and the falcons.[52]

The falcons fit neatly into a standard aristocratic model and involved a modest use of the network to secure an excellent Icelandic bird, but it was the decorative birds that involved the Medici in longer-distance patterns of exchange. The birds were principally parrots, ostriches, peacocks, ducks from India, turkeys, and a vague category of birds from the Indies, which typically meant the Americas. Parrots circulated regularly in Italian aristocratic networks of exchange. Duchess Eleonora of Toledo, for instance, received in 1551 a kitten and a parrot from Baldovino del Monte, count of Monte San Sevino and Pope Julius III's (1487–1555) brother.[53] Generally, though, parrots came to Tuscany from Spain. They seem to have done so more through aristocratic gift exchange than through agency relations, though the usual diplomatic channels served as a postal infrastructure. For example, Diego (el Africano) Fernández de Córdoba, marquis of Comares, wrote from Madrid to Francesco I on November 29, 1576, explaining that the prior Don Antonio de Toledo had given two parrots from the Indies to Ambassador Lenzi to send to Francesco I.[54] Likewise, in 1592, Ferdinando I received horses, dogs, and a parrot from Rodrigo de Castro Osorio (1523–1600), cardinal of Seville, and sent a return gift of a chest of glassware made using the grand duke's secret ("nostro secreto").[55] The substitution of a parrot for a falcon in the traditional hunting triad probably reflects the cardinal of Seville's presumably privileged access to items coming from Spain's American colonies to the official monopoly port for Spanish-American trade.

Exotic birds from the Americas feature quite regularly in the items sent to the Medici from Spain. For example, two letters sent from Madrid in June 1565 by Garces, the secretary to Ambassador de Nobili, "to the Prince of Florence and Siena" (the future Francesco I) discussed birds from the Indies.[56] Two years later, Ambassador de' Nobili sent another three birds from the Indies to Francesco, who instructed the ambassador, "try to find us some more of these birds."[57] Later that same year, Ambassador de Nobili also sent Cosimo I a Spanish goshawk and sought to find him some sparrow hawks from India.[58] On August 14, 1570, Francesco again asked Ambassador de Nobili, "see if it is possible to provide us with little birds from the Indies or sparrow hawks as you can find them and send them to us immediately."[59] Two weeks later, a letter from Francesco's secretary, Antonio Serguidi, reminded the ambassador about the desired birds.[60] Spectacular examples of birds from the Indies eventually made their way to Tuscany. On January 9, 1575, Ugolino Grifoni (1504–1576)—an old and trusted secretary of Cosimo I, member of an ancient family from San Miniato, and master general of the Hospital of S. Iacopo of Altopascio—wrote to Grand Duchess Johanna Habsburg de' Medici (1547–1578) and sent her Altopascio wine and cheese and two "galli d'India," which may have been turkeys.[61] As Lia Markey has shown, parrots and turkeys were sufficiently firmly established to enter Medici art commissions, from a tapestry based on Agnolo Bronzino's cartoon of circa 1545, La Dovizia, to Ludovico Buti's 1588 fresco of America at the Uffizi.[62]

The Medici avidly sought birds transported through Iberian networks, but their commitment to collecting and gift exchange was far too intense to be confined to this source. Rather, birds associated with India and Africa came to the Medici along quite a variety of channels. Ostriches came from North Africa, from which they arrived quite regularly. In 1547, Francesco Capponi wrote from Alexandria to Pier Francesco Riccio in Florence sending both carpets and a pair of gazelles to Cosimo I and indicating that upon his return he would bring ostriches.[63] Ostriches, like most animals, arrived in Livorno before being transported elsewhere in Tuscany. On July 10, 1565, for instance, Luigi Dovara wrote to Prince Francesco de' Medici in Florence explaining that Pompeo da Calci had sent an ostrich to Francesco addressed to the captain of Livorno.[64] Complicating the picture of conflict between Tuscany and the corsair ports of the Maghreb, ostriches were regularly dispatched across the Mediterranean. An April 11, 1581, bill of lading for the *Santa Anna* arriving from "Barbary" includes an ostrich for Francesco I.[65] The bey of Algiers's effort, a few years later, to send Ferdinando de' Medici an ostrich, among other presents, shows how, even over relatively short distances, several intermediaries were required. Specifically, the bey explained that through "Giacobo Brangia, scribe to our captain Arnaot Memi Bey, I send Geronimo Salvino *polsano* and the Pisan Sebastian de Paula, subjects of Your Most Serene Highness with two horses and two lions and an ostrich, also a pair of knives with two little gilt scabbards and two *marrama* [pickaxes?]."[66] In sending the ostriches as part of a group with other animals, the shipment was typical; the ostriches sent in 1547 and 1581 came, respectively, with a pair of gazelles and a single gazelle.[67]

The continuous arrival of such birds all over Europe meant that exotic birds might also be secured from quite close by. At the end of August 1591, for instance, Ferdinando I wrote from the Villa of Pratolino to the Bolognese senator Raffaello Riario in Bologna to thank him for sending a male peacock while commenting, "as I will be very grateful for the female, if she can be found."[68] The possibilities of breeding tacit in seeking the female pointed to a desire to secure a self-reproducing supply.[69] As with the seeds transferred and reproduced in Tuscany, having a breeding pair of peacocks would enable the Medici to be providers as well as recipients of diplomatic and aristocratic gifts. Whatever his source, by October of the next year, Ferdinando I wrote from Villa dell'Ambrogiana to his niece Eleonora de' Medici-Gonzaga (1567–1611), duchess of Mantua (1587–1611), "I saw with pleasure Your Highness's gardener and the things you sent me, as rare as curious, which are very dear to me, nor will I fail to send him back with the white peacocks you desire."[70]

The Medici do not seem to have been major bird suppliers, but this gift was not unique. Just under a year later, on September 29, 1593, the duchess of Mantua wrote again to her uncle, Ferdinando I, sending gifts with her gardener, Giovanni Radici, and requesting plant grafts. The duchess reminded her uncle of the promised white peacocks and asked also for some of his *"anitre d'India* [ducks of India]."[71] "Indian ducks" had long been a popular request. Decades earlier, on October 18, 1549, Cosimo I had written from his villa of Poggio a Caiano to Francesco Babbi (1507–1587), the Medici envoy in Naples, about Isabella di Capua-Gonzaga, princess of Molfetta, that "the promise will be observed of the *anatre d'India* [ducks of India] and the animals that are desired for her park."[72] It appears that the Medici were sometimes behind in sending their avian gifts.

Just as the Medici successfully participated in networks of gift exchange for hunting, exotic, and decorative birds, so also they received fine horses and dogs from around the Mediterranean. The ubiquity of horse exchanges, the comparatively marginal role of the Medici in equine culture highlighted in Montaigne's travel journal, and the relatively narrow ambit from which the Medici drew their stock make it possible to state the case briefly.[73] Some examples from 1539–1544, in the early years of Cosimo I's reign, illustrate the patterns. For instance, a query came from Rome about Cosimo I's interest in a fine Turkish horse (1539) and Eleonora of Toledo secured reluctant compliance from the Florentine senator Alessandro Antinori (1481–1558) to her request for his Turkish horse (1540).[74] The next year, Cosimo I received a letter from Octaviano de' Medici (1482–1546), Florentine senator and depositary general, reporting on the arrival of two Turkish horses in Ancona for him along with information about the price and quality of the horses.[75] Ancona was a natural place for Ragusan and other merchants trading in Turkish horses to land them, but the Medici could also negotiate for them closer to home, as Cosimo I's agents did with a Ragusan merchant resident in Florence in early 1544.[76]

Barb horses were likewise readily available to the Medici within Italy. A flurry of letters sent by Pirro Musefilo, count of Sassetta, in Naples to Cosimo I in November and December 1540, illustrates the point. Sassetta discussed horses imported from North Africa to Naples to be sent on to Tuscany and plans for gifts of barbs from Cosimo I's father-in-law, Viceroy Pedro Alvarez de Toledo (1484–1553), and by the viceroy's son and Duchess Eleonora's brother, Don Garcia de Toledo (1514–1577). Sassetta reported to Cosimo I on December 18 that Don

Garcia had sent five mares and five black slaves.[77] The Medici were very much involved in the culture of Mediterranean slavery, so much so that the slaves and horses were mentioned in the same sentence.[78] The Medici could also go straight to the suppliers in North Africa. For instance, Prince Francesco wrote on June 30 and September 9, 1568, to Giuseppe della Seta about buying a pair of barb racing horses—"very fast at the course"—from either Algiers or Bona (Annaba, Algeria), telling della Seta in his second letter to buy the horses at 80–100 *scudi* per horse.[79]

Just as the Medici secured horses from around the Mediterranean, so they also acquired hunting dogs. A pack of forty Corsican dogs arrived in 1546, and Francesco I wrote on December 14, 1581, to thank his father-in-law, Bartolomeo Cappello (1519–1594), in Venice for the gift of a Turkish dog.[80] The Medici collection of horses and hunting dogs seems not to have lacked for anything and yet neither does it seem to have been of the first order. Certainly, the Medici possessed extensive hunting grounds served by an array of villas, but their participation in the hunt seems to have lacked the vast commitment displayed by those from older aristocratic traditions.

Even so, the Medici remained attuned to the diplomatic opportunities presented by equine gifts. In 1540, Cosimo I was as busily engaged in giving away Turkish horses as receiving them. On August 23, 1540, Cosimo I heard from his ambassador in Rome, Giovanni di Filippo dell'Antella (1475–1548) about the delight of Charles V's cavalry general, the prince of Sulmona, Philippe de Lannoy (1514–1553), at receiving Cosimo I's gift of a Turkish horse.[81] A week later, Cosimo I wrote to the Florentine resident ambassador at the Imperial Court, Alessandro Giovanni di Pierantonio Bandini (1498–1568), about a gift of Turkish horses to Emperor Charles V.[82] Indeed, Turkish horses seem to have been a particularly appropriate diplomatic gift to the high nobility and royalty, being both appreciated and easily reciprocated. For instance, in 1545, Cosimo I sent gifts that included Turkish horses to Catherine de' Medici, then married to the dauphin, the future King Henry II (r. 1547–1559).[83] On September 19 of that same year, Duchess Eleonora of Toledo wrote to thank Catherine de' Medici for the five hackney horses and the little dogs she had sent.[84] Gifts of this sort seems to have remained common throughout the period. When Peter Paul Rubens

(1577–1640) passed through Livorno on the way to Spain bearing gifts from Duke Vincenzo I Gonzaga (1562–1612), he was prevailed on to bring an equipped *chinea* (hackney) horse to Juan de Vich in Alicante as a gift from the Medici court.[85] This participation in standard aristocratic practices of gift exchange is important to bear in mind, lest it be unduly overshadowed. Still, rare and exotic animals best reflect the diplomatic uses the Medici made of their long-distance connections, transforming themselves into suppliers of lions, tigers, and leopards to the princes of Europe. In this, the Medici emulated the Portuguese and Spanish practice of giving exotic animals. Yet the Medici also reached beyond the Iberian empires to find as many wondrous animals to collect and give as possible.

### Collecting and Diplomacy with Exotic Animals

As King Manuel I had so vividly shown at the beginning of the sixteenth century, exotic animals could make powerful diplomatic and cultural statements. To do so effectively in the world of spectacle that was a Renaissance court, however, Manuel understood that it helped if they were big, a principle he put into action with an elephant and a rhinoceros. The very scale of these animals—with the attendant costs, logistical difficulties, and vulnerability to mishap so vividly illustrated by their early deaths—meant that most Renaissance courts opted for somewhat smaller, if still large, animals. In a culture of continuous gift giving and intensive competitive collecting in which nobles like Montaigne visited, evaluated, and wrote about their experiences of courts, acquiring and giving prestige animals were closely linked symbolic acts. For Portugal and Spain, the symbolism was clear. Collecting and giving rare animals meant mobilizing their imperial administrations to transfer the animals to Europe. The ability to do so signified the vast extent of their domains and the lands to which they gave access. Tuscany had to work rather harder to play at this level. Its success, however, won Tuscany recognition among European courts, elites, and the broader public not just for magnificence, but also for the range of their connections. Always at risk of marginalization, the Medici used the spectacle of Florence's exotic animals to showcase their connections, both commercial and diplomatic.

Tuscany's relationships with the polities across North Africa, from Morocco to Ottoman Egypt, were often quite fraught. Corsair raiding,

galley slavery, diplomatic intrigue, and amphibious assaults complicated the maintenance of more peaceful ties. Even so, the Medici quite
regularly acquired African animals and often did so in North Africa.
Although the Maghreb, from Algiers to Tripoli, would have been the
easiest source logistically, the prevalence of corsair raiding from these
ports meant that Medici agents often turned to Ottoman Alexandria
as a source. Francesco Capponi sent gazelles to Cosimo I from there
in 1547, and Paolo Mancini sent one from Alexandria to Prince Francesco in 1566.[86] In 1581, Francesco I received another gazelle, this time
from Algiers.[87] On other occasions, the original location is unclear, but
the gazelles' arrival in Livorno for the Medici, as in a June 1559 case,
certainly allowed for a North African itinerary.[88] The gazelles were presumably intended for one of the Medici villas, though their small numbers suggests a decorative rather than hunting purpose. For instance,
Francesco I wrote from the villa of Poggio a Caiano on September 22,
1580, to Giovanni Battista Ricasoli to thank him for a variety of items
that included a pair of gazelles.[89] Like other imported and collected animals, gazelles also circulated in Italy, though perhaps primarily immediately after import. On July 16, 1582, Francesco I wrote from the
villa of Pratolino to thank Francesco Moro in Venice for his gifts, which
included an attractive nag, hounds, and a gazelle.[90] Presumably, the animals had not been housed for long in the maritime city but were trans-
shipped via Venice. Desirable as gazelles, parrots, and ostriches were,
their meanings were relatively muted, confined to their beauty or exot-
icism. More spectacular animals could be more heavily freighted with
symbolism and none more so for Florence than the lion.

Symbolic and actual lions had long been at the center of Florence.
The *Marzocco*, a statue of a lion holding the heraldic crest of Florence,
stood in the Piazza della Signoria, and lions had long lived nearby in a
den off the Via dei Leoni near Palazzo Vecchio; a pair of lions was born
there in 1331.[91] Quite typically, the Medici moved swiftly to appropriate
this symbolism, just as they moved into and took over the symbolic
center of Florence. Kurt W. Forster has shown that Cosimo I adopted
Herculean imagery that stressed his leonine character, connecting him
closely to Florence.[92] Also typically, the Medici continued the existing
Florentine tradition of keeping lions but now did so as part of their personal control of animals. Their attachment to real and symbolic lions

was doubtless familiar to Pope Julius III (1487–1555)—who had been born in Rome of a family from Monte San Savino near Arezzo and had studied in Perugia and Siena—when he dispatched two lionesses as gifts to Cosimo I in 1551.[93] Medici interest in receiving lions seems to have been widely known. The duke of Savoy sent Prince Francesco a particularly fine lion in 1568; an Algerian captain sent a horse, a lion, and a monkey to Cosimo I in 1569; and the bey of Algiers sent a lion in 1586.[94]

While they certainly were appreciated, Cosimo I did not entirely depend on such gifts. A December 30, 1553, note by Tomaso d'Iacopo de' Medici (1543–1584), then the under majordomo, authorized Pagolo di Romolo Baccegli to acquire musk and amber in Alexandria for Duchess Eleonora and a male lion for Duke Cosimo.[95] Administrative documents likewise track the arrival of lions, among other animals. Typically, tracking seems to have consisted of correspondence between the Medici or one of their senior officials and their senior officers in Livorno. On June 12, 1568, Prince Francesco wrote to Bernardo Baroncelli—*provveditore* of Livorno in 1563 and *provveditore* of the Customs of Livorno from 1564—that the Ragusan, "Tutolino, captain of our ship *Fenice*, gives us to understand he has brought three little domestic lions, a cat of Algalia, three dogs as big as pigs, four painted Guinea hens, two white turtledoves, and many little birds of *Caranà* and some Cordovans of Spain." These animals were to be brought to Florence.[96] Similar correspondence tracks the arrival of lions from Algiers in 1586. A letter from the *provveditore* of Livorno, Matteo Forestani, of January 4 notes that the merchants on the ship that brought the lions had been sent to quarantine and that three lions and four Christians from Algiers were going to Florence.[97] A letter dated a week later points out that Forestani had not been paid for the meat the lions had eaten at Livorno.[98] The next year, Forestani was appointed *provveditore* of the Customs of Livorno. Shipping animals from Livorno involved senior figures in the administration, whether or not the animals were diplomatic gifts.

Though Medici efforts seem to have focused on lions, they also collected other large cats, principally tigers and leopards. As with the lions, Medici supplies derived from a combination of purchase through North Africa or the ports trading with it, patrician gift exchange, and diplomatic gifts. Though less symbolically important to the Florentines, both tigers and leopards could play a similarly substantive diplomatic role, populate the grand ducal menagerie, and assist with the hunt. Indeed, Cosimo I seems to have considered leopards as being a reasonable substitute for a tiger. For instance, on December 3, 1556, Cosimo I wrote to Piero Gelido (1495–1569), the long-standing legation secretary to the Medici embassy in Venice, "Of the tiger, we have received advice by way of Alexandria that there will be one, being very expensive, we will not wait for it otherwise although we find certain leopards that are very pleasing and fast and animated in the hunt."[99] Cosimo I certainly was in a position to make such comparisons, for, five years earlier, he had received a report about the ill health and medical care of a tiger then living in the grand ducal menagerie.[100]

Structurally, the speculation about tiger and leopard purchases points to a second Medici diplomatic chain, stretching from Venice to Alexandria, to complement that operating on the Iberian peninsula. Although Florentines could operate directly in Egypt, they seem often to have relied on intermediaries. Perhaps Venice's better relationship with the Ottoman Empire offered more secure access. In any event, the Medici turned again to this same channel to buy leopards.[101] On November 27, 1567, Prince Francesco wrote to Cosimo Bartoli (1503–1572), an established Medici agent in Venice, authorizing the purchase of a leopard proposed by Alessandro Caravia, but only "if he is domestic and tractable," not if "wild or unpleasant."[102] Leopards were court and hunting animals and needed to behave as such. Bartoli seems ultimately to have decided not to risk it, for Prince Francesco wrote again on December 17 telling Bartoli, "if the leopard is as terrible as you write, it is not for us, therefore do not take the trouble to send it to us."[103] If the Medici declined to purchase this leopard, they did eventually receive a pair of leopards, a male and a female, as a diplomatic gift from Vincenzo I Gonzaga, duke of Mantua, in 1609.[104]

The Medici received lions from the pope, the duke of Savoy, and the bey of Algiers and leopards from the duke of Mantua, but they seem to have been more active suppliers than recipients of such diplomatic gifts. Even as they reciprocated with similar gifts in the Mediterranean, many of their big cats went beyond the Alps. In this, they followed King Manuel in understanding that charismatic animals are more appreciated the further they are from home. As befit the Medici symbolic appropriation of Florence's lions, the Medici gave lions widely. Having dispatched lions as a gift abroad in 1541, the Medici seem to have developed a reputation.[105] In January 1542, the duke of Bavaria, Wilhelm IV, wrote to Cosimo I to ask for a male and a female lion.[106] Twenty-three years later, some lions would escape from Bavaria and wreak havoc in the countryside of Friuli, as a report sent to Cosimo I from Venice explained.[107] Indeed, the Medici seemed to be the people to ask for advice on lions, but Cosimo had to write to Francesco Babbi in 1549 to convey to Cosimo's father-in-law, Pedro de Toledo, the long-serving viceroy of Naples, that he could not provide counsel on preventing captive lions from eating their cubs.[108] The Medici were, however, reasonably effective in preserving their own cubs, for Cosimo I sent a pair to Count Otto Heinrich von der Pfalz (1502–1559) in 1542.[109]

Six years later, a flurry of letters from Cosimo I to the Medici ambassador in Paris, Giovanni Battista Ricasoli, and the legation secretary, Piero Gelido, discussed the gift of a pair of lion cubs to King Henry II or Queen Catherine de' Medici. The missives explain that the Medici did not possess any less than a year old at that time.[110] The next year, Guidobaldo II della Rovere (1514–1574), duke of Urbino, wrote to ask for a lion. Down to their last good male lion, the Medici were able to offer only a female lion and a bear.[111] Even so, two years later, in 1551, Cosimo I asked that two lion cubs be sent to Pisa on February 23.[112] A letter summary of April 18, 1553, notes that lions had been sent away by sea.[113] On March 9, 1560, the long-time Medici agent in Milan, Fabrizio Ferrari, passed on the request of Alonso Pimentel, the castellan of Milan, for a male lion to breed with his female lion; a letter of October 2, notes that Pimentel had asked Ferrari about the lion Cosimo I had promised him.[114] The tradition of lion giving continued under Francesco I, who gave a pair in 1585 to his son-in-law, Prince Vincenzo Gonzaga; Vincenzo thanked Francesco for the gift and sent him live fish on May 17, 1585.[115] As the difficulties with captive lion breeding faced by the viceroy of Naples suggested, lions benefited from regular replenishment from North Africa. In this way, the Medici used their connections both to North Africa and to other courts to set themselves up as a reliable source of lions. Doing so built connections to major ultramontane princes and cemented ties in Italy.

The Medici appreciated the diplomatic utility of supplying a range of big cats to friendly courts. Their practices with tigers and leopards confirm the pattern, with the Medici profiting diplomatically from their role as intermediaries between North Africa and distant European courts. In 1581, Francesco I wrote to Wilhelm V von Wittelsbach (1548-1626), duke of Bavaria, having heard from Giulio Cesare Alidosio "that the Tiger having died there that had been sent from here, has felt great sorrow about her, with affirmation from him that being able to have another would one be most appreciated, I finding one that is very domestic and agreeable, I have resolved to send it to Your Excellency."[116] The Medici were certainly attuned to the value of a timely gift and to the ways that it could establish an enduring relationship. Just over a decade later, Cavaliere Hortentio Triachi, a court gentleman of the duke of Bavaria, arrived in Florence. He planned to take back with him a youth who had been sent by the duke of Bavaria to learn at length, but apparently not very successfully, how to hunt with and keep leopards.[117]

The complications of securing tigers and leopards for Holy Roman Emperor Rudolf II (1552-1612) a quarter of a century later illustrates both the role of the Medici and their sourcing habits.[118] The Emperor asked Ferdinando I to supply him with a tiger and four leopards. Ferdinando responded that he had a tiger and some leopards, which he would send, and that he would seek to find more of them.[119] On July 4, 1607, Ferdinando I wrote to his ambassador at the Imperial Court, Rodrigo Alidosi, saying that he was sending "Burrino, one of our muleteers, with two tigers for His Imperial Majesty" and explaining that it was not possible to send the third yet but that it would be sent when the leopards had come from Alexandria. These last were necessary because Ferdinando's own pair of leopards were unsuitable for transportation, being "most difficult to govern."[120] Ferdinando I's gift of a pair of tigers across the Alps was a spectacular one. It appears that the Tuscan court sought to advertise this, with the key Medici diplomat and state counselor, Belisario Vinta, writing on September 23, 1607, to the Medici ambassador in Spain, Sallustio Tarugi, about the gift to Rudolf II.[121] The communication seems to have had the desired effect. On July 3, 1611, Tarugi's replacement as Medici ambassador to the Spanish Habsburg court, Orso Pannocchieschi d'Elci, wrote to Belisario Vinta. The Tuscan ambassador explained that he had written to a senior Spanish diplomat and courtier, Rodrigo Calderón (1578-1621), who would become Count of Oliva de Plasencia, "saying that the lead hunter of Your Highness, my lord, had written to me about having two hunting leopards" and asking Calderón whether Philip III wanted them. Philip III was receptive to the Tuscan offer of leopards, and so Ambassador Pannocchieschi d'Elci wrote that it would be good for Cosimo II "to order that they come as soon as possible."[122] Tragically, the leopards did not survive.[123] As King Manuel had found out with the rhinoceros, large animals are vulnerable on long journeys.

Even as the Medici provided Europe's courts with diplomatically useful animals, they also received animals from the Americas through Spain. Typically, they were birds, as we have seen, but in 1584 Cardinal Rodrigo de Castro sent Francesco I "two bizarre birds, a wild pig from Peru, and a skull from those countries."[124] Sadly, the pig did not make it, though Francesco I was still happy with his gifts. Augusto Tizio, a courtier of Francesco I and secretary to Cardinal Rodrigo de Castro, explained that he would look for "other curiosities" and mentioned that the cardinal would appreciate it "if he was sent some gallantry like those glasses of crystal and similar sorts of things."[125] Medici projects to collect charismatic animals, rare seeds, and natural wonders meshed neatly with the fine productions of the Medici workshops to allow them to sustain a vast network of gift exchange linking them to political, social, and religious elites across Europe, especially its Catholic lands. Although the Peruvian pig did not make it, we can readily imagine where it might have ended up. After a stay at one of the villas, it would have been a prime candidate for further gifting. Just three years before the failed transfer of the Peruvian pig to Florence, Francesco I had sent Archduke Ferdinand von Habsburg (1529–1595), count of Tyrol, "a little animal that came to me from the Indies that they call hare of that country."[126]

Just as the Medici needed to replenish their stock of leopards and lions from Alexandria and Algiers to supply their northern European contacts, so also they had such a steady demand for American animals, principally birds, that they supplemented the stream of gifts received with orders from a Tuscan firm in Spain. On February 12, 1607, Belisario Vinta ordered from Alessandro and Luigi Federighi birds and medicinal plants from New Spain.[127] Raffaello Romena (1567–1625), a former Medici legation secretary in France and future Medici ambassador to Spain then serving as an agent of the Monte di Pietà and of the Medici, wrote to Belisario Vinta on November 24, 1609, about the hunting birds from the "Indies of the west" that Luigi Federighi was sending to Cosimo II from Cadiz. Just two of the five had survived; they were to go to Livorno with Luigi Federighi.[128] The Tuscan commercial and diplomatic networks intersected to provide the Medici with rare animals in much the same way that they did for luxury goods.

Lions, leopards, tigers, ostriches, and American birds all signified Medici access to the living beings of distant lands, embodying the web of purchase and gift exchange that allowed Florence to be the natural supplier for the Emperor, kings, and princes. To play this role, Tuscany required not only an extended network of agents and ambassadors but also institutions within Tuscany to support its charismatic fauna. The stables, kennels, lion pits—located in Piazza San Marco in 1551—and menageries were all familiar features of Florence and natural corollaries of Florence's animal diplomacy.[129] The primates, principally monkeys and baboons, seem to have been kept at villas.[130] In 1547, for instance, a pair of baboons that Michele di Paolo Olivieri asked to be given to Duchess Eleonora of Toledo had first recuperated and regained their lost coats at Olivieri's villa in the Mugello.[131] Other animals, like the bears requested for a hunt to celebrate Prince Francesco's wedding to Giovanna d'Austria, seem not to have been long for the world.[132] Perhaps the bears given by Giuseppe Godano, bishop of Sagona in Corsica, to Ferdinando I were retained.[133] Certainly, both bears and wolves were kept in the center of Florence for a time, for a pair of letters from November 1550 discuss the movement of the bears and wolves out of their rooms in Palazzo Vecchio to facilitate construction.[134] The center of Florence, then, held gardens on the roof of the Loggia dei Lanzi, lion pits in Piazza San Marco, and wolves and bears before they were moved from Palazzo Vecchio to Via del Maglio.[135]

In this context, the reindeer living in the Boboli Gardens come as less of a surprise. Four of the seventeen reindeer sent by Sigismund III Vasa (1566–1632), king of Sweden and of Poland, had survived the journey. The reindeer were recovering nicely in the Boboli Gardens in the winter of 1593, as indicated by a letter of February 11, which also explains that a pregnant female and two *gran bestie* were still awaited.[136] Remarkably, the *gran bestie* were already familiar in Florence, since three of the four that Lorenzo Cagniuoli sent to Francesco I had made it, as a June 5, 1587, letter from the grand duke indicates.[137] The safe arrival of the three allowed the grand duke to respond on July 1, 1587, to Michele Mercati's (1541–1593) gift of a *Granbestia* leg with generous thanks, before writing "and as you pass by here we can show you the whole animal of the *Granbestia*, having had three live ones from Sweden."[138] As to the king's reindeer from Sweden, according to a letter from Ferdinando I's majordomo, Enea di Domenico Vaini (1537–1612), to Belisario Vinta, one was to be harnessed to a carriage the next day.[139] In so doing, the Florentines combined the courtly, diplomatic, and exotic right at the heart of power.

Returning to the gift of the *Granbestia* leg, Michele Mercati's expectation that the Medici were interested in collecting animal products was exactly right. Sable furs came from Muscovy; bezoars from Spain, Portugal, and ultimately the Indies; an elephant tusk from a sailor; and "unicorn" horns from the Portuguese Indies that might have been borrowed from other collectors or received as a gift.[140] The Florentines could not only marshal an extraordinary array of naturalia but also sought to depict, analyze, and understand it. For that, they depended on expertise, whether Carletti's knowledge—he claimed to have taught the grand duke's physicians how to use bezoars—or Jacopo Ligozzi's artistic skill, on display in his extraordinary depictions of plants and animals made for Francesco I between 1577 and 1587.[141] The case of musk illustrates the dynamic. Duchess Eleonora wanted to have a cat to produce musk, which was to be purchased in Venice in 1546, and Marsilio degli Albizzi was to import fifty musk bladders from Venice for Cosimo I in 1566.[142] The goal in acquiring musk and civet cats was to make perfume, a skill that in 1557 an applicant for work with Duchess Eleonora's civet cats claimed to have had.[143] Characteristically, Carletti asserted expertise on the matter of musk, describing trade practices such as the profitable Chinese sale of adulterated musk to the Portuguese and Indians.[144] He asserted that "the which musk it is not true that it is made in the way that many have described, and I brought the skin of the whole animal to Your Highness with its bladder, which is none other than the same umbilicus of the animal, which it has outside under the body full of that odoriferous matter," likening it to a small European fox.[145] That Carletti thought to acquire an animal skin and bring it back halfway across the world to substantiate his contention points to the role of naturalia at the Medici court. In sum, the plants and animals flourishing at the Medici villas and urban palaces simultaneously served as natural wonders, as items enmeshed in court culture, as objects of aristocratic sociability and diplomatic gift exchange, and as specimens to be depicted and studied.

## The Pleasures of Thinking Globally

The Medici drew a quite direct connection between the items that came from around the world and knowledge of the world as a whole. Nowhere was this expressed more clearly than in the Guardaroba in Palazzo Vecchio. The extensive collection held there can perhaps be best understood by taking the example of New Spain, which has been the subject of several important art historical works. Detlef Heikamp and, recently, Lia Markey have studied the New Spanish objects that made their way to Tuscany along with the associated art. Typically for the Medici, these Mesoamerican items arrived early and were of high quality. Under Cosimo I, Francesco I, and Ferdinando I, the Medici acquired from New Spain onyx, agate, and amethyst dog's heads; a turquoise-and-shell mosaic mask; and a bishop's miter made of feathers. By 1539, the Guardaroba included an extensive collection of feather items from Mexico.[146]

The Guardaroba Nuova in Palazzo Vecchio centralized Medici collections of exotica with a strikingly ambitious artistic program of global scope. It was decorated with an extensive set of maps that covered drawers containing objects from around the world; naturally, this included a map of New Spain, probably completed by Egnazio Danti in 1564.[147] The room's program as a *mappa mundi* in a *Wunderkammer* was understood by contemporary visitors, as a Spanish account from 1593 suggests.[148] The visitor wrote, "In one of two very celebrated palaces that the grand duke has in Florence is the principal garde-robe, among other things there is a very beautiful frame, in the space above, all provided with paintings and portraits inlaid in place in good order, for the part below encompassed around with chests of drawers of two heights that when closed remove the desire to see what there is inside of them such that they entertain by themselves. Because in each door of the chest of drawers there are two spaces with their curious moldings each one nearly three yards square in circuit and in each space illuminated with great diligence a province of the world with the fortune that each is a piece of a Universal world map [*mapamundi*]most agreeable to the eyes."[149] That the Medici were in a position to compile such maps was not unique, even in Italy. Indeed, maps of and news about the Ottoman Empire, for instance, circulated quite widely in Renaissance Italy.[150] Even so, it is telling that a Spanish observer thought such a display remarkable. The impression was no doubt helped by pairing the maps with appropriate objects in the Medici collections, for the Spanish visitor observed, "The last chest of drawers is full of a thousand extravagances brought from foreign parts like shoes from China, things of the feather of Mexico, vases come from Turkey, and also thousands of most curious little boxes besides this garde-robe and other of lower quality that are almost infinite in number of silk hangings, tapestry, and like things."[151] The various luxury items that Medici affiliates like Sassetti had remitted made quite an impact. This fit well with the Spanish author's overall impression, "the Court that the Grand Duke has is very much of the first people all very noble and many of them very rich."[152] Ferdinando I's reputation as the King of Coin rested not only on his financial investments, but also on his opulent court, filled with the world's wonders and forever circulating among a large collection of villas and palaces.

Consistent with the intellectually lively world of late Renaissance Florence, the court's extensive collections were matched by an interest in the societies and cultures that produced them. Their interest can, perhaps, fit under the expansive rubric of human and natural geography. To the maps of the Guardaroba, the Medici could add the items held in its boxes, the plants at the villas and botanical gardens, and the animals held at the villas, the menagerie, and gardens. As we have seen, these beings and objects were complemented by resident experts. More enduringly, they were also matched by descriptive texts collected by or made for the Medici. In light of linguistic limitations, the texts sometimes straddled the line between beautiful or exotic objects and informative resources, but they clearly bespeak a wide-ranging curiosity. Perhaps the most spectacular of these were the Mesoamerican codices that began arriving in Italy through religious networks, as gifts to popes and cardinals. King Manuel of Portugal gave Giulio de' Medici, then a powerful cardinal, a book now known as the Codex Vindobonensis Mexicanus I along with a parrot-feather blanket. It has been argued that this was originally a gift from Emperor Charles V to King Manuel, probably on the occasion of his marriage to Charles V's sister, Eleonora, in 1518.[153] Renaissance regifting and sales constituted major avenues for the circulation of such plundered Mesoamerican cultural objects. The Codex Vindobonensis Mexicanus I made its way to Germany in 1537 and from thence to Vienna, from which it takes its modern name. The time lag for such transfers could be long indeed. The Codex Zouche-Nuttall, which had been in the library of San Marco in Florence, was sold to a visiting Englishman in the nineteenth century and eventually given to the British Museum.[154] Such transfers extended beyond codices. A turquoise mosaic Mixtec mask of extraordinary beauty, which seems to have been given to Pope Clement VII in 1533, entered the possession of the Medici grand dukes and was then transferred to the Bolognese naturalist Ulisse Aldrovandi.[155]

Perhaps the initial codices, being effectively illegible to the Medici, were slotted into the same category of beautiful curiosity that the mask was. The same did not apply, however, to the most important of the codices to make its way to Florence, where it still remains. The Florentine Codex is one of the most fundamental texts for the study of the history and culture of the Nahuatl-speaking peoples of Mesoamerica, most famous among them the Mexica. The twelve manuscript books of the *Historia general de las cosas de Nueva España*, held in the Michelangelo-designed Biblioteca Medicea Laurenziana in Florence, with their 2,468 illustrations, represent an extraordinary collaboration between Bernardino de Sahagún (1499–1590), the elders of various central Mexican towns, and students of the Colegio de Santa Cruz in Tlatelolco. After nearly three decades of work, a complete version of the manuscript was made in 1575–1577 and sent to Spain.[156] The era was one of grand imperial projects, as Mackenzie Cooley has shown, from the Francisco Hernández expedition (1570–1577) to the *Relaciones geográficas* (1577–1586); one might expect, therefore, that the Florentine Codex would have been the Simancas, Seville, or Madrid Codex.[157] As Lia Markey has shown, however, Philip II ordered the project halted and seized in 1577—a message Sahagún seems never to have received—apparently on religious grounds. Ironically, a parallel religious apparatus protected the manuscript, for Sahagún's supporter, Franciscan commissary general Rodrigo de Sequera, brought the manuscript to the cardinal

protector of the Franciscans. This official was, in fact, Cardinal Ferdinando de' Medici, who appreciated the text, having parts translated
and copied; Ferdinando then brought it with him to Florence on his
accession as grand duke in 1587.[158]

Francesco I and Ferdinando I seem to have been personally animated by intellectual curiosity about the wider world. Travelers like
Sassetti and Carletti could and did provide them with stories about
how other societies functioned. For instance, Carletti offered evalua-
tive thumbnail descriptions of the Spanish Americas, which ranged
from his disdain for the unhealthiness of Nombre de Dios to his commentary on the prosperous cattle-owning residents of Panamá City
to his astonishment at the immense riches and abundant silver of
Lima.[159] Among the worst, for Carletti, was Acapulco. He did acknowl-
edge the excellence of its harbor, but he stressed that its unhealthiness
meant that Spaniards inhabited it in huts and only part of the year.[160]
Warming to his subject, Carletti wrote, "similarly, this place is in effect
full of gnats and of scorpions and of other animals and bugs all very
poisonous the which biting, one dies, and the bugs, if one eats them by
some misfortune or if they were drunk in wine or water, they kill and
the gnats torment one in every way such that it is insupportable."[161] It
is hardly surprising that Carletti seems to have departed almost immediately for Mexico City. He would ultimately spend just under a year in
New Spain before leaving for Manila in March 1596.[162]

On his journey from Acapulco to Mexico City, Carletti was astonished by the low quality of the transport infrastructure on the way and
appalled by the poor treatment of the indigenous population, which he
linked quite directly to their gradual destruction.[163] After such depressing
initial experiences, Mexico City astonished and delighted the weary traveler.[164] Carletti described it as being "in a place as beautiful and delightful
and copious with every delight as can be imagined and seen in the whole
world, and the city is well placed besides, being built by the Spanish in the
modern way with houses of stone and lime, nearly all of them going with
the straight and large streets, even more so than those that Your Serene
Highness has had made in your new Livorno."[165] Attentive to his audience,
Carletti linked Mexico City, jewel of Spanish America, with the grand
duke's signature project at Livorno.[166] Carletti's description surpassed
a by-then canonical likening of Tenochtitlan-Mexico City with Venice,

which had been noted, for instance, in Egnazio Danti's map of New Spain in the Guardaroba Nuova.[167] Stressing ties between Mexico City and Livorno was certainly meant to flatter the grand duke by treating the massive viceregal capital as in some way comparable to Tuscany's still quite modest-sized new port. Certainly, Carletti's enthusiasm for Mexico City knew few bounds. Indeed, he claimed that "in this most beautiful city there is everything and every good in supreme perfection and abundance" and that "finally, the City of Mexico is an earthly Paradise, filled with every commodity and delight of every sort enjoying all that which comes from Spain, from China, and the other provinces of those countries."[168]

In Chapter 4, we saw how Carletti's assessments of the societies of the Spanish Philippines, Japan, China, and the Portuguese Estado da Índia contributed to the Medici stock of strategic information. Yet, for all its importance, these observations were only a fraction of the information he offered. Carletti also provided a survey of Japanese geography, food culture including chopsticks and cleanliness, silver mining, and low prices.[169] After his account of the persecution of the Christians, he returned to constructing a portrait of Japanese society, highlighting their building techniques and use of screens, social customs, clothing, trade routes, and even their fishing with cormorants.[170] Similar examples can be adduced for Carletti's assessment of Chinese society.[171] Some of this, like Carletti's comments on the role of fans in Chinese society, might have been useful in contextualizing objects.[172] Generally, though, the point was to satisfy curiosity.

Carletti's travels in China appear to have been minimal, but he did spend a year and a half in Macao.[173] That seems to have been enough time for him to gather information indirectly, relying in particular on a Chinese geographic text, which he brought back to Florence. Explaining that the number of materials exceeded the time available to describe them and asking pardon for the length of his presentation, Carletti stated, "the which came to pass as I have put in this my simple discourse part of the things that one finds written in the said books of the Geography of China, the which, together with the things that I have not had time to have interpreted, Your Highness will one day be able to have put in an orderly volume in the way that they contain them on the occasion when some Religious should come from those parts and who should know and understand those hieroglyphic characters."[174]

The specific content of the material taken from the Chinese books of geography and Carletti's method of presentation strongly suggest he intended at least part of the China section to act as a reference piece. Specifically, Carletti addressed the demographic, urban, and military statistics associated with each province in a systematic format that reads like a table.[175] In his decision both to embed reference materials in his text and to return with books that could not yet be read, Carletti's actions befit the intellectual ambition to know and collect the world that animated the Medici court.

The Medici ability to combine texts, which dove deeply into a place, with news reports, correspondence, and the visits of travelers, made their geographic knowledge much less imperfect than that of others. Connections to well-informed exiles, captives, and visitors gave the Medici the chance to extend and update the information provided by earlier texts and travelers. As we shall see in Part 3, Tuscany sought to support rebellions across the Ottoman Empire, including that of the Druze emir Fakhr-al-Dīn II (1572–1635). Upon the reassertion of Ottoman control, the emir went into exile in Tuscany in 1613, not returning to Lebanon till 1618.[176] Tuscany likewise played host to a renegade Syrian dragoman, Michelangelo Corai, who served as Tuscan ambassador in Syria and Safavid Iran.[177] Exiles and expatriates complemented Florentine travelers in informing the Medici court.

Even as Tuscany sheltered exiles, the Medici regularly hosted long-distance embassies, with all the opportunities for information and gift exchange that that entailed. A Safavid embassy led by Robert Sherley (c. 1581–1628), for instance, went to the Holy Roman Imperial Court in 1609 and spent a month in Florence on its way to Rome.[178] Indeed, diplomatic and religious missions to Rome from distant lands often intersected with Tuscany. In a letter of 1587, Filippo Sassetti commented on the return journey through India of the four young Japanese boys whom Alessandro Valignano, SJ, had sent to Rome in 1581; they had arrived in Livorno in 1585 and had been received by Francesco I in Pisa.[179] In receiving such far-off emissaries, the grand duke not only benefited from firsthand information but also mirrored the role of more important princes. Doing so was doubly important in a hierarchical world that carefully considered gradations of status and subordination in the accordance of honors. When another Japanese embassy

set off for Rome in 1614–1615, the Spanish Council of the Indies de-
liberated on the status to accord to the ambassador. They ultimately
decided that he should be given "the same treatment as those that come
from the inferior potentates of Italy."[180] Being accorded a similar status
was what the grand duke wanted to avoid, in part by himself hosting
ambassadors and exiles.

With nearly any globally ambitious project, understanding language presents a barrier. Typically, Tuscans acted in Tuscan Italian,
though other Romance languages and Germanic languages seem to
have posed no particular problem at court. With people from outside
Europe, the Medici faced challenges similar to those others faced, but
they benefited from a few signal advantages. The breadth of the Florentine network meant that Florentines were long practiced in operating
in other languages. As important, the close Medici ties to the Catholic
Church gave Florence access to probably the most linguistically versa-
tile organization in the sixteenth and seventeenth centuries. Finally,
Italian itself offered advantages in the sixteenth century that it slowly
lost only after centuries. In a sign of the prominence of Italian as a Mediterranean lingua franca, on April 30, 1545, Cosimo de' Medici specified that the safe conduct for the consul in Alexandria should be "in
Florentine language and not Latin"; the consul was in turn empowered
to issue his own safe conducts.[181] Indeed, Italian would remain an essential diplomatic language in the region throughout the early modern
period. As late as 1774, the official text of the Treaty of Küchük Kay-
narja between the Ottomans and Russians was the version in Italian,
even if the Ottomans and Russians relied on their own, differing translations.[182] As Paris and Madrid would be for French and Spanish, so
Florence would be for Italian, playing host as it did to the Accademia
della Crusca (1583/1585), whose dictionary (1612) played an important
role in the development of literary Italian.[183]

### Making Global Objects—Medici Porcelain

Medici efforts to collect and display naturalia, exotica, and information from around the world constituted an important part of their engagement with the first global age. Critically, however, the Medici did
not confine themselves to being collectors. Rather, they sought to turn
the sprawling array of palaces, villas, gardens, and institutions under

their control into sites of production for global goods. As we have seen, the Medici court supported the cultivation of plants and breeding of animals from around the world. They not only commissioned images incorporating global items and maps of the world's regions but also patronized *pietre dure* production, with its attendant demands for semiprecious stones. Displaying considerable bravura, they even transformed items imported from the Iberian empires into boxes of medicine to serve as diplomatic gifts. And, of course, the Medici sought to bring Brazilian sugar to Livorno to refine it there.

In the context of diligent efforts to transform Tuscany into a production center, the Medici sought to go one better and develop their own porcelain industry. In this, they were far ahead of European rivals. We have seen that Carletti sought to import Ming porcelain. As might be expected at this point, both Sassetti and Carletti provided clear accounts of porcelain, with Sassetti's based on a Portuguese book.[184] Carletti's account included a typically terse rebuttal of claims about the composition of porcelain, insisting that "it is nothing but earth having that quality" mined in certain locations in China. Tellingly, Carletti drew a direct comparison with Tuscany, explaining about porcelain that "as the potters do at Montelupo or somewhere else, the which [happens] according to the benefit that it gives it and according to the quality of the earth, it comes out finer or coarser." He went on to stress the variety of types and the abundance of porcelain such that "one could freight I do not say ships but fleets of it."[185] Carletti knew his audience, for not only did Tuscany have a robust pottery tradition, but the Medici had already sought to develop domestic porcelain production.

Medici porcelain was among Francesco I's projects carried out in the grand ducal workshops in the Boboli Gardens and the Casino di San Marco.[186] With his enthusiastic support, the workshop achieved a measure of success that was not to be equaled in Europe until the soft-paste technique used in Florence was matched in France almost a century later. Medici porcelain was not true porcelain of the sort produced at Jingdezhen in Ming China, but instead a form of soft-paste porcelain that followed a technique of long standing in the greater Middle East. A Venetian ambassador reported in 1575 that a "Levantine" was responsible for the development of the technique used to make Medici porcelain. True porcelain was not produced in Europe until 1710 at Meissen in Saxony.[187] The traditional dates provided for Medici porcelain are 1575–1587, with the latter date being sometimes hedged as a point of diminished production if not a stopping point, but Marco Spallanzani has confidently argued for uninterrupted production after Francesco I's death.[188] The porcelain workshop produced a considerable inventory, which the Medici retained into the eighteenth century; using inventories, Spallanzani estimates that there were 310 pieces at Francesco I's death in 1587 and also in 1735.[189] In sum, Medici porcelain was produced in an innovative court workshop that existed to serve Francesco I's curiosity and to provide court items and gifts.[190]

## Conclusion

Late Renaissance Florence and its immediate environs developed a series of mostly new sites and institutions that collectively provided the Medici and the Florentine patriciate with a formidable apparatus for the collection, analysis, and production of global things.[191] The world's luxuries and marvels went to the Guardaroba, the palaces, and villas. In the Guardaroba, the Medici displayed an ambition for global geographical knowledge, combining maps and objects. The experts held on retainer at the court, the exiles and diplomats passing through, and the books and letters now dispersed to libraries and archives would have complemented these objects with context to make them meaningful. Alternatively, global objects and information might be transformed into the ingredients of medicines, *pietre dure* pieces, or Medici porcelain.

Plants and animals from distant corners of the world populated the new botanical gardens and the extensive network of Medici villas. In so doing, they embodied global nature, providing accessible subjects for comparison, depiction, and analysis. Simultaneously, the Medici used plants and their collections of exotic animals to cut a fine figure on Europe's diplomatic stage, echoing the exploits of Iberian kings. Tuscan commitment to this project, both Medici and Florentine patrician, extended across decades and involved substantial financial outlays. As important, it required sustained organizational efforts, mobilizing the Medici network from Alexandria to Seville and well beyond.

In central Florence, the Medici fundamentally reshaped the republican city. The new Cappella dei Principi with its overwhelming display

of *pietre dure* stood in the same complex that housed the Biblioteca
Medicea Laurenziana, home of the Florentine Codex. The San Lorenzo
complex stood kitty-corner from the traditional family palazzo, now
the Palazzo Medici Riccardi. Overshadowing these changes, the Medici
seized the symbolic center of Florence, converting the Palazzo della Signoria into the Palazzo Vecchio and dragooning the guilds into forming
the ground floor of the new Uffizi (1560–1581) complex. The Vasari Cor-
ridor (1564) linked the Guardaroba in Palazzo Veccio, the Uffizi, and
Francesco's garden on the roof of the Loggia dei Lanzi with Palazzo Pitti
and the Boboli Gardens, crossing Ponte Vecchio without once touching
the street.[192] It was a dramatic symbolic repertoire that still stamps the
Medici image on the heart of the city. Combined with the villas, botanical gardens, and workshops, it also constituted a remarkably complete
apparatus for a capital. With respect to the Americas, Lia Markey has
argued that the artistic and collecting program pursued by the Medici
constituted a "vicarious conquest.[193] This chapter has sought to extend
that idea by showing that the breadth and depth of Tuscan engagement
with the wider world meant that Florence, far from receding into provincial decadence, became an intellectual and cultural capital for Europe's burgeoning overseas connections.

# Part III

## The Tail Wags the Dog

6

# The Tuscans in North Africa

$\mathcal{S}$uccessive Medici grand dukes believed deeply in the potential of Livorno as a gateway to the wider world. Their heavy investments in both its commercial and its military sides, however, showed an unwillingness to make a strategic choice between the new maritime policies that the port enabled. Housing religious refugees and law-abiding merchants, corsairs, and shackled slaves, the port represented ambivalence about Tuscany's role in the Mediterranean. In Part 1, we saw Livorno as a haven of religious tolerance and cross-cultural trade that received much-needed northern European grain ships even as it served as a nest of Dutch and English corsairs. This chapter turns to the Janus faces the new port showed to the Muslim polities of North Africa. The Tuscans engaged in a curious combination of open commerce, regular slave-taking, and occasional bouts of remarkably ambitious belligerence.

For a sense of the scope of Tuscan ambivalence toward the southern shore of the Mediterranean, let us recall the case of William Davies presented in Chapter 3. Davies was captured and enslaved by Tuscany's galleys for trading with Tunis, even though the grand duke patronized other English merchants and corsairs. This violent aggression against

North African trade stood in unreconciled contrast with Tuscany's commercial interest in trade with North Africa, which offered enticing prospects. Not only were the cities of the North African coast a large and proximate market, but they also offered access to ancient transit trades across the Sahara and up the Red Sea. As we have seen, the original *livornine* had envisioned North African merchants doing business in Livorno. That business tacitly depended on stable diplomatic relations with North African polities, which also constituted an essential source of exotic animals.

Even though the Medici fostered Livorno as a commercial center, they remained tempted by a more aggressive policy. In particular, Tuscany's new naval and amphibious assault forces offered an independent military option. Operating under the banners of the Order of Santo Stefano (1562) and of the Tuscan navy, Tuscany's two fleets enjoyed unusual strategic flexibility, which was enabled by the politically and militarily secure position of the Medici in Tuscany and the heavily fortified Tuscan naval base of Livorno.[1] Mirroring the activities of the corsair ports of North Africa, Tuscan galleys set off regularly on slaving voyages, capturing ships at sea and engaging in the occasional opportunistic amphibious assault. In the short run, the raids provided Tuscany with considerable diplomatic leverage and permitted it to play an outsized role. In the longer term, the naval raiding policy proved costly, alienating potential trading partners without covering the costs of the raids. Recognizing the long-term costs, the Medici made good on the original promise of Livorno such that, by 1620, Turkish merchants were allowed to trade in Livorno on Christian ships; in the following decade, the Medici also reined in privateering.[2]

This chapter considers Tuscany's fraught relationship with North Africa and the related issues of Tuscany's trade relationship with the Ottoman Empire and of the Grand Duchy's participation in slavery. Though certain patterns characterized Tuscan activity along the whole coast, a tripartite division serves as a useful heuristic for organizing Tuscany's activities. In the east, Tuscany's relationship with Egypt was driven primarily by commerce and collecting. Closest to Tuscany, from Libya to Algeria, a far more fraught relationship characterized by corsair raiding and military conflict prevailed; the chapter pauses its march westward to consider the issue of slavery raised by the conflict with the

Barbary coast. Finally, in the far west, Tuscany sought a much deeper engagement with Morocco, seeking to build political alliances and engage in more intensive commerce. Tuscany explored the boundaries of military conflict and commercial cooperation, carefully avoiding such dramatic action as to rupture its alliances or compromise its security. This approach gave the Medici numerous opportunities to intervene but ultimately left Tuscany with neither a strong and stable trading relationship nor a firm improvement in its geopolitical position. Reflecting the costliness of their ambivalent position, the Medici gradually withdrew from naval conflict and concentrated on promoting Livorno as a neutral center of trade.[3]

## Egypt

The Ottoman invasion of the Mamluk Sultanate (1516–1517) had brought Egypt and the entire mainland coast of the eastern Mediterranean into the Ottoman Empire.[4] Ottoman success presented distinct disadvantages to Medici Tuscany that mirrored some of the benefits that the empire provided to Egypt itself. The Ottomans could wield naval power beyond anything the Mamluks had been able to muster, credibly offering security to their new subjects. When Medici Tuscany broke with the Florentine Republic's long tradition of pacific commercial relations to join in the policy of naval aggression to which Tuscany's alliance with Spain and the papacy committed it, Tuscan merchants throughout the eastern Mediterranean faced the prospect of reprisals.[5] Only Ottoman patience with minor transgressions and willingness to allow private merchants to operate opened some scope for activity. This policy was particularly true of Alexandria, which was praised by contemporaries for its openness to trade by both friends and foes.[6]

In addition to the attractions to a Renaissance society that trading with a city founded by Alexander the Great offered, Egypt remained distinct in the imagination as the former heart of a major empire.[7] It was fascinating and familiar, its geography and wonders readily envisaged from the center of the Tuscan state in the Guardaroba Nuova.[8] The Guardaroba's program of maps naturally included several covering regions held by the Ottoman Empire, with separate maps of Egypt and of Anatolia.[9] The established quality of the commercial route between

Italy and Egypt ensured that the Medici stayed informed about Egypt and the regions of the Ottoman Empire to which it was closely connected.[10]

Part of Egypt's attraction for the Medici undoubtedly came down to its status as a source of desirable luxury goods and exotica. Much of its position derived from its traditional role as a center of transit trade. In the sixteenth century, for instance, both Chinese porcelain and İznik ware made their way to the Tuscan port of Livorno via Alexandria.[11] In the other direction, Tommaso de' Medici sent three boxes of corals via Livorno to the Egyptian city in 1571.[12] Naturally, then, the Medici regularly requested and received rare and exotic items from Alexandria. In 1545, Jacopo Capponi, the Florentine consul in the port, was informed of Duchess Eleonora of Toledo's desire for such goods: upon "finding something beautiful and rare from those parts of Egypt for women, do not omit to send it for Her Excellency."[13] The consul headed the Florentine community in Alexandria—a 1554 complaint sent from the city mentions a denunciation made to the "Florentine Nation" ("natione fiorentina") there—which, for better and worse, now had a relationship with a state that was much more active than when Florence was a republic.[14]

The change in political regime in Florence shaped trade patterns with Alexandria. As we have seen, Florentine imports especially included rare and exotic animals. Even so, the ship that carried a gazelle for Prince Francesco from Alexandria to Livorno in 1566 was also laden with spices, foods, fabrics, leather, and gum arabic for various others; it should be seen as part of a normal, if still notable, commerce.[15] With the creation of the Tipografia Medicea, this normal commerce was meant to include exports of books. As we shall see in Chapter 8, Giovanni Battista Vecchietti and Giovanni Battista Britti traveled to Alexandria in 1584, charged both with papal diplomatic missions and service to the Medici-patronized Tipografia Medicea. In subsequent years, the Medici state would continue the project of seeking avenues for the distribution of Arabic books in the eastern Mediterranean, receiving a report from Abraham Israel in Livorno, for instance, about distributing such books in İzmir, Syria, or Alexandria.[16]

The trade in exotic animals and plans for book distribution notwithstanding, violence lurked in the background, casting a pall on prospects for peaceful commerce. Part of the tension derived from the regular hazards of piracy and corsairs from which Tuscany suffered, although Tuscany contributed more to piracy than it was hurt by it. For all the liberal language of the *livornine* of 1591 and 1593, inviting not only a panoply of Europeans, but also Moors, Persians, and Turks to peaceful trade, Muslim merchants generally did not accept the offer.[17] Livorno's role as a notorious nest of corsairs rather compromised its attractiveness.

Cosimo I had sought to reopen Tuscan-Ottoman trade in 1547, but the move to open warfare in the 1560s had undermined commercial ties.[18] With the winding down of major Spanish-Ottoman confrontation, Francesco I made a new effort to establish peaceful commercial relations with the Ottoman Empire. As we have seen, Filippo Sassetti had dedicated his treatise *On Commerce between Tuscany and the Levantine Nations* to the Medici ambassador to the Sublime Porte, Bongianni Gianfigliazzi. Sassetti's proposals included guarantees for the security of Ottoman shipping to Livorno, new legal structures for the protection of Ottoman subjects, an efficient customs service, and a heavy investment in infrastructure for accommodating merchants.[19] Whether or not Sassetti's text had any direct impact, as F. Özden Mercan has recently shown, Francesco I had pursued a diplomatic opening with the Ottomans from 1574. Relations had progressed to such a point that Bongianni Gianfigliazzi was dispatched as Florentine ambassador in 1578.[20] Riguccio Galluzzi's classic account of the negotiations stressed Francesco I's effort to distance himself from the Order of Santo Stefano and the possibility that the Florentine *Bailo* might issue letters of protection.[21] Galluzzi reproduces a letter to Mehemet Bascià (presumably Grand Vizier Sokullu Mehmed Pasha) of April 29, 1577, in which Francesco I asked for open and reciprocal trade and diplomatic relations with the Ottomans.[22] The grand duke stated "that this enterprise is not ours, but an Order of Knights, founded by our father in the name of Saint Stephen for his devotion, and for the health of his soul, with express rules that it may be able to keep twelve armed galleys, that would be ready for any command of the Pope or the King of Spain. The Order cannot be annulled by us, or dismissed without incurring the ire of our Lord God, and with many alterations of Our States."[23] It is unclear what the Medici expected the Ottomans to think of the claim that God would be displeased with the grand duke for stopping anti-Muslim piracy by the Order of Santo Stefano. Still, Özden Mercan argues that Sokullu Mehmed Pasha accepted Francesco I's claims, considered the Order of Santo Stefano to be of secondary importance, and responded sufficiently positively to invite the dispatch of a Florentine ambassador.[24]

Bongianni Gianfigliazzi turns out to have been a poor choice. Though he was received courteously at the outset, he seems to have misjudged court politics and faced entrenched opposition from the French, the Venetians, and Grand Admiral Uluç Ali Pasha. In a set piece of court theater, the Tuscans were exposed as negotiating in bad faith through several reliable attestations that the galleys of the Order of Santo Stefano were indeed at the entire disposal of the grand duke. The final Ottoman response was that there could be no peace until the grand duke put aside the pretense about the galleys and stopped them.[25] Though Francesco I blamed the interests of various Ottoman officials for the failure of the negotiations, Özden Mercan also persuasively points to Gianfigliazzi's weaknesses as an ambassador including his failure to seek timely advice, rejection of compromise, and alienation of potential supporters.[26] Özden Mercan's insistence on the broader diplomatic context is a valuable corrective to the traditional focus on the role of the Order of Santo Stefano.[27]

Taking the broader context of trade with the Ottoman Empire into account, Daniel Goffman argues that the strength of the Venetian position was such that, except when Venetians were expelled and Florentines patronized by the Ottomans, as during the brief period 1462–1479, the Florentine and other Italian states' trade could flourish only with Ottoman support. After 1500, the rise of Ottoman subject and dependent merchants and the weakening of Venetian military power undermined the rationale for promoting other Italians at Venetian expense.[28] In particular, the Ottomans seem unlikely to have seen the Florentines as an attractive alternative as long as the Order of Santo Stefano existed. Its existence and activities were so structurally problematic and similar to that of the Knights of St. John—who had provoked massive Ottoman amphibious operations against them on Rhodes (1480 and 1522) and Malta (1565)—that it is hard to imagine how the Order of Santo Stefano could have remained active without constituting an obstacle.[29] This, at least, seems to have been Ferdinando I's conclusion when he opened a second attempt at negotiations two decades later.

Legalistic disingenuousness having failed under his brother, in 1598 Ferdinando I struck at the root of the problem by offering to suspend the activities of the Order of Santo Stefano as part of negotiations to establish friendly commercial relations.[30] Ferdinando I wrote in a conciliatory tone, "Most Glorious and Unconquerable Lord Sovereign Emperor and lord of the great Empire of Constantinople, Asia, Persia, Syria, Arabia, Egypt, etc. singular benefactor and very good health, etc. Signor Mustafa brought me your Majesty's most humane and courteous letter the which I very favorably received and accepted, with the prompt and affectionate will, which is worthy, vouchsafe to affirm for me true, sincere, and stable amity, for all the merchants of my states and to my subjects that will come to do business in your great and happy Empire."[31] Invoking the memory of past agreements, Ferdinando I then sought to restore Tuscan commercial privileges. To do so, he promised to "postpone the course of the galleys of the knights of Santo Stefano" and to rely on the Florentine *bailo*, Neri Giraldi (1560–1620), promising to accept whatever Giraldi agreed to.[32] Giraldi seems to have achieved an initial measure of success, as Florentine merchants living in Istanbul were to receive tax concessions on silk for which taxes had already been paid elsewhere.[33] In spite of this encouraging start, Galluzzi's account of the negotiations sees them as stymied by the same dynamics as the 1577–1578 talks. The negotiations were undermined by court intrigue fueled by greed, jealousy, and the animosity of the French ambassador and Venetian *bailo*. According to Galluzzi, Giraldi was imprisoned for climbing a minaret whence it was possible to see some of the *sultanas* of the seraglio; he was saved only by the intercession of the French ambassador and Venetian *bailo*, who, having achieved their end, sought to curry favor with the grand duke by saving Giraldi. Galluzzi asserted that, as a result of this incident, Ferdinando I resolved to use his galleys to wreak vengeance on the Turks and rejected further overtures from the Ottoman Sultan.[34] The position was anyway a fairly traditional one for the Medici and was well suited to Tuscany's institutions and alliances, if not necessarily to the prosperity of Tuscan merchants.

The decade after the failure of reconciliation with the Ottomans saw a rapid expansion of Tuscan military activity directed against the

Ottoman Empire. With mixed results, Tuscan forces raided Chios (1599), Algiers (1600), Preveza (1605), Turkey (1606), Famagusta (1607), Bona (Annaba) (1607), shipping off the coast of Rhodes (1608), and around the eastern Mediterranean (1609–1611).[35] Gregory Hanlon has tabulated the figures for the Tuscan fleet and the galleys of the Order of Santo Stefano, noting that in the half century from 1560 to 1609, "the Tuscan fleet captured 76 galliots, seven galleys, two large roundships and 67 minor craft, taking 9,620 slaves and liberating 2,076 Christians"; separately, the Order of Santo Stefano captured and lost 11 galleys between 1568 and 1599 and captured 17 between 1602 and 1635.[36] This battle record bespeaks a rapid tempo of activity in the face of significant losses for Tuscany's two small fleets. In 1604, for instance, the Order of Santo Stefano mustered a fleet of 6 galleys, 3 roundships, 2 *bastardelli*, 1 galleon, 1 galleass, and 2 transports.[37] In 1610, Tuscany commanded a fleet of 8 *bertoni*—typically northern European–style roundships of three to five hundred tons, with three masts and sixty sailors—bearing a total of two hundred guns and the capacity to transport eight hundred troops; they had been launched from Portoferraio on Elba and were commanded by Dutch or English captains.[38] The *bertoni* were crucial for Tuscany's long-range strike capacity, because galleys fleets faced severe technical and logistical challenges that largely confined them to fine-weather sailing and compelled them to resupply with water very frequently.[39] In sum, Tuscany's naval forces were of middling size, capable of mounting powerful raids but not of standing in open battle.

The pervasive violence perpetrated by Tuscan-sponsored ships colored Tuscan relations with Ottoman Egypt, bringing the sordid trade in captives to the fore. For instance, an anonymous 1618 memorandum values, for the purposes of a ransom, a forty-four-year-old galley slave named Nasser di Amor of Alexandria at 500 ducats because he was the nephew of an Alexandrian galley captain named Ametto di Mamett and the brother of Isuff, a Red Sea galley captain.[40] The ransom of galley slaves points to a dramatic change in Tuscany's relationship with Egypt and the broader Ottoman world from a century before. It is hard to imagine the Florentine republic either constituting the naval crusading Order of Santo Stefano or pursuing a militant policy of capturing trading partners. This, then, was a consequence of the creation of the Grand Duchy.

The routine horrors of galley slavery and the ransoming of prisoners that plagued the early-modern Mediterranean also incentivized more dramatic military interventions. With prisoners providing the labor service driving the galleys before their eventual ransom, sale, or death, even brief opportunistic attacks on a vulnerable shore might be advantageous. The hazards, however, of such aggression were obvious to a great empire with sprawling, vulnerable frontiers: retaliation that might escalate to enervating warfare. It was far better to rely on proxies, whether prodded to action or moving on their own initiative. The context may help explain a pair of letters from the distinguished Spanish governor and state counselor, Fernando Girón, to Ferdinando I.[41] Both are short missives signed informally, suggesting familiarity. The first recounts advice given by one Vinceguerra to Philip III about "the ease of the Enterprise of Ferraglioni."[42] This advice consisted of a plot to capture the poorly guarded Egyptian castle "because taking this castle which assures the port of Alexandria they would find the galleons of Constantinople loaded to return there."[43] The hostile intent was clear, with the objective starkly stated as "to sack Alexandria," which was vulnerable because Ottoman forces had been redeployed to the Persian front, put on the galleys, or were too far away in Cairo.[44] Girón reported that certain Spanish galleys had arrived in Naples for this enterprise or, perhaps, for another one directed not against Egypt but against Famagusta in Cyprus. The Famagusta objective had to recommend it the similarly inattentive Ottoman defense of Cyprus and the additional element of a large Christian population, "there being in the island twenty Christians against one Turk" and the neighboring mainland region of Caramania could not send men, being depopulated.[45]

Projects for opportunistic aggression against the Ottomans were remarkably common, especially when they were engaged in a war on two fronts against the Austrian Habsburgs and the Safavids and beset by extensive rebellions.[46] Most were nothing but overly optimistic memoranda that died on the overcrowded desks of princes and ministers. In 1605, Philip III's Spain was beset by chronic financial woes driven by its still ongoing war with the Dutch and only partially relieved by the recently completed peace with England after nearly two decades of war. Spain did not need the new costly war with the Ottoman Empire that a raid on Alexandria would certainly provoke. Medici Tuscany, by contrast, with its consistently dreadful relations with the Ottoman Empire and rather more robust financial position, was just then entering a period of remarkable bellicosity against the Ottomans, which may explain why Girón's brief missives were directed to the Medici. The combined strike force of the Tuscan navy and the Order of Santo Stefano was much better suited to this sort of brief amphibious operation than Spain's much larger forces precisely because Tuscany was both small and well protected from Ottoman retaliation. In 1605, the Tuscan fleet was busy elsewhere, but the logic of striking a distracted and war-weary Ottoman Empire had captured Ferdinando I's imagination. Two years later, Tuscany jumped into the fray. As we shall see in Chapter 7, in 1607 Tuscany intervened on a large scale with an amphibious strike on Cyprus and an alliance with the rebel Pasha of Aleppo, Canbuladoğlu Ali. Tuscany did not, ultimately, engage in direct military aggression against Egypt, but it did briefly pursue a belligerent policy of naval warfare that threatened Ottoman shipping lanes until Tuscany's gradual withdrawal that began in 1612.[47]

## The Corsair Coast: From Libya to Algeria

As we have seen, the Medici sought to use their enthusiastic commitment to the Spanish alliance both to deepen their relationship with the dominant regional power and to forward their own objectives in the central Mediterranean. The independent importance of this latter came into relief after the Spanish-Ottoman truce of 1581. As the exhausted Spanish and Ottomans came to a modus vivendi in the Mediterranean in the late 1570s, culminating in the truce of 1581, Tuscan ships continued their depredations unabated.[48] The matter was more complicated than managing relations with Ottoman Egypt, since Maghrebi politics and the relationship with the Ottomans could vary considerably from port to port and change substantially over time. Both in the era of joint operations with Spain and afterward, Tuscany required timely information about the shifting politics of the major ports, from Tripoli and Tunis to Algiers and Bona (Annaba).[49]

In the era of joint operations, Tuscany required not only an effective fleet, but also a sophisticated diplomatic network that both provided information and coordinated with essential allies. This they succeeded in building. Tuscan records closely follow the twists and turns of the struggle between the Spanish Habsburgs and the Ottomans for North Africa. Tunis, for example, fell to Emperor Charles V in 1535 in a celebrated operation, only for it to change hands twice before the decisive Ottoman conquest of 1574.[50] The Medici archives accordingly contain, for instance, information about Spanish arrangements with the king of Tunis in 1551 and a pair of *avvisi* and a translation of an Ottoman account discussing the fall of Tunis to the Ottomans in 1574.[51] Indeed, the Tuscans followed North African politics with an intensity similar to that they devoted to parts of Europe. A letter from Venice in June 1567 illustrates the point: it mentions an outbreak of the plague in Trent and the deposition of the so-called king of Algeria.[52] Likewise, a 1575 *avviso* from Venice recounts an intelligence coup in which an escaped slave arrived in Naples and drew the plan of Tripoli's fortifications.[53] In short, the Tuscan bureaucracy carefully compiled and retained recent information about political and military developments in North Africa.

When immediate military action threatened, the diplomatic machinery moved into high gear. Flurries of letters, for instance, tracked the movements of fleets, like that of the Algerian governor Alì-el-Uluk in the western Mediterranean in September 1581.[54] Beyond immediate defensive preparations, the obvious solution was to strike the headquarters of such fleets. A Catholic fleet's victory, as against Dragut's base near Tunis in 1550, occasioned public celebrations but did not change the fundamental dynamics of the situation.[55] In accordance with Tuscany's Spanish alliance, Tuscan ships eventually joined Spanish operations in North Africa, participating in the siege of Tripoli in 1559, as we saw in Chapter 1.

Tuscany's modest merchant marine, relative military security, and mostly inland population protected it from the worst of reciprocal raiding. This had not always been the case. In the 1550s, Tuscany suffered significant raids by the joint Franco-Ottoman fleet.[56] From 1559, however, France, having made peace with Spain and beset by recurring religious civil war, withdrew essential support for these operations, leaving the Spanish-led naval alliance in control.[57] With the end of major fleet operations two decades later, the epidemic of large-scale conflict subsided into a pattern of endemic raiding focused on captive taking.

Mediterranean slavery followed an ineluctable pattern in which captured slaves powered the galleys and provided prisoners for ransom and exchange. It was a true cycle of violence. In the 1560 ransoming of a Catalan ship captured by the Algerians off the coast of Tuscany, the provisions of the ransomed ship were sent to the ducal galleys.[58] Tuscany's galleys used such resources to pursue an aggressive policy, though doing so came with some risk of similar capture. The defeat of Tuscan warships in 1594 resulted in captives who were shipped off to Istanbul.[59] Likewise, a failed raid on Chios in 1599 led another group of Tuscans into captivity in the Ottoman capital.[60] Relative, if violent, equilibrium meant the tables were turned repeatedly. An inventory of the items taken in the August 1610 capture of three Algerian ships by the Order of Santo Stefano includes artillery, slaves, money, and various other items.[61] We can imagine that these were plowed back into this permanent, low-level war in which captives and booty became the resources of further conflict.

Thus far, we have a vision of Tuscany participating in the Catholic naval alliance, following political events in North Africa, and engaging in a long-running corsair war. At the same time, however, Tuscany always had the option of pursuing a strategy that deviated from the permanent belligerence implied by the Order of Santo Stefano. A July 1593 letter from Mehmet Pasha in Tripoli to Ferdinando I, for instance, sent a pair of horses.[62] A gift exchange might simply culminate with the accumulation of goodwill, but it also could accompany more substantive diplomacy. In the mid-1630s, Tuscany made a trade agreement with Tripoli guaranteeing the security of maritime commerce between Tripoli and Livorno; the draft of a letter affirming this agreement also thanks the pasha of Tripoli for sending a gift of horses.[63] They are likely to have been racehorses, the fastest available, probably for *palio* racing. Such equine gifts as accompanied Tripoli's trade agreement with Tuscany, however, could not guarantee lasting friendship. Indeed, Tuscany's relationship with Tripoli remained fraught, with Mehmet Pasha discussing not renewing the agreement in a letter of May 1639.[64]

Oscillation among violence, trade, and gift giving characterized Tuscany's relationship with ports from Tripoli and Tunis to Algiers and Bona. We have seen that Tuscany joined its Spanish allies and enthusiastically cheered as they engaged in military operations against Tripoli and Tunis. At the same time, the economic logic of trade with North Africa militated against constant conflict, resulting in periodic rapprochements. In

the case of Tunis, amity resumed quite quickly after the Ottoman recon-
quest in 1574. A pair of documents from February 1577, for instance, describe the arrival of the Marseillaise ship *Diana*, apparently from Tunisia,
in Livorno carrying spices and other goods.[65] A measure of amity seems
then to have prevailed, for a gift of a pair of *palio* horses from Mehmet
Pasha of Tunis in 1590 signaled the pasha's acceptance of Ferdinando I's
offer to renew the friendship that had existed in his brother Francesco's
reign.[66] For all the language of friendship, however, the Tuscan galleys
continued their depredations in later years, interdicting ships departing
from Tunis carrying contraband. As we have seen, one such operation at
the end of the century resulted in the capture of William Davies's ship
and his long enslavement.

A similar mixture of conflict and cooperation characterized Tuscany's relationship with Algiers, the largest corsair haven, and the other
ports of the Algerian coast. As we have seen, Tuscany imported lions, a
gazelle, and an ostrich from Algiers and sought to acquire racehorses
either from Algiers or Bona. As with Tunis, a regular, politicized trade
in horses existed in tension with the simultaneous persistence of captive taking and major military expeditions. In 1589, for instance, the
king of Algiers—as he was known to the Tuscans—returned the eight
mules taken from Don Pietro de' Medici in 1588.[67] The next year, Ali
Mamí (Arnaut Mamí) in Algiers wrote to Antonio Serguidi in Florence about sending him a horse, explaining that he had not sent the
animal to Livorno yet "because I would not want it to die from the bad
weather as happened to that of His Most Serene Highness."[68] Arnaut
Mamí was the captain who had captured the ship carrying Miguel de
Cervantes from Naples to Spain in 1575, and Antonio Serguidi not only
had served as Francesco I's secretary but also had been a Knight of the
Order of Santo Stefano since June 1567.[69] That two ostensibly permanent religious foes and at least nominal participants in the corsair war
could amicably exchange horses points to the complexity and shifting
quality of Tuscany's relationships.

Even as it wreaked devastation on countless lives, hampered trade,
and plagued coastal communities, simmering corsair warfare offered
sufficient benefits to the grand duke to encourage its continuance. Such
warfare permitted Tuscany, like its North African peers, to maintain an
unusually large fleet, garner religious prestige, and play a diplomatic

role out of all proportion to its slender resources.[70] For example, even after five Tuscan galleys served in a failed allied raid on Algiers, Tuscany could still play a useful role as a diplomatic mediator.[71] A January 1607 letter from the Medici envoy in Venice described a conversation with the Spanish ambassador. The pair discussed using Turkish slaves held by Tuscany to ransom English captives in Algiers whose freedom the king of England sought.[72] Tuscany's usefulness in these and other matters allowed it to thread a diplomatic needle, maintaining a working relationship with England even as it hosted English exiles and pursued militantly Catholic policies. Standing at the center of such exchanges encouraged Tuscany both to accumulate leverage against Algiers and the Ottomans in the form of captives and to work closely with the policy of ransoming captives in all directions.

## On Slavery

The persistent tension between gift exchange and trade, on the one hand, and piracy and warfare, on the other, can perhaps be seen most clearly in the case of Bona (Annaba; Bône), Algeria. In the 1560s we hear of Bona, as it is called in the Tuscan records, as the place whence a corsair came, but also as a possible location for purchasing Berber racehorses.[73] A memorandum from 1600 notes the quality of the surrounding land and the richness of the corals that the people of Bona harvest. Yet a note of menace emerged here, because the information was conveyed in a proposal to attack the city.[74] Unlike so many memoranda proposing ventures, this project came to fruition relatively quickly. After the failed raid on Algiers, the heart of Maghrebi corsair raiding, Tuscany's forces returned to Algeria to deliver a stinging blow.[75] The Tuscans took Bona in 1607. In so doing, they carried off a grim haul of fifteen hundred slaves.[76] Immensely satisfied with their slave raiding, the Medici proudly boasted of their exploit in various media. The victory was swiftly commemorated in a printed account, a map of the city sent to Philip III, and, within a couple of years, frescoes in the Sala di Bona in the Pitti Palace.[77] The booty from the conquest was still under discussion in 1610.[78]

This type of belligerence and its commemoration helped earn Tuscany a reputation both for unremitting aggression and for galley slavery. But activity on such a scale stretched Tuscany's resources. It could be sustained only with a pattern of military victories. Initially, it seemed possible to sustain the effort. In 1608, seven Tuscan warships attacked a Turkish convoy of forty-two ships off Rhodes, taking six hundred more slaves and one million ducats in booty. Long-distance raiding of this sort was quite risky. A follow-up expedition to the eastern Mediterranean in 1609–1611, with 1,800 men on seven roundships, resulted in eight hundred deaths and four disabled ships.[79] Tuscany's fleet and naval ambitions shrank from 1612, but the legacy of such warfare continued.[80] The warfare was commemorated most dramatically in the *Quattro Mori* (1626), commissioned by Cosimo II from Pietro Tacca in 1617 and still standing in Livorno. Tacca surrounded an earlier statue of Ferdinando I, standing in a commanding posture atop a column, with four dramatically chained bronze "Moors."[81] This male galley slavery, which the monument disturbingly celebrates, complemented a long-established but less visible practice of African slavery in Tuscany centered on the sale of captive women into domestic service.[82]

One member of the Tuscan court courageously took issue with this whole tradition of unabashed slavery and its bombastic celebration. Francesco Carletti had started his long circumnavigation with a slaving voyage of his own, from Seville to Cape Verde and thence to Cartagena.[83] Upon arriving in Cape Verde, Carletti and his father rented a house and made their interest in buying slaves known. Francesco Carletti described the process of buying slaves as being fundamentally similar to that of buying livestock, explaining that the Portuguese "keep them in the country in their villas as a herd like cattle, [and] ordered that they be conducted to the city to let us see them."[84] At some point, however, the younger Carletti suffered a crisis of conscience. After describing the branding of slaves, Carletti confessed that this was a "thing truly that I remember having done under the command of one who was in charge of me [his father], it causes me a certain sadness and confusion of conscience, because truly Most Serene Lord this always seems to me an inhuman traffic and unworthy of the Christian profession and piety inasmuch as there is not any doubt that it comes to trafficking in men or to put it properly human flesh and blood and even more disgusting, being baptized, that although they are of different color and in the fortune of the world, nonetheless they have the same Soul formed in them by the same maker that forms ours."[85] Carletti went on to "ask forgiveness of His Divine Majesty notwithstanding that I know very well that [He] knows that my intention and will were always repugnant to this business."[86]

Francesco Carletti's ethical stand and unquiet conscience put him at odds with much of the trading community of his age. The origins of Carletti's revulsion are not certain. If the crisis had not happened on Cape Verde, perhaps the trip to Cartagena was decisive. Carletti was a witness of and participant in the notorious Middle Passage, the grim results of which were not only the death of seven of the seventy-five slaves purchased, "but many of these were badly treated, and sick, and nearly half dead."[87] The specific point at which Francesco Carletti concluded that slavery was wrong may have been later, but he certainly did come to this decision not only rhetorically but in practice. Writing about the Japanese invasion of Korea and enslavement of Koreans, Carletti wrote of the Korean slaves: "and I bought five of them for little more than twelve scudi in all, which having had them baptized I conducted them to India to Goa, and there I left them free, and one of them I lead with me up to Florence, and today I believe he can be found in Rome named Antonio." [88] Carletti's purchase of Korean slaves in Japan might seem to undermine his critique of slavery, but two points bear consideration. First, the Korean slaves were war captives from a proximate war, which made them more like the slaves in which the Tuscans usually dealt. More important, the slave purchases happened while Carletti's father was still alive and presumably in charge. By the time Carletti reached Goa, his father was dead. Thus, there is cause to accept that Carletti truly did find the institution repugnant even in a place where it was firmly entrenched, Goa, and that he was willing, as it were, to put his money where his mouth was.[89] Certainly, having benefited from extensive Medici patronage, it took a rare courage to address the grand duke with such a clear denunciation of slavery.[90] The challenge to one's courage proved too much for subsequent generations. As an October 25, 1721, note appended to the Carletti manuscript explains, the 1701 edition published in Florence is "strangely changed and also castrated," in particular in relation to Carletti's discussion of slavery.[91] The Florentines may have failed in securing chattel slave sugar colonies, but they retained the underlying colonial attitude. By the eighteenth century, Carletti's cry of conscience had been enveloped in silence.

## Morocco

Even as the long legacy of the corsair war dominated Tuscany's interactions with central North Africa and ancient trade ties to Alexandria proved enduring, so also the Medici relationship with Morocco had a distinctive quality. In Morocco, Tuscany acted both in support of Iberian allies and independently, navigating the treacherous waters of Moroccan politics and the swirling currents of Iberian ambitions. The relationship began with the Medici popes. The many names of Leo Africanus bore the legacy of the complex ties between the Medici family, the papacy, the Iberian peninsula, and Renaissance Africa. As Natalie Zemon Davis has reconstructed, Leo Africanus (1494–1554) was originally al-Hasan ibn Muhammad ibn Ahmad al-Wazzan, a sometime diplomat in service of the ruler of Fez. Captured by a Spanish pirate and delivered in 1518 as a prisoner to the first Medici pope, Leo X, he was baptized Johannes Leo de Medicis in St. Peter's just over a year later.[92] His *Descrittione dell'Africa*, published by Giovanni Battista Ramusio in 1550, was subsequently translated into a number of European languages, quickly becoming perhaps the most famous account of Africa published in the early modern period.[93] Leo Africanus's book has long seemed to represent Italy's role as the receiver of the rare and exotic, the publisher of the wonders of the world. The Grand Duchy of Tuscany, however, went further, plunging deep into Moroccan politics.

Leo Africanus's Morocco was complex, characterized by diplomatic maneuver, religious fervor, imperialism, and dynastic intrigue. In the early sixteenth century, the most important external force was a surging, expansive Portugal. Unlike further south in West Africa, where Portuguese fortresses were primarily oriented to the export trade, Portuguese encroachments on the coast of Morocco included a strong element of unremitting *reconquista*.[94] Leo Africanus's account rhythmically resonates with the devastation wrought by Portuguese intervention along the coast of Morocco. The second book of his *History and Description of Africa: And of the Notable Things Therein Contained* includes written portraits of cities in the region of Hea that often end with devastation. According to Leo Africanus, for instance, Teduest was abandoned by its frightened inhabitants when their neighbors allied with the Portuguese.[95] The fate of Teculeth and of Hadecchis, destroyed or sacked and abandoned amid conflict with the Portuguese, vindicated such fears.[96] At this stage, Tuscany's role in all this Portuguese aggression and violence was of the most indirect sort, limited to the activities of the Florentine commercial community in Lisbon. Six decades later, the situation would be quite different. As we have seen, the Grand Duchy of Tuscany and the still sub-stantial group of Florentine merchants in Lisbon found themselves em-broiled in one of the great calamities of early modern Portuguese history when they helped finance the disastrous 1578 invasion of Morocco.

With the crushing defeat of Portugal, Morocco flourished under the reign of its most famous monarch, Sultan Ahmad al-Mansūr (1549–1603). Trade between Tuscany and Morocco grew on the basis of Mo-roccan cane sugar for marble from the Apuan Alps. Never reluctant to meddle when an opportunity presented itself, when al-Mansūr died, Tuscany supported the unpopular initial winner in the power struggle, al-Mansūr's eldest son, al-Mamūn. Kaled El Bibas has argued that al-Mamūn bid for both Spanish and Tuscan support and thought of Tus-cany as a potential site of exile if he was defeated in the civil war. Drawing on the services of two Florentines resident in Fez, Niccolò Giugni and Bastiano Acquisiti, al-Mamūn sought to renew al-Mansūr's treaty with Ferdinando I.[97] Niccolò Giugni (1585–1649), the marquis of Camporse-voli, served the Medici as a courtier and diplomat, and so these negotia-tions were taking place at a serious level.[98] As El Bibas argues and a series of letters from 1604 held in the Archivio di Stato di Firenze show, Fer-dinando wanted to transform the relationship into a full alliance with al-Mamūn.[99] Even as al-Mamūn set out to conquer the south of Morocco held by his brother, Tuscany provided him with both arms and an escape plan. Discovery in Fez of Giugni and Acquisti's involvement in the es-cape plan led to calls for their death, which in turn led to Spanish inter-vention. The episode shut down the use of Tuscan naval ships disguised as merchantmen, ending Tuscany's role in Morocco and requiring Tus-cany to smooth matters over diplomatically with Spain.[100]

This concession to the realities of power did not end Tuscan in-terest in Moroccan politics, however. Quite the contrary, the Venetian resident in Florence, Roberto Lio, wrote to the doge on March 11 and again on March 17, 1606, noting the large imports of dressed leather from Morocco to Livorno and reporting the grand duke's unsurprising support for his old ally, the ruler of Fez, in the Moroccan civil war. The Venetian resident noted that the grand duke had passed on the news that the king of Fez had benefited from defections from the king of Morocco involving the transfer of a large quantity of artillery and "300 camels laden with munitions." In Ferdinando I's view, the king of Fez "deserved every good, because he was a wise prince, elder, and the son of the wife; and the other [was] the younger and the son of a slave."[101] The grand duke's detailed knowledge of political developments in Morocco points to an enduring engagement with the region.

## Conclusion

Tuscany's disguised intervention in Morocco and raid on Bona constitute the highwater mark of Tuscany's activist policy in North Africa. The timing, late in Ferdinando I's reign, is telling. The grand duke then evinced a willingness to test the boundaries of the possible, sending teams of diplomats and agents to make deals with enterprising merchants and to offer support to embattled regimes and rebels willing to work with Tuscany. The lure of Livorno, Tuscany's expeditionary forces, and Tuscany's great power allies combined to make it an attractive potential partner.

This confident, ambitious Tuscany, heavily armed and itching for the chance to find some plan, any plan, that might change the political and economic status quo and unlock a better future, eventually found such an opportunity. The plan was simple in conception and well timed. It was also outrageously audacious. Tuscany set out to lead a grand coalition to destroy the Ottoman Empire. Far from a fantasy of crusade, Tuscany sought to pull together a coalition of rebels in Cyprus, Lebanon, and Syria to work with Tuscan naval forces and the Safavid Iranian invasion of a war-weary and rebellion-wracked Ottoman Empire to shatter Ottoman control in the Levant. To do this, Tuscany sought to create sufficient military momentum for the Tuscan tail to wag the dog of the Spanish alliance. It nearly worked. The Chapters 7 and 8 tell the story of the plot to destroy the Ottoman Empire.

# 7

# The Plot to Destroy the Ottoman Empire

*P*lans for Atlantic trade and colonies, a proposal to join the VOC, a Muscovite trade deal, a raid on Algeria, and intervention in Morocco's civil war—Ferdinando I's final decade witnessed an explosion of ventures. Although the Muscovy project was overwhelmed by the Time of Troubles and the Algerian raid proved a success on its own terms, nearly all the most ambitious projects eventually ran afoul of international politics, especially Spanish Habsburg and Dutch monopoly practices. Weakened as Spain was by decades of war with the Dutch and English, Tuscany was neither militarily nor politically prepared for a rupture with the Iberian empires over long-distance trade with Protestants. Having tested the boundaries of the possible within the framework of Tuscany's existing international position, Ferdinando I sought opportunity to act independently. The Ottoman Empire's existential crisis in the opening decade of the seventeenth century seemed to present just such a chance. Ferdinando leapt at it.

Tuscany had greater freedom of action in the eastern Mediterranean than it had elsewhere. Far from Spanish interests and bases, religious, commercial, political, and strategic priorities aligned to facilitate unmediated activity. Specifically, as a militantly Catholic power secure in its relationship with the papacy, Medici Tuscany needed no one's permission to pursue a bellicose policy toward the Ottoman Empire. The activities of the Order of Santo Stefano had foreclosed the alternative path of accommodation, but they had also demonstrated that no power would intervene to stop Tuscany from taking such a violent course. Tuscany's demonstrated expeditionary strike capabilities likewise gave the Medici regime the military option for the first time. Throughout the sixteenth century, its military had mattered very little. Ottoman naval and military power so overwhelmingly outmatched Tuscany's that Tuscan military strikes would be, at best, foolhardy raids of no lasting strategic consequence. War changed the situation. From 1603, the Ottoman Empire faced military exhaustion, ground down by an exhausting two-front war and a wave of large-scale revolts. For a brief moment in 1606–1607, Tuscany had the opportunity to make a major strategic difference by supporting the Ottomans' many opponents and dragging in the Spanish system of alliances. This chapter is the story of Tuscany's plot to destroy the Ottoman Empire by intervening in the eastern Mediterranean. The next chapter follows the story to Safavid Iran to consider Tuscany's relationship with its most powerful new friend.

## The Ottoman Crisis

In 1605–1607, Canbuladoğlu Ali Pasha, self-proclaimed Ottoman governor of Aleppo and scion of a powerful northern Syrian Kurdish clan, rebelled against an Ottoman Empire beset by foreign wars and other rebellions.[1] Before delving further, a brief account of the complex situation in Syria is in order.[2] Beset by a grinding two-front war with the Habsburgs in the Balkans and, from 1603, with the Safavids in northwestern Iran and the Caucasus, the Ottoman state began to buckle under the pressure. This allowed numerous disruptive rebel groups called *celâlîs* to wreak havoc in Anatolia. In northern Syria and eastern Anatolia, near the front with the Safavids, various tiers of the Ottoman military and political system—from the janissaries posted to Damascus and Aleppo through the *beylerbeyis* (provincial governors) of Aleppo, Damascus, and Tripoli to the *serdar* commanding the Ottoman army on the eastern front—proved fractious, engaging in violent personal rivalries and armed confrontations.[3] They were spurred on and exacerbated by the fraught relationship with figures outside the standard hierarchy, especially hereditary local emirs and *celâlîs*. The latter were usually a few dozen strong but sometimes could be much more numerous. Both the emirs and *celâlîs* possessed militarily potent but problematic forces that were sometimes coopted into the Ottoman military system to meet immediate threats. The *celâlîs* could be bandits. Competent with weapons, they were also undisciplined and self-seeking, making them unreliable on the battlefield. Emirs might possess more disciplined and effective forces, but such emirs usually had local ambitions for autonomy, resources, and recognition that did not always mesh well with the needs of grinding campaigns in the devastated lands on the empire's eastern frontier. Out of this welter of leaders claiming authority, a series of armed confrontations emerged in Syria, in Damascus, Aleppo, and elsewhere, concentrating on the right to hold governing posts in the Ottoman administration. In Aleppo—a city of more than two hundred thousand inhabitants—the dispute over the city's governorship between the Istanbul appointee Nasuh Pasha (d. 1614) and the Kurdish emir of Kilis, Canbuladoğlu Hüseyn Pasha (d. 1605), a friend of the *serdar* Cağalazade Sinan Pasha (d. 1605), resulted in a siege by the emir's forces in 1604 that ended in Nasuh Pasha's exit. With a hereditary Kurdish emir and his well-equipped forces now in charge of Aleppo, the *serdar* expected support for his campaigns against the Safavids. After the stinging, career-ending defeat of the Ottoman army under the *serdar*'s command by Shah 'Abbas I (1571–1629) at Sufiyan in November 1605, the retreating *serdar* encountered Canbuladoğlu Hüseyn Pasha, with his army intact, at Van. Rashly, the *serdar* had Canbuladoğlu Hüseyn Pasha executed for dilatoriness in the discharge of his duties.[4]

Faced with the legally dubious execution of his uncle, Canbuladoğlu Ali Pasha (d. 1610) raised a cry of vengeance that met with initial sympathy. Aligning himself with major *celâlîs* and local rebels, especially Çemsid, pasha of Adana, Ali quickly moved to assume his uncle's position in Aleppo. Through a rapid campaign against existing Ottoman leaders in Tripoli and Damascus, which included winning a pitched battle at Hama on July 24, 1606, Ali consolidated control of

Syria. Leading as many as sixty thousand troops in the summer of 1606 and surrounded by a network of allies and protégés, Ali played a double game, professing loyalty to the Ottoman Empire in some venues yet simultaneously taking the fateful step of proclaiming independence, in coinage, at Friday prayers, and even in a foreign treaty.[5]

## The Essential Exile

In 1606 and for much of 1607, the creation of an independent Syria ruled by Canbuladoğlu Ali Pasha seemed a real possibility. Well informed about Levantine affairs and keenly interested in all anti-Ottoman projects, Medici Tuscany sought to make Ali Pasha's new title of Prince and Protector of the Kingdom of Syria a reality in 1607.[6] Aware that the Austrian Habsburgs and Safavids had battered, but not seriously breached, Ottoman defenses, the savvy Ferdinando I appreciated the futility of a direct assault. Instead, the Medici state pursued a two-pronged strategy. Tuscany would assiduously seek to form a coalition to attack the Ottoman Empire on as many fronts as possible, stretching the empire's resources and preventing its preeminent army from concentrating its might against a single foe. Simultaneously, Tuscany would seek to ally with the local leaders of subject religious and ethnic communities to carve out independent or at least autonomous polities. In Tuscan plans, the empire would then crumble into its constituent pieces. These, grateful for outside support, would form manageable successor states granting favorable arrangements to the Tuscans. Preserved among the Medici state papers in Florence, a draft of the letter to the pasha of Aleppo, complete with its correction of the ambassador's title, concisely lays out the basis of Medici action:

> To the most high and powerful Lord Ali Pasha, of the most honorable lineage of Zambollat, Protector of Aleppo, Damascus, and Tripoli in Syria, and of all the Holy Land. After you declared yourself opposed to the tyranny of the Ottoman house, you so reconciled the spirits of the Christian Princes, which all are praising and honoring your generous resolution, desiring also the augmentation of your power and glory. And We that continually endeavor with Our galleys and ships to trouble this great Tyranny, we are also ready to help all those that seek to offend them. So that returning

in this same province ~~the honored man~~ Sir Michelag.[lo] Corai of the
City of Aleppo, very well known and loved by Us, we have given him
some commissions to treat secretly with you for the common service. Therefore, it will please you to listen to him, and then let us
understand that which from here we will be able to do for your service, and to end we salute you with all our spirit.

Most prompt for any service to you[7]

Who was this gentleman from Aleppo who braved civil war to return to
his homeland as Tuscany's ambassador?

Michelangelo Corai seems to have been born in Aleppo as Fathullah
Qurray. He may originally have been Syrian Orthodox, though it has
been plausibly suggested that he was a convert.[8] In other words, he was
initially a subject of the Ottoman sultan. He would not, however, remain one. As Federico Federici has recently shown with plausible assumptions about a few ambiguous references, Corai can be identified
as having been in the service of the Italian renegade Sinan Pasha before
falling out with him and apparently spending time in Safavid Iran. Arriving in Venice in 1597, Corai then seems to have served as a translator
for Vincenzo I Gonzaga, duke of Mantua, on campaign on the Balkan
front against the Ottomans during the Long Turkish War. Apparently
for this service, Corai was knighted by Vincenzo I on April 3, 1598.
Shortly thereafter, he met Anthony and Robert Sherley in Venice and
joined them on their adventurous expedition to Safavid Iran.[9] Two letters of 1599—in the first of which he is described as an escaped "Syrian
Dragoman"—note that "he had served as interpreter for a Sir Don Antonio," almost certainly the politically connected privateering rogue
Anthony Sherley (1565–c. 1636). At the time of the first letter, Sherley
was to set off as one of the ambassadors of Shah 'Abbas I to the courts
of Europe.[10]

As we shall see in Chapter 8, both Anthony and Robert Sherley
would serve as ambassadors to the courts of Europe for 'Abbas I. Here,
the critical point is that Corai visited Florence in 1599 and again in
1607 in the company of Anthony and Robert Sherley on their respective
diplomatic missions.[11] The timing of his second visit proved fortuitous.
Corai could not return to Ottoman Syria, doubly compromised as he
was by his service to the Safavids and to Europeans Christian foes of

the Sultan. Ali Pasha's rebellion, then, offered Corai his best chance to go home. To Ferdinando I, Corai must have seemed the ideal instrument of Tuscan policy. Formidably accomplished as a linguist, he was a native son of the rebel capital, a committed Christian, an Italian knight, and deeply tied to the Safavid court.[12] In short, Corai embodied everything that Ferdinando I wanted the Levant to become. In this context, it is hardly surprising that Corai should have accepted the grand duke's offer of the position of ambassador to the Ottoman rebels in greater Syria and to 'Abbas I.[13]

The transformation of an exiled Syrian dragoman into a Medici diplomat broke with Tuscan convention in regular embassies, signaling at the outset the risky and exceptional nature of a project bound up with the individual experience and skills of the ambassador. Traditionally, full-scale Medici embassies were staffed by Florentine patricians and supported and supervised by legation secretaries from the Medici bureaucracy.[14] For this operation, however, the only Tuscan involved was to be the legation secretary, Ippolito Leoncini. The closing of the treaty eventually signed with the pasha of Aleppo makes clear the relationship among the three individuals: "Sir MichelAngiolo Coraj Ambassador here present, with Sir Hippolito Lioncinj sent in his company by the aforesaid Highness and by the Secretary Giorgio Cruger."[15] Leoncini had ostensibly been appended to the embassy for his expertise. Indeed, a draft copy of the instructions for Corai commands that he depart from Livorno on the first available ship, "taking with you only your companion, and Ippolito Leoncini, who we send with you because he is an expert man who will help you in Our service in that which daily you judge good to serve you in it, and to communicate hand in hand any business."[16] Given the depth of Corai's knowledge and the brevity of his time in Tuscan service, Leoncini's primary role is likely to have been political.

Leoncini's task of acting as the reliable Tuscan representative relied on his discretion and ability to serve in a subordinate position. He appears to have been a poor choice for this role. Corai seems to have found Leoncini primarily useful for conveying messages and goods between Aleppo and Tuscany. Using him that way would have had the added advantage of freeing Corai to work more independently and with greater discretion. A draft letter to Corai, dated October 13, 1607, complained that he had sent only two brief letters since arriving in Aleppo and "~~His Highness~~ also marvels that Your Lordship writes nothing about Lioncino, and would like that you would be served by him, and might give him an opportunity to learn and to practice."[17] Later, in 1608, Leoncini set out with Angelo Bonaventura to secretly deliver artillery and personal firearms to the Levant. As Bonaventura complained in a letter to Belisario Vinta, Leoncini disclosed this information as soon as they left Livorno.[18] From this incident, it appears that Corai's reluctance to use Leoncini was well justified by Leoncini's lack of discretion.

Whereas Leoncini was, at best, a controversial member of the team, Corai's secretary seems to have proved loyal and invaluable. Giorgio Crüger (Georg Krieger) served as secretary to the Medici ambassador both in Syria and later in Iran from 1607 to 1610.[19] Originally from Dresden, Krieger would, by 1616, end up in India at the court of Ibrahim Adil Shah II (r. 1580–1627), sultan of Bijapur; there, he played generous host to his fellow German H.v. Poser.[20]

Before Krieger's sojourn in India, however, Corai, Leoncini, and Krieger set out from Livorno early in 1607. These envoys had to operate in the shadows, for their mission was inflammatory. The Tuscans sought the death of the Ottoman Empire by a thousand cuts, overwhelming it by coordinating and supporting numerous rebels and invaders. Once the Ottoman Empire had been shattered, its pieces would be reassembled into a new arrangement of successor states. For envoys bearing such a message, secrecy was of the utmost importance, as a draft copy of Corai's instructions stresses.[21] Upon arrival in Syria, Corai was to "show that you have gone for your particular service, and finding friends or relatives of yours, do not communicate to anyone the commission you have of Us, secrecy being necessary to not put the people in suspicion and to not break the business."[22] To maintain the fiction of traveling on private business, the envoys had to travel on private vessels, which required a frustrating, if productive, layover in Cyprus, as Corai outlined in a letter from Saline (Larnaca) on March 1, 1607.[23]

## The Cyprus Operation

Arriving in Cyprus, the Medici diplomatic team—a Syrian diplomat, a Tuscan legation secretary, and a German secretary—landed first at Saline.

There, they could find no ships heading to Alexandretta.[24] During their stay, Corai went to Famagusta, Nicosia, and Lamisson, at which port he failed to find a ship. He therefore returned to Saline, where he considered taking a "Turkish skiff" but distrusted it and then "was advised not to entangle myself with him," that is the skiff's captain. Corai's great hope, then, rested on the expected arrival of an English ship from Livorno heading to the port for Aleppo. Even so, expressing his frustration with the delays, Corai wrote, "it seems to me thousands of years to arrive in Aleppo." This, at least, is the innocent story that Corai reported in the plaintext of his letter to Tuscany. Partially enciphered and written under the guise of commercial travel, however, the letter cannot be read as a simple recital of Corai's activities. Indeed, it is intentionally internally contradictory, addressing both its intended recipient in Tuscany and the prying eyes of those who might peruse its contents with different stories.[25]

On a mission to undermine the Ottoman Empire, Corai could hardly allow his stay in Cyprus to go to waste.[26] As a result, while on the island, he assessed the receptivity of the Cypriots to Tuscan military intervention.[27] Suspicion of precisely such an intention in a time of turmoil would have made Ottoman officials wary. Dissimulation of his intentions, at least, appears to have been the dynamic at play during Corai's peregrinations through Cyprus. Between searching for ships heading to Syria, he went to Famagusta.[28] Discussing this trip, he wrote, "all this Kingdom is a land of great suspicion and evil for the Christians that come upon those shores, taking all of them for spies and it is often justified."[29] This plaintext reference to Christian spies in a letter filled with ciphertext marks the beginning of a campaign of explicit deception. Corai was, of course, a Christian spy. He acted as if he had nothing to hide by mentioning the suspicion of spies directly in plaintext. To avoid doing so might have been suspicious, for the Ottoman administration in Cyprus did in fact inquire into his business. Corai wrote that (the ciphertext is given in italics) "I was conducted to the Pasha who gave me a long examination and he wanted many particulars from me, but I for being a merchant did not know how to give him the satisfaction for which he was looking, and while he was talking with me, there appeared *the senior steward, and most secretly said that it is true the rebellion of 1500 Turks was newly united with the Christians,* he said it so quietly that I did not understand anything."[30] A plaintext passage punctuated by ciphertext can hardly have allayed suspicions. Still, Corai used the plaintext to assure a snooping reader that he was indeed just a merchant, which was, of course, untrue.

Corai's use of ciphertext adapted standard Tuscan diplomatic practice to the exigencies of his illicit role in Cyprus. The Grand Duchy of Tuscany used a nomenclator, a system that mixed a short codebook adapted to the specific assignment with a substitution cipher. The latter involved assigning one-digit or, more usually, two-digit numbers to each letter regularly used in Italian. The codebook assigned common words and proper names a two- or three-digit number, often accompanied by either a superscript character or punctuation.[31] Table 7.1 gives the cipher key inferred from the cipher secretary's decipherments of some of Corai's letters. Corai's practice of partially deploying the nomenclator matched that of permanent Medici embassies, though his difficult circumstances required greater subtlety in his use of the tool. Of course, the technically safest path would have been to encipher the letter completely. The cumbersome process of creating a totally enciphered text and the very secrecy of the document, however, would have attracted unwanted attention. Corai, then, sought to conceal essential information without compromising either his cover or his embassy's cipher.

This deception was difficult to sustain. Returning to the letter, in the following sentence Corai's use of cipher was less deft. He wrote, "Wherefore *I saw the Pasha most disturbed,* which was the reason rather that he dismissed me that I might go to do my deeds."[32] Small ciphertext sections like this are vulnerable to guessing. From there it is a short step to making suppositions about the cipher. A single slip would probably not have revealed the cipher. The attitude to security implicit in such slips, however, points to some features of early modern secret communication. Writing in cipher would have been laborious for an agent in the field. Carrying a cipher key or writing in plaintext before enciphering the secret pieces would have been risky. There must have been a desire to minimize the use of cipher to save work and maintain cover. Recognized ambassadors had a legitimate reason to write long enciphered inserts, but Corai's cover as a merchant would have been undermined by such blocks of ciphertext.[33] The technical security of the system and the demands of Corai's role were in structural tension.

*Table 7.1* This table captures a large part of a Tuscan diplomatic cipher operative in the Levant in the early seventeenth century. The table is primarily based on information taken from ASF, MdP 4275, 124r–127v, but also ASF, MdP 4275, 64–65 and 178–81.

| Plain text | Ciphertext* |
|---|---|
| A | 14, 30, 49 |
| B | 19, 35 |
| C | 24, 40 |
| D | 10, 37 |
| E | 23, 34, 52 |
| F | 18, 36 |
| G | 22, 41 |
| H | 28, 38 |
| I | 12, 32, 51 |
| J | |
| K | |
| L | 15, 43 |
| M | 20 |
| N | 25, 33 |
| O | 29, 53 |
| P | 26, 39 |
| Q | 11, 46 |
| R | 16, 42 |
| S | 21, 47 |
| T | 27, 44 |
| U/V | 17, 31, 50 |
| W | |
| X | |
| Y | |
| Z | 13, 45 |
| Aleppo | 59. |
| Alessandretta | 61 |
| Amà | 63 |
| Amicizia | 66 |
| Arme | 71 |
| Artiglieria | 72 |
| Babilonia/ Rinegato | 75. |
| Barberia | 76 |
| Bascia | 78 |
| Bertoni | 82 |
| Bursa | 84 |

*Table 7.1* (continued)

| Plain text | Ciphertext* |
| --- | --- |
| Caramusali | 91 |
| Carovana | 93 |
| Cavalli | 95 |
| Chiaus | 96 |
| Città | 98 |
| Compagnia | 99. |
| Constantinopoli | 14. |
| Damasco | 16. |
| Emir | 18. |
| Faccardino | 20. |
| Fortezza | 22. |
| Genti | 27. |
| Giannizzini | 28. |
| (Gran) Turco / Gran Signore | 33. |
| Guerra | 35. |
| Inglesi | 41. |
| Italia | 42. |
| Lega | 44. |
| Lui | 70. |
| Malta | 46. |
| Mancamento | 47. |
| Munizione | 51. |
| Papa | 62. |
| Persia | 63. |
| Porto | 65. |
| Presi | 66. |
| Questo/Quel | 71. |
| Qui/Qua | 72. |
| Re | 73. |
| Regno | 74. |
| Rinegato | 75. |
| Saccheggiato | 77. |
| Schiavi | 79. |
| Soldati | 82 |
| Sultanini | 86. |
| Turchi | 94. |
| Ungaria | 98. |
| (Qui)vi/Là | 15. |

*Table 7.1* (continued)

| Plain text | Ciphertext* |
|---|---|
| Veneziani | 96. |
| Vittoria | 97. |

\* Multiple numbers indicate alternative ciphertext renderings of the letter, which provided a measure of security against frequency analysis.

Corai's final statement on the overheard conversation is indicative of the general theme of his reports, which stress the discontents and rebelliousness of Ottoman subjects, *"I understood as well that it is true that a renegade Turk of the prince was united with perhaps 100 Christians of the country and with a Caramusali [pinnace] left in the night with great diligence on a course to Malta to pass from there* according as is said *to Spain.* In sum all the *island is topsy-turvy."*[34] Corai's report on the overhead conversation could hardly have been a more authoritative statement on events in Cyprus. By reporting a secret conversation between enemy officials heard at first hand, Corai gave his intelligence credibility; Ottoman officials were unlikely to inflate the strength of the rebels.

Corai's choice to recount the conversation in a summary format that emphasized setbacks to Ottoman rule is typical of his anti-Ottoman views. That is, Corai's letter was not an impartial assessment but instead fatefully reflected his and the grand duke's shared belief in intervention. The report confirmed the essential role Tuscany could play. As Corai summarized the views of *"the bishop of the Greeks,"* with whom he spoke on Cyprus, "The sum of which is that *many trust in Your Majesty but because they do not have people that come to treat with him, they are not able to find the easy way that they have to make them lose the whole country, and to depart from under such a tyranny, confessing that they ought not to trust in the Venetians,* for being too attached to the *Great Turk, and that the king of Spain who would be able to do much, is for them too far, so that Your Highness only would be able to console them."*[35] This was, of course, deeply flattering to the grand duke and his pretensions to influence. It may also have been true. The Cypriots can hardly have been enthusiastic about supporting the reinstallation of the old Venetian colonial regime and Spain was not interested in new commitments in the region.

If the links in the chain of causation are incomplete, a sketch out-line is suggestive of Corai's letter's role. He wrote his report on March 1, 1607, which was at the very beginning of the sailing season.[36] As we have seen, the Medici had already received a proposal to intervene in Cyprus from Fernando Girón in 1605. Because 1605 and 1606 were very difficult years for the Ottoman central administration, as the Medici knew well, the broader context for a Medici intervention had grown more propitious. Corai's report seems to have tipped the balance.[37] In 1607, Ferdinando I launched one of Tuscany's most ambitious military enterprises, dispatching the bulk of the ships at his disposal to Cyprus. With eight galleys, nine other ships, 2,200 men, and substantial amounts of weapons and munitions, the strike force was to join with 6,000 Greek rebels in an attack on Famagusta. After taking the island, Cyprus was to be a base for the execution of the plans for Syria. In the event, the fleet scattered, there was much less Greek support than had been hoped for, and the assault ladders were too short for the operation, thwarting the raid.[38]

Why did the Cypriots choose not to rebel? The usual preference for order and quiet aside, conquest had transformed Cyprus from a lonely Venetian outpost at the end of the empire into an Ottoman island in a sea in which the whole mainland coast was also firmly Ottoman. The Ottoman administration also offered relief from vexatious elements of Venetian rule. The long history of conflict between Latins and Greeks, especially over religious matters; the specific Venetian colonial legacy in Cyprus; and the likelihood that a rebellion would be a bloody failure that provoked retribution all militated against rebellion. The Grand Duchy of Tuscany, in particular, seemed an unlikely candidate for a long-term defense of Cypriot independence, not only because of its military weakness but also because of its forces' dealings with other Greek communities. Indicative of the problem with the raiding strategy, in 1608, the year after the failed intervention, Angelo Bonaventura wrote to Florence lamenting the depredations of Christian forces on the islands of Paros and Thasos. Of the Christian forces at Paros, Bonaventura wrote, "They finally put in such desperation those poor Greeks that they [the Greeks] wanted to flee to the mountains and leave the land, only saying that the Turks did not do a thousandth part of the damage that the Christians were doing to them, and they also said that they wanted to send ambassadors to His Serene Highness to lament this fact."[39] Tuscany's strategy of religiously inflected naval raiding and its close alliance with the papacy gave Greek islanders little reason to believe that their property or their faith would be respected.

## The Meeting with the Pasha

In the spring of 1607, however, Tuscany's prospects in the eastern Mediterranean seemed bright. Departing from Cyprus, Corai and his team successfully made their way to rebel Aleppo. The ambiguous position Corai assumed as merchant, spy, and ambassador illustrates the extent to which the Tuscans relied on his discretion and judgment for realizing their plans to destabilize the Ottoman Empire. As we have seen, he was instructed to act as if he were on private business upon his arrival in Syria.[40] Corai had been dispatched as ambassador to the pasha of Aleppo, but it was unclear that he would be received favorably. In light of the risks, the draft instructions urge a measure of caution. Corai was to "go without wasting time to find the Pasha of Aleppo where he will be, showing whereupon to all that you have gone upon your private affairs and look to approach and contact him moreover, under the pretext of giving him the news of Christendom."[41] Once in the pasha of Aleppo's presence to relate this news, the draft instructions envisage Corai maintaining his cover as he responded to questions, interlacing his responses with encouragement about the goodwill of the Christian princes and their willingness to provide assistance.[42] Corai was then to follow a decision tree laid out in the draft instructions, "if in these discourses you see that he does not lend an ear and shows that he does not warrant the help and the friendship of the Christian Princes, do not pass on to other things, and do not communicate that you have letters or an embassy from us."[43] Had the pasha repented of his rebellion, the Tuscans might have been vulnerable indeed, so this judgment was crucial. Fortunately for the Tuscans, judging by the subsequent treaty of alliance, the pasha was indeed receptive.[44] For this eventuality, Corai was to "then reveal all alone Our commission and present Our letter, making in conformity to that, the offer of Our friendship and correspondence and testifying to him ~~making him do~~, that not only We with Our maritime forces, will be ready to give him that help which we will be able [to offer], but we will endeavor also to persuade all the other Christian Princes of the same, the which do not have a greater desire than to see the tyrannical Ottoman Empire completely depressed."[45] In Syria, Corai was given wide discretion on how to proceed. Indeed, later in the instructions, Corai was granted considerable latitude in deciding with whom to conduct negotiations on the basis of whether the pasha was, as reports indicated, the "lord of all Syria."[46]

The reliance on Corai's discretion and judgment throughout his instructions clearly demonstrates how information and logistical problems prevented the grand duke and his government from controlling diplomacy from Tuscany. Tuscan dependence on the man on the spot seems to have been fairly general in all Tuscan long-distance ventures. There was little scope in such a situation for the sort of autocratic control that Alessandra Contini has argued the grand dukes exercised through their legation secretaries at the regular embassies.[47] Nor, for that matter, was there much choice of personnel. Only a handful of people had the linguistic skills, contacts, diplomatic abilities, and loyalties to function as an undercover ambassador.[48] Indeed, Corai's mission involved far more than fomenting rebellion in Cyprus and allying with the pasha of Aleppo, demanding as this was. The Medici archives retain a draft of a letter to the patriarch of the Maronites at Mount Lebanon. In it, the grand duke asked the patriarch to pray to God for him and for his operations, which were only directed to the service of God and Christendom. The grand duke then stated that he sought to gratify the patriarch and Christians in those countries before closing his brief letter by introducing his friend, Michelagnolo Corai.[49]

Corai's decision whether to proceed with his embassy rested on his own judgment, but once he decided to move forward, he had clear instructions for the terms of the alliance. A marginal insertion added to the draft instructions illustrates the centrality of the military component and Tuscany's role as supplier of specialist military assistance. Corai was to "offer him also, that if he should wish for four or six pieces of cannon in the fashion and form of Italy, We will willingly send them to him, on condition that he promises, that the men that will go for that purpose, would be well respected ∧ and preferred and would be able to live as Christians while they were in those countries, and that they will be able to return to our place."[50] This additional offer of artillery represented a deepening of Tuscany's commitment. Now Tuscan specialists wielding the most sophisticated military equipment of the day would be directly involved in the ground campaign under the command of an Ottoman rebel, firing on the main Ottoman field army in Ottoman territory. By offering his personnel, the grand duke not only undermined any prospect of disclaiming responsibility, he also ceded control of the decision to commit Tuscany to a new level of belligerence to Ali Pasha. In light of Tuscany's past history of attempting to disclaim the naval activities of the Order of Santo Stefano and the secrecy of the Tuscan embassy, the pasha might well have doubted the sincerity of Tuscany's professions of support; the offer of Tuscan artillery and experts would have served as a sign of commitment.

Having thus committed Tuscany to new belligerence against the vast Ottoman Empire in support of a rebel regime, basic concerns about the viability of the rebellion came to the fore. In particular, the Tuscans were deeply aware of the importance of rebel unity and the risk that the Ottomans would pursue a policy of divide and rule; as Spanish power in Italy had been established in just such a way, perhaps the Tuscans were especially cognizant of the risk. In any event, Ambassador Corai was exhorted in his instructions to "above all remonstrate and persuade him [the pasha] to be united,[51] and maintain a very good intelligence with all the other leaders that are alienated from the said Empire, to the end that surveying each one his forces, they would be able for the occasions of offensive or defensive war to join together. Because perceiving this union, the Turk will lose the hope of being able to suppress them, and the Christian Princes would be more easily persuaded to help them."[52] Beyond the fairly obvious military benefits, the initial argument for unity rested on an analysis of the means by which the European powers would decide on intervention. Only by presenting a united front could the rebels signal to the Ottoman government the futility of seeking to suppress the rebellion and to foreign powers the probability that the rebels would succeed in at least some measure. Because the Ottomans had, of course, successfully dealt with numerous rebellions and struggles with local potentates in the process of assembling and maintaining their vast empire, the initial presumption on the part of foreign powers would have been that the Ottomans would suppress the rebellion.[53] The Tuscan government was

cognizant of the fact that, in so doing, the Ottomans would employ their
standard rebellion suppression playbook, and so Corai was instructed to
explain, "And already it is understood here, that the Turk has been preparing himself with very large forces to overcome them and principally
the Pasha of Aleppo, for being of the lineage of the great lords of Syria, and
of those particularly that gave to the Ottoman House: whereby so much
the more the said union is necessary, because the Turk keeps presently to
separate them conceding to each leader all of the demands that they had
made, but will not maintain them later, as he has done to many, and as his
predecessors did."[54] Having pointed out that the Ottomans were taking
the rebellion seriously and that their tactics would predictably consist of
duplicitous divide and rule, Corai was to urge the advantages of staying
united.[55] Continuing with the positive effects of such unity, Corai was to
explain that "The princes of there [Europe] seeing that he [the Turk] has
lost Asia, it will encourage them, and with great ease they will overthrow
his power and We have much in hand, to make many people in Europe
rise up, and already there are the leaders here that wait for nothing other
than hearing of this union, having this intelligence of being able to have
in [their] hands one of the strongest places of the Turk and the Christian
princes that are aware of this will be prompt to help them."[56] The eager-
ness to urge unity on the rebels and to assure them of the probability of
Christian intervention reflected a fear that the Ottomans would succeed
in using divide-and-rule tactics to bring the rebels to heel. In light of this,
Corai was to vigorously oppose any representatives of the Turk who might
arrive, and he was to work to secure unity among the rebels in preparation
for the arrival of the Ottomans in force.[57]

The military viability of the alliance of rebel leaders that Corai was
to support depended on the unity of rebels as a necessary but not sufficient condition. To make good their rebellion, the main Ottoman field
army would have to be defeated. Doing so required major forces of the
sort that only a great power could provide. For all Tuscany's apparently
sincere desire to urge the Christian princes to play that role, the difficulty of mobilizing them meant that the Syrian rebels needed more
local allies, and in particular the assistance of the Safavid Iranian army
under Shah 'Abbas. Corai's instructions about these broader dimensions of the anti-Ottoman coalition, and in particular about Persia,
will be explored in Chapter 8.[58]

Returning to Corai's instructions vis-à-vis the pasha of Aleppo and his immediate allies, Corai was given the challenging task of assuring the pasha and his allies that the Christian princes would be unified, would intervene on their side, and would not seek unacceptable compensation as the price for their support.[59] Corai was therefore instructed, "And assure the said Pasha and all of the other leaders, that the Christian princes will not have any greediness to acquire countries in the land of Asia, but that their principal intention is, that everyone work together to finish the destruction of the said Ottoman Empire."[60] By disavowing territorial ambitions, the Medici could and did act effectively as a safe source of support. Tuscany's relatively modest military power would have lent credibility to the claim that the Medici simply sought the destruction of the Ottoman Empire and favorable commercial, diplomatic, and religious arrangements in the Levant. What Tuscany wanted above all was a legal architecture that permitted visiting Tuscans to conduct their affairs under attractive arrangements. In a marginal note, Corai was instructed to note the implied corollary of the disavowal of territorial ambitions, "and each of the said leaders will remain lords of their provinces, and of those that they will conquer."[61] This new Levant whose birth the Tuscans sought to midwife would be a fractured political terrain of fledgling successor states.

Recognizing the need for the support of the Christian powers, the grand duke's instructions to Corai return to the persistent problem of Christian disunity, with the grand duke expressing his hope of soothing the discord between the pope and the Venetians, arguing that the Christian princes needed to unite in support of the pasha.[62] Implicitly recognizing that unifying the forces of Christendom might take some time, Corai was again urged to secrecy on the grounds that the knowledge that the pasha sought friendship with the Christian powers might prompt the Ottomans to commit all their forces to Syria before the rebels had a chance to ally with Christendom.[63] Corai was instructed that after he had already discussed all these matters at least once with the pasha he was to tell the pasha that the grand duke and the Christian princes had only one other interest beyond suppressing the Ottoman Empire—though Tuscany in fact had another, as specified later in the letter—which was the ability for the Christians to visit and stay in Jerusalem. To that end, the grand duke desired that, upon its conquest by the pasha, the Christians might freely and securely exercise their religion there. The grand duke seems to have had a broad conception of this, for he asked for land for the Christians to farm around the city at least down to the port of Zaffo (probably Jaffa); for this the grand duke was willing to induce the Christian princes to pay an annual subsidy "according to what may be judged convenient"—a sense of what this might have been can be seen in the crossed out text indicating 25,000–30,000 *scudi*.[64] This willingness to pay an annual subsidy would perhaps have allowed Corai to make the request for land for Christians while nonetheless disavowing any territorial ambitions by the Christian powers.

To return to a point hinted at earlier, the Tuscans did indeed have one other, rather large request. Specifically, the grand duke asked Corai to secure access to Syrian ports for Tuscan shipping, especially the Tuscan fleet. Corai was to demonstrate to the pasha that such an arrangement would be advantageous to him, noting that seven heavily armed ships could be deployed to blockade a point on the coast at the pasha's need. The grand duke also specified in some detail how the information about access was to be conveyed out of Syria to the Tuscans.[65] Had the Cyprus strike been a success, the deployment might have been strategically critical, for it would have placed Tuscany's fleet on both sides of the main supply route to Egypt. With the overland route cut by the rebellion in Syria, Egypt would have been isolated.

As we have seen, Corai was also to carry an admirably concise and direct letter to the pasha of Aleppo, which would have served as a letter of introduction in addition to the general passport he would have been given.[66] Although the subsequent treaty between the powers is filled with commercial, legal, and religious articles that would have provided the rules that structured their day-to-day relationship, this letter highlights the underlying strategic purpose of the alliance, their common enmity to the Ottoman Empire. For Ali Pasha, defeating the Ottoman Empire was a sine qua non not only for future independence but also for dying a nonviolent death. For the Tuscans, while commercial advantage was certainly an important consideration, the general tenor of Tuscan policy toward the Ottoman Empire at this point was one of nearly unrestrained belligerence against an empire viewed as tyrannical and illegitimate. The Tuscan view is perhaps clearest in the consistency of Tuscan rhetoric. So central was the trope of Ottoman tyranny to the Tuscans that the Medici regime deployed it in at least four documents pertaining to this venture, including the draft instructions to Corai, the draft instructions to Leoncini, the letter to the pasha of Aleppo, and a draft letter to Shah 'Abbas I.[67]

The grand duke's instructions to Corai and letter to the pasha of Aleppo laid the groundwork for a relationship. Even so, the Syrian exile turned ambassador faced a formidable task in transforming these general terms into a specific alliance. An undated, unsigned, and unaddressed document preserved in the Medici archives, which appears to be a letter by Corai or, perhaps, Leoncini to Ali Pasha, shows how the transformation may have been accomplished.[68] The text begins by upgrading the salutation to "Most Serene and Most Worthy King," which could refer to any of several recipients.[69] Later, however, it discusses damaging the Turks with the "Enterprise of the Most Holy Sepulcher" and refers to the king of Persia.[70] In light of the terms of the treaty, discussed later herein, the phrase seems to be a close match for the pasha of Aleppo turned king of Syria. As to the content of the document, the letter begins not with the conquest of Jerusalem, but instead starts with trade. Specifically, the grand duke requested free and secure trade throughout Ali Pasha's kingdom and reciprocally offered free trade in Livorno and the other ports of the Grand Duchy of Tuscany.[71] This offer of open commerce rested on more than a principle of amity and a general openness to commerce. Rather, the document lists a whole series of specific types of textiles to be traded.[72] Turning to the strategic dimension, the document adds to its discussion of the enterprise of the Most Holy Sepulcher an offer that "the Serene Grand Duke will not only help with his forces, but also will procure help from other Christian Princes, who each will willing concur with this enterprise."[73] In pursuit of its anti-Ottoman strategy, the document continues by offering to bring in the "Persian most potent King."[74]

Supporting this general program of anti-Ottoman alliance with specific proposals, the document suggests that in order that "the Turks cannot seize it," the grand duke would offer at need "People, and Artillery, to guard well the said Ports and seashore."[75] After extensively invoking divine support, the document then reaffirms the goal was "to suppress, abase, and uproot as far as possible this Grand Turk, who disturbs and ravishes and not only is an enemy of the Christians, but infests, scourges, damages, and destroys the whole world as well."[76] To this denunciation of the Ottomans, the documents adds a ringing call to arms and a belief in divine support likened to the "submersion in an instant of Pharaoh with all his numerous army, for wanting to persecute the Hebrews against Divine will."[77] The document closes with an exhortation: "having said all this to the honor of God, and to satisfy the command of my Most Serene Prince and Lord, where one can see well the useful future and great benefit that you can bring to Your Majesty's Kingdom, going united in company with the Most Serene Grand Duke of Tuscany Ferdinando Medici my only Lord and Patron."[78] This construction identifies the author as a devoted servant of Grand Duke Ferdinando convinced of divine support for the great anti-Ottoman struggle. The rhetoric resonates with Corai's apparent views, and the terms proposed are consonant with the treaty eventually signed, suggesting that the document is most probably a clean copy of Corai's letter to Ali Pasha.

## The Syrian Alliance

Corai's message of anti-Ottoman alliance met with a warm reception. Indeed, Tuscan offers of material support were so acceptable to the rebel pasha that he signed a treaty of alliance with Tuscany. The opening sentences of the main body of the treaty recount its origins:

> According to the relation that we have from the Most Serene Grand Duke of Tuscany, and which was given by Sir Signor MichelAngiolo Corai[,] a Gentleman of Aleppo, sent to Us, as express ambassador of His Most Serene Highness in the name of whom he has presented to us a most cheerful letter, to Us the above letter [is] most gratifying for We have had great pleasure in this, the great desire that His Most Serene Highness has to contract with Us a perfect Friendship. We declare that about this, Our wish is not a minor point, and that we are most content. Therefore, we accept willingly his most powerful and inviolable Friendship, assuming that it is truly offered; of which we are certain, that he will accept Our lofty and irrevocable Friendship, the which we offer to

> him with those great chains of obligation and affection that
> tighten a true eternal Friendship, foreseeing the infinite
> good that ought to result for both parties.[79]

The treaty then outlines detailed commercial and diplomatic arrangements under the rubric of "capitulations," a standard term for such an
agreement; the terms gave Tuscany a remarkably privileged position.[80]
The desperateness of Ali Pasha's plight, the attractiveness of paper
promises when immediate material assistance accompanied the offer,
and the relatively low cost of privileging the Tuscans, led the pasha to
readily agree. Under the treaty, Tuscany's merchants and diplomats
would have the best position of any Europeans in the region, including
special rights of supervision of disputes in a Jerusalem open to Catholic
pilgrims and free commerce throughout the pasha's lands.[81] These
rights were conceded in part in the expectation that "if perhaps the
Most Serene Grand Duke condescends to such a great friendship with
Us, the Holiness of the Most Blessed Pope Paul V[th] vicar of the Omnipo-
tent God among the Christians, and the Majesty of the Most Glorious
and Catholic Don Philip III King of Spain Ze' and other Potentates and
Christian Princes, will all agree to make a League with Us."[82] Tuscany's
position in this arrangement was as a special interlocutor. No matter
how enthusiastic the Tuscans were in their support of Ali Pasha, they
lacked the forces to turn the tide against even a severely weakened Ottoman host. Among the Christian powers, only Spain, Venice, and
France had the combination of naval and ground forces to intervene in
strength in Syria. The immediate purpose of involving Tuscany's allies,
then, was clearly military.

Syria was not a remote frontier region the Ottomans could afford to let slip into the control of a local dynasty that only occasionally heeded the wishes of the sultan. Sitting at the crossroads among
continents, Syria possessed a central commercial and strategic importance for any empire with aspirations for control in the Middle East.
Aleppo, in particular, played a vital role in the lucrative silk trade.[83] As
the very existence of this treaty of friendship constituted an act of defiance against the Ottomans, the signatories had little reason to attempt
to conceal their goals. Accordingly, the treaty specifies the purpose of
this new league in no uncertain terms, "and this great Friendship and

League among Us, is not for any other effect, but to abase and destroy, as [much] can be with divine help, the Ottoman Empire, and to increase the Power of the House of Giampulat and particularly to raise up Our illustrious person."[84] The purpose of the treaty from the perspective of Ali Pasha, then, is clear. He and his house sought large-scale Christian intervention to defeat the Ottomans, which would allow the House of Giampulat (Canbulad) to become the ruling dynasty of an independent Syria. For the Tuscans, Ali Pasha's compromising defiance made true reconciliation with the Ottomans and betrayal of the Tuscans impractical. The assumption of this position by the pasha would have had the effect of signaling to Tuscany's allies, weary of endless overly optimistic reports of discontented locals ready to rebel, that Ali Pasha was fully committed. Whatever his later protestations to the Ottomans, his actions indicate that the rebellion was indeed in earnest.

The most immediate contribution of the House of Giampulat (the Canbulads) to the alliance was to be military action, the objective of which illustrates a key component of Tuscan interest in the Levant. Ali Pasha undertook

> For the furthering of which we adduce and promise to undertake the most arduous enterprise you wish to color such a powerful design. Giving irrevocable words of appeal for the first [i.e., promising], the acquisition of the Holy City of Jerusalem, moving war to all those Cities and Lands, which dare to oppose us and making use of every great force to become the lord of them, as we hope in God, which may most happily come to pass. For the which holy enterprise, and for any other more difficult, We engage Our faith and swear we will be most prompt to expose ourselves, whenever the said Most Serene Grand Duke will have subscribed the Friendship and League with Us, to the Holiness of the aforesaid Pope, and to the Catholic Majesty and with both agreed, and passed the articles or chapters pertaining to all of the provisions, for the notable enterprises that have to be made.[85]

The promised move to seize Jerusalem and the surrounding territories shows the ties that bound the allies and the shared strategic vision of the parties to the treaty. Tuscany and the major allies that the Tuscans hoped to bring into the league were interested generally in the destruction of the Ottoman Empire, but specifically in the religious and commercial rights in the Levant that might be acquired after the defeat of the Ottomans. Indeed, the acquisition of the Holy Land was a sine qua non of some critical subsequent provisions of the treaty, which assume that Ali Pasha rules there. Although any ruler of Syria might be interested in controlling the Levantine shore and its hinterland from Lebanon to Egypt, the planned move on the inland and commercially relatively unimportant city of Jerusalem seems to have been primarily a matter of alliance politics. A march on Jerusalem would draw the Syrian rebels away from their base of operation and from their two likeliest allies, the Anatolian rebels and the shah of Iran, and so it would have been a pure play for assistance. Having promised to seize the Holy Land and adhere to the generous terms of the treaty, the pasha of Aleppo called for papal and Spanish intervention:

> Deferring (concerning these) to the most prudent Providence and worth of His Most Serene Highness the which will have exquisite regard how this is the most important and greatest cause that in our age in all the world it is possible to undertake. And when the assistance will be greater, then we will have greater courage, and with more certain hope we will expose ourselves to attempt and overcome most virtuously (God favoring) every enterprise. We reply therefore that at the time when the said Most Serene Grand Duke will have advised us that the said two Princes, in particular, will have accepted us in Friendship and signed the League and the agreed chapters, and sends by express message authentic writing, and according to the content of this arriving here at the precise time the provisions and assistance at the maritime ports of our Dominion, where there will be order enough to receive all, and to make every provision for the Galleys or the *Brettoni* or the other vessels that for such effect will come: We will be most prompt to govern ourselves in conformance to the order, which it will give the said League, to give a beginning to the enterprise, without making any

> delay to the execution of it, to the end that, as soon as may
> be, in Christendom Our happy progress will be felt.[86]

This explicit exhortation to the papacy and Spain to join in the league and provide tangible military assistance cut to the heart of the projected alliance. Military assistance would lead to favorable access to the Holy Land. By providing naval support, Spain and the papacy would help ensure the survival of the new state and thereby ensure the implementation of the attractive terms agreed in the treaty. Militarily, the papacy had a considerably lower capacity to provide the sort of assistance contemplated than the Grand Duchy of Tuscany. The purpose of the pope's inclusion on an equal footing with the king of Spain, a ruler whose military forces were sufficient to tilt the scales on his own, must have rested on the pope's moral authority and ability to rally a broader Catholic coalition.

In practice, any assistance that the Tuscan-led alliance might be expected to provide would arrive by sea to one of the ports on the Levantine shore. Weakened though the Ottomans were, there was no prospect of a Christian army advancing overland. The dependence, perforce, of the Tuscan-led alliance on naval intervention on behalf of the Syrian rebels made it logistically difficult for the Catholic allies to make a significant strategic impact. Specifically, the survival of the rebels would be determined by their ability to stop an Ottoman field army marching across Anatolia from sweeping them out of Syria. Therefore, the most that might be accomplished directly by the naval forces of the Catholic allies would be to help complicate the Ottoman movement of troops and supplies to the theater of action and to distract some forces through amphibious raids. What the Syrian rebels truly needed, then, was not the fleets of the papacy, Tuscany, and Spain, but the supplies and perhaps troops that such fleets could escort to rebel ports on the Levantine shore.

The centrality of the Levantine ports to any prospect of European assistance for the Syrian rebels dovetailed with the economic interests of the lead power negotiating the alliance.[87] Specifically, any economic benefits that the Grand Duchy of Tuscany might hope to secure from dabbling in the Middle East would come through trade conducted in Levantine ports. In light of the economic and strategic importance of the ports, the second article of the treaty specifies that "now for the greater assurance of all the Princes of the League of Our inviolable faith and that Our desire to depress and frustrate the powerful enemy could not be greater: We promise to assign a Port of Our sea, according to which we will forward the agreement with the Highness of Tuscany, for all the galleys, ships, and vessels of the said League, to the which will be used every sort of kindness and which will have the commodity that they will show themselves to desire."[88] The offer of access to a port constituted one of the most immediately tangible benefits of the alliance. Reliable access to a secure anchorage in the eastern Mediterranean would have been helpful for all Tuscan shipping, both commercial and military, but absolutely essential for the use of Tuscany's galley fleet in the eastern Mediterranean. Galleys were inherently short-range warships; the large complement of men relative to the cargo capacity of the galley required very frequent resupply, especially of water.[89] In sharp contrast to Venice, Tuscany lacked a network of secure anchorages from its central port at Livorno to the eastern Mediterranean, which severely limited the range and operational effectiveness of Tuscan galleys. The Tuscans did possess substantial sailing vessels that might have reached the eastern Mediterranean in any event. Even so, galleys were central to the battle fleets of Mediterranean powers, and the ability to use a local port to support the galleys would have greatly enhanced Tuscany's deployable power in the eastern Mediterranean. Access to a safe harbor and necessary supplies therefore had a strategic importance to Tuscany that it would not have had for Venice, which had its bases, or for northern European powers that were less dependent on galleys.

Perhaps the single most important strategic objective for the Tuscans, once the new state was formed and its survival secured, was to ensure that the Syrian rebels did not simply content themselves with holding the territory in their possession but instead moved to secure the Holy Land. Only with control of the Holy Land could the Syrians provide the Tuscans with the promised religious benefits. Anticipating the success of the rebel invasion of the Holy Land and their capture of Jerusalem, the treaty specifies in substantial detail the arrangements governing access. The third article of the treaty states that

> And forasmuch as the first enterprise that We will grasp we
> intend to be that of the Holy City of Jerusalem, on the which

[enterprise] we wish to go in person, provided that the aforementioned Princes of the League would have made all of the
necessary provisions in conformance to the Capitulations
that will have been accepted by the Grand Duke of Tuscany.
And hoping with the grace of God to become the lord of it
[Jerusalem]: We desire that all Catholic Christians be able to
securely live there and to exercise their Catholic Religion as
also to receive hand in hand all those who wish to become
Christians; but in the matter of differences or other [con-
flicts] that may be born among them, they will have recourse
to the Consul or vice Consul of the Florentine Nation that
you will send to them, the Consul of the said nation dwelling
in Aleppo, to administer Justice in their disagreements.[90]

For all the formality of the treaty, the prospective and conditional character of the alliance emerges strongly in this article. The pasha of
Aleppo promised to take Jerusalem provided that the princes delivered
on their side of the bargain. Neither party was wholly convinced, it
would seem, of the other's commitment, which is perhaps unsurprising
in a treaty between a rebel and a hypothetical alliance. To turn this hypothetical alliance into a reality, the pasha of Aleppo offered extraordinarily attractive religious provisions; aside from direct rule, indeed,
Catholic Europe could hardly ask for more. The offer was not merely of
toleration, but of religious security on a discriminatory basis in favor of
Catholics. Even more striking, though, is the promise of security for
those who accept Christianity. This article explicitly embraced the possibility of conversion but made no reservations about which faith an
individual might be permitted to leave; because apostasy was a capital
offense under Islamic law, perhaps the assumption was that Muslims
would not be converting.[91]

The final provision of the article highlights the contrast between
the speculative nature of the relationship between the Syrian rebels and
Spain, the papacy, and other unnamed Christian princes and the so-
lidity of the ties that bound the Tuscans to the Syrian rebels. It was,
after all, Tuscan diplomats who had slipped into Syria, negotiated the
treaty, and promised, in great detail, specific assistance. Part of the reward for this prompt and solid assistance seems to have been a treaty

architecture that distinctly privileges Tuscans and the grand duke's diplomatic representatives in the planned future of the Levant. This privileged position was not granted, however, simply in gratitude for the promptness of Tuscan assistance—though that is mentioned as the rationale for a subsequent privilege—but involved an added contribution on the part of the grand duke of Tuscany.[92] In exchange for the grant of valuable privileges to Catholics in the Holy Land in general, the treaty called for a specific expenditure by the grand duke of Tuscany in particular, as laid out in Article 4:

> We intend as well and wish that conquering that Province and Holy City that not only the Florentines or Tuscans, but all of the Christians, the one and the other sex, which render obedience to the Holiness of the aforementioned Most Blessed Pope Paul V[th] coming to visit as pilgrims or otherwise the Most Holy Sepulcher in Jerusalem of Jesus Christ their Redeemer and God, as also all the other holy places that can be found in Palestine, be exempted from any sort of expense or tribute to visit, enter, or leave the said Holy places or to go there, and in particular the Most Holy Sepulcher, not paying anything, according as they were accustomed or it was typical to pay in the time that the Ottoman Empire has or had unworthily possessed it. Since for this ability or aforementioned exemption that we accord to all of the Pilgrims and residents in the Holy City[,] Signor Ambassador Corai has promised us in the name of the Most Serene Grand Duke of Tuscany that for recompense there will be made an annual subsidy according to what we will agree to be reasonable together with that Highness and Us.[93]

Continuing a shift that emerged toward the end of Article 3, Article 4 was primarily concerned with the architecture of an enduring relationship. The promises of action and exhortations to assistance having been made, the treaty now assumed success. The promise of financial transfers from the grand duke in exchange for privileges that constitutes the fourth article of the treaty is wholly typical of the general style of Tuscan diplomacy in this period. Had the rebellion been a success and the treaty gone into force, Tuscany would have been able to claim a prestigious and potentially influential position as the favored interlocutor with the ruler of the holy sites. In an era when prestige and precedence were valued highly, the title that Tuscany might claim by virtue of its privileged position would have been no small prize. Although no title is specified, it would have been hard for other Catholic powers to contest a claim by the grand duke to a title like Protector of the Holy Land.

In keeping with general Medici policy, the Tuscan government simultaneously pursued trade rights on the broadest basis possible. The Medici were willing to settle for commercial concessions for individuals or groups, but they seem to have been primarily interested in fostering trade by Tuscans and through Tuscany in general, as we saw in the case of the arrangements with Muscovy. The richly detailed commercial articles of the treaty with Ali Pasha are indicative of the seriousness of the Medici government's commitment to fostering economic prosperity for their subjects through the creation of a favorable international legal architecture. Article 5 lays the groundwork for the commercial articles, establishing the principle that open trade was a privilege granted in recognition of Tuscany's alliance with the rebel pasha, "And because of this powerful and inviolable Friendship and League We intend that the one part and the other has to give and draw out the opportunity for common benefit, for free commerce in the landing places, cities, and lands, which are under Our obedience, according as will happen to negotiate these, we having commanded that beyond the Chapters written above, the which we approve and swear to maintain, there might be written as well the following capitulations of the subject hereafter."[94] The phrasing of this article suggests that the grant of free commerce was to be of "common benefit." That the remaining commercial provisions of the treaty were exclusively concerned with privileges granted to the Tuscans to be exercised in Ali Pasha's domains, however, suggests that the mutual benefits envisioned may have been of different kinds. The tone of the treaty, the one-sided list of concessions, and the absence of reciprocal grants of privileges in Tuscany for either the merchants or diplomatic representatives of Ali Pasha suggests that the grant of open trade would have been considered a benefit accruing largely to Tuscany. The benefits for Ali Pasha—the other side of the ledger—were to be of a more personal and political kind, as will be discussed further on.

The linkage of political alliance with commercial privileges reappears in the most important commercial article of the treaty. It was in the spirit of the contemporary Ottoman practice of granting capitulations to resident foreign communities.[95] Whereas Article 5 laid out a general framework for mutually beneficial commerce, Article 7 provided specific, legally enforceable privileges: "That all the Florentines and Tuscans, and others that go under the banner of the grand duke of Tuscany will be able, with any sort of vessel, to come to the landing places of Our Dominion, to depart from there, and to go freely where they please, as also they will be able to traffic in all sorts of merchandise from those Cities and Lands that are under Our obedience contracting in Our bazaars, according as they will agree with the merchants, and most securely to sell and to buy, but that the Florentine Nation would be enabled more than the others that depend on that Highness, to whom, as the first friend, it is most dearly offered."[96] Article 7 is a sweeping opening of Ali Pasha's dominions to Tuscan trade. With a stroke of the pen, the article abjures restrictions on movement and commerce for Florentines and Tuscans. That both are specified illustrates the slippage between the terms at the time. Part of this slippage was historical, part political. Tuscany was a new, controversial polity created by force and authorized by the papacy, whereas Florence was an ancient, famous state. The English insisted, for instance, on calling the grand duke of Tuscany the duke of Florence.[97] Article 7 seems to recognize the ambiguity by giving both terms. For all the promises of Article 7, for open trade to become a commercially viable reality required settling a variety of detailed issues to shield Tuscan merchants from forms of restriction and harassment. Subsequent articles deal with the various points of contact where Tuscan merchants and diplomats might have faced opposition and restrictions.

Tuscan trade with the Levant was necessarily seaborne trade. Because Tuscany was a traditional foe of the Ottomans, Tuscan trade was also likely to violate commercial rules on the legitimate items of and parties to trade obtaining prior to the revolt. For the Tuscans, then, trade in Ali Pasha's ports would, in the absence of specific protections, have required running a risk of confiscation. Article 10 promised, therefore, "In consideration of the perfect Friendship that the Most Serene Grand Duke has contracted with Us, We wish that the Florentines that will traffic in the places of Our obedience will be able with their money to take contraband goods, and that being up to this prohibited, and that they be able to load aboard the galleys or other vessels of the said Grand Duke or aboard other vessels that they might bring for that purpose, without anyone being able to impede them."[98] In addition to necessary legal security, Article 10 provided the Tuscans with the sort of extraordinary privilege that might have sparked resistance from local merchants. The Tuscans were specifically permitted to trade in contraband goods; presumably, contraband included trade with the enemy. In case there was any uncertainty on this point, Article 12 stated "That the merchandise that will be loaded aboard the Galleys of the Grand Duke or the ships of the Florentines belonging to our Enemies, or, of Our Dominion, will not be able to be taken, under the pretense that it is of Our said enemies, thus being Our will."[99] The Tuscans' license to trade in goods that were, as contraband and enemy goods, usually forbidden to local merchants was a potentially profitable privilege. Even so, both this provision and Article 13 were mostly about protecting Tuscan merchants from harassment. As Article 13 specified, "The merchandise that the Florentines will bring to the landing places or ports of Our Dominion, or those that they will take away will not have to pay other commerce or imposition to be estimated at a higher price than that of the ancient custom."[100] With the promise of open trade, customary taxes, and protection against confiscation on the grounds of dealing in contraband, the primary remaining political risk lay in restrictions on foreign exchange. In light of the role of banking in Tuscan history and politics and its traditional position in the economy, it is hardly surprising that the Tuscans negotiated a favorable arrangement on currency issues. Article 11 states, "The coins that the Florentines carry or bring from their country, through all Our Dominion, will not be able to be taken by Our Treasurers, nor from those that mint the money, Ottoman or Ours, under pretense of wanting to make Ottoman or Giampulat coin, nor omitting we wish that they will be able to take any of the others, by reason of not deviating from the ancient usage, unless the same merchants will not be content with it."[101] The article invokes "ancient usage" as a precedent for currency policy, which glosses over the politically fraught character of the decision. At the most elevated level, conceding the right to trade using foreign coins reflected a concession in a critical area of sovereignty. Among the classic ways of proclaiming sovereignty at the onset of a rebellion was to strike new coinage, as perhaps the pasha had done.[102] Beyond the issues of sovereignty and symbolism, the currency concession insulated Tuscan merchants from local officials.

Operating under the expectation of a sustained commercial relationship, the treaty also outlines a series of maritime provisions meant to facilitate commerce. Article 20 offered general assurances of welcome and assistance as well as active support in the event of stress of weather, "wishing and commanding that they would be immediately helped" and "their vessels would be respected and cherished, providing them with their money for all of the means that they will request."[103] The promises of welcome and assistance in adverse circumstances would have lowered the risks of trade. Such risks nonetheless remained substantial even with the provisions of Article 20. Article 21 consequently provided assurances that, in the event of shipwreck, "we command that all that which will be able to be recovered would be restored and put in the power of the merchants to which they belong."[104] Having addressed a number of the specific impediments that might face Tuscan merchants, the treaty returned to general assurances. In Article 22 assurances were again accompanied by admonitions to respect Tuscan privileges as long as they paid their taxes: "That the Florentines, interpreters or other appertaining to them, coming to Our Countries, whether by sea or by land, to sell or to buy, and to do business, paying the dues of Our commerce, and the dues of the Residents of the Grand Duke and of the Consuls, as is the custom, without being molested, no less their vessels, nor their merchandise impeded by Our Captains nor by volunteers, nor by whom that may be there of Our Dominion, neither coming, nor going, nor meeting again."[105] Article 22 offered blanket assurance that the wide array of commercial privileges granted to the Tuscans and their dependents would not be negated by the initiative of truculent local officials.

Among the many potential points of conflict, perhaps the most salient were in the areas of debt and contracts. Commerce runs on credit and good faith; it slows to a relative crawl in their absence. For that reason, Tuscan merchants attempting to conduct business on any substantial scale with their Syrian counterparts were likely to find themselves in contractual arrangements that imposed obligations on the Tuscans. Even in the absence of malfeasance and ill intentions, business is inherently an uncertain matter. It might therefore be expected that some Tuscans who made contractual arrangements with local merchants would, in the course of time, fail to honor their obligations. Such a failure would have imposed a loss on the local merchant. Even before considering bad faith, miscommunication, fraud, and so on, unresolved financial obligations could be a recurrent point of friction between an aggrieved local and a foreigner of a different religion. The treaty, therefore, addresses the issue in three related articles. Article 23 states, "In any case when a Florentine was found to be a debtor, it would not be possible to ask for the debt from others than from him, or to which he will have obliged himself, and the same is intended for anyone who will walk under the banner of the Grand Duke of Tuscany[.] With this they would always be in the view of their competent judge, the Consul of the Florentine Nation."[106] In effect, the article repudiated any collective responsibility among Florentine merchants. Further, Florentine merchants as a whole were granted the privilege of being subject to Florentine legal jurisdiction under the aegis of the Florentine consul. Although the legal jurisdiction of the Florentine Consul was exalted in the noncommercial articles of the treaty, the primary point at issue in Article 23 and the closely related articles 25 and 27 was the limitation of the responsibility of the Florentines for contracts that they ostensibly made with local merchants. Article 27 reaffirmed the limitation of liability to the specific Florentines with whom a contract had been made or debt contracted, "There being any Florentine who is a debtor of anyone, or who would have committed any bad act, and if he would have fled, We wish and command, that the other Florentines that will not have consented thereto or stood surety for him, will not be able to be searched or harassed on anyone's account."[107] It is not difficult to imagine the frustration of the local merchant community when a Florentine debtor fled on one of the privileged Florentine galleys and the related temptation of a local official to court popular acclaim by seeking redress from the remaining Florentine merchants. At the same time, the Florentine merchant community would have had a great deal of difficulty operating in an open trade environment in which individual Florentines could come and go at will while leaving the entire community with unlimited liability for his debts or crimes. The treaty addressed the potential for outrage on the one hand and of unacceptably unlimited liability and collective responsibility on the other by tightly limiting liability to those explicitly responsible. The model of trade outlined in Articles 23 and 27 is individual, private, and grounded in personal responsibility. The provisions of the treaty envisioned this model being enforced by a resident community of Tuscan diplomats with juridical powers.

Even in a system of individual responsibility and Florentine consular jurisdiction in some debt cases, there remained a risk of contact with the local legal system. The provisions of the treaty, however, evinced a pervasive distrust of the honesty and goodwill of local officials and merchants in their dealings with the Tuscans. The distrust was rendered quite explicit in Article 25, which dealt with procedures for registering contracts to protect against fraudulent claims: "That the Florentines, their Consuls, Interpreters, and those of the places that depend on them ought in their selling, buying *plegorie,* and in every other point of Justice, to make contract before the Qadi, in the absence of the which those that will have any pretension against them would not be able to make it appear as a contract registered in the books of Our Judges, or wishing to produce false testimonies; we wish and command that these would not be heard, but if it is good to give faith to the contracts that will have been passed before Our Judges and not being any in the said registers, such requests in any account would not be admitted; and it is warned that nothing will be arrived at contrary to sacred Justice."[108] The insistence on following a bureaucratic process of contract registration was hardly surprising, but the phrasing is. The article emphasizes rooting out anticipated perjury and fraud by Ali Pasha's own subjects. It indicates Tuscan fears about the hazards of the local business environment and Ali Pasha's willingness to allow the provisions of the treaty to be phrased in an unflattering way to reassure the Tuscans. Just as the concessions in the treaty were almost all one-way, so the assumptions about who needed protection from whom were hardly reciprocal. The treaty did recognize the possibility of misbehavior by the Tuscans, but it was overwhelmingly preoccupied with restricting and restraining the actions of local officials and merchants against the Tuscans.

Restrictions on the actions of local officials were mirrored by privileges granted to Tuscan diplomats in the domains of the pasha of

Aleppo. The enumerated privileges included the usual diplomatic immunity but also extended far beyond, granting Tuscan diplomats almost complete extraterritorial jurisdiction over the resident merchant community. The foundational articles underlying this jurisdiction were the right of free movement and residence for the whole Tuscan diplomatic establishment outlined in Article 8, "That the extraordinary ambassadors of the Most Serene Grand Duke to Us sent as Consuls, vice Consuls of the Florentine Nation, interpreters and subjects, will be allowed to come, depart, go, and inhabit all of the places of Our Dominion most securely without being given any sort of disturbance, rather We intend that they be favored and helped in everything with which they have need."[109] This sweeping series of privileges would have permitted the Tuscans to establish a ubiquitous network of diplomatic employees with access to the entirety of the pasha of Aleppo's domains. The phrase "extraordinary ambassador" does seem to carry with it the implication that the Tuscan ambassador would be sent specially and occasionally, but the extensive and permanent legal obligations of the Tuscan ambassador (on which more later) make it clear that the Tuscans were expected to maintain a continuous diplomatic presence. The legal framework for a permanent diplomatic network was consonant with contemporary practice in the Ottoman Empire, in which France maintained an extensive network of consulates.[110] This Ottoman precedent presumably formed the basis for many, but not all, of the treaty's provisions.

The extensive and permanent model of diplomatic representation offers a clue to understanding an otherwise perplexing article of the treaty. Article 29 states, "For the establishment and change of the Florentine Consuls in the landing places of Our Dominion, no person would dare to oppose it or to meddle to such effect."[111] Implicit in Article 29 was the expectation that someone might wish to interfere in the composition of the Tuscan diplomatic network. In models of diplomatic representation focused on the attendance of the ambassador on the person of the sovereign, the diplomatic personnel selected to fill the relative handful of roles would have been of limited interest outside the inner circles of power. By contrast, Tuscan diplomatic representatives were granted such extensive judicial powers that the choice and establishment of Tuscan diplomatic officials would have become a matter of some importance to local communities and to other foreigners present in Ali Pasha's domains. Article 9 of the treaty, for instance, states that "all the Nations dependent on the said Princes and Potentates confederated with Us, in the matter of differences, business or otherwise, that they may have together, as well as for the Civil as for the Criminal, would always have a recourse to the Consul or Vice Consul of the Florentine Nation dwelling in Aleppo," restricting access to other courts and rendering the consuls' decisions final.[112] The right to run the high court for foreigners in the pasha of Aleppo's domains was a valuable privilege, both as a mark of status and as a practical means of serving Tuscan interests. It was also the sort of privilege to which Tuscany could not normally have hoped to lay claim, except as a result of alliance with a new political order.

The advantage of having a Tuscan government official as the highest judge in civil cases for Tuscan commerce is fairly clear. Jurisdiction in criminal law cases might seem less obviously advantageous for Tuscan commerce and influence, yet it was arguably more important. Otherwise, local judicial proceedings could have become sites of economic, political, or religious proxy conflicts. A similar set of concerns seem to underlie many of the articles of the treaty, but Article 26 states the matter clearly: "There being plotted any treachery against the Florentines or their dependents by accusing them of having injured or been blameworthy, producing false testimonies, to find a way to trouble them, We command that one most minutely view it in similar occasions and take care that these Florentines would neither be harassed nor pass the things too far before."[113] Presumably this last was to prevent too rapid a rendering of judgment and distribution of the items concerned in case the accusation was a calumny. The fear of calumny and the desire that judges avoid being taken in by it are expressed clearly here, but such exhortations would have provided precious little protection in actual cases of abuse. In apparent recognition of this, most cases in which the Tuscans might have been involved and in which there might have been a temptation for abuse were removed from the authority of local officials. Crimes committed within the resident Florentine community were to be settled internally as specified in Article 15, "That happening some homicide or other inconvenience among the Florentine Nation the Ambassador and the Consul will be allowed to follow their laws and statutes to do justice, without any one of Our officers or ministers being able to take information from anyone, nor impeding them."[114] This article promises full Florentine legal independence for all internal issues. In effect, if a pair of Florentine merchants fell out over a card game in Aleppo and came to blows, they might expect their conflict to be resolved with as much reference to Syrian law or officials as if they had been in Florence. A Florentine dealing only with other Florentines would therefore have been effectively immune from local law. While this provision can hardly have been popular with local judges—indeed the purpose seems to have been precisely to exclude local officials from the legal process completely—it would have given the Tuscan community greater confidence in living and doing business in Syria by offering a familiar, sympathetic, and predictable legal environment in which cases could be heard in Tuscan by Tuscans. In case there was any lack of clarity that such was the intention, Article 30—the final article of the treaty—states in no uncertain terms: "That if there is born any contention or controversy between two Florentines We wish that the Resident Ambassador of Tuscany or the Consul of their Nation would put an end to their differences, conforming to their laws and statutes, without anyone else and any of Our officers who wish to object to the contrary."[115] As in Article 15, the final clause of the sentence makes clear that Tuscan legal independence was to be complete, with Tuscan judicial powers supplanting those of local officials in internal matters. This legal independence covered Tuscan property all the way to the grave. So, to return to the hypothetical card game, if a Florentine had been killed in the affray, his estate would have been governed by Article 24, which states, "And it occurring that any Florentine or Tuscan should die, or whoever walks under the banner of Tuscany, We wish and command all Our officers and Commissaries, that they would not have to see the goods or wealth of the deceased, but they would be assigned without impediment from anyone, to whom he would have left as the Testator in his final will, and dying intestate, it would be conducted and assigned with the intervention and consent of the Consul, in the house or in the place of one of his Compatriots, without the commissaries being able to interpose a point or impede the execution."[116] Early modern trade could involve mortal peril, from disease and piracy to brigandage and warfare. To instill confidence that Tuscan property would be protected from the dictates of the local legal regime and reduce the risk of misappropriation of funds, the treaty excluded the distrusted local officials from every stage of the process and instead reposed the responsibility for handling the inheritance with the resident Tuscan diplomatic official.

Conceding a separate legal jurisdiction within the same geographic space occupied by the subjects of the pasha of Aleppo raised inevitable questions about which individuals, precisely, were to be subject to Tuscan jurisdiction. The question was of some moment, not only for the separate legal regime, but also for the various financial liabilities to which individuals would be subject, a point addressed by Article 28: "That the Florentines or those that depend on them, for those married or not married in Our Dominion, practicing as merchants, working with their art, or otherwise, would not have to pay tribute, nor to concur to any imposition."[117] The broad definition of membership of the Tuscan community in Syria seems to have been designed to minimize conflict and confirm the Tuscans in the security of their property.

For all this judicial independence to be real, however, it was not enough to grant jurisdiction to senior Tuscan diplomatic personnel; they required personal immunity as well. In a striking indication of the level of resistance expected of local officials, Article 16 states that "The Florentine Consuls that will be established in the landing places of Our Dominion, having care of the repose and security of the traders, would not be allowed to be made prisoners, nor to have their houses marked. And in case anyone might question them or there might be pretended something of these neither the Qadis, nor the Subashi, nor the Chechià, nor other officers either Criminal or Civil will be able to molest them at all but the cognizance [of the case] will be sent to Our presence and public Divan."[118] In contrast to the many articles in which the restraint on the action of local officials was confined to exhortation and prohibition, Article 16 offered a real and effective mechanism of appeal. By granting immediate recourse to the pasha's personal court, Article 16 effectively gave Tuscan diplomats faced with local harassment the ability to threaten local officials with appeal to a jurisdiction where the desire to maintain Tuscan alliance, trade, and subsidies would outweigh any resentment or wounded pride on the part of the local official.

Personal immunity for the Florentine consuls also tacitly affirmed the principle of diplomatic immunity as applicable to the person of the ambassador. Permanent embassies in the capital had a precedent in the Ottoman Empire, where the Dutch Republic, England, France, the Holy Roman Empire, and Venice, among others, kept them, but the principle of diplomatic immunity was less well respected. Indeed, at the outset of the Long Turkish War, the embassy of the Habsburg Holy Roman Emperor in Istanbul was taken and the staff enslaved.[119] With such hazards a part of the inherited Ottoman political culture, it is perhaps unsurprising that, in addition to the general protections offered by Article 16, the Tuscans negotiated further extensive and specific privileges and protections for diplomatic personnel and the community they headed. These privileges focused on probable points of friction with local officials centering on issues of the application of discriminatory religious law.

Although a reading of prescriptive legal and religious literature can create an unduly rigid impression of religious restrictions on both sides of the Mediterranean, the Ottoman Empire did officially embrace the long-standing tradition of according Christian and Jewish communities protected *dhimmi* status. The hierarchical Ottoman *millet* system accorded each protected religious community a large measure of autonomy in matters of religious and family law and custom on condition of acceptance of Sunni superiority and loyalty to the Ottoman state.[120] The foundational document for this protected minority status was the so-called Pact of Umar, ostensibly a seventh-century agreement between Syrian Christians and Caliph Umar.[121] Well over nine hundred years of Muslim rule in Syria had led to all manner of practical accommodations, but the pact's ban on new Christian structures or even repairs on existing ones made granting permission for new churches potentially controversial. In light of this, the concessions offered in Article 17 of the treaty with Tuscany were substantial: "That the Florentine Consuls and their Nation will have the ability to build and erect a Church in Aleppo, where it will seem best to them for the purpose or according as they will convene the owners of the site as therefore to make it they will have need, ordering Our subjects to facilitate it in what they will be allowed, to the end that they will rest pleased to make the said Church, to have the ability to be officiated by Religious in their way according to the laws and rites of their Catholic faith without anyone whatever they want or [whatever] conditions daring to molest them at all. Permitting as well that the said Florentines will be able to take effect, rent, buy and make houses, shops, and warehouses for their habitation and the accommodation of their merchandise."[122] The almost offhand inclusion of general rights to operate in the residential and commercial property market in the final sentence indicates that the religious article constituted the greater concession. This autonomous Tuscan community would constitute its own society, wherever it pleased, in Ali Pasha's capital, though we can readily imagine that the Florentines would have clustered around their church much as they did in Rome around San Giovanni dei Fiorentini.[123]

The potential for religious conflict was not confined to such apparent flashpoints as the construction of a new religious building but extended to the marks of status that Christians might bear. The Pact of Umar had prohibited Christians from riding and bearing weapons and required such deference as to hand over seats.[124] Ancient prescriptive literature aside, Christian Europeans in late-sixteenth-century Syria had been merchants and pilgrims permitted to visit, in a decidedly subordinate manner, the triumphant Ottoman Empire. In Ali Pasha's Syria, by contrast, the Tuscans were to have a new, officially recognized, status marked by visible symbols of personal position. Article 19 specifies that "Occurring to the Ambassador of the Grand Duke of Tuscany and to the Consuls and Vice Consuls of the Florentine Nation to go outside the City to come to Our audience or for business or otherwise or as well outside of the City for their own affairs or for pleasure they would be able to go on horseback, with accompaniment as well on horseback from their Nation, and with guard that they will have with them for their person dependent on Us, nor that anyone dare to provoke them, or to give them any impediment."[125] In effect, as a result of Tuscany's favored political position, local socioreligious scruples were to be ignored to honor Tuscan diplomats and their retinues not solely for official business but all the time. One can imagine the scandal that might have been caused, then, by a Tuscan consul riding from his grand house first to the newly built church in Aleppo and then off for a jaunt in the countryside, all accompanied by a crowd of mounted Tuscans, yet this was the future envisioned by the treaty. At the highest level of state—Ali Pasha's court—promises of future privileges to Tuscany, an ally willing to provide immediate assistance to a rebel government fighting for its survival, must have seemed an inexpensive price to pay indeed. Outside the elite court circle, however, the privileges accorded to the Tuscans would probably have seemed a violation of traditional social order.

The Tuscan community was, then, to be a self-governing affair practically immune to local laws and local officials and governed by resident diplomatic officials accorded extensive rights. To support this resident diplomatic corps, Article 14 states, "Everything that will be laden aboard the Florentine Vessels or [those] that will traffic under the banner of the Grand Duke of Tuscany will have to pay the right of the Ambassador or of his Resident or prescribed Minister of that Highness as well as the right of the Florentine Consul without encountering opposition."[126] At an initial level, the article functions simply as an agreement between the pasha of Aleppo and the grand duke that the grand duke's ministers will tax Tuscan-flagged shipping, presumably to help defray the cost of Tuscany's diplomatic presence. With the extent to which the pasha anticipated benefiting from the presence of Tuscany's diplomats and because the tax was to fall solely on Tuscan shipping, this article may seem a minor, uncontroversial concession on the part of the pasha. Yet, viewed in the context of the array of powers, privileges, and responsibilities granted to the permanent Tuscan diplomatic presence in Syria, Article 14 takes on a different complexion. Specifically, the power to collect revenue from Tuscan merchants added a right of independent taxation to the formidable array of privileges granted to the Tuscan ambassador. These, in aggregate, contribute to the impression that resident Tuscan diplomats were to function as a semiautonomous government of an expatriate state within a state.

A central component of Tuscan strategy for securing trade rights and other privileges at long distance was a willingness to be among the first to treat with figures of dubious legitimacy who had recently established de facto control. By 1607 Tuscany had already dabbled in a Moroccan civil war and reached an agreement with Boris Godunov's usurper regime in Muscovy. Not being a great power may well have been helpful in such adventures by allowing Tuscan diplomacy to be more agile and less risk-averse than that of the great powers.

For all Tuscany's enthusiastic early support and resulting special privileges, the elephant in the room remained the need to induce other European powers to adhere to the treaty.[127] To that end, the bilateral treaty between the grand duke of Tuscany and the pasha of Aleppo also functioned as a framework for a broader alliance. As we have seen, the opening articles called for Spanish and papal adhesion to a league, but the full ramifications of that become clearer later in the treaty. Article 6 illustrates clearly how nominally exclusively Tuscan privileges might be extended to new members of the league, "As the Most Serene Grand Duke of Tuscany was the first that desired and asked for Our Friendship, we wish that the Tuscan Nation of the aforementioned Highness, and in particular the Florentines, would have the authority to create a Consul or Vice Consul in the cities of Our Dominion, to whom in matters of business or otherwise, as near here we will have declared, will be subject all the other Nations; the Princes and Potentates of the other Kingdoms and Provinces will have as much as Tuscany if they unite in League with us, provided that it will not seem otherwise to that Highness of Tuscany."[128] The implications of the article ran beyond the issue of the future precedence of Tuscan diplomats in the prospective post-Ottoman Middle East. The treaty seems to have been predicated on the assumption that Spain and the papacy would join the league and that, upon joining, they would receive privileges akin to those granted to Tuscany; how Tuscan diplomatic primacy was to be shared is not entirely clear. In any event, the extensive and detailed list of commercial privileges with which much of the treaty was concerned functioned, then, not only as a reward to Tuscany, but as a demonstrative inducement. In the interim, Article 18 promised Tuscany primacy stating,

> And because the Most Serene Grand Duke has demonstrated to us acts of greatest Friendship, for the having of which with us with an express Ambassador requested and, before any other, offered to aggrandize Our Most Excellent House with the promise to acquire and league with us in Friendship, with the said Princes and other Potentates, we wish and command that their Ambassadors, Consuls, and Residents, coming to Our Great Divan, or going to the Palace of Our Qadi, Chechia, Subashi, or others of Our Principal Ministers and officers, they would have the ability, and it being in their arbitration to precede the other Ambassadors, Consuls and Residents of the other Princes and Potentates united with Us, so too all of the other Consuls of

other Nations that will abide in Aleppo, so long as that
Highness of Tuscany does not intend the contrary.[129]

In the event of a victorious outcome, the pasha of Aleppo's court would
have been that which presided over Jerusalem and the lucrative trade
flowing through the ports of the Levant. Precedence in such a court
would have been quite the diplomatic coup for Tuscany, reinforcing
Medici prestige and influence. In sum, Article 18, like so many articles
of the treaty, offered a generous paper concession to Tuscany, which
might have had great value in the event of success.

This extended analysis of the treaty arrangements between the
pasha of Aleppo and the grand duke of Tuscany reflects their importance for the shape of Tuscany's ambitions, not their practical implications. These latter were de minimis, as the realities of military power
and the stark result of defeat rendered them a dead letter. Though Tuscany's efforts were unsuccessful, the model of trading advanced weapons,
money, naval power, and diplomatic recognition for capitulations that
granted diplomatic, economic, and religious privileges amounting to
autonomy would become popular in succeeding centuries.

The treaty's provisions amount to a precise articulation of Tuscany's sweeping ambitions, ambitions that it backed with troops, ships,
money, and supplies. The Syrian adventure represented Tuscany's best
chance for reshaping its future as the leading European power in the
eastern Mediterranean. The window of opportunity was narrow, but
at just this moment Tuscany had relatively powerful naval forces and
unparalleled diplomatic connections to the new regime. With basing
rights in Lebanon and a successful revolt in Cyprus, Tuscany's fleet
would have had a chokehold on the central naval artery linking Istanbul and Alexandria. Tuscany's forces were powerful enough and the
Levantine shore was far enough from Ottoman bases that, with a little
help from Tuscany's allies, communications with Egypt could have
been effectively severed. Whether or not Egypt itself fell, it would have
been likely to drift from the Ottoman orbit, achieving Tuscany's objective of a fragmented empire. This was a plan that could have worked—
indeed, it nearly did—not the idle speculation of an armchair strategist.

The promises of military intervention by a broad coalition of Catholic
Christian allies envisaged by the treaty reflected not only Tuscany's hopes

but also a belief about what was in fact transpiring. Indeed, a month after Corai's stop in Cyprus, on April 6, 1607, a letter from the grand ducal court in Tuscany addressed to Michelangelo Corai recounts the gathering of the fleet of the Catholic alliance.[130] As in decades past, the Spanish ships from Sicily (12), Naples (12), and Spain (40), allied ships from Genoa (8), Don Carlo Doria (14), Malta (5), the papacy (5), and Savoy (2) were to gather in Messina; less Venice, this was the Lepanto coalition.[131] Tuscany was to provide its own force of eight galleys and fifteen galleons and *bertoni* (roundships) "armed with good men and many artillery."[132] On the basis of the information at his disposal, Ambassador Corai had negotiated in good faith. Optimism about the enthusiasm of the Spanish alliance for an all-out naval campaign against the Ottoman Empire proved to be misplaced, however, though not for lack of Tuscan effort.

## Gifts for the Pasha

The treaty Tuscany agreed with Ali Pasha amounted to the realization of a wish list of Tuscan desires. To achieve such a one-sided document, Tuscany offered diplomatic and military support in time of need. As important, Tuscany sought to use extensive and generous gift giving to acquire goodwill and contribute to Ali Pasha's transformation into a sovereign prince. To this end, Tuscany was to offer "items that were of necessity that Sir Michelangiolo agreed with this Most Serene Pasha." The list is among the Medici state papers; it includes "five pieces of field artillery and accompanying battery" and "a great barrel of marzolino," a type of Florentine cheese.[133] The list of diplomatic gifts offers a window into Tuscany's goals and methods in seeking to make a new prince.

Tuscany's ambitions throughout the Mediterranean relied not just on a willingness to deploy naval force, but also on an astute recognition of their partners' priorities. Benefiting from excellent information and an illustrious tradition of diplomacy, Tuscan diplomats soothed concerns and lined pockets even as they negotiated favorable treaty terms. To secure the extraordinarily generous provisions of the treaty between Tuscany and Ali Pasha, Ambassador Corai offered rich gifts.[134] Tuscany agreed to pay Ali Pasha with real items of value in exchange for nothing more than paper promises. Its success was doubtless facilitated by Tuscany's lead diplomat's origins in Aleppo. Ambassador Corai knew both what Tuscany could give and what Ali Pasha needed to make his court. Fortunately, the terms agreed have come down to us:

> Copy of the League and Chapters that were made and agreed in Aleppo between the Most Serene Grand Duke of Tuscany, the Third, and the Most Serene Prince Alij Giampulat Governor of the Kingdom of Syria[135]
>
> *List of the items that were of necessity that Sir Michelangiolo*
> *agreed with this Most Serene Pasha*
>
> Five pieces of field artillery and accompanying battery
>
> Barrel of the arquebus of the measure of 5 palms of a design that Hippolito[136] has in his trunk of -------------- number 1000 ---
>
> Jackets / Mail shirts of the fashion [or fashionable jackets] of the measure that the said Hippolito has in his trunk, that ten conform to the said measure and the others in the best fashion that can be found of ------------------- number 100 ---
>
> Columns of white marble and *marmo mischio* as knows the bearer that 4 white and the others motley [*mischie*] and having to serve as fountain columns 8 -----------
>
> A Lion carved in white marble that would have the two silver parts in front [ / ] above the body of an ox and the other a type of prey with the mouth open from where would be able to exit the water having to serve for a fountain
>
> Two robes of finished velvet on the outside and plush inside of the color as will be most liked, except for black or melancholy colors, having to serve for the Most Serene Pasha and the other for his married wife
>
> A great barrel of marzolino [a type of Florentine cheese]
>
> A gardener and a gunner
>
> Four marked for the *checchià* of rich velvet, in the hand of which remains everything and governs all, of the color green, peacock-colored, red, and sky blue
>
> A dozen gilded pistols of one palm that are found at Vienna of Hungary of the price of an *unghero* each
>
> Two wheel-lock arquebuses
>
> Cuts of ermine or satin for five, or six robes for various officials[137]

If the list of items to be transferred initially appears to be eclectic, ranging from gilded pistols to marble columns, as a group the items have a measure of coherence. Though not sufficient in and of themselves, the listed items represent a significant contribution to the equipment of a new royal court. This is most evident in the fine clothing—two batches, one for the pasha and his wife and another for five or six of the Pasha's officials—and in the carved lion and eight marble columns intended for an apparently elaborate fountain.[138] Yet even the seemingly more martial items—the five pieces of field artillery, the one thousand arquebus barrels, the dozen gilded pistols, and the two wheel-lock arquebuses—seem to be court pieces.[139] With the possible exception of the artillery, they represented a militarily trivial amount of weaponry for any confrontation with an Ottoman imperial field army, as must soon have been expected. A thousand arquebuses and five field guns may have served well, however, for a palace guard. Likewise, the ambiguously named jackets or mail coats may well have been war materiel, because the Tuscans agreed to transfer 100 of them; in the absence of the design referenced, it is difficult to tell.[140] As with the guns, though, the quantity seems to have been just enough for a court guard. The handful of fine pistols and arquebuses were presumably reserved for the pasha and those close to him. Interpreting the list as items for a fledgling court has the added attraction of explaining curious items—the great barrel of cheese and the gardener and gunner—that otherwise seem out of place. The barrel of cheese might have served for a feast, and the gardener and gunner would have served on a palace staff.[141]

Notably absent from the list of items, then, is a sense of urgency, of the need to prioritize military items to meet the coming military challenges. For instance, the cost and transport space required by the eight marble columns might, it would seem, have been replaced with weapons, ammunition, or money, any of which might have aided the rebellion's military fortunes.[142] Like the provisions of the treaty that laid out in detail the future framework within which Tuscans might trade, pray, and conduct diplomacy, this request for columns for a fountain seemed to assume success. For an established sovereign like the Safavid Shah, who might expect to have a court and empire even if the fortunes of war turned against him, such a request might simply have been part of the normal currency of diplomatic exchange. But for a rebel whose dominions were by no means securely held and who might expect an immediate invasion and dreadful consequences in case of defeat, the request for columns bespeaks a striking degree of insouciance. Perhaps the pasha thought to behave as a sovereign as part of his claim to legitimacy. Or perhaps he expected that the opportunity cost of requesting columns was acceptably low or that the Tuscan aid would arrive too late to make a military difference. But if he expected the latter, why begin with requests for weapons? In any case, the pasha certainly expected to enjoy the benefits of power through a flow of luxuries from the alliance.

The agreed items reveal the currency of Tuscan diplomacy and what was ultimately valued in the Levant. As in Tuscany's similarly dubious dealings in Morocco, Tuscan marble was prized.[143] The listed items allow us to conjure up a fountain with eight Tuscan marble columns, four white and four motley (marmo mischio), with a sculpted lion from which water was to emerge.[144] The Tuscans could offer to clothe and arm the sovereign and his household and to provide some of the experts with which to run his court and artillery train.[145] Of modest military utility, Tuscan aid was primarily political. As a partner during peacetime, then, Tuscany could offer luxury goods to help create a dazzling court. Relying on the Galleria dei Lavori, which Ferdinando I had established in the Uffizi as part of the Guardaroba, the Medici possessed both ample collections of court finery and the ability to produce high-quality clothing and luxury goods. Tuscany, therefore, was especially well prepared to equip a prince and his court.[146]

As it happens, we can follow this story a step further and see how Tuscany excelled at the luxury element of this exchange. A further list of items documents the contents of a chest, apparently to be sent to Ambassador Corai.[147] The items in the chest give a vivid impression of the beautiful equipment Ali Pasha and a companion would have had courtesy of the Florentines:

> A shield set with a point in the middle, and worked with foliage all damasked, trimmed with a fringe of silk of more colors, with silver thread and lined with plain linen worked with red, white, and azure silk with its red back case.
>
> A foot soldier's head piece worked with damasked gold similarly trimmed with gilded studs with its little ears [ear pieces] similarly worked and all lined with similar linen, with its red back case.

A breastplate proved by arquebus, grooved according to your list in white, and around the edges likewise trimmed with black velvet with laces of gold and black silk, with its red back case.

A similar backplate [proved] by pistol shot, trimmed similarly with its similar back case.

A similar gorget [proved] by arquebus fringed similarly, with its similar back case.

A headpiece with ear guards adorned with gilded studs in rosette form, [proved] by arquebus, similarly adorned and lined with red on the back, with its red back case.

A breastplate [proved] by arquebus with its two leather thongs covered with the said linen with its similar case.

A gorget for the said breastplate [proved] by arquebus, lined with similar linen, and trimmed with gold laces with its similar back case.

A wheel-lock arquebus with a barrel of length 62 worked from the mouth to the middle and to the breech in gold and adorned with silver with a wheel and tools similarly worked and the stock of newly made threads and perforated silver plate, with its linstock burnished and hunting balls and molds with two pouches for the said, one of black cordovan leather and the other of flesh tone linen. A gilded iron key and bored through with its cord of gold and red silk and azure.

A pistol with a violet colored barrel, worked from the mouth to the middle and to the breach adorned in gold, with wheel and similarly worked tools with boxes of pear dyed red with their instruments with two pouches of black cordovan leather and with bags lined with cloth of silver and red, white, and azure silk adorned with laces, with two red backed upper garments, With also the arquebus of Messer Michelagnolo that was there in the guardaroba.[148]

The items in the chest overlap only in a general sense with some of the items on the list Corai had agreed with Ali Pasha. Indeed, the generically elegant military items and the inclusion of Corai's gun give the impression that this was assembled in part by rummaging around in the Guardaroba. The careful description of the beautifully worked items reinforces the sense that Tuscany mobilized the resources of its grand ducal workshops and the stores of the Guardaroba to provide symbolically rich items to substantiate Ali Pasha's claim to status. These elegant objects were to constitute the opening gifts of an enduring alliance. The treaty detailing the terms and conditions of that alliance is dated "On the 10th of the Moon Giamadilacher. in the year 1016½," or about October 2, 1607.[149] Sadly for Tuscan hopes and Ali Pasha's fortunes, that was far too late. Ali Pasha's regime would not last the month.

## Defeat and Departure

> Then again, governments set up overnight, like everything in nature whose growth is forced lack strong roots and ramifications. So they are destroyed in the first bad spell. This is inevitable unless those who have suddenly become princes are of such prowess that overnight they can learn how to preserve what fortune has suddenly tossed into their laps, and unless they can then lay foundations such as other princes would have already been building on.[150]
>
> —NICCOLÒ MACHIAVELLI, *The Prince*, "VII: New principalities acquired with the help of fortune and foreign arms"

For a rebel to become a recognized prince, his regime must survive. This, Machiavelli warned, generally fails to happen. The Ottoman recovery showed decisively the difference between an enduring empire that drew on wells of prestige and loyalty centuries deep and an upstart local dynasty. The initially propitious set of circumstances that enabled Ali Pasha's bid for independence slowly disintegrated as the Ottomans came under the firm leadership of Kuyucu Murad Pasha (d. 1611). After negotiating peace with the Habsburgs at Zsitvatorok in 1606, Murad Pasha rose steeply in rank. The death of Lala Mehmed in June 1606 and the execution of his successor, Derviş Pasha, in December led to Murad Pasha's elevation to the grand vizierate. Proceeding carefully and skillfully, Murad Pasha assembled an overwhelming Ottoman field army using the newly available Ottoman forces in Europe. He proceeded to snuff out or neutralize the *celâlî*s of Anatolia as he marched relentlessly eastward. With the collapse of Ali Pasha's allies in Anatolia and a simultaneous rebellion in Baghdad, Ali Pasha was left to face the main Ottoman field army on unfavorable ground at Oruç Ovası on October 22–24, 1607. Though the

Ottoman force of 75,000 was nearly double his, Ali Pasha's army ac-
quitted itself well for two days. On the third, however, Ali's army was decisively defeated, sustaining catastrophic losses in battle and subsequent
executions. Ali Pasha fled, attempting to secure his family in Aleppo's
castle before making his way on a complex journey starting with Baghdad.
His plan failed. Canbulad property was confiscated, Aleppo fell swiftly,
and Ali's family and supporters suffered grievous losses in a wave of executions. Ali's own fate was more complicated, involving rejection by Shah
'Abbas, failed negotiations with the major *celâlîs* in Anatolia, and a nominal and controversial in-person reconciliation with Sultan Ahmed I
(1590–1617). Appointed beylerbeyi of Temeşvar, but never accepted as reconciled by substantial portions of the Ottoman elite, Ali fled to Belgrade
in April 1609. The end was near. Murad Pasha, returning west, ordered
Ali's execution, which took place around March 1, 1610.[151]

As for the Tuscans, things initially looked grim, but they soldiered
on with their plans. As Kaled El Bibas has shown, even as Ali Pasha's
regime fell in Aleppo, the Tuscan delegation led by Ippolito Leoncini
sought to pursue a similar treaty with the Lebanese Druze emir Fakhr-al-
Dīn II. Luxury goods, the support of the Tuscan fleet, and artillery
all featured, though with the difference that the matter of the Tuscan
prisoners captured in the fall of Ali Pasha were now added to the discussions. The emir was savvy enough to ask for artillery experts and
materials to produce ten to twelve artillery pieces, twice as many as the
pasha had requested. Agreeing to a treaty in 1608, Fakhr-al-Dīn was
eventually chased out of Lebanon by Grand Vizier Nasuh Pasha in 1613;
he fled to Tuscany. Fakhr-al-Dīn spent five years in exile there before
returning to Lebanon. Temporarily reconciled with the Ottomans, he
was eventually executed in 1635.[152] Just as Leoncini continued the mission to Lebanon, so also did Corai persist with his project, though at
considerable personal cost, as we shall see. Indeed, Corai reported from
Aleppo on December 6, 1607, that he was heading to Persia to continue
his embassy.[153] To Iran, therefore, we must proceed in Chapter 8.

## Conclusion

The first decade of the seventeenth century was perhaps the closest the
Ottoman state came to falling apart in the early modern period. The

Long Turkish War against the Austrian Habsburgs (1593–1606) left the Ottomans vulnerable to *celâlî* rebellion in Anatolia, Safavid invasion, rebellion in Syria, sedition in Lebanon and the Greek world, and political turmoil at the center.[154] The Ottoman Empire did not, of course, fall apart. Indeed, it may not have been all that close to it. Contemporaries, however, thought they smelled blood and felt that a final push might have done the trick. They could not have known toppling the Ottoman state would be a three-hundred-year chimera; for them it was new. Hopes for wrecking it ignored two key problems. First, nearly all dreams of destroying the power of the Ottomans depended on rallying an implausibly large group of allies, many of whom were perfectly happy to see the powerful Ottomans fighting someone else. Philip III of Spain, for instance, was in no need of new wars, having plenty of other problems. Second, in light of the Ottoman Empire's power and internal diversity, plans for its destruction nearly always featured optimistic expectations about the prospects for massive rebellion in support of outside intervention. Exiles kindled such hopes. Yet exiles can be dangerous guides to policy, as Machiavelli perspicaciously noted in his *Discourses* in the section "How Dangerous It Is to Believe Exiles": "As for vain promises and expectations, their desire to return home is so great that they sincerely believe many things that are false and add many things to them cunningly. Consequently, between what they believe and what they say they believe, they fill you with such expectations that, if you rely on them, either you incur futile expenses or you engage in an undertaking that destroys you."[155] Even in the case of its support for one of the largest rebellions that the Ottoman Empire faced in the early modern period, the Grand Duchy of Tuscany might have been wise to remember not just the examples from classical antiquity on which Machiavelli drew, but also the history of the many generations of illustrious Tuscan exiles produced by centuries of political turmoil. Dreams are powerful things, however, and exiles can be spellbinding. Lured by the dream of what a new Levant of friendly successor states would mean for their power, wealth, and faith, Tuscan diplomats and envoys sought to assemble coalitions to act in alliance with Ottoman rebels. If only they could fashion a new prince, then Florence could prosper in the way that Venice had once done—if only.

# 8

# Persian Dreams

## The Consequences of Defeat

Enduring war, defeat, and torture before his deliverance, the Tuscan envoy Michelangelo Corai reemerged on the path to Iran in early December 1607. Before departing from Aleppo, however, he dispatched three documents to Tuscany: a bill of exchange for a substantial sum, a concise letter to Ippolito Leoncini, and a long letter to the grand duke. The documents arrived in early February 1608. A brief letter, dated February 11, 1608, related how the three documents arrived in Europe. It stated that envelopes for "Your Lordship" and Ippolito Leoncini "from Timotteo Mayen, a merchant resident in Aleppo, were sent on the ship San Matteo that arrived here today."[1] The author of the note reports that a "bill of exchange of eight hundred pieces of eight Spanish *reales* from Sir Michelangelo Corai" had also arrived.[2] Aboard the *San Matteo* came news from the fallen rebel capital and a glimmer of hope for Tuscan projects.

A long, partially enciphered letter, dated December 6, 1607, and intended for the galleon *San Matteo* bound for Marseille, grippingly relates to Ferdinando I the last days of the rebellion in Syria.[3] Corai began the letter by recounting that "Now you will know that on 6 October, as soon as Signor Hippolito left, came news that the Vizier had arrived in Adana and was going to come by Baias." Ali Pasha, therefore, went to put his troops in order.[4] As we have seen, the pasha of Adana had been an important fellow rebel, guarding a major road from Istanbul to Aleppo. In short, the grand vizier's army's arrival there was grim news for Ali Pasha. Even before the major battle, matters had begun to deteriorate in Aleppo. The citizens closed their houses and shops to protect them from the depredations of the freebooters (probably *celâlîs*, or bandits) about to depart with the pasha's army. "The Pasha, hearing many rumors from the city, commanded their General and his Uncle Aiderbech and many other Captains to go into the city armed and prevent this evident peril, which was executed and they castigated them a great deal." Upon the departure of these forces, the freebooters returned and redoubled their lawlessness.[5] Ali Pasha had to return to restore order; he beheaded two of the freebooters. In all, the disorder in Aleppo had lasted six days.[6]

This settled, Ali Pasha left with thirty thousand troops, garrisoning the fortress in Aleppo to prepare it against a powerful siege. As Corai noted, it was "not for want of that" that the pasha's plans failed.[7] Denouncing the rumors and confusion surrounding the pasha's actions, Corai told the story of the decisive battle clearly and concisely. He explained that Ali Pasha's army had fought hard with that of the grand vizier starting on October 22. Having driven back the grand vizier's forces twice, the freebooters then pursued the Ottoman army as they retired toward a hill where the Ottoman artillery was positioned. This proved decisive. The artillery opened fire on the pasha's freebooters, who fled because they were "all surprised and also for the great fame" of the artillery. The grand vizier's forces, "following them [the freebooters] put them all to flight, and he who had a horse was saved by flight on it and he who did not have a horse was killed so that as they say eight thousand people died." Corai noted that the first two setbacks of the grand vizier's army had also entailed heavy losses and that the battle was fought "near a place called Amch," two days from Aleppo.[8]

The aftermath of the defeat came swiftly to Aleppo. "The same night after the news arrived, so also arrived the Pasha, entering the city with part of his army to put in order all his things and possessions for flight."

Naturally, discipline broke down with the arrival of the remaining soldiers, who, shut out of what had been their own city, proceeded to sack the suburbs.[9] The collapse of civil order caused "everyone to fortify himself in his house" and defend himself as well as he could. Considerable bloodshed ensued, including the burning of a nearby Jewish house, apparently with the inhabitants inside, when the plunderers failed to break in.[10] In other instances, once the plunderers sacked the house and stripped the inhabitants naked, they took their children, who they threatened in order to find out where their money was hidden. The inhabitants cried out for the speedy arrival of the grand vizier to deliver them from the depredations of the defeated army.[11] In Corai's account, the situation inside the city was even worse, with Ali Pasha's soldiers breaking into shops and houses and sacking them. The destruction stopped only when Ali Pasha, having left five hundred freebooters in the fortress, took his remaining forces in the direction of Antep (Gaziantep), and "in this way the city was also liberated from this terrible generation."[12]

After Ali Pasha's main army departed, the inhabitants of Aleppo rose up in rage. They beset those who remained with stones, killing many and so threatening Ali Pasha's uncle Aiderbech that he escaped only because of his good horse.[13] Lingering in the devastated city was most unwise. "In the following days, some Turks came to the city to see it and if any of the freebooters remained and all of these that they found they killed and drank their blood, of many they gouged out their hearts and livers and roasting them they ate them for their vendetta." Corai gives further details of the "horrendous cruelty," but that one image is clear enough.[14] On October 29, the grand vizier approached within two miles of the city and appointed a new governor. This new pasha of Aleppo entered the city on November 1 and "the same day the Vizier entered also" to offer a deal to those holed up in the fortress. He offered these rebels their lives and a pardon if they vacated the fortress. They did not respond, and the vizier ordered an attack.[15] The arrival of the artillery the next day broke the rebels' resistance, "and like men without faith" they sought terms of surrender that guaranteed their persons and goods. The fortress fell on November 4.[16] The grand vizier entered two days later and proceeded to seize the property of Ali Pasha and his relatives. His men found a large trove walled up underground in the house of Hussein Pasha, Ali Pasha's uncle.[17] The arrival of the Ottoman army ended Aleppo's role as a rebel capital and brought a measure of peace and order to its inhabitants.

This account of Ali Pasha's ignominious defeat and the terrible behavior of his troops cast Tuscan's putative ally in a grim light. Still, a measure of interpretative caution is in order. Corai used cipher strategically to convey a narrative consistent with his cover in plaintext and a more hopeful account of the rebels' actions in ciphertext. The foregoing narrative, although a fair account of the fall of Aleppo, was also written entirely in plaintext Italian. In the first portion of the letter detailed in the preceding account, the rebels come off badly, as perhaps they deserved to. The letter's tone shifts, however, once the cipher begins.

Having recounted the publicly available information about the fall of Ali Pasha and the horrifying damage inflicted on Aleppo, Corai switched to partial encipherment. He did so to recount that Ali Pasha had left with ten thousand horse and five thousand foot for Antep.[18] A messenger arrived from Constantinople with instructions for the grand vizier. Simultaneously, news also filtered to Aleppo that Ali Pasha had had twenty thousand soldiers, part on horseback and the others on donkeys at Antep, before heading to Malatya, which he "entered with cunning by having *counterfeit* letters in the name of and with the seal of *the Vizier* as if he had been sent by him" (italics represents ciphertext). In short, with breathtaking gall Ali Pasha pretended that he had been sent by the grand vizier, with whom he had in reality just fought a battle. Ali Pasha then proceeded to demand money for his troops from Malatya, threatening to sack the city.[19] Meanwhile, the grand vizier sent forces to clear the villages neighboring Aleppo of remaining freebooters and dispatched two armies against the rebels of Caramania (southern Anatolia). Ever hopeful, Corai reported that columns of ten thousand and twelve thousand Ottoman troops had been "*routed by the rebels* and cut in pieces" and that in response the vizier was sending part of his forces against the rebels and another to displace Ali Pasha from Malatya. The grand vizier's forces amounted to seventy thousand troops, though of low quality in Corai's estimation, and crippled by the death of so "many *horses*, mules, and camels" from "*cold* and *hunger*."[20]

As in his letter from Cyprus, Corai played a double game with the partial use of cipher, proving considerably more critical of Ali Pasha and his freebooters in the plaintext than he was in cipher. In ciphertext, by contrast, his message offered news of the continuing military hopes for Ali Pasha and the other rebels. Even so, Corai's letter continued to unblinkingly recount the strengthening of the Ottoman position. Responding quickly to the restoration of Ottoman imperial authority, local elites scrambled to declare their loyalty to the grand vizier, showering him with gifts and contributions to the army. Reporting the events by date, Corai noted the arrival of seven hundred with the son of the old pasha of Damascus on November 11.[21] On November 20, "the *Emir Giediit King* of the Arabs" gave the "*Vizier six beautiful horses,* sixty *Camels,* three thousands *geldings,*" and large quantities of grain, and his son the Emir Giosef arrived on November 24 with "money to the value of 100,000 *sultanini.*"[22] Likewise, "the same day, 1,500 *Janissaries of Damascus*" arrived in Aleppo having caught a rebel column sent by the Lebanese emir Fakhr-al-Dīn (Faccardino to the Tuscans) to the aid of Ali Pasha. These troops had arrived too late to aid Ali Pasha and seem to have returned to "*obedience to the Vizier.*"[23]

The defeat of Ali Pasha left Emir Faccardino in an impossible position. Faccardino sought to find a lost English *bertone* that had been loaded with presents for the Vizir by the emir, but another ship that went to find the English vessel had not succeeded. Reacting to this misfortune, Faccardino had imprisoned the European merchants in his port to force them to seek the lost ship. They were not successful and their failure to find it had put them in peril. In mixed plain and ciphertext, Corai then reported a rumor that Faccardino was putting some ships in order for a plan to flee to Italy.[24]

Even as the Lebanese emir sought to make his escape to Tuscany, the citizens of Aleppo were beset by an opposite fear. Corai reported that on December 1 the grand vizier had entered the city, but a rumor had arrived of a "*command from the Great Turk*" that ordered the grand vizier to return to the Hungarian front. His withdrawal would leave the city of Aleppo vulnerable to Ali Pasha's remaining forces. Such were the rebels' depredations on their earlier departure that the citizens of Aleppo went to petition the grand vizier to stay in Aleppo to protect them from another sack by Ali Pasha's forces.[25] Corai related news, or perhaps just promising rumors for the rebel side, that after the grand vizier's departure for Syria, the rebels and some forty thousand soldiers between Bursa and Constantinople had gone to seize Bursa and threatened Constantinople.[26] If true, the threat to the heart of the Ottoman state presented the grand vizier with a direct challenge to his position.

Closer to hand, Corai reported on the news from central Iraq. There, "the Son of the Zicala was named the *Pasha of Babylon* and on the 28th of November sent his lieutenant to these parts but some want to say that *that Pasha* will not surrender or give place, and that the slaves of *Babylon* would rather give it to the *King of Persia* than leave *their Pasha* and take a new one."[27] Even as the tide of war had turned against Ali Pasha and Emir Faccardino, the news in the east remained more encouraging. This, in turn, shaped both Corai's course of action and his sense of the direction of Tuscan policy. It was on Safavid Iran and its neighboring rebels in Iraq that Tuscan hopes would increasingly rest. From that quarter, Corai had most encouraging, if vague, news to report. "From *Persia* there is news that *that King makes very large*[28] preparations *for war* the which [king] understands that *the Great Turk ~~made~~ has commanded the Vizier* that after having reformed these countries *to go against him*."[29]

Corai ranged across the whole region with reports of military movements and plans for future operations, remaining nevertheless keenly engaged in Tuscan grand strategy. His ability to do so reflects the swift flow of information around the Mediterranean and Tuscany's reputation. Corai wrote, "you will understand better than I the success of *the enterprise of Bona in Barbary*," referring to letters from Marseille, but he then mentioned the perhaps even more damaging corsair enterprises of the English and Turkish ships.[30] Corai's inapposite comparison with the massive Tuscan raid on Bona, which was to be so extensively commemorated in Palazzo Pitti, points to an emerging risk for him. With every passing month he grew more distant from the Tuscan court. Not having spent much time there in the first place, his judgment about Tuscan interests would begin to drift. As Ferdinando I frenetically sought opportunities in Brazil and Sierra Leone and his successor celebrated Galileo's string of triumphs, Corai found himself a world away in Safavid Iran.[31]

Making it there, however, had required considerable travails. Corai disclaimed explaining in detail as "a too bothersome business, and it would seem that one wanted to recount the tears of death" before thanking God that he had been delivered.[32] In that Corai wanted to avoid revelations of his true identity, his brevity probably showed as much prudence as stoicism. As we shall see, he was certainly happy to complain at length about much lesser troubles with snow on the way to Iran. As to his travails, Corai remained remarkably brazen in lying under interrogation, blaming his putative Jewish enemies of falsely accusing him when his ciphertext throughout the letter confesses his guilt. Corai wrote,

> there being unfortunately spread the report by all that be-
> cause I came to these shores having brought *three arquebuses*
> *to the Pasha from* Christendom and that I having advised how
> *to recast* those *burst artillery* and also to make them anew,
> how after *the Pasha* was departed I was together with *his Ma-*
> *jordomo* to *provision the fortress* and order everything that was
> needed of *munitions* and of the other, which came to the ears
> *of the Vizier* who sent for me to call and he *examined* me and
> asked to account for all these particular things, but I who
> am nothing, am able to do nothing, and am worth nothing,
> excused and defended myself as well as I could marveling
> unfortunately that these things had been said of me, dem-
> onstrating that all of this had no other origin than the envy
> and malignity of those cursed Jews my enemies who had ac-
> cused me and that nobody could prove these things.[33]

More breathtaking audacity is hard to imagine. Distressingly using anti-Semitic rhetoric, Corai mobilized a shared prejudice to suggest that he had been falsely accused of the rebellion, treason, and espio-nage of which he was most definitely guilty.

The grand vizier had not risen to his position of prominence through credulity. His response to Corai consisted of an offer of com-mercial privileges for him and his family before consigning him to de-tention. There he was questioned about why he had come with a pair of foreigners, one of whom had left while the other remained.[34] Corai wrote in a mix of cipher and plaintext that, "one day I was taken to a house as if for other affairs, where there were *lying four soldiers* who *bound* me and wanted to get my *secrets* by giving me *torments*, I with the help of Our Lord supported them with patience and they seeing that they could not penetrate that which they desired and being tired of *tormenting me* left to chastise me in another way."[35] The soldiers switched to demanding

500 piasters (Spanish silver dollars), to which Corai protested that he
"not having 500 nor 50" had to rely on the help of the French merchant
Timoteo Moyen, who Corai called "a man most true, most honorably
beloved and praised by all," who paid the sum for him. Corai seems to
have taken Moyen into his confidence at this point.[36]

Freed from captivity but still precariously situated in Otto-
man-controlled Aleppo, Corai faced a choice. He might have risked
staying in his devastated hometown, abandoning the long career of adventure that had brought him so far. Having negotiated with princes,
played at the highest levels of international politics for a decade, and
survived ferocious interrogation, Corai instead embraced the travails
of pursuing his great project as the Tuscan ambassador at large. Doing
so from Ottoman Aleppo, however, left Corai with a decision. He decided "*to take myself to Persia* to dispatch *the embassy* and my commission
to *that Majesty*, as *the Caravan* had not yet left that three months before
ought to have left for these reasons of wars and I keep *the letter* still with
me, I was all the same resolved to present to *His Majesty* pleasing God,
the which seemed better to me than going to find *the Emir Faccardino*
or other, there being with him few men still on the balance and not
knowing to what there will be resolved."[37] Corai's decision to continue
to Iran reflected the insecurity of his situation in Aleppo, his sense of
mission, the presence of the detained caravan, and his assessment that
the prospects of the Lebanese emir were dim. Corai's choice remained
a bold one, all the same, for he intended to proceed to Iran without instructions from Tuscany and with a letter to Shah 'Abbas written in the
radically different political situation that had obtained while Corai
was in Tuscany.

His confidence in so doing rested not only on his expectations of
Tuscan approbation for his courageous conduct, but also on encouragement closer to him. Corai wrote,

> And all the more that *the Pasha* at this same time sent me a
> letter in secret *by a Persian Chiasbech* one of his favorites de-
> siring that I go when it was possible to find *the King of Persia*
> and treat with *His Majesty* about what we had many times
> discussed together that is to *league with him in friendship* in *I
> am taken* with that and if he *can* have *help from there* will be all

the more dear to him if at least he was persuaded to give it *his band comes with those greater forces* that may be possible to *damage the Turk* that he would not anyway fail to do the same because he having *sworn to have revenge* even if it would cost him his life would never abandon this *enterprise* and that he knows that none of his could do that which I can do if I *go there* he asked me to not fail *to go* when I could and to do that which I can and not to leave him in this extremity, that with time if God will help him he would recognize me saying that he would willingly have sent me that commodity that I ought to have to make *this journey* but I would excuse him on account of the distance and the dangers that he runs to come *here* the said *Persian* read me the letter showing *his handwriting* and the *seal of the Pasha.*[38]

As we have seen, Ali Pasha's rhetoric proved unreliable, for he did attempt a temporarily successful reconciliation with the Ottoman establishment before being executed. He may have done better to stand by his promises to Corai and Shah 'Abbas, but his situation was desperate either way. In any event, this secret message seems to have been quite persuasive to Corai, no doubt helped by its flattery of Corai's clearly remarkable abilities.

Corai's decision to recount Ali Pasha's missive in his own letter, including the story of the secret message delivered at great risk with its assertion of continuing defiance and confidence in the Safavid shah, acted to justify both Corai's decision to go to Iran and his continuing to adhere to the strategic logic of that alliance. If Ali Pasha were to continue his struggle in eastern Anatolia, the pasha of Babylon (probably Baghdad, Iraq) were to defect to the Safavids, and the grand vizier were to be forced to return to the Ottoman heartland to deal with threats from rebels and on the Hungarian frontier, then the prospects of a successful Safavid invasion looked bright. Corai simply needed to make it to Iran in time to persuade Shah 'Abbas to concentrate his energies for the next campaigning season. Tuscany's original plans may have failed miserably, but hope remained. To this end, Corai tapped his new friend for funds: "I went at once to the said Mr. *Moyen* [and] showed him my *patent from Your Highness* given to me and I asked him in virtue of that if he would help me again with 300 piasters which would be refunded by *Your Highness* which he willingly did both for the principal service to succeed for the praise of God, benefiting and *augmenting* of *all* Christendom as also to serve *Your Highness* for that which he can be obliged to serve even to the shedding of his blood in everything that you will command him."[39] This last may have normally been a formulaic phrase intended to profess loyalty, but Moyen's decision to fund Corai's expedition certainly put him at very real risk of his life. In profound gratitude for Moyen's intervention first to save his life and then to restore his embassy's prospects, Corai implored the grand duke to honor the debt of eight hundred pieces of eight in a bill of exchange directed to a Mr. Pesciolini in Marseille. Corai then promised to keep the grand duke informed of all that happened in these parts before his return to Tuscany, which he hoped would be quick.[40]

Finally, Corai returned to the subject of the treaty agreed with Ali Pasha. Far from believing the treaty to be a dead letter, Corai expressed firm hopes that Tuscany's dreams of a new Levant would be realized. He wrote, "as to the things *agreed* with *this Most Serene Pasha* in any case he has no other intention than *to revenge himself* and there is the opinion that the *Vizier* will not be able *to stay here* too long but will need to be in the Spring in Hungary or in Persia the which leaving from *here will make a road for the Pasha* to return here, and how very easily he will *become Lord* again of all as we hope in God he will be able to succeed."[41] In closing his letter, Corai explained that he hoped to leave in three or four days in a caravan of thirty people to Babylon. From there he planned to go swiftly to the domains of Shah 'Abbas with ten or twelve people.[42] Corai's hopeful, if formulaic, closing, included two further pieces of information, namely the constant presence of the secretary Georg Krieger and the plan to send the letter on the galleon *San Matteo* "that heads to Marseille and by the usual route of Pesciolini that serves for news."[43]

Three days later, Corai wrote another, much shorter, letter from Aleppo, apparently to Leoncini, who was expected to have returned to Tuscany by then, having been "saved and liberated from the awful perils and travails that after your departure came to find us."[44] Corai had, unfortunately, borne the brunt of these calamities. In this letter, though, he wrote that "The things of God from here your lordship will know that I leave to the worshipful counsel and prudence of His Most Serene

Highness who will know how to govern himself according to the news that will be sent from here by mister Tim.° M.ᵉⁿ our very dear, courteous, and loving [man] who will apprize you of all that will happen with me as I have asked him and he has promised me to want to do with all the commodity that he will be able to do it, because I go now on the way to Persia."⁴⁵ Corai continued by expressing his intention to carry out his mission to "the Majesty of Persia as much for the commission that I have from His Most Serene Highness as also for the part of God here."⁴⁶ Corai's sense of holy mission helps explain his perseverance. His ability to continue this journey, however, had required the assistance of a French merchant, whose expenses Corai asked to be reimbursed, for Moyen had "helped me in my extreme necessity at the time when I was abandoned by all, and liberated me, to say almost, from death and recovered my honor, life, and house"; helping his merchant savior, Corai also recommended him for any commercial business services the grand duke might need.⁴⁷

## Ambassadors and Grand Strategy

Trekking with the caravan from Iraq to Iran, Corai trod a path to an empire he knew well. Indeed, his embassy stood at the end of a long series of contacts stretching back decades. To understand what brought Corai to Iran and the situation he found there, we need to consider two intertwined issues: Tuscan-Safavid relations and the role of the ambiguous agents that tied them together in the late sixteenth and early seventeenth centuries. This tie, stretching several thousand miles, already inherently tenuous, was further frayed and twisted by the intertwined problems of uncertainty and ambiguity. The agents, adventurers, and envoys who made the long, perilous journey often served multiple masters and played many roles. As a result, Tuscany's relationship with Iran was embedded in larger stories, which bind together Tuscan forays overseas, the personal histories of the agents, and the activities of Tuscany's primary allies.⁴⁸

The centrality of individual envoys to the relationship between Tuscany and Iran and the ambiguity surrounding their position demand that attention focus not just on the content of the messages, but also on the mechanics of diplomacy. Much scholarship on Renaissance

Italian diplomacy has focused on its role as the precursor to the modern
system. There is considerable merit to this view when considering the
resident embassies in Europe and their emergent bureaucracies.[49] At
longer distance, however, matters were quite different. The envoys who
bound together the Safavid and Medici dynasties shared something of
the world of their Renaissance predecessors portrayed in paintings like
Hans Holbein's *The Ambassadors*, but they had more in common with
the charlatan adventurer Niccolò Vespucci or the English captain cum
ambassador to the Mughal court whose position he usurped in the fictional world of Salman Rushdie's *Enchantress of Florence*.[50] Returning
from the world of art—incidentally, never far from the scene at the glittering Medici and Safavid courts—a confluence of political interests
brought the Grand Duchy of Tuscany and Safavid Iran into periodic
contact. Shared dreams of destroying, or at least diminishing, the Ottoman Empire underpinned plans for military cooperation between
Tuscany and Iran from the 1580s to the 1610s.

The Medici were altogether fortunate in the timing of their interest
in cooperating with Safavid Iran, for the reigns of Ferdinand I (r. 1587–
1609), Cosimo II (r. 1609–1621), and Ferdinando II (r. 1621–1670) overlapped with that of the Safavid Empire's most dynamic ruler, Shah
'Abbas I (r. 1588–1629).[51] A very brief sketch of the regional power dynamics and political history, painted in broad strokes, may help elucidate the position of the Safavids in a wider imperial context.[52] To the
north, the Safavids faced a still distant but expanding Muscovy, whose
conquest of the khanates of Kazan (1552) and Astrakhan (1556) and
whose foundation of the port of Archangel (1583) created, as we have
seen in Chapter 3, a tenuous trade link between the Caspian and the
White Sea.[53] To the south and east, cultural and commercial possibilities opened with the expanding sultanates of the Deccan and maritime
southeast Asia, but they were constrained by Portuguese dominance
of Iran's maritime affairs through its control of Hormuz.[54] More substantially, the Safavids had a complex relationship with Mughal India,
from playing host (1544) to the temporarily exiled Mughal emperor
Humayun (r. 1530–1540 and 1555–1556) during the reign of Shah Tahmasp (r. 1524–1576) to a long Safavid-Mughal rivalry over control of
Kandahar.[55] Indicating the changing dynamics of the relationship, Humayun took Kandahar on his path to retaking India and then ceded

it to Tahmasp in exchange for his assistance in recovering his throne. The Mughals then retook Kandahar on the death of the Safavid governor and lost it to Tahmasp in 1558. The city was then betrayed to the Mughal emperor Akbar in 1595 before Shah 'Abbas recovered it in 1622. The Safavids lost the city again in 1638 and retook it in 1653.[56]

As commercially, culturally, and politically valuable as these links could be, Safavid Iran's primary challenge lay with its powerful Sunni neighbors. In the northeast, the Safavids engaged in a sometimes ferocious rivalry with the Uzbeks. This violence, the religious conflict between the Sunni Uzbeks and the messianic Shi'ism of the Safavids, and Uzbek territorial claims on Safavid lands made the Uzbeks foes of the Safavids and natural allies of the Ottomans against them. Both the Uzbeks and the Ottomans had fought the Safavids in the early years of the Safavid Empire's formation, and the expansive claims of all three states meant that the frontiers were always potentially fluid and in contention. In the earliest years of the Safavid Empire, it had appeared that the Safavids would be on the offensive, destabilizing their neighbors. As Abbas Amanat has argued, the founding Safavid shah, Ismail I (1487–1524), brought together a potent combination of Twelver Shi'ism with a messianic twist, leadership of the Safavi order, and a noble military inheritance to develop a power base in Iranian Azerbaijan. Ismail could draw on a legacy of regional political importance, for the Safavi had served as a rallying point for Turkomans displaced by the Ottomans. In northwest Iran, they built a Turkoman tribal confederacy, called Kizilbash by their enemies, in the 1480s. Starting in 1501, a decade of rapid expansion under the young Ismail Safavi and spearheaded by the Kizilbash, swept the Safavids into power across the Iranian plateau, including Iran and parts of eastern Turkey, Iraq, the Caucasus, Afghanistan, and Turkmenistan. In the west, Safavid-Ottoman relations had proved especially fractious, for the Ottomans perceived the Safavids as both a religious and a political threat to their lands and the loyalties of their subjects. Ottoman Sultan Selim I Yavuz, "the Grim" (r. 1512–1520) moved swiftly and decisively. Selim's crushing victory over the Safavids at the Battle of Chaldiran (August 23, 1514) shattered the momentum of the Safavids, secured Ottoman control of Anatolia, and paved the way for the extremely rapid Ottoman conquest of the Mamluks in 1516–1517. The Safavids held onto their power base in Iran as the Ottomans under Suleiman the Magnificent (Kanuni—the Lawgiver; r. 1520–1566) focused on conquests in the Balkans and the Mediterranean and extending Ottoman reach out to Yemen and Algiers. Even so, the Ottomans occasionally pummeled the Safavids, fighting a war with the Safavids from 1532 to 1535 in which the Ottomans took Tabriz, the Safavid capital at the time. Suleiman marched into Baghdad in 1534 and invaded again in 1546 and 1553 before concluding a treaty recognizing Ottoman control over Baghdad and Kurdistan in 1555; Basra had fallen in 1549. The Safavid central state remained relatively weak during the remainder of the reign of Ismail and during the long, culturally important reign of Shah Tahmasp I (r. 1524–1576), but the tribal confederation that the Safavids led maintained firm control over the Iranian plateau. The manifest vulnerability of Tabriz led Shah Tahmasp to move the capital to Qazvin, where it stayed until 'Abbas founded his new capital at Isfahan in 1598.[57]

When Shah 'Abbas came to the throne after the years of political turmoil that succeeded the death of Shah Tahmasp, the military situation was dire. Tabriz and Herat had been lost, civil war had devastated the empire, the central administration was weak, and various Kizilbash tribes had seized control of parts of the empire. Shah 'Abbas consolidated power, first by eliminating the power broker who had fatally underestimated the young shah and expected to control him. 'Abbas realized that foreign wars were feeding into domestic political weakness, empowering the Kizilbash tribes. His insight was that he needed peace, even on dreadful terms, to strengthen his state internally and consolidate his power. To this end, he conceded Azerbaijan and other territories to the Ottomans after a decade and a half of war (the treaty was signed on March 21, 1590), Herat to the Uzbeks, and Kandahar (1594/1595) to the Mughals. He turned to asserting royal power inside the Safavid Empire, seizing provinces for royal control that had effectively been run by tribes and building a powerful army loyal to him that prominently included gunpowder forces. This consolidation complete, he burst forth, retaking all the lost lands and presiding ultimately over a strongly governed, powerful Safavid Empire stretching from Tabriz (retaken 1603) and Iraq (taken in 1623–1624) to Herat (recaptured 1598) and Kandahar (recaptured 1622) and including the major Portuguese position of Hormuz (captured 1622). European allies, with their gunpowder weapons and ships, could be helpful in this effort; the English aided the Safavid conquest of Hormuz in 1622.[58] Domestically, the economic base was, in addition to the usual agricultural and transit revenues, the silk export industry. This flourished under 'Abbas, as did the merchant communities that marketed it, including especially the Armenians, who he patronized.[59] In 1604–1606, the Safavids forcibly transplanted the Armenian community from Julfa—which the Safavids destroyed during their retreat from the Ottoman front in northeast Anatolia—to northern silk-producing provinces and 'Abbas's new capital of Isfahan. From 1598, 'Abbas had started to move the capital from Qazvin to Isfahan, and the Armenians built an urban quarter there called New Julfa.[60]

In short, from the turmoil of the 1580s the Safavid Empire sank to its nadir around the beginning of Shah 'Abbas's reign. The empire's phoenix-like recovery involved such spectacular military, political, economic, and social reforms as to amount to a new foundation of the empire. Amid these dramatic developments, European adventurers, diplomats, priests, merchants, and statesman who saw both opportunity and peril in Safavid Iran dramatically increased their engagement with the empire. The difficulties of the journey, Ottoman hostility, and Portugal's fraught relationship with the Safavids, provoked by Portugal's possession of Hormuz, constrained both Safavid and European envoys to engage in challenging itineraries and to rely on those hardy individuals willing and able to serve. In the picaresque world of the late sixteenth and early seventeenth centuries, adventurers and agents with ambiguous, flexible identities rushed into the gap, with mixed consequences. In keeping with Tuscan practice, Medici affiliates were prominent among them.

## Books and Guns

As the Safavid Empire careened toward its nadir, beset by civil strife and foreign wars, Giovanni Battista Vecchietti made his way to Tabriz and the Safavid court in June 1586.[61] Before following Vecchietti on his diplomatic career, we need first to consider the Medici Oriental Press (Tipografia Medicea Orientale), for which he ostensibly worked. We have already met, in Chapter 4, Giovanni Battista Vecchietti and

Giovanni Battista Britti interacting with Sassetti in India. They had set out for Alexandria in 1584 as the first stop on their respective missions, which were part of a project to distribute the books printed by the press.[62] Both Britti and Vecchietti were from Cosenza; the Vecchietti of Cosenza, however, were by origin an important Florentine family.[63] Britti was charged with going to Ethiopia on behalf of the press and Pope Gregory XIII, but he chose a rather circuitous route from Alexandria, going via Tripoli in Syria, Aleppo, Baghdad, Basra, and Hormuz. He ran into trouble with pirates aboard a ship from Hormuz headed toward Ethiopia and ended up in Goa, where Sassetti wrote about him on January 23, 1586; Britti's story peters out there.[64] Vecchietti fared rather better on his voyage. Beyond the search for manuscripts for the press to print, he had two diplomatic missions. He was to hold discussions about reunion of the Coptic Church with Rome. Then he was to travel to Iran to meet with the shah to discuss anti-Turkish alliances. His route from Egypt was via Antioch, Damascus, and Aleppo, eventually reaching Tabriz. He reappeared in Hormuz in 1587. As we saw in Chapter 4, he was with Sassetti in Goa and Cochin in 1588 and honored his host with a funeral oration.[65]

As Margherita Farina and Sara Fani have shown, the Medici Oriental Press began as a Medici joint venture with the papacy. The press was founded in Rome in 1584 to disseminate knowledge, promote reunion with the Eastern churches, spread the Catholic faith, and seek profit.[66] Directed by the scholar Giovanni Battista Raimondi, the press was dedicated to printing works of scientific and religious value in the languages of the greater Middle East.[67] It was a pioneer in publishing, considerably antedating the more famous orientalism of the northern Europeans. As Timothy Brook has shown, John Selden's 1635 edition of *The Closed Sea* was "the first English book to print Arabic in metal type."[68] Granted that Selden's book was an important development in the history of English orientalism, it was not of course primarily written in either Hebrew or Arabic. The Tipografia Medicea, by contrast, had already operated on a large scale two generations before.

To work effectively, the press required three elements: texts in the desired languages; an editorial staff capable of reading, editing, and printing such texts; and a printing press equipped with types in the appropriate languages. Quite remarkably, all this was achieved in the first years of the press. To condense a complex story, the remarkable linguist and scholar Giovanni Battista Raimondi led the Tipografia Medicea and provided it with the necessary intellectual heft. His abilities and dedication to the project ensured the quality of the product. It also probably facilitated his interactions with others of remarkable linguistic abilities and who had engaged in long-distance travels.[69] Among these, three in particular were important sources of works: the exiled Syrian Orthodox Patriarch Na'matallah and the brothers Giovanni Battista and Girolamo Vecchietti, in particular the former.[70]

Medici interest in patronizing the press began with Cardinal Ferdinando's career before he became grand duke. Margherita Farina has pointed to the profit motivation for Ferdinando but also noted that he had been the cardinal protector of the Kingdom of Ethiopia, the Patriarchate of Alexandria, and the Patriarchate of Antioch in Syria.[71] As we have seen, under Ferdinando I the Medici developed deep political, religious, and military interests in the Islamic world from Morocco to Safavid Iran, and so his political and religious interests, not his financial interests, are likely to have been controlling. This is particularly likely to have been the case because the press was only tenuously a commercial venture. Unlike the supple structure of Florentine wool and silk firms designed to respond to the slightest ripples in demand the press continued to churn out huge numbers of unsold books.[72] Sara Fani has demonstrated that, although a substantial number of the press's books were eventually distributed, with print runs generally ranging from 1,500 to 3,500, a large number were still held by the press nearly two centuries later. A 1772 list of unsold books includes 1,967 of a print run of 3,000 of Euclid's *Elements*, 810 of 1,750 of Avicenna's *Canon*, and 1,039 of 3,500 Latin-Arabic Gospels.[73] The press produced editions of high editorial and production quality. Indeed, Pier Giorgio Borbone has cited the costliness of the editions and limited Western market as contributing to the large stocks of unsold books.[74]

Tuscan involvement in the press continued even after Ferdinando I's death. Three letters sent by Belisario Vinta from January to July 1610 reveal the continuing involvement of the Medici government. First Secretary of State Belisario di Francesco Vinta, a *dottore*, Florentine senator, and senior figure in the Order of Santo Stefano, had already completed a long career (1572–1605) in diplomatic service—as the Medici legation secretary at the Imperial court and repeatedly as an envoy to Ferrara, Mantua, Rome, France, and Innsbruck—and stood at the center of the Medici state.[75] To see him include comments on negotiations with Raimondi in a letter to Giovanni Battista Vecchietti or to write about the shipment of seven hundred books printed by the press, indicates continuing interest.[76] Indeed, in 1610 Vinta had Raimondi, resident in Rome, paid the comfortable, if not munificent, sum of 18 *scudi* monthly from the Florentine court roll.[77] Even so, the letters of 1610 represent the tail end of Medici interest. Indeed, unlike the Galleria dei Lavori in Pietre Dure, the Tipografia Medicea exhibited considerable institutional fragility. Ultimately, the press depended on Raimondi and on Ferdinando I's patronage or the immediate legacy of the latter. Vinta died in October 1613 and Raimondi in early 1614. Raimondi did not have a successor, and the Medici did not seek to institutionalize their support for the press, but instead allowed it to lapse.[78]

Returning to Iran and one of the press's first agents, Giovanni Battista Vecchietti's itinerary and loyalties involved the papacy, the Tipografia Medicea Orientale, and the Portuguese Estado da Índia, whose infrastructure he used, including returning to Europe bearing a letter from Shah Muhammad Khudabanda (r. 1578–1587).[79] Overlapping interests and loyalties of this sort could be mutually supporting, as long as interests converged. When they diverged—as they did with relations with the Safavids—multiple loyalties of the sort that Vecchietti had could be problematic. Before proceeding with the uncertain and often disappointing course of diplomacy between the Safavids and a group of ostensibly allied European powers, we need to consider how various strategic situations led the Austrian and Spanish Habsburgs and their allies to divergent relationships with the Safavids.

As we have seen, Medici Tuscany was embedded in an alliance network led by the Spanish Habsburgs and the papacy and including a large number of small polities. The Spanish alliance of the mid-sixteenth century frayed and shifted as the decades passed. Even as Spanish allies charted more independent courses and the Dutch and English fought with increasing effectiveness against Philip II, the Prudent King gained new reserves of strength. With the acquisition of the Portuguese Empire in 1580, Philip II acquired Hormuz, a large commercial city just outside the Safavid domains on the Persian Gulf.

Whereas in 1570 the Spanish alliance might be expected to be straightforwardly anti-Ottoman and therefore pro-Safavid, by the late 1580s, the Safavids also posed an important threat to Iberian interests. The Austrian Habsburgs and the Holy Roman Empire they led, by contrast, continued to maintain a clear focus on resisting the Ottoman Empire and its expansionist ambitions in the Balkans and so were inclined to see the Safavids primarily as potential allies in conflict with the Ottomans. Indeed, the Safavids expected rather more cooperation from the Austrian Habsburgs than they delivered. The Austrian Habsburgs and the Safavids fought the Ottomans together from 1603 until the Holy Roman Empire made a separate peace at Zsitvatörök in 1606, opening a rift with the Safavids.[80] Thus, although the two Habsburg systems generally cooperated with each other and the papacy on a broad array of policies, these alliance networks and their constituent pieces worked together only when it suited them. The curious and dynamic feature in the case of the Safavids, however, was that Rome and Florence also conducted their own, not wholly consonant, policy. The result was that ambassadors needed to stop in Prague, Florence, Rome, and Madrid. The tense balance among the allies as they pursued their overlapping, sometimes conflicting, interests forms a core of the story of Tuscany's relationship with the Safavid Empire.

With this context in mind, let us consider Giovanni Battista Vecchietti as a papal envoy to Persia and see what his connections to Tuscany show about multiple loyalties and alliance politics. Having left Vecchietti returning to Europe from Goa with a letter from Shah Muhammad Khudabanda, let us resume his story at the center of Iberian Empire, in Madrid. There, the relationship between Vecchietti and the Tuscan ambassador to Spain, Vincenzo di Andrea Alamanni, illustrates the complex interplay of loyalties within the Catholic alliance led by the Spanish Habsburgs and the papacy. Two reports sent from Madrid on December 10, 1588, to Ferdinando I, from Vecchietti and Alamanni respectively, recount a presentation to Philip II in which Vecchietti gave a detailed description of Persia, noted the shah's military forces, and presented a *relazione* on Persia; Alamanni confirmed that Philip II showed great interest in this presentation.[81] As well he might, for the security of Hormuz depended on Safavid developments. The case was not simply one of the pope's envoy reporting to the ultimate head of the Estado da

Índia, however, for Vecchietti's first meeting on December 10 had been preceded by correspondence between Ferdinando I and Vecchietti. On November 12, 1588, Vecchietti had undertaken to explain to Philip II what had been negotiated in Persia under Ferdinando I's instructions.[82] Thus, the December 10 meeting had been at Ferdinando I's behest and was recorded in two separate accounts sent to him afterward.

Ferdinando I and Pope Sixtus V had worked closely with Philip II on joint projects, most recently the Spanish Armada, which had met with disaster earlier in 1588. As Philip II settled into a long war with Elizabethan England, papal and Florentine attention had turned to the peril of an expanding Ottoman Empire, then in the process of soundly defeating the Safavid Empire. Spain, the papacy, and the Grand Duchy of Tuscany all shared a general interest in the defeat of the Ottomans and the spread and protection of Catholic Christianity, but their specific view of a possible role for the Safavid Empire diverged. The dynamic can be seen clearly in Vecchietti's proposal to provide military support to the shah. Vecchietti had been favorably received at the court of Philip II of Spain in late 1588, but Ambassador Alamanni had his doubts about a subsequent meeting in 1589. On May 27, 1589, Ambassador Alamanni wrote to Piero di Francesco Usimbardi explaining that Vecchietti had written to him. Vecchietti's missive to Alamanni apparently informed the ambassador that Ferdinando I wanted to know whether Philip II would object if Ferdinando I sent artillery experts and people to the king of Persia (that is, the shah of Iran) to superintend the construction of fortifications in response to the shah's request. In Alamanni's telling, the ostensible reason to make the request to Philip II was that the experts would be sent to Hormuz via Portugal. Alamanni dragged his feet on this project. He did so because he was unsure that such a move as proposed would be approved by Philip II or that, even if the experts were sent, they would not be retained for service in Philip II's domains; nonetheless, Alamanni protested that he would do as instructed.[83]

This disagreement between Alamanni and Vecchietti illustrates a tension that was masked in Vecchietti's original presentation. Vecchietti's proposal matched Tuscan and papal interests well. These powers had little to lose and much to gain from good relations with the Safavids. In particular, the shah could protect Eastern Christians and use

Safavid military might to smite the Ottomans. The resident Tuscan ambassador Alamanni's objections, by contrast, were grounded in an understanding of Portugal's differing strategic reality. The Portuguese possessed an anomalously large and militarily vulnerable trading city— Hormuz—right off the coast of Iran.[84] The Safavids were thus potential enemies of the Portuguese. Artillery and fortifications in particular were core areas of Portuguese advantage in the Estado da Índia. Tuscany artillery and fortifications, some of the finest in Europe, would certainly be useful in the struggle with the Ottomans; the same guns, however, might also be used against the Portuguese, in particular at Hormuz. Vecchietti's proposal clarified that one could serve multiple masters only up to a point. He could gather information for the whole alliance, but he could not set policy that was equally accepted by all.

## Ambiguous Agents

The problem of multiple loyalties can be seen even more clearly in the famous case of a pair of English brothers, Anthony and Robert Sherley, who had ties to the Safavids and spent time in Florence. We have already met their brother, Thomas Sherley, in the context of his failed raid on the Ottoman-ruled Cyclades. Remarkably, Thomas seems to have had the least adventurous itinerary of these three brothers. Some flavor of Anthony and Robert Sherley's complicated loyalties and tangled personal histories can be gleaned from the contrast between their place of birth and titles. Their respective *Oxford Dictionary of National Biography* entries note that they were one of Sir Thomas Sherley's nine children and "born at the family estate of Wiston in Sussex."[85] Yet the much older Anthony ended up as a Holy Roman Imperial count,[86] while his younger brother Robert became a count of the Papal States.[87] More remarkable still, they each separately served as ambassadors of Shah 'Abbas to Europe.[88] How did they end up as Persian ambassadors? And what does this have to do with Tuscany?

Anthony (1565–1636?) and Robert (c. 1581–1628) Sherley's stories have captured attention, both positive and negative, since their spectacular returns to Europe as Safavid ambassadors. In recent historiography, Anthony Sherley's expedition to Safavid Iran (1598–1599), his return to Europe with a Safavid diplomatic party (1599–1601), and the

role of Michelangelo Corai at this stage have been the subject of intensive research, especially by Sanjay Subrahmanyam, Richard Raiswell,
E. K. Faridany, and Federico Federici. In this context, I present only the
pith of the Sherleys' stories, focusing on the ways they contributed to
Tuscany's tangled ties to Iran.[89]

Educated at Oxford and the Inner Temple, Sherley served as an infantry captain under Robert Dudley (1532/3–1588), Earl of Leicester, in
the Low Countries for three years from 1586 and again as a regimental
commander under the Earl of Essex in 1591, displaying considerable
personal courage and distinction in a battle in Brittany. A subsequent
1593 diplomatic mission to France saw him awarded a noble order, his
acceptance of which without permission cost him a term in prison in
England and the loss of the order. His judgment seems not to have improved in the following year. As a result of a secret marriage to an Essex
cousin in 1594, Sherley was exiled from court and bound to the Earl
of Essex. The marriage was unhappy, however, and to escape it Sherley
raised 11 ships and 1,500 men for a raid on São Tomé, but he had to give
up 4 ships and 500 men to Essex's raid on Cádiz, leaving a smaller fleet
to depart on May 20, 1596.[90] For all Sherley's subsequent unscrupu-
lousness, this particular military foray was sanctioned, as can be seen
in a commission of April 9, 1596, signed by E[dward] Reynoldes that
authorized Sherley to raise and command a force of 1,500 men and the
accompanying ships.[91]

The raid on São Tomé did not work out, and a subsequent attack
on São Tiago in the Cape Verde Islands yielded minimal returns. An
attack on Ribeira Grande, also in Cape Verde, yielded a costly battle
that, while the English won, induced them to set out for the Caribbean,
arriving at Dominica on October 17, 1596. Sherley's forays went from
bad, with the mutiny of a ship off Colombia in February 1597, to disappointing, with a largely fruitless attack on Jamaica, and finally to
disastrous, with the mutiny of his fleet off Cuba, forcing his return to
Dover in July 1597. At this low ebb in 1597, Sherley wrote in humble
tones to a major figure, who was presumably his patron, Essex, since
the letter is held in the papers of Essex's intelligence master, Anthony
Bacon.[92] Sherley announced first that he would be going to secure fish
in Newfoundland before selling them in Turkey (the Ottoman Empire).
While there, relying on the advice of a Portuguese prisoner, he planned

to convince the Ottomans to use their galleys in the Red Sea to attack the Portuguese. He framed the proposal as part of a strategy to deprive Philip II of revenues from both the West and East Indies.[93] This Red Sea strategy was not wholly fanciful, but Sherley's imagined role was. Giancarlo Casale has argued that there was a faction in the Ottoman Empire interested in similar projects for much of the sixteenth century.[94] By the 1590s, however, the Ottomans lacked the requisite naval power. If the Ottomans had possessed such a powerful Red Sea fleet, they would surely have known what to do with it.

Essex, however, had other plans for Anthony Sherley. Heading to Venice, Sherley led a small contingent of volunteers to participate in the Ferrara crisis, but his plans came to naught, for they were too slow to aid Cesare d'Este's bid for control of Ferrara. Even so, the move to Italy drew on established Sherley family experience on the peninsula. By the time of Anthony's arrival, his brother Robert had spent the five years preceding 1598 at Ferdinando I's court in Tuscany. As we have seen in Chapter 3, Thomas Sherley also served the grand duke in 1602 and wrote an account of Florence and Livorno. These intimate ties to the Grand Duchy of Tuscany probably required a religious position rather more sympathetic to Catholicism than was consonant with official policy in England. In any event, Anthony eventually took the decisive step and converted to Catholicism in Venice.[95]

In Venice in search of opportunity, the Sherleys received advice from Giacomo Foscarini on the idea of heading east, but to a rather different purpose than Anthony Sherley had proposed in his letter. Rather than mobilize the Turk, the Sherleys were to meet his archenemy, the Shah. Essential to executing and perhaps conceiving of the Persian venture was none other than the recently (April 3, 1598) knighted Sir Michelangelo Corai. Anthony and Robert Sherley were accompanied by Corai as they traveled from Venice to Qazvin from May to December 1598. They set out from Venice on May 24 on a ship—called either the *Morizell* or the *Nana e Ruzzina*—also bearing Armenian and Italian merchants. This multinational ship seems to have been riven by tensions between the English and Venetians over insults and the legitimacy of the Englishmen's business, which culminated in Corai's arrest and the denunciation of the English. The accounts differ beyond this. For Subrahmanyam, the English were left on Zante to make their own way

after a violent quarrel with the Italians. For Federici, drawing on Corai's probably more reliable account to the Collegio dei Savi in Venice
in 1599, the Venetians denounced the English to the Ottoman governor
of Tripoli in Lebanon. A Greek had warned the English of the denunciation, but English protestations to the Ottoman governor were not
accepted, which led to Corai's detention; the Armenians eventually negotiated their release.[96] We saw in Chapter 7 how Corai returned to Italy
in 1599 and would remain entangled with the Sherleys.

A vain and boastful spendthrift of questionable loyalty and character, Anthony Sherley is not a sympathetic figure to modern scholars
nor is his appeal, beyond a vaguely defined charisma, well appreciated.
Upon his arrival in Iran, Sherley made claims to military expertise
helped by books on fortifications that he says he showed Shah 'Abbas.[97]
On this point, Sherley's career indicates he had a good case. He had
seen decorated service as a captain under the leading gentlemen of
Elizabeth's court, held a large independent naval command, and had a
decade of military experience mostly consisting of combat. A later century would have accorded a rank like rear admiral or brigadier general
to the leader of such a venture as Sherley's 1596 commission. Sherley
may have been an irresponsible rogue, but he was not a charlatan when
it came to his military record, but then irresponsible roguery was not
inconsistent with noble military culture. As Subrahmanyam points
out, we do not know whether Sherley made the courtly speech he claims
to have made to Shah 'Abbas nor how Michelangelo Corai translated
it if he did.[98] He did, however, receive the title of *mirza* (emir) and considerable favor from Shah 'Abbas.[99] The title of *mirza* needs to be taken
seriously. Sherley's appeal may be more intelligible if we recall not only
the story of the exiled Robert Dudley in Tuscany and Europe's continued reliance on military entrepreneurs, but also the construction
of power in the closely culturally linked Mughal Empire. In Emperor
Akbar's (r. 1556–1605) contemporary India, a highly multiethnic, multinational nobility of multiple religious traditions, including many
Persians, served as the backbone of the Mughal cavalry and political
order; they carried the general title of *amir*, along with specific numer-
ical ranks.[100] In Safavid Iran, Shah 'Abbas was just then building a new
gunpowder military to displace the old tribal cavalry. In this context,
Sherley's status as a noble with a considerable military record made

him something more than a technical expert or diplomat, but instead an attractive candidate for appointment as an emir.[101]

A letter of December 17, 1599, cited in Chapter 7, which characterizes Corai as Sherley's interpreter, also offers a clear sense of how Europeans perceived Sherley on his return journey to Europe. It notes that Corai had been "in Persia while he had served and treated with that King and now affirms that he has become his forerunner and the said Sir Don Antonio ^ sent from the Persian will carry letters from that Prince P̶e̶r̶s̶i̶a̶n̶ to the Pope, to the Emperor, to the King of Spain, to the King of France [,] to the Doge of Venice, and to the grand duke of Tuscany. And that the said Sir Don Antonio takes the road for Muscovy, because the Turk, having known of his coming, had put guards on the passes to detain him."[102] Abandoning his brother as a hostage in Persia, Anthony Sherley proceeded to demonstrate all the reasons that touchy aristocrats with delusions of grandeur can make poor diplomats. Sherley traveled north to Muscovy and on to Archangel, apparently following one of the critical silk routes. He managed in the process to use an accusation of sexual misbehavior against the Augustinian friar who was one of his traveling companions—and who had accused him of theft—to have the tsar dispose of the friar. Sherley then offended the tsar over an issuance of precedence. This was the same Tsar Boris Godunov with whom the Medici would negotiate just a couple of years later. Although the initial reception in Prague by Rudolf II had been favorable, Sherley's role in the embassy began to disintegrate as he wildly overspent, fell into severe debt, apparently stole, and fell out with his companion, Hasain Ali Beg Bayat, who was accorded more respect. In Florence in March 1601, Sherley heard news of the arrest of Essex and in April confirmation of Essex's execution. By mid-1601 in Rome, Sherley seems to have abandoned the embassy and begun other schemes. He did not, however, tell the shah or save his brother, whose status fell in Persia the longer Anthony Sherley was out of touch.[103] Anthony Sherley's continuing story is fascinating, but one whose numerous subsequent twists we can leave aside as we turn to his younger brother.

Robert Sherley was not left to languish indefinitely. His brother's disastrous performance notwithstanding, Robert was dispatched as Safavid ambassador in February 1608, spending the winter in Poland at the court of Sigismund III before proceeding to the Holy Roman Imperial court in

1609. From there he moved on to Rome after a month in Florence.[104] We may recall that Robert had lived for years in Tuscany, and so the court in Florence would have been a return to his youth. Shifting point of view, let us consider how the embassy would have looked from the Florentine perspective.

The adventures of the pair of English brothers presented issues of credibility and uncertain loyalties. Such issues turn out not to have been uncommon. Little flurries of activity surrounding the verification of identities and the credibility of projects happened fairly regularly. A year before Sherley's arrival in Florence, for instance, two letters of June 1608 explain that a Persian spy traveling undercover as a merchant in the Ottoman Empire had been captured by the Tuscans at sea, enslaved, and then set free by the grand duke in Livorno.[105]

People claiming to represent territories hostile to the Ottomans presented themselves regularly. Leaving the Persian connection briefly for context, let us consider two letters of March 1609. On March 8, 1609, Asdrubale Barbolani di Montauto wrote from Venice to Belisario di Francesco Vinta in Florence about an individual claiming to be a messenger from a Moldavian prince who ostensibly sought to correspond with Cosimo II. Deep skepticism pervades Montauto's characterization of the prince's story. Principal among the doubts was that he had long been imprisoned there but now sought to return with the support of the king of Great Britain ("Re della Gran Bretagna") to recover his state.[106] Following up on this same story, a March 29, 1609, letter from Montauto in Venice to Vinta in Florence accepted Vinta's instructions to tell the prince not to raise a new crusade against Constantinople.[107] Anti-Ottoman projects like this one, often of a dubious character, bubbled up frequently. Tuscany did not accept all of them and for good reason.

Mirroring these ambitious individuals with their projects were reports and requests for military intervention from around the eastern Mediterranean and the Balkans. In light of the tempo of Tuscan activity from Cyprus and Syria to the Aegean, the frequency of such requests is hardly surprising. Even so, their occurrence indicates that the failures in Syria and Cyprus had not doused hopes for Tuscan intervention. As we have seen, their hopes were not entirely misplaced, for the Tuscan fleet did engage in an aggressive campaign around the eastern

Mediterranean from 1608 to 1611, with a notable success off Rhodes in 1608 and heavy losses in the 1609–1611 campaign.[108] The Medici archives teem with reports of the kind from these years. Ferdinando I received a report on the fortifications of the island of Levkas and an appeal for military aid against the Ottomans.[109] Three further reports, all perhaps from 1609, describe Cyprus, Rhodes, and Macedonia, detailing their human and physical geographies.[110] As ever, renegades crossed the religious frontier. The Medici, for instance, received a pitch-perfect report on an Ottoman aga who, sent to strip Christian buildings in the Greek Isles of their marble and porphyries, instead converted to Christianity and defected.[111] Heart-warming stories within the framework of Counter-Reformation Europe's politico-religious outlook could slide into policy driven by the over-optimistic hopes of exiles. Tuscany experienced the perils of this in Cyprus and Syria. Wish fulfillment did not constitute a sound policy.

When receiving ambassadors from distant princes, then, questions of identity, credibility, motivation, and mutual comprehension rendered diplomacy fragile. Misbehavior, mistrust, confusion, and the accidents of travel and communications could lead an embassy to collapse. The possibilities, however, were correspondingly large. In the case of the Safavids, the scope of commercial and military opportunities justified a measure of risk taking and tolerance for figures like Anthony Sherley. Bearing this in mind, let us return to Robert Sherley's arrival in Florence. Grand Duke Cosimo II received Robert Sherley as ambassador from Shah 'Abbas on August 15 and 16, 1609.[112] Robert Sherley would of course have been a familiar figure, but perhaps not that familiar. He had been a teenager when he left Florence. Now he was a married man serving as ambassador for Shah 'Abbas. What is more, Ferdinando I had died earlier in 1609, at which point his nineteen-year-old son came to the throne as Cosimo II (1590–1621); Cosimo would have been a mere child when Robert Sherley had been at court. Robert Sherley's embassy seems nonetheless to have worked, for he continued to Rome and thence to Spain in 1610; problems began to proliferate for him, however, in 1611.[113] In Florence, the Sherley visits were remembered for some time. A July 7, 1622, note recounts the gold necklaces given to the shah in 1601—presumably in response to Anthony Sherley's visit—and the gift of a further necklace on the occasion of the Sherley visit in 1609.[114]

After Robert Sherley's departure, further issues of identity emerged to perplex the Tuscan state. On January 5, 1610, Belisario Vinta asked Giovanni Battista Vecchietti to translate a letter, ostensibly in Armenian, as part of an effort to verify the identity of a supposed Persian ambassador. Vinta explained his doubts with reference to the fact that the little pouch carrying the letter of reference was missing a lid that appeared on Count Robert Sherley's little pouch.[115] We met Vecchietti as the papal envoy to Persia and agent of the Tipografia Medicea Orientale more than twenty years before. The story concluded quickly. On January 16, 1610, Vinta wrote to Giovanni Bartoli, the Medici ambassador in Venice, explaining that safe passage had been granted to the Armenian, Cugè Sefer, who was going to Venice.[116] We will return to Sefer shortly, but here let us consider the role of Vecchietti in determining Sefer's identity. Whether Vecchietti determined the identity directly or relied on further experts, he was clearly the resident figure to ask. Experts with both the language skills and travel experience to verify identities were still quite rare in the early seventeenth century and they were often off on long journeys. Indeed, Giovanni Battista Vecchietti had spent the period 1597–1608 on an extended journey through Syria, Iraq, Iran, and India, ending up in Agra at the court of Akbar before returning to Italy in 1608 after significant travails.[117] Rarity meant that the pool of resident experts was largely coterminous with that of former or eligible future ambassadors. This, in turn, presented difficult principal-agent and power transfer problems, to which monarchs adapted largely by making the rewards and punishments involved in diplomatic activity particularly extreme. We can see this last in the case of the envoy sent after Robert Sherley.

Robert Sherley had arrived in Madrid in January 1610.[118] Back in Rome, he had written a plaintive letter to his brother on October 2, 1609, describing the success of his journey thus far, lamenting Anthony's silence, noting that Robert had picked up Anthony's debts in Prague for him, and desiring a meeting. In this note, he lamented the issue of entering the Spanish court in his state, writing, "and my iorny to the corrte of Spayne is not shortte, nether a place to eanter basly into; my trayne is small, not consistinge in aboue ten persons, I mustt be confydennt in you in this succor."[119] Whether or not Anthony provided any assistance, Robert's entry into court worked, at least for a while. Just

over a year later, however, Dengiz Beg and Father Gouvea, who had been
sent as part of a silk trade mission from the Safavid Empire, arrived
in Spain.[120] Upon his arrival in February 1611, Dengiz Beg disclaimed
Sherley's ambassadorial credentials.[121] Here the stories of Sherley and
Sefer entangle. The arrival of Dengiz Beg and the expectation of Sefer's
arrival led to a collapse in Robert Sherley's status at the Spanish court.
This led to an order for his papers to be reexamined and for his arrest.
Robert Sherley, like his brother, was nothing if not a survivor; he escaped.[122] Further adventures ensued for him, but he leaves our story
now. As for the corrupt, or unfortunate, Dengiz Beg, however, the whole
venture ended badly. Apparently guilty of embezzling silk entrusted to
his care, Dengiz Beg was executed upon his return to Isfahan in 1613
and his property handed over to, of all people, Michelangelo Corai.[123]
Royal ambassadors held high status, could reap substantial rewards,
and possessed a measure of discretionary power. The price they paid
was a fairly high risk of impoverishment, imprisonment, and untimely
death.

## Ambassador Corai in Safavid Iran

In light of the difficulties that Safavid ambassadors had faced in Europe about their status, Michelangelo Corai reciprocally confronted potentially serious problems about his identity as he fled east from the
fallen rebel capital of Aleppo. In addition to the memory of his prior
service as a dragoman with the Sherleys, Corai needed official validation. Establishing it required him to undertake the difficult task of secretly transporting his credentials. With respect to the Safavids, the
foremost such credential was a letter from Ferdinando I to Shah 'Abbas
I. A surviving draft copy held in the Medici archives in Florence provides a clear sense both of Medici objectives at this point and of the nature of the relationship with the shah.

> To the King of Persia. January 25, 1607
>
> Don Ferdinando Medici, by the grace of Omnipotent God Grand
> Duke of Tuscany, 4th Duke of the state of Florence, 3rd of the state
> of Siena, absolute Prince of the Republic of Pisa Prince of Capostrano,
> Grand Master of the Knights and Religion of St. Stefano, Lord of the
> Tyrrhenian Sea and of many islands of it . and Prince of the state of Capostrano

To the ~~the most high~~, Most Serene most puissant and invincible Lord
Shah Abbaz, King of Persia, of Tartary, of Arabia, and of Turkey, of a
most ancient lineage of Kings, lord of the Sea and of the Land, perse-
cutor and breaker of the Ottoman House, great friend of Christians,
that may God most happily preserve, together with all of Your Royal
progeny for many centuries. The name of Your Majesty is so glorious
among the Christian Princes for your happy progress against the tyranny of the Turk, as all are celebrating your enterprises and actions,
supposing that you have been born to the world as a scourge of the
Ottoman House, and therefore they wish you continuing victory,
with the entire destruction of your enemy. I among all the others
have double reason to rejoice, both for the affection and esteem that
I have for the supreme worth of Your Majesty, as also for my own old
observation of you, beginning from the time of the glorious memory
of your Lord father and growing from the great favor that a few years
since Your Majesty gave me with the sending to me of that noble Embassy. Therefore there being here <sup>the knight</sup> Michelagnolo Corai, who
was already Interpreter <sup>for Your Majesty with those of your Ambassadors</sup> and having
said to me that from Syria he thought of coming to this same Royal
court, I wanted with such an occasion to remind Your Highness with
this letter the prompt will that I will always have to serve you, if on
occasion you will favor us with your commands and I having given
the same <sup>sir</sup> Michelag<sup>lo</sup>. some commissions to negotiate with Your
Majesty for the public service, I refer myself to him; the which he will
also inform you of by voice, of that which I think and do to continually damage the Turks with the small maritime forces that God has
given me and to end I kiss most affectionately Your Majesty's hand.
From Your Majesty's most affectionate Servant.[124]

As it happens, we also have another letter from almost the same period
to the shah, this one from Philip III. Or rather, we have an undated copy
of that letter held in the archives of the old viceregal capital of Goa. The
letters have some similarities, but the differences are quite instructive
for what they say about the regular, continuous relations between
Philip III and Shah 'Abbas. To elucidate these differences, I quote the
copy of the letter (in my translation from the Spanish-inflected Portuguese) in full here:

Copy of the Letter that his Majesty wrote to
the King of Persia in which is mentioned the letter
that His Majesty wrote to the Viceroy[125]

Most Serene and Most Powerful Shah Abbá King of Persia Our
very dear and beloved friend: I Dom Phelippe by grace of God King
of the Spains and of the East and West Indies and of the Islands and
Provinces of the Ocean Sea, King of Naples and Sicily, of Jerusalem,
of the Algarves on this side and beyond the Sea in Africa, Archduke
of Austria, Duke of Milan etc.[126]

I saw the letter that your Serenity wrote me from which I received
very great contentment for the good correspondence and friendship
that you offer me, and of that I wrote to My Viceroy of India that I
wanted to have it with me and with all my states. And in conformity
with the same I have offered to Your Serenity by your ambassador
Cusen Alibey, to whom I gave warmly the good treatment as Your
Serenity has understood; and the same I gave now to the Secretary
of your other ambassador who had been sent to our Most holy Father Clement the Eighth who died in March. And to preserve and
augment this accord I sent you My Ambassador Luis Pereira de Laçerda nobleman of my house and of my Counsel, who I hope has
arrived at that Court of Your Serenity and that from this I would
have much more particular news of Your Serenity and of your prosperous successes for with these I am gladdened, as now I am made
happy with the news that my viceroy of India wrote me of the great
victories that Your Serenity had against your enemies; and all of
this quality will always please me greatly, the which I will be happy
to know more particularly from your ambassador who the said my
viceroy writes me had been sent to me from Your Serenity and by
chance that for that he was in Goa; and I wrote to him that otherwise to give him no hindrance and all that is necessary for his passage with the good treatment that I desire be given to all your envoys : And that Your Serenity ordered to your Court the Religious [,]
Friar Antonio de Gouvea, Friar Christovão the Friar Hieronymo, I
received much contentment; and I am for this, and for the house
that you gave to them to retire and do the divine offices of Christianity, Very grateful; and I will always hold this [?][127] of the grandeur
of Your Serenity the due recognition and to your person we wish

very affectionately to preserve and Your grace that for there to be people that for the service of our lord and of his Religion who will leave the goods of the World that the work offered They will be deserving of being kept in the protection of Your Serenity.[128]

And because last year I wrote to Your Serenity as is understood by Letters of the viceroy of India and of the Captain of Hormuz that the Sultan of Shiraz by a deal took the island of Bahrain from the King of Hormuz my vassal with the death of Guazil that was in his name and signifies to Your Serenity the obligation that I had to help the said King as my vassal principally in the Restitution of this Island that pertains to My state of India, for it having been taken from the common enemy the Turk with his forces and conserved from then until the present without Contradiction from anyone entrusting Your Serenity will be pleased that among our vassals there is the same good Correspondence and friendship that we have among us. I asked of Your Serenity by another letter of mine to send to give order that the said Island of Bahrain be restored freely to the said King of Hormuz so that he has and possesses it comfortably; and that those that in this case were guilty are given the punishment that they deserve the which I have confidence your serenity will order satisfied as they were; for it is understood to be the will of Your Serenity to preserve the peace and Friendship that you have offered me that I desire to be augmented each day; And because about this matter my ambassador Luis Pereira de Lacerda, to whom this letter is given, will speak more particularly to Your Serenity give entire credit to that which for my part he speaks.

Most Serene and Most Powerful Prince Shah Abbá King of Persia, Our Lord illuminate Your Serenity with his grace and with it have in his guard You [manuscript faded] and Royal state.[129]

The original letter appears to date from 1606, although 1605 is possible. The Luis Pereira de Lacerda embassy left from Spain in 1602, but he did not enter Iran until 1604.[130] These latter dates might have argued for an earlier date for the letter, but two further details strongly suggest 1606. A Persian embassy found itself stuck in Goa in late 1605.[131] A further reference to 1605 depends on how, in the sentence mentioning Clement VIII, one reads both the ambiguous referent and the abbreviation "Maz.," which I have translated as "March"; Clement VIII died in March 1605. The precise date is perhaps less important here than that the letter seems to have arrived a few years before the Corai embassy and that its contents differ quite substantially from those of the letter that accompanied Corai's embassy. As to the contents of the letters, the basic structure of the letters from Philip III and Ferdinando I were fundamentally similar. The list of titles of the constituent pieces of the composite monarchies over which they presided while referring to the recipient's domains by a briefer, more generalized list of titles appears to have been both typical and obligatory. Indeed, the practice was not confined to Western European sovereigns, for a letter from Tsar Boris Godunov to Ferdinando I, apparently of 1602, follows the same pattern, although the Tsar's list of titles was quite a bit longer.[132] The conclusions of the letters from Philip III and Ferdinando I to Shah 'Abbas are similar, entrusting the bulk of the negotiation to the verbal communication of the ambassador. Although the huge distances and slow transit times involved required granting discretion to the ambassador, the amount of discretion granted is still striking. The royal letters can be read in a few moments and state only the broadest outlines of a desired outcome. Philip III certainly could have sent a longer note, since the annual instructions to the viceroy still held in Goa are considerably longer; even so, they too tend to treat each subject concisely.[133] Perhaps the brevity of the letters to the shah reflected the smaller number of subjects to discuss than the numerous items that came up in administering the Estado da Índia. In any event, the practice seems to have been to mention and state in a few lines or perhaps a couple of sentences the monarch's view on each subject. Details were to be handled by the representative on the spot.

The structural similarity of the letters notwithstanding, the specific content of the two letters is strikingly different and suggests a major point of divergence between the Tuscans and their Iberian allies. The lesser divergence concerned religion. Tuscany was enthusiastic about Eastern Christians; Philip III was responsible for protecting a full-scale ecclesiastical establishment throughout the east, of which the Persia operation was a small branch. Thus, if Ferdinando I could choose to involve himself in these matters, he could also choose to ignore them; a brief compliment notwithstanding, he did so. Philip III, by contrast, had both the advantage of access to the services of friars on the ground and the disadvantage of supporting a mission at odds with the local political and religious order and therefore prone to disruptive crises.

More problematically, the military dynamics of the two letters could not have been more different. Admittedly, both letters recognized the Turk as the common enemy. But the primary purpose of the Tuscan letter was to offer full-fledged military alliance against the Ottomans, whereas the reference to the Turk as the common foe in Philip III's was by way of reproach to Shah 'Abbas. Where Philip III's letter diplomatically pretended that the issue was a dispute between vassals, the address of the letter to Shah 'Abbas was a clear acknowledgment that there was a territorial dispute between the Safavids and the Portuguese. This recognized the reality of the situation, for Shah 'Abbas had commanded Allah Verdi Khan, who ruled Shiraz, to take Lar province (now part of Fars province) in 1601; in 1602, he took Bahrain.[134] The history of the Persian Gulf and of Iberian-Safavid relations in this period is intricate. The latter is treated thoroughly in the two volumes of Luis Gil Fernández, *El imperio luso-español y la Persia safávida* and more recently in the work of Graça Almeida Borges.[135] For our purposes here, the critical point is that territorial disputes precluded Philip III from forging the sort of unreservedly enthusiastic military alliance that Tuscany offered.

In comparison with the regular exchange of ambassadors and frequent contacts permitted by the Portuguese outpost at Hormuz, one can imagine how disruptive the Tuscan letter might have been, appearing from Ottoman Syria with its message of war. What is more, Corai did not content himself with delivering the letter, but instead became the resident Tuscan ambassador in Iran. To make it there required an arduous caravan journey across the frontier from the Ottoman domains to Safavid Iran. Corai's first letter from Iran begins in a way that Sassetti would have appreciated. Just as Sassetti had complained at length and in detail about the sufferings and mismanagement aboard the *Carreira da Índia*, so Corai's June 26, 1608, letter from Isfahan recounts in detail each stage of the journey, lamenting the state of the roads, the arduousness of the mountain crossing, and the challenges of managing the mules and their burdens with the snow.[136] Corai traced the path by the number of days between each stage past Tartena, the first Persian fortress, through the snowy mountain passes to Hamadan and thence to Qazvin; he arrived on March 19, 1608.[137]

    After the lengthy journey, Corai reported concisely that he arrived at the court of Shah 'Abbas on April 8, 1608. There he presented the grand duke's letter and was warmly received.[138] This timing put Corai at the Safavid court just two months after Robert Sherley had left on his long embassy to Europe. As to the content of the meeting, Corai summarized the strategic discussion, which ran along the lines that might be expected at this point. The seizure of a port in Syria would enable the Christian powers to supply the Safavids. As ever, the greater plan involved the capture not only of Jerusalem, but also of Syria and Palestine.[139] The discussion turned briefly to commercial prospects before Corai reported on what he had negotiated with Ali Pasha. Displaying the acumen that might be expected of such an experienced ruler, Shah 'Abbas and Corai then moved beyond the general descriptor, Christian princes, to the specific roles of the pope, the Spanish, the grand duke of Tuscany, the Holy Roman Emperor, and the Venetians, with concern concentrating on the prospects of a peace agreement.[140] Such a separate peace, which the Emperor had already made in late 1606, threatened to undermine all plans for anti-Ottoman alliance. Having surveyed the general political situation, 'Abbas then asked about the galleys of the grand duke of Tuscany. Corai, who had been instrumental in calling in their strike on Cyprus, put a positive spin on Tuscan actions. He reported saying that the Tuscan ships "have this last year two times damaged a great deal *the Kingdom of Cyprus* the first time they disembarked at *Famagusta* they made many *slaves* and *destruction* the second time at *Saline* where they threw down the *fortress* and with *the Emir* who *took* made many other *slaves* and they have preyed on that *sea* happily."[141] This naval raiding involved targeting the tribute of Alexandria. Corai boasted of the Tuscans' having taken two Turkish galleons by Damietta, carrying a million and a half in gold and generally preying on all traffic with Alexandria. He likewise pointed with pride to the sacking of Bona and that raid's rich haul of slaves and plunder.[142] Skillfully weaving together the full gamut of Tuscan naval activities, Corai remarkably managed to present the plunder and enslavement of Muslim civilians as virtuous indicators of Tuscan commitment to causing *"very great damage to the Turk"* and hoped for more in future.[143] Stretching a point, Corai claimed that the Tuscans had al-

ready agreed to a league with the pope and the king of Spain against the
"*common enemy.*"[144] Concluding his account of this discussion of grand
strategy, Corai reported that "*The King* listened to me with the utmost
attention."[145] Corai then spent a month in Mazandaran, following the
king "from one villa to the next" as the shah pursued truly massive-scale
hunts—involving some forty-five thousand people and conducted like a
military campaign—that left him little time to speak to Corai.[146]

Corai then briefly touched on the subject of the Sherley brothers,
which is hardly surprising in light of his old connection with them.[147]
After his strategic audience with the king, Corai's letter reports news
and observations, including their arrival at Isfahan on May 24 and the
presence of the discalced Carmelites sent by the pope, which latter information he chose to encipher.[148] Entirely in keeping with his reputation, Anthony Sherley seems to have left significant debts, which had
caused difficulties for the friars. Indeed, Anthony Sherley continued
to cast a long shadow. As Corai reported, apparently one of Anthony
Sherley's servants had published a treatise in Italy "under the name
of Domenico Stoppeni" that had claimed that Sherley—which Sherley
is ambiguous, but Robert makes more sense—had served as a general
responsible for Persian victory, when in fact Robert had been merely a
courtier long held hostage for his brother.[149]

Corai turned next to the strategic position of the shah in the Persian Gulf. Here Corai captured strategic dynamics different from those
of the grand anti-Ottoman coalition he had long sought to rally. Shah
'Abbas had a long-standing project to secure an expansive vision of the
frontiers of his realm, frontiers that had frequently been challenged
during periods of Safavid weakness. Expansion put him in direct conflict with the Portuguese over political power in the Persian Gulf. Specifically, Shah 'Abbas had moved to assert lordship over Bahrain, an advance that threatened the Portuguese position in Hormuz and caused
Corai to speak of the Portuguese interest in having the king of Spain
dispatch a large armada to protect them in the event of war. In Corai's
telling, Robert Sherley had been responsible for informing Shah 'Abbas
of the power of the king of England's navy and it was to James I that
'Abbas looked for help in such a conflict.[150] This particular moment of
tension would pass, but, as we have seen, the English would indeed help
the Safavids under Shah 'Abbas capture Hormuz in 1622.

For all Corai's dismay about these tensions and their potential to distract from the anti-Ottoman struggle, Shah 'Abbas responded to the arrival of "the fathers," sent by Pope Clement VIII (r. 1592–1605) and confirmed by Pope Paul V (r. 1605–1621), by sending an ambassador to the pope, the king of Spain, the emperor, the grand duke of Tuscany, and other "Christian princes to ask for *union and league* among them and animate them anew against *the Turk*."[151] Corai, however, seemed to doubt the diplomatic prospects either with England or with Spain. Turning again to the Sherleys, Corai reported answering 'Abbas's question about Anthony Sherley's whereabouts by saying that he was in service to the king of Spain before returning anew to hopes for Robert Sherley's embassy.[152] This recurrent preoccupation with the Sherleys suggests that they stayed rather more important to Shah 'Abbas than might have been expected, though Corai's close personal connection to them cautions against making too much of this. Far from being solely concerned with the Sherleys or the struggle over the Persian Gulf, Corai's letter continued at length to consider the situation of the English ambassador, the Catholic fathers sent to Iran, the prospects for commerce between Tuscany and Iran by way of Muscovy and the Caspian Sea, and the political situation of the Europeans in relation to the war with the Turk.[153] Finally, after reporting on the news from Babylon (Iraq), Corai concluded by explaining that he would send the letter by way of an Armenian caravan heading to Aleppo; Moyen in Aleppo would then send it via Marseille.[154]

Although Corai could not have known it, the tide of anti-Ottoman activity that gave coherence both to his diplomatic venture and to Tuscany's burst of military activity in the Mediterranean had crested. The Ottoman central state proved effective in crushing the rebellions that had beset it, benefiting from the focus that peace on the Balkan frontier permitted. For all the excited talk, no significant threat to the Ottomans emerged in the Mediterranean. Tuscany persisted in naval raiding, but the death of Ferdinando I in early 1609 deprived the forward policy of its leading source of momentum. Tuscany's ongoing overseas actions by no means came to an immediate halt, but projects from the Amazon expedition to the Medici Oriental Press were not renewed after the early years of Cosimo II's reign. The same trajectory tracks Corai's evolution into a resident ambassador. In 1608 he was a newly arrived envoy at the court of Shah 'Abbas I who brought news from behind enemy lines and a message of military alliance. Thereafter, Corai regularly if infrequently wrote long letters to Tuscany, starting with the letter of June 26, 1608, reviewed earlier. On August 10, 1609, he sent another report from Isfahan; in an indication of the difficulties of communication, four copies of the letter were sent.[155] Corai seems already to have been quite firmly established as a resident ambassador in 1609. He was still in Iran in 1611, since on October 29, 1611, he wrote to Vinta in Florence asking for money to maintain his status at court.[156] This long residence and his precarious relationship to Tuscany appear to have opened the way for a further evolution in his role. By 1612, Corai seems to have become so integrated into the shah's court that he was appointed commissioner of mining operations in Persia. The news came to Florence in the form of two letters, one from Corai on July 9, 1612.[157]

To carry this story to its conclusion, I turn to the E. K. Faridany's reconstruction of Corai's departure from Iran.[158] Corai's appointment as mining commissioner gave him freedom of movement close to the border.[159] This need for freedom of movement was the unfortunate side effect of Corai's success at the court of Shah 'Abbas. Faridany argues that the benefits showered on Corai came with the implicit expectation of Corai's conversion to Islam.[160] It was a time for choosing. Corai chose to flee, in an exploit worthy of a spy novel; he had, after all, been a successful spy before. Corai quietly arranged for asylum in Portuguese Hormuz and traveled to the Persian Gulf coast under the pretext of his mining responsibilities. His efforts to complete the transfer to Hormuz led to his arrest, but the wily Corai drugged his captors at a dinner party and fled to Portuguese-held Comorão, losing one of his party in the chase. He was whisked off to Hormuz and then went to Goa, where he was in 1616.[161]

Stepping back from the excitement of the chase, what happened here? By taking a government position at the Safavid court Corai muddied his status as ambassador. As ambassador of a very Catholic state, his Christianity was expected. As a Safavid official who had received exceptional favor, however, his Christianity had apparently become a problem. Issues of belief aside, conversion was a difficult choice. It is hard to see how conversion to Shia Islam would not have cut Corai off from the grand duke of Tuscany, from Europe, and from his contacts in Syria. It would have been a bigger defection than his first move from Ottoman subject to Tuscan agent. In the end, the flexible identities and loyalties that had served Corai for so long put him in a dreadful position.

The regular, bureaucratic diplomacy that grew out of Renaissance Italy and eventually flourished throughout early modern Europe coexisted with a type of diplomacy at long distance that differed in almost every way. The ad hoc envoys I have been describing were men with extraordinary abilities and willingness to take risks; they were also rare, difficult to control, and of variable competence, honesty, and loyalty. The structural fragility of the diplomatic ties between Tuscany and the Safavid Empire meant that envoys faced not only slow, dangerous, and expensive journeys, but also questions over their identity, status, and negotiating powers. Such challenges were exploited both by charlatans claiming unwarranted positions and actual agents who saw tactical advantage for themselves or their monarch in working with the possibilities created by the uncertainty. These ambiguous agents, whose status and loyalties were variable, multiple, and subject to tactical change, were both essential and risky, which was not simply a matter of the deficiencies of technology. Rather, monarchs used the possibilities of ambiguity for purposes like deniability and flexibility, and agents took advantage of uncertainty to enhance their status, enrich themselves, and provide themselves with a measure of security by creating options.

Often, ambiguity is used to highlight the agency and creativity of agents. In the case of Ambassador Corai, however, monarchs played on the malleability of his status to serve their own ends. After the death of Ferdinando I, the Tuscan regime gradually disengaged from its long-distance ventures, allowing Corai to drift away from Tuscan service. Shah 'Abbas, by contrast, found Corai if anything too valuable for Corai's comfort. The change of circumstances and Corai's eventual flight from both roles marked the end of an era. For Tuscany, the attractions of a Safavid alliance dissipated with Tuscany's effective withdrawal from major participation in the contest with the Ottomans. With the failure of the plot to destroy the Ottoman Empire, the need to find fellow enemies of the Ottomans became less urgent. The costs and complications of long-distance diplomacy could be sloughed off. The Medici regime remained an active player, especially in Europe and the Mediterranean, but its global ambitions receded for a time. Florence awoke from its Persian dream to find itself confined politically.

# Epilogue

$\mathcal{I}$n the final years of Ferdinando I's reign, the whole world seemed open to Tuscany. Working with the Dutch, Tuscany might join the VOC in reaping the profits of the spice trade, transforming Livorno into one of Europe's premier ports. Deals with Portuguese nobles might result in Tuscan colonies in Brazil and Sierra Leone, mirroring in miniature the grim logic of slavery and sugar that linked Portuguese possessions on both sides of the Atlantic. Alternatively, working with English adventurers, a Florentine outpost on the Amazon might mirror its contemporary in Jamestown, for better and for worse. Dovetailing neatly with the growth of the Tuscan fleet of northern European–style warships, the expansion of trade and investment these transoceanic ventures entailed might combine to make Tuscany a naval and colonial power. Closer to home, Tuscany pursued an extraordinary campaign of raiding across the length and breadth of the Mediterranean to reshape the political, religious, and commercial landscape from Algeria to Syria. For a time, it seemed that by working with Cypriot, Lebanese, and Syrian rebels, Tuscany might help tip the balance against an Ottoman Empire facing widespread rebellion in eastern Anatolia and Iraq. Above all, Tuscany hoped that a Safavid alliance based on shared anti-Ottoman animosity would deal the coup de grâce to Ottoman power in the Levant, rolling back the Ottoman conquest of the Mamluks and returning the empire to its early-sixteenth-century boundaries. In this new world of Ottoman successor states sponsored by a friendly Safavid Empire, Tuscan pilgrims, merchants, and diplomats would safely journey from Livorno to Jerusalem, Aleppo, and Isfahan.

In all ages, international affairs are beset by illusions and unrealized hopes, perhaps rarely more so than in periods of instability and shifting power balances like the early seventeenth century. Not all unrealized hopes are chimeras, however. Often, they represent other facets of the possible. In Tuscany's case, consideration of alternative futures serves an important analytical point, suggesting not only the stakes of choices made and the importance of the contingencies of battle, but also the persistent structures that ultimately played such a powerful role in shaping the path Tuscany eventually took. For such a consideration to remain firmly grounded in the historical record, it is essential to distinguish sites where individual contingencies had a clear impact on developments and where the alternative path is plausible.

Perhaps the clearest case of contingency can be found on the battlefield. For all Tuscany's late bellicosity, however, only two operations showed any prospects of making a substantial difference to Tuscany's long-term future. Had the Cyprus campaign been a success, Tuscany might well have sought to entrench itself and hold on for a time. Yet it is hard to imagine a recovering Ottoman Empire tolerating the loss of territory. In the end, then, the only battle that truly shaped Tuscany's prospects was one in which the Tuscans did not participate. This was the battle of Oruç Ovası on October 22–24, 1607, between Ali Pasha and the grand vizier's Ottoman imperial army. A decisive victory for an outnumbered and outgunned Ali Pasha was always unlikely, but the length of the battle suggests that it was possible. The Tuscans were already deeply involved in plotting European and Safavid intervention. Victory by Ali Pasha might well have made that military intervention possible.

Leaving aside the fortunes of war, Tuscany's primary path to direct engagement with the wider world rested on negotiations. Here, two features are immediately striking. First, for nearly forty years, Tuscany pursued numerous projects for long-distance trade and cooperative empire. Some were generated internally, and many responded to external offers. Tuscany's prospects of participation in imperial partnerships were not, then, a pipe dream, but rather a staple of international diplomatic discussions. On paper, the projects always seemed clearly attractive and mutually beneficial. Yet their equally persistent failure points to a second, structural element. Tuscany's geopolitical situation rendered any arrangements with a non-Iberian power a direct challenge to the dominance of the Spanish Habsburgs. With Spanish forces in Milan, Naples, and the Presidial States, Spanish allies on all frontiers, and close familial, religious, and economic ties with the Iberian peninsula, decisively breaking with the Spanish Habsburgs would have been costly and very risky. Ferdinando I teetered on the brink of making that choice repeatedly, but equally regularly he pulled back. Had he taken the plunge, Tuscany would have been swept into a much more violent and dangerous world without the protection of encircling seas and dikes that could close the entry routes. Spanish armies had toppled two Florentine regimes in the last century and made equally plain to the popes where power lay. Certainly taking a path of confrontation would have put Tuscany center stage in early-seventeenth-century politics, a venture that worked so poorly for Parma, Mantua, Savoy, and the Palatinate in the Thirty Years' War that it is hard to gainsay Ferdinando I's choice.

The obvious alternative was to work with the Spanish and Portuguese Empires. This the Tuscans sought to do with remarkable consistency. Developing a dense web of family connections linking the Florentines and other Medici affiliates to the highest echelons of the Spanish and Portuguese nobility, Florentines successfully embedded themselves in the Iberian empires. By serving as a most faithful ally, supplying ships and money to Spanish projects as varied as the naval war in the Mediterranean, the invasion of Portugal, and the Spanish Armada, the Medici sought to create bonds of mutual obligation that would result in protection and privileged access. In the discussions of spice contracts in the 1570s and 1580s, in the Brazilian sugar-refining projects of the 1590s and 1600s, in the proposals for having the Medici take up a subimperial role in Brazil or Sierra Leone in the 1600s—in all their aspirations, the Medici sought to build on private Florentine precedents and connections to join the Portuguese imperial project. At some level, the outcome of all these ventures was contingent. Tuscany could have bid more for the spice contract and secured it. Philip II or Philip III could have said yes to any of the Tuscan proposals, overriding the objections of privileged Iberians on the grounds that the empire needed Tuscan money for its defense. Francesco I and Ferdinando I clearly hoped, if not expected, that this would in fact happen, but it never did.

Tuscany faced hard structural constraints on its engagement in high politics, empire, and transoceanic trade. In a mercantilist age, even the relatively free-trading Dutch violently insisted on monopoly in their commerce with Asia, if not elsewhere. All other European maritime powers were more restrictive. Tuscany possessed the ships, the men, the money, the information, and the ambition to build a global position, either in cooperation with allies or on its own. What it did not possess was the political security to do so in defiance of the great powers. Only in the exceptional circumstances of the Ottoman Empire's near-death experience in the first decade of the seventeenth century could Tuscany make a major move. Even there, success depended less on the gunboat tactics and swashbuckling bravado so common in this picaresque era and more on the skill of Tuscan diplomats and the success of rebel armies. Tuscany could certainly have taken bigger risks, committing larger forces and investing more heavily in the maritime venture, but there a second key difference emerges.

Unlike the Dutch and English, officially excluded from Iberian empire by virtue of warfare, political rivalry, and religious conflict, the Tuscans had peaceful, if partial, access to the Spanish and Portuguese Empires. What is more, the limited militancy of the small Tuscan nobility, the absence of a large body of restless mariners, and a stable and prosperous commercial society did not engender a large number of adventurers. Meanwhile, the religious fervor of the committed could be easily channeled within the existing structures of the Church, especially after the establishment of the Order of Santo Stefano and the founding of the Jesuits. Indeed, Tuscany's close and ancient relationship with Rome and the essential Medici dynastic ties to the Habsburgs and then to France embedded Tuscany firmly at the heart of the Counter-Reformation Catholic world. Florentines would certainly have much preferred unfettered access to the Iberian empires and to have realized Carletti's vision of free nations able to trade anywhere. But they were not, ultimately, willing to go to war for the point. We can imagine a different future in which the Iberians loosened their hugely economically inefficient restrictions on commerce and trusted their allies to join them in the project of empire. A more creative monarch than the Habsburgs at hand might have seen the logic in Tuscany's proposals, especially as the wars with the English and Dutch lengthened and Spanish finances repeatedly collapsed. As it was, Tuscany was neither sufficiently embedded in the Iberian empires to be truly trusted nor sufficiently outside them to challenge them directly.

Even as Tuscany bumped against the structural limits of its position, Florentines made the most of their political position to engage deeply with the wider world. Medici affiliates gathered exotica, naturalia, luxury goods, and information from around the world and remitted it to Tuscany. There the world's wonders would be collected, analyzed, depicted, displayed, and, often enough, regifted. Botanical gardens, villas, libraries, palaces, and fledgling museums housed the collections and provided a site for intensive intellectual engagement with the flora, fauna, cultural artifacts, and anthropological, linguistic, and geographic information pouring into Tuscany. Medici-sponsored entities such as the workshops of the Casino di San Marco, the Fonderie, the Galleria dei Lavori in Pietre Dure, and the Tipografia Medicea Orientale—the latter patronized jointly with a resurgent papacy—not only participated in networks of intellectual exchange and gift giving, but also sought to use knowledge and raw materials from around the world to create global objects. Medici porcelain, Latin-Arabic gospels, spectacular creations with inlaid semiprecious stones, and ebony boxes of medicine depended on long-distance contacts. In Tuscany, sitting beneath the banyan trees; watching the reindeer, lions, parrots, and ostriches; enjoying one of Carletti's demonstrations of Bengali cotton; or seeing one of Sassetti's purchases, perhaps the embroidered Chinese silks, Florentines could enjoy the fruits of Tuscany's engagement with the wider world. The show made quite the impression, above all in the Guardaroba with its walls of maps and cabinets brimming with things from around the world.

To achieve all this, Florentines had to go out into the world, indeed, to travel all around it. That the Grand Duchy of Tuscany never possessed any overseas territories may have actually helped, requiring Tuscans to negotiate access wherever they went, but also freeing them from a heavy commitment to any one place. Indeed, precisely because the primary barriers to global engagement that the Grand Duchy of Tuscany faced were political, private Florentines succeeded in going where the state could not. Becoming donatary captains in Brazil, dominating the Mexican cochineal trade, working for the pepper contractors in Goa, settling in Macao, or traveling all the way around the world, private Florentines prospered in the first global age. We have touched on their stories here insofar as they connected with the Medici and the Tuscan state. Another book will be needed to tell the story of these private global Florentines.

The Grand Duchy of Tuscany's long-distance efforts varied widely in their scope and success. Colonies and direct trade proved ever illusory. The plot to destroy the Ottoman Empire came closer to fruition but ultimately ended in defeat. Although the Tuscans maintained Ferdinando I's projects for a few years after his death, new initiatives were not begun. Tuscany turned away from its naval activities and indeed from the ambition of charting an independent policy, seeking in neutrality and the free port a peaceful path to enjoying the benefits of long-distance trade. By contrast, Tuscany's cultural and intellectual engagement with the wider world was at the cutting edge. Having sought to understand all of this world, Cosimo II welcomed Galileo to study those other worlds his telescope revealed.

# ABBREVIATIONS

NB: MAP database files are abbreviated "MAP Doc ID, ASF, MdP..."

At reader's request, abbreviations in transcriptions have been expanded when the meaning is clear, except in transcriptions of partially or completely enciphered documents. So, V.A.S. has been rendered as Vostra Altezza Serenissima and S. M$^{tà}$ Catt:$^{ca}$ as Sua Maestà Cattolica. I have likewise expanded abbreviations for common words like che, per, non, questo, etc. In cases of ambiguity, I have left the abbreviation.

| | |
|---|---|
| ANTT | Arquivo Nacional da Torre de Tombo |
| ASF | Archivio di Stato di Firenze |
| ASV | Archivio di Stato di Venezia |
| BNE | Biblioteca Nacional de España en Madrid |
| CM | Camden Miscellany |
| DBI | *Dizionario Biografico degli Italiani* (accessed through Treccani.it) |
| DSC | Department of Special Collections, Charles E. Young Research Library, UCLA |
| HAG | Historical Archives of Goa |
| Ins. | Insert |
| OFP | Orsini Family Papers, Department of Special Collections, Charles E. Young Research Library, UCLA |
| LPL | Lambeth Palace Library |
| MAP | Medici Archive Project |
| Misc. Med. | Miscellanea Medicea, Archivio di Stato di Firenze |
| MdP | Mediceo del Principato, Archivio di Stato di Firenze |
| SP | State Papers, National Archives at Kew |
| YRL | Charles E. Young Research Library, UCLA |

# NOTES

## INTRODUCTION

1. Variously known as the Guardaroba Medicea or the Sala delle Carte Geografiche, we shall return to this important site in Chapter 6. Mark Rosen, "A New Chronology of the Construction and Restoration of the Medici Guardaroba in the Palazzo Vecchio, Florence," *Mitteilungen des Kunsthistorischen Institutes in Florenz* 53, nos. 2–3 (2009): 285–308; Mark Rosen, *The Mapping of Power in Renaissance Italy: Painted Cartographic Cycles in Social and Intellectual Context* (New York: Cambridge University Press, 2015).

2. Paul Barolsky and William E. Wallace, "The Myth of Michelangelo and Il Magnifico," *Notes in the History of Art* 12, no. 3 (Spring 1993): 16–21; Mary Ann Jack, "The Accademia del Disengo in Late Renaissance Florence," *Sixteenth Century Journal* 7, no. 2 (Oct. 1976): 3–20; Edward A. Parsons, "At the Funeral of Michelangelo," *Renaissance News* 4, no. 2 (Summer 1951): 17–19; J. L. Heilbron, *Galileo* (New York: Oxford University Press, 2010); Mario Biagioli, *Galileo Courtier: The Practice of Science in the Culture of Absolutism* (Chicago: University of Chicago Press, 1994).

3. An anonymous reader of the manuscript kindly noted that Cosimo I handed significant power over to Francesco I on May 1, 1564. Cosimo I remained an active player, however, and retained his titular preeminence until his death, and so I follow historiographic convention in matching the end of his reign with the year of his death.

4. For a digitized collection of Tuscan *stemme*, see Archivio di Stato di Firenze, *Ceramelli Papiani:* Blasoni delle famiglie toscane descritte nella *Raccolta Ceramelli Papiani*, accessed 11/9/19 and 7/8/2020, http://www.archiviodistato.firenze.it/ceramellipapiani/index.php?page=Home. For a sense of the scale of patrician involvement, the following are some of the Tuscan, principally Florentine, families that appear in the text: Alamanni (fasc. 34), Albizzi (56), Alidosi (83), Bardi (389), Baroncelli (409–410), Baroncini (412), Bartoli (423–430), Battaglini (5088), Bonaventuri (809 and 810), Bondelmonti (827), Del Caccia (1076), Canigiani (1166), Capponi (1209), Carletti (1229), Carnesecchi (1243), Cavalcanti (1347), Concini (1621), Dovara (1808), Federighi (1957), Forestani (2084), Gaddi (2175 and 2176), Gianfigliazzi (2341), Giraldi (2401), Giugni (2409), Grifoni of San

Miniato, Pisa, and Florence (2487), Guicciardini (2570), Guidi (2581, 2582, 2585), Guidotti (2589 and 2590), Lenzoni (2747), Leoncini (2750 and 2751), Macinghi (2865), Mancini (2923–2926 and 5906), Medici (3130), Mercati (3158, 3159, and 7826), Migliorati (3181–3183), Nasi (3349), Neretti (3374), Nobili (3419; de' Nobili of Lucca: 6106, 6107, and 6108), Orlandini (3477–3479 and 3483), Pagni (3532–3536), Pannocchieschi d'Elci (6194), Parenti (3613), Ricasoli (3959), del Riccio (3978–3983), da Romena (4054–4057), Sassetti (4270), Serguidi (4354), Serristori (4369), Strozzi (4515), Tarugi (4571), Usimbardi (4765), Valori (4791), Vecchietti (4825), Velluti (4827), Vespucci (4886), Vinta (4885). Many, but not all, of these families had been officially accepted in the patriciate by the period in question.

5.  John M. Najemy, *A History of Florence: 1200–1575* (Malden, MA: Blackwell, 2008), 468–473; J. G. A. Pocock, *The Machiavellian Moment: Florentine Political Thought and the Atlantic Republican Tradition* (Princeton, NJ: Princeton University, 1975); Quentin Skinner, *The Foundations of Modern Political Thought*, 2 vols. (Cambridge: Cambridge University Press, 1978).

6.  Noel Malcolm, *Useful Enemies: Islam and the Ottoman Empire in Western Political Thought, 1450–1750* (New York: Oxford University Press, 2019), 352.

7.  R. Burr Litchfield, *Emergence of a Bureaucracy: The Florentine Patricians 1530–1790* (Princeton, NJ: Princeton University Press, 1986); Jean-Claude Waquet, *Corruption: Ethics and Power in Florence, 1600–1770*, trans. Linda McCall (University Park, PA: Pennsylvania State University Press, 1992).

8.  On the state and absolutism in Italy, see Litchfield, *Emergence of a Bureaucracy*, 4–9; Giovanni Botero, *Della ragione di stato: Libri dieci* (Rome: Vincenzio Pellagallo, 1590); Romain Descendre, "Ragion di stato," *Enciclopedia machiavelliana* (2014), online ed., accessed June 22, 2019, http:// www.treccani.it/enciclopedia/ragion-di-stato_%28Enciclopedia-machi avelliana%29/. On the relationship between Machiavelli and reason of state in the context of the Ottoman Empire, see Malcolm, *Useful Enemies*, 159–183.

9.  For two recent engagements with this large subject, see Mark Greengrass, *Christendom Destroyed: Europe 1517–1648* (New York: Penguin, 2014), esp. xxv–xxix, 1–5, 24–30, and 675–680; Malcolm, *Useful Enemies*, esp. 57–75; Martin W. Lewis and Kären Wigen, *The Myth of Continents: A Critique of Metageography* (Berkeley: University of California Press, 1997); Fernand Braudel, *The Mediterranean and the Mediterranean World in the Age of Philip II*, 2nd rev. ed., 2 vols., trans. Siân Reynolds (Berkeley: University of California Press, 1995), esp. chapter 3, "Boundaries: The Greater Mediterranean," 1: 168–231.

10.  A. R. Disney, *A History of Portugal and the Portuguese Empire: From Beginnings to 1807*, 2 vols. (New York: Cambridge University Press, 2009), 1: 196–200;

James C. Boyajian, *Portuguese Trade in Asia under the Habsburgs, 1580–1640* (Baltimore, MD: Johns Hopkins University Press, 1993), 65 and 132–134. For Francesco Carletti's evasion of such restrictions, see Biblioteca Angelica ms. 1331, 3r–3v; Filippo Sassetti, *Lettere dall'India (1583–1588)*, ed. Adele Dei (Rome: Salerno, 1995), Letter 26, 215; António Galvão, *Tratado: Que compôs o nobre & notavel capitão Antonio Galvão, dos diversos & desuayrados caminhos, por onde nos tempos passados a pimenta & especearia veyo da India ás nossas partes, & assi de todos os descobrimentos antigos & modernos, que são feitos ate a era de mil & quinhentos & cincoenta; com os nomes particulares das pessoas que os fizeram, & em que tempos & as suas alturas, obra certo muy notavel & copiosa*, 31. The Lilly Library at Indiana University, where I read this, gives the date of the treatise as December 15, 1563.

11. Céline Dauverd, *Imperial Ambition in the Early Modern Mediterranean: Genoese Merchants and the Spanish Crown* (New York: Cambridge University Press, 2015), has quite persuasively argued for "symbiotic imperialism" (2) as characteristic of Genoa's relationship with imperial Spain; Dauverd focuses on the role of Genoa's merchants in developing a mercantile and financial empire entwined with Spain's political one, concentrating on southern Italy. Although Florence and Genoa both contributed ships and loans to the Spanish alliance, Tuscany's relationship with Spain differed sharply by virtue of its scale, dynastic ties, and political structure and thus Tuscany's objectives. The Tuscan state's offer of symbiotic relations outside the Mediterranean was thus more politically threatening and less successful than that of Genoa's merchants even as the latter were closely entwined with the Genoese state.

12. Michael S. Laver, *The Sakoku Edicts and the Politics of Tokugawa Hegemony* (Amherst, NY: Cambria, 2011); Ronald P. Toby, *State and Diplomacy in Early Modern Japan: Asia in the Development of the Tokugawa Bakufu* (Stanford, CA: Stanford University Press, 1991); Victor Lierberman, *Strange Parallels: Southeast Asia in Global Context, c. 800–1830*, 2 vols. (New York: Cambridge University Press, 2009), 2: 453 and 453n247 citing Toby; Timothy Brook, *Vermeer's Hat: The Seventeenth Century and the Dawn of the Global World* (London: Bloomsbury, 2008), 84–116 and 198–202; Erika Monahan, *The Merchants of Siberia: Trade in Early Modern Eurasia* (Ithaca, NY: Cornell University Press, 2016), 47.

13. Dagmar Eichberger describes Naturalia as follows: "for so-called *Naturalia*, a category which included specimens of rare plants, minerals and exotic animals, and for *Exotica*, a term used for ethnographic material and artefacts from distant countries" (18). Dagmar Eichberger, "*Naturalia* and *artefacta*: Dürer's Nature Drawings and Early Collecting," in *Dürer and His Culture*, eds. D. Eichberger and C. Zika (Cambridge: Cambridge University Press, 1998): 13–37 and 212–216.

14. For an accessible standard definition of these terms in the early modern context, see *Google Arts and Culture*, "Cabinet of Curiosities," accessed July 30, 2019, https://artsandculture.google.com/theme/4QKSkqTAGnJ2LQ.

15. On Genoa's centrality as a financial center for the Spanish Empire, see Dauverd, *Imperial Ambitions*, 68–71. P. 69, table 2.1, for instance, shows that in a survey of banks in the Kingdom of Naples from 1509 to 1571, seven were Genoese and two Florentine and from 1572 to 1636, twelve were Genoese banks and five Florentine. See also Thomas Allison Kirk, *Genoa and the Sea: Policy and Power in an Early Modern Maritime Republic, 1559–1684*, (Baltimore, MD: Johns Hopkins University Press, 2005), 29–32 and 84–99.

16. Thanks to Professor Cécile Fromont of Yale who, as respondent to a paper I gave at the American Academy in Rome, proposed "shadow capital" as a description; responsibility for any problems with usage rests with me. Since then, I have found Thomas J. Barfield's imperial taxonomy and characterization of shadow empires to be particularly helpful. Thomas J. Barfield, "The Shadow Empires: Imperial State Formation along the Chinese-Nomad Frontier," in *Empires: Perspectives from Archaeology and History* (New York: Cambridge University Press, 2001), ed. Susan E. Alcock, Terence N. D'Altroy, Kathleen D. Morrison, and Carla M. Sinopoli, 10–41, esp. 29 and 33–36. Barfield defines shadow empires as an internally differentiated class of empires that exist as responses to primary empire formation. For Barfield, such shadow empires depend on their relationship with primary imperial states, mimicking their forms, but lacking their whole substance. In various ways, this relationship often seems to have been parasitic. Barfield suggests four types of shadow empire—mirror, maritime trade, vulture, and nostalgia—but does not argue that the list should be limited to these types.

17. Sally McKee, *Uncommon Dominion: Venetian Crete and the Myth of Ethnic Purity* (Philadelphia: University of Pennsylvania Press, 2000); John Martin and Dennis Romano, eds., *Venice Reconsidered: The History and Civilization of an Italian City-State, 1297–1797* (Baltimore, MD: Johns Hopkins University Press, 2002); Eric Dursteler, *Venetians in Constantinople: Nation, Identity, and Coexistence in the Early Modern Mediterranean* (Baltimore, MD: Johns Hopkins University Press, 2006); Monique O'Connell, *Men of Empire: Power and Negotiation in Venice's Maritime State* (Baltimore, MD: Johns Hopkins University Press, 2009); Natalie E. Rothman, *Brokering Empire: Trans-Imperial Subjects between Venice and Istanbul* (Ithaca, NY: Cornell University Press, 2011); Maria Fusaro, *Political Economies of Empire in the Early Modern Mediterranean: The Decline of Venice and the Rise of England, 1450–1700* (New York: Cambridge University Press, 2015); Frederic C. Lane, *Venice: A Maritime Republic* (Baltimore, MD: Johns Hopkins University

Press, 1973); Robert Finlay, "The Immortal Republic: The Myth of Venice during the Italian Wars (1494–1530)," *Sixteenth Century Journal* 30, no. 4 (1999): 931–944; James S. Grubb, "When Myths Lose Power: Four Decades of Venetian Historiography," *Journal of Modern History* 58 (1986): 43–94. See also Braudel, *The Mediterranean*, 1: 500–508 and 535; 2: 960–962; Henry Kamen, *Empire: How Spain Became a World Power, 1492–1763* (New York: Harper Collins, 2003), 89–90 and 173.

18. Corey Tazzara, *The Free Port of Livorno and the Transformation of the Mediterranean World, 1574–1790* (New York: Oxford University Press, 2017), importantly contrasts Livorno and Venice and has been influential in my thinking; all errors remain my own. See also Francesca Trivellato, *The Familiarity of Strangers: The Sephardic Diaspora, Livorno, and Cross-Cultural Trade in the Early Modern Period* (New Haven, CT: Yale University Press, 2009); Molly Greene, *Catholic Pirates and Greek Merchants: A Maritime History of the Mediterranean* (Princeton, NJ: Princeton University Press, 2010), 78–95.

19. Tuscans diplomatic texts regularly referred to the Ottoman Empire; for instance, ASF, MdP 4275, 114r, "l'Impero Ottomań[n]o."

20. *Oxford English Dictionary*, online ed., accessed August 2, 2019, s.v. "empire," https://www-oed-com.libezproxy2.syr.edu/view/Entry/61337?isAdvanced=false&result=1&rskey=tx8oTW&.

21. McKee, *Uncommon Dominion*; Dursteler, *Venetians in Constantinople*; O'Connell, *Men of Empire*; Rothman, *Brokering Empire*; Samuel K. Cohn Jr., *Creating the Florentine State: Peasants and Rebellion, 1348–1434* (Cambridge: Cambridge University Press, 1999); Elena Fasano Guarini, "Center and Periphery," in "The Origins of the State in Italy, 1300–1600," Supplement, *Journal of Modern History* 67 (1995): S74–S96; William Connell and Andrea Zorzi, eds., *Florentine Tuscany: Structures and Practices of Power* (New York: Cambridge University Press, 2000); Najemy, *History of Florence*; Marvin Becker, *Florence in Transition*, vol. 2, *The Rise of the Territorial State* (Baltimore, MD: Johns Hopkins University Press, 1968); Jean Boutier, Sandro Landi, and Olivier Rouchon, eds., *Firenze e la Toscana: Genesi e trasformazione di uno stato (xiv–xix secolo)* (Florence: Mandragora, 2010).

22. Peter H. Wilson, *Heart of Europe: A History of the Holy Roman Empire* (Cambridge, MA: Harvard University Press, 2016).

23. This is concisely put in Gaines Post, review of *Tudor Royal Proclamations*, vol. 1, *The Early Tudors (1485–1553)*, by Paul L. Hughes and James F. Larkin, *American Journal of Legal History* 9, no. 4 (Oct. 1965): 369.

24. See, for instance, Mike Mason, *Turbulent Empires: A History of Global Capitalism since 1945* (Chicago: McGill-Queen's University Press, 2018).

25. Charles H. Parker, *Global Interactions in the Early Modern Age, 1400–1800* (New York: Cambridge University Press, 2010), 2–8.

26. Margaret Meserve, *Empires of Islam in Renaissance Historical Thought* (Cambridge, MA: Harvard University Press, 2008); John F. Richards, *The Mughal Empire* (Cambridge: Cambridge University Press, 1993); Douglas E. Streusand, *Islamic Gunpowder Empires: Ottomans, Safavids, and Mughals* (Boulder, CO: Westview, 2011); Stephen F. Dale, *The Muslim Empires of the Ottomans, Safavids, and Mughals* (New York: Cambridge University Press, 2010).

27. While Imperial China is used ubiquitously in the literature, the term has recently been contested. Although Timothy Brook, *The Troubled Empire: China in the Yuan and Ming Dynasties* (Cambridge, MA: Belknap, 2010), uses the term *empire* in a conventional sense, he has recently sought to substitute "great state" in Brook, *Great State: China and the World* (London: Profile Books, 2019). Even books with revisionist approaches have traditionally used "empire" or a variant: F. W. Mote, *Imperial China, 900–1800* (Cambridge, MA.: Harvard University Press, 1999) and Valerie Hansen, *The Open Empire: A History of China to 1600* (New York: Norton, 2000).

28. For the statistic, see Simon Sebag Montefiore, *The Romanovs: 1613–1918* (New York: Alfred A. Knopf, 2016), xix. For Peter the Great's adoption of an imperial title, see James Cracraft, *The Revolution of Peter the Great* (Cambridge, MA: Harvard University Press, 2003), 27 and 171; Robert K. Massie, *Peter the Great: His Life and World* (New York: Ballantine, 1980), 741-742. On the assertion of sovereignty and the idea of Muscovy as the Third Rome, see Catherine Evtuhov, David Goldfrank, Lindsey Hughes, and Richard Stites, *A History of Russia: People, Legends, Events, Forces* (New York: Houghton Mifflin, 2004), 114–117.

29. Wilson, *Heart of Europe*, esp. chapter 1, 19–76. Geoffrey Parker's deeply erudite new biography of Emperor Charles V foregrounds the term: Geoffrey Parker, *Emperor: A New Life of Charles V* (New Haven, CT: Yale University Press, 2019).

30. For example, Portugal: Sanjay Subrahmanyam, *The Portuguese Empire in Asia, 1500–1700: A Political and Economic History* (New York: Longman, 1993); A. R. Disney, *A History of Portugal and the Portuguese Empire: From Beginnings to 1807*, 2 vols. (New York: Cambridge University Press, 2009); Glenn J. Ames, *Renascent Empire?: The House of Braganza and the Quest for Stability in Portuguese Monsoon Asia, ca. 1640–1683* (Amsterdam: Amsterdam University Press, 2000). Spain: J. H. Elliott, *Imperial Spain, 1469–1716*, rev. ed. (New York: Penguin, 2002), and Elliott, *Empires of the Atlantic World: Britain and Spain in America, 1492–1830* (New Haven, CT: Yale University Press, 2006). Dutch Republic: C. R. Boxer, *The Dutch Seaborne Empire, 1600–1800* (London: Hutchinson, 1965). Multiple: Jonathan I. Israel, *Conflicts of Empires: Spain, the Low Countries and the Struggle for World Supremacy, 1585–1713* (London: Hambledon, 1997); Anthony Pagden, *Lords of All the World: Ideologies of Empire in Spain, Britain and France c. 1500–c.*

*1800* (New Haven, CT: Yale University Press, 1995); James D. Tracy, ed., *The Rise of Merchant Empires: Long-Distance Trade in the Early Modern World, 1350–1750* (New York: Cambridge University Press, 1993); James D. Tracy, ed., *The Political Economy of Merchant Empires: State Power and World Trade, 1350–1750*, 1991 (New York: Cambridge University Press, 1997).

31. For a recent use of the term for the Mexica, see Stuart B. Schwartz, *Victors and Vanquished: Spanish and Nahua Views of the Fall of the Mexica Empire: A Brief History with Documents*, 2nd ed. (Boston: Bedford / St.Martin's, 2018). In a book that is very attentive to the use of language, Camilla Townsend, *Fifth Sun: A New History of the Aztecs* (New York: Oxford University Press, 2019), 60, 72, and 79, refers to the late fifteenth and early sixteenth century polity centered in Tenochtitlan with imperial terminology. On the Inka, see Izumi Shimada, ed., *The Inka Empire: A Multidisciplinary Approach* (Austin: University of Texas Press, 2015).

32. Disney, *History of Portugal*, 2: 19–20.

33. John O. Hunwick, *Timbuktu and the Songhai Empire: Al-Sa'Dī's Ta'rīkh al-Sūdān down to 1613 and Other Contemporary Documents* (Boston: Brill, 1999); Kevin Shillington, *A History of Africa*, 3rd ed. (New York: Palgrave Macmillan, 2012), 174–175 and 187–189.

34. Navina Najat Haidar and Marika Sardar, *Sultans of Deccan India, 1500–1700: Opulence and Fantasy* (New York: Metropolitan Museum of Art, 2015), 45; Richard M. Eaton, *A Social History of the Deccan, 1300–1761: Eight Indian Lives* (New York: Cambridge University Press, 2005), 97–99.

35. Shillington, *History of Africa*, 114–122 and 170–173.

36. See, for instance, Gregory Hanlon, *The Twilight of a Military Tradition: Italian Aristocrats and European Conflicts, 1560–1800* (New York: Holmes and Meyer, 1998), maps 2.1 and 2.3, 48 and 55; Guarini, "Center and Periphery," esp. S74n2. and S83–85.

37. Nicholas Scott Baker, *The Fruit of Liberty: Political Culture in the Florentine Renaissance, 1480–1550* (Cambridge, MA: Harvard University Press, 2013); Eric Cochrane, *Florence in the Forgotten Centuries 1527–1800: A History of Florence and the Florentines in the Age of the Grand Dukes* (Chicago: University of Chicago Press, 1973), book 1, 11–92; Giorgio Spini, *Cosimo I e l'indipendenza del principato mediceo*, 2nd ed. (Florence: Vallecchi, 1980); Stefano dall'Aglio, *The Duke's Assassin: Exile and Death of Lorenzino de' Medici*, trans. Donald Weinstein (New Haven, CT: Yale University Press, 2015).

38. See, for instance, J. R. Hale, *Florence and the Medici* (London: Phoenix, 2001); Cochrane, *Florence*. On Siena, see DSC, Min Z233.I8 S67i 1557, "Inuestitura Senensis MDLVII"; Najemy, *History of Florence*, 467–468 and 484; Simon Pepper and Nicholas Adams, *Firearms and Fortifications: Military Architecture and Siege Warfare in Sixteenth-Century Siena* (Chicago: University of Chicago Press, 1986); E. Fasano Guarini, "Lo stato regionale,"

in *Storia della Toscana: 1. Dalle origini al Settecento*, ed. E. Fasano Guarini, G. Petralia, and P. Pezzino (Rome: Laterza, 2004), 148 (fig. 11) and 161. Florence's fifteenth-century conquest of Pisa and siege of Siena in Lauro Martines, *Furies: War in Europe, 1450–1700* (New York: Bloomsbury, 2013), 103–112, serve as archetypal examples of brutality.

39. On population, see Richard Goldthwaite, *The Economy of Renaissance Florence* (Baltimore, MD: Johns Hopkins University Press, 2009), 337, table 4.3. Florence's recovery: Cochrane, *Florence*. Vauban comparison: Hanlon, *Twilight*, 62; Hale, *Florence and the Medici*, 130; Robert Dallington, "A suruey of the great dukes state of Tuscany In the yeare of our Lord 1596," (London: Printed [by George Eld] for Edward Blount, 1605), 8 (5) (the pagination is eccentric and repetitive, so I give the Early English Books Online pdf page parenthetically); Niccolò Capponi, "Le Palle di Marte: Military Strategy and Diplomacy in the Grand Duchy of Tuscany under Ferdinand II de' Medici (1621–1670)," *Journal of Military History* 68 (October 2004): 1129.

40. Hale, *Florence and the Medici*, 130–132.

41. On the title, see Elena Fasano Guarini, "Cosimo I de' Medici, duca di Firenze, granduca di Toscana," *DBI* 30 (1984).

42. Ingrid D. Rowland, *The Scarith of Scornello: A Tale of Renaissance Forgery* (Chicago: University of Chicago Press, 2004), 26, 30–31, 67–68, 76, and 98–100.

43. Gregory Murry, *The Medicean Succession: Monarchy and Sacral Politics in Duke Cosimo dei Medici's Florence* (Cambridge, MA: Harvard University Press, 2014).

44. William J. Bouwsma, "The Renaissance and the Drama of Western History," *American Historical Review* 84 (1979): 1–15; Edward Muir, "The Italian Renaissance in America," *American Historical Review* 100 (1995): 1095–118; Anthony Molho, "The Renaissance: Made in the USA," in *Imagined Histories: American Historians Interpret the Past*, ed. Anthony Molho and Gordon Wood (Princeton, NJ: Princeton University Press, 1998): 263–294; John Jeffries Martin, "The Renaissance: Between Myth and History," in *The Renaissance: Italy and Abroad*, ed. John Jeffries Martin (New York: Routledge, 2003): 1–23; Paula Findlen, "The Renaissance in the Museum," in *The Italian Renaissance in the Twentieth Century*, ed. Allen Grieco, Michael Rocke, and Fiorella Superbi (Florence: Olschki, 2002): 93–116.

45. Jacob Burckhardt, *The Civilization of the Renaissance in Italy*, trans. S. G. C. Middlemore (New York: Modern Library, 2002); Hans Baron, *The Crisis of the Early Italian Renaissance* (Princeton, NJ: Princeton University Press, 1966); Gene Brucker, *Florentine Politics and Society* (Princeton, NJ: Princeton University Press, 1962); Brucker, *Renaissance Florence* (New York: Wiley, 1969); Brucker, *Florence: The Golden Age, 1138–1737* (Berkeley: Uni-

versity of California Press, 1998); Brucker, *Living on the Edge in Leonardo's Florence* (Berkeley: University of California Press, 2005), esp. 1–21.

46. Dale Kent, *The Rise of the Medici Faction in Florence, 1426–1434* (New York: Oxford University Press, 1978); Dale Kent, *Cosimo de' Medici and the Florentine Renaissance* (New Haven, CT: Yale University Press, 2000); Nicolai Rubinstein, *The Government of Florence under the Medici (1434–1494)*, 2nd ed. (Oxford, UK: Clarendon, 1998); Anthony Molho, "Cosimo de' Medici: *Pater Patriae* or *Padrino?*," *Stanford Italian Review* 1 (1979): 5–33; Hale, *Florence and the Medici*; Christopher Hibbert, *The Rise and Fall of the House of Medici* (London: Folio Society, 1998).

47. Samuel K. Cohn Jr., *Creating the Florentine State: Peasants and Rebellion, 1348–1434* (Cambridge: Cambridge University Press, 1999); Guarini, "Center and Periphery"; John M. Najemy, *Corporatism and Consensus in Florentine Electoral Politics, 1280–1400* (Chapel Hill: University of North Carolina Press, 1982); Najemy, *History of Florence*; Richard C. Trexler, *Public Life in Renaissance Florence* (Ithaca, NY: Cornell University Press, 1980); Connell and Zorzi, *Florentine Tuscany*; Boutier, Landi, and Rouchon, *Firenze e la Toscana*. For social history, see Samuel K. Cohn Jr., *The Laboring Classes in Renaissance Florence* (New York: Academic Press, 1980); Cohn, *Death and Property in Siena, 1205–1800* (Baltimore, MD: Johns Hopkins University Press, 1988).

48. Paula Findlen, Michelle M. Fontaine, and Duane J. Osheim, eds., *Beyond Florence: The Contours of Medieval and Early Modern Italy* (Stanford, CA: Stanford University Press, 2003). On lordships and courts, see John Larner, *The Lords of Romagna: Romagnol Society and the Origins of the Signorie* (Ithaca, NY: Cornell University Press, 1965); Cecilia Ady, *The Bentivoglio of Bologna: A Study in Despotism* (London: Oxford University Press, 1969); Werner Gundersheimer, *Ferrara: The Style of a Renaissance Despotism* (Princeton, NJ: Princeton University Press, 1973); Trevor Dean, "Lords, Vassals and Clients in Renaissance Ferrara," *English Historical Review* 100, no. 394 (January 1985): 106–119; Trevor Dean, "The Courts," in "The Origins of the State in Italy, 1300–1600," Supplement, *Journal of Modern History* 67, (December 1995): S136–S151; Trevor Dean, *Land and Power in Late Medieval Ferrara: The Rule of the Este, 1350–1450* (New York: Cambridge University Press, 2002); Trevor Dean and Chris Wickham, eds., *City and Countryside in Late Medieval and Renaissance Italy* (London: Bloomsbury Academic, 2003); Louis Green, *Castruccio Castracani: A Study on the Origins and Character of a Fourteenth-Century Italian Despotism* (New York: Oxford University Press, 1986); Benjamin Kohl, *Padua under the Carrara, 1318–1405* (Baltimore, MD: Johns Hopkins University Press, 1998). On communes and city-states, see William Bowsky, *A Medieval Commune: Siena under the Nine, 1287–1355* (Berkeley: University of California Press, 1981); Lauro Martines, *Power and Imagination: City-States in Renaissance Italy* (Baltimore,

MD: Johns Hopkins University Press, 1988); Philip Jones, *The Italian City-State: From Commune to Signoria* (New York: Clarendon, 1997); Ronald Musto, *Apocalypse in Rome: Cola di Rienzo and the Politics of the New Age* (Berkeley: University of California Press, 2003); Daniel Waley and Trevor Dean, *The Italian City Republics*, 4th ed. (New York: Routledge, 2010); Chris Wickham, *Sleepwalking into a New World: The Emergence of Italian City Communes in the Twelfth Century* (Princeton, NJ: Princeton University Press, 2015). On Renaissance states, see M. E. Bratchel, *Medieval Lucca and the Evolution of the Renaissance State* (New York: Oxford University Press, 2008); Andrea Gamberini and Isabella Lazzarini, eds., *The Italian Renaissance State* (New York: Cambridge University Press, 2012).

49. David Herlihy and Christiane Klapisch-Zuber, *Tuscans and Their Families: A Study of the Florentine Catasto of 1427* (New Haven, CT: Yale University Press, 1989); Gene Brucker, ed., *Two Memoirs of Renaissance Florence*, trans. Julia Martines (Long Grove, IL: Waveland, 1991); Sergio Tognetti, "Mercanti e libri di conto nella Toscana del basso medioevo: le edizioni di registri aziendali dagli anni '60 del Novecento a oggi," *Anuario de Estudios Medievales* 42, no. 2 (July–Dec. 2012): 867–880; Duccio Balestraccci, *The Renaissance in the Fields: Family Memoirs of a Fifteenth-Century Tuscan Peasant* (State College: Pennsylvania State University Press, 1999); Dale V. Kent and F. W. Kent, *Neighbours and Neighbourhood in Renaissance Florence* (Locust Valley, NY: J. J. Augustin, 1982). By comparison: James S. Grubb, "Memory and Identity: Why the Venetians Didn't Keep Ricordanze," *Renaissance Studies* 8 (1994): 375–386.

50. Edwin S. Hunt, *The Medieval Super-Companies: A Study of the Peruzzi Company of Florence* (New York: Cambridge University Press, 1994); Edwin S. Hunt, "A New Look at the Dealings of the Bardi and Peruzzi with Edward III," *Journal of Economic History* 50, no. 1 (March 1990): 149–162; Richard Goldthwaite, *Private Wealth in Renaissance Florence: A Study of Four Families* (Princeton, NJ: Princeton University Press, 1968); Goldthwaite, "The Medici Bank and the World of Florentine Capitalism," *Past and Present* 144 (1987): 3–31; Goldthwaite, *Wealth and the Demand for Art in Italy, 1300–1600* (Baltimore, MD: Johns Hopkins University Press, 1993); Philip Jacks and William Caferro, *The Spinelli of Florence: The Fortunes of a Renaissance Merchant Family* (University Park: Pennsylvania State University Press, 2001); Francesco Guidi Bruscoli, *Papal Banking in Renaissance Rome: Benvenuto Olivieri and Paul III, 1534–1549* (New York: Routledge, 2016); Iris Origo, *The Merchant of Prato* (London: Folio Society, 1984). On the economy, see Goldthwaite, *Economy of Renaissance Florence*; Paolo Malanima, "L'economia toscana dalla pesta nera alla fine del seicento" in Guarini et al., *Storia della Toscana*, 183–197.

51. Felix Gilbert, *Machiavelli and Guicciardini: Politics and History in Sixteenth-Century Florence* (Princeton, NJ: Princeton University Press, 1965); Pocock,

*Machiavellian Moment*; Melissa Bullard, *Lorenzo il Magnifico: Image, Anxiety, Politics and Finance* (Florence: Leo S. Olschki, 1994); Mark Jurdjevic, *A Great and Wretched City: Promise and Failure in Machiavelli's Florentine Political Thought* (Cambridge, MA: Harvard University Press, 2014); Lucio Biasiori and Giuseppe Marcocci, eds., *Machiavelli, Islam and the East: Reorienting the Foundations of Modern Political Thought* (New York: Palgrave Macmillan, 2018).

52. Najemy, *History of Florence*.

53. Riguccio Galluzzi, *Storia del Granducato di Toscana*, new ed., 11 vols. (Florence: Leonardo Marchini, 1822); Luciano Berti, *Il principe dello studiolo: Francesco I dei Medici e la fine del Rinascimento fiorentino* (Pistoia, It.: Artout Maschietto, 2002). Berti remained in dialogue with Galluzzi's work (25–27) and drew the distinction between Francesco I as a late mannerist prince and Ferdinando I as a truly Counter-Reformation one (32). See also Furio Diaz, *Il granducato di Toscana: I Medici* (Turin, It.: UTET, 1976).

54. Cochrane, *Florence*.

55. Archivio di Stato di Firenze, *Archivio Mediceo del Principato: Inventario Sommario* (Rome: Ministero dell'Interno publicazioni degli archivi di stato I, 1966), http://www.archiviodistato.firenze.it/asfi/fileadmin/risorse/allegati _inventari_on_line/s17_inventario.pdf.

56. Claudia Conforti, ed., *Vasari, gli Uffizi e il duca* (Florence: Giunti, 2011); Paula Findlen, "The 2012 Josephine Waters Bennett Lecture: The Eighteenth-Century Invention of the Renaissance: Lessons from the Uffizi," *Renaissance Quarterly* 66, no. 1 (Spring 2013): 1–34. On the Tuscan elite, see Litchfield, *Emergence of a Bureaucracy*; Waquet, *Corruption*; Giovanna Benadusi, *A Provincial Elite in Early Modern Tuscany: Family and Power in the Creation of the State* (Baltimore, MD: Johns Hopkins University Press, 1996). On absolutism, see Biagioli, *Galileo Courtier*; Perry Anderson, *Lineages of the Absolutist State* (New York: Verso, 1979).

57. Konrad Eisenbichler, ed., *The Cultural Politics of Duke Cosimo I de' Medici* (Burlington, VT: Ashgate, 2001); Murry, *Medicean Succession*; Kathleen M. Comerford, *Jesuit Foundations and Medici Power, 1532–1621* (Boston: Brill, 2017). Thanks to Philip Davis for bibliographic information and many stimulating conversations.

58. Trivellato, *Familiarity of Strangers*; Tazzara, *Free Port*; Greene, *Catholic Pirates*, 78–95.

59. Capponi, "Palle di Marte"; Hanlon, *Twilight*; Alberto Tenenti, *Piracy and the Decline of Venice: 1580–1615*, trans. Janet and Brian Pullan (Berkeley: University of California Press, 1967); Giovanna Fiume, *Schiavitù mediterranee: Corsari, rinnegati e santi di età moderna* (Milan: Bruno Mondadori, 2009); Franco Angiolini, "L'Ordine di Santo Stefano, i Toscani e il mare," in *Atti del Convegno, l'Ordine di Santo Stefano e il Mare* (Pisa, It.: ETS, 2001), 31–50; Giovanna Benadusi, "Career Strategies in Early Modern Tuscany:

The Emergence of Regional Elite," *Sixteenth Century Journal* 25, no. 1 (Spring 1994): 85–99.

60. Michael Mallett, *Florentine Galleys of the Fifteenth Century* (Oxford, UK: Clarendon, 1967); Cesare Ciano, *I primi Medici e il mare: Note sulla politica marinara toscana da Cosimo I a Ferdinando I* (Pisa, It.: Pacini, 1980); Gino Benvenuti, *Le repubbliche marinare: Amalfi, Pisa, Genova e Venezia: La nascita, le vittorie, le lotte e il tramonto delle gloriose città-stato che dal Medioevo al XVIII secolo dominarono il Mediterraneo* (Rome: Newton Compton, 1989); Marco Tangheroni, ed., *Pisa e il Mediterraneo: Uomini, merci, idee dagli Etruschi ai Medici* (Milan: Skira, 2003). On Tuscany in allied fleets, see Colin Martin and Geoffrey Parker, *The Spanish Armada*, rev. ed. (New York: Manchester University Press, 2002); Niccolò Capponi, *Victory of the West: The Great Christian-Muslim Clash at the Battle of Lepanto* (Cambridge, MA: Da Capo, 2007).

61. Giorgio-Giòrs Tosco, "In Pursuit of the World's Trade: Tuscan and Genoese Attempts to Enter Trans-oceanic Trade in the Seventeenth Century," PhD diss., European University Institute, 2020.

62. Thanks to Lucio Biasiori of the University of Padua for the opportunity to meet Alessandro Favatà of the University of Padua and Luca Calzetta of the Scuola Normale while presenting remotely to his class.

63. Marco Spallanzani, *Mercanti fiorentini nell'Asia portoghese (1500–1525)* (Florence: S.P.E.S., 1997); Nunziatella Alessandrini, "Contributo alla storia della famiglia Giraldi, mercanti, banchieri fiorentini alla corte di Lisbona nel XVI secolo," *Storia Economica* 14, no. 3 (2011): 377–407; Francesco Guidi Bruscoli, *Bartolomeo Marchionni, "Homem de Grossa Fazenda" (ca. 1450–1530): Un mercante fiorentino a Lisbona e l'impero portoghese* (Florence: Olschki, 2014); William J. Connell, "Italians in the Early Atlantic World," in *The Routledge History of Italian Americans*, ed. William J. Connell and Stanislao G. Pugliese (New York: Routledge, 2018), 17–41; Sergio Tognetti, "Firenze, Pisa e il mare (metà XIV–fine XV sec.)," in *Firenze e Pisa dopo il 1406: La creazione di un nuova spazio regionale* (Florence: Olschki, 2011): 151–175; Tognetti, "Gli uomini d'affari toscani nella Penisola Iberica (metà XIV secolo—inizio XVI secolo)," *eHumanista* 38 (2018): 83–98. Of course, not all of this research is recent: Sanjay Subrahmanyam, "'Um Bom Homem De Tratar': Piero Strozzi: A Florentine in Portuguese Asia, 1510–1522," *Journal of European Economic History* 16, no. 3 (Winter 1987): 511–526; Gustavo Uzielli, "Piero di Andrea Strozzi Viaggiatore Fiorentino," *Memorie della Società Geografica Italiana*, vol. 5 (Rome: G. Civelli, La Società Geografica Italiana, 1895), 136–138.

64. Sara Fani and Margherita Farina, eds., *Le vie delle lettere: La Tipografia Medicea tra Roma e l'Oriente* (Florence: Mandragora, 2012); Margherita Farina, "Uno scambio epistolare fra Mario Schepani e Giovanni Battista Raimondi: Lo studio della lingua araba nel tardo rinascimento, interesse

scientifico e curiosità," *Egitto e Vicino Oriente* 36 (2013): 63–72; Margherita Farina, "Giovanni Battista Raimondi's Travel in the Middle East: A Case of Sixteenth-Century Portuguese-Italian Interference," *Oriente Moderno* 98, no. 1 (2018): 52–72; Alexander Bevilacqua, *The Republic of Arabic Letters: Islam and the European Enlightenment* (Cambridge, MA: Harvard University Press, 2018); Mario Casari, "This Language Is More Universal Than Any Other: Values of Arabic in Early Modern Italy," in *City, Court, Academy*, ed. Eva Del Soldato and Andrea Rizzi (New York: Routledge, 2018): 173–198; Mario Casari, "Raimondi, Giovanni Battista," *DBI* 86 (2016). The international roundtable "Creating the Digital Republic of Letters, Rome: Early Modern 'Orientalism,'" held at the Istituto Storico Austriaco in Rome in October 2019, showcased numerous projects in progress that bode well for the future vitality of the field.

65. Daniela Degl'Innocenti and Tatiana Lekhovich, eds., *Lo stile dello zar: Arte e moda tra Italia e Russia dal XIV al XVIII* (Geneva-Milan: Skira, 2009); Fani and Farina, *Le vie delle lettere*.

66. P. E. H. Hair and Jonathan D. Davies, "Sierra Leone and the Grand Duchy of Tuscany," *History in Africa* 20 (1993): 61–69; Kaled El Bibas, *L'emiro e il granduca: La vicenda dell'emiro Fakhr ad-Dīn del Libano nel contesto delle relazioni fra la Toscana e l'Oriente* (Florence: Le Lettere, 2010).

67. Detlef Heikamp with contributions by Ferdinand Anders, *Mexico and the Medici* (Florence: Edam, 1972); Lisa Jardine, *Worldly Goods: A New History of the Renaissance* (New York: W. W. Norton, 1998); Lisa Jardine and Jerry Brotton, *Global Interests: Renaissance Art between East and West* (Ithaca, NY: Cornell University Press, 2000); Brian Curran, *The Egyptian Renaissance: The Afterlife of Egypt in Early Modern Italy* (Chicago: University of Chicago Press, 2007); Anna Contadini and Claire Norton, eds., *The Renaissance and the Ottoman World* (Burlington, VT: Ashgate, 2013); Sean Roberts, *Printing a Mediterranean World: Florence, Constantinople, and the Renaissance of Geography* (Cambridge, MA: Harvard University Press, 2013).

68. R. W. Lightbown, "Oriental Art and the Orient in Late Renaissance and Baroque Italy," *Journal of the Warburg and Courtauld Institutes* 32 (1969): 228–279; Rosamond Mack, *Bazaar to Piazza: Islamic Trade and Italian Art, 1300–1600* (Berkeley: University of California Press, 2002); Francisco Zamora Rodríguez, "Interest and Curiosity: American Products, Information, and Exotica in Tuscany," in *Global Goods and the Spanish Empire, 1492–1824: Circulation, Resistance and Diversity*, ed. Bethany Aram and Bartholomé Yun-Casalilla (New York: Palgrave Macmillan, 2014); Maurizio Arfaioli and Marta Caroscio, eds., *The Grand Ducal Medici and the Levant: Material Culture, Diplomacy, and Imagery in the Early Modern Mediterranean* (London: Harvey Miller, 2016); Lia Markey, *Imagining the Americas in Medici Florence* (University Park: Pennsylvania State University Press, 2016); Marilena Mosco and Ornella Casazza, *The Museo degli Argenti Collections*

*and Collectors*, MIBAC (Florence: Giunti, 2004); Martin, *Renaissance*; Lia Markey and Elizabeth Horodowich, eds., *The New World in Early Modern Italy, 1492–1750* (New York: Cambridge University Press, 2017).

69. Paula Findlen, *Possessing Nature: Museums, Collecting, and Scientific Culture in Early Modern Italy* (Berkeley: University of California Press, 1996); Claudia Lazzaro, *The Italian Renaissance Garden: From the Conventions of Planting, Design, and Ornament to the Grand Gardens of Sixteenth-Century Italy* (New Haven, CT: Yale University Press, 1990); Lucia Tongiorgi Tomasi and Gretchen A. Hirschauer, *The Flowering of Florence: Botanical Art for the Medici* (Burlington, VT: Lund Humphries, 2002); Helena Attlee, *Italian Gardens: A Cultural History* (London: Frances Lincoln, 2006); Isabella Lapi Ballerini with Mario Scalini, *The Medici Villas: Complete Guide*, trans. Michael Sullivan and Eleonor Daunt, rev. ed. (Florence: Giunti, 2010); Mariachiara Pozzana, *The Gardens of Florence and Tuscany: A Complete Guide* (Florence: Giunti, 2011); Markey, *Imagining the Americas*; Cristina Bellorini, *The World of Plants in Renaissance Tuscany: Medicine and Botany* (Burlington, VT: Ashgate, 2016); Angelica Groom, *Exotic Animals in the Art and Culture of the Medici Court in Florence* (Leiden, Neth.: Brill, 2018).

70. Alessio Assonitis and Brian Sandberg, eds., *The Grand Ducal Medici and Their Archive (1537–1743)* (London: Harvey Miller, 2016). See the Medici Archive Project's mission statement, accessed October 27, 2020: http://www.medici.org/mission/. The figures provided suggest that in 2015 the project had cataloged 292 of the 6,429 volumes in Mediceo del Principato. The scale of the challenge is massive, as the project (http://www.medici.org/mediceo-del-principato-2/) estimates that the Mediceo del Principato contains about four million letters.

71. I am editing this book during a pandemic that has brought travel to a standstill and thrown so much into doubt, and it remains unclear at the time of writing whether this period has now come to an end or is merely paused.

72. A few examples cannot be more than indicative, but see, for instance, John F. Richards, *The Unending Frontier: An Environmental History of the Early Modern World* (Berkeley and Los Angeles: University of California Press, 2003); Kenneth Pomeranz and Steven Topik, *The World That Trade Created: Society, Culture, and the World Economy, 1400 to the Present*, 3rd ed. (New York: Routledge, 2012); Bruce Mazlish, "Comparing Global History to World History," *Journal of Interdisciplinary History* 28, no. 3 (Winter 1998): 385–395; Immanuel Wallerstein, *The Modern World-System*, vol. 1, *Capitalist Agriculture and the Origins of the European World-Economy in the Sixteenth Century* (New York: Academic, 1974); vol. 2, *Mercantilism and the Consolidation of the European World-Economy, 1600–1750* (New York: Academic, 1980); and vol. 3, *The Second Great Expansion of the Capitalist World-Economy, 1730–1840s* (San Diego: Academic, 1989).

73. This historiographic debate is covered extensively in a recent special supplement: John-Paul Ghobrial, ed., "Global History and Microhistory" *Past and Present* 242, Supplement 14 (Nov. 2019). Notably cited are the Princeton critiques of global history by David Bell and Jeremy Adelman: David A. Bell, "Questioning the Global Turn: The Case of the French Revolution," *French Historical Studies* 37, no. 1 (2014): 1–24, and Jeremy Adelman, "What Is Global History Now?" *Aeon* 2017 (Mar. 2, 2017), cited in John-Paul Ghobrial, "Introduction: Seeing the World like a Microhistorian," in John-Paul Ghobrial, ed., "Global History and Microhistory," 4n12 and 5n14.

74. Angelo de Gubernatis, ed., *Storia dei Viaggiatori Italiani nelle Indie Orientali* (Livorno, It.: Franc. Vigo, 1875); Giuseppe Tucci, *Italia e Oriente*, reissue, ed. Francesco d'Arelli (Rome: Istituto Italiano per l'Africa e l'Oriente, 2005); Gabriela Airaldi, *Dall'Eurasia al Nuovo Mondo: Una storia italiana (sec. XI– XVI)* (Genoa: Fratelli Frelli, 2007). For an explicitly nationalist piece that nonetheless contains important research, see Giuseppe Gino Guarnieri, *Un'audace impresa marittima di Ferdinando I dei Medici (Con una tavola fuori testo, documenti e glossario indo-caraibico): Contribuito alla storia della marina mercantile Italiana* (Pisa, It.: Nistri-Lischi, 1928), published in Fascist Italy.

75. The Carletti manuscript is ms. 1331 in Biblioteca Angelica (Rome). Francesco Carletti, *My Voyage around the World: The Chronicles of a 16th Century Florentine Merchant*, trans. Herbert Weinstock (New York: Pantheon, 1964), xiv; "Carletti, Francesco," *DBI* 20 (1977); Stefania Pineider, *"In così immense pellegrinatione": La scrittura del viaggio nei Ragionamenti di Francesco Carletti* (Rome: Vecchiarelli, 2004); Sassetti, *Lettere dall'India*; Francesco Surdich, "Sassetti, Filippo," *DBI* 90 (2017); Marica Milanesi, *Filippo Sassetti* (Florence: Nuova Italia, 1973); Nunziatella Alessandrini, "Images of India through the Eyes of Filippo Sassetti, a Florentine Humanist Merchant in the 16th Century," in *Sights and Insights: Interactive Images of Europe and the Wider World*, ed. Mary N. Harris and Csaba Lévai (Pisa, It.: Pisa University Press, 2007), 43–58. On precedents, see Spallanzani, *Mercanti fiorentini*.

76. Sanjay Subrahmanyam, *Three Ways to Be Alien: Travails and Encounters in the Early Modern World* (Waltham, MA: Brandeis University Press and the Historical Society of Israel, 2011); Federico Federici and Dario Tessicini, eds., *Translators, Interpreters, and Cultural Negotiators: Mediating and Communicating Power from the Middle Ages to the Modern Era* (New York: Palgrave Macmillan, 2014); E. K. Faridany, "Signal Defeat: The Portuguese Loss of Comorão in 1614 and Its Political and Commercial Consequences," in *Acta Iranica: Portugal, the Persian Gulf and Safavid Persia*, ed. Rudi Matthee and Jorge Flores (Leuven, Belg.: Peeters, 2011), 119–141.

77. Rothman, *Brokering Empire*; Natalie Zemon Davis, *Trickster Travels: A Sixteenth-Century Muslim between Worlds* (New York: Hill and Wang, 2007);

Brook, *Vermeer's Hat*; Eric R. Dursteler, *Renegade Women: Gender, Identity and Boundaries in the Early Modern Mediterranean* (Baltimore, MD: Johns Hopkins University Press, 2011); Noel Malcolm, *Agents of Empire: Knights, Corsairs, Jesuits, and Spies in the Sixteenth Century Mediterranean World* (New York: Oxford University Press, 2015); thanks to Corey Tazzara for recommending this last.

78. Paula Findlen, ed., *Early Modern Things: Objects and Their Histories, 1500–1800* (New York: Routledge, 2013); Anne Gerritsen and Giorgio Riello, eds., *The Global Lives of Things: The Material Culture of Connections in the Early Modern World* (New York: Routledge, 2016); Daniela Bleichmar and Peter C. Mancall, eds., *Collecting across Cultures: Material Exchanges in the Early Modern Atlantic World* (Philadelphia: University of Pennsylvania Press, 2011); Renato Ago, *Gusto for Things: A History of Objects in Seventeenth Century Rome*, trans. Bradford Bouley and Corey Tazzara with Paula Findlen (Chicago: University of Chicago Press, 2013); Frank Trentmann, *Empire of Things: How We Became a World of Consumers, from the Fifteenth Century to the Twenty-First* (New York: Harper Collins, 2016).

79. Steven Topik, Carlos Marichal, and Zephyr Frank, eds., *From Silver to Cocaine: Latin American Commodity Chains and the Building of the World Economy, 1500–2000* (Durham, NC: Duke University Press, 2006); Sophie D. Coe and Michael D. Coe, *The True History of Chocolate*, 2nd ed. (New York: Thames and Hudson, 2007); Marcy Norton, *Sacred Gifts, Profane Pleasures: A History of Tobacco and Chocolate in the Atlantic World* (Ithaca, NY: Cornell University Press, 2008); Irene Fattacciu, "The Resilience and Boomerang Effect of Chocolate: A Product's Globalization and Commodification," in Aram and Yun-Casalilla, *Global Goods*, 255–273; Amy Butler Greenfield, *A Perfect Red: Empire, Espionage, and the Quest for the Color of Desire* (New York: HarperCollins, 2005). On the Silk Road, see Valerie Hansen, *The Silk Road: A New History* (New York: Oxford University Press, 2012). Peter Frankopan, *The Silk Roads: A New History of the World* (New York: Alfred A. Knopf, 2016). On the spice trade, see John Keay, *The Spice Route: A History* (Berkeley: University of California Press, 2006); Paul Freedman, *Out of the East: Spices and the Medieval Imagination* (New Haven, CT: Yale University Press, 2008); Gary Paul Nabhan, *Cumin, Camels, and Caravans: A Spice Odyssey* (Berkeley: University of California Press, 2014); Lizzie Collingham, *The Taste of Empire: How Britain's Quest for Food Shaped the Modern World* (New York: Basic Books, 2017). On Asian trade, see Janet L. Abu-Lughod, *Before European Hegemony: The World System a.d. 1250–1350* (New York: Oxford University Press, 1991); Patricia Risso, *Merchants and Faith: Muslim Commerce and Culture in the Indian Ocean* (Boulder, CO: Westview, 1995); Stewart Gordon, *When Asia Was the World* (Boston, MA: Da Capo, 2008). On long-distance trade, see Niels Steensgaard, *Carracks, Caravans and Companies: The Structural Crisis in the European-Asian Trade in*

*the Early 17th Century* (Copenhagen: Studentlitteratur, 1973); *The Organization of Interoceanic Trade in European Expansion, 1450–1800*, ed. Pieter Emmer and Femme Gaastra (Brookfield, VT: Variorum, Ashgate, 1996).

80. Braudel, *Mediterranean*; Peregrine Horden and Nicholas Purcell, *The Corrupting Sea: A Study of Mediterranean History* (Malden, MA: Blackwell, 2000); Molly Greene, *A Shared World: Christians and Muslims in the Early Modern Mediterranean* (Princeton, NJ: Princeton University Press, 2000); John Julius Norwich, *The Middle Sea: A History of the Mediterranean* (New York: Vintage, 2007); Faruk Tabak, *The Waning of the Mediterranean, 1550–1870: A Geohistorical Approach* (Baltimore, MD: Johns Hopkins University Press, 2008); Kenneth McPherson, *The Indian Ocean: A History of People and the Sea* (Delhi: Oxford University Press, 1993); Michael Pearson, *The Indian Ocean* (New York: Routledge, 2003); K. N. Chaudhuri, *Trade and Civilisation in the Indian Ocean: An Economic History from the Rise of Islam to 1750* (Cambridge, UK: Cambridge University Press, 1999); Ashin Das Gupta, *The World of the Indian Ocean Merchant, 1500–1800: Collected Essays of Ashin Das Gupta* (New Delhi: Oxford University Press, 2001); Anthony Reid, *Southeast Asia in the Age of Commerce: 1450–1680*, 2 vols. (New Haven, CT: Yale University Press, 1988); Benjamin Arbel, *Trading Nations: Jews and Venetians in the Early Modern Eastern Mediterranean* (New York: Brill, 1995); Sebouh David Aslanian, *From the Indian Ocean to the Mediterranean: The Global Trade Networks of Armenian Merchants from New Julfa* (Berkeley: University of California Press, 2011).

81. Annemarie Jordan Gschwend and K. J. P. Lowe, eds., *The Global City: On the Streets of Renaissance Lisbon* (London: Paul Holberton, 2015); Junko Thérèse Takeda, *Between Crown and Commerce: Marseille and the Early Modern Mediterranean* (Baltimore, MD: Johns Hopkins University Press, 2011).

82. Victor Lierberman, *Strange Parallels: Southeast Asia in Global Context, c. 800–1830*, 2 vols. (New York: Cambridge University Press, 2003 and 2009); Francis Fukuyama, *The Origins of Political Order: From Prehuman Times to the French Revolution* (New York: Farrar, Straus, and Giroux, 2011); Walter Scheidel, *Escape from Rome: The Failure of Empire and the Road to Prosperity* (Princeton, NJ: Princeton University Press, 2019); Tonio Andrade, *The Gunpowder Age: China, Military Innovation, and the Rise of the West in World History* (Princeton, NJ: Princeton University Press, 2016). The military revolution thesis was global in implications, but its focus was on Europe: Geoffrey Parker, *The Military Revolution: Military Innovation and the Rise of the West, 1500–1800*, 2nd ed. (New York: Cambridge University Press, 1996); Clifford Rogers, ed., *The Military Revolution Debate: Readings on the Military Transformation of Early Modern Europe* (San Francisco: Westview, 1995).

83. Kenneth Pomeranz, *The Great Divergence: China, Europe, and the Making of the Modern World Economy* (Princeton, NJ: Princeton University Press,

2000); Ronald Findlay and Kevin H. O'Rourke, *Power and Plenty: Trade, War, and the World Economy in the Second Millennium* (Princeton, NJ: Princeton University Press, 2007); Prasannan Parthasarathi, *Why Europe Grew Rich and Asia Did Not: Global Economic Divergence, 1600–1850* (New York: Cambridge University Press, 2011); Ian Morris, *Why the West Rules—For Now: The Patterns of History, and What They Reveal about the Future* (New York: Farrar, Straus and Giroux, 2010).

84. Sanjay Subrahmanyam, *Explorations in Connected History: From the Tagus to the Ganges* (New Delhi: Oxford India Paperbacks, 2011); Subrahmanyam, *Explorations in Connected History: Mughals and Franks* (New Delhi: Oxford India Paperbacks, 2011).

85. Meera Juncu, *India in the Italian Renaissance: Visions of a Contemporary Pagan World 1300–1600* (New York: Routledge, 2016); Sanjay Subrahmanyam, *Europe's India: Words, People, Empires, 1500–1800* (Cambridge, MA: Harvard University Press, 2017); Jonathan Gil Harris, *The First Firangis: Remarkable Stories of Heroes, Healers, Charlatans, Courtesans and Other Foreigners Who Became Indian* (New Delhi: Aleph, 2015); Donald F. Lach, *Asia in the Making of Europe*, vol. 1, *The Century of Discovery* (Chicago: University of Chicago Press, 1965).

86. Joan-Pau Rubiés, *Travel and Ethnology in the Renaissance: South India through European Eyes, 1250–1625* (New York: Cambridge University Press, 2000), 381–383 (Sassetti); Antonello Gerbi, *Nature in the New World: From Christopher Columbus to Gonzalo Fernández de Oviedo*, trans. Jeremy Moyle (Pittsburgh, PA: University of Pittsburgh Press, 2010), 154 (Sassetti) and 289 (Carletti); Anthony Pagden, *The Fall of Natural Man: The American Indian and the Origins of Comparative Ethnology* (New York: Cambridge University Press, 1982); Surekha Davies, *Renaissance Ethnography and the Invention of the Human: New Worlds, Maps and Monsters* (New York: Cambridge University Press, 2017); Ivo Kamps and Jyotsna G. Singh, eds., *Travel Knowledge: European "Discoveries" in the Early Modern Period* (New York: Palgrave, 2001).

87. See, for instance, Palmira Fontes da Costa, ed., *Medicine, Trade and Empire: Garcia de Orta's Colloquies on the Simples and Drugs of India (1563) in Context* (Burlington, VT: Ashgate, 2015); Mark Harrison, *Climates and Constitutions: Health, Race, Environment and British Imperialism in India, 1600–1850* (New Delhi: Oxford University Press, 2002); Pamela H. Smith and Paula Findlen, eds., *Merchants and Marvels: Commerce, Science, and Art in Early Modern Europe* (New York: Routledge, 2002); Londa Schiebinger and Claudia Swan, eds., *Colonial Botany: Science, Commerce, and Politics in the Early Modern World* (Philadelphia: University of Pennsylvania Press, 2005); Schiebinger, *Plants and Empire: Colonial Bioprospecting in the Atlantic World* (Cambridge, MA: Harvard University Press, 2004); Valeria Finucci, *The Prince's Body: Vincenzo Gonzaga and Renaissance Medicine* (Cambridge, MA: Harvard University Press, 2015).

88. Orlando Figes, *Natasha's Dance: A Cultural History of Russia* (New York: Picador, 2002); Evtuhov et al., *History of Russia*; Robert O. Crummey, *The Formation of Muscovy, 1304–1613* (New York: Longman, 1987); Marius B. Jansen, *The Making of Modern Japan* (Cambridge, MA: Belknap, 2000); Conrad Totman, *Early Modern Japan* (Berkeley: University of California Press, 1993); Toby, *State and Diplomacy*; Michael Cooper, *The Japanese Mission to Europe, 1582–1590: The Journey of Four Samurai Boys through Portugal, Spain, and Italy* (Kent, UK: Global Oriental, 2005); Anthony Reid, *Southeast Asia in the Age of Commerce*; Anthony Reid, ed., *Southeast Asia in the Early Modern Era: Trade, Power, and Belief* (Ithaca, NY: Cornell University Press, 1993); Tara Alberts, *Conflict and Conversion: Catholicism in Southeast Asia, 1500–1700* (New York: Oxford University Press, 2013); Barbara Watson Andaya and Leonard Y. Andaya, *A History of Early Modern Southeast Asia, 1400–1830* (Cambridge: Cambridge University Press, 2015).

89. Jerry Brotton, *Trading Territories: Mapping the Early Modern World* (London: Reaktion, 1997); Timothy Brook, *Mr. Selden's Map of China: Decoding the Secrets of a Vanished Cartographer* (New York: Bloomsbury, 2013); Brook, *The Confusions of Pleasure: Commerce and Culture in Ming China* (Berkeley: University of California Press, 1998); Brook, *Troubled Empire*; Palmira Brummett, *Mapping the Ottomans: Sovereignty, Territory, and Identity in the Early Modern Mediterranean* (New York: Cambridge University Press, 2015); John W. O'Malley, *The First Jesuits* (Cambridge, MA: Harvard University Press, 1993); R. Po-Chia Hsia, *A Jesuit in the Forbidden City: Matteo Ricci, 1552–1610* (Oxford: Oxford University Press, 2012); Liam Matthew Brockey, *Journey to the East: The Jesuit Mission to China, 1579–1724* (Cambridge, MA.: Belknap, 2007); Brockey, *The Visitor: André Palmeiro and the Jesuits in Asia* (Cambridge, MA: Belknap, 2014); Ray Huang, *1587: A Year of No Significance: The Ming Dynasty in Decline* (New Haven, CT: Yale University Press, 1981); Jonathan D. Spence, *The Search for Modern China* (New York: W. W. Norton, 1991); Mote, *Imperial China*; Richards, *Mughal Empire*; Sanjay Subrahmanyam, *The Political Economy of Commerce: Southern India, 1500–1650* (New York: Cambridge University Press, 2002); John Keay, *India: A History* (New York: Grove, 2000); Mark A. Burkholder and Lyman L. Johnson, *Colonial Latin America*, 7th ed. (New York: Oxford University Press, 2010); Matthew Restall and Kris Lane, *Latin America in Colonial Times* (New York: Cambridge University Press, 2011); Ruggiero Romano, *America latina: Elementi e meccanismi del sistema economico coloniale (secoli xvi–xviii)*, trans. Marcello Carmagnani (Milan: UTET, 2007).

90. Halil İnalcık, *The Ottoman Empire: The Classic Age 1300–1600* (London: Phoenix, 2000); William J. Griswold, *The Great Anatolian Rebellion: 1000– 1020 / 1591–1611* (Berlin: Laus Schwarz Verlay, 1983); Karen Barkey, *Bandits and Bureaucrats: The Ottoman Route to State Centralization* (Ithaca, NY: Cornell University Press, 1994); Caroline Finkel, *Osman's Dream: The Story*

*of the Ottoman Empire 1300–1923* (New York: Basic Books, 2007); Suraiya Faroqhi, *The Ottoman Empire and the World around It* (New York: I. B. Tauris, 2006); Jane Hathaway with contributions by Karl K. Babir, *The Arab Lands under Ottoman Rule, 1516–1800* (New York: Pearson, 2008); Baki Tezcan, *The Second Ottoman Empire: Political and Social Transformation in the Early Modern World* (New York: Cambridge University Press, 2010); Ali Yaycıoğlu, *Partners of the Empire: The Crisis of the Ottoman Order in the Age of Revolutions* (Stanford, CA: Stanford University Press, 2016); Alan Mikhail, *Under Osman's Tree: The Ottoman Empire, Egypt, and Environmental History* (Chicago: University of Chicago Press, 2017); Selçuk Akşin Somel, *Historical Dictionary of the Ottoman Empire* (Lanham, MD: Scarecrow, 2003); Edhem Eldem, Daniel Goffman, and Bruce Masters, *The Ottoman City between East and West: Aleppo, Izmir, and Istanbul* (New York: Cambridge University Press, 1999); Philip Mansel, *Aleppo: The Rise and Fall of Syria's Great Merchant City* (New York: I. B. Tauris, 2016); Palmira Brummett, *Ottoman Seapower and Levantine Diplomacy in the Age of Discovery* (Albany: State University of New York Press, 1994); Giancarlo Casale, *The Ottoman Age of Exploration* (New York: Oxford University Press, 2010).

91.  Rudolph P. Matthee, *The Politics of Trade in Safavid Iran: Silk for Silver, 1600–1730* (New York: Cambridge University Press, 1999); Rudi Matthee and Jorge Flores, eds., *Acta Iranica: Portugal, the Persian Gulf and Safavid Persia* (Leuven, Belg.: Peeters, 2011); Willem Floor and Edmund Herzig, eds., *Iran and the World in the Safavid Age* (New York: I. B. Tauris, 2012); Luis Gil Fernández, *El imperio luso-español y la Persia safávida*, 2 vols. (Madrid: Fundación Universitaria Española, 2006 and 2009); Michael Axworthy, *A History of Iran: Empire of the Mind* (New York: Basic Books, 2010); Abbas Amanat, *Iran: A Modern History* (New Haven, CT: Yale University Press, 2017); Thomas Barfield, *Afghanistan: A Cultural and Political History* (Princeton, NJ: Princeton University Press, 2010).

92.  L. P. Harvey, *Muslims in Spain, 1500 to 1614* (Chicago: University of Chicago Press, 2005); Stuart B. Schwartz, *All Can Be Saved: Religious Tolerance and Salvation in the Iberian Atlantic World* (New Haven, CT: Yale University Press, 2008); Andrew C. Hess, *The Forgotten Frontier: A History of the Sixteenth-Century Ibero-African Frontier* (Chicago: University of Chicago Press, 2010); Tamar Herzog, *Frontiers of Possession: Spain and Portugal in Europe and the Americas* (Cambridge, MA: Harvard University Press, 2015); Nancy E. van Deusen, *Global Indios: The Indigenous Struggle for Justice in Sixteenth-Century Spain* (Durham, NC: Duke University Press, 2015); Thomas James Dandelet, *Spanish Rome: 1500–1700* (New Haven, CT: Yale University Press, 2001); Michael J. Levin, *Spanish Ambassadors in Sixteenth-Century Italy* (Ithaca, NY: Cornell University Press, 2005); Gabriel Guarino, *Representing the King's Splendour: Communication and Reception of Symbolic Forms of Power in Viceregal Naples* (New York: Manchester University

Press, 2010); John A. Marino, *Becoming Neapolitan: Citizen Culture in Baroque Naples* (Baltimore, MD: Johns Hopkins University Press, 2011); Geoffrey Parker, *The Army of Flanders and the Spanish Road, 1567–1659: The Logistics of Spanish Victory and Defeat in the Low Countries' War*, 2nd ed. (New York: Cambridge University Press, 2004).

93. Henry Kamen, *Philip of Spain* (New Haven, CT: Yale University Press, 1998); Geoffrey Parker, *The Grand Strategy of Philip II* (New Haven, CT: Yale University Press, 2000); Parker, *Imprudent King: A New Life of Philip II* (New Haven, CT: Yale University Press, 2014); Hugh Thomas, *World without End: Spain, Philip II, and the First Global Empire* (New York: Random House, 2014); Robert Goodwin, *Spain: The Centre of the World 1519–1682* (New York: Bloomsbury, 2015).

94. Pagden, *Lords of All the World*; Elliott, *Empires of the Atlantic World*; J. H. Elliott, *Spain, Europe, and the Wider World, 1500–1800* (New Haven, CT: Yale University Press, 2009); Israel, *Conflicts of Empires*.

95. Luis Alonso Álvarez, *El costo del imperio asiático: La formación colonial de las islas filipinas bajo dominio español, 1565–1800* (A Coruña: Universidade da Coruña, 2009); Arturo Giraldez, *The Age of Trade: The Manila Galleons and the Dawn of the Global Economy* (New York: Rowman and Littlefield, 2015); Tatiana Seijas, *Asian Slaves in Colonial Mexico: From Chinos to Indians* (New York: Cambridge University Press, 2015); Aram and Yun-Casalilla, *Global Goods*; Serge Gruzinski, *The Eagle and the Dragon: Globalization and European Dreams of Conquest in China and America in the Sixteenth Century*, trans. Jean Birrell (Malden, MA: Polity, 2014).

96. Henry Kamen, "The Decline of Spain: A Historical Myth?," *Past and Present* no. 81 (Nov. 1978): 24–50; J. I. Israel, "The Decline of Spain: A Historical Myth?," *Past and Present* no. 91 (May 1981): 170–180; Henry Kamen, "The Decline of Spain: A Historical Myth? A Rejoinder," *Past and Present* no. 91 (May 1981): 181–185. On the eighteenth-century empire's vitality, see Stanley J. and Barbara H. Stein, *Apogee of Empire: Spain and New Spain in the Age of Charles III, 1759–1789* (Baltimore, MD: Johns Hopkins University Press, 2003).

97. Kamen, *Empire*, xxi–xviii; Henry Kamen, *Spain, 1469–1714: A Society of Conflict*, 3rd ed. (Harlow, UK: Pearson, 2005). By contrast, see Elliott, *Imperial Spain, 1469–1716*.

98. Kamen, *Empire*, 65.

99. G. V. Scammell, "Indigenous Assistance in the Establishment of Portuguese Power in Asia in the Sixteenth Century," *Modern Asian Studies* 14, no. 1 (1980): 1–11; A. J. R. Russell-Wood, *The Portuguese Empire, 1415–1808: A World on the Move* (Baltimore, MD: Johns Hopkins University Press, 1998); Boyajian, *Portuguese Trade*; Subrahmanyam, *Portuguese Empire*; Disney, *History of Portugal*; Ernst van Veen, *Decay or Defeat? An Inquiry into the Portuguese Decline in Asia, 1580–1645* (Leiden, Neth.: Leiden University, Research

School CNWS, 2000); Malyn Newitt, "Formal and Informal Empire in the History of Portuguese Expansion," *Portuguese Studies* 17, no. 1 (January 2001): 1–21.

100. P. J. Marshall, "Western Arms in Maritime Asia in the Early Phases of Expansion," *Modern Asian Studies* 14, no. 1 (1980): 13–28; George Raudzens, "Military Revolution or Maritime Evolution? Military Superiorities or Transportation Advantages as Main Causes of European Colonial Conquests to 1788," *Journal of Military History* 63, no. 3 (July 1999): 631–641; Armando da Silva Saturnino Monteiro, "The Decline and Fall of Portuguese Seapower, 1583–1663," *Journal of Military History* 65, no. 1 (Jan. 2001): 9–20; Boxer, *Dutch Seaborne Empire*; Simon Schama, *The Embarrassment of Riches: An Interpretation of Dutch Culture in the Golden Age* (New York: Vintage, 1987); Jonathan I. Israel, *The Dutch Republic: Its Rise, Greatness, and Fall: 1477–1806* (Oxford, UK: Clarendon, 1998); Lissa Roberts, ed., *Centres and Cycles of Accumulation in and around the Netherlands during the Early Modern Period* (Münster, Ger.: LIT, 2011); Kenneth R. Andrews, *Trade, Plunder and Settlement: Maritime Enterprise and the Genesis of the British Empire, 1480–1630* (New York: Cambridge University Press, 1984); Robert Brenner, *Merchants and Revolution: Commercial Change, Political Conflict, and London's Overseas Traders, 1550–1630* (New York: Verso, 2003); Alison Games, *Web of Empire: English Cosmopolitans in an Age of Expansion, 1560–1630* (New York: Oxford University Press, 2009); Philip Lawson, *The East India Company: A History* (New York: Longman, 1993); Jean Sutton, *Lords of the East: The East India Company and Its Ships (1600–1874)* (London: Conway Maritime, 2000); Emily Erikson, *Between Monopoly and Free Trade: The English East India Company, 1600–1757* (Princeton, NJ: Princeton University Press, 2014). For a locally oriented view, see Keith Wrightson, *Earthly Necessities: Economic Lives in Early Modern Britain* (New Haven, CT: Yale University Press, 2000).

101. Lucette Valensi, *The Birth of the Despot: Venice and the Sublime Porte*, trans. Arthur Denner (Ithaca, NY: Cornell University Press, 1987); Nancy Bisaha, *Creating East and West: Renaissance Humanists and the Ottoman Turks* (Philadelphia: University of Pennsylvania Press, 2004); Meserve, *Empires of Islam*; Malcolm, *Useful Enemies*, esp. 201–228; Edward W. Said, *Orientalism* (New York: Vintage, 2003)—originally published in 1978—has come under sustained criticism, most recently in Malcolm, *Useful Enemies*, 415–417.

102. Dallington, "Suruey of the great," 8 (5). See also Hanlon, *Twilight*, 62; Capponi, "Palle di Marte," 1129; Hale, *Florence and the Medici*, 130.

103. Dallington, "Suruey of the great," 8 (5).

104. Carletti, *My Voyage*, 12–13; Antonio Forte, "About Carletti's Attitude towards Slavery," *East and West* 42, no. 2 / 4 (Dec. 1992), 511–513; Lionello Lanciotti, "About Carletti's Attitude towards Slavery: A Rejoinder" *East*

*and West* 42, no. 2 / 4 (Dec. 1992), 515; T. F. Earle and K. J. P. Lowe, eds., *Black Africans in Renaissance Europe* (New York: Cambridge University Press, 2005); David Bindman and Henry Louis Gates Jr., eds., *The Image of the Black in Western Art*, vol. 3, *From the "Age of Discovery" to the Age of Abolition, Part I: Artists of the Renaissance and Baroque* (Cambridge, MA: Harvard University Press, 2010); David Wheat, *Atlantic Africa and the Spanish Caribbean, 1570–1640* (Chapel Hill, NC: University of North Carolina Press, 2016).

## 1. FINANCE AND THE SPANISH ALLIANCE

1. Alessandra Contini, "Medicean Diplomacy in the Sixteenth Century," in *Politics and Diplomacy in Early Modern Italy: The Structure of Diplomatic Practice, 1450–1800*, ed. Daniela Frigo, trans. Adrian Belton (Cambridge: Cambridge University Press, 2000), 49–94. J. R. Hale, *Florence and the Medici* (London: Phoenix, 2001), 144.

2. Hale, *Florence and the Medici*, 151 and 164.

3. Francesco Guidi Bruscoli, *Papal Banking in Renaissance Rome: Benvenuto Olivieri and Paul III, 1534–1549* (New York: Routledge, 2016); Richard Goldthwaite, *The Economy of Renaissance Florence* (Baltimore, MD: Johns Hopkins University Press, 2009), 170–175 and 245–255. On early-sixteenth-century Rome, see Peter Partner, *Renaissance Rome, 1500–1559: A Portrait of a Society* (Berkeley: University of California Press, 1979); Elizabeth S. and Thomas V. Cohen, *Words and Deeds in Renaissance Rome: Trials before the Papal Magistrate,* (Toronto: University of Toronto Press, 1993); Silvio A. Bedini, *The Pope's Elephant* (Nashville, TN: J. S. Sanders, 1998); Catherine Fletcher, *Our Man in Rome: Henry VIII and His Italian Ambassador* (London: Bodley Head, 2012); Gianvittorio Signorotto and Maria Antonietta Visceglia, eds. *Court and Politics in Papal Rome, 1492–1700* (New York: Cambridge University Press, 2002).

4. Elisabeth G. Gleason, "Confronting New Realities: Venice and the Peace of Bologna, 1530," in *Venice Reconsidered: The History and Civilization of an Italian City-State, 1297–1797*, ed. John Martin and Dennis Romano (Baltimore, MD: Johns Hopkins University Press, 2002), 168–184.

5. "Discorso sopra il potere, e habilità che hà il Duca di Bracciano, di servire la Corona di Spagna. Di come habbi in ogni occasione mostrato la sua devotione con gran finezza. E qua[n]to poco sia stato riconosciuto," Stati Esteri, Spagna 2, box 10, folder 10, Vecchia Segnatura: I.DA. LXXVI.53, Orisini Family Papers (OFP) 902, Department of Special Collections (DSC), Charles E. Young Research Library (YRL), University of California Los Angeles (UCLA). Document descriptions are quoted from the finding guide, "Orsini Family Papers, ca. 1150–1950 (bulk 1500–1900)," "Processed by Guendalina Ajello Mahler; machine-reading

finding aid created by Caroline Cubé," Online Archives of California (Los Angeles: UCLA Library Special Collections, 2007), Stati Esteri, Grandato di Spagna 1708–1871, box 11, folder 1, OFP 902, DSC, YRL, UCLA.

6. To Grand Duke Francesco I from Bernardo Canigiani in Madrid, dated March 14, 1582, ASF, MdP 4911, 312r.

7. "Relatione a Sua Maestà del' Duca di Bracciano, et del Cardinal'Orsino suo Fratello in Roma à x di xbre [dicembre] 1620," ASF, MdP 5080, 493r–494v. "Si deve ancora considerare, che i Duchi di Bracciano, et suoi successori possono essere efficaci strumenti per aiutare Vostra Maestà in qual' si voglia occasione di revolutione in Italia, et per assicurare il Regno di Napoli," 494r. All translations are mine unless otherwise indicated.

8. Vanna Arrighi, "Orsini, Clarice," *DBI* 79 (2013). Ingeborg Walter, "Medici, Lorenzo de'," *DBI* 73 (2009). Maria Grazia Pernis and Laurie Schneider Adams, *Lucrezia Tornabuoni de' Medici and the Medici Family in the Fifteenth Century* (New York: Peter Lang, 2006), 71–77.

9. Patrizia Meli, "Medici, Piero de," *DBI* 73 (2009), and Vanna Arrighi, "Orsini, Alfonsina," *DBI* 79 (2013).

10. "Minuta. Mandato di procura di D.a Francesca Orsini Marchesa di Padula favore di D.a Alfonsina Orsini de' Medici e Lorenzo de' Medici di lei figlio per contrarre matrimonio in suo nome con Lorenzo de' Conti di Ceri e dell'Anguillara," 1516, Città, Stati, Feudi e Castelli [hereafter, Città, Stati, Feudi], Anguillara 1, box 20, folder 1, Vecchia Segnatura: I.E.II.24, OFP 902, DSC, YRL, UCLA; "Minuta. Mandato di procura di D.a Francesca Orsini Marchesa di Padula favore di D.a Alfonsina Orsini de' Medici e Lorenzo de' Medici di lei figlio per contrarre matrimonio in suo nome con Lorenzo de' Conti di Ceri e dell'Anguillara," Città, Stati, Feudi, Anguillara 1, box 22, folder 1, Vecchia Segnatura, I.E.II.16, 1516, OFP 902, DSC, YRL, UCLA; Gaspare de Caro, "Anguillara, Lorenzo," *DBI* 3 (1961).

11. Elena Fasano Guarini, "Cosimo I de' Medici, duca di Firenze, granduca di Toscana," *DBI* 30 (1984). Elisabetta Mori, "Medici, Isabella de'," *DBI* 73 (2009); MAP Person ID 408, "Medici-Orsini, Isabella di Cosimo I de'." Elisabetta Mori, "Orsini, Paolo Giordano," *DBI* 79 (2013); MAP Person ID 417, "Orsini, Paolo Giordano I (I Duca di Bracciano)." For a useful family tree, see Genealogie, box 15, folder 3, item 10/8, OFP 902, DSC, YRL, UCLA.

12. "Donazione causa mortis fatta da Paolo Giordano Orsini Duca di Bracciano in D.a Isabella Medici sua consorte di tutto l'usufrutto di Bracciano e Vicovaro, e a Felice Orsini sua sorella moglie di Don Marc'Antonio [Marco Antonio] Colonna di [scudi] 80,000. Per atti di Giovanni Battista Giordani not[aio] fiorentino not[aio] in Livorno," January 1, 1561, Città, Stati, Feudi , Bracciano 4, box 31, folder 3, Vecchia Segnatura, I.A.IV.69,

OFP 902, DSC, YRL, UCLA. Grand Duke Ferdinando I and his representative are mentioned in a 1589 instrument concerning Vicovaro: "Istr[ument]o di transazione tra D. Olimpia de Valle v[edov]a di Giovanni Paolo Orsini, e Caterina erede di esso, e D. Virginio Orsini rappresentato da Giovanni Nicolino Medici di Ferdinando, sopra i castelli di Vicovaro e parti di Seracinesco [Saracinesco], che ad evitar questioni rinunzia, riservato il diritto di donazione fatta ad essa da Paolo Giordano Orsini sopra Cantalupo e Bordella. Atti di Francesco Pechinoli di Civita Castellana," Città, Stati, Feudi, Vicovaro 1, box 174, folder 2, Vecchia Segnatura: I.A.VII.12, 1589, OFP 902, DSC, YRL, UCLA.

13. Mori, "Orsini, Paolo Giordano."

14. "Patti circa l'affitto dello Stato di Bracciano, e sue entrate, fatto da D. Paolo Giordano Orsini al Duca di Firenze," Città, Stati, Feudi, Bracciano 5, box 31, folder 4, Vecchia Segnatura: I.A.V.II. March 8, 1563, OFP 902, DSC, YRL, UCLA. This was in exchange for control of the revenue of Bracciano for three years: Barbara Furlotti, *A Renaissance Baron and His Possessions: Paolo Giordano I Orsini, Duke of Bracciano (1541–1585)* (Turnhout, Belg.: Brepols, 2012), 18. A note on currencies is perhaps in order. In light of the prominence of the Portuguese to this story, I rely on van Veen, *Decay or Defeat?*, Appendix 0.1 (p. 243), Appendix 1.1 (p. 244), Appendix 1.2 (p. 245), and Appendix 3.2 (pp. 252–253) for currencies. 1 Spanish ducat = 375 *maravedís* (about 35.3 g of silver); 1 *escudo* = 400 *maravedís* (about 37.65 g of silver); 1 Spanish *real* = 34 *maravedís* (about 3.2 g of silver); 1 Spanish *real* of eight = 272 *maravedís* (about 25.5 g of silver); 1 *cruzado* = 360 *réis* (sixteenth century) and 400 *réis* (seventeenth century); 1 *xerafim* = 300 *réis*; 1 pagoda = 360 *réis*. The value of a *cruzado* varied from 27.45 g–32.92 g of silver.

15. "1564–1571, Proposte, petizioni, comparse, repliche, per Paolo Gio. Orsini contro i Cavalcanti e i Giraldi," Città, Stati, Feudi, Bracciano 5, box 31, folder 4, Vecchia Segnatura: I.CA.IX.37, OFP 902, DSC, YRL, UCLA. On the Cavalcanti-Giraldi, see Bruscoli, *Papal Banking*; Simona Feci, "Pio V, papa, santo," *DBI* 83 (2015).

16. This is the title used in the first page of the file containing the dispute with the Cavalcanti-Giraldi: Città, Stati, Feudi, Bracciano 5, box 31, folder 4, Vecchia Segnatura: I.CA.IX.37, OFP 902, DSC, YRL, UCLA. On the Grand Ducal title, see Fasano Guarini, "Cosimo I de' Medici, duca di Firenze, granduca di Toscana," *DBI* 30 (1984). This was a famous and extensively commemorated event. For instance, Cesare Nebbia's drawing "Pope Pius V Crowns Cosimo I de' Medici Grand Duke of Tuscany" from the late 1580s is posted at the Rhode Island School of Design website, accessed October 26, 2020, https://risdmuseum.org/sites/default/files/styles/scaled_600_w/museumplus/90066.jpg?itok=Io6Pi2Ye.

17. Città, Stati, Feudi, Bracciano 5, box 31, folder 4, Vecchia Segnatura: I.A.V.39a (Tomo XXII, N. 6), OFP 902, DSC, YRL, UCLA; "γζς [ / ] pius

pp v$^s$ [ / ] Dilecte fili nobiles vir, salutem, et ap.cam ben'. Perche noi tenemo il signor Duca di Fiorenza per una delle più savie teste d'Italia, laudaremo se'[m]pre tutte quelle deliberationi, che farete con il prudentissimo conseglio, et volontà di sua Eccellenza, pregando insieme il signor Dio, che accompagni di continui con il favore della gratia sua tutte le vostre attioni; In tanto vi mandiamo la nostra benedittione, non ci occorrendo per hora dire altro alla vostra lettera. Dat[i]s Roma apud P.$^{um}$ Petru', Die xx Apriles M. D. Lxvij Anno 2.$^{do}$." N.B. In transcriptions, clear abbreviations like s.$^{or}$ (signor) and s. Ecc.$^{za}$ (sue Eccellenza) have been expanded, but Latin titles and anything ambiguous have been left in their abbreviated form, for ease of reading. Even so, it should be borne in mind that even formal documents were heavily abbreviated and writing out the full form risks making the text appear more ponderous and ornate than it does in the original. Finally, direct quotations from catalogues and printed texts are left as printed.

18. For property action related to Isabella's dowry, see "Consenso di D. Isabella Medici a D. Paolo Giordano Orsini suo marito per la vendita dei diritti e giurisdizioni sui castelli di Formello e Isola e suoi territori, sui quali era ipotecata la sua dote,", Varie Legali 9, box 247, folder 1, OFP 902, DSC, YRL, UCLA; "Assenso prestato da Donato dell'Antella maestro di casa del Card. Medici, che ritenuti li frutti di Formello, Monterano e le erbe di Bracciano, nonche per render libera Galera D. Paolo Giordano Orsini assegni agli eredi di Filippo Serlupie Bernardino Olgiati tutte le rendite dell'Anguillara e della tenuta di Spanoro a tutto il 1584," December 16, 1582, Bracciano 06, box 32, folder 1, Vecchia Segnatura, I.A.VI.52, OFP 902, DSC, YRL, UCLA.

19. Furlotti, *Renaissance Baron*, 19–20 and 20n64.

20. Furlotti, *Renaissance Baron*, 20; Mori, "Orsini, Paolo Giordano"; Mori, "Medici, Isabella de'." Mori argues quite robustly that the story that Paolo Giordano murdered Isabella de' Medici out of jealousy and with the connivance of Francesco I is false, an anti-Medici libel picked up in the nineteenth century.

21. Mori, "Orsini, Paolo Giordano." Giovanni Orioli, "Accoramboni, Vittoria," *DBI* 1 (1960); MAP Person ID 881, "Orsini, Virginio di Paolo Giordano I (II Duca di Bracciano)." On Virginio Orsini, his role as the model for Shakespeare's Orsino in *Twelfth Night* (p. 53), and his movement to Rome with Flavia Peretti, his wife (p. 53), see Valerio Morucci, "Poets and Musicians in the Roman-Florentine Circle of Virginio Orsini, Duke of Bracciano (1572–1615)," *Early Music* 43, no. 1 (Feb. 2015): 53–61; Elena Fasano Guarini, "'Rome, Workshop of All the Practices of the World': From the Letters of Cardinal Ferdinando de' Medici to Cosimo I and Francesco I," in Signorotto and Visceglia, *Court and Politics*, 67–68.

22. "Addizione all'eredità della buo[na] me[moria] di Paolo Giordano Orsini fatta da Virgilio suo figlio col beneficio della legge," December 13, 1585, Bracciano 6, box 32, folder 1, Vecchia Segnatura: I.A.VI.77, OFP 902, DSC, YRL, UCLA.

23. "Testamento di D. Virginio Orsini Duca di Bracciano Codicillo e particola di testamento di Virginio Orsini del 1594," July 26, 1594, Bracciano 6, box 32, folder 2, Vecchia Segnatura: I.A.VII.61, OFP 902, DSC, YRL, UCLA; Stefano Boero, "Peretti Damasceni, Flavia," *DBI* 82 (2015). MAP Person ID 3211, "Usimbardi, Lorenzo di Francesco."

24. "Istr[ument]o di creazione di un censo di scudi cento mila fatto da D. Virginio Orsini a favore di D. Ferdinando Medici Duca di Toscana da restituirsi al med[esim]o [Duca] nel termine di anni quattro. E dichiarazione del pred[ett]o D. Virginio di liberare le varie persone a suo favore obligate. Atti di Barnaba fu Orazio Baccelli notaro," June 14, 1599, Censi, Censo 1, box 226, folder 1, Vecchia Segnatura: I.A.VII.97, OFP 902, DSC, YRL, UCLA; "Restituzione di prima rata di scudi 25 mila dei cento mila dati da D. Ferdinando de Medici a D. Virginio Orsini e da restituirsi da questo in quattro rate ugual," July 3, 1600, Città, Stati, Feudi, Bracciano 9, box 32, folder 4, Vecchia Segnatura: I.A.VII.101, OFP 902, DSC, YRL, UCLA; "Istromento di dichiarazione di Vincenzo de Medici senatore fiorentino e tesoriere generale circa la restituzione di [scudi] 100 mila fatta da D. Virginio Orsini al Gran Duca," July 2, 1601, Bracciano 9, box 32, folder 4, Vecchia Segnatura: I.A.VII.115, OFP 902, DSC, YRL, UCLA. The financial entanglements would seem to have continued; see Fideiussione di Duccio Mancini a favore di Virginio Orsini per scudi cento mila avuti da Cosimo Medici Duca di Firenze. Antimo Palmieri di Aspro not[aio].' 1 pezzo, 4 carte, Ms., 2 sigilli," May 10, 1613, , Varie Legali 7, box 246, folder 3, Vecchia Segnatura: I.A.VIII.101, OFP 902, DSC, YRL, UCLA.

25. Not all their children had Medici names: Raimondo, Paolo Giordano II, Carlo, Felice Maria, and Maria Camilla followed other naming conventions, but the presence of four Medici names is unlikely to be a coincidence. For the children's names, see MAP Person ID 881, "Orsini, Virginio di Paolo Giordano I (II Duca di Bracciano)."

26. On Rome and the Papal States in the late sixteenth and seventeenth centuries, see Thomas James Dandelet, *Spanish Rome: 1500–1700* (New Haven, CT: Yale University Press, 2001); Renato Ago, *Gusto for Things: A History of Objects in Seventeenth Century Rome*, trans. Bradford Bouley and Corey Tazzara (Chicago: University of Chicago Press, 2013); Laurie Nussdorfer, *Civic Politics in the Rome of Urban VIII*, (Princeton, NJ: Princeton University Press, 1992); Tessa Storey, *Carnal Commerce in Counter-Reformation Rome* (New York: Cambridge University Press 2008); Rose Marie San

Juan, *Rome: A City Out of Print* (Minneapolis: University of Minnesota Press, 2001); Gauvin Alexander Bailey, *Between Renaissance and Baroque: Jesuit Art in Rome, 1565–1610,* (Toronto: University of Toronto Press, 2003); Bradford A. Bouley, *Pious Postmortems: Anatomy, Sanctity, and the Catholic Church in Early Modern Europe* (Philadelphia: University of Pennsylvania Press, 2017).

27. "Congiura di D. Alessandro Orsini ed Angelo Fraschini da Siena col Duca di Firenze [Cosimo I de Medici] per uccidere D. Nicola Orsini Conte di Pitigliano, ed invadere i suoi stati, colle deposizioni del Fraschini," July 1, 1560, Città, Stati, Feudi, Pitigliano, box 114, folder 2, Vecchia Segnatura: I.A.IV.57, OFP 902, DSC, YRL, UCLA. This item contains two linked documents, with the second starting on the verso side of the last page of the first document; both are dated July 1, 1560. The first document ends with a confession, the second involves the duke of Florence's denial.

28. Irene Fosi, "Orsini, Niccolò," *DBI* 79 (2013). MAP Person ID 9697, "Orsini, Nicola (IV Conte di Pitigliano), Signore di Sorano."

29. On the marriage to the Capponi, see Genealogie, box 15, folder 3, item 7, OFP 902, DSC, YRL, UCLA; Guarini, "Rome, Workshop," 68; Opera postuma del Dott. Giuseppe Bruscalupi, *Monografia Storica della Contea di Pitigliano,* (Florence: Martini, Servi, 1906), 405–406. A full scanned copy in many hyperlinked sections of Bruscalupi's monograph is available at the Pitigliano website, accessed October 26, 2020, http://pitigliano.altervista.org/monografia/index1.htm edited by Paolo Liberati (2010). For a subsequent dispute, see "Nullius Status Pitiliani. Causa agitata tra la March[e]sa Maddalena Orsini Capponi e Girolamo Orsini [lettura errata] sulla successione al feudo di Pitigliano.' La causa é agitata da Girolama o Geronima Orsini, sorella di Alessandro Orsini, moglie di Scipione Capponi," 1622, Città, Stati, Feudi, Pitigliano, box 114, folder 2, Vecchia Segnatura: I.B.XXIX.6., OFP 902, DSC, YRL, UCLA.

30. Geoffrey Parker, *Emperor: A New Life of Charles V* (New Haven, CT: Yale University Press, 2019), 408–10; quotations on 410 citing the *Political Testament.*

31. Fernand Braudel, *The Mediterranean and the Mediterranean World in the Age of Philip II,* 2nd rev. ed., 2 vols., trans. Siân Reynolds (Berkeley: University of California Press, 1995), 2: 1125.

32. For "our side," see Braudel, *Mediterranean,* 2: 1061 and 1154.

33. Vincenzo Pitti, *Esseqvie della sacra cattolica real maesta del re di Spagna d. Filippo II d'Avstria: celebrate dal serenissimo D. Ferdinando Medici, gran duca di Toscana nella città di Firenze / descritte da Vincentio Pitti* (Florence: Sermartelli, 1598), 75.

34. Benvenuti, *Repubbliche marinare;* Michael Mallett, *Florentine Galleys of the Fifteenth Century* (Oxford, UK: Clarendon, 1967); John H. Pryor, *Com-*

*merce, Shipping and Naval Warfare in the Medieval Mediterranean* (London: Variorum Reprints, 1987); Pryor, *Geography, Technology, and War: Studies in the Maritime History of the Mediterranean 649–1571* (New York: Cambridge University Press, 1992); Susan Rose, "Islam versus Christendom: The Naval Dimension, 1000-1600," *Journal of Military History* 63, No. 3 (July 1999): 561–578; Rose, *Medieval Naval Warfare, 1000–1500* (New York: Routledge, 2002); Marco Tangheroni, ed., *Pisa e il Mediterraneo: Uomini, merci, idee dagli Etruschi ai Medici* (Milan: Skira, 2003); Helen Nicholson, *Medieval Warfare: Theory and Practice of War in Europe: 300–1500* (New York: Palgrave Macmillan, 2004).

35. Gregory Hanlon, *The Twilight of a Military Tradition: Italian Aristocrats and European Conflicts, 1560–1800* (New York: Holmes and Meyer, 1998). Cesare Ciano, *I primi Medici e il mare: Note sulla politica marinara toscana da Cosimo I a Ferdinando I* (Pisa, It.: Pacini, 1980).

36. Hanlon, *Twilight*, 37–39.

37. For all these figures, see Hanlon, *Twilight*, 21, 30 and 39; Braudel, *Mediterranean*, 2: 1083.

38. Braudel provides detailed fleet lists based on Genoese and Spanish archival sources from the 1560s: *Mediterranean*, 2: 1008n252, 1011–1012, and 1021. See also Roger Crowley, *Empires of the Sea: The Siege of Malta, the Battle of Lepanto, and the Contest for the Center of the World* (New York: Random House, 2008). The Lepanto contributions are instructive: Niccolò Capponi, *Victory of the West: The Great Christian-Muslim Clash at the Battle of Lepanto* (Cambridge, MA.: Da Capo, 2007), appendix 1, "Battle Arrays," 325–331. Summing the figures provided for each component of the Holy League fleet (ignoring Capponi's figures for lanterns): Genoa (private): 25 galleys, 75 guns; Genoa (public): 3 galleys, 13 guns; Malta: 3 galleys, 15 guns; Naples: 31 galleys, 95 guns; Savoy: 3 galleys, 5 guns; Sicily: 7 galleys, 25 guns; Spain: 12 galleys, 44 guns.

39. Braudel, *Mediterranean*, 2: 841n15.

40. Braudel, *Mediterranean*, 2: 841n15.

41. Cost estimate from Braudel, *Mediterranean*, 2: 841. See also John Francis Guilmartin, *Gunpowder and Galleys: Changing Technology and Mediterranean Warfare at Sea in the 16th Century* (Annapolis, MD: Naval Institute Press, 2003), 130; Geoffrey Parker, "Ships of the Line 1500-1650," in Geoffrey Parker, ed., *The Cambridge History of Warfare*, 117–130; Ennio Concina, "La costruzione navale," in *Storia di Venezia: Dalle origini alla caduta della serenissima*, 10 vols., ed. Alberto Tenenti and Ugo Tucci (Rome: Istituto poligrafico e zecca dello stato, 1991), 10: 211–258; Frederic Chapin Lane, *Venetian Ships and Shipbuilders of the Renaissance* (Baltimore, MD: Johns Hopkins University Press, 1934).

42. Geoffrey Parker, *The Grand Strategy of Philip II* (New Haven, CT: Yale University Press, 2000); Parker offers a table on p. 135, "The Cost of War on

Two Fronts, 1571–1577," that compares the money received, rather than the expenses, by the Mediterranean fleet and the Army of Flanders. The year 1572 marked the highpoint for the Mediterranean fleet, which received 1,463,000 ducats in that year; in 1577 the fleet received only 673,000, the lowest total in the years covered. In both 1571 and 1576, the fleet received more than the army, but the army received so much from 1572 to 1575 that its total receipts were 11,692,000 to the fleet's 7,063,000 in the period 1571–1577.

43. "Magnifico nostro carissimo: Aspettavamo pure, che cotesti ministri Regij, havessino dato qualche ordine per il pagamento delle nostre Galere, poiche non ci hanno assegnato cosa alcuna, et vedendo, che il negotio và in lungo più che mai, et che mostrano poca voglia di sodisfarci, havendo già un'anno passato chiesto le rassegne, procure, et altra lungagnole senza venirne alla conclusione vogliamo, che con buona occasione ne diate conto alla Maestà Sua, et la supplichiate à nome nostro à voler dar' ordine per l'intero pagamento d'esse quanto prima, mostrandole che come non, è, alcuno, che più prontamente et volentiere spenda La rob[manuscript damaged] li stati, et la vita istassa di noi per servizio suo, cosi disideriamo, ch'ella faccia conoscere al mondo, che ci tiene per quelli divoti servitori, che inverità Le siamo,: con ordinari à quei suoi ministri, che le cose nostre, che pur son proprie della Maestà Sua, sieti trattati d'altra maniera da loro, che non fanno, soggiugnendole, che se ella non ci provide con li effetti, non potremo à tempo nuovo mettere in essere Le nostre Galere per servizio di lei, ilche pure ci dispiacerebbe, non havendo[]noi altra mira, che servirla" (Francesco de' Medici in Florence to Cavaliere de Nobili, December 20, 1565, ASF, MdP 4901, unnumbered). On Francesco's assumption of some power, see Luciano Berti, *Il principe dello studiolo: Francesco I dei Medici e la fine del Rinascimento fiorentino* (Pistoia, It.: Artout Maschietto, 2002), 35–36.

44. From Cosimo I de' Medici in Florence to Pedro Afán de (Perafán) Ribera in Napoli, August 12, 1559, MAP Doc ID 8648, ASF, MdP 211, 32. From Cosimo I de' Medici in Florence to Juan de la (Duque de Medinaceli) Cerda y Silva in Palermo, August 7, 1560, MAP Doc ID 8742, ASF, MdP 211, 84.

45. From Leonardo di Antonio de Nobili in Madrid to Francesco I de' Medici in Florence, January 25, 1568, MAP Doc ID 14372, ASF, MdP 4902, ins. 1, 2.

46. "[G]ravi danni cosi per il piccolo stipendio assegnato loro," ASF, MdP 4898, P. I, 176. ASF, MdP 4898, P. I, 170–171, is dated from Madrid, January 25, 1567 (171v). Braudel, *Mediterranean*, 2: 841n15 cites "Simancas E° 1446, f° 107" for an asiento for the Tuscan galleys.

47. "Io sono stato sempre d['] oppenione, che 'sia di molta riputatione, et grandezza di V[ostro] E[ccellenza] I·. tener buon numero di galere, et di

non piccola utilità ancora, ogni volta che'questa Maestà le voglia pagare,"
ASF, MdP 4898, P. I, 204-206. 204r.

48. "[I]l che' causa molta intelligenza, et confidenza con lei: perche 'farà
    sempre conto non piccolo di ta[n]te forze di mare appiccate con la pre-
    stezza delle genti Toscane in ogni suo bisogno," ASF, MdP 4898, P. I,
    204r.

49. "[E]t d'onde si vede nascer' il benifitio, quivi molte volte corre l'affettione,
    et per consegue[n]te si fà ogni opera di mantenerselo amico, massime
    quando il numero delle galere di Vostra Eccellenza venga tale, che 'per
    bontà, et per numero fosse quasi il nervo dell'armata andando crescendo
    di mano in mano sin' al numero di venti: il quale crederei, che fosse
    bastante à patroneggiar que mari. onde per queste," ASF, MdP 4898,
    P. I, 204r.

50. ASF, MdP 4898, P. II, 413-415, 429-430, and 450-55.

51. ASF, MdP 4897, 88; ASF, MdP 4898, P. I, 23-28. Writing in 1566, Ambas-
    sador Nobili recounted that he had explained to Philip II and Ruy
    Gomez that the Medici galleys had served Philip II for three years with
    grossly insufficient compensation, leaving the Medici in debt. Braudel,
    *Mediterranean*, 1: 488 and 488nn173-176, discusses, using various docu-
    ments from the ASF, how Nobili assembled and dispatched with some
    difficulty 280,000 *reali* in eight chests, which were to travel by galley
    from Spain.

52. Braudel, *Mediterranean*, 2: 1154-1166.

53. Colin Martin and Geoffrey Parker, *The Spanish Armada*, rev. ed. (New
    York: Manchester University Press, 2002), 112n4.

54. Martin and Parker, *Spanish Armada*, 89; Parker, *Grand Strategy*, 179, states
    that the grand duke sent Dovara in Feburary 1585, while Martin and
    Parker (89), stress that it was Sixtus V who worked through Dovara.
    Diana Toccafondi Fantappiè, "Dovara, Luigi," *DBI* 14 (1992) gives
    Dovara's embassy in Spain as being in June 1585. "Dovara, Luigi," MAP
    Person ID 666, lists him as envoy to or ambassador in Rome, Milan, Fer-
    rara, Venice, Naples, and Spain.

55. Harry Kelsey, "Drake, Sir Francis, (1540-1596)," *Oxford Dictionary of Na-
    tional Biography* (Oxford: Oxford University Press, 2004 / 2009). Parker,
    *Grand Strategy*, 180.

56. Braudel, *Mediterranean*, 1: 106 and 106n17; Eladi Romero García, *El impe-
    rialismo hispanico en la Toscana durante el siglo XVI* (Lleida, Spain: Dilagro,
    1986), 126. For earlier mentions of the Tuscan galleon, see the letters
    from Bernardo Canigiani in Madrid dated January 9, 1581, and October
    17, 1580, ASF, MdP 4911, 160v and 205r (out of order).

57. Romero García, *Imperialismo hispanico*, 126.

58. Martin and Parker, *Spanish Armada*, 20, and Appendix I, 261. I draw the
    comparative claims from the figures provided in Appendix I, "Table of

the opposing fleets," 261–268. On the Tuscan name, see from Madrid to Florence in 1588, MAP Doc ID 26921, ASF, MdP 5037, 615r.

59. Martin and Parker, *Spanish Armada*, 16 and 20.

60. On the Tuscan envoy, see Parker, *Grand Strategy*, 211. Avviso from Madrid to Florence on May 28, 1588, MAP Doc ID 22866, ASF, MdP 5037, 611.

61. For the letter see ASF, MdP 4919, P. II, 456r–462r; MAP Person ID 848, "Guidi, Camillo di Francesco." In 1588, Guidi was relatively early in a long and accomplished career of Medici service.

62. Romero García, *Imperialismo hispanico*, 126. Tuscany's experience with galleons traveling through Spanish domains in Tuscan service was not, however, over. See ASF, MdP 5080, 410, for a copy of a Spanish passport from the Catholic king for the grand duke's galleon called *Liorno* dated from the Prado on November 29, 1607.

63. John M. Najemy, *A History of Florence: 1200–1575* (Malden, MA: Blackwell, 2008), 474–475. Hale, *Florence and the Medici*, 160.

64. On Florence's high taxes in 1582, see Braudel, *Mediterranean*, 1: 535.

65. This follows Hale's summary of Ferdinando I's advice (Hale, *Florence and the Medici*, 152).

66. Eric Cochrane, *Florence in the Forgotten Centuries 1527–1800: A History of Florence and the Florentines in the Age of the Grand Dukes* (Chicago: University of Chicago Press, 1973), book 2, 112.

67. Hale, *Florence and the Medici*, 160.

68. Robert Dallington, "A suruey of the great dukes state of Tuscany In the yeare of our Lord 1596," (London: Printed [by George Eld] for Edward Blount, 1605) 41 (25) (Early English Books Online pdf page is given parenthetically); C. S. Knighton, "Dallington, Sir Robert (1561-1636x8)," *Oxford Dictionary of National Biography*.

69. Dallington, "A suruey of the great dukes," 41 (25).

70. Dallington, "A suruey of the great dukes," 41–42 (25–26).

71. Quotations: Niccolò Machiavelli and Francesco Guicciardini, *The Sweetness of Power: Machiavelli's* Discourses *and Guicciardini's* Considerations, trans. James B. Atkinson and David Sices (DeKalb: Northern Illinois University Press, 2002), Machiavelli, II: 10, 185–87. Machiavelli's opposition to *pecunia nervus belli* and the *condottieri* who embodied its principles pervades the *Discourses*. See (all from the *Discourses*) Machiavelli, I: 21, 79–80; I: 43, 120–121; II: 3, 170–171; II: 4, 171–174; II: 6, 178–179; II: 12, 192; II: 19, 215–218; II: 30, 247–250; III: 31, 346 for Machiavelli's insistence on the virtue of having one's own troops (especially a citizen militia); the deficiencies of reliance on mercenaries; the structural weakness of the military systems of Athens, Sparta, Florence, and Venice; and the weakness of states that rely on money including to buy territory. On *pecunia nervus belli*, see Michael Howard, *War in European History* (New York: Oxford University Press, 2001), 27. For a use of the term by Ambassador Thomas Spinelly in describing one opinion in

Charles V's council in 1520, see Parker, *Emperor*, 113; Roger B. Merriman, "Charles V's Last Paper of Advice to his Son," *American Historical Review* 28, no. 3 (April 1923): 491. Merriman drew a specific connection on p. 490. On the origins of the phrase, see C. F. Konrad, "Marius at Eryx (Sallust, P. Rylands 473.1)," *Historia: Zeitschrift für Alte Geschichte* 46 (1997): 62n124.

72. For Guicciardini's critique in his *Considerations on the Discourses of Machiavelli*, see Guicciardini, II:12, 427, and II: 19, 431-432.

73. Gasparo Contarini, *The Commonwealth and Government of Venice*, trans. Lewes Lewkenor (London, 1599) [originally published as *De magistratibus et republica Venetorum* (1543)], 108 (quotation) and 131-132 (use of mercenaries).

74. Dallington, "A suruey of the great dukes," 42 (26).

75. Dallington, "A suruey of the great dukes," 42 (26).

76. Dallington, "A suruey of the great dukes," 42-43 (26).

77. Goldthwaite, *Economy of Renaissance Florence*, 243-244; Goldthwaite, "The Medici Bank and the World of Florentine Capitalism," *Past and Present* 144 (1987): 3-31; Goldthwaite, *Private Wealth in Renaissance Florence: A Study of Four Families* (Princeton, NJ: Princeton University Press, 1968); Raymond de Roover, *The Rise and Decline of the Medici Bank, 1397–1494* (New York: W. W. Norton by arrangement with Harvard University Press, 1966); Melissa Bullard, *Lorenzo il Magnifico: Image, Anxiety, Politics and Finance* (Florence: Leo S. Olschki, 1994); Anthony Molho, "Cosimo de' Medici: Pater Patriae or Padrino?," *Stanford Italian Review* 1 (1979): 5-33.

78. Braudel, *Mediterranean*, 1: 342.

79. Braudel, *Mediterranean*, 1: 393. For an explicit comparison between the Florentines and Genoese, see Céline Dauverd, *Imperial Ambition in the Early Modern Mediterranean: Genoese Merchants and the Spanish Crown* (New York: Cambridge University Press, 2015), 127-133.

80. Braudel, *Mediterranean*, 1: 391n181.

81. Goldthwaite, *Economy of Renaissance Florence*, 48, quotes the *Cinque Savi alla Mercanzia*.

82. The fairs actually took place in Piacenza (Braudel, *Mediterranean*, 1: 322). The document Braudel cites is from January 1607, which was 1606 in the Venetian system. Even so, the report seems to be a different one than that cited by Goldthwaite, who cited its quotation in Isabella Cecchini, "Piacenza a Venezia: La ricezione delle fiere di cambio di Bisenzione a fine Cinquecento nel mercato del credito lagunare," *Note di Lavoro* (Dipartimento di Scienze Economiche, Università Ca' Foscari Venezia), no. 18 (2006):14 (Goldthwaite, *Economy of Renaissance Florence*, 48n8), since Cecchini, 14nn65 and 66 cites "ASV, Cinque Savi alla Mercanzia, *Seconda serie*, b. 13, fasc. 229 / 1, 16 gennaio 1606," while Braudel (322n232) cites A.d.S. Venice, *Cinque Savii*, Risposte 1602-1606, f° 189, v°, 195." Cecchini's article

is online at http://www.unive.it/media/allegato/DIP/Economia/Note_di
_lavoro_sc_economiche/NL2006/NL_DSE_Cecchini_18_06.pdf.

83. Braudel, *Mediterranean*, 1: 503. I have Italianized Braudel's translator's
spelling.

84. Braudel, *Mediterranean*, 1: 463.

85. Braudel, *Mediterranean*, 1: 498.

86. Goldthwaite, *Economy of Renaissance Florence*, 257–258.

87. Thanks to Corey Tazzara and Paula Findlen for conversations about the
Florentine elite's uninterrupted commercial engagement; errors remain
my own. On Cosimo I as a merchant prince, see Najemy, *History of Florence*, 474–475.

88. Braudel, *Mediterranean*, 2: 1201.

89. Najemy, *History of Florence*, 474–475.

90. Najemy, *History of Florence*, 474.

91. See Najemy, *History of Florence*, 475, for the increase in Cosimo I's personal patrimony.

92. Najemy, *History of Florence*, 475.

93. Braudel, *Mediterranean*, 1: 485.

94. Najemy, *History of Florence*, 475.

95. Stephan Skalweit, "Caterina de' Medici, regina di Francia," *DBI* 22
(1979).

96. On the short-term debt suspension, see Braudel, *Mediterranean*, 1: 535.
On settlement of the 1596 default in 1597, see Braudel, *Mediterranean*, 1:
514. Figures showing military spending as causal are from Geoffrey
Parker, *The Army of Flanders and the Spanish Road, 1567–1659: The Logistics of
Spanish Victory and Defeat in the Low Countries' War*, 2nd ed. (New York:
Cambridge University Press, 2004), 116, and Parker, *Grand Strategy*, 134.
Parker notes that there were at least forty-five mutinies in the Army of
Flanders in the years 1573–1607 and that nearly half of these took place
after 1596 (Parker, *Army of Flanders*, 157). The years 1596 and 1607 were
both dates of Spanish default. On the rising costs of war that drove this,
see Braudel, *Mediterranean*, II, 842. See also I. A. A. Thompson, "Money,
Money, and Yet More Money!' Finance, the Fiscal-State, and the Military
Revolution: Spain 1500–1650," in Clifford Rogers, ed., *The Military Revolution Debate: Readings on the Military Transformation of Early Modern Europe*
(San Francisco: Westview, 1995), 273–298. For an alternative perspective
on Philip II's defaults and debt situation, the story of which has been
mobilized in recent sovereign debt debates, see Mauricio Drelichman
and Hans-Joachim Voth, "The Sustainable Debts of Philip II: A Reconstruction of Spain's Fiscal Position, 1560–1598," CEPR Discussion Paper
No. DP6611, https://papers.ssrn.com/sol3/papers.cfm?abstract_id=1373750.

97. Braudel, *Mediterranean*, 1: 490.

98. Braudel, *Mediterranean*, 2: 1181. See also ASF, MdP 4912, 99–101. This letter, of March 7, 1579, from Dovara in Madrid, discusses a possible grand ducal loan of 250,000 *scudi*. There is a much messier, probably original, copy of the same letter on 104r et seq.

99. Braudel, *Mediterranean*, 1: 557; Marica Milanesi, *Filippo Sassetti* (Florence: Nuova Italia, 1973), 36–37.

100. ASF, MdP 4911, 68r–69r, is a proclamation in Portuguese by King Philip to the Portuguese secular and clerical elite stating his claim to be the legitimate king and denouncing the claim of dom Antonio, the illegitimate son of Philip's uncle, the Infante Don Luis (68r). The proclamation is dated from Badajoz on June 26, 1580 (69r). 73r–74v, is a proclamation in Portuguese from King Philip; 78r–79v, in Castilian, and 80r–80v, in Portuguese, also pertain to this. On 150r–150v, Bernardo Canigiani reports on the prohibition of the commerce of Portugal with England, France, and Flanders in a December 12, 1580, letter from Madrid. Tuscan diplomats also took particular care to report on Italian soldiers on the Portugal campaign, from the raising of the troops and their transportation to casualties sustained with attention to notable Tuscans (ASF, MdP 4911, 18v). See, for instance, ASF, MdP 4912, 40, 52v, 71r, 79r, and 149r, and ASF, MdP 4911, 16–18, 37–38, and 87r.

101. Henry Kamen, *Empire: How Spain Became a World Power, 1492–1763* (New York: Harper Collins, 2003), 294 and 302. On the *tercio* cost, see Braudel, *Mediterranean*, 2: 842.

102. Braudel, *Mediterranean*, 1: 490.

103. Romero García, *Imperialismo hispanico*, 120; Cochrane, *Florence in the Forgotten Centuries*, 113; and Milanesi, *Filippo Sassetti*, 39–40. Romero García gives 1,416,667, but I follow Cochrane here as it seems preferable to give the lower figure. See also Carmen Sanz Ayán, "Prestar, regalar y ganar' Dinero y mecenazgo artístico-cultural en las relaciones entre la Monarquía Hispánica y Florencia (1579-1647)," in *Banca, crédito y capital: La monarquía hispánica y los antiguos Países Bajos (1505–1700)*, ed. Carmen Sanz Ayán and Bernardo José García García (Madrid: Fundación Carlos de Amberes, 2006), 459–482.

104. Braudel, *Mediterranean*, 1: 492 and 492nn213–214.

105. Goldthwaite, *Economy of Renaissance Florence*, 236–245.

106. Capponi, "Palle di Marte," 1112. On the Genoese, see Braudel, *Mediterranean*, 1: 500–508 and 535, 2: 960–962; Kamen, *Empire*, 89–90 and 173.

107. Hale, *Florence and the Medici*, 151 and 164.

108. Hale, *Florence and the Medici*, 164. Luisa Bertoni, "Cristina di Lorena, granduchessa di Toscana," *DBI* 31 (1985).

109. Skalweit, "Caterina de' Medici."

110. The major source for the following is "Maria de' Medici, regina di Francia," *DBI* 70 (2008).

111. Hale, *Florence and the Medici*, 173–174.

112. Braudel, *Mediterranean*, 2: 1220.

113. Braudel, *Mediterranean*, 2: 1213; Hale, *Florence and the Medici*, 161–162.

114. "Maria de' Medici, regina di Francia." Hale, *Florence and the Medici*, 174.

115. Hale, *Florence and the Medici*, 151.

116. Gregory Hanlon, *The Hero of Italy: Odoardo Farnese, Duke of Parma, His Soldiers, and His Subjects in the Thirty Years' War* (New York: Oxford University Press, 2014); Giampiero Brunelli, "Odoardo Farnese, duca di Parma e di Piacenza," *DBI* (2015). On Mantua, see R. A. Stradling, "Prelude to Disaster; the Precipitation of the War of the Mantuan Succession, 1627–29," *Historical Journal* 33, no. 4 (Dec. 1990): 769–785; David Parrott, "The Mantuan Succession, 1627–31: A Sovereignty Dispute in Early Modern Europe," *English Historical Review* 112, no. 445 (Feb. 1997): 2–65; Gino Benzoni, "Carlo I Gonzaga Nevers, duca di Mantova e del Monferrato," *DBI* 20 (1977).

117. Hale, *Florence and the Medici*, 164.

118. Contini, "Medicean Diplomacy," 70; R. Burr Litchfield, *Emergence of a Bureaucracy: The Florentine Patricians 1530–1790* (Princeton, NJ: Princeton University Press, 1986).

119. Contini, "Medicean Diplomacy," 70. See also Daniela Frigo, "Introduction" in Frigo, *Politics and Diplomacy in Early Modern Italy*, 13.

120. This follows Contini, "Medicean Diplomacy," 59 and 64–66, and Frigo, "Introduction," 14.

121. ASF, MdP 4911, 52, 54 and 58, "con tutto ch'io non m'intenda di leggi, nè intenda interame[n]te la lingua spagnuola" (54r). On Canigiani, see Fabio Troncarelli, "Canigiani, Bernardo," *DBI* 18 (1975); MAP Person ID 3283, "Canigiani, Bernardo di Lorenzo."

122. Contini, "Medicean Diplomacy," 70 (legation secretaries from p. 70 onward).

123. Contini, "Medicean Diplomacy," 73.

124. Frigo, "Introduction," 17.

125. ASF, MdP 4897, 156r–164v. Cavalier de Nobili's plaintive requests for more money to pay for his expenses can be found among the documents appearing between 156r and 164v inclusive. MAP Person ID 416, "Nobili, Leonardo di Antonio de'," and Vanna Arrighi, "De Nobili, Leonardo," *DBI* 38 (1990).

126. ASF, MdP 4897, 156r–v (currency is the *scudo*); 159r–160r (account of expenses); 189–190. From Cavaliere de Nobili in Alcalá on December 14, 1565. 190r is a copy of 157r, but not an exact one. Beneath the original text of the manuscript there is "ha havuto [a symbol for *scudi*] 500 del donativò et sei˙ mesi delle sue provis̓[ione]: 771·3." This would seem to imply that sixth months of *provisione* were equivalent to either 271.3 or 771.3 *scudi* depending on whether the colon was intended to indicate a

summation. I am inclined to think that the writer intended the colon to signify a summation, which would leave the ambassador's annual salary in excess of 500 *scudi*, hardly a trifling sum. This lower figure is consistent with the ambassador's evident stress over a shortfall of 685 *scudi*, which would have amounted to more than his annual *provisione*.

127. ASF, MdP 4897, 162r–164v. From Cavalier de Nobili in Alcalá, November 29, 1565 (162r, 163v) to Bartolomeo Concini, first secretary to the prince of Florence. 162v: "sua eccellenza Illustrissima sa benissimo la carestia di questo paese, et la spesa di questa corte, et cò [n]forme alla sua grandezza vorrà çhe io tenga la riputationę." He mentions "et la mia provisione cominciassi il primo d[']ottobre, che parti io alli 10, o, dodici" (163r).

128. ASF, MdP 4898, P. I, 29, 34v (address). The letter is dated from Madrid on January 25, 1566 [1567].

129. Frigo, "Introduction," 16–18, on honors and expenses.

130. I draw this generalization from reading ASF manuscripts. Compare with Venice: Filippo de Vivo, *Information and Communication in Venice: Rethinking Early Modern Politics* (New York: Oxford University Press, 2007).

131. Braudel, *Mediterranean*, 2: 1015n293.

132. Hale, *Florence and the Medici*, 151, quotes Ferdinando I's direct instructions, which I paraphrase here. See also Braudel, *Mediterranean*, 2: 1094–1095.

133. Parker, *Emperor*, xviii, 431–432.

134. MAP Doc ID 16555, ASF, MdP 3108, 235. From Fabrizio Ferrari in Milan to Cosimo I de' Medici in Florence on August 6, 1561. MAP Person ID 491 "Ferrari, Fabrizio." At this time, Ferrari was a Medici agent in Milan.

135. ASF, MdP 4897, 7r–9v. This appears to be MAP Person ID 736, "Garçes, Gabriel"; Garçes was a secretary in the court of Philip II.

136. ASF, MdP 4898, P. I, 127–132.

137. See, for instance, ASF, MdP 5080, 442r, 443r, and 590r.

138. From Bongianni di Piero (Fra) Gianfigliazzi in Madrid to Francesco I de' Medici in Florence on June 16, 1586, MAP Doc ID 16129; ASF, MdP 5046, 193.

139. From Cosimo Bartoli in Venice to Francesco I de' Medici in Florence on October 15, 1569, MAP Doc ID 21910; ASF, MdP 3080, 630.

140. MAP Doc ID 10010, ASF, MdP 5080, 412 (from Spain on October 15, 1607).

141. To Felipe III de Austria in Madrid on July 17, 1609, MAP Doc ID 16566, ASF, MdP 5080, 1018.

142. On the Genoese advantage of access to bullion and the superior level of Genoese high finance, see Goldthwaite, *Economy of Renaissance Florence*, 45; Braudel, *Mediterranean*, 1: 496.

143. Braudel, *Mediterranean*, 1: 486–488.

144. Braudel, *Mediterranean*, 1: 491.

145. Braudel, *Mediterranean*, 1: 493n219, 495, and 500.
146. Toskana 3, 18r, Österreichisches Staatsarchiv, Vienna. The letter begins by noting the death of the grand duke of Tuscany, Cosimo II, on February 28, 1620, before turning to the contents of his most secret testament: "Il detto Testamento è pieno d'avvertimenti, et ricordi amorevoli, sustantiali, et di mole' importanza, tanto per i Capi risguardanti il buon governo dello Stato, et amministratione della buona giustizia, et beneficio de sua figliuoli et Casa, quanto per la conservazione et augumento dell'entrate, riformando i Ruoli, resecando et diminuendo le spese; Et quanto al Tesoro, con molte prohibitioni, et gravi peni ordinò, che non si toccassi in modo nessuno, se non in certi casi di necessità da lui dichiarati, risguardanti il bisogno et interesse della propria Casa, Prohibendo espressamente, che dalle Tutrici, nè meno con autorità del Consiglio, durante la minora età del Principe, non si potessi imprestare danari ad' alcun Principe, Republica, ò, Potentato, ò, altra persona, nè meno si potessi consentire, ch'à simili Personaggi si prestassi dal Monte di Pietà della Città di Fiorenza, ancorche s'offerissero sicurtà, et mallevadori nelli stati di Sua Altezza nè le medesime Tutrici potessero entrare sicurtà, con molte considerationi, et ricordi." Prince Ferdinando is then named as universal heir and a regency council is ordered until he reaches the age of eighteen. The document is enclosed in a letter that extends from 17r to 20v. The address on 20v seems to indicate that the letter is from March 13, 1621.
147. Capponi, "Palle di Marte," 1105-1141.

### 2. COOPERATIVE EMPIRE

1. See Henry Kamen, *Empire: How Spain Became a World Power, 1492-1763* (New York: Harper Collins, 2003), and Kamen, "The Decline of Spain: A Historical Myth?," *Past and Present* no. 81 (Nov. 1978): 24-50; J. I. Israel, "The Decline of Spain: A Historical Myth?," *Past and Present* no. 91 (May 1981): 170-180; Henry Kamen, "The Decline of Spain: A Historical Myth? A Rejoinder," *Past and Present* no. 91 (May 1981): 181-185.
2. Fernand Braudel, *The Mediterranean and the Mediterranean World in the Age of Philip II*, 2nd rev. ed., 2 vols., trans. Siân Reynolds (Berkeley: University of California Press, 1995), 1: 560-61; James C. Boyajian, *Portuguese Trade in Asia under the Habsburgs, 1580-1640* (Baltimore, MD: Johns Hopkins University Press, 1993), 18-20.
3. Michael Mallett and Christine Shaw, *The Italian Wars, 1494-1559: War, State, and Society in Early Modern Europe* (New York: Routledge, 2014), 280.
4. Richard Goldthwaite, *The Economy of Renaissance Florence* (Baltimore, MD: Johns Hopkins University Press, 2009), 152-161; A. R. Disney, *A History of Portugal and the Portuguese Empire: From Beginnings to 1807*, 2 vols.

(New York: Cambridge University Press, 2009), 2: 241; Nunziatella Alessandrini, "Images of India through the Eyes of Filippo Sassetti, a Florentine Humanist Merchant in the 16th Century," in *Sights and Insights: Interactive Images of Europe and the Wider World*, ed. Mary N. Harris and Csaba Lévai (Pisa, It.: Pisa University Press, 2007), 46; Francesco Guidi Bruscoli, *Bartolomeo Marchionni, "Homem de Grossa Fazenda" (ca. 1450–1530): Un mercante fiorentino a Lisbona e l'impero portoghese* (Florence: Olschki, 2014).

5. For Filippo Sassetti's famous account (p. 39) in the context of European views of Lisbon, see Kate Lowe, "Foreign Descriptions of the Global City: Renaissance Lisbon from the Outside," in *The Global City: On the Streets of Renaissance Lisbon*, ed. Annemarie Jordan-Gschwend and Kate Lowe (London: Paul Holberton, 2015), 36–55. Brad Bouley graciously found, photographed, and shared a Sassetti autograph letter praising Lisbon on these grounds, ASF Carte Strozziane, Prima Serie, b. 324, n. 17, esp. 77r–78r. Francesco Surdich, "Sassetti, Filippo," DBI 90 (2017); Goldthwaite, *Economy of Renaissance Florence*, 109; Francesca Trivellato, *The Familiarity of Strangers: The Sephardic Diaspora, Livorno, and Cross-Cultural Trade in the Early Modern Period* (New Haven, CT: Yale University Press, 2009), 215–217 and 229.

6. Andréa Doré, "Cristãos na Índia no século XVI: A presença portuguesa e os viajantes italianos," *Revista Brasileira de História* 22, no. 44 (2002): 311–339; Marco Spallanzani, *Mercanti fiorentini nell'Asia portoghese (1500–1525)* (Florence: S.P.E.S., 1997); Sanjay Subrahmanyam, *The Portuguese Empire in Asia, 1500–1700: A Political and Economic History* (New York: Longman, 1993), esp. 113–117; Eric Cochrane, *Florence in the Forgotten Centuries 1527–1800: A History of Florence and the Florentines in the Age of the Grand Dukes* (Chicago: University of Chicago Press, 1973), 108.

7. Filippo Sassetti, *Lettere dall'India (1583–1588)*, ed. Adele Dei (Rome: Salerno, 1995), Letter 1, 30 n. 8. On Piero Strozzi, who had traveled to India earlier in the century, see Sanjay Subrahmanyam, "'Um Bom Homem De Tratar': Piero Strozzi: A Florentine in Portuguese Asia, 1510–1522," *Journal of European Economic History* 16, no. 3 (Winter 1987): 511–526; Gustavo Uzielli, "Piero di Andrea Strozzi Viaggiatore Fiorentino," *Memorie della Società Geografica Italiana*, vol. 5 (Rome: G. Civelli, La Società Geografica Italiana, 1895), 136–138.

8. R. Burr Litchfield, *Emergence of a Bureaucracy: The Florentine Patricians 1530–1790* (Princeton, NJ: Princeton University Press, 1986).

9. Stefano Tabacchi, "Giraldi, Luca," *DBI* 56 (2001); Nunziatella Alessandrini, "Contributo alla storia della famiglia Giraldi, mercanti, banchieri fiorentini alla corte di Lisbona nel XVI secolo," *Storia Economica* 14, no. 3 (2011): 377–407. Luca Giraldi was the nephew of Luca Capponi (Alessandrini, 380).

10. A. J. R. Russell-Wood, *The Portuguese Empire, 1415–1808: A World on the Move* (Baltimore, MD: Johns Hopkins University Press, 1998).

11. Tabacchi, "Giraldi, Luca."

12. Alessandrini points out the strong connection between Luca's son Francesco and his cousin Giovanni's son Vincenzo. This genealogical information derives from Alessandrini, "Contributo alla storia," 380-381. On Luca Giraldi's interest in the bank and the strength of the family connection to the branches of the Cavalcanti and Giraldi in Florence, see Alessandrini, "Contributo alla storia," 393-394.

13. Mickaël Augeron and Laurent Vidal, "Creating Colonial Brazil: The First Donatary Captaincies or the System of Private Exclusivity (1534-1549)," in *Constructing Early Modern Empires: Proprietary Ventures in the Atlantic*, ed. Louis H. Roper and Bertrand van Ruymbeke (Boston: Brill, 2007), 22-30 and 33-43; Mark A. Burkholder and Lyman L. Johnson, *Colonial Latin America*, 7th ed. (New York: Oxford University Press, 2010), 104. Disney, *History of Portugal*, 2: 204-207, 210-216, and 235-236; Kenneth Pomeranz and Steven Topik, *The World That Trade Created: Society, Culture, and the World Economy, 1400 to the Present*, 3rd ed. (New York: Routledge, 2012), 31-34; John F. Richards, *The Unending Frontier: An Environmental History of the Early Modern World* (Berkeley: University of California Press, 2003), 377-411.

14. Augeron and Vidal, "Creating Colonial Brazil," 35-36 and 50-51; Tabacchi, "Giraldi, Luca." The authorization to sell was granted in 1560 and received royal confirmation in 1561 (Alessandrini, "Contributo alla storia," 391-392). See also Stuart B. Schwartz, "A Commonwealth within Itself: The Early Brazilian Sugar Industry, 1550-1670," in *Tropical Babylons: Sugar and the Making of the Atlantic World*, ed. Stuart B. Schwartz (Chapel Hill: University of North Carolina Press, 2004), 159-160.

15. Bahia had been turned into a royal captaincy as the Portuguese reined in the captains in 1548-1549 (Augeron and Vidal, "Creating Colonial Brazil," 43-48 and 50). The Portuguese Crown continued to create captaincies, dissolving them only with the Pombaline reforms of 1753 (Disney, *History of Portugal*, 2: 213, and Burkholder and Johnson, *Colonial Latin America*, 105).

16. Alessandrini, "Contributo alla storia," 400.

17. Alessandrini, "Contributo alla storia," 399 and 401.

18. Alessandrini, "Contributo alla storia," 403 and 403n105 (transcription).

19. "Quando le venisse alle mani qual'che curiosita ò semi di cose, che no[n] sien quà," ASF, MdP 270, 7r. Francesco I de' Medici to Francesco Giraldi, December 26, 1586. This register contains condensed contents of letters. All translations are mine unless otherwise indicated. MAP Doc ID 19301, ASF, MdP 270, 6-7.

20. Vincenzo di Andrea Alamanni in Madrid to Ferdinando I de' Medici in Florence, April 30, 1588, MAP Doc ID 8238, ASF, MdP 4919, 222; MAP Person ID 133, "Alamanni, Vincenzo di Andrea."

21. Angelo de Gubernatis, ed., *Storia dei Viaggiatori Italiani nelle Indie Orientali* (Livorno, It.: Franc. Vigo, 1875), 27–28. De Gubernatis cited "Lettera inedita, negli archivii toscani (Carte di Spagna)" at 28n1).

22. Goldthwaite, *Economy of Renaissance Florence*, 68–78.

23. The interaction of business travel and political exile was already old when Alessandra Strozzi composed her famous letters to her sons: Alessandra Strozzi, *Selected Letters of Alessandra Strozzi*, trans. and ed. Heather Gregory (Berkeley: University of California Press, 1997).

24. On the Cavalcanti, I rely on the manuscript history, ASF, Manoscritti, 382: "ISTORIA Della Famiglia de Cavalcanti scritta da Scipione Ammirato l'Anno 1586"; the title notwithstanding, it was updated through 1626. Thanks to Beth Coggeshall of Stanford University for introducing me to this document, which she found as part of her work on the friends of Dante. The original title of the published Florentine family histories was *Delle famiglie nobili fiorentine*. For this and other information on Scipione Ammirato, see Rodolfo de Mattei, "Ammirato, Scipione," *DBI* 3 (1961). See also Cochrane, *Florence in the Forgotten Centuries*, 147–148.

25. ASF, Manoscritti, 382. Both the Albuquerque and the Vasconcelos coats of arms appear in António Godinho, *Livro da Nobreza e da Perfeição das Armas do Reis Cristãos e Nobres Linhagens dos Reinos e Senhorios de Portugal*, c. 1521, ANTT, PT / TT / CR / D / A / 001 / 20, 30 and 31 (f. 10v and 11r). Franco Cardini, "Cavalcanti," *Enciclopedia Dantesca* (1970) terms this branch of the Cavalcanti "di Albuquerque"; the encyclopedia is available online at http://www.treccani.it/enciclopedia/elenco-opere/Enciclopedia_Dantesca. On the power of the Cavalcanti Albuquerque, see Stuart B. Schwartz, *Sovereignty and Society in Colonial Brazil: The High Court of Bahia and Its Judges, 1609–1751* (Berkeley: University of California Press, 1973), 179–180.

26. "Antonio Cavalcanti, che habita nel Verzino mi ha fatto mostrare una lettera del Gran Duca nostri Signore nella quale Sua Altezza dice, che teneva ordinato al signor Roderigo Alidosi suo Ambasciatore in quel tempo che con il nome, autorità et favore dell'Altezza Sua aiutasse et favorisse certa pretensione di detto Cavalcanti; et in virtu' della medesima lettera et ordine vorrebbe hora che a' suo tempo io parlassi à questi Signori del Consiglio di Portogallo et dove bisognasse per la buona speditione della sua pretensione, che deve esser' per quanto intendo di esser' dichiarato naturale di questi Regni et capace di tutte le gratie e privilegij che soglion' godere i naturali et hidalghi; et havendo risposto a' chi men' ha parlato, che io non posso metter' la mano in questo negotio senza nuovo ordine di Sua Altezza per compiacere a' questo gentilhomo, desidero sapere da Vostra Signore Illustrissima se l'Altezza Sua gusterà, che io parli a favor' suo, che secondo il suo avviso mi governerò, non sapendo, chi sia il Cavalcanti, e se Sua Altezza tien' piu quella volonta' verso di lui, et a Vostra Signore Illustrissima bacio le mani," ASF, MdP 4937, 506r.

27. ASF, MdP 4937, 506r.
28. MAP Person ID 147, "Alidosi de Mendoza, Rodrigo."
29. Much of the demand for spices remained local, though it is the long-distance trade that has captured the imagination. See John Keay, *The Spice Route: A History* (Berkeley: University of California Press, 2006), xiii–xiv; Janet L. Abu-Lughod, *Before European Hegemony: The World System a.d. 1250–1350* (New York: Oxford University Press, 1991); Barbara Watson Andaya and Leonard Y. Andaya, *A History of Early Modern Southeast Asia, 1400–1830* (Cambridge: Cambridge University Press, 2015), esp. 134–135; Giancarlo Casale, *The Ottoman Age of Exploration* (New York: Oxford University Press, 2010); Paul Freedman, *Out of the East: Spices and the Medieval Imagination* (New Haven, CT: Yale University Press, 2008); Victor Lierberman, *Strange Parallels: Southeast Asia in Global Context, c. 800–1830*, 2 vols. (New York: Cambridge University Press, 2003 and 2009); Kenneth McPherson, *The Indian Ocean: A History of People and the Sea* (Delhi: Oxford University Press, 1993); Gary Paul Nabhan, *Cumin, Camels, and Caravans: A Spice Odyssey* (Berkeley: University of California Press, 2014); Michael Pearson, *The Indian Ocean* (New York: Routledge, 2003); Anthony Reid, *Southeast Asia in the Age of Commerce: 1450–1680*, 2 vols. (New Haven, CT: Yale University Press, 1988); Reid, ed., *Southeast Asia in the Early Modern Era: Trade, Power, and Belief* (Ithaca, NY: Cornell University Press, 1993); Patricia Risso, *Merchants and Faith: Muslim Commerce and Culture in the Indian Ocean* (Boulder, CO: Westview, 1995); Niels Steensgaard, *Carracks, Caravans and Companies: The Structural Crisis in the European-Asian Trade in the Early 17th Century* (Copenhagen: Studentlitteratur, 1973); James D. Tracy, *Rise of Merchant Empires* and *Political Economy of Merchant Empires; The Organization of Interoceanic Trade in European Expansion, 1450–1800*, ed. Pieter Emmer and Femme Gaastra (Brookfield, VT: Variorum, Ashgate, 1996); Tracy, ed., *The Political Economy of Merchant Empires: State Power and World Trade, 1350–1750* (New York: Cambridge University Press, 1997); Ronald Findlay and Kevin H. O'Rourke, *Power and Plenty: Trade, War, and the World Economy in the Second Millennium* (Princeton, NJ: Princeton University Press, 2007); Prasannan Parthasarathi, *Why Europe Grew Rich and Asia Did Not: Global Economic Divergence, 1600–1850* (New York: Cambridge University Press, 2011).
30. Boyajian, *Portuguese Trade in Asia*, 12.
31. Boyajian, *Portuguese Trade in Asia*, 42, Table 2.
32. Boyajian, *Portuguese Trade in Asia*, 44, Table 3. Boyajian deals separately and in detail with issues of smuggling and underreporting, but the point is clear from these figures.
33. This is one of my primary takeaways from Boyajian, *Portuguese Trade in Asia*.
34. The gross state revenues from the Carreira da Índia and of the Portuguese state are given in metric tons of silver (14,700 kg and 62,800 kg of

silver respectively) in Ernst van Veen, *Decay or Defeat? An Inquiry into the Portuguese Decline in Asia, 1580–1645* (Leiden, Neth.: Leiden University, Research School CNWS, 2000), appendix 1.1, 244.

35. Subrahmanyam, *Portuguese Empire*, 113.

36. Boyajian, *Portuguese Trade in Asia*, 19–20.

37. Boyajian, *Portuguese Trade in Asia*, 19–20; Braudel, *Mediterranean*, 1: 560–561.

38. Boyajian, *Portuguese Trade in Asia*, 20.

39. The monopoly excluded royal and charitable allocations of sugar (Alessandrini, "Contributo alla storia," 382). Sergio Bertelli, "Affaitati, Giovan Carlo," *DBI* 1 (1960), gives 1528 as the date of death; Alessandrini, whose scholarship is more recent and of impeccable quality, gives April 29, 1529, and so deference is given to her judgment.

40. Bertelli, "Affaitati, Giovan Carlo."

41. This account is based on Alessandrini, "Contributo alla storia," 384–385.

42. Alessandrini, "Contributo alla storia," 386.

43. Boyajian, *Portuguese Trade in Asia*, 8–9.

44. Alessandrini, "Contributo alla storia," 388–389; for Niccolò as the younger brother, see 383n16.

45. Alessandrini, "Contributo alla storia," 396 and 401.

46. Alessandrini, "Contributo alla storia," 392–393.

47. Alessandrini, "Contributo alla storia," 398 and 398n80.

48. Subrahmanyam, *Portuguese Empire*, 113. Marica Milanesi, *Filippo Sassetti* (Florence: Nuova Italia, 1973), 35.

49. This follows Milanesi, *Filippo Sassetti*, 35–36.

50. Milanesi, *Filippo Sassetti*, 25 and 35.

51. Subrahmanyam, *Portuguese Empire*, 113.

52. Milanesi, *Filippo Sassetti*, 36.

53. Oliverotto Guidotti in Madrid to Antonio Serguidi in Florence on December 26, 1576, MAP Doc ID 805, ASF, MdP 4906, 9; MAP Person ID 1027, "Serguidi, Antonio."

54. MAP Person ID 852, "Guidotti, Oliverotto."

55. Oliverotto Guidotti in Madrid to Antonio Serguidi in Florence on December 26, 1576, MAP Doc ID 805, ASF, MdP 4906, 9. Rivalry between Florence and Genoa was open. Céline Dauverd, *Imperial Ambition in the Early Modern Mediterranean: Genoese Merchants and the Spanish Crown* (New York: Cambridge University Press, 2015), 129–130, cites a 1622 letter from Genoa's doge to Genoa's ambassador in Spain in which the doge asserted that Genoa ought to have been accorded primacy over Florence and a 1595 letter from the Genoese consul in Palermo deploring the granting of a triumphal arch to a Florentine and not a Genoese galley.

56. Braudel, *Mediterranean*, 1: 557 and 557n113. Braudel's archival reference in this passage is "Abbe Brizeño to the king, Florence, 26th November 1576, Simancas E° 1450."

57. Antonio Vecchietti in Lisbon to Francesco I de' Medici in Florence on September 27, 1576, MAP Doc ID 14225, ASF, MdP 4906, 157.

58. Tommaso di Iacopo de' Medici in Florence to the "Strozzi (Family)" in Venice on June 19, 1570, MAP Doc ID 5119, ASF, MdP 221, 79.

59. Frederic C. Lane, *Venice: A Maritime Republic* (Baltimore, MD: Johns Hopkins University Press, 1973), 290-295; Milanesi, *Filippo Sassetti*, 25; Braudel, *Mediterranean*, 1: 561-562; Boyajian, *Portuguese Trade in Asia*, 7; Subrahmanyam, *Portuguese Empire*, 62-74; Casale, *Ottoman Age*.

60. Braudel, *Mediterranean*, 1: 557. Braudel's archival reference: "Ch. de Salazar to the king, Venice, 11th September, 1577, Simancas E° 1336." See also 1: 557n112.

61. Milanesi, *Filippo Sassetti*, 37 and 37n79.

62. Boyajian, *Portuguese Trade in Asia*, 20-21; van Veen, *Decay or Defeat?*, appendix 3.2, 252-253.

63. Dei, "Nota biografica," in Sassetti, *Lettere dall'India (1583–1588)*, 22; Surdich, "Sassetti, Filippo"; Milanesi, *Filippo Sassetti*, 42-46, 49, and 67.

64. Sassetti, *Lettere dall'India*, Letter 4, 46.

65. Sassetti, *Lettere dall'India*, Letter 4, 46-47.

66. Boyajian, *Portuguese Trade in Asia*, 124-127.

67. Sassetti, *Lettere dall'India*, Letter 4, 47.

68. Subrahmanyam, *Portuguese Empire*, 62-74; Lane, *Venice*, 284-294.

69. Sassetti, *Lettere dall'India*, Letter 14, 110.

70. Sassetti, *Lettere dall'India*, Letter 14, 110.

71. Sassetti, *Lettere dall'India*, Letter 14, 109-110. The translation of <u>gauro</u> comes from Salvatore Battaglia, *Grande Dizionario della Lingua Italiana*, 21 vols. (Turin, It.: Unione Tipografico-Editrice Torino, 1961-), which, circularly, cites this passage from Sassetti for one of its definitions. The star symbols appear in Dei's edition of Sassetti's letters from India.

72. For the complicated religious, economic, and ideological ties that entwined the Portuguese in Sri Lanka see Zoltán Biedermann, *(Dis)Connected Empires: Imperial Portugal, Sri Lankan Diplomacy, and the Making of a Habsburg Conquest in Asia*, (Oxford: Oxford University Press, 2018).

73. Adele Dei in Sassetti, *Lettere dall'India*, Letter 14, 110n8 identifies Dacem as Pacem on the Northeast coast of Sumatra. On Pacem in Sumatra as a site of a Portuguese fortress or *feitoria* see, Russell-Wood, *The Portuguese Empire*, 22. On Pasai see, Reid, *Southeast Asia in the Age of Commerce*, vol. 2, 1, 7, 12, 69-70, and 111-112. Biedermann, *(Dis)Connected Empires*, 35.

74. Sassetti, *Lettere dall'India*, Letter, 25, 208 and 212.

75. Sassetti, *Lettere dall'India*, Letter 25, 212.

76. Braudel, *Mediterranean*, 1: 558-559.

77. Braudel, *Mediterranean*, 1: 559-560.

78. MAP Doc ID 22857, ASF, MdP 5037, 581. MAP suggests perhaps 1587.

79. MAP Person ID 133, "Alamanni, Vincenzo di Andrea." Alamanni was a Medici diplomatic envoy in France (1568), Venice (1578), and Savoy (1580) and ambassador to France (1572-1576) and Spain (1586-1590).

80. "Siamo Auti persuasi, et invuitati a dovesi pigliare da Sua Maestà Cattolica tutta quella quantità delle Pepi, che da India sono condotti a' Portogallo; et farne l'appalto in nostro nome; et poi secondo il solito distribuirli come à noi piacerà per le parti ove giudicheremo habbino spaccio, et dare parte di detto appalto a' nostri Vasalli, et altri secondo che ci sarà di piacere, et comodo," ASF, MdP 270, 148v, August 4, 1587.

81. "Et perche habbiamo caro di trattare con quella Al.ᵗᵃ ci ricolveremo facilmente attenderci se potremo convenire perche cose honeste, et ragionevole; ma perche non siamo per al passate à pieno informati in che termine sia il negotio; desideriamo avanti di venire alla resolutioni sapere le cose, et li capi apresso, cio è," ASF, MdP 270, 148v.

82. "Veder di sapere la somma precisa, ò poco appresso delli Pepi che Sua Maestà Cattolica vuol dare all'Appaltatore," ASF, MdP 270, 148v-149r.

83. ASF, MdP 270, 149r.

84. "Pigliare più certa informatione che si possa quanta somma di Pepi [149v:] resta oggi in essere in Lisbona si in mano della casa della contrattione, com in mano d'altri particolari," ASF, MdP 270, 149r-149v.

85. "Pigliare informatione particolare quali sono l'mercanti soliti d'interessanti nelli Appalti seguiti da un tempo in qua in Lisbona, et particolarmente si desidera informatione di Girolamo Duarte Jiminez, et di Andrea Jiminez portoghesi di Lisbona; ciòè che qualità di Persone siano circa alle facultà, et circa il credito, et circa il buon modo, et reale, che hanno nel loro negʳᵉ," ASF, MdP 270, 149v.

86. "Intendere se di passate si pratica, et tratta di fare partito di questi Pepi, et con chi si sia praticato, et si pratichi questo appalto, et che speranza si tenga nella conclusione d'esso et potendosi intendere qualche particolare de pregi, tempi, et altre conditioni haremo caro d'esserne avvisati," ASF, MdP 270, 149v.

87. "Intendere se doppo li Appaltatori hanno ricevuto li pepi, volendoli estrarre di Lisbona, ò, del Regno per qualsi voglia luogo per mare, ò, per terra che spesa vi è di diritti, ò, gabelle, ò, altro," ASF, MdP 270, 149v.

88. Braudel, *Mediterranean*, 1: 557.

89. Milanesi, *Filippo Sassetti*, 43-46. Van Veen, *Decay or Defeat?*, appendix 3.2, 252-253, offers a detailed explanation of the consortium.

90. Gino Benzoni, "Francesco I de' Medici, granduca di Toscana," *DBI* 49 (1997).

91. Vincenzo di Andrea Alamanni in Madrid to Ferdinando I de' Medici in Florence on April 13, 1589, MAP Doc ID 8744, ASF, MdP 4919, 863.

92. Braudel indicates that Venice and Florence played this role, citing a letter of Simón Ruiz of May 4, 1589 (Braudel, *Mediterranean*, 1: 562).

93. See, for instance, a 1567 bill of lading, MAP Doc ID 17315, ASF, MdP
    529a, 822, sent from Livorno on May 26, 1567; a 1577 ship's inventory,
    MAP Doc ID 12585, ASF, MdP 695, 199, sent from Livorno to Francesco
    I de' Medici in Florence on March 20, 1577; and *avvisi* from 1606, MAP
    Doc ID 16443, ASF, MdP 5080, 400, sent from Madrid to Florence on
    December 20, 1606.

94. Braudel, *Mediterranean*, 1: 106n18, cites ASF, MdP 2080 (November 29,
    1581). Braudel gives the ship as "probably Portuguese (the *Santo Antonio*,
    captain Baltasar Dias) loaded in Brazil and carrying notably 460 cantars
    of *pau brasil*" (635n547).

95. Braudel, *Mediterranean*, 1: 635 and 635n548, which cites ASF, MdP 2079,
    337 and 365. Braudel explains that "the first ship, *Nuestra Señora do Monte
    del Carmine*, from Goa, had a cargo of 4000 cantars of pepper and her ar-
    rival is dated merely 1610 without details; on 14th August 1610, arrived
    *Nostra Signora di Pietà*, from the East Indies, carrying 4170 cantars of
    pepper, precious stones and 145 cantars of Indian fabrics" (636n548).

96. Braudel, *Mediterranean*, 1: 641 and 641n575. In the seventeenth century,
    crates weighed about 200–300 kilograms according to Schwartz, "Com-
    monwealth within Itself," 180.

97. Burkholder and Johnson, *Colonial Latin America*, 171.

98. "Essendo impossibile si per li ordini *di Portogallo*," ASF, MdP 492i, c. 405,
    transcribed as document no. 1 in Sérgio Buarque de Holanda, "Os Pro-
    jetos de Colonização e Comércio Toscanos no Brasil ao Tempo do Grão
    Duque Fernando I (1587-1609)," *Revista de História* 142-143 (2000), 114.
    See also MAP Person ID 918, "Lenzoni, Francesco di Girolamo."

99. ASF, MdP 4921, 516-517, transcribed as document no. 2 in Buarque de
    Holanda, "Os Projetos de Colonização," 115-116. A further round: ASF,
    MdP 4921, cc. 57071, transcribed as document no. 3 in Buarque de Hol-
    anda, "Os Projetos de Colonização," 116-117.

100. Sugar provided less than 5 percent of Portuguese crown revenues in 1619
    (Disney, *History of Portugal*, 2: 238; Burkholder and Johnson, *Colonial Latin
    America*, 164 and 171).

101. MAP Person ID 775, "Vinta, Belisario di Francesco"; MAP Person ID
    842, "Guicciardini, Francesco di Agnolo."

102. "I nostri Mercanti vorrebbono far qui Una raffineria di Zuccheri, la qual
    sarebbe loro di grande utile, et à i nostri stati di gran commodo, et dove la
    si fà hora à Venetia con andarne tutto l'utile in mano d'Infedeli si addi-
    rizzerebbe qui con utilita de Christiani purche cotesta. Maestà si conten-
    tasse, et facesse gratia che otto Navi per lo meno et fino in x al piu cariche
    di Zuccheri potessino venire dal Brasil à linea diritta verso lo stretto di
    Zibilterra, et di quivi à Livorno, fuggendo il lungo circuito, et il pericolo
    dell'andare à Lisbono, et del haver dipoi di quivi à venire à Livorno: Et
    quanto à diritti et Gabelle di cotesta Maestà gli si obbligherebbono, et

darebbono sicurta di pagarle, et le pagherebbono alla Maestà Sua non altrimenti che se passassino p[er] Lisbona propria con tutte quelle cautioni maggiori, che ricercassino i Ministri di cotesta Maestà et perche fino al tempo dell'Ambasciatore Lenzoni che pero mai non messe mano à questo negotio sene scrisse costa, et sene mandorno à nome de [1145v:] i Mercanti, i, memoriali," ASF, MdP 5080, 1145r–1145v; Belisario di Francesco Vinta in Florence to Francesco di Agnolo Guicciardni in Madrid on February 5, 1594 (adjusted), MAP Doc ID 16585, ASF, MdP 5080, 1145; MAP Person ID 918, "Lenzoni, Francesco di Girolamo." Adjusted indicates that a correction has been made to convert the date to the modern calendar from the Florentine one, which started the year on March 25.

103. ASF, MdP 5080, 1145.

104. "Et la farebbono i Mercanti senza che sene facesse romore ne apparenza" and "Et però verremmo, che con destrezza senza nominar noi voi tenteste in qualche bel modo se l'Ambasciatore accettasse questa impresa," ASF, MdP 5080, 1145v.

105. Buarque de Holanda, "Os Projetos de Colonização," 96; P. E. H. Hair and Jonathan D. Davies, "Sierra Leone and the Grand Duchy of Tuscany," *History in Africa* 20 (1993): 62.

106. Augeron and Vidal, "Creating Colonial Brazil," 32, 39, 48, and 50–51 (Table 8). On sugar, see Buarque de Holanda, "Os Projetos de Colonização," 96; Burkholder and Johnson, *Colonial Latin America*, 162–165 and map 6 (168). Schwartz, "Commonwealth within Itself," 158–200, is immensely informative.

107. ASF, MdP 4939, 638, transcribed as document no. 7 in Buarque de Holanda, "Os Projetos de Colonização," 119–120; MAP Person ID 873, "Tarugi, Sallustio."

108. ASF, MdP 4939, 638, transcribed as document no. 7 in Buarque de Holanda, "Os Projetos de Colonização," 120.

109. ASF, MdP 4939, 638, transcribed as document no. 7 in Buarque de Holanda, "Os Projetos de Colonização," 120.

110. Rio de Janeiro to Ferdinando I de' Medici in Florence on August 20, 1601, ASF, MdP 4275, 20 and 21, MAP Doc ID 9952; Guarnieri, *Un'audace impresa marittima*, ASF, MdP 5080, 315, 7 and 7n4, which cites ASF, MdP 949, 1346r, of July and August 1608.

111. Hair and Davies, "Sierra Leone," 62. Buarque de Holanda, "Os Projetos de Colonização," 96.

112. Hair and Davies, "Sierra Leone," 61.

113. Hair and Davies, "Sierra Leone," 62. In their study, Hair and Davies cite ASF, MdP 960, 363 / 412; ASF, MdP 951, 609; ASF, Miscellanea Medicea, 29, Ins. 36, 1; ASF, Miscellanea Medicea, 29, Ins. 36, 3–5; ASF, Miscellanea Medicea, 29, Ins. 36, 6; ASF, MdP 3762 A; ASF, MdP 960, 364 / 411; and ASF, MdP 960, 362 / 413.

114. Hair and Davies, "Sierra Leone," 63.

115. The translations are mine from "io havrei molto desiderio di procurarne una relazione più minuta che fosse possibile" and "e che forse sia oggi in Roma alcuno di detti Padri che vi sia stato," transcribed in Buarque de Holanda, "Os Projetos de Colonização," 121, document no. 8, a short letter from Ferdinando I to Cardinal Maria Francesco del Monte Santa Maria in Rome of December 29, 1608. For the timing point, I draw on the information Hair and Davies, "Sierra Leone," 67, provided in the document list; this is their document no. 6.

116. Hair and Davies, "Sierra Leone," 65.

117. Hair and Davies, "Sierra Leone," 64; ASF, Misc. Med. 29, Ins. 3, Doc 2, 5r.

118. "Questo è un sito che mette in mano la Chiave dell'Indie orientali, et occidentali, et di tutta la navigatione, et che il Re viene a restare molto impegnato con chi ne sarà Patrone, et quasi dependente, di maniera che il Re voglia nel darla qualche Cautela," ASF, Misc. Med. 29, Ins. 3, Doc 2, 5r. The transcription is mine from the original, but I follow Hair and Davies's notes about the document's role. Hair and Davies, "Sierra Leone," 67, lists it as document 4, tacitly suggesting that the undated document belongs to a set from December 28–29, 1608. They describe it as an "unsigned, undated, account of Sierra Leone and terms to be sought, concluding with the name of Francisco Pereira, perhaps the informant."

### 3. THE NORTHERN EUROPEAN ALTERNATIVE

1. Simon Pepper and Nicholas Adams, *Firearms and Fortifications: Military Architecture and Siege Warfare in Sixteenth-Century Siena* (Chicago: University of Chicago Press, 1986).

2. J. R. Hale, *Florence and the Medici* (London: Phoenix, 2001), 130–132.

3. Richard Goldthwaite, *The Economy of Renaissance Florence* (Baltimore, MD: Johns Hopkins University Press, 2009), 168.

4. Corey Tazzara, *The Free Port of Livorno and the Transformation of the Mediterranean World, 1574–1790* (New York: Oxford University Press, 2017); Francesca Trivellato, *The Familiarity of Strangers: The Sephardic Diaspora, Livorno, and Cross-Cultural Trade in the Early Modern Period* (New Haven, CT: Yale University Press, 2009).

5. Trivellato, *Familiarity of Strangers*, 74; Tazzara, *Free Port of Livorno*, 26–27. Figure 1.1 on p. 27 reproduces Buontalenti's plan for Livorno (Ida Maria Botto, "Buontalenti, Bernardo," *DBI* 15 [1972]).

6. Trivellato, *Familiarity of Strangers*, table 2.1, 54–56, and the main text on 57.

7. This summarizes Trivellato, *Familiarity of Strangers*, 108.

8. Trivellato, *Familiarity of Strangers*, 50–51; Fernand Braudel, *The Mediterranean and the Mediterranean World in the Age of Philip II*, 2nd rev. ed., 2 vols.,

trans. Siân Reynolds (Berkeley: University of California Press, 1995), 1: 641.

9. Quoted in Trivellato, *Familiarity of Strangers*, 76.

10. Tazzara, *Free Port of Livorno*, 41.

11. Trivellato, *Familiarity of Strangers*, 53.

12. Braudel, *Mediterranean*, 1: 419, cites figures of thousands of tons of wool in 1580 and 150,000 tons arriving at the port in 1592–1593.

13. Goldthwaite, *Economy of Renaissance Florence*, 42 and 124; Trivellato, *Familiarity of Strangers*, 107.

14. Tazzara, *Free Port of Livorno*, 50; Goldthwaite, *Economy of Renaissance Florence*, 38 and 114–115.

15. Tazzara, *The Free Port of Livorno*, 50; Braudel, *Mediterranean*, 1: 629–636. See esp. the table "Northern Grain at Leghorn in 1593" on p. 630 and figure 54, "The Increasing Numbers of Northern Boats at Leghorn 1573–1593," 632–633.

16. National Archives, Kew, State Papers Foreign, Tuscany 98 / 1, f. 24.

17. For the figures, see Tazzara, *Free Port of Livorno*, 50.

18. Trivellato, *Familiarity of Strangers*, 78–79 and 106.

19. S[r]. Tho: Sherley, *Discours of the Turkes*, The Royal Historical Society, ed. E. Denison Ross, 1936, held as MS 514 in Lambeth Palace Library, London, it was printed in *The Camden Miscellany* [hereafter CM], vol. 16, Camden third series, vol. 52 (London: Offices of the Society, 1936). I worked with both the manuscript and the printed edition. The printed version will be "Sherley, *Discours of the Turkes* (CM)." Sherley, *Discours of the Turkes* (CM), vi–vii. There is some disagreement about Sherley's date of death, c. 1630: History of Parliament: J.E.M., "Shirley, Thomas II (1564–c.1630), of Wiston Suss.; later of the I.o.W." in P. W. Hasler, ed., *The History of Parliament: The House of Commons 1558–1603* (London: Published for the History of Parliament Trust by H.M.S.O., 1981), online ed. On the date 1630, see MAP Person ID 20662, "Shirley, Thomas". For 1633 / 1634 see Richard Raiswell, "Sherley, Sir Thomas (1564–1633 / 4)," *Oxford Dictionary of National Biography*. On c. 1634, see Lambeth Palace Library Catalogue, Code: GB / 109 / 19067.

20. Sherley, *Discours of the Turkes* (CM), 24–25n3. On Sir Thomas Sherley I, see Janet Pennington, "Sherley, Sir Thomas (c. 1542–1612)," *Oxford Dictionary of National Biography*; J.E.M., "Shirley, Thomas I (c. 1542–1612), of Wiston, Suss.," in P. W. Hasler, ed., *The History of Parliament*, online ed.; MAP Person ID 19219, "Shirley, Thomas."

21. I rely here on the History of Parliament biography, J.E.M., "Shirley, Thomas II (1564–c.1630), of Wiston, Suss.; later of the I.o.W." See also Anthony D. Alderson, "Sir Thomas Sherley's Piratical Expedition to the Aegean and His Imprisonment in Constantinople," *Oriens* 9, vol. 1 (Aug. 1956): 1–40.

22. Sherley, *Discours of the Turkes* (CM), vi–vii; J.E.M., "Shirley, Thomas II."

23. For ease of reading, I have modernized and regularized the spelling. The original is "Ligorna is a fayre harbor, but exeedinge open to all the westerne poyntes of the compas. The towne is not yett finished, but it wyll bee the finest smalle towne of Itali, all builte at the Duke his owne chardges. The fortification is one of the best that euer I sawe, for there wanteth noe mannor of thinge to it that the wytte of a soldyare can deuise, it is soe exellentelye well flanked with bulwoorkes of rare forme & strengthe, the ditche deepe & broade. To these there is added a cittadelle within the rampiere, yf the towne shoulde bee taken. There is a moate within the walles for the sauffe keepinge of the gallyes, but it is toe shallowe for shyppes. They haue grounde inoughe within the towne to make a newe fortification yf this shoulde bee loste. There are 1200 foote in garrison in it, but noe ordinans yett mounted, saue onelye in the olde castell, whyche serueth to noe purpose but to commaunde the harbor. This place was once subiecte to the Genoases, & it hathe in the harbor sutche a lanterne as that of Genoa" (Sherley, *Discours of the Turkes*, 23–24 [CM]). This corresponds to f. 42 of the Lambeth Palace Library manuscript; the handwriting in the manuscript is appalling.

24. Sherley, *Discours of the Turkes* (CM), 24; f. 44 of the Lambeth Palace Library manuscript. Modernized orthography. The original is "Florens is one of the finest townes in Itali for the exacte buildinge, cumlines of the streetes, & neatenes; & it is greate, thoughe inferior to manye for biggenes ; the riuer of Arne runneth thoughroughe the middle of it."

25. Sherley, *Discours of the Turkes*, 24 (CM); f. 44 of the Lambeth Palace Library manuscript. Modernized orthography. The original is "The Duke of Florens is one of the moste politique & prudentest princes in the woorlde, & iusteste in his gouernemente; not giuen ouer to to manye passions, yett a man ; & (in myne opinion) I fynde noe prince in anye courte where I haue bynne soe true a frynde to the kinge as hee, for hee seemeth to loue his personne, his honor, & his realme, & hee is bounde to this louinge respect but onelye in affection to his royalle person ; for hee hathe not sutche causes of state to moue him to this profession as other princes haue, for the kinge can les offende him (yf hee wer at enmitye with him) then hee can doe moste other princes, his territory beinge alltogither in terra firma & farre remote from Englande ; & the Englishe trade in Toscan is of leaste profitte to him & his cuntrye of anye other."

26. William Davies, *True Relation of the Travailes and most miserable Captivitie of William Davies, Barber-Surgion of London, under the Duke of FLORENCE.: Wherein is truly set downe the manner of his taking, the long time of his slaverie, and meanes of his deliverie, after eight yeeres, and ten moneths Captivitie in the Gallies.: Discovering many mayne Landes, Ilandes, Rivers, Cities, and townes, of the Christians and Infidels, the condition of the people, and the manner of their*

*Countrey: with many more strange things, as in the Booke is briefly and plainely expressed.: By William Davies, Barber-Surgion of London, and borne in the Citie of Hereford* (London: Nicholas Bourne, 1614), 5 (pagination of EEBO pdf), right (Br); 9, left (v); 9, right. Davies's orthography is more legible, so I have not modernized it.

27. Davies, *True Relation*, 5, right (Br).

28. Davies, *True Relation*, 9, left (v).

29. Davies, *True Relation*, 9, left (v).

30. For the foregoing account and quotations, see Davies, *True Relation*, 9, left (v).

31. Davies, *True Relation*, 9, right.

32. Davies, *True Relation*, 10, left (Cv).

33. Davies, *True Relation*, 9, left (v) then right (Cr).

34. Braudel, *Mediterranean*, 2: 865 and 867, for the quotations; see also 870. "Leghorn" is apparently from the rendition of Livorno as "Ligorne" in early-seventeenth-century English. See, for instance, William Davies, *True Relation*, 9, left (v).

35. Braudel, *Mediterranean*, 2: 867, 878, and 889.

36. Braudel, *Mediterranean*, 1: 636, and 2: 865, 867, 870, 878, and 889; Hale, *Florence and the Medici*, 154; Alberto Tenenti, *Piracy and the Decline of Venice: 1580–1615*, trans. Janet and Brian Pullan (Berkeley: University of California Press, 1967).

37. Gregory Hanlon, *The Twilight of a Military Tradition: Italian Aristocrats and European Conflicts, 1560–1800* (New York: Holmes and Meyer, 1998), 41.

38. Tazzara, *Free Port of Livorno*, shows how this confluence played an essential role in defining the free port.

39. On Don Giovanni's mother, see MAP Person ID 4949, "Albizzi-Panciatichi, Eleonora degli." The critical point here is that Eleonora (b. 1543) was the young lover of the aging Cosimo I de' Medici and bore him a daughter in 1566 and a son in 1567. The daughter died as an infant, but the son survived as Don Giovanni (MAP Person ID 556, "Medici, Giovanni di Cosimo I de' [Don Giovanni])." Born in Florence on May 13, 1567, he was general of the imperial artillery (from April 26, 1595), Medici ambassador in Spain (1598), captain general of the Republic of Venice (from 1610), and "Accademico degli Inconstanti" (from 1618). He was married to Livia Vernazza-Granara de' Medici from 1619 and had a son and daughter, and he died in Murano, Venice on July 19, 1621.

40. Giovanni di Cosimo I de' Medici (Don Giovanni) in Antwerp to Ferdinando I de' Medici in Florence on January 10, 1602, MAP Doc ID 9046, ASF, MdP 5155, 127. I infer the modern date to be 1603 on the basis of MAP's calendar correction later in this correspondence (MAP Doc ID 11668).

41. Stuart B. Schwartz, "A Commonwealth within Itself: The Early Brazilian Sugar Industry, 1550-1670," in *Tropical Babylons: Sugar and the Making of*

*the Atlantic World*, ed. Stuart B. Schwartz (Chapel Hill: University of North Carolina Press, 2004), 172–175; on Dutch exclusion in 1605, see p. 166.

42. James C. Boyajian, *Portuguese Trade in Asia under the Habsburgs, 1580–1640* (Baltimore, MD: Johns Hopkins University Press, 1993), 10; A. R. Disney, *A History of Portugal and the Portuguese Empire: From Beginnings to 1807*, 2 vols. (New York: Cambridge University Press, 2009), 2: 221. Amsterdam's refineries grew rapidly in this period. The first was set up in 1597, there were three in 1605, and twenty-five in 1622; by 1661, there were fifty or sixty according to Eddy Stols, "The Expansion of the Sugar Market in Western Europe," in *Tropical Babylons: Sugar and the Making of the Atlantic World*, ed. Stuart B. Schwartz (Chapel Hill: University of North Carolina Press, 2004), 273.

43. Cosimo Baroncelli in Antwerp to Belisario di Francesco Vinta in Florence on January 24, 1602 (1603), MAP Doc ID 17618, ASF, MdP 5155, 155; MAP Doc ID 17619, ASF, MdP 5155, 156. MAP transcription: "sugette alla corona di Spagna o altri potentati"; MAP Person ID 10215, "Baroncelli, Cosimo"; Giovanni di Cosimo de' Medici (Don Giovanni) in Antwerp to Ferdinando I de' Medici in Florence on February 28, 1602 (1603), MAP Doc ID 17622, ASF, MdP 5155, 166; Cosimo Baroncelli in Antwerp to Belisario di Francesco Vinta in Florence on March 7, 1602 (1603), MAP Doc ID 9185, ASF, MdP 5155, 376; Ferdinando de' Medici in Florence to Giovanni di Cosimo I de' Medici (Don Giovanni) in Flanders on February 2, 1602 (1603), MAP Doc ID 11668, ASF, MdP 5153, Ins. 2, 39; Cosimo Baroncelli in Antwerp to Belisario di Francesco Vinta in Florence on April 25, 1603, MAP Doc ID 9219, ASF, MdP 5155, 444.

44. Giuseppe Gino Guarnieri, *Un'audace impresa marittima di Ferdinando I dei Medici (Con una tavola fuori testo, documenti e glossario indo-caraibico): Contribuito alla storia della marina mercantile Italiana* (Pisa, It.: Nistri-Lischi, 1928), 22–23, transcribes ASF, Miscellanea Medicea 97, Ins. 89, 3r-3v.

45. ASF, Miscellanea Medicea 97, Ins. 89, 3r-3v / 4r.

46. Buarque de Holanda, "Os Projetos de Colonização," 97–98. I infer that this is the same one described in the memorandum.

47. Guarnieri, *Un'audace impresa marittima*, 23–24.

48. Stols, "The Expansion of the Sugar Market," 274–275.

49. MAP Person ID 9841, "Godunow, Boris Fyodorovich."

50. Thanks to Corey Tazzara for introducing me to Lussio and providing references. In 2011, the Museo degli Argenti in Florence held an exhibition, The Treasures of the Kremlin, that proved very informative, http://www.polomuseale.firenze.it/en/mostre/mostra.php?t=4ebd73e0f1c3bce410001f6b, accessed October 26, 2020.

    The letter of credentials from Tsar Boris Godunov to Grand Duke Ferdinando I of 1602 was exhibited (ASF Miscellanea Medicea 102, Ins.

9, 1). The Cyrillic letter of credentials is reproduced in Daniela Degl'Innocenti and Tatiana Lekhovich, "Mercanti, diplomatici e viaggiatori fra Russia e Italia (XIV–XVI secolo)" in *Lo stile dello zar: Arte e moda tra Italia e Russia dal XIV al XVIII* , ed. Degl'Innocenti and Lekhovich (Geneva-Milan: Skira, 2009), 195; the informative caption is on 194.

51. ASF, Miscellanea Medicea 102, Ins. 9, 2r–3r, is an early modern translation of the letter from Moscow. Because the draft response letter, of May 1603, refers to the tsar's letter as having been sent the last June, this would have been 1602 (8r–8v). The original is Miscellanea Medicea 102, Ins. 9, 1. An excerpt of the translation, with the abbreviations expanded, follows: "Là Vostra Altezza Serenissima nell'ultima parte della lettera fa Riverenza alla Imperial maestà nostra et il detto Abramo Lussio attùalmente ne ha fatto Riverenza in nome di Vostra Altezza Serenissima la qual Riverenza é stato da noi accetto molto Amorevolmente et mosso da gli preghi di Vostra Altezza Serenissima· habbiamo Concesso secondo la Domando di esso Abramo, Al Padre Sione lussio et a soi figliùoli Abramo: Isaach et matia di poter venir nel nostro Imperio, et arrivare, stare Intrare et partire@ i nostri porti di moscovia et Castel Archangelo con le navi Cariche d'ogni sorte di marcantie et fare ogni libero traffico et la nostra Sacra Imperial maestà Col serenissmo Fedro Borissovizo: signore di tutta la Russia Con Vostra Altezza Serenissima Ferdinando Gran' Dùca di Toscana et Dùca di fiorenza, vogliamo tenere Amicitia, havendo a Caro e laudando la Vostra Altezza Serenissima Ferdinando che nel nostro Imperio, cerchi la nostra Amicitia et Cortese Amorevolezza per la qùal richiesta di Vostra Altezza Serenissima habbiamo Concesso al detto sion lussio et a suoi figliùoli Abramo Isach é matio di poter venire. con le navi Cariche di ogni sorte di marcantie nel nostro Imperio al Porto di moscòvia et di Castel' Archangelo a far ogni sorte di traffico libero e secùro senza Impedimento alcùno per il chè la nostra Imperial maesta, al detto Abramo habbiamo dato per maggior securezza un nostro previleggio per venire andare ad Arivare. @ i sopra nominati Porti di moscòvia et Castel'Archangelo. senza alcuno Impedimento Con salvezza di tutta la sua marcantia é huominj," Miscellanea Medicea 102, Ins. 9, 2v.

52. Catherine Evtuhov, David Goldfrank, Lindsey Hughes, and Richard Stites, *A History of Russia: People, Legends, Events, Forces* (New York: Houghton Mifflin, 2004), 128–129.

53. Evtuhov et al., *History of Russia*, 126–129 and 136–137.

54. "Serenissimo et Potentessimo Grand' Imperatore et Gran Duca signore Boriso Fedroviso [ / ] Rendo à Vostra Imperial Maestà affettuosissime gratie della cortese humanissima risposta, ch'ella mi hà data con la lettera sua scritta nel Mese di Giugno, ~~l'anno doppo la pace~~ prossimo passato ~~fatta 7110~~, et ne ringratio ancora il Serenissimo Fedro Borisoviso figliuolo di

<u>Vostra Maestà</u>, et singolarissima gratia mi è stata quella del suo favore, et della sua Amicitia ,et cosi del <u>Serenissimo Fedro Borisoviso Signore di tutta la Russia,</u> et prego <u>Vostra Maestà</u> à mantenermela, et in specie per il traffico libero, et sicuro de' miei Vassalli ,et Popoli di Toscana in tutti i Luoghi, et Porti dello <u>Imperio, et Dominio di Vostra Maestà;</u> Rendendole ancora particolari gratie del bellissimo Dono inviatomi del Timbre di Zibellini, et del Privilegio, che à mia instanza ella hà fatto à Sion Lussio, et à i suoi figliuoli, Abraam, Isac, et Mattias, di poter venire con le lor Navi cariche d'ogni sorte di robe in tutti li stati <u>della Maestà Vostra,</u> et precipuamente nel Porto di Moscovia, et di Castell'Arcangiolo, et mi sarà carissimo, che detto Privilegio sia, non solo conservato, ma anche dalla cortese amorevolezza <u>di Vostra Maestà</u> ogni di più ampliato; Et io <u>Serenissimo Boriso Fedroviso, et Serenissimo Fedro Borisoviso</u> voglio essere affettionatissimo del continuo, insieme con il mio figliuolo Don Cosimo di ₍Don Ferdinando Medici Principe di Toscana·<u>all'Imperiale Maestà Vostra, et al Serenissmo [8v:] suo figliuolo Fedro Borisoviso Signore di tutta la Russia,</u> et se dì quà possiamo ne' Luoghi de' nostri Dominij di Terra, et di Mare far loro commodo, et servitio, <u>Vostra Maestà; et il signore Fedro Borisoviso</u> ci hanno sempre alla libera à comandare ; et di nuovo raccomando alla cortesia, et favore <u>di Vostra Maestà.</u> Sion Lussio, et i suoi figliuoli, Abraam, Isac, et Mattias, et anche tutti li miei Huomini, et suddeti Toscani, che ₍volessino venire ~~capitino~~ <u>nelle Ditioni, et stati della Maestà Vostra,</u>F. [See insertion "F" below] ~~Alla quale mando una Acquasanta, che miracolosamente este del Corpo di sto Niccolao, et è efficacissimo remedio quasi contra ogni malattia.; et una scatola di certa polvere, appropriatissimo remedio contra la peste~~ ; et alla <u>Vostra Imperiale Maestà faccio affettionatissimamente reverenza.</u> Dat Nella mia Città di Pisa nel Mese di Maggio alli xij l'anno della nostra salute. <u>1603.</u> <u>Di Vostra Imperiale Maestà</u> [Insertion F:] F et se ella se ne contentera dirizzeranno ssi s'in[?] ạnno con mercantie, et Traffico," ASF, Miscellanea Medicea 102, ins. 9, 8r–8v.

55. ASF, Miscellanea Medicea 102, Ins. 9, 10r–10v. The quotation is from 10v: "l'allarghi in concedere loro facultá di poter mandare un huomo loro á fare il caviale, et la Morona in Astracan, et di qui[vi] estrarla per Italia, et in particulare per la Toscana." Florio's dictionary—Iohn Florio, *Queen Anna's New World of Words or Dictionarie of the* Italian *and* English *tongues* (London: Printed by Melch. Bradwood for Edw. Blount and William Barret, 1611)—links "Moróna" to "Muréna" to "Muríce": "an engine of warre with sharpe points to cast in the enemies way called Caltrops. Also a kind of hard shell-fish or winkle called a Benet-fish, which some think will stay a ship if it sticke unto it, of whose liquor a purple colour is made." All translations are mine unless otherwise stated.

56. Evtuhov et al., *History of Russia*, 139–140 and 147–149.

57. From Arkhangelsk to Florence on July 7, 1605, MAP Doc ID 24387, ASF, MdP 4294, Ins. 1, 49.

58. Evtuhov et al., *History of Russia*, 139-157.

59. Jan van der Neesen in the Hague to Abraham Lus in Livorno on September 12, 1606, MAP Doc ID 26930, ASF, MdP 4259, Ins. 1, 7r. The MAP synopsis provides essential context and references to other letters about this affair: Jan van der Neesen in the Hague to Abraham Lus, perhaps in Livorno, on December 10, 1606, MAP Doc ID 26929, ASF, MdP 4259, Ins. 1, 7; Signor Papenburch in the Hague to Abraham Lus in Livorno on December 11, 1606, MAP Doc ID 26932, ASF, MdP 4259, 7; Jan van der Neesen in the Hague to Isach Lus, perhaps in Livorno, perhaps in 1606, MAP Doc ID 26935, ASF, MdP 4259, 7; Jacques Lores in Amsterdam to Francesco di Ferdinando I de' Medici on January 16, 1607, MAP Doc ID 26975, ASF, MdP 4750.

60. Jacques Lores in Amsterdam to Francesco di Ferdinando I de' Medici on January 16, 1607, MAP Doc ID 26975, ASF, MdP 4750.

61. Giovanni di Cosimo I de' Medici (Don Giovanni) in Paris to Ferdinando I de' Medici in Florence on November 10, 1606, MAP Doc ID 8843, ASF, MdP 5157, 541.

62. Francesco Carletti, *My Voyage around the World: The Chronicles of a 16th Century Florentine Merchant*, trans. Herbert Weinstock (New York: Pantheon, 1964), 243-244.

63. Carletti, *My Voyage*, 265.

64. Carletti, *My Voyage*, 257.

65. "l'interesse del quale depende tutto dal mare e per ciò no[n] è maraviglia se hanno cercato nuovi traffichi, e nuove navicationi in nuovi mondi," Biblioteca Angelica, Rome, ms. 1331, 206v; Carletti, *My Voyage*, 261.

66. Carletti, *My Voyage*, 260.

67. MAP Doc ID 23017, ASF, MdP 4256, 166. Document year: 1602.

68. Unknown writer in Amsterdam to Ferdinando I de' Medici in Florence on April 6, 1603, MAP Doc ID 23020, ASF, MdP 4256, 174. MAP transcription: "questa nova compagnia." MAP adds a bracketed insertion in the transcription to suggest that the referent is "[the VOC]."

69. Guarnieri, *Un'audace impresa marittima*, 22-23, transcribes the Brazil proposal, which transcription he ends with "1608—Neg. per le Indie occidentali," which makes sense in context.

70. ASF, Miscellanea Medicea 97, Ins. 89, 3r-3v / 4r. See Appendix 4.2 (pp. 549-553) of Brian Brege, "The Empire That Wasn't: The Grand Duchy of Tuscany and Empire, 1574-1609," PhD diss., Stanford University, 2014, for a transcription of the original; I offer a full translation in the main text (pp. 341-343).

71. "Serenissimo Gran Duca." "Piacendo à Sua Altezza Serenissima negotiar per via de mar de Hollanda nelle Indie—orientalj, che fin qui e riuscito

negotio dj grand utilitá, et—per principiar il ditto traffico, besognerebbe fabricar o Comprar, quatro nave bŭone, L['̌]una piu grande de l[']altra Insieme Incirca de Salme Sej millia o puoco manco, qualj deverebbino partire nel mese de Decembre o al piu tardj in Gennaro, il quale è il vero tempo, ben provistj dj vinj olej et altre vett[o]vȧglie Arteleria et amunitione àbastansa p[er] un Simile voẙagio, dj doj annj Incirca, Con ducento marinarj à soldo de mese," ASF, Miscellanea Medicea 97, Ins. 89, 2r. My thanks go to Brett Auerbach-Lynn from Berkeley who, in the course of conversation about this document in the reading room at the ASF, offered helpful suggestions about the currency symbols. Any errors are nonetheless my own.

72. "Coe hanno costatj quellj—della Compagnia olandesia mandate p[er] India," ASF, Miscellanea Medicea 97, Ins. 89, 2r.

73. "In ogni modo Con un Scudo vengano—a guadagnare quatuor____Et quando piacesse a Sua Altezza Serenissima. de farle assecŭrare del tutto. se le farȧ per Andata con 18 p[er].co et per ritorno per quanto . piacera ,sene troverȧ da fare a 20 In 22 percento," ASF, Miscellanea Medicea 97, Ins. 89, 3v.

74. "Per av̌ansare, besognerebbe. Comprar o far fabricar le nav̌e In Holanda et spedire di la del tŭtto, et mandarle, e spedite che fussero, di la a drittura per dette Indie Orientalj, con pienissimo ordine et prŏvisione, qualj poj si farebbino alla tornata far venir de drittŭra qui à Livorno con lor pieno Carico de pepj et altre droghe et specerie, vª vero per non caŭssar Smavo, Se poterebbe far andar dŭe nav̌e In Holanda de drittura delle Indie, ma tutti verrebbino della Compagnia fin alla Altessa de Spagna, ch[e] Suj se partirebbino l[']un de l[']altro," ASF, Miscellanea Medicea 97, Ins. 89, 2v.

75. "Et à Livorno Scarricatj che fŭssero se poterebbino recaricar per Holanda Londra o Halle de grace, Con Alumj, o per Holanda Con Sale risi et oleo et altre mercansie, et dipoi lor ritorno In detti lŭochj farle allestir et Spedir di nov̌o per diette Indiě," ASF, Miscellanea Medicea 97, Ins. 89, 2v.

76. "che, Ivj si farà quasi con la meta delle Spese, manco che che Se farebbe In queste bande, õ al manco Si Avanserà in ditta Speditione il terso, cosi nelle vittualie gente et altro, qui solamente Se farebbe Comprar tutto il Corallo tondo lustro che Se trov̌asse per mand̈ar In dette Indie, che Ivj se vende Con grandissimo av̌antagio et essitŭ," ASF, Miscellanea Medicea 97, Ins. 89, 2v.

77. Trivellato, *Familiarity of Strangers*, 224–232.

78. Trivellato, *Familiarity of Strangers*, 229.

79. "Et Resolv̌endosi Sua Altezza Serenissima far ditto negotio, pregiamo de valersi de l'opera nostra promettendela de servire A. Sua Altezza Serenissima. Con ogni affectione et fidelà, et casŭ che Sua Altezza Serenissima trov̌asse buono, di mandare in ditta Holanda uno o doj di soj fidelj min-

istrj per haṽerne Cuřa del tŭtto, et aministrar il ditto In Compagnia nostra, le poterà fare, et accio il tŭtto restj Secreto, et per non scoprir il dissegno de Sua Altezza Serenissima, Le potera far allogiar In casa nostra Sotto nome de mercantj forestierj, racommandatj da me, o per passagerj, ancora che non Sia solito d['] allogiar nissuno In case nostra, -------- Et per maggior Secretess se cosi piacerà a Sua Altezza Serenissima Le robe che verrano a Livorno se poterano far consignar à me, et il proposto negotio da noj Sarà tenŭto molto Secreto et aministrato con ogni realta, et Avantagio ---- Casu che Sua Altezza Serenissima non volesse principiar ditto negotio con tanto gran Capitale pọtera Solamente per la prima volta Comminciar con dŭe naṽe grande et una naṽetta qualj con ogni cosa Spedito alla vela, comprese le mercansie verrano a Costar Cento millia Scudj Incirca, et con beneplacito de Sua Altezza Serenissima Si Contentiamo de tener un qŭarto, ----------," ASF, Miscellanea Medicea 97, Ins. 89, 3r.

80. Niccolò Capponi, "Le Palle di Marte: Military Strategy and Diplomacy in the Grand Duchy of Tuscany under Ferdinand II de' Medici (1621–1670)," *Journal of Military History* 68 (October 2004): 1105–1122 and 1138–1139.

81. Disney, *History of Portugal*, 2: 206 and 215–216, and Mickaël Augeron and Laurent Vidal, "Creating Colonial Brazil: The First Donatary Captaincies or the System of Private Exclusivity (1534–1549)," in *Constructing Early Modern Empires: Proprietary Ventures in the Atlantic*, ed. Louis H. Roper and Bertrand van Ruymbeke (Boston: Brill, 2007), 22–23, cite Portugal's other commitments as limiting early investment in Brazil.

82. Joyce Lorimer, ed., *English and Irish Settlement on the River Amazon, 1550–1646*, Hakluyt Society, series 2, vol. 171 (London: Hakluyt Society, 1989), xiv–xxv; Alan Gallay, *Walter Ralegh: Architect of Empire* (New York: Basic Books, 2019). On the French presence, see Disney, *History of Portugal*, 2: 215.

83. I infer the distinction from Lorimer's historical maps. Lorimer, *English and Irish Settlement*, xviii–xxv.

84. Augeron and Vidal, "Creating Colonial Brazil," 44n44.

85. Disney, *History of Portugal*, 2: 214–215, 221, 235, and 267–277; Lorimer, *English and Irish Settlement*, xx–xxv. Outposts: Irish (1612, 1620), English and Irish (1613), English (1612, 1620, 1629, 1631), Dutch and English (1616, 1623), Dutch and Irish (1629), Dutch (1615), French (1612; captured by the Portuguese in 1615), and Portuguese (1616, 1623, 1625, 1637–1638); Belém founded (1616).

86. Felipe Fernández-Armesto, *Amerigo: The man Who Gave His Name to America* (New York: Random House, 2007), map (xxiii) and 141, among other places. For Vespucci as a self-publicist, see also Seymour Phillips, "The Outer World in the European Middle Ages," in Joan-Pau Rubies,

ed., *Medieval Ethnographies: European Perceptions of the World Beyond* (New York: Routledge, 2016), 1.

87. Simon Adams, "Dudley, Sir Robert (1574–1649)," *Oxford Dictionary of National Biography*.

88. Buarque de Holanda, "Os Projetos de Colonização," 100–101; Guarnieri, *Un'audace impresa marittima*, 32.

89. Adams, "Dudley, Sir Robert."

90. Belisario di Francesco Vinta in Cafaggiolo, Tuscany, to Sallustio Tarugi in Valladolid, Spain, MAP Doc ID 16933, ASF, MdP 5052, 71.

91. MAP Person ID 13169, "Gifford, Richard (Captain)." MAP suggests that Gifford had controversially seized the ship *Prospera* but did not transfer its content to Ferdinando I in 1604. See, however, unknown writer in Tuscany to Robert Cecil, Earl of Salisbury, in London on January 1, 1606, MAP Doc ID 13416, ASF MdP 4184, 39. The portion of the document that MAP transcribes suggests that Gifford's ships were seized in England as pertaining to him, but that they actually pertained to the grand duke and ought therefore to have been released along with their merchandise. In any event, the Tuscans seem to have felt they needed more information, for a February 22, 1606, letter from a Tuscan agent in Amsterdam reports paying a bribe for information (MAP Doc ID 26017, ASF, MdP 4256, 329). As to Gifford's trouble with the authorities, a brief document of 1609 permits Robert Dudley, Count of Warwick, to enter the Belvedere fortress to talk to Captain Robert Gifford (Belisario di Francesco Vinta in Florence to Eustachio Fannelli at the Fortezza San Giorgio in Florence on October 28, 1609, MAP Doc ID 12532, ASF, MdP 302, 30). One did not tend to end up in the Belvedere requiring permission to be visited from the first secretary without being in trouble. As to the English side, a December 17, 1610, letter notes that Gifford had been pardoned (Ottaviano di Lotti in London to Belisario di Francesco Vinta in Tuscany on December 17, 1610, MAP Doc ID 13201, ASF, MdP 4189).

92. Adams, "Dudley, Sir Robert." For the book, see Belisario di Francesco Vinta in Livorno to (Sir) Robert Dudley on January 8, 1607, MAP Doc ID 13503, ASF, MdP 300, 4.

93. MAP Person ID 1043, "Barbolani di Montauto, Asdrubale"; Asdrubale Barbolani di Montauto in Venice to Belisario di Francesco Vinta in Florence on May 26, 1607, MAP Doc ID 14188, ASF, MdP 3000, 107; MAP Person ID 775, "Vinta, Belisario di Francesco."

94. Asdrubale Barbolani di Montauto in Venice to Ferdinando I de' Medici in Florence on August 4, 1607, MAP Doc ID 14271, ASF, MdP 3000, 154. (The judgment that the Robert was probably Robert Dudley is MAP's.) Asdrubale Barbolani di Montauto in Venice to Belisario di Francesco Vinta in Florence on August 18, 1607, MAP Doc ID 14312, ASF, MdP 3000, 163.

95. Guarnieri, *Un'audace impresa marittima*, 32–35; Thornton's instructions are at 32–39, Dudley's map at 39–50.

96. Guarnieri, *Un'audace impresa marittima*, 8, and section 2, 14–20. Guarnieri highlighted three documents: (1) ASF, MdP 1829, 459r (8n2); (2) *"Dell'Arcano del Mare: Di D. Ruberto Dudleo Duca di Nortumbria, e conte di Warvich.* Tomo secondo, contenente il libro sesto, nel quale si tratta delle Carte sue geografiche e particolari. Impressione seconda ecc., Firenze, M. D. C. L. I. Nella nuova stamperia, per Giuseppe Cocchini, all'insegna della Stella. Ad istanza di Jacopo Bagnoni et Antonfrancesco Lucini. Parte quarta, libro 6.°, pag. 33 e seguenti" (8n3); (3) "A. S. C. L.; n. 5—*Capitaneria del porto. Magistrati al Governo. Rescritti per la contumacia, anno* 1606 *al* 1611, c. 142 r." (8n4).

97. Davies, *True Relation*, 10 left (Cv).

98. Davies, *True Relation*, 10 left (Cv), 10 right (C2r), 11 left (C2v).

99. Davies, *True Relation*, 10 right (C2r).

100. Davies, *True Relation*, 11 left (C2v).

101. Davies, *True Relation*, 11 left (C2v) and 11 right (C3r).

102. Davies, *True Relation*, 11 right (C3r).

103. Davies, *True Relation*, 4, right ([A4]r).

104. Davies, *True Relation*, 14, left (Dv), 14 right (D2r), 15 left (D2v), and 15 (D3r).

105. Davies, *True Relation*, 15 (D3r); Guarnieri, *Un'audace impresa marittima*, section 2, 14–20.

106. Guarnieri, *Un'audace impresa marittima*, 50–53; 50n1; "A. S. C. L. *Capitaneria del Porto*, n. 5: 'Magistrali al Governo ; Rescritti per la Contumacia ; anno 1606 al 1611' c.142," Appendix, document 14, pp. 77–78.

107. Gregory Hanlon, *The Hero of Italy: Odoardo Farnese, Duke of Parma, His Soldiers, and His Subjects in the Thirty Years' War* (New York: Oxford University Press, 2014).

### 4. THE USES OF ACCESS

1. Riccardo Fubini, "Diplomacy and Government in the Italian City-States of the Fifteenth Century (Florence and Venice)," in *Politics and Diplomacy in Early Modern Italy: The Structure of Diplomatic Practice, 1450–1800*, ed. Daniela Frigo, trans. Adrian Belton (Cambridge, UK: Cambridge University Press, 2000), 25–48; Catherine Fletcher, *Diplomacy in Renaissance Rome: The Rise of the Resident Ambassador* (New York: Cambridge University Press, 2015).

2. The Capponi appear among the "principali casati della nostra Città" on the verso side of the first page of Valerio Ruggieri, "Lettera all'illvst.mo et eccell.mo signor Don Pietro Medici di Valerio Ruggieri sopra la festa fatta dal duca di Carroccio, nella festività di San Giouambatista in Firenze" (Florence: ["Heredi di Bernardo Giunta"], 1588), held at DSC,

YRL, UCLA, Ahmanson-Murphy Collection of Early Italian Printing, call number: Z233.G45 R829le 1588; the quoted bibliographic information is from UCLA's catalog.

3. See Adele Dei's note on Sassetti in Filippo Sassetti, *Lettere dall'India (1583–1588)*, ed. Adele Dei (Rome: Salerno, 1995), at Letter 20, 157n6.

4. Marica Milanesi, *Filippo Sassetti* (Florence: Nuova Italia, 1973), 34; Francesco Surdich, "Sassetti, Filippo," *DBI* 90 (2017).

5. Francesco Guidi Bruscoli, "Sassetti, Francesco," *DBI* 90 (2017).

6. Surdich, "Sassetti."

7. Surdich, "Sassetti." Milanesi, *Filippo Sassetti*, 23–31 and 52–77; MAP Person ID 1240, "Sassetti, Filippo"; Bernard Weinberg, "The Accademia degli Alterati and Literary Taste from 1570 to 1600," *Italica* 31 no. 4 (Dec. 1954): 207–214; Eric Cochrane, *Florence in the Forgotten Centuries 1527–1800: A History of Florence and the Florentines in the Age of the Grand Dukes* (Chicago: University of Chicago Press, 1973), 108 and 116–121. On Sassetti's membership in the Accademia degli Alterati, see Dei, "Nota biografica," in Sassetti, *Lettere dall'India*, 21. Many of Sassetti's correspondents were also members of the Alterati: Sassetti, *Lettere dall'India*, Letter 17, 122–123n13; Letter 18, 132n1; and Letter 21, 161n4. The society was revived as a literary wine blog in February 2012: https://accademiadegli-alterati.com/, accessed October 26, 2020.

8. Surdich, "Sassetti."

9. The original title is *Sul commercio tra la Toscana e le Nazioni levantine*; for a recent analysis, see Corey Tazzara, *The Free Port of Livorno and the Transformation of the Mediterranean World, 1574–1790* (New York: Oxford University Press, 2017), 32–37. See also Surdich, "Sassetti"; Milanesi, *Filippo Sassetti*, 23–31; MAP Person ID 1240, "Sassetti, Filippo"; Vanna Arrighi, "Gianfigliazzi, Bongianni" *DBI* 54 (2000); MAP Person ID 430, "Gianfigliazzi, Bongianni di Piero (Fra)."

10. Surdich, "Sassetti."

11. A. R. Disney, *A History of Portugal and the Portuguese Empire: From Beginnings to 1807*, 2 vols. (New York: Cambridge University Press, 2009), 2: 19–20.

12. Milanesi, *Filippo Sassetti*, 38–40.

13. Disney, *History of Portugal*, 1: 192–199.

14. Surdich, "Sassetti"; Milanesi, *Filippo Sassetti*, 38 and 40–41.

15. Milanesi, *Filippo Sassetti*, 23, 33–34, 38–46, and 69; Sassetti, *Lettere dall'India*, Letter 20, 157n6; Surdich, "Sassetti"; Ernst van Veen, *Decay or Defeat? An Inquiry into the Portuguese Decline in Asia, 1580–1645* (Leiden, Neth.: Leiden University, Research School CNWS, 2000), Appendix 3.2, 252–253. For more on the Rovellasca, see Benedetta Crivelli, "Pepper and Silver between Milan and Lisbon in the Second Half of the Sixteenth Century," in *Commercial Networks and European Cities, 1400–1800*, ed. Andrea Caracausi and Christof Jeggle (New York: Routledge, 2014), 195–

196, and Benedetta Crivelli, "Conflicts in Global Trade: The Tale of a Milanese Firm in the Monopolistic Business Sphere of the Iberian Monarchies (1570–1610)," in *Mediterranean Doubts: Trading Companies, Conflicts and Strategies in the Global Spaces (XV–XIX Centuries)*, ed. Daniele Andreozzi (Palermo, It.: New Digital Frontiers, 2017), 21–44.

16. "et per molto che si sieno affaticatj Filippo Sassettj et L$^r$ mio figl[abbreviation]o con la lettera in mano de i Capponj et Spina di Lione, che me[]l['] appuntano: non sen' è cavato alt° dà q° benedi[abbreviation] Cor$^{re}$ Maiore et suoij ministri, Car$^{mi}$ nostri più di 30. B per lira, se non che non hà portato coluj che hà condotto l'ultimo viaggio d'Italia quì cassett'a Cs$^a$ ne sà che chi condusse le lettere dà Airun à Burgos (che sempre si scabia cor.$^{re}$) ò, dà Burgos, et à Airun, che la si rinverrà. Ho'ne scr'o questo à mè co' pochiss$^a$ speranza circa il ritrovarla: et di più ne hò dato conto ai Capponi, et Spina à Lione et i' corte al signor Dovara à ogni buono effetto, et ritrovandosi (il che io non credo) ne seguirò questo . Vostra Altezza Serenissima comanda, la quale m'è parso bn' i' tanto advertir di questo et per hora, et per in futuro di similj occasionj," Bernardo Canigiani in Madrid to the grand duke, June 26, 1581, ASF, MdP 4911, 224r–v.

17. "Il primo del presente scrissi à Vostra Altezza Serenissima due versi più perche ella fusse ragguagliata de progressi della peste di Siviglia, che per altre occorenze. Di poi per lettere de 30. ho visto che non ne moriva piu che 18. o 20. il giorno, ma mi dice il Sassetti che le sue più fresche non ne parlono, et in altri di luglio ne ha viste, ch'accusono notabil peggioramento," Bernardo Canigiani in Madrid to the grand duke, July 10, 1581, ASF, MdP 4911, 243r–v.

18. Sassetti was mentioned in the context of news at court that Don Pietro had been in danger from arquebus fire (268r): "confermandomi massime il Sassetti pratichissimo di Lisbona, che dal Castello al luogo dove fu percosso Salvestrino, non è manco che costà del cimitero di S. Franc.° alla casa del Nero in su la piazza de Mozzi," Bernardo Canigiani in Madrid to the grand duke, October 16, 1581, ASF, MdP 4911, 268r–271r. All translations are mine unless otherwise indicated.

19. Surdich, "Sassetti"; Dei, "Nota biografica," 22; Milanesi, *Filippo Sassetti*, 67.

20. "La nave Caragial della flotta d'India di Portogallo, dove andò il Sassetti è arrivata salva al cavo di S. Vinc.° ma della Cap.$^{na}$ et dell'altre due che sciolsero della costa d'India x giorni innanzi à lei, non ha mai veduto ne' sentito segno," Bernardo Canigiani in Madrid to the grand duke, August 6, 1582, ASF, MdP 4911, 342v. For further news about the Caragial, see Bernardo Canigiani in Madrid to the grand duke, August 6, 1582, ASF, MdP 4911, 344r–345r.

21. "Tutte le navi della Flotte cominciono à rinvenirsi, et à comparire, fra le quali la Caragial che fu la prima ha pur condotto à Lisbona un liofante

puledro di quei del Zilan, che dicono è si piacevol cosa: Ma la S. Filippa che partì per all' inlà alli 5. d'Aprile, ci ha riportato alli 5. di Settembre dentro al Rio Tagio à Cascais il nostro Sassetti, dove anche hebbe à gittar le robbe in mare, e fu la nave per sommergersi; ma scampò per voto, et miracolo di Nostra Donna: doppo 5. mesi, et circa 2500. leghe di viaggio pericoloso e pauroso d'esser divorati, hor dagli Antropofagi, hor dai Tuberoni, o dalli Scioni dell'onde, nonostante i quali disagi et timori sofferti, et il brutto cenno della Fortuna, che l'ha balestrato d'un colpo rarissimo e insolito, egli si prepara per passar' al Cocchin destinatosi, con la medesima compagnia alla fine di Marzo prossimo, havendo dic'egli imparato dall'esperienza qualcosa di più che non sapeva, et vedute molte stelle dell'altro Polo, sendo stato di là dall'equinottiale nella costa del Bresil sopra il Rio di S. Agostino, nei minori giorni che sieno lì, più di 13. giorni," ASF, MdP 4911, 348r–v, Bernardo Canigiani in Madrid to the grand duke, September 17, 1582. I have rendered "Tuberoni" as sharks from the Spanish "tiburón" and Portuguese "tubarão." Alternatively, one could follow Florio's definition for "Tuberóne" as "the starre-royall." I have opted for the former on the basis of context. For further on the ship on which Sassetti returned with such travail to Lisbon, see Bernardo Canigiani in Madrid to the grand duke, December 20, 1582, ASF, MdP 4911, 365r–v: "A questi dì è tornata una nave di quelle che partirno al principio d'Aprile per all'Indie di Portogallo con quella del Sassetti, et anch'ella è stata per sommergersi nell'entrar' in Lisbona."

22. "come la sup.co ancora à legger con buono occhio la lettera che frà con questa del suo virtuoso e da bene servitore Filippo Sassetti, che è ben' resoluto, per non dire ostinato di ritornarsene á India alla fine di Marzo," Bernardo Canigiani in Madrid to the grand duke on November 22, 1582, ASF, MdP 4911, 362r–363v.

23. Surdich, "Sassetti"; Dei, "Nota biografica," 22; Milanesi, *Filippo Sassetti*, 67.

24. Milanesi, *Filippo Sassetti*, 42–46 and 49; Meera Juncu, *India in the Italian Renaissance: Visions of a Contemporary Pagan World 1300–1600* (New York: Routledge, 2016); Sanjay Subrahmanyam, *Explorations in Connected History: From the Tagus to the Ganges* (New Delhi: Oxford India Paperbacks, 2011); Subrahmanyam, *Europe's India: Words, People, Empires, 1500–1800* (Cambridge, MA: Harvard University Press, 2017); Jonathan Gil Harris, *The First Firangis: Remarkable Stories of Heroes, Healers, Charlatans, Courtesans and Other Foreigners Who Became Indian* (New Delhi: Aleph, 2015).

25. Sassetti, *Lettere dall'India*, Letter 1, 31–32n16, 34–35, and 34n24; Letter 4, January 22, 1584, 45–47; Milanesi, *Filippo Sassetti*, 42–46, 49, and 67; Cochrane, *Florence in the Forgotten Centuries*, 262; Jean-Claude Waquet, *Corruption: Ethics and Power in Florence, 1600–1770*, trans. Linda McCall (University Park, PA: Pennsylvania State University Press, 1992); James C.

Boyajian, *Portuguese Trade in Asia under the Habsburgs, 1580–1640* (Baltimore, MD: Johns Hopkins University Press, 1993), 124–127.

26. MAP Person ID 430, "Gianfigliazzi, Bongianni di Piero (Fra)."

27. Surdich, "Sassetti."

28. Bongianni di Piero Gianfigliazzi to [Grand Duke Francesco I de' Medici], July 9, 1584, ASF, MdP, 5046, 56v–57r; Bongianni di Piero (Fra) Gianfigliazzi in Madrid to Francesco I de' Medici in Florence on July 9, 1584, MAP Doc ID 16081, ASF, MdP 5046, 56.

29. Bongianni di Piero (Fra) Gianfigliazzi in Madrid to Francesco I de' Medici in Florence on July 28, 1584, ASF, MdP 5046, 58v–60v, MAP Doc ID 14540.

30. Giulio Battaglini in Madrid to Pietro di Francesco Usimbardi in Rome on July 28, 1584, MAP Doc ID 15682, ASF, MdP 5113, Ins. 1, 217. MAP Person ID 256, "Battaglini, Giulio," notes that Battaglini was born in 1548, died on December 26, 1600, in Naples, and served as an agent in Naples from 1599. MAP Person ID 469, "Usimbardi, Pietro di Francesco" notes that Usimbardi was born in 1539 in the Colle di Val d'Elsa and died on May 28, 1612, in Arezzo. He served as bishop of Arezzo, Cortona, and Borgo San Sepolcro (June 9, 1589–May 28, 1612), first secretary of state for Ferdinando I de' Medici, and bishop of Colle Val d'Elsa.

31. "Habbiamo rice[v]uto il pregi del Sassetti, et intro da lui molti particulari di quelli° bandi°, alli quali non ci ou$^{re}$: rispondiri°, ma si beni° al migliorati, chi° ci° l' ha' m'diritti," ASF, MdP 5046, 385r–386v.

32. Ugo Tucci, "Buondelmonti, Giovanni, detto il Vecchino," *DBI* 15 (1972).

33. Filippo Sassetti, *Lettere edite e inedite di Filippo Sassetti*, ed. Ettore Marcucci (Florence: Felice Le Monnier, 1855), 301, Sassetti's letter to Francesco I from Santa Croce of Cochin on February 11, 1585.

34. Margherita Farina, "La nascita della Tipografia Medicea: Personaggi e idee," in *Le vie delle lettere: La Tipografia Medicea tra Roma e l'Oriente*, ed. Sara Fani and Margherita Farina (Florence: Mandragora, 2012), 48–49 and 60–63.

35. Sassetti, *Lettere dall'India*, Letter 25, 203–204.

36. Farina, "Nascita della Tipografia Medicea," 63–65; Angelo de Gubernatis, ed., *Storia dei viaggiatori italiani nelle Indie orientali* (Livorno, It.: Franc. Vigo, 1875), 25 and 25n1; Joan-Pau Rubiés, *Travel and Ethnology in the Renaissance: South India through European Eyes, 1250–1625* (New York: Cambridge University Press, 2000), 381–383; Subrahmanyam, *Explorations in Connected History: Mughals and Franks* (New Delhi: Oxford India Paperbacks, 2011), 83.

37. Francesco Carletti, *My Voyage around the World: The Chronicles of a 16th Century Florentine Merchant*, trans. Herbert Weinstock (New York: Pantheon, 1964), 142–144 and 143nn. The translator's notes on 143 point out that Neretti was a friend of Sassetti's, had been present at Sassetti's death,

and had served as his executor. See also De Gubernatis, *Storia dei viaggiatori italiani*, 26-27.

38. De Gubernatis, *Storia dei viaggiatori italiani*, 26-27. See also Rev. Father H. Hosten, S.J, "Notes and Queries," *Bulletin of the School of Oriental Studies, University of London* 4, no.1 (1926): 207, on the letter from Giuseppina Maranca and response by "Very Rev. Fr. J. D. Alberti, S.J".

39. Sassetti, *Lettere dall'India*, Letter 26, 213-214.

40. Liam Matthew Brockey, *Journey to the East: The Jesuit Mission to China, 1579-1724* (Cambridge, MA.: Belknap, 2007), 29; F. W. Mote, *Imperial China, 900-1800* (Cambridge, MA.: Harvard University Press, 1999), 721-722.

41. Mark A. Burkholder and Lyman L. Johnson, *Colonial Latin America*, 7th ed. (New York: Oxford University Press, 2010), 167; Henry Kamen, *Empire: How Spain Became a World Power, 1492-1763* (New York: Harper Collins, 2003), 202-227; Charles C. Mann, *1493: Uncovering the New World Columbus Created* (New York: Vintage, 2011), 23-30; Timothy Brook, *The Troubled Empire: China in the Yuan and Ming Dynasties* (Cambridge, MA: Belknap, 2010), 226-231; Arturo Giraldez, *The Age of Trade: The Manila Galleons and the Dawn of the Global Economy* (New York: Rowman and Littlefield, 2015).

42. Boyajian, *Portuguese Trade*, 13; Disney, *History of Portugal*, 1: 198-200; Marius B. Jansen, *The Making of Modern Japan* (Cambridge, MA: Belknap, 2000); Conrad Totman, *Early Modern Japan* (Berkeley: University of California Press, 1993).

43. Sassetti, *Lettere dall'India*, Letter 26, 215.

44. António Galvão, *Tratado: Que compôs o nobre & notavel capitão Antonio Galvão, dos diversos & desuayrados caminhos, por onde nos tempos passados a pimenta & especearia veyo da India ás nossas partes, & assi de todos os descobrimentos antigos & modernos, que são feitos ate a era de mil & quinhentos & cincoenta; com os nomes particulares das pessoas que os fizeram, & em que tempos & as suas alturas, obra certo muy notavel & copiosa*, 31. The Lilly Library at Indiana University, where I read this, gives the date of the text as December 15, 1563.

45. Disney, *History of Portugal* 1: 196-200; Boyajian, *Portuguese Trade*, 132-134.

46. Boyajian, *Portuguese Trade*, 65.

47. Biblioteca Angelica, ms. 1331, 2v-3r; MAP Person ID 4431, "Carletti, Francesco"; "Carletti, Francesco," *DBI* 20 (1977). For the dates of Carletti's journey, see Carletti, *My Voyage*: Florence (5/20/1591)—Seville [pp. 3-4]; Seville (1/8/1594)—Cape Verde [pp. 4-6]; Cape Verde (4/19/1594)—Cartagena de Indias [p. 16]; Cartagena de Indias (8/12/1594)—Nombre de Dios [pp. 24-26]; Nombre de Dios—Casa de Cruces [pp. 27-29]; Casa de Cruces—Panamá City (9/1594) [pp. 29-31, 33]; Panamá City (11/1594)—Lima via Callao (1/1595) [pp. 31-39, 48]; Decided to leave Lima (5/1595)—Acapulco

(6/1595) [pp. 48, 51–55]; Acapulco–Mexico City (6/1595) [pp. 55–57, 69]; Mexico City (3/1596)–Acapulco (3/1596) [pp. 69–70]; Acapulco (3/25/1596)–The Velas / Ladrones / Marianas Islands (~5/30/1596) [pp. 69–71]; The Velas / Ladrones / Marianas Islands–Cavite near Manila (6/1596) [pp. 78–81]; Manila (5/1597)–Nagasaki (6/1597) [pp. 90–91, 99]; Nagasaki (3/3/1598)–Macao (probably 3, not later than 7/1598) [pp. 135–142]; Macao (12/1599)–Malacca [pp. 183–187]; Malacca–Cochin (3/1600) [pp. 196–200]; Cochin–Goa (3–4/1600) [p. 200]; Goa (12/25/1601)–Saint Helena (3/14/1602) [pp. 226–229, 249]; Saint Helena (3/14–16/1602)–Fernando de Noronha (4/6/1602) [pp. 229–243]; Fernando de Noronha (5/2/1602)–Middleburg, Zeeland (7/7/1602) [pp. 243–244]; Brielle near The Hague (12/1605)–Paris (12/9/1605) [pp. 267–268]; Paris (probably 5–6/1606)–Florence (7/12/1606) [pp. 3, 270].

48. Biblioteca Angelica, ms. 1331, 2v–4r, esp. 3v; Carletti, *My Voyage*, 4–5. On the *salma*, Iohn Florio, *Queen Anna's New World of Words or Dictionarie of the Italian and English Tongues* (London: Printed by Melch. Bradwood for Edw. Blount and William Barret, 1611) gives for "sálma" "a soame, a lode, a burthen, a fraught. Also a mans bodie, weight or carcase. Also a kind of weight." The *Enciclopedia italiana* (1936), "Salma," online, ed., accessed December 3, 2020, https://www.treccani.it/enciclopedia/salma_%28 Enciclopedia-Italiana%29/ gives it as a unit of dry capacity used in Italy, especially Sicily. The Sicilian *salma* = 275.08 liters and that of Alessandria = 213.25 liters. Carletti's little ship, then, would have been between 20.35- and 26.5-tons capacity using the liter to shipping tonnage calculator provided at https://m.convert-me.com/en/convert/volume/liter/liter-to-ton nage.html?u=tonnage&v=1, accessed December 3, 2020.

49. Kamen, *Empire*, 472–474, makes this point forcefully for the eighteenth century.

50. Biblioteca Angelica, ms. 1331, 4r–15v; Carletti, *My Voyage*, 5–19. On Cape Verde, see A. J. R. Russell-Wood, *The Portuguese Empire, 1415–1808: A World on the Move* (Baltimore, MD: Johns Hopkins University Press, 1998), 40–41. On Carletti in Cape Verde, see Malyn Newitt, ed., *The Portuguese in West Africa, 1415–1670: A Documentary History* (New York: Cambridge University Press, 2010), 155–158.

51. Biblioteca Angelica, ms. 1331, 15r–v; Carletti, *My Voyage*, 20–21.

52. MAP Person ID 919, "Medici, Pietro di Cosimo I de'"; Paola Volpini, "Medici, Pietro de'" *DBI* 73 (2009). Volpini explains that Pietro's relationship with Ferdinando I had broken down over the matter of inheritance.

53. Carletti, *My Voyage*, 23–24.

54. Carletti, *My Voyage*, 50–51. On the Panama route and the maroons, see Mann, *1493*, 442–458.

55. Carletti, *My Voyage*, 69.

56. Carletti, *My Voyage*, 70.

57. Biblioteca Angelica, ms. 1331, 53r, mentions "ritornammo con il nostro argento verso il pred.° Porto d'Acapulco"; the Carlettis sailed from Manila to Nagasaki carrying only silver bars (Carletti, *My Voyage*, 91).

58. Carletti, *My Voyage*, 70. As it happens, Mann, *1493*, 198, recounts the findings of an underwater investigation of a Manila galleon shipwrecked in 1654 that offers confirmation of this, with 418,323 pesos registered and 1,180,865 recovered from the wreck. On silver in this period, see Paula Findlen, "Early Modern Things: Objects in Motion, 1500–1800" in *Early Modern Things: Objects and Their Histories, 1500–1800*, ed. Paula Findlen (New York: Routledge, 2013), 18 and 18nn70–71; Burkholder and Johnson, *Colonial Latin America*, 156–171; Timothy Brook, *Vermeer's Hat: The Seventeenth Century and the Dawn of the Global World* (London: Bloomsbury, 2008), chapter 6; Mann, *1493*, chapters 4 (157–209) and 5 (210–247).

59. Carletti, *My Voyage*, 89–90.

60. Carletti, *My Voyage*, 91.

61. "e[]que não haja de nenhuà das partes que estão sob o[]governo, e[]administração dos Castilhanos para as dos Portuguezes, nem de hûas a[] outras Sem espeçial liçença minha dada por provizão por mim assinada, e[]não por meus VReis, ou Gov.ʳᵉˢ, por q[ue] elles hej por bem que não possão dar as[]taes liçenças!" HAG, Archive Number 7, Livros das Monções do Reino, no. 5, 44r–45r.

62. "Se[]não tendo o tal Religiozo, ou Religiozos, expressa liçença minha passada pellos Ministros da[]dita Coroa de Portugal para poderem ir as[]ditas partes," HAG, Archive Number 7, Livros das Monções do Reino, no. 5, 44r–45r. Sanjay Subrahmanyam, reading my dissertation that transcribes this document in full, kindly noted in correspondence in the summer of 2020 that a transcription was published in J. H. Cunha Rivara, ed. *Archivo Portuguez-Oriental*, 6 fasc. in 10 parts (Nova Goa: Imprensa Nacional, 1861), fasc. III, part 1, no. 147, 450–451.

63. "o qual se publicara nos lugares publicos de Goa, Cochim, Malaca, e Macao," HAG, Archive Number 7, Livros das Monções do Reino, no. 5, 44r–45r.

64. Carletti, *My Voyage*, 103–104.

65. Carletti, *My Voyage*, 91.

66. Carletti, *My Voyage*, 96–99.

67. Carletti, *My Voyage*, 102–103; John Heilbron, *The Sun in the Church: Cathedrals as Solar Observatories* (Cambridge, MA: Harvard University Press, 2001), 39.

68. Boyajian, *Portuguese Trade*, 13.

69. Brook, *Vermeer's Hat*, 87–116.

70. Brockey, *Journey to the East*; Brockey, *The Visitor: André Palmeiro and the Jesuits in Asia* (Cambridge, MA: Belknap, 2014).

71. Biblioteca Angelica, ms. 1331, 103r; Carletti, *My Voyage*, 135–142.

72. Carletti, *My Voyage*, 141.

73. Carletti, *My Voyage*, 141.

74. Disney, *History of Portugal* 2: 67–68, 163, and 201.

75. Carletti, *My Voyage*, 140–141; Brockey, *Journey to the East*, 30–33; Brockey, *The Visitor*, 15–16; Ronnie Po-chia Hsia, "Ricci, Matteo," *DBI* 87 (2016); "Ruggièri, Michele," *Treccani Enciclopedia* online, accessed August 11, 2019, http://www.treccani.it/enciclopedia/michele-ruggieri/.

76. "Noi rispondemmo esser' venuti dall' Isole Filippine, à quelle del Giappone e poi in questa d'Amacao: di dove era nostro pensiero, e desiderio passare all'India orientale [108r:] per nostro spasso e curiosità e no[n] per altro interesse ó altro, che contrafacesse, ó preterisse alli ordini Regi dell'una, ne dell'altra Corona, inoltre ch'eramo di natione Italiana, e che venivamo d'un Paese libero, come era il Giappone no[n] punto suggetto nè all'una, ne all'altra natione spagnola, e che l'andare per il mondo era cosa, che si permetteva à tutte le natione," Biblioteca Angelica, ms. 1331, 107v–108r, Carletti, *My Voyage*, 141–142.

77. Carletti, *My Voyage*, 142 and 150.

78. "Ruẏ Lourenço de[]tavora Visorey amigo, Eu el Reẏ vos envio muito saudar Pello que tenho mandado por minhas provisões, e Instrucoes, sobre se prohibir o Comerçio das Indias occidentaes com as Orientais como tereis visto, Entendereis muito que deseẏo seguarde o[]que acena disso tenho provido p.ª que nenhu[]d [corrections in the manuscript render the transcription of the foregoing three words uncertain] forma ajao[]ditto Comercio nem se permita de huà e[]outra parte, E por[]ser materia esta detanta importançia vos eẏ por muẏ encarregado fazerdes que a seẏ se[]cumpra inviolavelm.ᵗᵉ sem conceder em[]quando a isto dispensaçaõ algu[m]à , E porque por não haver outra parte donde comodam.ᵗᵉ se possa acodir à falta q̇ nas Phelippinas se padeçe de Moniçoes se[]não de Cidade de Machao, eser conviniente e devido valerense, e[]ajudarense meus estados humȯ de[]outros nas[]cousas que p.ª defensa e[]conservação delles for neçess.º ordeneẏ por minha carta de 23 de jan.ʳᵉ de <u>608</u> a forma em que da[]dita cidade de Machao se[]proverão as monicões que o Gover.ⁿⁿ das Phelippinas mandar pedir com as personas e[]pella mat.ª que[]vereis pella dita carta e minha provisão que tambem sobre isso," HAG, Archive Number 12, Livros das Monções do Reino, 9, 10, and 11, 167r–v.

79. Carletti, *My Voyage*, 142.

80. Carletti, *My Voyage*, 142–143; Elisabetta Colla, "16th Century Japan and Macau Described by Francesco Carletti (1573?-1636)," *Bulletin of Portuguese–Japanese Studies* 17 (2008), 135–136. Colla's information on Neretti primarily derives from Gemma Sgrilli, *Francesco Carletti, mercante e viaggiatore fiorentino, 1573 (?)–1636* (Rocca S. Casciano, It.: Licinio Cappelli, 1905), 78–79n2.

81. Carletti, *My Voyage*, 143.

82. Orazio Neretti in Macao to Cosimo II de' Medici in Florence on January 8, 1617, ASF, MdP 5080, 464r, MAP Doc ID 14216.

83. "Havessi piaciuuto a Dio che l'ardor giovenile el' disio di veder paesi e gente nuova non m' haveßi mai fatto lassar Thoscana sono già trenta otto annj de quali consumaj alcuni nel' Indie Orientali nel' servitio del' Re di Spagna altri passai in quest'ultime parti del' mondo nella Cina e Giappone, e finalmente carico d'annj e inutile d'una gamba con una archibusata, combattendo in' mare con li mori Malabari, restai cittadino in' questa Città di Maccao, porto della Cina con casa moglie, e figliuoli tutti Vassalli di Vostra Altezza Serenissima," ASF, MdP 5080, 464.

84. Sgrilli, *Francesco Carletti*, 78–79n2.

85. Carletti, *My Voyage*, 229–244.

86. Carletti, *My Voyage*, 241.

87. Carletti, *My Voyage*, 239.

88. Biblioteca Angelica, ms. 1331, 190v–191r, "fortificato le mie ragioni per indurli á farmi [191r] questo servitio et commodo con il dire, che si ricordaveno de cortesi trattamenti et carezze, che Vostra Altezza Serenissima fa loro continuamente, quando vengono nel suo Porto di livorno, della qual cosa molti ricordevoli mi favoriorno, et accordorno di compiacermene." The Angelica manuscript is an early copy of Carletti's book. Whenever the manuscript is cited and a transcription given, quotations are my translation from my transcription of the manuscript held in Rome. I often also list the page of the Weinstock translation for reference. References to the Weinstock edition without the manuscript are references just to that edition. Carletti, *My Voyage*, 242.

89. Carletti, *My Voyage*, 148–149.

90. Carletti, *My Voyage*, 244–245.

91. Carletti, *My Voyage*, 4 and 247. The MAP entry—MAP Person ID 14372, "Franceschi, Paolo"—refers to a single letter of 1616, from Paolo Franceschi in Brussels to Giovanni di Cosimo I de' Medici (Don Giovanni). which is MAP Doc ID 14983, ASF MdP 2355, Ins. 1, 8.

92. Carletti, *My Voyage*, 247.

93. Biblioteca Angelica, ms. 1331, 199r, "et l'altre curiostià, che portavo per Vostra Altezza Serenissima." Carletti, *My Voyage*, 252.

94. Carletti, *My Voyage*, 148–149.

95. Biblioteca Angelica, ms. 1331, 188r, "questi come che sieno heretici Calvinisti la maggior Parte non voglione vedere pitture di santi ne dell'istesso Iddio crocifisso." Carletti, *My Voyage*, 239.

96. Carletti, *My Voyage*, 243–244 and 267–268.

97. Biblioteca Angelica, ms. 1331, 200r, "quando Vostra Altezza Serenissima scrisse quella lettera, che se non mi rendevono le mie robbe e curiosità, che portava per Vostra Altezza, che sarebbe forzata à rivalersene dalle loro Navi, mercantie, et persone, che venissero et trattessero in queste

suoi Porti. Sopra di che la Provincia di Hollanda si risenti, et fece fare un solenne Protesto à quella di Zellananda, che mi dovessero re[n]dere il mio." Carletti, *My Voyage*, 253.

98. Richard Goldthwaite, *The Economy of Renaissance Florence* (Baltimore, MD: Johns Hopkins University Press, 2009), 96–98 (esp. 96), discusses this issue mostly with respect to the fourteenth and fifteenth centuries.

99. Biblioteca Angelica, ms. 1331, 205r–v, "Aministratori della compagnia de Mercante che negotiano all'India orientale"; "non perche diffidassero della giustitia, mediante le loro buone ragioni, ma per compiacerni li detti stati Generali, et per respetto del favore delle lettere della Regina di francia, e di quelle del Gran Duca di Toscana" ; [205v] "quella Compagnia ò d'altre à fare il simile ad altri per una certa consequentia et obligo, ma solo per li suddetti rispetti." Carletti, *My Voyage*, 259–260.

100. The classic statement of the importance of the VOC is Niels Steensgaard, *Carracks, Caravans and Companies: The Structural Crisis in the European-Asian Trade in the Early 17th Century* (Copenhagen: Studentlitteratur, 1973), 10. See also Ronald Findlay and Kevin H. O'Rourke, *Power and Plenty: Trade, War, and the World Economy in the Second Millennium* (Princeton, NJ: Princeton University Press, 2007), 177–179.

101. Jonathan I. Israel, *The Dutch Republic: Its Rise, Greatness, and Fall: 1477–1806* (Oxford, UK: Clarendon, 1998), 321–322.

102. Carletti, *My Voyage*, 260.

103. Carletti, *My Voyage*, 260.

104. Carletti, *My Voyage*, 266–270 and 266n. On the French offer, see "Carletti, Francesco," *DBI* 20 (1977).

105. Biblioteca Angelica, ms. 1331. See the October 25, 1721, note on the first page concerning the distortions of the 1701 edition. The relevant Weinstock translation of this manuscript has been cited as well because it is the only accessible English translation at present. See the translator's note in Carletti, *My Voyage*, xiv, for a manuscript history. See also MAP Person ID 4431, "Carletti, Francesco." Carletti was "Maestro di Casa" from 1609 and "Salariato di Cosimo II de' Medici" from 1609 to 1613. "Carletti, Francesco," *DBI* 20 (1977), states that Carletti retained a Medici pension until his death. Weinstock gives his date of death as 1636 (xiii), with which the *DBI* entry concurs.

106. Malyn Newitt, "Formal and Informal Empire in the History of Portuguese Expansion," *Portuguese Studies* 17, no. 1 (January 2001): 1–21; Russell-Wood, *Portuguese Empire*; Sanjay Subrahmanyam, *The Portuguese Empire in Asia, 1500–1700: A Political and Economic History* (New York: Longman, 1993); Disney, *History of Portugal*.

107. Saturnino Monteiro, "The Decline and Fall," 9–20. P. J. Marshall, "Western Arms in Maritime Asia," 13–28. Raudzens, "Military Revolution or Maritime Evolution?" 631–641.

108. Subrahmanyam, *Portuguese Empire*, 2–8 and 157.

109. Sassetti, *Lettere dall'India*, Letter 4, 47.

110. Geoffrey Parker, *The Military Revolution: Military Innovation and the Rise of the West, 1500–1800*, 2nd ed. (New York: Cambridge University Press, 1996); Simon Pepper and Nicholas Adams, *Firearms and Fortifications: Military Architecture and Siege Warfare in Sixteenth-Century Siena* (Chicago: University of Chicago Press, 1986); F. L. Taylor, *The Art of War in Italy, 1494–1529*, repr. (Westport, CT: Greenwood Press, 1973); Bert S. Hall, *Weapons and Warfare in Renaissance Europe: Gunpowder, Technology, and Tactics* (Baltimore, MD: Johns Hopkins University Press, 1997); J. R. Hale, *Renaissance Fortification: Art or Engineering*, Walter Neutrath Memorial Lecture (London: Thames and Hudson, 1977); M. E. Mallet and J. R. Hale, *The Military Organization of a Renaissance State: Venice, c. 1400 to 1617* (New York: Cambridge University Press, 1984).

111. Sassetti, *Lettere dall'India*, Letter 14, 108 and 108n2, Sassetti's editor Dei proposes in her footnote that this engineer was perhaps Filippo Magrera, mentioned in Letter 23 to Lorenzo Canigiani.

112. Sassetti, *Lettere dall'India*, Letter 14, 108–109.

113. Sassetti, *Lettere dall'India*, Letter 25, 197–198 and 197n11.

114. Sassetti, *Lettere dall'India*, Letter 25, 198.

115. MAP Doc ID 22713, ASF, MdP 5037, 289, from Goa, perhaps in 1572.

116. Cammillo Guidi in Madrid to the grand duke, ASF, MdP, 4919, P. II, 456–462r, August 21, 1588. The relevant part of the *avviso* is at 462r. See also MAP Person ID 848, "Guidi, Camillo di Francesco." MAP lists him as legation secretary in Spain in 1586, 1590, 1593, and 1597 and legation secretary in Rome in 1587; it seems likely that he was legation secretary in Madrid in 1588.

117. ASF, MdP 4937, 518r. The acquisition of the island of Ternate, where the cloves are grown, with much bloodshed among the Dutch and Portuguese, is briefly recounted.

118. John Keay, *The Spice Route: A History* (Berkeley: University of California Press, 2006), 207–208, 217–218, 233–234, and 237. Russell-Wood, *Portuguese Empire*, 127.

119. Sassetti, *Lettere dall'India*, Letter 25, 210.

120. Sassetti, *Lettere dall'India*, Letter 25, 210–211.

121. Sassetti, *Lettere dall'India*, Letter 25, 211.

122. Sassetti, *Lettere dall'India*, Letter 25, 202–203.

123. Sassetti, *Lettere dall'India*, Letter 25, 203.

124. Sassetti, *Lettere dall'India*, Letter 25, 203.

125. Peter Robb, *A History of India* (New York: Palgrave, 2002), 62–65, 78–86, 90–92, 96, 112–113; John F. Richards, *The Mughal Empire* (Cambridge: Cambridge University Press, 1993); Sanjay Subrahmanyam, *The Political Economy of Commerce: Southern India, 1500–1650* (New York: Cambridge

University Press, 2002); Navina Najat Haidar and Marika Sardar, *Sultans of Deccan India, 1500–1700: Opulence and Fantasy* (New York: Metropolitan Museum of Art, 2015); Richard M. Eaton, *A Social History of the Deccan, 1300–1761: Eight Indian Lives* (New York: Cambridge University Press, 2005); John Keay, *India: A History* (New York: Grove, 2000).

126. Sassetti, *Lettere dall'India*, Letter 4, 50–51.

127. For the study of Tacitus by Bernardo Davanzati, one of Sassetti's correspondents and a member of the Accademia degli Alterati, see Cochrane, *Florence in the Forgotten Centuries*, 117–121. Sassetti wrote to Davanzati from Cochin on January 22, 1586: Sassetti, *Lettere dall'India*, Letter 22, 165-180. On European travel writing and ethnography in south India see Rubiés, *Travel and Ethnology*.

128. Sassetti, *Lettere dall'India*, Letter 4, 51–52. According to Dei (Sassetti, 51n20), the term *amocchi* is derived from *amok*, a depressed state that culminates in improvised homicidal folly and therefore in forgetfulness.

129. The *zamalucco* was the king of Ahmadnagar. For the etymological evolution, see "Ralph Fitch, 1583–91," 13n1, in William Foster, ed., *Early Travels in India, 1583–1619* (New York: Oxford University Press, 1921).

130. Sassetti, *Lettere dall'India*, Letter 25, 201–202. On the king of Narsinga as "Narasinha raja" king of Vijayanagara, see Sassetti, *Lettere dall'India*, Letter 22, 166n3. This would seem to be a reference to the Battle of Talikota (1565).

131. Sassetti, *Lettere dall'India*, Letter 25, 201–202.

132. Sassetti, *Lettere dall'India*, Letter 25, 200, noted that the Javanese were particularly renowned for their *amocchi*.

133. Sassetti, *Lettere dall'India*, Letter 25, 199.

134. Sassetti, *Lettere dall'India*, Letter 25, 199–200 and 200n15.

135. Sassetti, *Lettere dall'India*, Letter 25, 200.

136. For Sassetti's letters to the Medici from India, all of which were sent from Cochin, see Sassetti, *Lettere dall'India*. To Francesco I: January 22, 1584 (Letter 4); February 11, 1585 (Letter 15); February 10, 1586 (Letter 25). To Cardinal Ferdinando: January 1584 (Letter 5); February 10, 1585 (Letter 13); February 10, 1586 (Letter 26). See also Carletti, *My Voyage*, 270. For the dates of Carletti's journey, see Carletti, *My Voyage*, 3–4, 243–244, and 270. Carletti's presentations to the grand duke (pp. 3 and 11) were from memory because his notes had been lost (pp. 95–96 and 124).

137. Stanford University Special Collections, MSS Codex 0462, *Cose Diverse del Toscana*. The catalog entry for this varied collection of documents dates it to the 1590s. On Piero Vettori, who Sassetti admired and to whom he was related through his mother, see Sassetti, *Lettere dall'India*, Letter 9, 76n1. Vettori was a Florentine senator, a reader in the humanities at the university of Florence, a count palatine, an eques auratus, and a Medici envoy to Rome (MAP Person ID 527, "Vettori, Piero di Iacopo";

Renzo Negri, "Vettori, Pietro," *Enciclopedia Dantesca* [1970]), online ed., accessed December 4, 2020, https://www.treccani.it/enciclopedia/pietro -vettori_%28Enciclopedia-Dantesca%29/.

138. Filippo Sassetti in Kochi to Francesco I de' Medici in Florence on January 20, 1584, MAP Doc ID 22796, ASF, MdP 5037, 508; Filippo Sassetti in Kochi to Ferdinando I de' Medici in Rome on February 10, 1585, MAP Doc ID 15581, ASF, MdP 5113, Ins. 1, 354; Filippo Sassetti in Kochi to Francesco I de' Medici in Florence on February 11, 1585, MAP Doc ID 22813, ASF, MdP 5037, 523; Filippo Sassetti in Kochi to Francesco I de' Medici in Florence on January 23, 1586, MAP Doc ID 22838, ASF, MdP 5037, 533.

139. Biblioteca Angelica, ms. 1331, 156v, "terra, e paese suggetto all Gra' Magor Monarca della meglio e della maggior parte di tutta quell'India,"; "di 200 mila huomini, e 200 mila Cavalli, sei mila elefanti"; "e piu di 40 mila Cammeli et di buoi." Carletti, *My Voyage*, 203.

140. Carletti, *My Voyage*, 226–227, 243–244, and 267–268.

141. Carletti, *My Voyage*, 83–84.

142. Carletti, *My Voyage*, 182 and 182nn.

143. Anthony Reid, *Southeast Asia in the Age of Commerce: 1450–1680*, 2 vols. (New Haven, CT: Yale University Press, 1988), 1: 148–150 and 151, fig. 21; the reference to Carletti is on 149.

144. Carletti, *My Voyage*, 95–96 and 124.

145. Biblioteca Angelica, ms. 1331, 61v–62r. "la qual Città di Manila è habitata da spagnoli, che l'hanno conquistata, e vi stanno con molti commodi agiatamente, padroni assoluti [62r:] delle Terre, e delli huomini e delle donne ancora, i quali tutti li pagano tributo, e molti ne hanno sotto di se cinquecento, e mille, che pagano almeno otto giulij per ciascuno l'anno." Carletti, *My Voyage*, 82.

146. Carletti, *My Voyage*, 88–90.

147. Carletti, *My Voyage*, 56–57, 70–71, 82, 88–90, 127, 129, 153–154.

148. Carletti, *My Voyage*, 187, 193, and 193n.

149. Biblioteca Angelica, ms. 1331, 90v. "mentre ch'io stetti in detta Città di Nangasacchi Popolata tutta di Giapponesi christiani con alcune poche case di mercante Portoghesi, che quivi stantiano sotto il governo di quel Rè." Carletti, *My Voyage*, 120. The king to whom Carletti referred was "King Taico Sama" (Carletti, *My Voyage*, 118), which Carletti's translator identifies on 113n1 as "Toyotomi Hideyoshi (1536–1598), who took the title of Taiko in 1591, pretending to retire from power, but actually holding it until his death."

150. Carletti, *My Voyage*, 114–116 and 114nn.

151. Biblioteca Angelica, ms. 1331, 61v, "e quelle del Giappone, che sono da temersi più dell'altre si per essere vicine, comè per essere quei popoli

gente bellicosa, e deita á guereggiare sempre tra di loro, e con li Vicini." Carletti, *My Voyage*, 82.

152. Carletti, *My Voyage*, 114–116.

153. Carletti, *My Voyage*, 114–115.

154. Jansen, *The Making of Modern Japan*, 20, cites a figure of some 158,0000 for Japan's 1592 invasion of Korea and adds that another 140,000 were sent in 1597.

155. Carletti, *My Voyage*, 139.

156. Carletti, *My Voyage*, 160–163; Mote, *Imperial China*; Timothy Brook, *The Confusions of Pleasure: Commerce and Culture in Ming China* (Berkeley: University of California Press, 1998); Brook, *Troubled Empire*; Kenneth Pomeranz, *The Great Divergence: China, Europe, and the Making of the Modern World Economy* (Princeton, NJ: Princeton University Press, 2000); Jonathan D. Spence, *The Search for Modern China* (New York: W. W. Norton, 1991); Francis Fukuyama, *The Origins of Political Order: From Prehuman Times to the French Revolution* (New York: Farrar, Straus, and Giroux, 2011).

157. Carletti, *My Voyage*, 163–164.

158. Biblioteca Angelica, ms. 1331, 126r–v. "et sono tante antiche queste inventioni nella Cina che passano migliaia d'anni et si può senz'alcun dubbio credere, che tutte venghino da loro, et io concorrerei á dire che non solamente queste ma ogn'altra inventione che di buono, ò di cattivo, ò di bello, ò di brutto fussero venute da quel paese ó almeno si può affermare che habbino il conoscimento d'ogni cose da loro medesemi et non da noi ne da Greghi, ó altre nationi, che le hanno insegnate á noi, ma d'autori nativi in quello cosí gran paese, et cose antico dicono, il quale sopravanza di molti migliaia d'anni della creatione del mondo descrita da Moisè; cosa la loro non meno fa[manuscript damaged; perhaps "v"] olosa, che falsa, se bene creduta da essi, che abbondano d'ogni cose, et d'ogni arte meccanica, et Pulitica, e fanno professione di filosofia morale, di mattematica, d'Astrologia, di Medicina, et d'altre scientie, nelle quali si tengono li primi huomini nel Mondo, e non pensano, che sia sapere fuora della loro natione, tenendo tutti gl'altri per gente barbara." Carletti, *My Voyage*, 164.

159. Carletti, *My Voyage*, 164.

160. Carletti, *My Voyage*, 164–169.

161. Carletti, *My Voyage*, 166.

162. Carletti, *My Voyage*, 167.

163. For the dates, see Carletti, *My Voyage*, 90–91, 99, and 183–187.

164. Maurizio Arfaioli and Marta Caroscio, eds., *The Grand Ducal Medici and the Levant: Material Culture, Diplomacy, and Imagery in the Early Modern Mediterranean* (London: Harvey Miller, 2016); Anna Contadini and Claire Norton, eds., *The Renaissance and the Ottoman World* (Burlington, VT: Ashgate, 2013);

Brian Curran, *The Egyptian Renaissance: The Afterlife of Egypt in Early Modern Italy* (Chicago: University of Chicago Press, 2007); Detlef Heikamp, *Mexico and the Medici* (Florence: Edam, 1972); Lisa Jardine, *Worldly Goods: A New History of the Renaissance* (New York: W. W. Norton, 1998); Lisa Jardine and Jerry Brotton, *Global Interests: Renaissance Art between East and West* (Ithaca, NY: Cornell University Press, 2000); R. W. Lightbown, "Oriental Art and the Orient in Late Renaissance and Baroque Italy," *Journal of the Warburg and Courtauld Institutes* 32 (1969): 228–279; Rosamond Mack, *Bazaar to Piazza: Islamic Trade and Italian Art, 1300–1600* (Berkeley: University of California Press, 2002); Lia Markey, *Imagining the Americas in Medici Florence* (University Park: Pennsylvania State University Press, 2016).

165. Antonio Vecchietti in Lisbon to Francesco I de' Medici in Florence on September 27, 1576, MAP Doc ID 14225, ASF, MdP 4906, 157; MAP Person ID 997, "Orlandini, Bartolomeo di Piero (Baccio)."

166. Bartolomeo di Piero (Baccio) Orlandini in Madrid to Francesco I de' Medici on October 10, 1576, MAP Doc ID 14215, ASF, MdP 4906, 128. MAP transcription: "per quella miglior strada che mi paressi, et uno per volta per scompartire il risico."

167. Bartolomeo di Piero (Baccio) Orlandini in Madrid to Francesco I de' Medici in Florence on October 15, 1576, MAP Doc ID 14217, ASF, MdP 4906, 137. See MAP Person ID 995, "Lenzi, Filippo." Lenzi would become quartermaster to Francesco I in 1579. Bartolomeo di Piero (Baccio) Orlandini in Madrid to Francesco I de' Medici in Florence on October 27, 1576, MAP Doc ID 810, ASF, MdP 4906, 142. MAP transcription: "I diamanti mi risolveró poi alla fine mandarli per il Lenzi, parendomi via piú sicuro di quante si possa tenere." Bartolomeo di Piero (Baccio) Orlandini in Madrid to Francesco I de' Medici in Florence on December 6, 1576, MAP Doc ID 811, ASF, MdP 4906, 167.

168. Cammillo di Francesco Guidi in Madrid to Ferdinando I de' Medici in Florence on October 29, 1590, MAP Doc ID 962, ASF, MdP 4920, 763; MAP Person ID 848, "Guidi, Camillo di Francesco."

169. Ferdinando I de' Medici in Ambrogiana, Montelupo, to Francesco di Girolamo Lenzoni in Madrid on October 30, 1592, MAP Doc ID 16749, ASF, MdP 282, 158; MAP Person ID 918, "Lenzoni, Francesco di Girolamo."

170. Niccolò Bartoli in Lisbon to Ferdinando I de' Medici in Florence on April 23, 1588, MAP Doc ID 8240, ASF, MdP 4919, 245. MAP transcription: "Le perle le mandai in un mazetto di lettere per un tal Cap.no Nasachi raugeo al'inbasciador."

171. Niccolò Bartoli in Lisbon to Ferdinando I de' Medici in Florence on April 23, 1588, MAP Doc ID 8240, ASF, MdP 4919, 245. MAP transcription: "e lui le consegnassi a l'ordine di Vostra Alteza al [Giulio] Bataglino con una mia lettera con ordine ne segua la volontà di V. A., come la mi ordinò più tempo fa."

172. Vincenzo di Andrea Alamanni in Madrid to Ferdinando I de' Medici in Florence, April 30, 1588, MAP Doc ID 8238, ASF, MdP 4919, 222.

173. Vincenzo di Andrea Alamanni in Madrid to Ferdinando I de' Medici in Florence on May 28, 1588, MAP Doc ID 8261, ASF, MdP 4919, 301. MAP transcription: "ho scritto a Lisbona a un Giulio Nesi et raccomandatogli molto caldamente questo servizio."

174. Vincenzo di Andrea Alamanni in Madrid to Ferdinando I de' Medici in Florence on July 28, 1588, MAP Doc ID 8324, ASF, MdP 4919, 414. MAP transcription: "Giulio Nesi mi scrisse che comperò l'ebano bellissimo, et per l'ultima sua mi dice che l'invierà alla volta di Livorno."

175. Vincenzo di Andrea Alamanni in Madrid to Ferdinando I de' Medici in Florence on October 15, 1588, MAP Doc ID 8424, ASF, MdP 4919, 504. MAP transcription: "L'ebano di V. A., per quanto mi scrive Giulio Nesi di Lisbona, si caricò per Livorno sopra una saettia di Ponzetto Martinez da San Torpè, con la poliza di carico per Firenze indiritta a Napoleon Cambi depositario, perchè egli lo faccia ricevere. Valendosi il Nesi del costo dal detto Depositario, che monta scudi 59.2.1 d'oro."

176. MAP Person ID 3657, "Cambi, Napoleone di Girolamo." The synopsis for MAP 8424 translates the title as "treasurer," but Florio expresses some of its importance in describing it as "Depositório, a secret trustie friend, a feoffie, one that takes in trust."

177. J. R. Hale, *Florence and the Medici* (London: Phoenix, 2001), 154–155 and 160.

178. Annemarie Jordan Gschwend and K. J. P. Lowe, eds., *The Global City: On the Streets of Renaissance Lisbon* (London: Paul Holberton, 2015).

179. Sassetti, *Lettere edite e inedite*, 235–236, Letter LXXVII, to the grand duke of Tuscany, Francesco I, from Lisbon February 7, 1583.

180. On Sassetti's purchases of items for the Medici, see Lightbown, "Oriental Art," 237–238; Sassetti, *Lettere dall'India*, Letter 13, 102–107.

181. Filippo Sassetti in Cochin on January 22, 1584, to Grand Duke Francesco I in Florence, Sassetti, *Lettere dall'India*, Letter 4, 55. Editor Dei explains in 55n33 the error in the figures and the issue of currency conversions with reference to a postscript. On Sassetti's description of goods available and his purchases for the Medici, see Lightbown, "Oriental Art," 235–238.

182. Sassetti, *Lettere dall'India*, Letter 13, 102–107; Letter 14, 113; Letter 15, 114. Andrea Migliorati was from Prato and Sassetti knew him in Lisbon, where he took care of Florentine merchant interests according to Letter 4, 54n30.

183. Filippo Sassetti in Cochin on February 10, 1586, to Francesco I de' Medici, grand duke of Tuscany, in Florence, Sassetti, *Lettere dall'India*, Letter 25, 210.

184. Sassetti, *Lettere dall'India*, Letter 25, 210. With reference to the bed canopy, Lightbown's translation of Sassetti's description, in a different

passage, of the object in question resolves the ambiguity inherent in the passage quoted here: Lightbown, "Oriental Art," 237.

185. Carlo Velluti in Lisbon to Grand Duke Ferdinando I in Florence, ASF, MDP 4919, P. I, 281r–284v, May 21, 1588. See also MAP Doc ID 8256, ASF, MdP 4919, 281. Sassetti died on September 3, 1588, in Goa (Surdich, "Sassetti").

186. Lightbown, "Oriental Art," 237, reconstructs this affair.

187. "la quale era di diversi et fantastichi animali et uccellami, et fiori, de quali abonda questo Paese estimonli più per la vista che per l'odore," Biblioteca Angelica, ms. 1331, 113v (quotations)–114r; "fogliami, e tutto molto al naturale" (Carletti, *My Voyage*, 148–149 [quotation], 229–243, and 252); Lightbown, "Oriental Art," 237.

188. Carletti, *My Voyage*, 149–150.

189. Biblioteca Angelica, ms. 1331, 203v. "una catena d'oro di v$^{-di}$ . 40. quella che volse Vostra Altezza Serenissima fatta nella Cina, alla quale erano appiccati due Reliquiarij pur d'oro." Carletti, *My Voyage*, 257–258.

190. Biblioteca Angelica, ms. 1331, 169r. "che entravano nel pregno della mano." Carletti, *My Voyage*, 217.

191. On Carletti as a consultant, see "Carletti, Francesco," *DBI* 20 (1977).

192. This paragraph paraphrases information from ASF, MdP 4898, 77v–78r. ASF, MdP 4898, 61v, is a letter from Madrid of May 30, 1567, and ASF, MdP 4898, 65r, is from June 18, 1567.

193. The New York Metropolitan Museum of Art holds a "Medal: Bust of Bernardo Nasi" from ca. 1500, in the Robert Lehman Collection, 1975. I draw the information on this Bernardo Nasi from the Met's online catalog 1251, accessed October 26, 2020, https://www.metmuseum.org/art/collection/search/461247.

194. "Nón voglio proterire di dire a Vostra Eccellenza Illustrissima come a Lisbona io trovai ů [n] Bernardo Nasi fratello di messer francesco nasi che sta in fiorenza il quale bernardo ę tenuto la ů [n] valentissimo huomo delle cose del maŗe et da molto ben conto di quelle parte et della professine marittiṃa . era gia molto riccho ma tornando dall Indie li affondo uña nave cón tutta la sua roba con molta disgratia di maniera che e venuto in poverta et desidera molto venire al servitio di · Vostra Eccellenza Illustrissima [78r:] nelle cose del mare et cón ogni sorte di cónditione. Io lo propongo ą · Vostra Eccellenza Illustrissima per quanto tocca al servitio di lei et nón a benifitio di Bernardo del quale mi fu detto tanto che se fussi la meṭą sarebbe huomo piu che ordinario," ASF, MdP 4898, 77v–78r. Francesco di Alessandro Nasi appears as assessed for "f. 500–f. 500" according to the MAP transcription of part of a list of Florentine taxpayers from 1563, MAP Doc ID 27208, ASF, MdP 616, Ins. 19, 346r, 1563.

195. MAP Person ID 15444, "Nasi, Bernardo." Cosimo I de' Medici in Florence to Bernardo Nasi in Livorno on May 19, 1572, MAP Doc ID 19673, ASF, MdP 238, 122.

196. For two brief and clear museum catalog accounts, see J. Paul Getty Museum's Galleria de'Lavori in Pietre Dure, accessed October 26, 2020, http://www.getty.edu/art/collection/artists/3545/galleria-de'lavori-in -pietre-dure-italian-active-1588-present/, and The Gilbert Collection: Pietre Dure at the Los Angeles County Museum of Art, accessed October 26, 2020, http://www.lacma.org/gilbert-collection-pietre-dure. The official website of the Opificio delle Pietre Dure, accessed October 26, 2020, http://www.opificiodellepietredure.it/, likewise traces its origins to Ferdinando I. On the Cappella dei Principi see the official site, accessed October 26, 2020, http://www.operamedicealaurenziana.org/il-complesso/le -cappelle-medicee/. See also Lucia Tongiorgi Tomasi and Gretchen A. Hirschauer, *The Flowering of Florence: Botanical Art for the Medici* (Burlington, VT: Lund Humphries, 2002), 59–61.

197. Ornella Casazza, "Ferdinando I and Florentine 'commesso,'" in *The Museo degli Argenti Collections and Collectors*, MIBAC, ed. Marilena Mosco and Ornella Casazza (Florence: Giunti, 2004), 87.

198. Casazza, "Ferdinando I," 87.

199. Cosimo Baroncelli in Antwerp to Belisario di Francesco Vinta in Florence, MAP Doc ID 8766, ASF, MdP 5157, 322. MAP transcription: "Essendo giunta qua la fama del superbo tempio che fa fare il P.rne Ser.mo [Ferdinando I de' Medici] per riporre le felici et honorate ceneri de' Serenissimi Gran Duchi suoi antecessori mi è venuto a trovare un mercante principale portoghese, e dice che ha un bellissimo pezzo di diaspro orientale di tutto paragone, e di tal grandezza da poterne fare una pila per tenere l'aquasanta, e voleva che io l'andassi a vedere in sua casa." The bracketed insertion is MAP's.

200. ASF, Miscellanea Medicea, 97, Ins. 89, 4.

201. "Carletti, Francesco," *DBI* 20 (1977).

202. Belisario di Francesco Vinta in Florence to Sallustio Tarugi in Madrid on December 16, 1608, MAP Doc ID 643, ASF, MdP 5052, 676. MAP transcription: "vuol Sua Alt.za [Ferdinando I] che si faccia ogni sforza di impetiarla loro, perché veramente vanno per rinvestire balasci in pietre per la cappella di S.Alt.a [Ferdinando I] et non in altro nè per altro. Et andaranno a Cambaia [Khambayat] che non debbe esser ne i dominii di cotesta Maestà [Felipe III], et la licenza ha da servir loro per solo passaggio." Bracketed text is MAP's. See also MAP Person ID 873, "Tarugi, Sallustio." On this episode, see also De Gubernatis, *Storia dei viaggiatori italiani*, 28.

203. MAP Person ID 670, "Pannocchieschi d'Elci, Orso"; Cosimo II de' Medici in Florence to Orso Pannocchieschi d'Elci in Madrid on August 27, 1610,

MAP Doc ID 2991, ASF, MdP 4943, 143; Francesco Bigazzi, "Pannocchieschi d'Elci, Orso Niccolò," *DBI* 80 (2014).

204. Hans Cools, Marika Keblusek, and Badeloch Noldus, eds., *Your Humble Servant: Agents in Early Modern Europe* (Hilversum, Neth.: Verloren, 2006). For the idea of agency as a function more than an occupation, see Marika Keblusek, "Introduction, Profiling the Early Modern Agent," in Cools et al., *Your Humble Servant*, 9.

205. Keblusek, "Introduction," 9–15.

206. Tomasi and Hirschauer, "Flowering of Florence," 38; Milanesi, *Filippo Sassetti*, 69; Sassetti, *Lettere dall'India*, Letter 4, 50n17; Cochrane, *Florence in the Forgotten Centuries*, 129. On Tuscany, botany, exotica, and collecting, see Cristina Bellorini, *The World of Plants in Renaissance Tuscany: Medicine and Botany* (Burlington, VT: Ashgate, 2016); Francisco Zamora Rodríguez, "Interest and Curiosity: American Products, Information, and Exotica in Tuscany," in *Global Goods and the Spanish Empire, 1492–1824: Circulation, Resistance and Diversity*, ed. Bethany Aram and Bartholomé Yun-Casalilla (New York: Palgrave Macmillan, 2014); William Eamon, *Science and the Secrets of Nature: Books of Secrets in Medieval and Early Modern Culture* (Princeton, NJ: Princeton University Press, 1994), 270. The classic account of the effort remains Paula Findlen, *Possessing Nature: Museums, Collecting, and Scientific Culture in Early Modern Italy* (Berkeley: University of California Press, 1996).

207. See Mackenzie Cooley, "Animal Empires: The Perfection of Nature between Europe and the Americas, 1492–1640," PhD diss., Stanford University, 2018, 356. Thanks to Mackenzie Cooley for permission to cite her dissertation. Bernardo di Lorenzo Canigiani in Madrid to Antonio Serguidi in Florence on December 6, 1582, MAP Doc ID 4263, ASF, MdP 1212, Ins. 3, 551; MAP Person ID 1027, "Serguidi, Antonio."

208. Bongianni di Piero (Fra) Gianfigliazzi in Madrid to Francesco I de' Medici in Florence on July 9, 1584, MAP Doc ID 16081, ASF MdP 5046, 56. On Gianfigliazzi's status as ambassador, see MAP Person ID 430, "Gianfigliazzi, Bongianni di Piero (Fra)."

209. Bongianni di Piero (Fra) Gianfigliazzi in Madrid to Francesco I de' Medici in Florence on May 29, 1584, MAP Doc ID 14532, ASF, MdP 5046, 49.

210. MAP Person ID 1028, "Santoyo, Sebastián de."

211. Bongianni di Piero (Fra) Gianfigliazzi in Madrid to Francesco I de' Medici in Florence on June 9, 1584, MAP Doc ID 14535, ASF, MdP 5046, 51; Bongianni di Piero (Fra) Gianfigliazzi in Madrid to Francesco I de' Medici in Florence on June 14, 1584, MAP Doc ID 16080, ASF, MdP 5046, 52.

212. Francesco I de' Medici in Florence to Bongianni di Piero (Fra) Gianfigliazzi in Madrid on July 19, 1584, MAP Doc ID 16149, ASF, MdP 5046,

352. MAP transcription: "il quale faremo seminare in molte maniere per provare se sarà posssibile di farlo nascere."

213. Bongianni di Piero (Fra) Gianfigliazzi in Madrid to Francesco I de' Medici in Florence on August 25, 1584, MAP Doc ID 14705, ASF, MdP 5046, 63. MAP transcription: "mi disse che volea scrivere a V. A. per supplicarla che gli facesse grazia del suo olio contro a veleno e di quello da stomaco, dell'acqua da petecchie e dello elisir." For another reference to Santoyo's efforts with the Moglis tree, see Pedro Luengo, "China in the European Baroque Culture: The Andalusian Role in Its Diffusion," *European Network for Baroque Cultural Heritage*, doi: 10.14615/enbach16, n. 42, which cites "AGI, INDIFERENTE, 1956, L. 2, F. 16r–17r."

214. Bellorini, *World of Plants*, 18–45; an image of one such box is reproduced as figure 1.3 (p. 22).

215. MAP Doc ID 4284, ASF, MdP 1212, Ins. 5, 821. MAP dates the document as "1580 (Unsure)" and in the "Date Notes" gives "c. 1580–1588." Happily, MAP provides a very extensive transcription of the inventory, which is written in Spanish. The quoted section comes from "una caja blanca pequeña sobre cubierta de papel en que van tres piedras beçares de las de la Yndia de Portugal metidas las dos en su guarniçion de oro de feligran y la otra sin guarniçion metida en una cajilla de madera; mas van en la dicha cajilla çinco piedras beçares de las de la Yndia de Castilla grandes y quatro o cinco pequeñas." The inventory includes yet further bezoars.

216. Ferdinando I de' Medici in Florence to Vincenzo di Andrea Alamanni in Madrid on September 8, 1588, MAP Doc ID 4298, ASF, MdP 5042. MAP transcription: "Di Portogallo vorremmo una pianta dell'albero che fa il sangue di drago che quivi si trova, però vedrete che con l'aiuto d'alcuno costì et con l'opera di quelli di Lisbona ci sia provista et mandata con ogni buona cura et diligenza; et che con essa ci venghino ancora semi, cipolle et piante di tutte le sorte che più notabili mandi l'India di Portogallo et quella di Spagna et che perciò alcuno supplisca alla spesa che bisognasse, perchè si rimborsarà subito." See also MAP Person ID 133, "Alamanni, Vincenzo di Andrea."

217. Vincenzo di Andrea Alamanni in Madrid to Ferdinando I de' Medici in Florence on February 4, 1589, MAP Doc ID 8585, ASF, MdP 4919, 723. MAP transcription: "Giulio Nesi m'ha mandato quei semi dell'arbor che fa il sangue di drago in certe coccole che saranno con questa, le quali, non 'sendo certo se nasceranno, dice che procurerà d'haverne due piante dalla Terzera et le manderà per il primo commodo."

218. Peter Holmes, "Clifford, George, third earl of Cumberland," *Oxford Dictionary of National Biography*.

219. Sassetti, *Lettere dall'India*, Letter 5, 57–58.

220. Sassetti, *Lettere dall'India*, Letter 5, 58.

221. Sassetti, *Lettere dall'India*, Letter 5, 57.

222.  Sassetti, *Lettere dall'India*, Letter 4, 48–49.

223.  Milanesi, *Filippo Sassetti*, 42–46.

224.  Filippo Sassetti in Cochin on February 11, 1585, to Grand Duke Francesco I de' Medici in Florence (Sassetti, *Lettere dall'India*, Letter 14, 111). On colonial bioprospecting, see Schiebinger, *Plants and Empire: Colonial Bioprospecting in the Atlantic World* (Cambridge, MA: Harvard University Press, 2004).

225.  Sassetti, *Lettere dall'India*, Letter 14, 112.

226.  Sassetti, *Lettere dall'India*, Letter 21, 160–161 and 161n2. See Sassetti, *Lettere dall'India*, Nota biografica, 21, Letter 1, 29n1, and Letter 3, 42n1, for the friendship between Sassetti and Francesco Valori and the relationship between the Valori. See also MAP Person ID 2309, "Valori, Bartolomeo di Filippo (Baccio)." In Dei's edition, Sassetti's letters to Francesco and Baccio Valori are his first and third from India. Dottore Baccio Valori was a knight of the Order of Santo Stefano and Florentine senator and would become a secret counsellor to Ferdinando I, and so he was firmly embedded in the Medici regime.

227.  Sassetti, *Lettere dall'India*, Letter 14, 111.

228.  For later developments, see Mark Harrison, *Climates and Constitutions: Health, Race, Environment and British Imperialism in India, 1600–1850* (New Delhi: Oxford University Press, 2002). On natural history, discovery, and the Iberian empires, see Antonio Barrera-Osorio, *Experiencing Nature: The Spanish American Empire and the Early Scientific Revolution* (Austin: University of Texas Press, 2006); Pamela H. Smith and Paula Findlen, eds., *Merchants and Marvels: Commerce, Science, and Art in Early Modern Europe* (New York: Routledge, 2002); Londa Schiebinger and Claudia Swan, eds., *Colonial Botany: Science, Commerce, and Politics in the Early Modern World* (Philadelphia: University of Pennsylvania Press, 2005); Antonello Gerbi, *Nature in the New World: From Christopher Columbus to Gonzalo Fernández de Oviedo*, trans. Jeremy Moyle (Pittsburgh, PA: University of Pittsburgh Press, 2010), 154 (Sassetti) and 289 (Carletti); Ivo Kamps and Jyotsna G. Singh, eds., *Travel Knowledge: European "Discoveries" in the Early Modern Period* (New York: Palgrave, 2001).

229.  Sassetti, *Lettere dall'India*, Letter 22, 175, 175n34, 177, and 177n41. On Mattioli, see Sassetti, *Lettere dall'India*, 175n34, and Cesare Preti, "Mattioli, Pietro Andrea," *DBI* 72 (2008). On Garcia de Orta, see Palmira Fontes da Costa, ed., *Medicine, Trade and Empire*; Vasco Resende, "Garcia de Orta, Garcia d'Orta," in *Christian-Muslim Relations 1500–1900*, ed. David Thomas, accessed July 31, 2018, http://dx.doi.org/10.1163/2451-9537 _cmrii_COM_27764, and C. R. Boxer, *Two Pioneers of Tropical Medicine: Garcia d'Orta and Nicolás Monardes* (London: Wellcome Historical Medical Library, 1963). For informative sketch biographical pages on Acosta, Mattioli, and Orta, see Rice University's Galileo Project, accessed October 26,

2020, http://galileo.rice.edu/Catalog/NewFiles/acosta_cri.html; http://galileo.rice.edu/Catalog/NewFiles/mattioli.html; and http://galileo.rice.edu/Catalog/NewFiles/orta.html. On Davanzati, see Sassetti, *Lettere dall'India*, Letter 21, 161n4.

230. Sassetti, *Lettere dall'India*, Letter, 22, 179–180 and 180n52.

231. For one of Sassetti's botanical reports, see Sassetti, *Lettere dall'India*, Letter 4, 48–49. For Sassetti's discussion of the connection between Greek, Latin, and Sanskrit, see Sassetti, *Lettere dall'India*, Letter, 22, 179–180 and 180n52. For grudging recognition of Sassetti's insight, see Jarl Charpentier, "The Original Home of the Indo-Europeans: Two Lectures Delivered at the School of Oriental Studies, London, on 10th and 17th June, 1925," *Bulletin of the School of Oriental Studies, University of London* 4, no.1 (1926): 149. For Sassetti's connection with Mercator, see Sassetti, *Lettere dall'India*, Letter 19, 147n17 and Letter 31, 239n7, and for his possible connection with Ortelius, see Sassetti, *Lettere dall'India*, Letter 19, 147n18. See also Milanesi, *Filippo Sassetti*, 2. For more on Sassetti in India, see Rubiés, *Travel and Ethnology*, 381–383, and Subrahmanyam, *Explorations in Connected History: Mughals and Franks*, 83.

232. Sassetti, *Lettere dall'India*, Letter 9, 82; Sassetti, *Lettere dall'India*, Letter 21, 161.

233. Sassetti, *Lettere dall'India*, Letter 21, 161.

234. Sassetti, *Lettere dall'India*, Letter 22, 179 and 179n50. His editor Dei suggests that Sassetti misidentified the name of the book, the word for dictionary, with the name of the author. According to Mario Rossi, *Un letterato e mercante fiorentino del secolo XVI: Filippo Sassetti* (Città di Castello: S. Lapi, 1899), 147 and 147nn1 and 2, Niganto may be identified with "*Dhanvantaryo nigant.uh* o *Dizionario di Dhavantari*," apparently a part of the Ayurvedic tradition.

235. Sassetti, *Lettere edite e inedite*, 389–390. Sassetti, *Lettere dall'India*, Letter 27, 218–220, does not reproduce the Discourse on Cinnamom, so I refer to the older Marcucci edition, as Dei does (Letter 21, 163n9, and Letter 27, 219n8).

236. Since the two terms used to describe cinnamon—*cannella* and *cinnamomo*—both translate to cinnamon in English, I give them in the original. Sassetti, *Lettere edite e inedite*, 384–385. The "Discorso sopra il Cinnamomo" (384–398) was included in the letter to Baccio Valori (382–384). For "cannella," Florio gives "a little cane, reede or pipe. Also a flute or recorder. Also a tap or spiggot. Also the ame-bone a man." Also Florio defines "cinamómo" as "the spice Cinamond," "Cinamomíno" as "the oyle of Cinamond," and "cinnamológo" as "a bird that buildeth her nest of Cynamond twigges."

237. Sassetti, *Lettere edite e inedite*, 393–394.

238. Sassetti, *Lettere dall'India*, Letter 27, 219.

239. Sassetti, *Lettere dall'India*, Letter 31, 238–239.

240. See Amy Butler Greenfield, *A Perfect Red: Empire, Espionage, and the Quest for the Color of Desire* (New York: HarperCollins, 2005), for a similar dynamic around the slow diffusion of information about cochineal.

241. Farina, "Nascita della Tipografia Medicea," 50.

242. Bellorini, *World of Plants*, 47; Giuseppe Olmi, "La rivoluzione scientifica: i domini della conoscenza. Collezionismo e viaggi scientifici," in *Storia della Scienza* (2002), online ed., accessed December 4, 2020 https://www .treccani.it/enciclopedia/la-rivoluzione-scientifica-i-domini-della-cono scenza-collezionismo-e-viaggi-scientifici_%28Storia-della-Scienza%29/. For "semplicista," see the MAP synopsis of Giovanni Francesco Ripa in Florence to Pietro di Francesco Usimbardi in Rome on February 16, 1586, MAP Doc ID 15109, ASF, MdP 1234a, Ins. 2.

243. Carletti, *My Voyage*, 108–109.

244. Carletti, *My Voyage*, 170–171, 170n, and 171n.

245. Carletti, *My Voyage*, 5 (*pagros*); 8 (civet cats and apes / mandril cats / *bugios*); 17–18 (flying fish); 18 (dorados, albacoras, bonitos); and 19 (dolphins).

246. Carletti, *My Voyage*, 5–6 (plantains and coconuts); 21 and 21n (cassava).

247. Carletti, *My Voyage*, 37 (potatoes), 44 (cucha), 45–46 and 46n (coca and llamas). On Carletti and the llamas, see Cooley, "Animal Empires," 265–266.

248. Carletti, *My Voyage*, 51–55. The traditional claim that Carletti was the first to introduce chocolate to Italy is rebutted by Sophie D. and Michael D. Coe, *The True History of Chocolate*, 2nd ed. (New York: Thames and Hudson, 2007), 139–140 and 145–146. For what must have been one of the origins of this story, see Galluzzi's account, Riguccio Galluzzi, *Storia del Granducato di Toscana*, new ed., 11 vols. (Florence: Leonardo Marchini, 1822), vol. 6, book 5, chapter 13, 130, year 1609 (as indicated in the printed marginal note).

249. Carletti, *My Voyage*, 53–54.

250. Marcy Norton, *Sacred Gifts, Profane Pleasures: A History of Tobacco and Chocolate in the Atlantic World* (Ithaca, NY: Cornell University Press, 2008), 161. On the matter of diffusion, this follows Irene Fattacciu, "The Resilience and Boomerang Effect of Chocolate: A Product's Globalization and Commodification," in Aram and Yun-Casalilla, *Global Goods*, 257.

251. Biblioteca Angelica, ms. 1331, 49r, "Giardino delle stalle." Carletti, *My Voyage*, 63–64 and 63n.

252. Biblioteca Angelica, ms. 1331 43v, "Il seme di quest'Albero è rinchiuso in una foglia in figura d.' Drago con tutte le sue parte dissegnatevi dalla natura maestrevolmente, cosa d'ammiratione e degna d'esser vista." Carletti, *My Voyage*, 55–56. On the New World dragon blood tree, Ezquahuitl, see Mackenzie Cooley, "Southern Italy and the New World in the Age of Encounters," in *The New World in Early Modern Italy, 1492–1750*, ed.

Lia Markey and Elizabeth Horodowich (New York: Cambridge University Press, 2017), 169, 171, 182n61, 184, and 187.

253. Carletti, *My Voyage*, 64 and 64n. On cochineal, see Greenfield, *Perfect Red*; Carlos Marichal, "Mexican Cochineal and the European Demand for American Dyes, 1550-1850," in *From Silver to Cocaine: Latin American Commodity Chains and the Building of the World Economy, 1500–2000*, ed. Steven Topik, Carlos Marichal, and Zephyr Frank (Durham, NC: Duke University Press, 2006), 76–92.

254. Carletti, *My Voyage*, 64 and 64n.

255. Biblioteca Angelica, ms. 1331, 50v; Carletti, *My Voyage*, 65–66 and 66n.

256. Biblioteca Angelica, ms. 1331, 49r, "Pianta veramente degna d'essere commendata da altri, che da miei semplici ragionamenti." Carletti, *My Voyage*, 64.

257. Biblioteca Angelica, ms. 1331, 50r, "nulla dimeno non ci,è piànta, ch'io credessi dover essere piu grata a vedersi in questi paesi, che questa se si potesse condurre." Carletti, *My Voyage*, 65.

258. Goldthwaite, *Economy of Renaissance Florence*, 124, for Simón Ruiz's business agent in Florence trading in New Spanish cochineal.

259. Bongianni di Piero (Fra) Gianfigliazzi in Madrid to Francesco I de' Medici in Florence on November 15, 1586, MAP Doc ID 16141, ASF, MdP 5046, 228, perhaps December 19, 1598, MAP Doc ID 22768, ASF, MdP 5037, 458, and from Antwerp to Florence on August 12, 1605, MAP Doc ID 23066, ASF, MdP 4256, 354.

260. Bernardo di Bartolomeo (il Baroncello) Baroncelli in Livorno to Francesco I de' Medici in Tuscany on February 11, 1571 (MAP adjusted from 1570), MAP Doc ID 18759, ASF, MdP 557, 57, and from Livorno, March 1577, MAP Doc ID 12736, ASF, MdP 695, 94.

261. Goldthwaite, *Economy of Renaissance Florence*, 160–161.

262. Greenfield, *Perfect Red*, 77–78. See also Carlos Marichal, "Mexican Cochineal and European Demand for a Luxury Dye, 1550-1850," in Aram and Yun-Casalilla, *Global Goods*, 204–207.

263. The seminal work is Alfred Crosby, *The Columbian Exchange: Biological and Cultural Consequences of 1492* (Westport, CT: Greenwood, 1972). See also Alfred W. Crosby, *Ecological Imperialism: The Biological Expansion of Europe, 900–1900*, 2nd ed. (New York: Cambridge University Press, 2004); Mann, *1493*; Richard H. Grove, *Green Imperialism: Colonial Expansion, Tropical Island Edens and the Origins of Environmentalism, 1600–1860* (New York: Cambridge University Press, 1996).

264. Carletti, *My Voyage*, 52–54 (cacao and tobacco), and 61–66 (maize, pepper, agave, and *nopales*).

265. Carletti, *My Voyage*, 80–81 (bananas and *giaca* (breadfruit)), 87–88, 87n and 216–217 (betel and areca).

266. Carletti, *My Voyage*, 99–102, 100n, and 175 (tea); 99–100 and 169 (rice wine); 108–109 (Japanese citrus and melons); 110 (*misol* sauce); and 170–171 and 170n (Chinese oranges, mangoes, and lychee).

267. Carletti, *My Voyage*, 187–190, 187n, 188n, 189n (durians, pineapples, rose apples, and mangosteen); and 190–192 and 204 (pepper, cloves, nutmeg, and mace).

268. Carletti, *My Voyage*, 197 (cinnamon), 224–225 (coconuts and Maldive coconuts), and 225–226 ("sad flowers").

269. Sassetti, *Lettere dall'India*, Letter 6, 68–69. On Piero Spina, see Sassetti, *Lettere edite e inedite*, 266.

270. "L'ananas mi pare a me la piú gustosa frutta che ci sia," Sassetti, *Lettere dall'India*, Letter 4, 48–49.

271. Tomasi and Hirschauer, "Flowering of Florence," 40; MAP Person ID 567, "Ligozzi, Iacopo di Giovanni."

272. Carletti, *My Voyage*, 188–189 and 188n.

## 5. THE SHADOW CAPITAL

1. Céline Dauverd, *Imperial Ambition in the Early Modern Mediterranean: Genoese Merchants and the Spanish Crown* (New York: Cambridge University Press, 2015), 68–71.

2. Bruno Latour, *Science in Action: How to Follow Scientists and Engineers through Society* (Cambridge, MA: Harvard University Press, 1987), 215–257.

3. The collections are now separated into specialist institutions: La Specola (anatomy and natural history); Museo Galileo (science, especially instruments); Tesoro dei Granduchi (rare and exquisite objects; previously called the Museo degli Argenti); Museo delle Porcellane (porcelains); and so forth. See Paula Findlen, *Possessing Nature: Museums, Collecting, and Scientific Culture in Early Modern Italy* (Berkeley: University of California Press, 1996); Findlen and Pamela Smith, eds., *Merchants and Marvels: Commerce, Science and Art in Early Modern Europe* (New York: Routledge, 2002); Findlen, "The Museum: Its Classical Etymology and Renaissance Genealogy," *Journal of the History of Collections* 1, no. 1 (1989): 59–78; Findlen, ed., *Early Modern Things: Objects and Their Histories, 1500–1800* (New York: Routledge, 2013).

4. For the World Digital Library's high-quality digitization of the text, accessed October 26, 2020, see https://www.wdl.org/en/item/10096/. See also Monica Fintoni, Andrea Paleotti, and Paola Vannucchi, eds., *The World of the Aztecs: In the Florentine Codex*, trans. Jeremy Carden and Andrea Paoletti (Florence: Mandragora, 2007).

5. Cristina Bellorini, *The World of Plants in Renaissance Tuscany: Medicine and Botany* (Burlington, VT: Ashgate, 2016), 33–35, esp. figure 1.6. The classic

work is Luciano Berti, *Il principe dello studiolo: Francesco I dei Medici e la fine del Rinascimento fiorentino* (Pistoia, It.: Artout Maschietto, 2002).

6. Findlen, *Possessing Nature*, remains the classic text. Aldrovandi's correspondence with Francesco I in the spring of 1586—MAP Doc IDs: 1414, 16304, and 16319—will be discussed further on. See also Bellorini, *World of Plants*, 45–46; Giuseppe Montalenti, "Aldrovandi, Ulisse," *DBI* 2 (1960). Galileo also held a life appointment in mathematics at the University of Pisa without teaching responsibilities (Ugo Baldini, "Galilei, Galileo," *DBI* 51 [1998]); Mario Biagioli, *Galileo Courtier: The Practice of Science in the Culture of Absolutism* (Chicago: University of Chicago Press, 1994), 104.

7. Sara Fani and Margherita Farina, eds., *Le vie delle lettere: La Tipografia Medicea tra Roma e l'Oriente* (Florence: Mandragora, 2012); Kathleen M. Comerford, *Jesuit Foundations and Medici Power, 1532–1621* (Boston: Brill, 2017).

8. Lia Markey, *Imagining the Americas in Medici Florence* (University Park: Pennsylvania State University Press, 2016); Detlef Heikamp, *Mexico and the Medici* (Florence: Edam, 1972).

9. Lucia Tongiorgi Tomasi and Gretchen A. Hirschauer, *The Flowering of Florence: Botanical Art for the Medici* (Burlington, VT: Lund Humphries, 2002); Tomasi, "The Flowering of Florence: Botanical Art for the Medici," in Tomasi and Hirschauer, *The Flowering of Florence*, 31–32 and 38; Findlen, *Possessing Nature*, 256–261. Franco Aurelio Meschini, "Ghini, Luca," *DBI* 53 (2000). Paula Findlen, "Natural History," in Katharine Park and Lorraine Daston, eds. *The Cambridge History of Science, Volume 3: Early Modern Science*, 8 vols. (New York: Cambridge University Press, 2006), 435–468.

10. Marzio di Girolamo Marzi Medici, Bishop of Marsico in Poggio a Caiano to Pier Francesco Riccio in Florence on February 24, 1543, MAP Doc ID 5977, ASF, MdP 1170, 324r; Tomasi, "Flowering of Florence," 31 and 108n38; the note specifies that the book was the 1544 Venice edition. The *Commentaries* were on Dioscorides's *De materia medica*. Bellorini, *World of Plants*, 25 (figure 1.4) reproduces a page of Mattioli's *Discorsi* with Cosimo's marginal annotations. See also Bellorini, *World of Plants*, 40–41, on Cosimo's knowledge. See also Cesare Preti, "Mattioli, Pietro Andrea," *DBI* 72 (2008); Fabrizio Cortesi, "Mattioli, Pierandrea," *Enciclopedia Italiana* (1934), accessed July 15, 2020, http://www.treccani.it/enciclopedia/pierandrea-mattioli_%28Enciclopedia-Italiana%29/.

11. Tomasi, "Flowering of Florence," 32.

12. Vanna Arrighi, "Eleonora de Toledo, duchessa di Firenze," *DBI* 42 (1993). On the villa, husbandry, breeding, and the developing sciences of nature, see Mackenzie Cooley, "Animal Empires: The Perfection of Nature between Europe and the Americas, 1492-1640," PhD diss., Stanford University, 2018, 11-12, 145-146, 157-162, 212-213, 229, 347-348, and 353-368.

See also Cooley's extensive footnote—p. 11 n. 30—on the historiography of the villa.

13. Isabella Lapi Ballerini, *The Medici Villas: Complete Guide*, trans. Michael Sullivan and Eleonor Daunt, rev. ed. (Florence: Giunti, 2010), 30 and 32.

14. Tomasi, "Flowering of Florence," 32–33; Alessandra Giannotti, "Pericoli, Niccolò, detto il Tribolo," *DBI* 82 (2015); Isa Belli Barsali, "Ammannati, Bartolomeo," *DBI* 2 (1960); Ida Maria Botto, "Buontalenti, Bernardo," *DBI* 15 (1972).

15. Bellorini, *World of Plants*, 44–45; MAP Person ID 1813, "Fortuna, Simone."

16. Lapi Ballerini, *Medici Villas*, 116.

17. Bellorini, *World of Plants*, 41. Tomasi, "Flowering of Florence," 32.

18. Bellorini, *World of Plants*, 46–47.

19. The speculation about distance is mine. On the villas: Bellorini, *World of Plants*, 47.

20. Bellorini, *World of Plants*, 49.

21. Lapi Ballerini, *Medici Villas*.

22. Eugenio Albèri, ed., *Relazioni degli Ambasciatori Veneti al Senato*, 15 vols. in 3 series (Florence: Fiorentina, 1839–1863), series 2, vol. 1, "Relazione di Firenze del clarissimo Marco Foscari tornato ambasciatore da quella repubblica l'anno 1527," 22–23.

23. On the history of the villa, see the Tuscan Region website, accessed October 26, 2020, http://www.regione.toscana.it/en/-/villa-capponi. For a brief family history of the villa in the twentieth century by Nicholas Clifford, a historian of China, whose family owned it for many years, see "A Backwards Glance at Villa Capponi," *The Florentine*, July 26, 2006 (Lifestyle section), http://www.theflorentine.net/lifestyle/2006/07/a-backwards -glance-at-villa-capponi/. The Capponi have had many properties in Florence. Their downtown palazzo, directly across the Arno from the Uffizi, houses the Stanford Center in Florence and a further Capponi property by Sesto Fiorentino, acquired in the eighteenth century, has recently been transformed into a series of expensive apartments; it is also called Villa Capponi. See the Villa Capponi website, accessed October 26, 2020, http://www.villa-capponi.com/history/, or http://www.villa-capponi .com/; or Miles Thompson, "Tuscany's Storied Villa Capponi Is Transformed into Apartments," at *The Spaces* website, accessed October 26, 2020, https://thespaces.com/2017/08/07/tuscanys-storied-villa-capponi -transformed-apartments/.

24. Lapi Ballerini, *Medici Villas*, 38.

25. Claudia Lazzaro, *The Italian Renaissance Garden: From the Conventions of Planting, Design, and Ornament to the Grand Gardens of Sixteenth-Century Italy* (New Haven, CT: Yale University Press, 1990); Mariachiara Pozzana, *The Gardens of Florence and Tuscany: A Complete Guide* (Florence: Giunti, 2011).

26. Bellorini, *World of Plants*, 44. The Ruccellai Gardens—the Orti Orcellari—were famously the setting for Machiavelli's dialogue, *The Art of War*: Niccolò Machiavelli, *The Art of War*, trans. and ed. Christopher Lynch (Chicago: University of Chicago Press, 2005), I.8, 8, and n5.

27. Cristiano Pagni in Pisa to Pier Francesco Riccio in Florence on May 5, 1548, MAP Doc ID 23901, ASF, MdP 1170a, 720r; MAP Person ID 905, "Pagni, Cristiano"; MAP Person ID 197, "Riccio, Pier Francesco."

28. UNESCO claims primacy for Padua in 1545—see "Botanical Garden (Orto Botanico), Padua" at the UNESCO website, accessed October 26, 2020, https://whc.unesco.org/en/list/824—but Pisa's garden antedates that (Tomasi, "Flowering of Florence," 32). On the origins of botanical gardens and Pisa's in particular, see Findlen, *Possessing Nature*, 256-261. See also Brian W. Ogilvie, *The Science of Describing: Natural History in Renaissance Europe* (Chicago: University of Chicago Press, 2006).

29. Tomasi, "Flowering of Florence," 42.

30. Tomasi, "Flowering of Florence," 38; Bellorini, *World of Plants*, 47; Paula Findlen, "Inventing Nature: Commerce, Art, and Science in the Early Modern Cabinet of Curiosities," in Smith and Findlen, *Merchants and Marvels*, 304.

31. Tomasi, "Flowering of Florence," 52.

32. Augusto (da Castiglione) Tizio in Seville to Pietro di Francesco Usimbardi in Rome on November 9, 1584, MAP Doc ID 15219, ASF, MdP 1234a, Ins. 5; Augusto (da Castiglione) Tizio in Madrid to Pietro di Francesco Usimbardi in Rome on January 13, 1585, MAP Doc ID 15651, ASF, MdP 5113, Ins. 1, 339; MAP Person ID 944, "Tizio, Augusto (da Castiglione)"; MAP Person ID 469, "Usimbardi, Pietro di Francesco." Usimbardi would eventually become bishop of Arezzo and of Colle Val d'Elsa and first secretary of state to Ferdinando I.

33. Niccolò Gaddi in Florence to Pietro di Francesco Usimbardi in Rome on March 9, 1585, MAP Doc ID 15063, ASF, MdP 1234a, Ins. 1. MAP transcription: "Ma nel foglio chela mi manda, vi sono molte piante che non solo non ne habbiamo qui, ma manco credo che habbino visto Italia, pure io farò ogni diligentia di haverne il più che potrò." All translations are mine unless otherwise indicated.

34. Francisco Zamora Rodríguez, "Interest and Curiosity: American Products, Information, and Exotica in Tuscany," in *Global Goods and the Spanish Empire, 1492–1824: Circulation, Resistance and Diversity*, ed. Bethany Aram and Bartholomé Yun-Casalilla (New York: Palgrave Macmillan, 2014), 187.

35. Bellorini, *World of Plants*, 45. Bellorini cites and quotes extensively from MAP Doc ID 1414, ASF, MdP 269, 18, a letter from Francesco I de' Medici in Florence to Ulisse Aldrovandi in Bologna on April 7, 1586. She then quotes from the next letter, MAP Doc ID 16304, ASF, MdP 269, 29, from

Francesco I de' Medici in Florence to Ulisse Aldrovandi in Bologna on April 24, 1586.

36. Francesco I de' Medici in Florence to Ulisse Aldrovandi in Bologna on May 29, 1586, MAP Doc ID 16319, ASF, MdP 269, 64. MAP transcription: "Ho ricevuto li semi con le note, et informationi venute con essi, et potete credere, che mi siano stati carissimi così per la rarità, et qualità loro, come per venirmi da voi, che io tanto amo."

37. Bellorini, *World of Plants*, 45.

38. Francesco I de' Medici in Florence to Guglielmo I Gonzaga in Mantua on March 22, 1586, MAP Doc ID 16289, ASF, MdP 269, 9. Further details are provided in the reply, which sends reciprocal gifts: Guglielmo I Gonzaga in Goito, Mantua, to Francesco I de' Medici in Florence on April 11, 1586, MAP Doc ID 4518, ASF, MdP 2939. See also MAP Person ID 826, "Gonzaga, Guglielmo I."

39. Bellorini, *World of Plants*, 20-22.

40. MAP Doc ID 912, ASF, MdP 5080, 313 (Madrid, August 15, 1600). MAP transcription: "due cassette d'ebano con medicinali."

41. On the relationship among animals, the history of science, Renaissance Italy, and the Spanish Empire, see Cooley, "Animal Empires."

42. Silvio A. Bedini, *The Pope's Elephant* (Nashville, TN: J. S. Sanders, 1998); Roger Crowley, *Conquerors: How Portugal Forged the First Global Empire* (New York: Random House, 2015), 283.

43. Bedini, *Pope's Elephant*, chapter 5, "The Ill-Fated Rhinoceros," 111-136. See p. 122 for Dürer's representation and 128-129 for the storm. See also Crowley, *Conquerors*, 282-283.

44. Angelica Groom, *Exotic Animals in the Art and Culture of the Medici Court in Florence* (Leiden, Neth.: Brill, 2018), was published on 10/22/2018, several months after this section was written. Appendix I, "*Medici Archive Project* Database of Documents Relating to 'Exotic and Unusual' Animals" (pp. 267-278), offers an excellent color-coded table summarizing the relevant MAP entries. This chapter independently uses these same entries as key sources. For Groom's note on the Medici Archive Project as a source, see p. 38n6.

45. *Montaigne's Travel Journal*, trans. Donald M. Frame (San Francisco: North Point, 1983), 65.

46. See Cooley, "Animal Empires," chapter 1, 30-90, and chapter 2, 91-140.

47. *Montaigne's Travel Journal*, 68.

48. Agnolo di Matteo Niccolini in Rome to Cosimo I de' Medici on February 5, 1539, MAP Doc ID 19535, ASF, MdP 3261, 219.

49. Paolo di Agnolo del Bufalo to Cosimo I de' Medici, perhaps in 1557, MAP Doc ID 16876, ASF, MdP 465, 445.

50. Rocco Galletti in Florence to Francesco I de' Medici in Florence on December 13, 1572, MAP Doc ID 22122, ASF, MdP 582, 60; Marco III Pio di

Savoia in Brussels to Belisario di Francesco Vinta in Florence on October 28, 1591, MAP Doc ID 28902, ASF, MdP 4253, 170r; MAP Person ID 15319, "Pio di Savoia, Marco III." On Icelandic gyrfalcons as diplomatic gifts of Danish kings, see Sigurður Ægisson, *Icelandic Trade with Gyrfalcons: From Medieval Times to the Modern Era* (Siglufjörður, Iceland: Sigurður Ægisson, 2015), 10.

51. Cristiano Pagni in Poggio a Caiano to Pier Francesco Riccio in Florence on July 29, 1547, MAP Doc ID 6361, ASF, MdP 1170a, 690r.

52. Just from October to December 1547, see, for example, Vincenzo Ferrini in Pisa to Pier Francesco Riccio in Florence on October 28, 1547, MAP Doc ID 8254, ASF, MdP 1173, 783r; Vincenzo Ferrini in Pisa to Pier Francesco Riccio in Florence on November 1, 1547, MAP Doc ID 8262, ASF, MdP 1173, 795r; Francesco di Niccolò de' Medici in Pisa to Pier Francesco Riccio in Florence, perhaps on December 8, 1547, MAP Doc ID 2505, ASF, MdP 1173, 915r; Francesco di Niccolò de' Medici in Pisa to Pier Francesco Riccio in Florence on December 19, 1547, MAP Doc ID 8343, ASF, MdP 1173, 947r.

53. Tommaso di Iacopo de' Medici at Poggio a Caiano to Pier Francesco Riccio in Florence on September 14, 1551, MAP Doc ID 3205, ASF, MdP 1176, 972r. The MAP synopsis identifies the giver from later correspondence. See also Averardo di Antonio Serristori in Rome to Pier Francesco Riccio in Florence on October 24, 1551, MAP Doc ID 3221, ASF, MdP 1176, 1021r; MAP Person ID 1640, "Ciocchi del Monte, Giovanni Maria (Julius III)"; MAP Person ID 1725, "Ciocchi del Monte, Baldovino."

54. Diego (el Africano) Fernández de Córdoba in Madrid to Francesco I de' Medici in Florence on November 29, 1576, MAP Doc ID 17354, ASF MdP 693, 101; MAP Person ID 640, "Fernández de Córdoba, Diego (el Africano)"; MAP Person ID 1285, "Alvarez de Toledo, Antonio"; Bartolomeo di Piero (Baccio) Orlandini in Madrid to Francesco I de' Medici in Florence on November 10, 1576, MAP Doc ID 14222, ASF, MdP 4906, 144.

55. Ferdinando I in Pisa to Augusto (da Castiglione) Tizio in Seville on March 5, 1592, MAP Doc ID 712, ASF, MdP 282, 126. Ferdinando I de' Medici in Florence to Giulio Brunacci in Cádiz on April 30, 1592, MAP Doc ID 16739, ASF, MdP 282, 135. MAP transcription: "^un^ nuovo lavoro di cristalli concerto nostro secreto," MAP Person ID 543, "Castro Osorio, Rodrigo de (Cardinale)."

56. "Sono stato aspettať piu giorni per che il sig.ʳ Dò[n] Antonio mi facci cò[n] segniare los, Passeros, dell Indie. quali nel presentarli la lettera di Vostra Eccellenza Illustrissima mi disse manderebbe a procaviarli, con quelli maggior presteiza che fussi possibile. ma perche non li debbe havere. in ordine non potro avanti la mia partita inviarli a Vostra Eccellenza Illustrissima ma lasciare questo negotio a Grazes, che quanto puo lo solleciti, et nella medesima maniera l'invij che, io havevo di commissione," ASF, MdP 4897, 118–19

(quotation in the endnote: 118v); Garces from Madrid on June 13, 1565 to the Prince of Florence and Siena, ASF, MdP, 4897, 122–23. "Los pajaros delas Indias solicito al signor don Antonio dize ha scrito por ellos ẏ los va procurando. y q responderia alas cartas de Vostra ex" (122v). For Garces's status, *Archivio Medicio*, vol. 3, 1, v–362, 739–748. "4897. 4. Spain: Letters from Garces, secretary of Cavalier de Nobili Ambassador to the Catholic Court from the year 1564 up until the year 1565. 4898" (my translation).

57. Francesco I de' Medici in Florence to Leonardo di Antonio de' Nobili in Madrid on April 1, 1567, MAP Doc ID 14311, ASF, MdP 4901. MAP transcription: "Procurate di trovarci qualche altri di questi uccelli et riuscendovi il poterli havere inviateceli."

58. Leonardo di Antonio de' Nobili in Madrid to Cosimo I de' Medici in Florence on May 5, 1568, MAP Doc ID 14380, ASF, MdP 4902, Ins. 1, 27.

59. Francesco I de' Medici in Florence to Leonardo di Antonio de' Nobili in Madrid on August 14, 1570, MAP Doc ID 14336, ASF, MdP 4901. MAP transcription: "Vedete se fusse possibile di provederci, o uccellini dell'Indie o sparvieri come potrete trovare, et inviateci subito."

60. Antonio Serguidi in Florence to Leonardo di Antonio de' Nobili in Madrid on August 28, 1570, MAP Doc ID 14345, ASF, MdP 4901; MAP Person ID 1027, "Serguidi, Antonio."

61. The MAP synopsis suggests turkeys are probable. Ugolino Grifoni in Pisa to Johanna von Habsburg-de' Medici in Florence on January 9, 1575, MAP Doc ID 3499, ASF, MdP 5923, 215. MAP transcription: "le mando dua galli d'India"; MAP Person ID 404, "Habsburg-de' Medici, Johanna von." The Archivio di Stato di Firenze provides a brief and very informative family history: Alida Caramagno, "Grifoni," August 30, 2006, first version, accessed October 26, 2020, http://www.archiviodistato.firenze .it/siasfi/cgi-bin/RSOLSearchSiasfi.pl?_op=printsprod&id=FIDD00010 5&_cobj=yes&_language=eng&_selectbycompilationdate=. See also MAP Person ID 512, "Grifoni, Ugolino."

62. Lia Markey, *Imagining the Americas*, 16–18 and 105–106. The tapestry is reproduced as figure 5 on pages 16 and 18. The fresco detail is figure 66 on page 106.

63. Francesco Capponi in Alexandria, Egypt, to Pier Francesco Riccio in Florence, June 15, 1547, MAP Doc ID 2486, ASF, MdP 1173, Ins. 5, 228; MAP Person ID 580, "Capponi, Francesco."

64. Luigi Dovara in Livorno to Francesco I de' Medici in Florence on July 10, 1565, MAP Doc ID 21513, ASF, MdP 516a, 681.

65. MAP Doc ID 16969, ASF, MdP, 746, 205, April 11, 1581. MAP transcription: "Portata della saettia nominata Santa Anna padrone Antonio Ribau di Marsilia carico in Barberia."

66. Mehmet (Pasha) in Algiers to Ferdinando I de' Medici in Florence on (perhaps) October 20, 1586, MAP Doc ID 26410, ASF, MdP 4279, 36. MAP

transcription: "Giacobo Brangia scrivano del nostro capitano Arnaot Memi bei, mando Geronimo Salvino polsano et Sebastiano de Paula pisano sudditi di Sua Altezza Serenissima con doi cavalli et doi leoni et uno struzzo parimenti uno paro di coltelli con doi mandili piccoli indoratti et doi marrama." MAP gives the date as "alla nostra inditione adì 20 ottobre 996." This mixed Gregorian / Islamic calendar makes this complicated, but using the "Conversion of Hijri AH (Islamic) and AD Christian (Gregorian) dates" tool provided by Zurich University's Institute of Oriental Studies "Islamic Philosophy Online: Philosophia Islamica," accessed October 26, 2020, http://www.muslimphilosophy.com/ip/hijri.htm. October 10, 1586, would have been Dhu'l Qa'dah (11) 6, 994 AH. October 20, 1588, would have Dhu'l Qa'dah (11), 29, 996 AH. This latter seems more probable, because Ferdinando was a cardinal in 1586 and grand duke in 1588 and the MAP transcription uses "Sua Altezza Serenissima" as his title.

67. MAP Doc ID 16969, ASF, MdP, 746, 205; MAP Doc ID 2486, ASF, MdP 1173, Ins. 5, 228.

68. Ferdinando I de' Medici at Pratolino to Raffaello Riario in Bologna on August 31, 1591, MAP Doc ID 7359, ASF, MdP 280, 88. MAP transcription: "sicome mi sarà gratissima la femmina, se ella la potrà trovare, gliene aggradisco con molto affetto." See also MAP Person ID 4871, "Riario, Raffaello." MAP Person ID 21568, "Salvino, Geronimo," gives Salvino's birthplace as the island of Ponza. On the peacock, see Cooley, "Animal Empires," 175 and 350–353.

69. On Renaissance breeding programs, see Cooley, "Animal Empires," esp. chapters 1 and 2.

70. MAP Person ID 550, "Medici-Gonzaga, Eleonora de'"; Ferdinando I de' Medici at Villa dell'Ambrogiana to Eleonora de' Medici-Gonzaga in Mantua (perhaps) on October 9, 1592, MAP Doc ID 16779, ASF, MdP 282, 187. MAP transcription: "Ho visto volentieri il giardiniero di V.A. et le cose mandatemi che come rare, et curiose, mi sono state carissime, né mancherò di rimandarnelo con li pavoni bianchi desiderati da lei." MAP identifies the gardener as Giovanni Radici.

71. Eleonora de' Medici Gonzaga in Mantua to Ferdinando I de' Medici in Florence on September 29, 1593, MAP Doc ID 4916, ASF, MdP 2942. MAP transcription: "et anco di quelle sue Anitre d'India."

72. Cosimo I de' Medici at Poggio a Caiano to Francesco (Il Babbi) Babbi in Naples on October 18, 1549, MAP Doc ID 20978, ASF, MdP 13, 70. MAP transcription: "Et della Principessa di Molfetta [Isabella di Capua-Gonzaga] s'osserverà la promessa dell'anatre d'India et d'altri animali che le desidera per il suo barcho." The parenthetical is MAP's. The MAP synopsis suggests that the park was the villa of Ottaviano. MAP Person ID 223, "Babbi, Francesco (Il Babbi)"; MAP Person ID 827, "Capua-Gonzaga di Guastalla, Isabella di."

73. The Medici seem to have had a smaller and less active equine network than the Gonzaga rulers of the much smaller Duchy of Mantua, on which see Cooley, "Animal Empires," chapter 1.

74. Agnolo di Matteo Niccolini in Rome to Ugolino Grifoni in Florence on January 22, 1539. MAP Doc ID 18649, ASF, MdP 345, 96; Ottaviano di Lorenzo de' Medici in Florence to Cosimo I de' Medici in Florence July 7, 1540, MAP Doc ID 19518, ASF, MdP 3162, 188; Ottaviano di Lorenzo de' Medici in Florence to Cosimo I de' Medici in Cafaggiolo on July 8, 1540, MAP Doc ID 18653, ASF, MdP 345, 143; MAP Person ID 171, "Antinori, Alessandro di Niccolò." Thanks to Mackenzie Cooley for teaching me what I know about horses; all remaining errors are, of course, my own.

75. Summary of letters for Cosimo I, Ottaviano de' Medici in Florence to Cosimo I de' Medici in Florence on July 8, 1541, MAP Doc ID 22815, ASF, MdP 617, 190; MAP Person ID 1172, "Medici, Ottaviano di Lorenzo de'."

76. Ugolino Grifoni in Pisa to Pier Francesco Riccio in Florence on January 9, 1544, MAP Doc ID 5973, ASF MdP, 1170, 306r; Pier Francesco Riccio in Florence on January 10, 1544, MAP Doc ID 5527, ASF, MdP 1169, 445r.

77. Pirro Musefilo, Conte della Sassetta, in Naples to Cosimo I de' Medici in Florence, perhaps November 12, 1540, MAP Doc ID 22337, ASF, MdP 652, 78; Pirro Musefilo, Conte della Sassetta, in Naples to Cosimo I de' Medici in Florence on November 16, 1540, MAP Doc ID 26636, ASF, MdP 653, Ins. 11, 287. Pirro Musefilo, Conte della Sassetta, in Naples to Cosimo I de' Medici in Florence on December 18, 1540, MAP Doc ID 26637, ASF, MdP 635, Ins. 11, 294; MAP Person ID 1308, "Alvarez de Toledo, Pedro (Marqués de Villafranca)"; MAP Person ID 366, "Alvarez de Toledo y Osorio, Garcia." On *barberi* (barb) horses, see Cooley, "Animal Empires," 65, 68-75, 77, and 80-86. On Renaissance horses and horse breeding, see Cooley, "Animal Empires," chapters 1 and 2; see chapter 2 in particular for the role of Naples in horse breeding and gift exchange.

78. Pirro Musefilo, Conte della Sassetta, in Naples to Cosimo I de' Medici in Florence on December 18, 1540, MAP Doc ID 26637, ASF, MdP 635, Ins. 11, 294.

79. Francesco I de' Medici in Florence to Giuseppe della Seta on June 30, 1568, MAP Doc ID 19135, ASF, MdP 229, 207. MAP transcription: "et velocissimi al corso." Francesco I de' Medici in Florence to Giuseppe della Seta on September 9, 1568, MAP Doc ID 19209, ASF, MdP 229, 257. On palio racing, see Cooley, "Animal Empires," 38-43 and esp. 61-72.

80. Vincenzo Ferrini in Pisa to Pier Francesco Riccio in Florence on December 29, 1546, MAP Doc ID 20510, ASF, MdP 1172, 703r; Francesco I de' Medici in Florence to Bartolomeo Cappello in Venice on December 14, 1581, MAP Doc ID 19280, ASF, MdP 257, 89; MAP Person ID 2621, "Cappello, Bartolomeo."

81. Giovanni di Filippo dell'Antella in Rome to Cosimo I de' Medici in Florence on August 23, 1540, MAP Doc ID 19157, ASF, MdP 3263, 202; MAP Person ID 2358, "Lannoy, Philippe de Charles de"; MAP Person ID 168, "Antella, Giovanni di Filippo dell'."

82. Cosimo I de' Medici in Florence to Alessandro Giovanni di Pierantonio Bandini at the Imperial Court on August 30, 1540, MAP Doc ID 7426; MAP Person ID 12903, "Bandini, Alessandro Giovanni di Pierantonio"; MAP Person ID 253, "Habsburg, Karl V von."

83. Lorenzo di Andrea Pagni in Lecceto to Piero Francesco Riccio in Florence on March 20, 1545, MAP Doc ID 2447, ASF, MdP 1171, 566r; MAP Person ID 348, "Medici-Valois, Caterina de'."

84. Leonor de Toledo-de' Medici (Eleonora da Toledo) in Florence to Caterina de' Medici-Valois in France on September 19, 1545, MAP Doc ID 12575, ASF, MdP 6, 232.

85. Alessandro Risaliti in Livorno to Belisario di Francesco Vinta in Florence, March 31, 1603, MAP Doc ID 21952, ASF, MdP 4275, 495; MAP Person ID 1215, "Rubens, Peter Paul." On Vincenzo Gonzaga, see Valeria Finucci, *The Prince's Body: Vincenzo Gonzaga and Renaissance Medicine* (Cambridge, MA: Harvard University Press, 2015); MAP Person ID 547, "Gonzaga, Vincenzo I (Duca di Mantova)."

86. Francesco Capponi in Alexandria to Pier Francesco Riccio in Florence, June 15, 1547, MAP Doc ID 2486, ASF, MdP 1173, Ins. 5, 228. Bernardo di Bartolomeo (il Baroncello) in Livorno to Francesco I de' Medici in Florence, May 27, 1566, MAP Doc ID 9834, ASF, MdP 521a, 773. See also Giovanni Compagni in Livorno to Francesco I de' Medici in Florence, May 13, 1566, MAP Doc ID 20545, ASF, MdP 521a, 586; Bernardo di Bartolomeo (il Baroncello) in Livorno to Francesco I de' Medici in Florence, May 27, 1566, MAP Doc ID 9838, ASF, MdP 521a, 779.

87. MAP Doc ID 16969, ASF, MdP, 746, 205, April 11, 1581, refers to a bill of lading for the ship *Santa Anna*.

88. Bastiano Campana in Livorno to Cosimo I de' Medici in Florence on June 3, 1559, MAP Doc ID 9567, ASF, MdP 479, 173.

89. Francesco I de' Medici at Poggio a Caiano to Giovanni Battista di Giuliano Ricasoli on September 22, 1580, MAP Doc ID 21252, ASF, MdP 254, 118.

90. Francesco I de' Medici at Pratolino to Francesco Moro in Venice on July 16, 1582, MAP Doc ID 13951, ASF, MdP 257, 177. Iohn Florio, *Queen Anna's New World of Words or Dictionarie of the* Italian *and* English *Tongues* (London: Printed by Melch. Bradwood for Edw. Blount and William Barret, 1611), gives for "Ronzíno" "a handsome prettie nag or tit."

91. Kurt W. Forster, "Metaphors of Rule. Political Ideology and History in the Portraits of Cosimo I de' Medici," *Mitteilungen des Kunsthistorischen Institutes*

*in Florenz* 15, no. 1 (1971): 79. See also Yvonne Elet, "Seats of Power: The Outdoor Benches of Early Modern Florence," *Journal of the Society of Architectural Historians* 61, no. 4 (Dec. 2002), 446, figure 2, for a detail of Domenico Ghirlandaio's *Pope Honorius Confirming the Franciscan Rule* showing the Marzocco in front of the Palazzo della Signoria.

92. Forster, "Metaphors of Rule," 79.

93. Giampiero Brunelli, "Giulio III, papa" *DBI* 57 (2001); Giovanni Battista Galletti in Rome to Cosimo I de' Medici in Florence on February 26, 1551, MAP Doc ID 19600, ASF, MdP 401, 476; Florence to Cosimo I de' Medici in Livorno on March 6, 1551, MAP Doc ID 6911, ASF, MdP 401, 555; Lorenzo di Andrea Pagni in Livorno to Pier Francesco Riccio in Florence on March 8, 1551, MAP Doc ID 3232, ASF, MdP 1176, 1037r.

94. Francesco I de' Medici in Florence to Antonio Scaramuccia in Turin on March 31, 1568, MAP Doc ID 19085, ASF, MdP 229, 136; Francesco I de' Medici in Florence to Antonio Scaramuccia in Turin on April 11, 1568, MAP Doc ID 19092, ASF, MdP 229, 143; Emanuele Filiberto di Savoia in Vercelli to Francesco I de' Medici in Florence on May 6, 1568, MAP Doc ID 23495, ASF, MdP 2960, 176; Caragiali in Algiers to Cosimo I de' Medici in Florence, September 12, 1569, MAP Doc ID 9519, ASF, MdP 58, 50; Cosimo I de' Medici in Florence to Caragiali in Algiers, perhaps December 10, 1569, MAP Doc ID 9516, ASF, MdP 58; Mehmet (Pasha) in Algiers to Ferdinando I de' Medici in Florence on (perhaps) October 20, 1586, MAP Doc ID 26410, ASF, MdP 4279, 36.

95. MAP Doc ID 3333, ASF, MdP 5922b, 17, December 30, 1553; MAP Person ID 350, "Medici, Tommaso di Iacopo de'."

96. Francesco I de' Medici in Florence to Bernardo di Bartolomeo (il Baroncello) Baroncelli in Livorno on June 12, 1568, MAP Doc ID 19124, ASF, MdP 229, 193. MAP transcription: "Il Tutolino Capitano della nostra nave Fenice ci fa intendere haver portato tre leoni piccoli domestichi, un Gatto d'Algalia, tre cani grossi da porci, quattro Galline di Ghinea pintate, due tortole bianche, et molti uccellini di Caranà et alcuni Cordovani di Spagna," MAP Person ID 4555, "Tutolini, Salvestro (Raugeo)." See also MAP Person ID 4408, "Baroncelli, Bernardo di Bartolomeo (il Baroncello)."

97. Matteo Forestani in Livorno to Antonio Serguidi in Florence on January 4, 1586, MAP Doc ID 17434, ASF, MdP 1198, Ins. 3, 540; MAP Person ID 15111, "Forestani, Matteo."

98. Matteo Forestani in Livorno to Antonio Serguidi in Florence on January 11, 1586, MAP Doc ID 17435, ASF, MdP 1198, Ins. 3, 542.

99. Cosimo I de' Medici in Pisa to Piero (Il Pero) Gelido in Venice, December 3, 1556, MAP Doc ID 9471, ASF, MdP 521a, 314. MAP transcription: "Della tigre ne habbiamo per via di Alessandria havuto adviso che cene sarà menata una, essendo cotesta assai cara, non ci attenderemo altrimenti ancorché vi

troviamo certi pardi [proposed reading: ora] che son tanto piacevoli e veloci e animosi nella caccia." The bracketed text is MAP's. See also MAP Person ID 492, "Gelido, Piero (Il Pero)."

100. Pier Francesco Riccio in Florence to Cosimo I de' Medici in Livorno on March 10, 1551, MAP Doc ID 18081, ASF, MdP 613, Ins. 6, 14.

101. For Giovanni Battista della Porta's decision to rely on live observation rather than a portrait of a leopard from Florence, see Cooley, "Animal Empires," 166-167.

102. Francesco I de' Medici in Florence to Cosimo Bartoli in Venice on November 27, 1567, MAP Doc ID 19019, ASF, MdP 229, 47. MAP transcription: "Il Caravia [Alessandro Caravia] vi parlerà d'un gatto pardo, se egli è domestico et agevole noi lo comperremo volentieri; ma se è salvatico o spiacevole non se ne parli, et advertite che sia agevole et domestico bene." The bracketed text is MAP's. See also MAP Person ID 202, "Bartoli, Cosimo."

103. Francesco I de' Medici in Florence to Cosimo Bartoli in Venice on December 17, 1567, MAP Doc ID 19031, ASF, MdP 229, 59. MAP transcription: "Se il leopardo è così terribile come scrivete, non fa per noi, però non pigliate briga di mandarcelo." For another example of the Medici declining to acquire leopards from Venice on different grounds, see Cooley, "Animal Empires," 167-168.

104. Vincenzo I (Duke of Mantua) Gonzaga in Mantua to Cosimo II de' Medici in Florence on April 25, 1609, MAP Doc ID 5114, ASF, MdP 2944, 673.

105. From Cosimo I de' Medici in Florence on June 12, 1541, MAP Doc ID 12664, ASF, MdP 4, 83.

106. Summary of letters for Cosimo I de' Medici in Florence on January 18, 1542, MAP Doc ID 22786, ASF, MdP 617, 133.

107. Cosimo Bartoli in Venice to Cosimo I de' Medici in Florence on September 22, 1565, MAP Doc ID 27204, ASF, MdP 2977, 180r.

108. Cosimo I de' Medici at Poggio a Caiano to Francesco (Il Babbi) Babbi in Naples on February 9, 1549, MAP Doc ID 20922, ASF, MdP 12, 253.

109. MAP Doc ID 6738, ASF, MdP 600, 9, March 31, 1542, refers to a ricordo of Pierfrancesco Riccio noting payment for transporting the lion cubs. MAP Doc ID 22879, ASF, MdP 617, 307, May 31, 1542, refers to a summary of letters including thanks for the lions. MAP Person ID 14823, "Pfalz, Otto Heinrich von der."

110. Cosimo I de' Medici in Pisa to Giovanni Battista di Simone Ricasoli in France on March 6, 1548, MAP Doc ID 7469, ASF, MdP 9, 478; Cosimo I de' Medici in Pisa to Giovanni Battista di Simone Ricasoli in France on perhaps March 26, 1548, MAP Doc ID 4845, ASF, MdP 9, 561; Cosimo I de' Medici to Piero (Il Pero) Gelido in Paris on April 16, 1548, MAP Doc ID 6942, ASF, MdP 11, 48; Cosimo I de' Medici in Pisa to Giovanni Battista di Simone Ricasoli in Paris on May 12, 1548, MAP Doc ID 19754,

ASF, MdP 11, 154; MAP Person ID 972, "Ricasoli, Giovanni Battista di Simone."

111. Guidobaldo II della Rovere in Pesaro to Cosimo I de' Medici in Florence on March 23, 1549, MAP Doc ID 22211, ASF, MdP 4050, 113; Cristiano Pagni in Florence to Pier Francesco Riccio in Florence on March 29, 1549, MAP Doc ID 2352, ASF, MdP 1169, 395r; Cristiano Pagni in Livorno to Pier Francesco Riccio in Florence on April 12, 1549, MAP Doc ID 514, ASF, MdP 1175, 198r; MAP Person ID 420, "Rovere, Guidobaldo II della."

112. Iacopo (da Volterra) Guidi in Pisa to Pier Francesco Riccio in Florence on February 23, 1551, MAP Doc ID 3212, ASF, MdP 1176, 1005r.

113. To Cosimo I de' Medici in Florence on April 18, 1553, MAP Doc ID 22975, ASF MdP 617, 751.

114. Fabrizio Ferrari in Milan to Cosimo I de' Medici in Florence on March 9, 1560, MAP Doc ID 12282, ASF, MdP 3108, 27; Fabrizio Ferrari in Milan to Cosimo I de' Medici in Florence on October 2, 1560, MAP Doc ID 17319, ASF, MdP 3108, 119; MAP Person ID 491, "Ferrari, Fabrizio"; MAP Person ID 9393, "Pimentel, Alonso."

115. Vincenzo I (Duca di Mantova) Gonzaga in Quingèntole, Mantua, to Francesco I de' Medici in Florence on May 17, 1585, MAP Doc ID 4471, ASF, MdP 2939.

116. Francesco I de' Medici in Florence to Wilhelm V von Wittelsbach in Munich on September 9, 1581, MAP Doc ID 13978, ASF, MdP 257, 30. MAP transcription: "Havendo inteso da Giulio Cesare Alidosio [. . .] che essendo morta costì la Tigre che già se le mandò di qua, ella n'habbia sentito gran dispiacere, con affirmarsi da lui che il poterne havere un altra le sarebbe gratissimo, ritrovandomene io una assai domestica, et agevole, mi son resoluto d' inviarla all' Ecc.za V.ra." Francesco I de' Medici in Florence to Baldassar staffiere (tedesco) on August 9, 1581, MAP Doc ID 16090, ASF, MdP 257, 30; MAP Person ID 259, "Wittelsbach, Wilhelm V von"; MAP Person ID 2810, "Alidosi, Giulio."

117. Enea di Domenico Vaini in Florence to Marcello degli Accolti in Pisa on February 9, 1593, MAP Doc ID 14496, ASF, MdP 831, 377.

118. MAP Person ID 782, "Habsburg, Rudolf II von."

119. Belisario di Francesco Vinta in Pisa to Rodrigo Alidosi de Mendoza in Prague on May 5, 1607, MAP Doc ID 1847, ASF, MdP 300, 39. Vinta explained to the Medici ambassador the grand duke's reaction to the Emperor's request.

120. Ferdinando I de' Medici in Florence to Rodrigo Alidosi de Mendoza at the Holy Roman Imperial Court on July 4, 1607, MAP Doc ID 13811, ASF, MdP 300, 67. MAP transcription: "Mandiamo Burrino, uno de' nostri mulattieri, con due tigre per la M.tà dell'Imp.re"; "per esser difficilissimi a governarsi." See also MAP Person ID 147, "Alidosi de Mendoza, Rodrigo."

121. Belisario di Francesco Vinta in Florence to Sallustio Tarugi in Madrid on September 23, 1607, MAP Doc ID 14860, ASF, MdP 5052, 471.

122. Orso Pannocchieschi d'Elci in Madrid to Belisario di Francesco Vinta in Florence on July 3, 1611, MAP Doc ID 14317, ASF, MdP 4941, 878. MAP transcription: "dicendoli che il cacciatore maggiore di Sua Altezza [Cosimo II de' Medici] mio signore mi scriveva di havere due gatti pardi cacciatore"; "Da questo aviso potrà Sua Altezza ordinare che venghino quanto prima." The bracketed insertion is MAP's. See also MAP Person ID 465, "Calderón, Rodrigo de (Marqués de Siete Iglesias)." Calderón became the marquis of Siete Iglesias in 1614.

123. Orso Pannocchieschi d'Elci in Madrid to Belisario di Francesco Vinta in Florence on August 28, 1611, MAP Doc ID 2846, ASF, MdP 4941, 918.

124. Augusto (da Castiglione) Tizio in Seville to Antonio Serguidi in Florence on April 17, 1584, MAP Doc ID 4269, ASF, MdP 1212, Ins. 4, 676. MAP transcription: "dua ucelli [uccelli] bizarri, un porchetto salvatico del Perù, et un tescion [teschione] di quei paesi." The bracketed insertion is MAP's.

125. Augusto (da Castiglione) Tizio in Seville to Antonio Serguidi in Florence on July 20, 1584, MAP Doc ID 4273, ASF, MdP 1212, Ins. 4, 712. MAP transcription: "Vederò d'inviare altre curiosità"; "se gl'inviassi qualche galanteria come di quelli vetri di cristallo et simil sorte di cose, che di più d'essere tanto amico et servitore di cotesti signori ritornerano in costà mille curiosità."

126. Francesco I de' Medici in Florence to Ferdinand von (Tirol) Habsburg in Prague (perhaps) on September 9, 1581, MAP Doc ID 13969, ASF, MdP 257, 30. MAP transcription: "mandandole ancora un animaletto venutomi dell'Indie che chiamano lepre di quel paese." See also MAP Person ID 784, "Habsburg, Ferdinand von (Tirol)."

127. Belisario di Francesco Vinta in Livorno to Luigi Federighi in Spain (perhaps) on February 12, 1607, MAP Doc ID 13560, ASF, MdP 300, 18.

128. Raffaello Romena in Madrid to Belisario di Francesco Vinta in Florence on November 24, 1609, MAP Doc ID 14088, ASF, MdP 4941, 335. MAP transcription: "dall'Indie di ponente." See also MAP Person ID 1206, "Romena, Raffaello."

129. Francesco Seriacopi in Florence to Pier Francesco Riccio in Pisa on February 10, 1551, MAP Doc ID 3163, ASF, MdP 1176, 775r.

130. For a monkey shipment, see Bernardo di Bartolomeo (il Baroncello) Baroncelli in Livorno to Francesco I de' Medici in Florence on October 19, 1568, MAP Doc ID 14767, ASF, MdP 538a, 926.

131. Michele di Paolo Olivieri in the Mugello to Pier Francesco Riccio in Florence on October 12, 1547, MAP Doc ID 8169, ASF, MdP 1173, 727r.

132. Cosimo I de' Medici in Florence to Leonardo Bertelli in Bagno di Romagna on November 1, 1565, MAP Doc ID 8054, ASF, MdP 225, 18.

133. Ferdinando I de' Medici in Florence to Giuseppe Godano in Corsica on July 26, 1591, MAP Doc ID 391, ASF, MdP 280, 76.

134. Pier Francesco Riccio in Florence to Cosimo I de' Medici in Pisa on November 2, 1550, MAP Doc ID 18202, ASF, MdP 613, Ins. 6, 51; Pier Francesco Riccio in Florence to Cosimo I de' Medici in Livorno on November 17, 1550, MAP Doc ID 18099, ASF, MdP 613, Ins. 6, 81.

135. MAP Doc ID 18202, ASF, MdP 613, Ins. 6, 51. Pier Francesco Riccio in Florence to Cosimo I de' Medici in Pisa on November 2, 1550.

136. Neri Giraldi in Florence to Biagio Pignata in Tuscany January 2, 1593, MAP Doc ID 14424, ASF, MdP 831, 4; Neri Giraldi in Florence to Marcello degli Accolti in Pisa on February 9, 1593, MAP Doc ID 14499, ASF, MdP 831, 378; Neri Giraldi in Florence to Marcello degli Accolti in Pisa on February 11, 1593, MAP Doc ID 14544, ASF, MdP 831, 431; Enea di Domenico Vaini in Florence to Belisario di Francesco Vinta in Pisa on February 20, 1593, MAP Doc ID 14602, ASF, MdP 831, 610; MAP Person ID 4876, "Wasa, Zygmunt III."

137. Francesco I de' Medici in Florence to Lorenzo Cagniuoli in (perhaps) Sweden on June 5, 1587, MAP Doc ID 16527, ASF, MdP 270, 110. MAP Person ID 14156, "Cagniuoli, Lorenzo," notes that Cagniuoli was a captain and in service to the king of Sweden in 1591. The MAP synopsis suggests an identification with elk.

138. Francesco I de' Medici in Florence to Michele Mercati in Rome on July 1, 1587, MAP Doc ID 16540, ASF, MdP 270, 126. MAP transcription: "et come passiate di qua vi potremo mostrare l'animale intero della Granbestia, havendone havuti tre vivi di Svetia." See also MAP Person ID 966, "Mercati, Michele."

139. Enea di Domenico Vaini in Florence to Belisario di Francesco Vinta in Pisa on February 24, 1592 [1593; see the following note], MAP Doc ID 14622, ASF, MdP 831, 645; MAP Person ID 772, "Vaini, Enea di Domenico." For the other documents on these reindeer—Doc IDs 14424, 14499, 14544, and 14602—MAP modernizes the "Date as written" to account for the March beginning of the Florentine calendar. It omits doing so for ID 14622, but it seems clear that it too corresponds to a modern calendar date of 1593.

140. On the sable (1544): Florence to Cosimo I de' Medici in Florence on January 8, 1544, MAP Doc ID 22898, ASF, MdP 617, 406. On the bezoars (1582): Luigi Dovara in Setubal, Portugal, to Antonio Serguidi in Florence on April 23, 1582, MAP Doc ID 4254, ASF, MdP 1212, Ins. 3, 468. The postscript to the Dovara letter contains an inventory of items in a Portuguese writing desk sent to Florence; the postscript is Luigi Dovara in Setubal, Portugal, to Antonio Serguidi in Florence on April 21, 1582, MAP Doc ID 4255, ASF, MdP 1212, Ins. 3, 470. It is interesting to note that the postscript antedates the letter (MAP Doc ID

4254) by two days. The other bezoars (1588 and 1592): Giulio Battaglini in Madrid to Pietro di Francesco Usimbardi in Florence on February 6, 1588, MAP Doc ID 8276, ASF, MdP 4919, 111; Giovanni di Cosimo I de' (Don Giovanni) Medici in Livorno to Ferdinando I de' Medici in Pisa on March 17, 1592, MAP Doc ID 8483, ASF, MdP 5154, 173. On the elephant tusk (1587): Bastiano Balbiani in Livorno to Antonio Serguidi in Florence on April 11, 1587, MAP Doc ID 17542, ASF, MdP 1198, Ins. 7, 1604. On Cosimo I's unhappiness about the insistence on collateral for the loan of a unicorn horn: Cosimo I de' Medici in Florence to Averardo di Antonio Serristori in Rome on January 11, 1546, MAP Doc ID 19968, ASF, MdP 3, 714. On a unicorn horn as gift to Cardinal Ferdinando (1587): Matteo Forestani in Livorno to Pietro di Francesco Usimbardi in Rome on May 6, 1587, MAP Doc ID 15201, ASF, MdP 1234a, Ins. 4; Matteo Forestani in Livorno to Pietro di Francesco Usimbardi in Rome on May 6, 1587, MAP Doc ID 15202, ASF, MdP 1234a, Ins. 4.

141. Francesco Carletti, *My Voyage around the World: The Chronicles of a 16th Century Florentine Merchant*, trans. Herbert Weinstock (New York: Pantheon, 1964), 196. On Carletti as a consultant, see "Carletti, Francesco," *DBI* 20 (1977); Tomasi, "Flowering of Florence," 38-50.

142. Lorenzo di Andrea Pagni in Pisa to Pier Francesco Riccio in Florence on December 17, 1546, MAP Doc ID 7769, ASF, MdP 1172, 646r. Cosimo I de' Medici in Florence to Isidoro di Lorenzo da Montauto in Florence on October 29, 1565, MAP Doc ID 7841, ASF, MdP 225, 17.

143. Lorenzo di Andrea Pagni in Florence to Bartolomeo Concini in Pisa on November 4, 1557, MAP Doc ID 16822, ASF, MdP 465, 203.

144. Carletti, *My Voyage*, 145-146.

145. Biblioteca Angelica, ms. 1331, 110v. "il qual musco non è vero che si faccia nel modo, che molti hanno descritto, et io ne portavo la pelle intera di tutto l'Animale a Vostra Altezza con la sua Vesciga, che non, è altro che lo stesso ombellico dell'Animale, che li esse in fuora sotto il corpo piena di quella materia odorifera." Carletti, *My Voyage*, 145.

146. Heikamp, *Mexico and the Medici*, 11-12 and 39-40. The items are mask (items 5 and 6; plates on 56-57); onyx dog's head (item 7, plate on 58); green agate dog's head (item 8, plate on 58); amethyst dog's head (item 9, plate on 59); and bishop's miter (item 18, plate on 68).

147. Heikamp, *Mexico and the Medici*, 10-11; Markey, *Imagining the Americas*, 37-45.

148. BNE, MSS/19698/78. Opening Page: "Relación delas cosas más notables delos palacios, servicio y recámara del Gran Duque de Florencia. a Florencia 23 Dic.ᵉ 1593 5 lny. Fol." The handwriting of this preliminary note is evidently that of a librarian, archivist, or secretary who filed the letter; the letter itself is in a different, early modern hand.

149. BNE, MSS/19698/78, 68/2r. Thanks to Eduardo Martinez for help with the translation; all remaining errors and infelicities are of course my own: "En uno de dos palacios çeleberrimos que[]tiene el gran Duque en Florençia esta la guarda Ropa principal entre otras puças ay una quadrada muy hermosa, Por[]la[]parte de[]arriba adereçada toda de quadros y[]Retratos senbrados a[]trechos por buen orden por[]lo[]baxo çercada alrrededor de Caxones de dos estados en alto que çerrados quitan la gana deber lo[]que ay en ellos según entretienen ellos solos, Porque en cada puerta de Caxon ay dos[]espacios Con[]sus molduras curiosas cada uno de Casi tres[]varas en quadro de circuyto y en Cada espaçio yluminada con[]suma diligençia Una provincia del mundo de suerte que[]toda a questa[] pieça es una mapamundi Universal agradablisimo a los ojos, ariaden ornato a[]estos Caxones mil Urnas y vasos por encima de[]piedras diversas y alabastros con hechuras estrabagantes debajo de[]tan onrada cubierta no fuera Raçon que." For a brief account of the history and function of the Guardaroba Medicea, see the explanation of the Archivio di Stato di Firenze, accessed October 26, 2020, http://www.archiviodistato.firenze.it/siasfi/cgi-bin/RSOLSearchSiasfi.pl?_op=getsprod&id=IFDB1058XX&_language=eng&curwin=thirdwindow.

150. Palmira Brummett, *Mapping the Ottomans: Sovereignty, Territory, and Identity in the Early Modern Mediterranean* (New York: Cambridge University Press, 2015), 66–74. Suraiya Faroqhi, *The Ottoman Empire and the World around It* (New York: I. B. Tauris, 2006), 179–210.

151. BNE, MSS/19698/78, 68/2v: "El Ultimo Cajon esta lleno de[]mil estrabagançias traydas de[]partes estrangeras como çapatos de la[]china cossas de Pluma del Mexico vasos venidos de Turquia y otras mil buxerias curiosisimas sin[]esta guarda Ropa a y otras de[]menos calidad en[]q̂. es casi ynfinito el numero de[]telas doseles tapiçeria y cossas semejantes."

152. BNE, MSS/19698/78, 67/1v. "La Corte que el Gran Duque[]tiene es muy de Principe gente toda muy noble y muchos dellos muy Ricos."

153. Heikamp, *Mexico and the Medici*, 8–9. King Manuel must have given the codex to Giulio de' Medici before he was Clement VII, because Manuel died in 1521 and Clement came to the throne only in 1523. This, at least, is Heikamp's interpretation of a sixteenth-century Latin inscription indicating that the codex had been given by King Manuel to Clement VII. Markey, *Imagining the Americas*, 13, presents much the same interpretation, adding the connection to the 1518 marriage.

154. Heikamp, *Mexico and the Medici*, 9–10; Natalie Zemon Davis, *Trickster Travels: A Sixteenth-Century Muslim between Worlds* (New York: Hill and Wang, 2007), 247–248; Bedini, *Pope's Elephant*, 143. Heikamp argues that the Florentine collections benefited from the closeness of the Medici to the Habsburgs.

155. Markey, *Imagining the Americas*, 13. The British Museum's website, accessed October 26, 2020, for the codex briefly explains its provenance: http://www.britishmuseum.org/research/collection_online/collection _object_details.aspx?objectId=662517&partId=1. It is museum number: Am1902,0308.1.

156. This follows the description of the texts' origin accompanying the World Digital Library's high-quality digitization of the text: World Digital Library, accessed October 26, 2020, https://www.wdl.org/en/item/10096/. See also Fintoni et al. *World of the Aztecs*.

157. On the Hernández expedition, see Cooley, "Animal Empires," chapter 5, 275–305. See also David Freedberg, *The Eye of the Lynx: Galileo, His Friends, and the Beginnings of Modern Natural History* (Chicago: University of Chicago Press, 2002), esp. chapter 9, 245–274. On the *Relaciones geográficas*, see Cooley, "Animal Empires," 227, 230–239, 246–247, 299–301, and 322–325.

158. Markey, *Imagining the Americas*, 96–97.

159. Carletti, *My Voyage*, 26 (Nombre de Dios), 32 (Panamá City), and 39–40 and 46–47 (Lima).

160. Carletti, *My Voyage*, 55.

161. Biblioteca Angelica, ms. 1331, 43v, "Similmente questo luogo e ripieno in effetto di zanzare e di scorpioni, e d'altri animali e cimice tutto molto velenose i quali mordendo se ne muore, e le cimice se si mangiano per qualche disgratia ò che fussero bevute in vino, ò acqua ammazzano, e le zanzare to\u02b3mentano di tal sort che sono insoportabili." Carletti, *My Voyage*, 56.

162. Carletti, *My Voyage*, 270.

163. Carletti, *My Voyage*, 57 and 60–61.

164. Carletti, *My Voyage*, 57 and 60–61.

165. Biblioteca Angelica, ms. 1331, 44v–45r, "in un luogo tanto bello e dilettevole, e copioso d'ogni delitia quanto immaginar si possa, e vedere nel mondo tutto è la Città bene collocata, oltre all'essere fabricata dalli spagnoli alla moderna con le case di pietre e calcina quasi tutte à un'andare con le strade dritte e larghe piu di quelle che Vostra Altezza Serenissima ha fatto fare nel suo livorno nuovo." Carletti, *My Voyage*, 57–58.

166. Carletti compared the Jesuits' use of a particular type of light stone in their building to avoid subsidence to the stones used to build Livorno (Carletti, *My Voyage*, 58–59).

167. Federica Ambrosini, "Venetian Diplomacy, Spanish Gold and the New World in the Sixteenth Century," in Horodowich and Markey, eds., *The New World in Early Modern Italy*, 58–59. On the Danti map's comparison of Venice and Mexico City see Heikamp, *Mexico and the Medici*, 10–11.

168. Quotation 1 is from Biblioteca Angelica, ms. 1331, 46r, "che in questa belliss.\u1d43 Città ci,è d'. ogni cosa, e d'ogni bene in suprema perfettione e

abondanza." See also Carletti, *My Voyage*, 59. Quotation 2 is from Biblioteca Angelica, ms. 1331, 51r, "finalm^e La Città del Messico e un Paradiso
in terra, ripiena d'ogni commodità e delitie d'ogni sorte godendosi tutto
quello che viene di spagna, della Cina, d'altre Provincie di quei Paesi."
See also Carletti, *My Voyage*, 66–67.

169. Carletti, *My Voyage*, 108–112.

170. Carletti, *My Voyage*, 120–122 (Christians and persecution; building techniques and screens), 123 (shoes off inside), 123–126 (clothing), 124
(bowing), 125 (suicide, infanticide, abortion, and hierarchy), 126 (standards of beauty), 126–128 (sexual mores), 129–132 (trade routes), and
134–135 (cormorant fishing).

171. Carletti, *My Voyage*, 146 (gold as a commodity), 146–147 (alchemy, astrology, physiognomy, and divination), 147–148 (clothing), 148–153 (payment, pricing, and counting), 153 (demand for silver), 153–154 (dimensions and measurement), 169–171 (Chinese crops), 171–174 and 177
(religion), 174–175 (food culture), 175–176 (language), 175–176 and 179
(entertainment). On social practices: 176 (arranged marriage and concubinage), 176–177 (slaves as brides / bride purchasing), 177 (slavery, infanticide, suicide, men giving dowries), 177–178 (incest taboos), 178 (foot-
binding, restrictions on women, hairstyles), and 178–179 (long nails).

172. Carletti, *My Voyage*, 178–179.

173. Carletti, *My Voyage*, 135–142 and 183–187.

174. Biblioteca Angelica, ms. 1331, 138r-v. "il che è seguito mediante l'haver
io messo in questo mio [138v:] semplice ragionamento parte di quelle
cose che si trovano scritte nelli detti libri della Geografia della Cina, le
quali insieme con quelle che io non hebbi tempo di fare interpretare,
potrà un giorno Vostra Altezza farne uno ordinato volume nella maniera
che quivi si contengono con l'occasione di qualche Religioso che venissi
da quelle Parti, et che conoscesse et intendere quei caratteri Ieroglifici."
Carletti, *My Voyage*, 179. The atlas, which Giorgio Riello, Alexander
Statman, and I consulted as part of the Carletti project, is Biblioteca Na-
zionale Centrale di Firenze (BNCF) ms.II.I.225 and ms.II.I.226.

175. Carletti, *My Voyage*, 154–159. Indeed, in my dissertation I assembled a
such table as appendix 3.3 (pp. 536–537), Brian Brege, "The Empire That
Wasn't: The Grand Duchy of Tuscany and Empire, 1574-1609," PhD diss.,
Stanford University, 2014.

176. El Bibas, *L'Emiro e il Granduca* is primarily concerned with this episode.
See also Caroline Finkel, *Osman's Dream: The Story of the Ottoman Empire
1300–1923* (New York: Basic Books, 2007), 179.

177. A pair of letters from 1599—ASF, MdP 4275, 3r-5r—almost certainly
refer to Corai. Federico M. Federici, "A Servant of Two Masters: The
Translator Michel Angelo Corai as a Tuscan Diplomat (1599-1609)," in

*Translators, Interpreters, and Cultural Negotiators: Mediating and Communicating Power from the Middle Ages to the Modern Era,* ed. Federico Federici and Dario Tessicini (New York: Palgrave Macmillan, 2014), 81–82.

178. Richard Raiswell, "Shirley, Sir Robert, Count Shirley in the papal nobility (c. 1581–1628)," *Oxford Dictionary of National Biography*; E. K. Faridany, "Signal Defeat: The Portuguese Loss of Comorão in 1614 and Its Political and Commercial Consequences," in *Acta Iranica: Portugal, the Persian Gulf and Safavid Persia,* ed. Rudi Matthee and Jorge Flores (Leuven, Belg.: Peeters, 2011), 125.

179. This was the Tenshō embassy (1582–1590), R. W. Lightbown, "Oriental Art and the Orient in Late Renaissance and Baroque Italy," *Journal of the Warburg and Courtauld Institutes* 32 (1969), 233 and 235; Michael Cooper, *The Japanese Mission to Europe, 1582–1590: The Journey of Four Samurai Boys through Portugal, Spain, and Italy* (Kent, UK: Global Oriental, 2005).

180. Lilly Library, call number LMC1962, Spain History mss., Jan. 3, 1614–Dec. 27, 1615, 111r: "acerca del Tratamento que se prodia hazer al enbax.ᵒʳ del xapon y pareçe al consejo, que supuesto que el rey de Boxu que le embia. es Uno de los sujetos al emp.ᵒʳ del xapen. se le prodria hazer el mismo tratamiento que a los que vienen de parte de los potentados inferiores de Italia, quedo advertido desto." The page is from December 29, 1614, and January 15 and 16, 1615. The embassy was the Keichō embassy (1613–1620), Koichiro Yaginuma, "Trasfondo histórico del envío del embejador Hasekura a España y la Nueva España en 1614," *Análisis* 17, no. 50, special edition on Japan [May 2014]: 17–42.

181. Pier Francesco Riccio in Florence to Lorenzo di Andrea Pagni in Livorno, April 30, 1545, MAP Doc ID 7205, ASF, MdP 1171, 718. MAP transcription: "in lingua fiorentina, et non latina."

182. Bernard Lewis, *From Babel to Dragomans: Interpreting the Middle East* (New York: Oxford University Press, 2004), 30.

183. The academy's statutes were compiled in 1583, but the inaugural ceremony took place in 1585. See the Accademia della Crusca website, accessed October 26, 2020, http://www.accademiadellacrusca.it/it/laccademia/storia/primordi-fondazione for the Crusca's description of its own history.

184. Lightbown, "Oriental Art," 231, makes the comparison between Carletti and Sassetti's accounts.

185. Biblioteca Angelica, ms. 1331, 114v. "perche no[n], è altro che terra presa di quella qualità"; "che si fanno i Vassellami à Montelupo ó altrove la quale secondo il benefitio che se li fà et secondo la qualitá del Terreno riesce o più fino ò più grossa"; "et se ne caricherebbono non dico le Nave, ma le flotte d'esse." Carletti, *My Voyage,* 149–150 and 150n.

186. Arthur Lane, "A Rediscovered Cruet of Medici Porcelain," *Bulletin of the Museum of Fine Arts* 56, no. 304 (Summer 1958), 79.

187. The foregoing summarizes the accounts provided in W. B. Honey, "The Origin and Affiliations of the European Porcelain-Factories," *Burlington Magazine for Connoisseurs* 87, no. 511 (Oct. 1945): 246, and esp. of Lane, "Rediscovered Cruet," 79–80. The Victoria and Albert Museum in London and the Metropolitan Museum of Art in New York exhibit pieces of Medici porcelain.

188. Lane, "Rediscovered Cruet," 79–80; Marco Spallanzani, "Medici Porcelain in the Collection of the Last Grand-Duke," *Burlington Magazine for Connoisseurs* 132, no. 1046 (May 1990): 317. The Met's account of "Medici porcelain" accompanying its case containing six pieces of Medici porcelain asserts that "manufacture is believed to have ceased or at least significantly diminished with the death of Francesco in 1587."

189. Spallanzani, "Medici Porcelain," 316–317. By comparison, losses appear to have been heavy since then. The digital display accompanying the exhibit containing the Victoria and Albert's Medici porcelain claimed, when I visited, that there are only fifty-seven surviving pieces; the Victoria and Albert has at least two of them. The Met agrees with the Victoria and Albert that surviving Medici porcelain is extremely rare but claims that fifty-nine pieces survive, of which it displays six in one case. The figure fifty-nine appears to come from a 1936 Italian catalog. Lane explains that, in addition, Ulrich Middeldorf had found evidence for three more pieces and Lane's article added a further three; Lane, "Rediscovered Cruet," 80–81.

190. The Victoria and Albert Museum explains, in reference to its collection of Medici porcelain, that Francesco gave his porcelain as a valued gift.

191. Findlen, *Early Modern Things*; Anne Gerritsen and Giorgio Riello, eds., *The Global Lives of Things: The Material Culture of Connections in the Early Modern World* (New York: Routledge, 2016); Frank Trentmann, *Empire of Things: How We Became a World of Consumers, from the Fifteenth Century to the Twenty-First* (New York: Harper Collins, 2016).

192. Claudia Conforti, ed., *Vasari, gli Uffizi e il duca* (Florence: Giunti, 2011).

193. Markey, *Imagining the Americas*, 159–161.

### 6. THE TUSCANS IN NORTH AFRICA

1. Gregory Hanlon, *The Twilight of a Military Tradition: Italian Aristocrats and European Conflicts, 1560–1800* (New York: Holmes and Meyer, 1998), 62; J. R. Hale, *Florence and the Medici* (London: Phoenix, 2001), 130; Robert Dallington, "A suruey of the great dukes state of Tuscany In the yeare of our Lord 1596" (London: Printed [by George Eld] for Edward Blount, 1605), 8 (5) (the pagination is eccentric and repetitive, so I give the Early English Books Online pdf page parenthetically); Niccolò Capponi, "Le Palle di Marte: Military Strategy and Diplomacy in the Grand Duchy of

Tuscany under Ferdinand II de' Medici (1621-1670)," *Journal of Military History* 68 (October 2004): 1129; Cesare Ciano, *I primi Medici e il mare: Note sulla politica marinara toscana da Cosimo I a Ferdinando I* (Pisa, It.: Pacini, 1980); Franco Angiolini, "L'Ordine di Santo Stefano, i Toscani e il mare," in *Atti del Convegno, l'Ordine di Santo Stefano e il Mare* (Pisa, It.: ETS, 2001); Giovanna Benadusi, "Career Strategies in Early Modern Tuscany: The Emergence of Regional Elite," *Sixteenth Century Journal* 25, no. 1 (Spring 1994): 85-99; Michael Mallett, *Florentine Galleys of the Fifteenth Century* (Oxford, UK: Clarendon, 1967); Richard Goldthwaite, *The Economy of Renaissance Florence* (Baltimore, MD: Johns Hopkins University Press, 2009), 150-151.

2. Capponi, "Palle di Marte," 1123-1125, gives the negative balance sheet for 1626. Of course, there were profitable years, as we shall see.

3. Capponi, "Palle di Marte," 1121.

4. Palmira Brummett, *Ottoman Seapower and Levantine Diplomacy in the Age of Discovery* (Albany: State University of New York Press, 1994); Giancarlo Casale, *The Ottoman Age of Exploration* (New York: Oxford University Press, 2010); Jane Hathaway, *The Arab Lands under Ottoman Rule, 1516–1800* (New York: Pearson, 2008); Alan Mikhail, *Under Osman's Tree: The Ottoman Empire, Egypt, and Environmental History* (Chicago: University of Chicago Press, 2017).

5. Goldthwaite, *Economy of Renaissance Florence*.

6. Corey Tazzara, *The Free Port of Livorno and the Transformation of the Mediterranean World, 1574–1790* (New York: Oxford University Press, 2017), 248.

7. Brian Curran, *The Egyptian Renaissance: The Afterlife of Egypt in Early Modern Italy* (Chicago: University of Chicago Press, 2007); Margaret Meserve, *Empires of Islam in Renaissance Historical Thought* (Cambridge, MA: Harvard University Press, 2008).

8. On the Guardaroba, see Lia Markey, *Imagining the Americas in Medici Florence* (University Park: Pennsylvania State University Press, 2016), 37-45; Mark Rosen, *The Mapping of Power in Renaissance Italy: Painted Cartographic Cycles in Social and Intellectual Context* (New York: Cambridge University Press, 2015); Anna Contadini and Claire Norton, eds., *The Renaissance and the Ottoman World* (Burlington, VT: Ashgate, 2013).

9. Brummett, *Mapping the Ottomans*, 64-65. The official Florence website listing the countries covered by the various maps is at http://museicivici-fiorentini.comune.fi.it/palazzovecchio/visitamuseo/sala_delle_carte_geografiche.htm, accessed October 26, 2020.

10. They heard, for instance, about an Ottoman fleet heading to Egypt in 1559, a rebellion in Yemen in 1568, and plague in Egypt in 1599 (Leonardo Corsini in Venice to Cosimo I de' Medici in Florence, June 24, 1559, MAP Doc ID 20255, ASF, MdP 479, 325; Curzio Bartoli in Venice to Francesco I de' Medici in Florence, January 10, 1568, MAP Doc ID 21571,

ASF, MdP 3080, 5; Giulio Battaglini in Naples to Lorenzo di Francesco Usimbardi in Florence, October 19, 1599, MAP Doc ID 17582, ASF, MdP 4087, 429).

11. Marta Caroscio, "Blue Daisies and Red Tulips: Chinese Porcelain, Iznik Ware and Early Modern Taste at the Medici Court," in *The Grand Ducal Medici and the Levant: Material Culture, Diplomacy, and Imagery in the Early Modern Mediterranean*, ed. Maurizio Arfaioli and Marta Caroscio (London: Harvey Miller, 2016), 150–151 and 155–156.

12. Tommaso di Iacopo de' Medici in Florence to Salvatore Quaratesi, in Livorno, May 31, 1571, MAP Doc ID 13878, ASF, MdP 221, 96.

13. Cristiano Pagni in Colle Val d'Elsa to Pier Francesco Riccio in Florence, May 18, 1545, MAP Doc ID 7212, ASF, MdP 1171, Ins. 8, 389. MAP transcription: "che trovando qualcosa bella et rara da quelle parti d'Egitto per donne non manchi mandarla per Sua Ecc.a:." All translations are mine unless otherwise indicated.

14. Gugliermo Guarduzza in Alexandria to Cosimo I de' Medici, November 9, 1554, MAP Doc ID 27376, ASF, MdP 437, 148r. Both "natione fiorentina" and "la Natione" appear in the MAP transcription.

15. Bernardo di Bartolomeo (il Baroncello) in Livorno to Francesco I de' Medici in Florence, May 27, 1566, MAP Doc ID 9834, ASF, MdP 521a, 773. See also Giovanni Compagni in Livorno to Francesco I de' Medici in Florence, May 13, 1566, MAP Doc ID 20545, ASF, MdP 521a, 586; Bernardo di Bartolomeo (il Baroncello) in Livorno to Francesco I de' Medici in Florence, May 27, 1566, MAP Doc ID 9838, ASF, MdP 521a, 779.

16. Abraham Israel in Livorno to Lorenzo di Francesco Usimbardi in Florence, probably December 1593, MAP Doc ID 27254, ASF, MdP 1245, 113.

17. Francesca Trivellato, *The Familiarity of Strangers: The Sephardic Diaspora, Livorno, and Cross-Cultural Trade in the Early Modern Period* (New Haven, CT: Yale University Press, 2009), 51 and 76; Tazzara, *Free Port*, 55–56 and 81–84.

18. Cosimo I de' Medici in Poggio a Caiano to Alfonso Berardi in Istanbul on September 16, 1547, MAP Doc ID 7916, ASF, MdP 186, 46; Niccolò Capponi, *Victory of the West: The Great Christian-Muslim Clash at the Battle of Lepanto* (Cambridge, MA.: Da Capo, 2007), 85–86.

19. Marica Milanesi, *Filippo Sassetti* (Florence: Nuova Italia, 1973), 23–31; Tazzara, *Free Port*, 32–37.

20. F. Özden Mercan, "Medici-Ottoman Diplomatic Relations (1574–1578): What Went Wrong?" in Arfaioli and Caroscio, *Grand Ducal Medici*, 19–22.

21. Riguccio Galluzzi, *Storia del Granducato di Toscana*, new ed., 11 vols. (Florence: Leonardo Marchini, 1822), vol. 4, book 4, chapter 3, 66–67, year 1577. For brief biographies of Galluzzi, see the website of the *Storia di Firenze*, a project begun at the University of Florence, accessed October 26,

2020, http://www.storiadifirenze.org/?p=627; Carla Sodini, "Jacopo Riguccio Galluzzi," accessed October 26, 2020, http://www.storiadifirenze
.org/?storici=galluzzi-jacopo-riguccio; and Orsola Gori Pasta, "Galluzzi,
Jacopo Riguccio," *DBI* 51 (1998).

22. Özden Mercan, "Medici-Ottoman Diplomatic Relations," 22.

23. Galluzzi, *Storia del Granducato di Toscana*, vol. 4, book 4, chapter 3, 67–68,
year 1577; the quotation is from p. 68. Galluzzi reproduces the entire
letter, the quoted portion of which is "che questa impresa non è nostra,
ma una Religione di Cavalieri, fondata dal padre nostro nel nome di S.
Stefano per sua devozione, e per salute dall'anima sua, con espresso ordine che ella possa tenere sino in dodici Galere armate, che sieno pronte
ad ogni comandamento del Papa, e del Re di Spagna, la quale Religione
non potrebbe da noi essere annullata, o dismessa senza incorrere nell'ira
del nostro Signore Iddio, e con molta alterazione delli Stati nostri."

24. Özden Mercan, "Medici-Ottoman Diplomatic Relations," 22.

25. Galluzzi, *Storia del Granducato di Toscana*, vol. 4, book 4, chapter 3, 68–71,
years 1577 and 1578; Özden Mercan, "Medici-Ottoman Diplomatic Relations," 23–28.

26. Özden Mercan, "Medici-Ottoman Diplomatic Relations," 27–28.

27. Özden Mercan, "Medici-Ottoman Diplomatic Relations," 28.

28. Daniel Goffman, *The Ottoman Empire and Early Modern Europe* (New York:
Cambridge University Press, 2002), 176–177.

29. Thomas F. Arnold, *The Renaissance at War* (London: Cassel, 2001), 129–
134 and 145–147.

30. This followed the advice of a 1589 memo suggesting suspension of the
activities of the Order of Santo Stefano to secure market access, Capponi, "Palle di Marte," 1123 and 1123n78.

31. National Archives at Kew, SP 98/1, bundle 1, 122r–v. There is another
copy of the letter on 123r–v, which was used as a reference for points of
uncertainty in the transcription. "Gloriosissimo et Invictissimo Signore
Sommo Imperatore et signore del grande Imperio di Constantinopoli,
Asia, Persia, Soria, Arabia, Egitto etc. benefatore singularissimo et clem-
entissimo salute etc. Il signor Mustafa, mi ha portato, l'humanissima et
cortesissima lettera, di vostra Magestà la quale si come mi é stata di
molto favore, et accetata da me, con quella pronta et affetuosa volonta,
che conviene, sendosi degnata d'affermarmi vera, sincera, et stabile
amicitia, per tutti gli merchanti delli stati miei, et a me suggetti, che verrano a contrare nel suo grande et fellice Imperio, [.]Nel modo che al
tempo delli suoi grandi Aví havevano fatto, per tanti anni, cosi con
fermo, stabile, proposito puo esser sicura vostra Magestà che sara da loro
et da me continuata, et osservata inviolabilmente con quelle condicioni,
et capitoli, che altra volta furono trattati, et interoti da certi maligni,
come molto bene scrive vostra Magestà a piedi delle quale mando. Neri

Giraldi uno dei mij [miei] gentilhuomini, et mercanti Florentini, acciochе le dichiari apertamente l'intentio mia, et di tutta questa natione molto inclinata al nome et grandezza di vostra Magestà et ne riporti non solo firmata la capitulatione che mando dala invitissima mano di vostra Magestà et suo Imperiale sigillo: Ma ancora l'assicuri d'una constante, ferma, sincera, et stabile amicitia, et fede; Postposto il corso delle Gallere cavaglieri di santo Stephano che non hanno che [122v:] fare in conto alcuno con li merchanti ne con la natione, come ha potuto vedere il signor Mustafa, et le sara detto dal Giraldi al quale piaccera a vostra Magestà dara intiera fede, et credenza, come che io stessi le parlassi, perche tutto quello che si fermara con lui, sara fermo et stabilito da me, et da tutti li mercanti della provincia à me suggetta; Al ritorno del quale non mancaro mandare il Bailo a honorare in nome di questa natione, et risedere sotto il suo invittissimo Imperio. Però rimet[t]endo mi a lui, le baccio con ogni reverenza le sue potentissime et invitissime mani. Di Fiorenza il Di primo di Luglio 1598 Ferdinando Gran Duca di Toscana."

32. National Archives at Kew, SP 98/1, bundle 1, 122r, "Postposto il corso delle Gallere cavaglieri di santo Stephano"; MAP Person ID 14155, "Giraldi, Neri."

33. From Neri Giraldi, perhaps in 1598, MAP Doc ID 21075, ASF, MdP 4275, 315.

34. Galluzzi, *Storia del Granducato di Toscana*, vol. 5, book 5, chapter 8, 212–214, year 1598.

35. Hanlon, *Twilight*, 11 and 39–41.

36. Hanlon, *Twilight*, 40–41. The quotation is from 40. See also Fernand Braudel, *The Mediterranean and the Mediterranean World in the Age of Philip II*, 2nd rev. ed., 2 vols., trans. Siân Reynolds (Berkeley: University of California Press, 1995), 2: 876–879.

37. See Hanlon, *Twilight*, 30, for the figures.

38. I take this from Hanlon, *Twilight*, 13 and 40.

39. For the importance of logistics to galley warfare, see Geoffrey Parker, "Ships of the Line," in Parker, ed., *The Cambridge History of Modern Warfare* (New York: Cambridge University Press, 2005), 119–120; Hanlon, *Twilight*, 10–11; John H. Pryor, *Geography, Technology, and War: Studies in the Maritime History of the Mediterranean 649–1571* (New York: Cambridge University Press, 1992).

40. MAP Doc ID 12465, ASF, MdP 2951, June 10, 1618 (perhaps).

41. MAP Person ID 11185, "Girón, Fernando" (1564–1631). While I rely on the original ms. from ASF, MdP 4759, I draw on the following relevant Medici Archive Project entries for reference: Fernando Girón to Ferdinando I de' Medici, in Florence, 1605, MAP Doc ID 26648, ASF, MdP 4759; Fernando Girón, in Alexandria (perhaps), to Ferdinando I de' Medici, in Florence, 1605 (perhaps), MAP Doc ID 26794, ASF, MdP 4759.

42. "a Sua Maesta Catolica de la facilita dell'Impresa delli Ferraglioni," MAP Doc ID 26648, ASF, MdP 4759. The MAP entry for this letter specifies that the giver of the advice was Jacques de Vinceguerre.

43. ASF, MdP 4759: "perche pigliando questo castello che assigura Il porto d'Alessandria trovarebono gli anche gallioni di Constantinopoli cargati per ritornarsene."

44. ASF, MdP 4759.

45. ASF, MdP 4759: "che sono dentro dell'isola vinti Christiani contra un Turco."

46. On the Long Turkish War (1593-1606), see Peter H. Wilson, *The Thirty Years War: Europe's Tragedy* (Cambridge, MA: Harvard University Press, 2009), 76-115. On the rebellions, see William J. Griswold, *The Great Anatolian Rebellion: 1000–1020 / 1591–1611* (Berlin: Laus Schwarz, 1983); Karen Barkey, *Bandits and Bureaucrats: The Ottoman Route to State Centralization* (Ithaca, NY: Cornell University Press, 1994). On the Safavid front, see Colin Imber, "The Battle of Sufiyan, 1605: A Symptom of Ottoman Military Decline?" in *Iran and the World in the Safavid Age*, ed. Willem Floor and Edmund Herzig (New York: I. B. Tauris, 2012), 96-98.

47. Hanlon, *Twilight*, 40-41, for the decline in Tuscan naval activity.

48. Braudel, *Mediterranean*, 2: 1154-1166.

49. This last has been Hippo Regius, then Bona, then Bône, now Annaba, Algeria.

50. Halil İnalcık, *The Ottoman Empire: The Classic Age 1300–1600* (London: Phoenix, 2000), 213-216, offers a useful chronology. See also Arnold, *Renaissance at War*, 143-144; Parker, "Ships of the Line," 121 (map 5).

51. Francesco di Paolo Vinta in Milan to Cosimo I de' Medici in Florence, March 14, 1551, MAP Doc ID 17824, ASF, MdP 3102, 302; Venice to Florence, October 4, 1574, MAP Doc ID 26967, ASF, MdP 3082, 151r; Venice to Florence, October 19, 1574, MAP Doc ID 26973, ASF, MdP 3082, 154r; Koca (Pasha) Sinan to Mehmet (Pasha) Sokollu in Istanbul, 1574, MAP Doc ID 22743, ASF, MdP 5037, 413.

52. Cosimo Bartoli in Venice to Cosimo I de' Medici in Florence, June 7, 1567, MAP Doc ID 27206, ASF, MdP 2978, 207r.

53. Venice to Florence, May 21, 1575, MAP Doc ID 27166, ASF, MdP 3082, 259r.

54. Francesco I de' Medici in Poggio a Caiano to Pedro de Mendoza in Genoa, September 11, 1581, MAP Doc ID 13989, ASF, MdP 257, 34; Francesco I de' Medici in Florence to Pedro de Mendoza in Genoa, September 23, 1581, MAP Doc ID 16098, ASF, MdP 257, 50; Francesco I de' Medici in Poggio a Caiano to Luigi Dovara in Lisbon, September 24, 1581, MAP Doc ID 14018, ASF, MdP 257, 54.

55. Cristiano Pagni in Poggio a Caiano to Pier Francesco Riccio in Florence, September 24, 1550, MAP Doc ID 7815, ASF, MdP 1176, Ins. 6, 9.

56. Capponi, *Victory of the West*, 84.

57. Braudel, *Mediterranean*, 1: 135-136.

58. Cosimo I de' Medici in Florence to Piero di Niccolò Machiavelli in Pisa, August 19, 1560, MAP Doc ID 8770, ASF, MdP 211, 95; Cosimo I de' Medici in Florence to Luca Martini in Livorno, August 20, 1560, MAP Doc ID 8773, ASF, MdP 626b, 96.

59. Giulio Battaglini in Naples to Lorenzo di Francesco Usimbardi in Florence on July 29, 1594, MAP Doc ID 17832, ASF, MdP 4085, 120.

60. Istanbul to Belisario di Francesco Vinta in Florence, perhaps in 1600, MAP Doc ID 21127, ASF, MdP 4275, 553. On the raid, see Hanlon, *Twilight*, 39. On the ransom of a prisoner from the same site—the Torre del Mar Nero—in 1601, see Iacopo Tonti in Torre del Mar Nero, Turkey, to Aurelio Tonti in Pistoia on November 4, 1601, MAP Doc ID 26942, ASF, MdP 4275, 506r; Francesco Marini in Istanbul to Aurelio Tonti in Pistoia, September 13, 1601, MAP Doc ID 26943, ASF, MdP 4275 521r.

61. The inventory is dated August 31, 1610, MAP Doc ID 17056, ASF, MdP 1305, 283.

62. Mehmet (Pasha) in Tripoli to Ferdinando I de' Medici in Florence, July 24, 1593, MAP Doc ID 26431, ASF, MdP 4279, 54.

63. Masseo Massei in Luri, Corsica, to Ferdinando II de' Medici in Florence, perhaps December 1636, MAP Doc ID 22172, ASF, MdP 4724, Ins. 4, 349; Ferdinando II de' Medici in Florence to Mamet (Pascià) in Tripoli, perhaps 1637, MAP Doc ID 18106, ASF, MdP 4274, Ins. 4, 124. For an account of the complexities of multiple legal jurisdictions and international trade involving Corsica, Genoa, Tunis, and Tuscany, see Guillaume Calafat, "Jurisdictional Pluralism in a Litigious Sea (1590–1630): Hard Cases, Multi-sited Trials and Legal Enforcement between North Africa and Italy," in John-Paul Ghobrial, ed., "Global History and Microhistory," Supplement 14, *Past and Present* 242 (Nov. 2019): 142-178.

64. Mamet (Pascià) in Tripoli to Ferdinando II de' Medici in Florence, May 22, 1639, MAP Doc ID 18094, ASF, MdP 4274, Ins. 4, 117.

65. Livorno to Florence on February 27, 1577 (MAP adjusted date), MAP Doc ID 16010, ASF, MdP 694, 103; Alessandro Puccini in Livorno to Francesco I de' Medici in Florence, February 27, 1577 (MAP adjusted date), MAP Doc ID 16012, ASF, MdP 694, 102.

66. Mehmet (Pasha) in Tunis to Ferdinando I de' Medici in Florence on May 28, 1590, MAP Doc ID 26422, ASF, MdP 4275, 48.

67. Emilio de' Cavalieri in Florence to Christine de Lorraine-de' Medici in Tuscany, October 3, 1589 (perhaps), MAP Doc ID 3641, ASF, MdP 5926, 226.

68. Ali (Arnaut Mamí) Mamí in Algiers to Antonio Serguidi in Florence on December 4, 1590, MAP Doc ID 26430, ASF, MdP 4279, 50. MAP tran-

scription: "perché non vorriei che per il mal tempo se morisse come fece colui di Sua Altezza Serenissima."

69. MAP Person ID 15211, "Mamí, Ali" (Arnaut Mamí). I draw this information from the research notes. See also MAP Person ID 1027, "Serguidi, Antonio."

70. Braudel, *Mediterranean*, 2: 878.

71. Hanlon, *Twilight*, 39.

72. Asdrubale Barbolani di Montauto in Venice to Ferdinando I de' Medici in Florence, January 19, 1607, MAP Doc ID 13987, ASF, MdP 3000, 13.

73. Bernardo di Bartolomeo (il Baroncello) Baroncelli in Livorno to Francesco I de' Medici, May 28, 1565, MAP Doc ID 21828, ASF, MdP 515a, 1030; Francesco I de' Medici in Florence to Giuseppe della Seta, September 9, 1568, MAP Doc ID 19209, ASF, MdP 229, 257.

74. Marin Malleville in Florence to Ferdinando I de' Medici in Florence, April 25, 1600, MAP Doc ID 18968, ASF, MdP 4759, 9.

75. Hanlon, *Twilight*, 39-51.

76. Hanlon, *Twilight*, 40.

77. Belisario di Francesco Vinta at Pratolino to Sallustio Tarugi in Madrid, October 16, 1607, MAP Doc ID 17132, ASF, MdP 5052, 483. My information on the Sala di Bona in the Pitti Palace comes from a personal visit and from a British Museum online collection entry for a drawing by Bernardino Poccetti, accessed February 15, 2016, http://www.britishmuseum .org/research/collection_online/collection_object_details.aspx?objectId =715690&partId=1&people=111237&peoA=111237-2-9&page=1. This preparatory drawing for a fresco depicting the siege of Bona was done for a 1608-1609 commission for the Sala di Bona—a remarkably rapid pace of commemoration for a victory that had taken place on September 16, 1607.

78. Cesare Ciardelli in Livorno to Lorenzo di Francesco Usimbardi in Florence, February 8, 1610, MAP Doc ID 17058, ASF, MdP 1305, 295.

79. Hanlon, *Twilight*, 40-41.

80. On the shrinkage of the Tuscan fleet, see Hanlon, *Twilight*, 40-41, and Capponi, "Palle di Marte," 1125-1126 and 1131.

81. On the *Quattro Mori* (*Monument of the Four Moors*), see Paul H. D. Kaplan, "Italy, 1490-1700," in *The Image of the Black in Western Art*, vol. 3, *From the "Age of Discovery" to the Age of Abolition, Part I: Artists of the Renaissance and Baroque*, ed. David Bindman and Henry Louis Gates Jr. (Cambridge, MA: Harvard University Press, 2010), 183.

82. Sergio Tognetti, "The Trade in Black African Slaves in Florence," in *Black Africans Renaissance Europe*, ed. T. F. Earle and K. J. P. Lowe (New York: Cambridge University Press, 2005), 213-224.

83. Francesco Carletti, *My Voyage around the World: The Chronicles of a 16th Century Florentine Merchant*, trans. Herbert Weinstock (New York: Pantheon, 1964), 4-20.

84. Biblioteca Angelica, ms. 1331, 9r. "che li tengono alla campagna nelle loro ville á branchi come il bestiame ordinorno che fossero condotti alla Città per farceli vedere." Carletti, *My Voyage*, 12-13.

85. Biblioteca Angelica, ms. 1331, 9v-10r. "cosa [10r:] veramente, che a ricordarmi di haverla fatto per commandamento di chi poteva in me, mi causa una certa tristezza e confusione di conscientia, perche veritieramente Serenissimo Signore questo mi parve sempre un traffico inhumano et indegno della professione et pietà christiana poiche non è dubbio alcuno, che si viene á fare incettà ó huomini, ó per dire piu propriamente di carne e sangue humano, e tanto piu repugna, essendo Battezzati, che se bene sono differenti nel colore, e nella fortuna del mondo, nulla dimeno hánno quella medesima Anima formatali d[e]ll'istesso fattore che formò le nostre." Carletti, *My Voyage*, 13.

86. Biblioteca Angelica, ms. 1331, 10r. "Io me ne scuso appresso á Sua Divina Maestà nonostante che io sappia molto bene, che sapendo quella, la mia intentione, et volontà esser stata sempre repugna[n]te á questo negotio non occorra." Carletti, *My Voyage Around the World*, 13.

87. Biblioteca Angelica, ms. 1331, 16r. "ma molti di essi venivano mal trattati, e infermi, e quasi mezzi morti." Carletti, *My Voyage*, 13-17 and 21.

88. Biblioteca Angelica, ms. 1331, 86v. "e io ne comprai cinq. per poco più di dodece scudi tutti che fattoli battezzare li Condussi nell'India in Goa, e quivi li lassai liberi, e uno d'essi lo menai con me sino in fiorenza, e hoggi credo si ritrovi in Roma nominato Antonio." Carletti, *My Voyage*, 115.

89. Carletti, *My Voyage*, 12-17, 21, 115, and 142-143; Antonio Forte, "About Carletti's Attitude towards Slavery," *East and West* 42, no. 2/4 (Dec. 1992), 511-513; Lionello Lanciotti, "About Carletti's Attitude towards Slavery: A Rejoinder" *East and West* 42, no. 2/4 (Dec. 1992), 515.

90. Carletti, *My Voyage*, 13.

91. Biblioteca Angelica, ms. 1331, 1r, "ma stranamente mutati e ancora castrati." Carletti, *My Voyage*, xiv. The 1701 edition is Francesco Carletti, *Ragionamenti di Francesco Carletti fiorentino sopra le cose da lui veduti ne' suoi viaggi: Si dell'Indie occidentali, e orientali come d'altri paesi* (Florence: Giuseppe Manni, 1701).

92. Natalie Zemon Davis, *Trickster Travels: A Sixteenth-Century Muslim between Worlds* (New York: Hill and Wang, 2007), 3 and 62-66.

93. Zemon Davis, *Trickster Travels*, 4.

94. See A. R. Disney, *A History of Portugal and the Portuguese Empire: From Beginnings to 1807*, 2 vols. (New York: Cambridge University Press, 2009), 2: 1-20 and esp. 5-10; Andrew C. Hess, *The Forgotten Frontier: A History of the Sixteenth-Century Ibero-African Frontier* (Chicago: University of Chicago Press, 2010).

95. Leo Africanus (Al-Hassan ibn-Mohammed al-Wezaz al-Fasi), *The History and Description of Africa: and of the Notable Things Therein Contained*, trans.

John Pory (1600), ed. Robert Brown, 3 vols. (New York: Cambridge University Press, 2010), vol. 2., 230–231.

96. Leo Africanus, *History and Description of Africa*, 232–234.

97. Kaled El Bibas, *L'emiro e il granduca: La vicenda dell'emiro Fakhr ad-Dīn del Libano nel contesto delle relazioni fra la Toscana e l'Oriente* (Florence: Le Lettere, 2010), 48.

98. MAP Person ID 3347, "Giugni, Niccolò di Vincenzo." MAP notes that Giugni was "Cameriere segreto di Cosimo II de' Medici," a knight of the Order of Santo Stefano, a Florentine senator (from 1625), and the Marchese di Camporsevoli. He served the Medici as an envoy to the Levant (1604), Morocco (1604), and Mantua (1609).

99. ASF, MdP 4274, Ins. 3. The insert consists of copies of the letters. The April 1604 letter from Fez is 83r–84r. The grand ducal letters are January 20, 1604 (87r–88r), March 15, 1604 (88r–89v), June 11, 1604 (85v–87r), June 12, 1604 (84r–85v), and June 2, 1605 (89v–90r). See El Bibas, *L'emiro e il granduca*, 48–49 and 49 n. 38.

100. El Bibas, *L'emiro e il granduca*, 49. For discussion of the escape of the king of Fez, see ASF, MdP 4274, Ins. 3, Doc. 7, 100r. On the Tuscan arms supply, see ASF, MdP 4274, Ins. 3, Doc. 7, 101.

101. ASV, Dispacci degli Ambasciatori al Senato, Lettere Ambasciatori e Rettori, Firenze XXI (1606–1607), 9–11. The relevant passage is on 9v–10r. ASV, Dispacci degli Ambasciatori al Senato, Lettere Ambasciatori e Rettori, Firenze XXI (1606–1607), 12r–15v. I quote from the comments on Morocco at 14r, "Poi passò à dirmi, che era seguita qualche fattione tra le genti delli Rè di Fetz, et di Maroco con avantaggio grande di quelli di Fetz, il quale haveva guadagnato molt'artigliaria, et , 300, camelli carichi di munitioni, che, non sapendosi come, erano passati da quel di Maroco, à quel di Fetz, il quale meritava ogni bene, perche era Principe savio, il maggiore di età, et figliuolo di moglie; et l'altro il minore, et figliuolo di schiava; et ricercato da me, come fusse, che questo havesse tutto il Tesoro rispose, che caduto il grande in disgratia del padre lo fece imprigionare. in Fetz, et che sendo in quel tempo morto, l'altro restò patron di Maroco, et del Tesoro." MAP calls Lio "the Venetian resident in Florence" in the synopsis of Asdrubale Barbolani di Montauto in Venice to Ferdinando I de' Medici in Florence on August 4, 1607, MAP Doc ID 14271, ASF, MdP 3000, 154. MAP Person ID 13878, "Ruberto, Lio," lists him as having been the Venetian resident since 1606.

## 7. THE PLOT TO DESTROY THE OTTOMAN EMPIRE

1. Colin Imber, "The Battle of Sufiyan, 1605: A Symptom of Ottoman Military Decline?" in *Iran and the World in the Safavid Age*, ed. Willem Floor and Edmund Herzig (New York: I. B. Tauris, 2012), 96–98; Caroline Finkel,

*Osman's Dream: The Story of the Ottoman Empire 1300–1923* (New York: Basic Books, 2007), 179; Edhem Eldem, Daniel Goffman, and Bruce Masters, *The Ottoman City between East and West: Aleppo, Izmir, and Istanbul* (New York: Cambridge University Press, 1999), 29–33.

2. For this I rely primarily on William J. Griswold, *The Great Anatolian Rebellion: 1000–1020/1591–1611* (Berlin: Laus Schwarz, 1983), but also on Finkel, *Osman's Dream*. Griswold also discusses the activities of the Grand Duchy of Tuscany, but I rely instead on my own research and Federico M. Federici's recent chapter, "A Servant of Two Masters: The Translator Michel Angelo Corai as a Tuscan Diplomat (1599–1609)," in *Translators, Interpreters, and Cultural Negotiators: Mediating and Communicating Power from the Middle Ages to the Modern Era*, ed. Federico Federici and Dario Tessicini (New York: Palgrave Macmillan, 2014), 81–82.

3. A *beylerbey (beglerbeg)* served as governor of the largest Ottoman administrative unit, the *beylerbeylik (beglerbegilik)*; there were more than thirty in the Ottoman Empire at the end of the sixteenth century. A *serdar (serdâr)* was usually the ranking general officer on the military frontier. Appointed by the sultan to lead a campaign, he had sweeping powers of appointment and was accountable to the sultan (Selçuk Akşin Somel, *Historical Dictionary of the Ottoman Empire* (Lanham, MD: Scarecrow, 2003), 6, 41, 43, and 268; Jane Hathaway, *The Arab Lands under Ottoman Rule, 1516–1800* (New York: Pearson, 2008), 296.

4. The foregoing relies primarily on Griswold, *Great Anatolian Rebellion*, chapters 3 and 4, but it also draws on Griswold's chapters 1 and 2 for reference. Chapter 3 provides the detail on Ottoman administration and the conflicts in Syria up to Canbuladoğlu Hüseyn Pasha's execution shortly after the Battle of Sufiyan in 1605. Husëyn's name is alternatively rendered "Canpoladzade Husëyin Pasha"; for this spelling, further discussion of the family's activities, and the transformation of the Ottoman Empire, see Baki Tezcan, *The Second Ottoman Empire: Political and Social Transformation in the Early Modern World* (New York: Cambridge University Press, 2010), 145, 149–151, 161–162, 173. For the *celâlîs*, banditry, and the Ottoman state, see Karen Barkey, *Bandits and Bureaucrats: The Ottoman Route to State Centralization* (Ithaca, NY: Cornell University Press, 1994), esp. chapter 5. For the Long Turkish War, see Peter H. Wilson, *The Thirty Years War: Europe's Tragedy* (Cambridge, MA: Harvard University Press, 2009), 76–115. On the Safavid situation, see Imber, "Battle of Sufiyan," 96–98; Abdul-Rahim Abu-Husayn, *The View from Istanbul: Ottoman Lebanon and the Druze Emirate in the Ottoman Chancery Documents, 1546–1711* (New York: I. B. Tauris in Association with the Centre of Lebanese Studies, 2004), 94.

5. Griswold, *Great Anatolian Rebellion*, 110–156, provides the basis for this narrative, which will be continued at the end of this chapter.

6. This is the title given in the treaty between Tuscany and Ali Pasha. See "Casa Giampulat, e in particolare di Noi Alij Giampulat, Principe e Protettore del Regno di Soria," ASF, MdP 4275, 113r. All translations are mine unless otherwise indicated.

7. "Al molto alto et potente Signore Halj Bascia, della honoratissima stirpe di Zambollat, Padrone di Aleppo, Damasco, e Tripoli di Sorìa, et di tutta la Terra Santa. Doppo che voi vi dichiaraste contro alla tirannide della casa Ottomåna, vi sete talmente conciliato gli animi de Principi christiani, che tutti lodando et magnificando la vostra generosa risoluzione, vi desiderano ancora augume[n]to di potenza et di gloria. et Noi ch[e] tuttavia ci ingegniamo con le Nostre Galere et Navi di travagliare questo gran Tiranno, siamo anch pronti ad aiutare tutti quelli ch[e] corcano di offenderlo. onde torna[n]dosene in cotesta provincia [56v] il Cavaliere ~~li honorato huomo m~~ Michelag.<sup>lo</sup> Corai della Città di Aleppo, molto conosciuto et amato da Noi, gli habbiamo dato alcune commessioni da trattar segretamente con esso voi per servizio comune. Però vi piacerà d'ascoltarlo, et farci poi intendere quello che di qui potremo fare per vostro servizio, et per fine vi salutiamo con tutto l[']animo. Prontissimo p[er] ogni vostri servizio," ASF, MdP 4275, 56r-v. The word <u>corcano</u> poses certain problems for translation. Florio translates "Corcáre" as "to lie downe or along, to squat downe. Also to doubt. Also to bray as a stag or bucke." Because this makes little sense in the context of the rest of the sentence, I have assumed for the purposes of the translation that "cercano" was intended.

8. As with much about Corai, his origins are disputed. For Aleppo, see Federici, "Servant of Two Masters," 81–85. For Damascus, see Kaled El Bibas, *L'emiro e il granduca: La vicenda dell'emiro Fakhr ad-Dīn del Libano nel contesto delle relazioni fra la Toscana e l'Oriente* (Florence: Le Lettere, 2010), 49. For Corai as originally Syrian Orthodox, see E. K. Faridany, "Signal Defeat: The Portuguese Loss of Comorão in 1614 and Its Political and Commercial Consequences," in *Acta Iranica: Portugal, the Persian Gulf and Safavid Persia*, ed. Rudi Matthee and Jorge Flores (Leuven, Belg.: Peeters, 2011), 128n32, for which Faridany cited "*Fondo Gonzaga, Libri dei Decreti*, 52, f. 56." Thanks to Maria Graça Almeida Borges for introducing me to this volume. The spelling of Ambassador Corai's name is also a vexed issue. The name is sometimes rendered Michel Angelo, though Corai himself seems to have preferred Michelangiolo. I generally compromise among the variants with a slight Anglicization, Michelangelo, though I retain the documents' spelling of the name in quotations and paraphrases. In the draft instructions to Ambassador Corai, his name is spelled, "Michelagnolo Corai" (ASF, MdP 4275, 49r); it is spelled "MichelAngiolo Corai" (ASF, MdP 4275, 113r) and "MichelAngiolo Coraj" (ASF, MdP 4275, 115r and 117v) in the treaty with the pasha of Aleppo. Because the

surviving manuscript of this treaty is in fact a formal translation done by Corai (ASF, MdP 4275, 115r), the spelling in this document is likely to have been what Corai preferred. Further, the enciphered signature on his letter from Aleppo of December 6, 1607 (ASF, MdP 4275, 127v), which, as it was enciphered letter by letter, is likely to have been carefully done, reads *Michelag.*lo *Corai* [Michelangiolo Corai]: "2012242823151425223229lo 2453161412." The text in italics is my transcription of the decipherment that appears in the manuscript; the bracketed text is the decipherment implied by the inferred cipher key. The name appears as "Michel Angelo Corai" in Faridany, "Signal Defeat," 125. A similar usage is present in Federici, "Servant of Two Masters." MAP Person ID 18063, "Corai, Michelagnolo," prefers the version used by the grand ducal court.

9. Federici, "Servant of Two Masters," 82–88. On Vincenzo I Gonzaga, see Valeria Finucci, *The Prince's Body: Vincenzo Gonzaga and Renaissance Medicine* (Cambridge, MA: Harvard University Press, 2015).

10. "Scapitato quì un Dragomanno Soriano, che hà servito d'Interpetre ad un seg.or Don Antonio, Gentilh[manuscript damaged at this point] Christiano, ma non dire di qual Provincia di Christianita," ASF, MdP 4275, 3r–5r. See also Richard Raiswell, "Sherley, Anthony, Count Sherley in the Nobility of the Holy Roman Empire (1565–1636?)," *Oxford Dictionary of National Biography*. On dragomans, see Natalie E. Rothman, *Brokering Empire: Trans-imperial Subjects between Venice and Istanbul* (Ithaca, NY: Cornell University Press, 2011).

11. Federici, "Servant of Two Masters," 92–93.

12. On Corai's impressive accomplishments as a polyglot, see Federici, "Servant of Two Masters," 82–83.

13. Federici, "Servant of Two Masters," 93–94.

14. Alessandra Contini, "Medicean Diplomacy in the Sixteenth Century," in *Politics and Diplomacy in Early Modern Italy: The Structure of Diplomatic Practice, 1450–1800*, ed. Daniela Frigo, trans. Adrian Belton (Cambridge: Cambridge University Press, 2000), 49–94. On legation secretaries, see pp. 70ff.

15. The treaty (ASF, MdP 4275, 117v) states, "Signor MichelAngiolo Coraj. Ambasciatore quì presente, col Signor Hippolito Lioncinj mandato in sua conpagnia dalla sudetta Altezza e dal Segretario Giorgio Crüger" N.B. The treaty is heavily abbreviated, but the abbreviations have been expanded here as elsewhere. Griswold, *Great Anatolian Rebellion*, 129, has Leoncini as the lead figure, but Federici, "Servant of Two Masters," 91–96, is right to see Corai as the head of the mission (ASF, MdP 4275, 49r).

16. "Partirete di livorno con la prima commodità di Nave che vadia verso quelle parti, menando solamente con voi il vostro compagno, et Ippolito Leoncini ,il quale mandiamo con esso voi, perche come huomo esperto vi aiuti nel servizio Nostro in quello che alla giornata giudicherete bene di

valervene, et gli comu= [at this point the sentence continues in the block of text in the left hand margin] nicherete [comunicherete] di mano in mano ogni negozio, accio che egli tanto piu si vadià esercitando nelle cose di quei paesi," ASF, MdP 4275, 49r.

17. "Si maraviglia anche S. A. che Vostro Signore non scriva nulla del Lioncino, et vorrebbe che ella si servisse di lui, et gli desse occasione di imparare et di esercitarsi," ASF, MdP 4275, 145r.

18. Angelo Bonaventura to Belisario di Francesco Vinta in Florence, perhaps 1608, MAP Doc ID 21036, ASF, MdP 4275, 155.

19. MAP Person ID 18098, "Krieger, Georg," research notes adds, "He was secretary to Michelagnolo Corai during his visit to Syria and Iran in 1607-10. Frequently referred to as 'Giorgio Criger' in documents found in MP 4275."

20. Faridany "Signal Defeat," 129n36 reads "A 29 January 1616 letter exists to Corai in Goa from George Criger, his faithful assistant then employed as an adviser at 'Adil Shah's court. Valladolid, Archivo General de Simancas, *Estado Legajos*, 437, ff. 149-151." See also Franz Übleis, "Deutsche in Indien 1600-1700: Entstehung, Struktur und Funktion des Indienbildes der deutschen Reiseberiche des 17. Jahrhunderts," *Zeitschrift für Religions- und Geistesgeschichte* 32, no. 2 (1980): 127-151.

21. For the draft instructions, see ASF, MdP 4275, 49-55; on both 49r and 49v secrecy is stressed. As so often with Tuscan activities in the Middle East, I have yet to find the final copies of the instructions. Inbound letters and treaties have been retained in final form, but it would appear that outbound documents, like letters and instructions, were often retained only in draft form; perhaps, though, they are simply retained in a location unknown to me.

22. "Similmente. sbarcato che sarete in Sorìa, mostrate d'esser andato per vostri servizij particolari, et trovando amici ò parenti vostri, [49v] non comunicherete à nessuno le commessioni che havete da Noi, essendo necessaria la segretezza, per non mettere le genti in sospetto, et per non guastare il negozio," ASF, MdP 4275, 49r-v.

23. ASF, MdP 4275, 64r-64v. I reproduce a full transcription, full translation, and cipher key for Corai's letter in appendix 5.2 of Brian Brege, "The Empire That Wasn't: The Grand Duchy of Tuscany and Empire, 1574-1609," PhD diss., Stanford University, 2014.

24. ASF, MdP 4275, 64r-v.

25. ASF, MdP 4275, 64r-v. 64v reads "C'è un Caiscio Turchescho delquale per le cose che habbiamo non m'è parso bene fidarsi"; "ma poi fu consigliato non m'intrigar con lui"; and "parendomi mille anni d'arrivare in Aleppo."

26. Cyprus had been Ottoman territory since an Ottoman invasion had captured the island during the 1570-1574 war with Venice. There are numerous accounts of the Venetian loss of Cyprus, for the Ottoman inva-

sion led to the war in which the battle of Lepanto took place. Hanlon, *Twilight of a Military Tradition*, 19–25, for instance, provides a brief account of the war and how Venice came to accept the loss of Cyprus even after the victory at Lepanto.

27. ASF, MdP 4275, 64r–v and 65r.

28. ASF, MdP 4275, 64r.

29. "è per tutto questo Regno fra terra in grandissimo sospetto, ε male per li Christiani che capitano in quelle bande, havendoli tutti per ispie è n'e stati giustificati parecchi," ASF, MdP 4275, 64r.

30. "Io fui condotto dal Bascià che mi fece un'esamina grande ε voleva molti particolari da me, ma io per esser mercante non gli seppi dare la sadisfazion che cercava, e mentre che ragionava meco, gli comparve 12152014 32291610532029,2030224151534223,3421522242522749202325273441 15123732214752232147344217231614153042121934154351533323 1034150094·2428523712331729315347231614252917333244514029 1224381632212751303312, ne disse si piano che io non intendessi ogni cosa," ASF, MdP 4275, 64r. The cipher secretary provided a combination of short interlineal decipherments and a page (65r) of decipherments for longer passages keyed using letters a through g. The text in italics in the main text consists of my translations of these decipherments checked against the inferred cipher key. The decipherment reads: "il Maiordomo maggiore, et segretam.^te gli disse esser vera la ribellione de 1500. Turchi che di nuovo s'erano uniti con i Christiani" (65r).

31. David Kahn, *The Codebreakers*, 2nd ed. (New York: Simon and Schuster, 1996), xvii–xviii, 108–111, and 150–151. Kahn's chapters 3 and 4 outline the early modern European development of ciphers.

32. "Onde 242823322917231037511243782053432729405325443142354916 2132, che fu la causa che più tosto mi licenzio che io andassi à fare i fatti miei" (64r); the decipherment reads: "onde che io viddi il Bascia molto conturbarsi" (65r). ASF, MdP 4275, 64r and 65r.

33. For an example of a lengthy enciphered insert sent with a letter, see ASF, MdP 4898, P. II, 408r–415r, from "Il Cavalier de Nobilij" in Madrid on January 16, 1569; a note on 408r gives 1568, presumably converting the date to the traditional Florentine start of the new year in March. The enciphered insert is on 415r. ASF, MdP, 4898, P. II, 429r–430r, contains an enciphered text (429r), that corresponds so closely to that on 415r that one is probably an imperfect but very close copy of the other and a decipherment (430r).

34. "123327232132142524291630,2321473442172316292438343125445042 405375·102326161225403239301551215217331244292453331829162123 100243816322127513033121023152614234734524029251733914712533 339494244322751,3712255327445251332216303310121532412325

13143015434917291544143712462623163930214749422123334, secondo che si dice 513384˙ Insom[m]a tutta l'122129151423212927445 34729264249" (64r); the decipherment reads: "Intesi ancora esser vero che un Turco rinegato de principali s'è unito con forse cento christiani del paese, e con un Caramusali sian partiti di notte in gran diligenza alla volta di Malta per passarsene, secondo ch[e] si dice, in Spagna" (65r). ASF, MdP 4275, 64r and 65r.

35. ASF, MdP 4275, 64r–64v and 65r. "Passai ancora à Nicosia per accertarmi meglio delle nove è trovai esser veriss.^me. 171221322714511215312 3472429505310231543322216342451121511171443232030263416 2152 2242303340532152 La somma delquale è che 20291527532112242925 1832373033531233 17.14.2014262316403823252933283025335326 3442 212933234028523134332228512553494416142744304240293315 34322 55333262921471225532124293916124234121518144012432 0291053403834224332284925335337513630423952161023423 427172744533243261423473452172140124210324729274453142 73033 44492732161425335.1492429253623214730333753402834105296 25533 32112373419353025531832103016 34 per esser troppo affettionati al 33˙23242834324373˙di 84˙402823262927163419355214214730122 32634 1615294253271629"; the decipherment reads: "Visitai il Vescovo delli Greci, il quale m'aperse gran cose. La somma del quale è ch[e] molto si confidano in V.A. ma perche non hanno persone ch[e] venghino à trattar con lei, no[n] possono scoprire il facil modo ch[e] gli hanno di far perdere tutto il paese, e uscir di sotto à tanta tirannia, con̄fessando ch[e] de Veneziani no[n] si debbano fidare, p[er] esser troppo affezzionati al Gra' Turco, et ch[e] il Rè di Spagna che potrebbe assai, èo per loro troppo lontano, si ch[e] V.A. sola gli potrebbe consolare" (65r).

36. ASF, MdP 4275, 64v. On the sailing season, see Fernand Braudel, *The Mediterranean and the Mediterranean World in the Age of Philip II*, 2nd rev. ed., 2 vols., trans. Siân Reynolds (Berkeley: University of California Press, 1995), 1: 137.

37. Riguccio Galluzzi pointed to the role of secret intelligence dispatched from Cyprus. Corai's letter is the most likely candidate for the information (Riguccio Galluzzi, *Storia del Granducato di Toscana*, new ed., 11 vols. (Florence: Leonardo Marchini, 1822), vol. 6, book 5, chapter 11, year 1607, 77–78).

38. Galluzzi, *Storia del Granducato*, vol. 6, book 5, chapter 11, year 1607, 77–78; Capponi, "Palle di Marte," 1109; and Hanlon, *Twilight of a Military Tradition*, 39–41.

39. Angelo Bonaventura to Belisario di Francesco Vinta in Florence, perhaps in 1608, MAP Doc ID 21040, ASF, MdP 4275, 164. MAP transcription: "Si erano finalmente posti in tanta disperatione quelli poveri Greci che

se ne volevano fugire alla montagna et lasciare la terra, sola dicendo che li Turchi non le facevano la millesima parte del danno che gli facevano li Christiani, et anco dissero che volevano mandare ambasciatori a S. A. S. a dolersi di questo fatto."

40. See ASF, MdP 4275, 49r–v, the draft instructions to Corai.

41. "Anderete senza perder tempo à trovare il Bascia d'Aleppo dove egli sarà, mostrando però ad ogni altro, ch[e] vi andate per vostri affari privati. et cercherete adito et entratura appresso di lui, sotto pretesto di dargli delle nuove di christianità. et questo vi sarà facile, perche egli medesimo haurà entro d'intendere et di domandarvi di molte cose di questi paesi, quando saprà che ci sete stato," ASF, MdP 4275, 49v.

42. "Dinanzi à lui anderete solo, et senza alcuna pompa nè apparenza [50r] et nel principio non entrerrete à ragrinar d'altro che delle cose de Principi christiani, secondo gli interrogatorij che da lui vi saranno fatti. mostrandogli quanto i detti Principi habbiano sentito et sentino volentieri i progressi che egli ha fatto contro alla tirannide Ottomàna, et che havete conosciuto et credete, che essi gli darebbono con molta prontezza aiuto et favore, ogni volta che egli si lasciasse intendere di desiderarlo," ASF, MdP 4275, 49v–50r.

43. "Se in questi ragiunamenti voi vedessi che egli non desse orecchie, et mostrasse di non sicurare delli aiuti et dell'amicizia di Principi christiani, non passate piu oltre, et non gli comunicate d'haver lettere nè ambasciate da Noi," ASF, MdP 4275, 50r.

44. See ASF, MdP 4275, 113r–117v for the treaty.

45. "Ma vedendocelo voi inclinato , come è verisimile che sarà, allora gli scoprirete à solo à solo, le Nostre commessioni, et gli presenterete la Nostra lettèra, facendogli in conformita di essa, l'offerta della Nostra amicizia et corrispondenza, et testificandogli facendogli fate, che non solamente Noi con le' Nostre forze marittime sarremo pronti à dargli quelli aiuti che potremo, ma c'ingegneremo ancora d'persuader l'istesso à tutti gli altri Principi christiani, i quali non hanno il magior desiderio, che veder de primere affatto il tirannico Imperio ottomanno," ASF, MdP 4275, 50v.

46. "Et poi che il detto Bascià di Aleppo, per gli avvisi che si sentono, è oggi si puo dir padrone di tutta la Soria, et voi stesso giudicate di far capo a˙ lui solo, et non trattar con altri, non vi si danno lettere per altri capi di quella provincia. Ma se pure a˙ lui paresse, che voi andassi a˙ trattar con qualcuni altro, potrete farlo con l˙ accompagnatura d˙un huomo suo ,o˙ con sue lettere . et in tal caso la Nostra Patente vi potra˙ servire come per lettera credenziale," ASF, MdP 4275, 53v.

47. On the issue of unfettered discretionary power, see Daniela Frigo, "Introduction," in *Politics and Diplomacy in Early Modern Italy*, 13. Alessandra

Contini, "Medicean Diplomacy in the Sixteenth Century," in *Politics and Diplomacy in Early Modern Italy*, 49–94 (especially 70).

48. Corai seems to have personally translated the treaty he negotiated with Ali Pasha (ASF, MdP 4275, 113r–117v). 115r begins "Traduttione della soscrizione del Serenissimo Principe sotto li presenti capitoli." This is followed by the pasha of Aleppo's ratification of the treaty and the conclusion of the league (written in Italian). After this, the following appears: "Traduttione della soscrizione del signor MichelAng<sup>lo</sup>io:Coraj." This in turn is followed by "Io affermo ε fortifico tutto il contenuto di questa scrittura autentica - Il humile servo di Dio MichelAngiolo Coraj." Corai's confirmation of the authenticity of the pasha of Aleppo's ratification, presumably written in the same language, does not in itself serve to indicate conclusively who translated the treaty, but Corai's previous work as a professional translator would make him the most likely candidate. Federici, "Servant of Two Masters," 83, notes that estimates of the number of languages Corai had mastered ranged from six to twenty-four.

49. ASF, MdP 4275, 23.

50. "Offritegli ancora, che se egli havesse gusto di 4. ò, 6. pezzi di cannoni all'usanza e forma d'Italia, Noi gliene manderemo volontieri, pur che egli prometti, che gli homini che vi andranno per questo effetto, siano ben visti ∧ <sup>et avanzzati</sup> et possin viver alla christiana mentre staranno in quei paesi, et che possino tornare à posta loro, con essergli da [?] nodi [?] et sicurezza di venirsene, et la promessa sia inscritto," ASF, MdP 4275, 50v.

51. ASF, MdP 4275, 50v. In the manuscript the word fragment "~~tan~~" appears at this point; I have omitted it from the translation. Perhaps the writer had begun to write the word "tanto," which might be translated as, "as well as."

52. "Sopratutto havete da rimostrargli et persuadergli l'esser unito, ~~tan~~ et mantenere una benissima intelligenza con tutti gli altri capi che si sono alienati dal detto Imperio, accio che riconoscendo ciascuno le sue forze, possino alle occasioni di guerra offensiva o˙ defensiva congiugnerle insieme. perche sentendosi questa unione, il Turco perderá la speranza di poterli opprimeri, et i Principi Christiani s'indurranno tanto piu volentieri ad aiutarli," ASF, MdP 4275, 50v–51r.

53. The general point is mine, but El Bibas, *L'emiro e il granduca*, 51, points to Spain's other commitments and sense of the challenges and advantages of the project.

54. Beginning with some uncertain marks, which I have transcribed as bracketed question marks, the passage continues in a long note in the left-hand margin of the manuscript, "et già s'è inteso qui, che il Turco si preparava con grandissime forze per debellargli [??] et principalmente il Bascia d'Aleppo, per esser di stirpe di grandi signori della Sorìa, et di

quei proprij che la diedero alla Casa Ottomanna, onde tanto piu è necissaria la detta unione, perche il Turco conservi instantemente di separarli concedendo à ciascun Capo tutte le condizioni che chiederanno, per non le mantener poi loro, come fu à molti, et come hanno fatto i suoi Antecessori," ASF, MdP 4275, 51r.

55. ASF, MdP 4275, 51r. The following derives from the same marginal note as the foregoing quotation. "Ma stando essi uniti, che haver p.ª concertato quello che hanno da fare, oˑ il Turco. non passerà innanzi, oˑ essi lo romperanno per haver miglior soldatesca di lui, et lo rintuzzeranno in europa."

56. ASF, MdP 4275, 51r. The beginning of the following derives from the same marginal note as the foregoing, but after "potenza" it shifts to a second, nested marginal note that appears below the first in the manuscript; the shift is signaled by a mark in the text in the first marginal note and a corresponding mark at the beginning of the second marginal note. "I Principi della quale vedendo che egli habbia perduto l'Asia, si solleveranno anch'essi, e con gran facilità abbatteranno la sua potenza et Noi habbiamo tanto in mano, da far sollevare in euŕopa molti popoli, et già son qui i capi, che non aspettano altro sendo di sentir questa unione, havendo essi intelligenza da poter haver nelle mani delle piu forti piazze dl Turco, et i Principi christiani che ne sono consapevoli, son punti ad aiutarli."

57. ASF, MdP 4275, 51r. The following derives from the same marginal note as the first part of the quoted material in the foregoing footnote. The text here quoted begins immediately after the mark indicating the point where the text of the second, nested marginal note was to have been inserted. "Per questi considerazioni ci parrebbe, che il Bascia d' Aleppo et i suoi collegati, non dovessero ammettere ambasciata oˑ negoziazione alcuna dl Turco, anzi ~~trattar mala~~ ₍far rigorosa dimostrazione contro à₎ quelli che vi venissero per simili trattamenti, per spavento degli altri .et voi ~~m~~ ᶜᵃᵛᵃˡⁱᵉʳᵉ Michelag.ˡᵒ vi offerirete al detto Bascia, dˑ impiegar l[']opera vostra, per ristrigner l'amicizia et unione di quelli che non si fussero ancora collegati seco . perche quando il Turco viene, bisogna haver prima concertato insieme botte le cose, et non haver allora aˑ far altro, che adoperar l'arme."

58. See ASF, MdP 4275, 51r–52r and 53v–54r for the Persian connection and 54v for Corai's instruction concerning the Patriarch of the Maronites.

59. ASF, MdP 4275, 51v and 52v–53v.

60. ASF, MdP 4275, 51v. "Et assicurate pure il detto Bascia et ognˑaltro di quei capi, che i Principi ₍christiani₎ non havranno mai avidità di guadagnar paesi ne` Terre in Asia, ma che la principal intenzione loro è, che ognuno concorra à finir di distruggere il detto Imperio Ottommanno."

61. ASF, MdP 4275, 51v. The quoted text is drawn from a marginal note. Corresponding marks in the manuscript indicate that the text in the marginal note was to be inserted directly after that quoted in the foregoing note, "et ciascuno di detti capi resterà padrone delle sue provincie, et di quelle che conquisteranno."

62. ASF, MdP 4275, 51v–52r. Returning to the main text: "Et che in queste buone congiunture Noi habbiamo speranza, che quietandosi ben presto le differenze che hora seno tra'l Papa et i Veneziani, debbino tutti i Principi della christianità voltarsi contro al Turco, con aiutar principalmente il detto Bascia' d'Aleppo, et quelli che saranno seco uniti et collegati."

63. "Di tutte queste negoziazioni, si come ricordiamo à voi la segretezza, cosi la ricorderete ancora al detto Bascia' d'Aleppo, perche se venisse agli orecchi del Turco, che egli cercasse di fare amicizia con i Principi christiani, et trattasse d' haver aiuti da queste parti, tanto piu si moverebbe à voltar tutte le sue forze in Soria, per cercare di dissipar quei Capi, innanzi che essi facessero collegazioni in Christianità," ASF, MdP 4275, 52r–52v.

64. "Et doppo che voi havrete piu d'una volta discorso col detto Bascia di tutte le sopradette cose, gli direte che Noi, et gli altri Principi christiani, oltre al desiderare la depressione dell·. Imperio del Turco, come di nostro nimico comune, non havremo altro interesse nè voglia particolare, se non che i christiani possino andare et stare sicuramente in Hierusalem, et che il desiderio Nostro sarebbe, che conquistando egli quella provincia et quella Città, si contentasse di concederà, che ella potesse esser habitata di' Christiani, i qùali sotto la protezzionè di lui fussero sicuri, et potessero esercitarvi la Nostra Religione, et raccottarvi di mano in mano tutti quelli che di christianità vi volessero andare . et che. per ricompensa ː di questo, Noi procureremmo che questi Principi unitamente gli farebbono un donativo annuo di 25. ò, 30 ͫ scudi, à secondo quello che fusse giudicato conveniente, purche assegnassero ai Christiani tanto territorio dintorno alla Città, che potessero serminarvi grano et altre cose, al meno fino al porto del Zaffo," ASF, MdP 4275, 52v–53r.

65. ASF, MdP 4275, 53v and 54v–55r. The relevant passages are from the marginal note on 53v that was to have been inserted immediately after the end of the passage quoted in the foregoing note: "Ristretta che havrete la pratica col detto Bascià, procurate che egli si contenti, che i Nostri vasselli possino andàre iṅ Tripoli di Soria ᴧ Alessandretta et altri Porti che siano, sotto L suo comando come anco le Nostre Galere, mostrandoli, che questo ᴧ traffico porterebbe a' lui et à' tutta quella provincia molto utile. et che particolarmente vi potessero andare sette Navi che hora usciranno fuora, benissimo armate, le quali, quando bisognasse per lor servizio, anderebbono anche ad assediar le bocche di cost.ˡⁱ accio che il Turco non potesse mandar fuora provedi-

menti contro di loro. i quali vasselli non harebbono paura, quando ben vi fusse un'armata grossa dl Turco. et oltre alle robe che queste Navi potrebbono portare ò in Tripoli, ò in Alessandretta, comprerebbono˙ anche con denari contanti delle cose di quei paesi, e massimamente del grano se ven 'avanzasse. Et se troverete facilita˙ d'introdurre il detto commerzio, et ne facciate le capitulazioni inscritto, con haverle voi in mano, ingegnatevi di darne avviso al Conte Alfonso Montecuccoli capo delle dette Navi, se s'intenda che capitino in quei mari, come potrebbono capitare alla Finica a˙ far acqua. et scrivetegliene con lettere duplicate, condennandole in dugento pezze da otto, che dal detto Conte saranno pagati à chi gli presentera˙ la lettera con la nuova di poter andar liberamente a̶ ̶l̶i̶ ̶p̶o̶l̶i̶ ᴧ in quei porti. et quà a˙ Noi scrivete per via d˙Alessandretta, col mezzo del Consolo de Franzesi, et per tutti i vasselli Franzesi che partiranno per Marsilia, ó per Venezia con far indirizzar le lettere all˙Ambasciatore di Francia in Venezia ò ai Pesciolini in Marsilia, et anche in Messina a˙ Cosimo del Sera . et scrivendo per via di Cipri, s'indirizzino a˙ Bartolomeo Munter Fiammingo che sta alle Saline di Cipri, il quale le manderà a˙ livorno a˙ Matteo d Terenlio" and the postscript on 54v–55r and its attendant marginal note on 55r: "Postscritta . Intorno à quello che habbiamo detto di sopra del commerzio che havete da ingegnarvi di introdurre ,avio che i Nostri vasselli possino andare liberamente nel porto di Tripoli di Sorìa; vogliamo che o̶l̶t̶r̶e̶ concludeṅdosi questo negotio et cavandone voi scrittura autentica, cerchiate di darne anche avvjso al Nostro Ammiraglio, quando intendiate che egli possa trovarsi con le Galere n̶e̶l̶l̶e̶ ̶n̶o̶n̶ in quei mari vicini, come alle Finica, ò in altro luogo . et le lettere che scriverete ò à lui, o al Conte Montecuccoli, siamo in cifra" (54v–55r) at this point there is a mark that indicates that the following marginal note should be inserted: "perche essi hauråno la copia di quella medesima che s' e data à voi." (55r) The main text then resumes: "facendo anche lor sapere, se potranno sicuramente p̶o̶r̶t̶a̶r̶e̶ condurre à vendere in Tripoli delle robe che havessero predate ᴧ ò schiavi da risenttare et nel condennar le lettere che manderete loro, anderete ate destreggiando, con quelle somme di denari, piu ò meno, secondo che ,˙ à voi parrà a̶ v̶o̶i̶ conveniente, et secondo le _ . commodità che troverete per li ricapiti della lettere."

66. ASF, MdP 4275, 56r–56v. For the draft of the passport, see ASF, MdP 4275, 57r.

67. For the trope of Ottoman or Turkish tyranny, see the draft letter to the king of Persia, Shah 'Abbas, at ASF, MdP 4275, 22v; the draft instructions to Ipolito Leoncini at ASF, MdP 4275, 29r; the draft instructions to Michelagnolo Corai at ASF, MdP 4275, 50r and 50v; and a copy of a letter to the pasha of Aleppo at ASF, MdP 4275, 56. On the rhetoric of tyranny, see Lucette Valensi, *The Birth of the Despot: Venice and the Sublime Porte*, trans. Arthur Denner (Ithaca, NY: Cornell University Press, 1987).

68. ASF, MdP 4275, 146r–147r.
69. "Serenissimo, et Degnissimo Re Iddio gli conceda salute, et ogni maggiore grandezza, è contento, Augurando li vita vitto'riosa, è felice: Salutandola affezionatissimamente per parte del Serenissimo Gran Duca di Toscana mio Signore et io ubbidiente Servo, genuflesso à I[ ]piedi, gli bacio con' ogni umilta, et Ossequio la sua Regale Veste," ASF, MdP 4275, 146r.
70. "per'andare insieme uniti, a'i danni del' Gran Turco con' fare. L'impresa del'Santissimo Sepolcro, se cosi sarà contenta Vostra Maestà Regia: E il Serenissimo Gran Duca non sollo aiuterà con' le sue forze, ma ancora procurera aiuto da altri Principi Christiani, che ciascuno volentieri a tale Impresa ci concorrera: Offerendosi di più di fare negoziare col Persiano potentissimo Re, che voglia ancorà Esso Combattere, per disturbare dall'altra parte; et tutto questo debba seguire principalmente per servizio di Vostra Maestà Regia," ASF, MdP 4275, 146r.
71. "Serenissimo Re. Essendo Io' stato mandato alla sua Regale presenza; dal Serenissimo Gran' Duca di Toscana mio Signor per ricercarla di potere ottenere Scala franca di Mercanzia, à tutti i suoi Porti della sua Spiaggia marittima, accio possino andare i suoi Mercanti et Sudditi per il suo Regno, franchi, e sicuri; Essendo che—questo di gran lunga apporterà, al suo Serenissimo Stato, benifizio, et reputazione, con' fare copiosi, i suoi Popoli di mercanzie, et di commerzo honorevolissimo, da potere cavare molto utile, et profitto:—Si come all'incontro, se cosi vorrà accettare. Vostra Maestà Regia gli offerisce il Serenissimo Gran Duca tale Commerzio et Scala franca A Livorno, et in tutti i suoi Porti, et Spiagge; come ancora per tutto il suo Felicissimo Stato: promettendo ricevere, i Mercanti, et Mercanzie, e ciascuno de suoi Sudditi, con ogni sorte di amorevolezza: et saranno accarezzati, et Amati," ASF, MdP 4275, 146r.
72. "Le marcanzie saranno Rascie, Perpignani, Saie, Accordellati, Panni fini, di piu sorte, et di ciascuno colore Drapperia, Velluti, Rasi, Dommaschi, Ermisini puri senza opera, et drappi variati con' opere, Drappi d'oro Signorili, et ricchi, con opere rare, et di tutte queste cose ne verrà quantita; Essendo Mercanzie tali ch[e]' i suoi Sudditi con grandezza, et con' molta reputazione sene serviranno: Ancora ci verrann Risi, et molte altre cose particulari," ASF, MdP 4275, 146r.
73. "E il Serenissimo Gran Duca non sollo aiuterà con' le sue forze, ma ancora procurera aiuto da altri Principi Christiani, che ciascuno volentieri a tale Impresa ci concorrera," ASF, MdP 4275, 146r.
74. "Offerendosi di più di fare negoziare col Persiano potentissimo Re, che voglia ancorà Esso Combattere, per disturbare dall'altra parte; et tutto questo debba seguire principalmente per servizio di Vostra Maestà Regia Essendo cosa verisimile che con tale buon'ordine, tutto doverrà supire à bene; Et massimo invocando l'aiuto Divino, che voglia essere favorevole à tale Impresa, In concederne Vittorioso fine," ASF, MdP 4275, 146r.

75. "Accio [146v:] i Turchi non possino impadronirsi, per date disturbo allo sbarco, nell'andare ò tornare; E quando in questo fatto Vostra Maesta Regia gli occorressi bisogno di Genti, et Artiglieria, per guardare bene gli detti Porti, et Spiaggia, Il Serenissimo Gran' Duca gliene offera, et largisce, si come ancora ogni altra cosa che sia giusta, et convenevole. E Se Vostra Maestà Regia si volesse allargare meco lo potria fare liberamente; In denotarmi i dubbi che Essa potesse tenere in tal' fatto. narrando in che meglio modo giudica si possa muovere tal' negozio con' piu suo vantaggio, et sicurezza," ASF, MdP 4275, 146r–v.

76. "A honore d'Iddio, che per tale causa il Serenissimo Gran Duca ha' mosso' tale Negozio per Divina spirazione, per occultare, abbassare, è spiantare per quanto può; questo Gran Turco, che si disturba, et rapisce, et non solo, è nemico à Christiani, ma tutto il mondo ancora, infesta, flagella, danneggia, e distrugge," ASF, MdP 4275, 146v.

77. "Ne possendo tutto il Mondo insieme contrastare contro al suo Divino volere ne pure opporsegli, che non sia vinto superato, et disperso: Si come fu Vinto Inghiotte [obscured by the binding; =?] to, et Summerso in uno stante Faraone con' tutto il suo numeroso Esercito; per volere perseguire gli Hebrei contro al'Divino volere," ASF, MdP 4275, 146v.

78. "Havendo tutto questo detto, à honore d'Iddio, et per saddisfare al' comandamento del' mio Serenissimo Principe, et Signore Dove si puo scorgere benissimo il Future utile, et benefizio grande che puo apportate à Vostra Maeste Regia; Andando unita incompagnia del Serenissimo Gran Duca di Toscana Ferdinando Medici. Unico mio Signore et Patrone," ASF, MdP 4275, 147r.

79. "Per la relazione che Noi habbiamo havuta del Serenissimo Gran Duca di Toscana, e che c'è stata data dal Cavaliere Signor MichelAngiolo Corai Gentilhuomo d'Aleppo, spedito à Noi, per Ambasciatore espresso da Sua Altezza Serenissima à nome della quale ci ha presentato una giocondissima lettera, à Noi sopramodo gratissima per haver visto con gran piacer Nostro in essa, il grandissimo desiderio che ha Sua Altezza Serenissima di contrarre con esso Noi una perfetta Amicizia. Noi dichiaramo che intorno à questo, non punto minore è il desiderio Nostro, et che ne siamo contentissimi. Però accettiamo volontieri la sua potentissima & inviolabile Amiciza, secondo che la c'è stata realmente offerta; si come siam sicuri, che l'accettarà l'eccelsa & inrévocabil Amicizia Nostra, la quale le offeriamo con quei maggiori vincoli d'obligo & affezione, che possino stringere una vera Amicizia eterna, antivedendo dover risultarne per ambele parti infinito bene," ASF, MdP 4275, 113r.

80. The treaty uses the word Capitolazioni in article 3 and again in Article 5, ASF, MdP 4275, 113v–114r. See Griswold, *Great Anatolian Rebellion*, 128–132; see also Federici, "Servant of Two Masters," 91–96.

81. ASF, MdP 4275, 113–117. For a brief account of the treaty, see Galluzzi, *Storia del Granducato di Toscana*, vol. 6, book 5, chapter 11, 75–76, year 1607.

82. "si fa forse il Serenissimo Gran Duca di far condescendere à tanta Amcizia Nostra la Santità del Beatissimo Papa Paolo V.º vicario dell' Omnipotentissimo Dio fra Christiani, e la Maiestà del Gloriosissimo ε Cattolico Don Filippo iij Re di Spagna Ze'. et altri Potentati e Principi Christiani, i quali tutti concorderanno à far una Lega con esso Noi," ASF, MdP 4275, 113r.

83. For a sense of the scale of this trade, see Faridany, "Signal Defeat," 123n15, who estimates annual raw silk exports from Iran to Europe via Aleppo at above two hundred metric tons in 1600.

84. ASF, MdP 4275, 113r.

85. "Perilche Noi maggiormente ce n'allegriamo, e promettiamo intrapender qual si voglia Impresa più ardua, per colorire così possente disegno. Dando inrevocabil parola d'impugnar per la prima, l'acquisto della Santa Città di Hierusalemme, col mover guerra à tutte quelle Città ε Terre, che ardiranno contraporcisi & far ogni sforzo maggiore per impadronircene, come speriamo in Dio, che ci habbia felicemente à riuscire. Perlaquale Santa impresa, & ad ogni altra ancora più difficile, Noi impegniamo la fede Nostra, e giuriamo voler esser prontissimi ad esporci, ogni volta che il detto Serenissima Gran Duca haurà fatto soscriver l'Amicizia e Lega con esso Noi, all Santità del predetto Pontefice, & alla Maiestà Cattolica e con amendue accordato, e passati gli Articoli ò capitoli appartenenti à tutte le provisioni, che à si notabili imprese ci hanno ad esser fatte," ASF, MdP 4275, 113r.

86. "Rimettendoci (in quanto à esse) alla prudentissima Providenza e valore di Sua Altezza Serenissima la qua haurà riguardo squisito come questo è il più importante e maggior: moto, che all' eta Nostre le in tuttol Mondo si possa fare. E che quanto l'aiuto sarà più grande, ce ne ingagliardiremo con maggior: corraggio, e con più certa speranza ci esporremo tentare e superare virtuosamente (favente Deo) ogni impresa. Replichiamo adunque che all'hora che il detto Serenissima Gran Duca ci farà avvisati che li suddetti dua Principi in particolare ci habbino accettati in Amicizia e segnata la Lega e li capitoli accordati, e et ne mandi per messaggio espresso scrittura autentica, e che secondo il contenuto di essa, ci arrivino al preciso tempo le provisioni & aiuti alli Porti di marina del Nostro Dominio; dove sarà ordine bastante ricevere il tutto, e fare havere ogni comodità alla Galere ò Brettoni ò altri Vasselli che per tal effetto vi capiteranno: Noi saremo prestiss:[ni] à governarci conforme all'ordine, che ne darà detta Lega, per dar principio all'imprese, ne mettere indugio alcuno à tanta essecuzione, acciòche quanto prima si senta in Christianità li Nostri felici progressi," ASF, MdP 4275, 113v.

87. Finkel *Osman's Dream*, 179, sees the economic role of Aleppo as the motivating factor behind Tuscan involvement.

88. "Hora per assicurare maggiormente tutti li Principi della Lega della Nostra inviolabil fede, e che il Nostro desiderio non può esser maggiore per deprimere e annullare si potente nemico: Noi promettiamo assegnare un Porto delle Nostre marine, secondo che per avanti Noi hauremo convenuto col Altezza di Toscana, à tutte le Galere, Navi ε vasselli della detta Lega, alliquali sarà usata ogni sorte d'amorevolezza, e fatte havere le comodità che le mostreranno desiderare," ASF, MdP 4275, 113r.

89. Geoffrey Parker, "Ships of the Line", in *The Cambridge History of Warfare*, Geoffrey Parker, ed., (New York: Cambridge University Press, 2005), 119.

90. "E perche la prima impresa che Noi impugneremo, intendiamo che habbia da essere quella della Città Santa di Hierusalemme, alla quale vogliamo andare in persona, sempre che li predetti Principi della Lega, ci habbino fatto havere tutte le provisioni. Necessarie conforme alle Capitolazioni che le haurà fatto passare il Gran Duca di Toscana. E speriamo con la grazia di Dio d'impatronircene: Noi vogliamo che tutti li Christiani Cattolici possino sicuramente habitarla, & essercitarvi la loro, Cattolica Religione, come ancora raccettare di mano in mano tutti quelli che di Christianità vi volessero andare; ma che in materia di differenze ò altro che nascesse infra di loro, habbino à ricorrere al Console ò vice Console della Nazion Fiorentina, che vi manderà il Console di detta Nazione dimorante in Aleppo, per amministrar la Giustizia nelle lore differenze," ASF, MdP 4275, 113v.

91. Bernard Lewis, *The Middle East: A Brief History of the Last 2,000 Years* (New York: Scribner, 1995), 229.

92. ASF, MdP, 4275, 114r, Article 6.

93. "Intendiamo ancora e vogliamo che conquistando quella Provincia e Citta Santa che non solamente li Fiorentini ò Toscani, ma che tutti li Christiani dell'uno e dell'altro sesso che rendono obedienza alla Santità suddetta del Beatissimo P.P.Vº andando à visitare come Pellegrini ò altrimente il Santissimo Sepolcro in Hierusalemme di Giesu Christo lor Redentore ε Dio, come ancora tutti gli altri luoghi santi che per tutta la Palestina si ritrovano, sieno esenti d'ogni sorte di spesa ò tributo tanto nel visitare e entrare, che nell'uscire da detti Santi luoghi ò andarci, é in particolare al detto Santissimo Sepolcro, non paghino cosa alcuna, secondo, che gli hanno accostumati ò erano soliti di pagare, nel tempo che l'Impero Ottomanno gli ha ò haveva indegnamente posseduti. Poiche per questa abilità ò esenzione suddetta che Noi accordiamo à tutti li Pellegrini e commoranti nella Città Santa ci ha promesso il Signor Ambasciatore Corai à nome del Serenissimo Gran Duca di Toscana, che per ricompensa ci sarà fatto un donativo annuale, secondo che conveniremo insieme quell'Altezza e Noi essere ragionevole," ASF, MdP 4275, 114r.

94. "E perche da si potente & inviolabil Amicizia e Lega, Noi pretendiamo che l'una parte e l'altra habbia da dare e cavare della comodità à beneficio comune, per il commerzio libero nelle Scale Città ε Terre, che sono all'obedienza Nostra, secondoche gli occorrerà negoziare, habbiamo comandato, che oltre alli Capitoli scritti di sopra, iquali approviamo e giuriamo di mantenere, sia scritto ancora le sequenti capitolazioni del tenore quì appresso," ASF, MdP 4275, 114r.

95. Finkel, *Osman's Dream*, 127; Halil İnalcık, *The Ottoman Empire: The Classic Age 1300–1600* (London: Phoenix, 2000), 133–139.

96. "Che tutti li Fiorentini ε Toscani, & altri che camineranno sotto la bandiera del Gran Duca di Toscana possino con ogni sorte di Vasselli venire nelle scale del Nostro Dominio, partirsene, e andare liberamente dove più piace loro, così ancora possino trafficare in tutte le sorti di mercanzie, per quelle Città ε Terra che sono all'obedienza. Nostra contrattandole per Nostri bazarri, secondo che gli accorderanno coi mercanti, & sicuramente [114v] venderne e comperare, ma che la Nazion Fiorentina sia abìlitata più dell'altre per dependere da quell' Altezza che per primo amico ci s'è caramente offerto," ASF, MdP 4275, 114r–v.

97. Sir Thomas Sherley, *The Discours of the Turkes*, 44r, LPL, ms. 514.

98. "In considerazione della perfetta Amicizia, che il Serenissimo Gran Duca ha contratta con Noi, Noi vogliamo che li Fiorentini che trafficheranno nelli luoghi della Nosra obedienza, possino con lor danari levar robe di contrabando, e che sieno fino à qui proibite, ε che possino farle caricare sopra le Galere ò altri Vasselli del detto Gran Duca ò sopra altri Vasselli che venisse loro à proposito, senza che alcuno possa darne loro impedimento veruno," ASF, MdP 4275, 114v.

99. "Che le mercanzie che saranno caricate à nolo sopra Galere del Gran Duca ò navi de Fiorentini appartenenti alli nemici Nostri ò, del Nostro Dominio, non possino esser prese, sotto pretesto che le sieno di detti Nostri nemici, essendo così la Nostra volontà," ASF, MdP 4275, 114v.

100. "Le mercanzie che saranno de Fiorentini portate nelle Scale ò Porti del Nostro Dominio, ò quelle che essi leveranno non habbino à pagare altro commerzio ò dazio in essere stimate, à più alto prezzo che quello dell'antica costuma," ASF, MdP 4275, 114v.

101. "Le monete che portano li Fiorentini ò faran venire dal Paese loro, per tuttol Nostro Dominio, non possino essere prese da Nostri Tesaurieri, ne da quelli che battono le monete, Ottomanne òle Nostre, sottopretesto di voler far moneta Ottomanna ò Giampulat, ne manco vogliamo che ne possino pigliare alcune d'altri, per non traviare dell'antico uso, se già li mercanti stessi non se ne contentassero," ASF, MdP 4275, 114v.

102. Finkel, *Osman's Dream*, 179.

103. "Che li Fiorentini che vengano con lor Vasselli e mercanzie per le scale & Porti del Nostro Dominio, possino andare, stare, e ritornare sicuramemte

sotto la fede publica. Et accadendo che la fortuna ò tempestà gettasse alcuno di essi per traverso, havendo bisogno dell'aiuto di coloro che sono alla Nostra obedienza, vogliamo e comandiamo che sieno subito aiutati, & che li Capitani, & altri de loro Vasselli sieno rispettati e carezzati, provedendoli coi lor danari di tutte le comodità che richiederanno, tanto per il viver loro che per altro," ASF, MdP 4275, 116v.

104. "Che in caso che li sudetti Vasselli Fiorentini dessino per fortuna in qualche scoglio ò in terra e naufragassero, Noi comandiamo che tutto quello, che si potrà ricuperare sia restituito, e messo in potere de mercanti à quali l'attengono, senza che Li Nostri Governatori et altri si ponghino loro in contrario, ma che debbino soccorrergli ne loro bisogni. Volendo commerzij, e li dritti de' Residenti del Gran Duca e de Consoli, com'è il costume, non sieno molestati, ne meno li loro Vasselli, ne le loro mercanzie impedite da Nostri Capitani ne da volontarij, ne da chi che sì sia, del Dominio Nostro, ne venendo, ne andando, ne riscontrando," ASF, MdP 4275, 116v.

105. "Che li Fiorentini Interpetri ò altri appartenenti à loro, venendo ne Nostri Paesi, sia per ˋmare ò per terra, per vendere ò comprare, e far mercanzie, pagando li dritti de Nostri commerzij, e li dritti de' Residenti del Gran Duca e de Consoli, com'è il costume, non sieno molestati, ne meno li loro Vasselli, ne le loro mercanzie impedite da Nostri Capitani ne da volontarij, ne da chi che sì sia, del Dominio Nostro, ne venendo, ne andando, ne riscontrando," ASF, MdP 4275, 116v.

106. "In caso álcuno Fiorentino si trovasse debitore, non si possa domandare il debito ad altri che à lui, ò à quello che si sarà obligato, e L'istesso s'intenda per queiche camineranno sotto la bandiera del Gran Duca di Toscana Con questo che gli habbino sempre à riconoscere per loro Giudice competente, il Console della Nazion Fiorentina," ASF, MdP 4275, 116v.

107. "Essendo alcuno Fiorentino debitore d'alcuno, ò havesse commesso qualche tristo atto, e' se ne fuggisse, Noi vogliamo et comandiamo, che gli altri Fiorentini che non ne saranno consenzienti ò assicurato per lui, non possino essere ricercati ne molestati in conto veruno," ASF, MdP 4275, 117r.

108. "Che li Fiorentini lor Consoli Interpetri, e quelli de lochi che da essi dependono debbino nelle loro vendite, compre plegorie, et in ogni altro punto di Giustizia, farne contratto dinanzi al Cadij, in mancamento del quale, quelli che hauranno qualche pretensione contra di essi, non facendol'apparire per contratto registrato ne'libri de Nostri Giudizij, ò volendo produrre falsi testimonij; vogliamo e comandiamo che non sieno ascoltati, ma si bene che sia data fede alli contratti che saranno passati avanti li Nostri Giudizij e non essendo nessuno nelli detti registri, talidomandai in conto alcuno non sieno ammesse; e s'avverta che non arrivi cosa contra la sacra Giustizia," ASF, MdP 4275, 117r.

109. "Che gli Ambasciatori straordinari del Serenissima Gran Duca. à Noi spediti Consoli, vice Consoli, della Nazion Fiorentina Interpetri e sudditi, possino venire, partirsi, andare, e habitare per tutti i luoghi del Nostro Dominio, sicuramente, senza che sia dato loro alcuni disturbi, anzi Noi intendiamo che sieno favoriti & aiutati in tutto quello che fa loro di bisogno," ASF, MdP 4275, 114v.

110. İnalcık, *Ottoman Empire*, 137.

111. "Che allo stabilimento e cambiamento delli Consoli Fiorentini nelle scale del Nostro Dominio, nessuna persona ardisca opporsi ò mettersi à tal effetto," ASF, MdP 4275, 117r.

112. "Tutte le Nazioni dependenti da detti Principi e Potentati collegati con Noi, in materia di differenze, per negozij ò per altro che potessino havere insieme, tanto per il Civile che per il Criminale, habbino sempre à ricorrere al Console ò Vice Console della Nazion Fiorentina dimorante in Aleppo, ne ad altro foro ò magistrato d'altri fianchi, ò Turchesco s'habbino à rappresentare, & sieno in appellabili ε validissime tutte le sue sentenze," ASF, MdP 4275, 114.

113. "Che essendo tramato qualch' insidia contro li Fiorentini ò loro dependenti per accusargli 'havere ingiuriato ò biasimato, producendo falsi testimonij, per trovar modo di travagliarli, Noi comandiamo che si riguardi minutamente in simili occasioni, e s'habbi cura che essi Fiorentini non ne venghino molestati, ne passino le cose più avanti," ASF, MdP 4275, 117r.

114. "Che accadendo qualche homicidio ò altro inconveniente tra la Nazion Fiorentina l'Ambasciatore e il Console possino seguendo le lor leggi e statuti far giustizia, senza che alcuno de Nostri offizieri ò ministri ne possino pigliare informazione veruna ,ne che gli impedischino," ASF, MdP 4275, 116r.

115. "Che se nascesse qualche contenzione ò controversia fra dua Fiorentini Noi vogliamo che l'Ambasciatore Residente di Toscana ò Console della Nazion loro habbi da terminare le loro differenze, conforme alle lor leggi e statuti, senze che altri, e sia chi si vuole de Nostri offizieri s'apponga in contrario," ASF, MdP 4275, 117r.

116. "Et occorrendo che alcuno Fiorentino morisse ò Toscano, ò chi camina sotto la bandiera di [117r] Toscana, Noi vogliamo e comandiamo à tutti li Nostri offizieri e Commessarij, che non habbino da vedere le sue robe ò facoltà del defunto, ma che le sieno consegnate senza impedimento veruno à coloro, à quali l'havesse lasciato per sua ultima volontà il Testatore, e morendo ab intestato, sieno condotte e consegnate con l'intervento e consentimento del Console, in casa ò in luogo d'uno de' suoi Compatriotti, senza che li Commessari, se ne possino punto interporre ò impedire l'essecuzione," ASF, MdP 4275, 116v–117r.

117. "Che li Fiorentini ò quelli che dependano da essi maritati ò non maritati nel Dominio Nostro, essercitando le mercanzie, lavorando col arti loro, ò

altrimenti, non siano tenuti à pagare tributo, ne concorrere à impo-sizione alcuna," ASF, MdP 4275, 117r.

118. "Li Consoli Fiorentini che saranno stabiliti nelle scale del Nostro Do-minio, per haver cùra del riposo e sicurtà de trafficanti, non possino es-sere fatti prigioni, ne le lor case bollate. E caso che si facesse loro domanda alcuna, ò fosse preteso qualcosa da essi, che ne Cadij, ne Sub-assij, ne Chechià, ne altri offizieri tanto Criminali che Civili possino dar lor molestia nessuna ma che la cognizione sia mandata alla Nostra pre-senza e Divano publico," ASF, MdP 4275, 116r. For a substantial defini-tion of qadi (kadı), see Somel, *Historical Dictionary*, 199–200. For short definitions, see Douglas E. Streusand, *Islamic Gunpowder Empires: Otto-mans, Safavids, and Mughals* (Boulder, CO: Westview, 2011): "Qazi (kadi): Shariah judge; in the Ottoman Empire, he had administrative as well as judicial responsibilities" (304); "Subashi (subaşî) (O): subdistrict gov-ernor; company-grade officer in the field" (305).

119. Wilson, *Thirty Years' War*, 77 and 97.

120. Somel, *Historical Dictionary*, 248–249, and Streusand, *Islamic Gunpowder Empires*, 306, for short definitions of *dhimmi* status.

121. For a clear translation of the Pact of Umar, see Fordham University's In-ternet Medieval Source Book, accessed July 17, 2020, http://www.fordham.edu/halsall/source/pact-umar.asp; I have also benefited from the background information provided there.

122. "Che li Consoli Fiorentini ε la sua Nazione habbino facultà di fabbricare & erigere una Chiesa in Aleppo, dove meglio parrà loro à proposito, ò secondo che converranno con li Patroni del sito, che perciò fare gli hauranno di bisogno, ordinando à Nostri sudditi facilitargli in quello che potranno, acciòche restino compiaciuti à far detta Chiesa, la quale habbino abilità di fare offiziare da Religiosi à modo loro, secondo le leggi e ritti della loro fede Cattolica senza che persona di qual si voglia ŝotto ò condizione ardisca darne loro molestia nessuna. Permettendo ancora di più che detti Fiorentini possino prendere affetto, affittare, comprare e fabbricare case, botteghe, e magazini, per loro abitazione & accommoda-mento delle loro mercanzie," ASF, MdP 4275, 116r.

123. On San Giovanni dei Fiorentini and the Florentine community in Rome, see Richard Goldthwaite, *The Economy of Renaissance Florence* (Baltimore, MD: Johns Hopkins University Press, 2009), 170–175.

124. Pact of Umar, Fordham University, Internet Medieval Source Book.

125. "Occorendo à gli Ambasciatori del Gran Duca di Toscana e à Consoli ε vice Consoli della Nazion Fiorentina andare fuori per la Città, per venire alla Nostra udienza, ò per negozij, ò per altro, ò pur fuori della Città per suoi affari, ò per diporto, possa andare à cavallo, con accompagnatore pur à cavallo di sua Nazione, e col guardiano, che gli haurà per la sua

persona dependente da Noi, ne che alcuno ardisca di concitarlo, ò dargli impedimento veruno," ASF, MdP 4275, 116v.

126. "Tutti quelli che caricheranno sopra Vasselli Fiorentini ò trafficheranno sotto la bandiera del Gran Duca di Toscana habbino à pagare il diritto dell' Ambasciatore [116r; 115 is a small insert, with text on the recto side] ò d'un suo Residente ò Ministro ordinato, da quell' Altezza così ancora il dritto del Console Fiorentino senza opporsi incontrario," ASF, MdP 4275, 114v and 116r. As elsewhere in the treaty, 114v ends with two hanging words, which represent the beginning words of the next page (in this case, 116r); I omit them here to avoid repetition while quoting across pages.

127. ASF, MdP 4275, 113.

128. "Che per essere stato il Serenissimo Gran Duca di Toscana il primo che habbia desiderato e domandato la Nostra Amicizia, vogliamo che della Nazion Toscana à quell'Altezza sottoposta, & in particolare della Fiorentina, gli habbia l'autorità di creare un Console ò vice Console nelle città del Nostro Dominio, alquale in materia di negotij ò altro, come quì appresso dichiaremo sieno sottoposte tutte le altre Nazioni, tanto di Toscana che delli altri Regni e Province, i cuì Principi e Potentati si sono per unire adesso in Lega con esso Noi, Sempre che à quell'Altezza di Toscana non parrà altrimenti," ASF, MdP 4725, 114r.

129. "E perche il Serenissimo Gran Duca ci ha dimostrato atti di grandissima Amicizia, per havercela con Ambasciatore espresso richiesta, e prima d'ogni altro offertosi ad aggrandire L'Eccellentissima Casa Nostra, con promessa di farci acquistare e legare in Amicizia, con li suddetti Principi & altri Potentati, vogliamo e comandiamo che li suoi Ambasciatori Consoli, ε Residenti venendo al Nostro gran Divano, ò andando al Palazzo de Nostri Cadij, Chechia, Subassij ò altri Nostri Principali Ministri e offizieri, habbino potestà, e sia in arbitrio loro di precedere à gli altri Ambasciatori Consoli e Residenti, delli altri Principi e Potentati uniti con Noi, così à tutti gli altri Consoli che dimoreranno d'altre Nazioni in Aleppo, mentre che l'Altezza di Toscana non l'intenda incontrari," ASF, MdP 4275, 116r.

130. Unsigned letter from the grand ducal Court in Florence to Michelagnolo Corai, April 6, 1607, MAP Doc ID 21027, ASF, MdP 4275, 134.

131. Niccolò Capponi, *Victory of the West: The Great Christian-Muslim Clash at the Battle of Lepanto* (Cambridge, MA: Da Capo, 2007), 331, appendix 1; Roger Crowley, *Empires of the Sea: The Siege of Malta, the Battle of Lepanto, and the Contest for the Center of the World* (New York: Random House, 2008); Victor Davis Hanson, *Carnage and Culture: Landmark Battles in the Rise of Western Power* (New York: Anchor, 2002), 238.

132. Unsigned letter from the grand ducal court in Florence to Michelagnolo Corai, April 6, 1607, MAP Doc ID 21027, ASF, MdP 4275, 134. The rele-

vant portion of the MAP transcription is "8 galere armate et 15 tra galeoni et bertoni armati di brava gente et di molta artigliera." On the Tuscan *bertoni*, see Hanlon, *Twilight of a Military Tradition*, 13 and 40.

133. "Listra delle robe ch' è stato di necessità che l signor Michelang:ᵗᵒ accordi con questo Serenissimo Bascia." "Cinque pezzi d'Artiglierie da campagno ε batteria scompartito" and "Un bariglione di marzolini." Multiple versions of this list appear in ASF, MdP 4275; ASF, MdP 4275, 103r–104r appears to be the final version. Florio defines "Marzolino" as "that is sowed or groweth in March. Also a kind of daintie cheese made about Florence." On Italian cheese, see Suraiya Faroqhi, *The Ottoman Empire and the World around It* (New York: I. B. Tauris, 2006), 141. Faroqhi cites Benjamin Arbel, who shows that the Venetians exported fine Italian (though the example is not Florentine) cheese to Istanbul for Ottoman pashas: Benjamin Arbel, *Trading Nations: Jews and Venetians in the Early Modern Eastern Mediterranean* (New York: Brill, 1995), 15–16 and 16n12, in turn citing Marin Sanuto, *I diarii* (Venice: 1879–1903), vol. 58.

134. ASF, MdP 4275, 103r–104r.

135. ASF, MdP 4275, 103r–104r.

136. This is Ippolito Leoncini, the legation secretary.

137. "Copia della Lega˙ ε Capitoli che s'è fatta ε accordata In Aleppo fra 'l [il] Serenissimo Gran Duca di Toscana iií ε l Serenissimo Principi Alij Giampulat Governatʳ˙ ch[']l Regno di Soria ------- Listra d[el]le robe ch' è stato di necessità che l sʳ Michelang:ᵗᵒ accordi con questo Serenissimo Bascia Cinque pezzi d'Artiglierie da campagno ε batteria scompartito Canne d'archibuso della misura che $\widehat{5}$ palmi che n' ha un disegno Hippolito nel suo tamburo d -------------- nʳᵒ 1000 ------ Giachi alla foggia delle misuro che ha il detto Hippolito nel suo tamburo, che dieci conforme alla detta misura & gli altri nel miglior modo che si troveranno d-------------- numero 100 ------- Colonne di marmo bianco ε mischie come sa il latore che 4 bianche ε l'altre mischie εt hanno a˙ servire per una fontana cⁿᵉ 8 ------ Un Lione scolpito in marmo bianco c'habbia le due bianche avanti sopra la trita d'un Bue ε l'altre un modo di predare con la bocca aperto per dove possa uscire l'acqua havendo à servire per una fontana Due veste di velluto à op[er]a di fuori ε felpa dentro di colore come piu piacerà fuor che nro [nero] o colore maninconico havendo à servire una per il serenissimo )—ᴵ Bascia ε l'altra per la sua moglie sposa Un bariglione di marzolini Un Giardinero ε un Bombardiero Quattro visto per il checchià di velluto riccio, in man del quale sta ogn.˜ cosa ε governa tutto, di coloro verde paonazzo rosso εt azurro celeste Una dozina di pistoli d'un palmo indorate che sono trova a Vienna d' Ungheria di prezzo d'un unghero l'una Dua archibusi à ruota Tagli di Ermisino ò raso per cinque, ò sei veste per diversi offizialj," ASF, MdP 4275, 103r–104r.

138. ASF, MdP 4275, 104r.

139. ASF, MdP 4275, 104r.
140. ASF, MdP 4275, 104r.
141. ASF, MdP 4275, 104r.
142. ASF, MdP 4275, 104r.
143. Bibas, *L'emiro e il granduca*, 48.
144. ASF, MdP 4275, 104r.
145. ASF, MdP 4275, 104r.
146. Thanks to Francesco Freddolini for this information.
147. "Listra delle appie robe in cassate," ASF, MdP 4275, 142r.
148. "Uno scudo d'aviaio con una punta in mezzo, è fogliami lavorato tutto alla Zimina, guarnito di frangia di seta di piu colore, con argento filato, è foderato di telitta piana à opera rossa con seta rossa, bianca, et turchina, con sua custodia di rovescio rosso. Un morione d'appie lavorato tutto d'oro carg.^to alla Zimina, simile guarnito di bullette dorate con sua orecchini lavorati simile e foderato tutto di teletta simile, con sua custodia di rovescio rosso. Un petto à botta d'archibuso provato, scanalato à tue listre di bianco, et attorno alli orli similmente guarnito di velluto nero, con passamano d'oro è seta nera, con sua custodia di rovescio. Una schiena simile à botta di pistola, guarnita simile con sua custodia di rovescio simile. Una goletta simile à botta d'archibuso guarnita simile, con sua custodia di rovescio simile. Una celata con sua orecchini guarnita di bullettine dorate à rosetta, à botta di archibuso, guarnita simile, et foderate di rovescio rosso, con sua custodia di rovescio rosso. Un petto à botta d'archibuso con dua coreggine di corame coperte di teletta suddetta con sua custodia simile. Una goletta per detto petto à botta di archibuso, foderata di teletta simile, è guarnita di passamano d'oro, et seta nera con sua custodia di rovescio simile [142v] Un' archibuso à ruota con canna lung^a 62 [or perhaps br] lavorata alla bocca in mezzo, et alla culatta d'oro, et d'argento à tausia con ruota, è ferri lavorati simile, è cassa di nove commessa di filetti, è piastrette d'argento straforata, con sua bacchetta rastatoio, è caccia palle, è forme, con due saccocce per detto, che una di cordovano nero, et l'altra di tela incarnata. Una chiave di ferro dorata, è traforata, con suo cordone d'oro, et seta rossa, et turchina. Una pistole con canna con colore à vivola mammola, lavorate alle bocche, in mezzo, et alle culatte d'oro à tausia, con ruote, è ferri lavorati simile con casse di pero tinto di rosso, con lor fornimenti, con dua saccoccie di cordovano nero, et borse foderate di teletta à opera d'argento, di seta rossa bian.° et turchino, guarnito di passamano, con dua sopraveste di rovescio rosso, Con più l'archibuso di m_r. Michelagnolo, che era qua in guardaroba," ASF, MdP 4275, 142r–v.
149. ASF, MdP 4275, 115r. This reads "Giamadilacher," corresponding to the sixth Islamic month: Jumada II / Jumādá al-Ākhirah / Jumada al-Thani. The date cited is based on inputting the 10th of Jumada II—6, 1016 AH

into the calendar conversion provided by Islamic Philosophy Online http://www.muslimphilosophy.com/ip/hijri.htm. This yields October 2, 1607, in the Gregorian calendar, itself a relatively new system at the time.

150. Niccolò Machiavelli, *The Prince*, trans. George Bull (New York: Penguin Classics, 2003), 22-23.

151. Griswold, *Great Anatolian Rebellion*, 110-156, provides the basis for this narrative. See also ASF, MdP 4275, 124r-v, which will be discussed in detail in Chapter 8. Murad Pasha took Aleppo almost immediately after arriving on November 8, 1607, but the castle fell only after a treacherous negotiation led to its surrender and the execution of many of its occupants (Griswold, *Great Anatolian Rebellion*, 148). See also Finkel, *Osman's Dream*, 179; Barkey, *Bandits and Bureaucrats*, 215-17; and Hathaway, *Arab Lands*, 72. For a recent work on Aleppo that briefly mentions Tuscany's role, see Philip Mansel, *Aleppo: The Rise and Fall of Syria's Great Merchant City* (New York: I. B. Tauris, 2016). See also Eldem et al., *Ottoman City*, esp. Bruce Master's section, "Aleppo: The Ottoman Empire's Caravan City," 17-78.

152. Bibas, *L'emiro e il granduca*, esp. 75-79. Finkel, *Osman's Dream*, 179, offers a concise English summary of the emir's story, on which I draw here.

153. ASF, MdP 4275, 124-127. Corai's capture and torture are on 126r-v; his ransom is on 126v. For Corai's subsequent move to Persia, see ASF, MdP 4275, 126v-127.

154. On the Long Turkish War, see Wilson, *Thirty Years War*, 97-103.

155. Niccolò Machiavelli and Francesco Guicciardini, *The Sweetness of Power: Machiavelli's* Discourses *and Guicciardini's* Considerations, trans. James B. Atkinson and David Sices (DeKalb: Northern Illinois University Press, 2002), *Discourses* II.31, 251.


## 8. PERSIAN DREAMS

1. "Da timotteo mayen mercante residente in aleppo cie stato inviati con la nave san matteo arrivata qui oggi li aclusi pieghi per Vostra Signoria e per il cavalieri Ipolito Leoncinj," ASF, MdP 4275 176r. The document gives no location information, but it was likely composed in Livorno.

2. "Insieme una lettere di cambio di otto cento pezze da otto reali di spagni del signor Michelangelo coraij," ASF, MdP 4275 176r.

3. "La presente le mandò con il Galeon di S.ᴸ Matteo che passa per Marsilia e per la solita via di Pesciolinj serve l'avviso," ASF, MdP 4275, 127v. There is an address on 123v, "Al Serenissimo Gran Duca di Toscana unico mio Signore," which may apply to this letter. In any event, the references on 127r to "l'1417," which the cipher secretary gives as "A.V" or to "171421," which the cipher secretary gives as "V.A." (but the cipher says VAS), clearly indicates an address to "Your Highness" or "Your Serene High-

ness." The regular enciphering of the letter's recipient's title also indicates a desire to obscure his identity, which is consistent with Corai's situation in writing to the grand duke.

4. "Hora la saprà che li 6. d'ottobre, appena partitosi il signor Hippolito venne nuove che il Visir era giunto à Adena et era per venire à Baias, imperò il Bascià stimando essere hormai tempo d'andargli incontro comandò alli suoi soldati, che si metessino in ordine et egli dalla banda sua fece il medesimo," ASF, MdP 4275, 124r. Adana is a large city in southeastern Turkey near the Syrian border.

5. "Li Saccomeni intendendo la partenza loro, .cominciorno andare per la città come altre volte havevano fatti con far mille insolenze & angarie à tutti quei che si riscontravano, si che per questo fatto tutte le botteghe si serrorno, ogn'uno si ritirò à casa sua, ma non lasciorno per questo li Saccomeni i lor'antici costumi, perche molte case e botteghe ne apersono e messino à sacco. Il Bascià udito tanti romori per la città comandò al lor Generale e al suo Zio Aiderbech e à molti altri Capitani d'andar intorno la città armatamente e proveder si evidenti pericoli, ilche fù eseguito, & farno gastigati assai, ma partiti che erano li capitani ritornorno i Saccomeni à far peggio che mai," ASF, MdP 4275, 124r.

6. "Si che il Bascià s'è risoluto d'andar in persona attorno, con gastigar tutti quei malfattori ch'erano trovati, dua de'quali ei medesimo ha tagliato le teste Zi'. e questo tumulto ha durato sei giorni continui che non s'attese à altro che à guardarsi di non esser saccheggiato ciascuno si fece forte nella casa sua ne usciva punto fuori," ASF, MdP 4275, 124r.

7. "Li 12 d'ottobre doppò haver il Bascià finito tutti li suoi affari, e lasciato buon ordine al suo Chechia, e à tutti, si partì con 30. mila buoni soldati, e così si liberò lo città di questi indomite bestie. Partito che fù il Bascià il suo Chechia incominciò à provisionare la fortezza, di tutto quello che stimava esser bisognio e bastante per difenderla da qual si vogli potentissimo assedio, ch'egli indovinò c'haveva à seguire, ma il suo disegno non gli rivocì per mancamento di quello che più d'ogni altro bisognava come poi l'intenderà," ASF, MdP 4275, 124r.

8. "Intanto si sentiva sempre qualche nuova hora buona hora cattiva secondo à chi si parlava, hora ch'il Bascià era andato all'obedienza del Visir, hora che gli haveva dato rotta, chi diceva ch'il Bascià era andato à pigliare Damasco, chi parlava in altra maniera, e tanti diversi avvisi correvano più che li gassetti di Venezia ma in effetto più bugia che verità, che durò insin' alli 24 del suddetto arrivò la nuova che alli 22 .passati, li soldati del Bascià trovandosi appresso l'esercito del Visir, hanno volsuto combattere insieme, e contr'il volere del Bascià son' andati in buon ordine à trovar il nemico che non aspettava altro, il quale se ben era assai più forte di loro, nondimeno l'hanno dato due rotte grandissime il che vedendo li nemici si son ritirati à dietro verso una collina, dove havevano le lor' arti-

glierie alliquali seguitando li Saccomeni, & appressati ch'erano quelli alle artiglieri s'hanno spartiti in que parti, e sparati l'artiglierie addesso à questi che n'hanno sentito pur troppo e tutti spaventati si com'anco per il gran famo ch'andava loro addesso che non vedevano più li nemici, si son ritirati e tornati à dietro, il nemico seguitando loro l'ha messo in fuga tutti, e chi haveva cavallo s'è salvato con fuggirsene chi non haveva cavallo è stato ammazzato si che come si dice, sono morti più di 8 mila persone cioe pedoni, e delli nemici si giudica che in questi 2. rotti ^sono stati ammazzati altri tanto, e questa battaglia è stata fatta in Lunedì dua giornata lon [124v] tano d'Aleppo di là di Chilles vicino à un luogo chiamato Amch," ASF, MdP 4275, 124r-v.

9. "La medesima notte doppò esser arrivata la nuva, arrivò anco il Bascià, entrò nella città con parte del suo esercito, per metter in ordine tutta la sua roba e facultà à fuggirsene, il giorno appresso arrivò il resto delli suoi soldati, e per esser stati serrati tutte le porte della città che non potevano entrarvi dentro, cominciorno à saccheggiar tutte le case di fuori," ASF, MdP 4275, 124v.

10. "Che fù causa ch'ogn'uno si fece forte in casa sua, con murar le porte e difendersi con armi chi l'haveva, chi nò, adoperò sassi, e per questo sono stati ammazzati assai persone, d'ambele sessi, dalli saccomen c'hanno voluto difendersi, una casa in Iudaica vicino à noi dove non potevano entrare, impizzorno e abbruciorno con tutta la roba che v'era dentro," ASF, MdP 4275, 124v.

11. "Molti altri doppò haver saccheggiati le case che non vi restò cose nessuna e spogliati le persone ignude gli bastonavano per confessar dove erano li danari, iquali si dissero d'haver seppeliti e nascosti, altri ancora ligavano e portavano à vendere per riscattare danari, à chi pigliavano figliuoli e menavano via con esse loro, di che si vedeva inaudita crudeltà e miseria e si sentiva grandissimi romori per tutto, da una banda gridare lamentare e piangere, dall'altra, mormorar, romoreggi e fracassare le porte delle case, si che molti che p:ᵃ non havevano mai volsuto sentire nominar' il Visir, hor pregavano Iddio che lo mandasse presto per liberar una volta il paese da questo grandissimo ne mai sentito travaglio, che durò dalla mattina fina la sera, all hora ogn'uno si messe à fuggire con quello c'haveva robato Zi," ASF, MdP 4275, 124v.

12. "Se intanto questi fuori della Citta hanno fatto del mal assai, peggior hanno fatto quelli di dentro entrati col Bascià, iquali hanno aperti per forza rotti e fracassati e guastati tutte le botteghe e messino à sacco, com'ancora molte case, et ha durato quel giorno intierò e la notte, fin'all'altro mezzo giorno, doppò haver il Bascià finito e messo insieme tutte le cose sue, e lasciato il suo Generale Giummabech per Govenatore dentro la fortezza con 500 Saccomeni si partì con quelli soldati ch'erano venuti con esso lei, alla volta d'Antap, e in questo modo si liberò anco la Città di questa pessima generazione," ASF, MdP 4275, 124v.

13. "Partito che fù il Basci questi ch'erano tardati dentro la città furno accompagnati con infinite sassate, dalliquali molti restono mortalmente feriti, e in particolare il Zio del Bascià Aiderbech toccò la parte sua, e se non fosse stat tanto presto à salvarsi con la fuga senza fallo sarebbe stato lapidato e ammazzato, ma il buon cavallo che gli haveva gli salvò la vita ˏ Zi," ASF, MdP 4275, 124v.

14. "Li giorni seg[ue]nti alcuni Turchi andorno per la Città à vedere se v'erano restati delli Saccomeni e tutti quei che sono stati ritrovati n'hanno ammazzati e bevuti il lor sangureda molti hanno cavato li cuori e fegati, e arrostiti n'hanno mangiati, per lor vendetta, da altri hanno cavato li fieli e messi per memoria nelle case loro, li corpi morti hanno butato avanti li cani che n'hanno mangiati, e questa horrenda crudeltà è stata causa che molti s'hanno stravestiti come nostrani, donne et ebrei per fuggirsene, ma pur come conosciuti sono stati ammazzati," ASF, MdP 4275, 124v.

15. "Li 29. del suddetto s'appressò il Visir à 2. miglia alla Città e s'accampò con suoi genti sotto padiglionj e mandò il suo luogotenente per Governatore dentro la città. Il primo di Novembre entrò il Bascià che di nuovo era stato fatto dal Visir Bascià d'Aleppo, il medesimo giorno entrò ancò il Visir per veder se quelli della fortezza si gli volevano rendere, mandò dua Blucbassj ch'erano stati nascosti quei giorni & hora furono trovati, dentro la fortezza, con lettere è promesse che se quelli di dentro gli rendessero la fortezza, egli prometterebbe loro sicurtà della vita, e perdenarebbe à tutti quei ch'erano dentro, ma loro non gli diedero altra risposta per hora, perciò si risolvè il Visir di combatterla e pigliarla per forza, dando ordine à quello che si doveva fare e tornò fuori sotto li padiglioni," ASF, MdP 4275, 124v.

16. "Li huominì del Visir e'andorno verso la fortezza apparecchiavano d'impir la fossa per dar l'assalto, e à far mine per minar la cerchavano anco l'acque ch'entravano dentro per insalarle e tagliarle, ilche redendo quei di dentro cominciorno à tirar tante Cannonate e archibusate ch'ogn'uno temeva che questa impresa doveva andare [125r:] alla lunga, ma durò poco, perche il giorno sequente, doppo haver visto sparar alcune pezze d'artiglierie che il Visir haveva mandato dentro la città per dar paura loro come si volesse batter la fortezza benche non haveva nessuno pezze da batteria e loro vedendosi privi di buona artiglierie s'incominciorno à dubitare, e come huomini senza fede e parole il giorno appresso hanno mandato fuori un Bluchbassj al Visir per accordarsi con esso lei, che s'egli darebbe loro sicurtà della vita e della roba, e prometterebbe à non molestiarle che gli renderebbono la fortezza, Il Visir che non desiderava altro, vedendo che à pigliarla per forza gli costerebbe assai, s'ha volontieri accordato con esse loro, e giurato fedeltà à tutto quello che desideravano, e così s'hanno reso il giorno sequente cioe li 4. di 9$^{re}$ [novembre]," ASF, MdP 4275, 124v–125r.

17. "Alli 6. del detto entrò il Visir nella fortezza à vederla, e avvertendo il mancamento delle artiglierie che l'haveva, fece metter dentro ali.<sup>e</sup> pezze di quelle ch'egli haveva portato seco, e rimesse di nuovo dentro quei Castellani che l'Alij Bascià haveva cazziato fuori, e rinforzato di nuovo il presidio torno fuori, e comandò à bellare tutte le magazini dove erano le monezioni e altre robe che l'Alij Bascià haveva mandato dentro à salvare, si come fece anco alle case del Bascià e di tutti li suoi parenti, dallequali l'ha poi cavato danari gioie, robe, e altre cose infinite, e in particolare della casa d'Ussein Bascià suo Zio nel[]quale ha trovato sotto la terra murato gran quantità d'oro con molto altre gioie, e delizie, appartenenti alla madre e donne d'Alij Bascià," ASF, MdP 4275, 125r.

18. Corai uses the terms cavalli and pedoni to convey numbers of cavalrymen and foot soldiers. As with all seventeenth-century armies, there would also have been a large number of noncombatants and support staff. Cavalry forces would conventionally have included many more horses than the number of cavalrymen, but after a defeat such as the pasha had suffered, there may not have been any reserve horses with his fleeing army.

19. ASF, MdP 4275, 125r. The quoted text in italics represents ciphertext. Bracketed insertions in italics are transcriptions of the cipher secretary's decipherments; double brackets are my insertions based on my decipherment of the underlying cipher. In light of the ciphertext, abbreviations in the transcription are left as in the original and not expanded as elsewhere. "ilquale 212326141627124429 [*s'e partito*] di 72· [*qui*] 242925 [*con*] dieci 2012 [*mila*] 151494 [*cavalli*] e cinq2012 [*mila*] 1514262310292512 [*pedoni*] alla volta 101425272326 [*d'Antepubia*]vt si<sup>a</sup> e giunto 15·[*vi*] 152814772717442729 [*l'ha saccheggiato tutto*] e ha cavato m.<sup>ti</sup> dan:<sup>ri</sup> e robe insom[m]a no[n] ha lasciato cosa ness:<sup>a</sup> Un 96 [*Chiaus*] ch'era venuto 101214· [*di Constantinopoli con*] con 24292014251030202333712 [*comandamenti*] d[e]ll 33· [*Gran Turco*] e altre lrè partic:<sup>re</sup> passando per quelle bande ha dato nelli 82·10231578 [*soldati del Bascia*] iquali l'hanno privato d[e]lli 2429201425103020,<sup>ti</sup> [*comandamenti*] e di tt° q[ue]llo c'haveva e mandato à dire 14151712213216 [*al Visir*] che gli aspetterebbono. Costui arrivò quì e disse q[ua]nto gli era occorso e fra altro confessò che 1215 [78?] [*il B*[[obscured by page damage: ascia?]] 213216 [[sir]] si trovava con 17122527322012151482· [*venti* [vinti] *mila soldati*] parte à 95 [*cavallo*] e parte 2029252714441221926 [*montati sopra*] 1630 4921322551 [*asini*] D'1425272326 [*Antep*] poi sen'e'andato 121578 [*il Bascia*] verso 20141530271249 [*Malatia*] dentro laq<sup>a</sup>le dicesi è entrato con astuzia per hav<sup>r</sup> 2429252716141830274429 [*contraffatto*] lre sottol nome e sigillo 102315 [*del*] 1712213216 [*Visir*] come si fosse stato mandato da lui quelli 101220141530273249 [*di Malatia*] vedendo le lre credendo che così fosse l'hanno accettato volont<sup>ri</sup> 121578 [*il Bascia*] dopo ch'è entrato ha mandato à chiamare li p[ri]ncipali della 98 [*Città*] d[e]lli quali ha domandato 40 V<sup>di</sup>

per 151426302249 [*la paga*] d[e]lli suoi 82· [*soldati*], minattiando loro ,se non gli facessero hav.ᵗᵉ questa som[m]a di dan.ʳⁱ che saccheggiarebba 27174427 [*tutta la*] 14153098 [*Citta*] diche spaventati quei huomini e per non ess.ʳᵉ saccheggᵗⁱ l'hanno portato tt° q[ue]llo c'havevano e 15· [*quivi*] si trova egli anc:ʳᵃ come si dice, con ᵐ40 82·[*soldati*]."

20. "L' ha di piu à sapere che doppò che 12151732215116 [*il Visir*] è giunto 72· [*qui*] ha mandato 10171419·ᵗⁱ [*due eserciti*] contr'a 1117231216321934154351 [*quei Ribelli*] che di 241416302049251214 [*Caramania*] lo seguitavano ,& havendo inteso che molti 211424402920232512 [*Saccomeni*] erano restati per le villaggie intorno 1059 [*d'Aleppo*] mandò fuori 82· [*Soldati*] à ttᵉ le bande à proibir[e] li passi e am[m]azzare t[ut]ti quei 211424402920232512 [*Saccomeni*] che si trovava, ò menarle 72· [*qui*] li villani vedendo l'aiuto che fù mandato si messino ancor loro in arme, e n'hanno am[m]azzati assai parte presi vivi e menati 72· [*qui*] avanti 12151732215116 [*al* [il] *Visir*] li quali anco fa 142030134549162717442712 [*ammazzar tutti*] et questo dura ancora perche ogni dì si 26291627142529 [*menano* [portano]] d[e]lli nuovi, si che si crede che di quel giorno ch'12151732215116 [*il Visir*] e giunto quì fin hoggi di ne sono 2029162712 [*morti*] dentro e fuori 59 [*d'Aleppo*] poco manco che nella 191427443022153249 [*battaglia*] un giorno mando 12151732215116253415431498 [*il Visir nella Città*] insie[m] e [125v:] in una volta 42, e fece tagliar in pezze avanti 1215 [*il*] castello in conspette d'ogn'uno per esempio che per l'avvenire ness:ⁿᵒ più ardisca à prender 15712429252716121573· [*l'arme contro il Re* [l'arme contr il Re]] li 1017291219ᵗⁱ [*due* [duoi] *eserciti*] l'uno di 10 e l'atr di 12 2012153 082· [*mila soldati*] sono stati 1629274412101415431216321925154312 [*rotti dai Ribelli* [dalli ribnlli]] e tagᵗⁱ in pezze t[ut]ti di che 121517322 15116 [*il Visir*] s'è risoluto à maniarne delli altri, come ha fatto la settimana pass.ᵗᵃ sendone partite assai iquali si dicono vanno parte 242925271614151216321923154351 [*contro* [contra] *li Ribelli*] e parte 2429252716141514151278 [*contro l'Aly* [Ali] *Bascia*] à rimoverlo da 20141530273249 [Malatia] dove lui s'è risoluto à suernare, ma come riuscirà loro, sentiremo alla giornata basta che 1519·1023151712213216 [*l'esercito del Visir*] che al n.° era di 70 2012151482· [*mila soldati*] in circa, ma huomini malsani di poca forza e valore sempre va consumando adagiamᵗᵉ. Sono anc fin hora 2029162712 [*morti*] assai 95 [*cavalli*] muli e cam[m]elli per ɨla grandᵐᵃ 18142023 e 181623103729 [*fame e freddo*] c'hanno patito per il viaggio e 202916122529 [*ne muoiono* [morino]] sempre più, e ttⁱ dicono se 71·78 [*questo Bascia*] havesse fermato ancora altri 6 ò 8 giorni senza 24292019142744231634 [*combattere*] era convenuto 14151712213216 [*al Visir*] di 161227291625144221233334 [*ritornarsene*] à 101223271629 [*dietro*] sendosi stati insin' à 3 giorni 212325131420302522124916 [*senza mangiare*]e bere ma l'ha sentito che ness.° altro che li 21172912 [*suoi*] medᵐⁱ 82· [*soldati*] sono stato la causa di

si 221614251629274430 [*gran rotta*] d'animo di combatt^re non mancava loro ma ben la forza e 47· [*mancamento*] d 72 [*d'artiglieria*] perche corre la voce publicam^te per tt° 1519·1023151732475142 [*l'esercito del Visir*] c'hanno 24292019142744172729 [*combattuto*] sì 261614173020 [*bravamente* [pravam]], che loro havevano dubitato 102315431497· [*della vittoria*] ma 242920232623162112 [*come perduti* [persi]]," ASF, MdP 4275, 125r–v.

21. "Li 11. del sud° arrivò 72 [*qui*] il fig^lo d[e]l Zicala che era stato 78101216· [*Bascia di Damasco*] con 700. cavalli," ASF, MdP 4275, 125v.

22. "Alli 20 del detto mandò l'18·[*Emir*]~~221229242318~~ [*Giocef*] 221223101 2512773·[*GiediitRe*] d[e]lli Arabià p̃nt ar al 1712213216,212312193415435195 [*Visir sei belli cavalli*] sessanta 241420231512 [*Camelli*] tre mila 241421271 6304432 [*Castrati*] cinq[ue]cento som[m]e 1029161329 [*d'orzo*] e 32·[*grano*] e sei 20121530 [*mila*] p^re Li 24 mandò l'18·2212292123181215211729 [*Emir Giosef il suo*] fig.^lo 72·[*qui*] con pn̄ti e danari alla valuta di ^m100 86· [*sultanini*]," ASF, MdP 4275, 125v.

23. "Il med.^mo giorno arrivorno 1500 28·101216·[*Giannizzini di Damasco*] iquali per la Strada havevano ricontrato 12152429151421471221 [*il Colassis*] uno de' i pncipali 16121923154332 [*Ribelli*] mandato 10141518·20· [*dal' Emir Faccardino*] per dar soccorso 71·78·[*al Bascia*] ma sendo venuto troppo tardi e vedendo li passi serrati à seguitare 1215 [*il*] 78 [*Bascia*] sen'è tornato à dietro e app[re]sso 63 [*Amà*] ha dati in q[ue]lli 10142014212428122532 [*Damaschini*] e volontariam^te s' ha reso senza combatt.^re con 500 211424402920232512 [*saccomeni*] parte à 95 [*cavallo*] e parte a 2612231032 [*piedi*] & è venuto all' 291923101223251330102311517 12213216 [*ubbidienza* [obedienza] *del Visir*] insieme con 152321173427· [*le sue genti*] ilquale l' ha accolto volont.^ri e donatogli una vesta con promessa che gli sia perdonato tt° q[ue]llo c'ha fatto mai, ma com'egli mantenirà li suoi giuram^ti che lo fà à questi 211424402920232512 [*Saccomeni*] e 16121934154351 [*et Ribelli*] si sentirà al fine perche la causa ch'egli hora si mostra così pietoso a ttj coloro che vengano alla sua 291923101223251330 [*ubbidienza* {obedienza}] non e per altri come publicam^te se dice, che d'hav^r 2525154334201433321514431278 [*nelle mani Aly Basica*] capo di tt° e non mira ad altro che à lui e acquistando 70·[*lui*] all hora taglierà in pezzi l'uno con l'altro, ma io spero in Dio che no[n] gli riuscirà il suo pernizioso disegno," ASF, MdP 4275, 125v.

24. "Li 6. di 9bre venne nuove 1061 [*d'Alessandretta*] come era comparso in 71·65· [*quel porto*] una barcha che andava à cerchare un 82·41· [*Bertone Inglese*] ch'era stato caricato 14213012274449101415 18·20· [à Saitta dall' [dal] *Emir Faccardino*] con molti presenti per 71·1712213216 [*questo Visir*] ma è stato perso è ness.° sà dove è andato, ilche' udito quel 18· [*Emir*] ha messo in prigione ttj li Franchi che trafficano in 71·65· [*quel porto*] minacciando loro che non ritrovandosi quel 82·^ne [*Bertone*] ch'egli sen 'appagherà con il lor sanġue e perciò li mercanti di 15· [*quivi*] hanno spedito q^a barch [126r]

per vedere se v'era giunto ò in 61 ò in 1914123021 [*Alessandretta ò in Baiàs*] ma in ness.° di questi 2629162712 [*porti*] s'è trovato, si che saranno in gran pericoli li mercanti del detto luogo hora corre la voce che quel 18· [*Emir*] mette in ordine alc. vasselli per 152317141621I1012I1530, e 18172241121621232534122S 42· [*levarsi 32 di la e fuggirsene in Italia*] s'egli sentirà che 12151732213216 [*il Visir*] vorrà andàrgli incontro perch'egli non vuol combattere altrim<sup>te</sup>," ASF, MdP 4275, 125v–126r.

25. "Il primo dizembre pass:˙ è entrato 12151732215116 [*il Visir*] dentro 151498 [*la Città*] per suernare 72· [*qui*] riformare e guardare il paese staṅdòsi per tt° in gran paura che s'egli 211226141627321630, 242823252933 [*si partirà* [che] *non vi torni*] vi torni 1514421278 [*L'Aly* [Ari] *Bascia*] 24292520142241322916185342133O [*con maggior forze* [forza]] che p:ª e faccia peggio che mai li giorni pass:<sup>ti</sup> si diceva ch'era venuto un 2429 20142510302023252729102315SS· [*un comandamento del Gran Turco*] ch'egli doveva ritornare à dietro per andar 122598· [*in Ungaria*] li pncipali 102315431498 [*della Città*] udito questo andorno unitam<sup>te</sup> 14151712213216 [*al Visir*] pregandolo à non partirsi perche facendo altrim<sup>te</sup> lascierebbe loro in gran riscio che non sarieno di nuovo sacchegg<sup>ti</sup> e forsi am[m]azzati tt<sup>i</sup> d‸ 14151278 [*Aly* [Ali] *Bascia*] il quale tornerebbe subito sentendo la sua partenza volendo loro con questo indovinare q[ue]llo c'ha à seguire Ze'," ASF, MdP 4275, 126r.

26. "Q[ua]nto à nuove corre voce che intorno 148498 [*à Bursa Città*] app[re] sso 14· [*Costantinopoli*] se trovano 16121923154332 [*Ribelli*] che dopò la partenza del 1712213216 [*Visir*] si sono di nuovo uniti insieme con 40<sup>m</sup> 82· [*soldati*] e fanno infiniti danni oltre che si dice c'habbino à impronirsi di 84 [*Bursa*]. e se q sara 14· [*Costantinopoli*] stara in gran pericolj_," ASF, MdP 4275, 126r.

27. "Il Fig<sup>lo</sup> d[e]l Zicala è dichiarato 78101275 [*Bascia di Babilonia*] & ha mandato li 28 di 9.<sup>bre</sup> il suo luogotenente per quelle parti ma alc<sup>i</sup> vogliono dire che 1117231578 [*quel Bascia*] no[n] gli cederà ne darà luogo, e che li schiavi di 75 [*Babilonia*] piu tosto si daranno al 73·101263· [*Re di Persia*] che lasciar il 15291678 [*lor Bascia*] e pig<sup>r</sup> uno di nuovo," ASF, MdP 4275, 126r.

28. There is a stray "mi" after the enciphered text that corresponds to the end of "grandissimi." This violated optimal practices of secrecy by offering a hint to the enciphered text. I have omitted it for clarity here.

29. "Di 63· [*Persia*] s'ha nuova che 1117231573·18142216302510122147 [*quel Re fa grandissimi*]<sup>mi</sup> preparamenti 101235· [*di guerra*] ilq<sup>a</sup>le ha inteso che 12 1533·2814262920302510492729141517122115116 [*il Gran Turco fa ha comandato* [ha pomandato] *al Visir*] che dopò hav<sup>r</sup> riformato questi paesi 17141030242925271614101215SSS2 [*vadia* [vada] *contro di lui*]," ASF, MdP 4275, 126r.

30. "L'haurà inteso meglio di me come riuscì 1512202616232130101219292S 14322576 [*l'impresa di Bona in Barberia*], le lre di Marsilia che d[e]lli 20.

giorni pass.<sup>ti</sup> dalli 3. vasselli arrivati in capo di 4. giorno insieme à 61 [*Alessandretta*], sono mandate quì, dicono che il 82 [*Bertone*] d[e]lli 41· [*Inglesi*] ch'andava corseggiando, e la 2514172327171624282321402814 [*nave Turchesca* [Turchescha]] l'uno e l'altro 66· [*presi*] dalli 2117291282 [*suoi Bertoni*] è stato mig<sup>r</sup> impresa che il 2114244129101219292549 [*sacco di Bona*]," ASF, MdP 4275, 126r.

31. Mario Biagioli, *Galileo Courtier: The Practice of Science in the Culture of Absolutism* (Chicago: University of Chicago Press, 1994).

32. "Q[ua]nto alli pericoli e travagli che noi habbiamo pass<sup>ti</sup> in quelle 2.º saccheggiam<sup>ti</sup> com ancora dal p.º giorno doppò ch'è giunto 72·12151712213216 [*qui il Visir*] fin hoggidì à descriverle tt<sup>i</sup> sarebbe una impresa troppo fastidiosa, e parerebbe che s' uno volesse raccontare le lagrime della morte, imperò senza perder più tempo lasciamo al giudizio di chi s'ha trovato in simili occ.<sup>ni</sup> ma veram<sup>te</sup> habbiamo altiss<sup>mo</sup> cagione di ringrare Iddio Benedetto che cosi ci ha salvato," ASF, MdP 4275, 126r.

33. Continuing without a break from the last quotation: "sendo purtroppo sparso la fama per tt°, perche io sono venuto in queste bande com'io havevo portato 271623141624281219172132141578102315434 [*tre archibusi al Bascia dalla*] Chr[isti]anità e come l'havevo consig<sup>to</sup> à 181416423 218292510231634 [*far rinfondere*] q[ue]lle 72 [*artiglieria*] 24162326142734 [*crepate*] e farle ancora di nuovo, come dopoi ch'era partito 121578 [*il Bascia*] io sono stato insie[me] col 2117292014322916105320 29 [*suo Maiordomo*] à 26162917122132292514421514 22· [*provisionar la fortezza*] & ordinare tt° quello che bisognava di 51· [*munizioni*] e d'altro ilche è venuto insin' alle orecchie 1023151712213216 [*del Visir*] ilquale m'ha mandato à chiamare, e m'ha 232114201225302729 [*esaminato*] e domandato di tt<sup>e</sup> queste cose partic:<sup>r</sup> conto, ma io che nulla sono nulla posso e nulla vaglio, m'ho scusato e difeso q[ua]nto meglio [126v] io ho potuto maravigliandomi pur troppo che queste cose si dicesse di me ,dimostrando che tt° questo non nascerebbe d'altro che d'invidia e malignità de quelli maledetti ebrei miei nem:<sup>ci</sup> che m' havevano accusato, e che ness° potrebbe provar queste cose Ze," ASF, MdP 4275, 126r–v.

34. "12151712213216 [*Il Visir*] che conosceva ben<sup>mo</sup> mi e tt<sup>i</sup> i miei parenti alliquali ci sempre era stato affett.<sup>mo</sup> non solo approvò per vere li miei ragioni ma offertosi ancora à favorirmi in tt° q[ue]llo ch'io desiderarebbe, mi fece 21261614171223161032153 3· [*Spravier del Gran Signore* [Turco]] con entrada annuale, mi dette ancora 26161217321534221232 [*privilegij*] per la casa mia e mi fece libero & esente d'ogni sorte di 27161219174429 [*tributo*] si per 35· [*guerra*] come per altro ma ttj erano inganni, alla fine per 2429201425103020232 52729 [*comandamento*] d[e]lli suoi 2216142 51012 [*grandi*] io fù messo in 22171416101230 [*guardia*] d'un 96 [*Chiaus*] che sottopretesto d'altro in' 23211420322529 [*esamina*] piu u.<sup>te</sup> perche causa io era venuto in queste bande accompag.<sup>to</sup> da 2. 18161425242812

[*Franchi*] l'uno delliquali s'era partito e l'atro restato con esso meco," ASF, MdP 4275, 126v.

35. Continuing without a break from the quotation in the foregoing note: "io gli risposi ben alla rima quello che la si può imaginare, ma con questo il tristo non si contentò, un giorno mi condusse in una casa come si fosse per altri affari, ove erano 1426393016232440281249271211171427444 229 [*apparecchiati quattro*] p[er] [*soldati*] ~~sort~~ che mi ł 1512221417302529 [*legarono* [ligavano] e volevano cavar li miei 21232216342732 [*segreti*] con darmi 2729162023254412 [*tormenti*], io con aiuto di NS. l'ho supportato con patienza, e loro vedendo che non potevano penetrare à q[ue]llo che desid[er]avano e' essendosi stra[c]cati a 27291620232544144422012 [*tormentarmi*] mi lasciorno con gastigarmi poi in altra," ASF, MdP 4275, 126v.

36. Florio gives "piastra d'argento" as "a dollar of silver in Spaine worthe five shillings three pence of ours." Continuing without a break from the quotation in the foregoing note: "maniera e far patir la borsa perche domandavano di me 500 p$^e$. io che n[on] havevo ne 500 ne 50 cercai per tt$^o$ questa som[m]a di dan.$^{ri}$ ma ness$^o$ era che mi l'imprestasse anzi ciasc$^o$ si scandale[z]za à me e mi fugg~~ìvì~~, all'ultimo trovai il s$^r$ 27122029442 3532029122325 [*Timoteo Moyen* [Moien]] mercante franzese, huomo veram$^{te}$, honoratiss.$^{mo}$ amato e lodato da ttj, ilquale havendo inteso la mia disgrazia, mosso à compass.$^{ne}$ verso di me vedendomi in tanti travagli e tormenti m'aiutò con la$_{\wedge}$$^{detta}$ som[m]a di 500 p.$^e$ per mez[z]o de'quali io ho liberato riscattato e ricuperato, l'honor, la vita e la casa mia, & se non fosse stato lei, io havrei corso qualch'altri magg$^{ri}$ pericoli e non sarei scappato così come per gra d'Iddio, & aiuto del detto s$^r$ 2029122325 [*Moyen* [Moien]] sono scappato alquale io son'obligato mentre io vivrò, Ze' & havendolo in questa mia estrema necessità conosciuto per vero et sincero amico e sig.$^{re}$ l'ho poi scoperso la causa che 20'28141830274 42917232512163233 [*m'ha fatto venire in*] questa disgratiss.$^{ma}$ paese, e destramente l'ho accennato le cose mie, e per levarmi mai più di questi sì gran travagli e pericoli avanti che non si 21241729261614 [*scuopra*] qual ch'altra cosa," ASF, MdP 4275, 126v.

37. "e 142510301620233334,122563· [*andarmene in Persia*] à spedir l'14201930 212412492714 [*ambasciata*] e la comession mia à 1117231543142030 34212749 [*quella Maestà*], poiche per non ess$^r$ per ancora partito 151493 [*la Carovana*] che di 3. mesi avanti doveva partire per questi motivi di guerre, & io tengo 151443232744341630· [*la lettera*] ancora meco, io med.$^{mo}$ sono risoluto d'andar à pntar à 2120 [*S.M.*$^{ta}$ [SM]] piacendo Iddio, ilche mi pareva miglior che l'andar à trovare ò 1518·20· [*l'Emir Faccardino*] ò altro, stando lui con pochi genti ancora su la bila[n]za e non sà à q[ue]llo c'ha à risolversi," ASF, MdP 4275, 126v.

38. "E tanto più che 121578 [*il Bascia*] in questo med.$^{mo}$ tempo ha mandat[i] quì una l$\dot{r}$a in segreto 141524281214211923403826231621323025 29 [*al*

*Chiasbech persiano*] uno de'suoi favoriti desiderando ch'io vada q[ua]nto p:ª sia possib.ᵉ à trovar 121573·101263·eà [*il Re di Persia*] trattar con 2120 [*S.M.*ᵗᵃ [SM]] di q[ua]nto più volte habbiamo discorso insieme cioè à 15232214161534 [*legarlo in amicizia*] in 66 [presi] con essa e s'egli 2629214714 [*possa*] havʳ 301217272910121514 [*aiuta di là*] gli sarà tanto più caro se no[n] almeno persuaderla che darla 1914251030211714172325223 0,2429251117231543492014224112291618291 61330 [*banda sua venga con quelle maggiori forze*] che sia possib.ᵉ à 1014253312 [*danni*] [127r] 10231533 [*d[e]l Turco*] ch'anco egli non mancherebbe à far il med.ᵐᵒ perch'egli haveva 2 2 1 2 1 7 1 6 1 4 2 7 2 9 1 0 1 2 1 8 3 0 1 6 4 2 3 2 2 1 2 3 2 5 2 7 5 1 2 0 3 4 3 3 ₍₄₎4429 [*giurato di far risentimento*] se gli costarebbe la sua propria vita no[n] abbandonerà mai quest 12202616232130 [*impresa*] e com'egli sà che ness:ⁿᵒ d[e]lli suoi può far queltanto che possa far io se io 14251034162915·[*anderà la*] così mi pregą di non mancar d'1425103016 [*andar*] q[ua]nto p:ª e far q[ue]llo io posso e non lasciarlo in questa estremità, che con tempo se Iddio gli aiuterà riconoscerà da me Ze. dicendo che volont.ʳᵉ m'havesse mandato q[ue]lla comodità ch'io debba havʳᵉ à far 71·17121422411229 [*questo viaggio*] ma io lo scusarebbe per la lontananza e per li pericoli che si corre per venir 72· [*qua*] il detto 2623162112302529 [*Persiano*] m'ha letto la lra ,mostrato il 2117292014252124161227 4429 [*suo manscritto*] e il 191715432910231578 [*bollo del Bascia*]," ASF, MdP 4275, 126v–127r.

39. "diche io havːʳ visto ciò come spronato sono andato subito al d.ᵗᵒ sʳ 2029122325 [*Moyen*] ho mostrato il 2012292614272325 4434,1014172114 [*mia patente da V.A.* [mio patente da VSA]] datomi e l'ho pregato che in virtù di quella m'aiutasse di nuovo co[n] 300 pᵉ che gli sarieno rifatte da 171421 [*V.A.* [VAS]] ilche l'ha fatti volont.ʳⁱ si per il servizio pncipale c'ha à riuscir à laude di Dio, benefizio & 1417222023252729 [*augmento*] di 27174427141530 [*tutto la*] Chr[isti]anità, com'ancora à serʳᵉ l'1417 [*V.A.*] alla qᵃle ci s'obliga à serːʳᵉ insin'al spargimento del suo sangue in ttᵒ q[ue]llo che gli sarà comandato," ASF, MdP 4275, 127r.

40. "l'ha fatto di più per aiutarmi & liberarmi di sì evidenti pericoli avanti che non m'avvenga qualch'altro magg.ʳᵉ Imperò supplico 151417 [*V.A.* [LAV]] à comandare che'l sia q[ua]nto prima rifatto e sia pagato la detta som[m]a di dan.ʳⁱ di ottocento pᵉ cioè reali di Spag.ª d'otto pezze l'uno al sʳ Pesciolini in Marsilia conforme alla lra di cambio Ze & s'egli sarà buon à serʳᵉ l'[14{the manuscript is damaged here; the "14" is inferred from the decipherment}]17 [*A.V.*] in queste è altre parti la supp:ᶜᵒ à impiegarlo e sia certa che con ogni maggʳ contentezza sarà sempre fedelissimamᵗᵉ servità. Intanto ci con ogni occ:ⁿᵉ di vasselli avvisarà l'1417 [*A.V.*] di ttᵒ q[ue]llo che passarà in queste parti insin' al mio ritorno che prego Dio sia presto perche l'intenzion mia è di no[n] perder tempo in quelle bande ma di tornarmene q[ua]nto p:ª mi sarà possibile," ASF, MdP 4275, 127r.

41. "Q[ua]nto alle cose 142440291610302723 [*accordate*] àl 71·212316mo78 [*Ser.moBascia* [questo Ser.mo Bascia]] tanto ch'egli no[n] ha altra intenzion che 101217232510322430162151 [*di vendicarsi*] e c'è openion che il 1712213216 [*Visir*] no[n] potrà troppo 182316203016213272· [*fermarsi qua*] ma bisognerà ch'alla Primavera sia ò 122598· ò in 63· [*in Ungaria o in Persia*] ilquale partendosi di 72·18141630212716141030141578 [*qua, farà strada al Bascia*] di ritornarsene, e come faciliss<sup>mo</sup> gli sarà 101220261427162925124221233334 [*d'impadronirsene*] di nuovi de tt° come speriamo in Dio che gli habbia à riuscire," ASF, MdP 4275, 127r.

42. "allora bisognerà che quelle cose siano pronti & apparecchiati, ma l'1417· [*A.V.*] sapeà meglio q[ue]llo che la deva fare, intanto lasciamo al ~~onde scritti nuovo~~ [marginal insertion: prudent<sup>mo</sup> consig° e providenza· di ~~171421~~ [*V.A.* [VAS]] la quale saprà à governarsi secondo l'avvisi che l'haurà di 72· [*qua*]. La partenza nostra sarà piacendo à Dio Bened.<sup>to</sup> fra 3· ò 4. giorni alpiù e andiamo in compag.<sup>a</sup> di 30. altre persone in 75. [*Babilonia*] non sendo per adesso comodità d'andar per altre bande di dove poi s'andarà con p:<sup>a</sup> occ:<sup>ne</sup> se haueremo 99 [*compagnia*] sè no[n] bisognerà che per nri dan.<sup>ri</sup> pig.<sup>mo</sup> qualch[e] 10 ò 12 persone per accompagnarci insino che passiamo li confine· e arriviamo nel paese del 73·101263·[*Re di Persia*] per laquale si pass.<sup>rà</sup> con ogni celerità magg<sup>re</sup> alla Corte di 2120 [*S.M.*<sup>ta</sup> [SM]]. dove la sarà," ASF, MdP 4275, 127r.

43. "Con[]che io mi p[re]parò alla partenza mia con allegra occ:<sup>ne</sup> da uscirmene una volta da q<sup>ti</sup> travagli e si evidenti pericoli e con deliberato animo di far cose che siano conforme alla buona & ottima volontà di 171421 [*V.A.* [VAS]] per felicitar la nra sorte. E con speranza che Dio Bened.<sup>to</sup> degni anc.<sup>ra</sup> benedir l'impresa si come à suo tempo solo à SD.M.<sup>tà</sup> ne restarà e sarà l'honore e la gloria, la quale io prego che mantenga e prosperi l'1417 [*A.V.*] in sanita & allegrezza e l'essalti ad ogni contentezza magg<sup>re</sup> [127v] Inchinandomi con ogni affetto à baciar la vesta 1012171421 [*di V.A.* [VAS]] così à 20. e. il 21 [*Madama et al*] mio 221614252616122524322623 [*Ser.*<sup>mo</sup> [Gran] *Principe*] come humilissimam<sup>te</sup> fa lo scre Giorg° Di 59 [*Aleppo*] li 6. di Dicembre 1607 La pnte le mandò con il Galeon di S.<sup>L</sup> Matteo che passa per Marsilia e per la solita via di Pesciolinj serve l'avviso 201224282315142522322 9<sup>lo</sup>2453161412 [*Michelag.*<sup>lo</sup> [Michelangio<sup>lo</sup>] *Corai*]," ASF, MdP 4275, 127r-v.

44. "Io aspetto sentir il salvo arrive di VS. e che felicem<sup>te</sup> goda cotesto feliciss.<sup>mo</sup> paese e la sua cara patria . . . ha salvato e liberato da si grand.<sup>mi</sup> pericoli e travagli che dopo la partenza sua e venuto a trovarci," ASF, MdP 4275, 177r. On the issue of the addressee, the volume separates the letters from their envelopes into groups; the addressee must therefore be inferred from the titles used, internal evidence, and the addressees of the remaining envelopes. ASF, MdP 4275, 182v is addressed to Leoncini "Al

Molto Ill^{re} sig^r Cav^r oss^{mo} Il sig.^r Hippolito Lioncinj" and then further down the page "Alla Corte." 177r begins "Molto Ill^{re} Cav^r oss^{mo}." Judging by a scan of "oss" terms in the 1611 edition of Florio's dictionary, "oss^{mo}" probably signifies "osservandissimo," which Florio gives as "right worshipfull or most worthy of regard."

45. "Le cose del Dio di quà Vostro Signore saprà ch'io l'ho lasciato all' ottimo Consiglio e Prudenza di Sua Altezza Serenissima la quale saprà governarsi secondo l'avvisi che ne manderà di quì il signor Timoteo Moyen nostro tanto caro cortese e amorevole il quale ne avviserà di tutto che passarà com'io l'ho pregato e lei m'ha promesso di voler fare con tutte le comodita che si rappresenteranno di poterlo fare, perche io me ne vago hora all volta di Persia e Vostro Signore non si moverà di là in nessuno modo," ASF, MdP 4275, 177r.

46. "la maestà di Persia tanto per la comessione ch'io ho da parte di Sua Altezza Serenissima come anco da parte del Dio di qua, accioche quanto p^a. venghi consolato e aiutato," ASF, MdP 4275, 177r.

47. "la quale m'ha aiutato nella mia estrema necessita allhora ch'io fui abbandonato da tutti, e liberatomi, a dire quasi, della morte e recuperato l'honor, la vita e la casa mia," ASF, MdP 4275, 177r.

48. Margherita Farina, "La nascita della Tipografia Medicea: Personaggi e idee," in *Le vie delle lettere: La Tipografia Medicea tra Roma e l'Oriente*, ed. Sara Fani and Margherita Farina (Florence: Mandragora, 2012), 63–65, and Giuseppe Tucci, *Italia e Oriente*, reissue, ed. Francesco d'Arelli (Rome: Istituto Italiano per l'Africa e l'Oriente, 2005), 64–66.

49. The classic accounts are Donald E. Queller, *The Office of Ambassador in the Middle Ages* (Princeton, NJ: Princeton University Press, 1967), and Garrett Mattingly, *Renaissance Diplomacy* (New York: Cosimo Classics, 2008). For more recent historiography see Daniela Frigo, ed., *Politics and Diplomacy in Early Modern Italy: The Structure of Diplomatic Practice, 1450–1800*, trans. Adrian Belton (Cambridge: Cambridge University Press, 2000); Catherine Fletcher, *Diplomacy in Renaissance Rome: The Rise of the Resident Ambassador* (New York: Cambridge University Press, 2015); Fletcher, *Our Man in Rome: Henry VIII and His Italian Ambassador* (London: Bodley Head, 2012); Filippo de Vivo, *Information and Communication in Venice: Rethinking Early Modern Politics* (New York: Oxford University Press, 2007). See also Monica Azzolini and Isabella Lazzarini, eds., *Italian Renaissance Diplomacy: A Sourcebook* (Durham, UK: Durham University; Toronto: Institute of Medieval and Early Modern Studies, Pontifical Institute of Mediaeval Studies, 2017). Thanks to Philip Davis for excellent bibliographic recommendations (on which I gratefully draw here) and many stimulating conversations on early modern diplomacy in the context of discussing his Syracuse University dissertation on Anglo-Italian diplomacy.

50. Salman Rushdie, *The Enchantress of Florence* (New York: Random House, 2009). On *The Ambassadors*, see Lisa Jardine, *Worldly Goods: A New History of the Renaissance* (New York: W. W. Norton, 1998), 425-436.

51. On the Safavids, see Willem Floor and Edmund Herzig, eds., *Iran and the World in the Safavid Age* (New York: I. B. Tauris, 2012); Rudolph P. Matthee, *The Politics of Trade in Safavid Iran: Silk for Silver, 1600–1730* (New York: Cambridge University Press, 1999); Stephen F. Dale, *The Muslim Empires of the Ottomans, Safavids, and Mughals* (New York: Cambridge University Press, 2010). On the Ottomans, see Baki Tezcan, *The Second Ottoman Empire: Political and Social Transformation in the Early Modern World* (New York: Cambridge University Press, 2010); Caroline Finkel, *Osman's Dream: The Story of the Ottoman Empire 1300–1923* (New York: Basic Books, 2007); Halil İnalcık, *The Ottoman Empire: The Classic Age 1300–1600* (London: Phoenix, 2000).

52. Though focused on the nineteenth and twentieth centuries, Abbas Amanat, *Iran: A Modern History* (New Haven, CT: Yale University Press, 2017), is sufficiently capacious to offer a substantial account of the Safavids. See also Michael Axworthy, *A History of Iran: Empire of the Mind* (New York: Basic Books, 2010), and Matthee, *Politics of Trade*. On Iberian-Safavid relations, see Luis Gil Fernández, *El imperio luso-español y la Persia safávida*, 2 vols. (Madrid: Fundación Universitaria Española, 2006 and 2009). For broader temporal and regional context, see Janet L. Abu-Lughod, *Before European Hegemony: The World System a.d. 1250–1350* (New York: Oxford University Press, 1991); Thomas Barfield, *Afghanistan: A Cultural and Political History* (Princeton, NJ: Princeton University Press, 2010). For a rich fictional account of the shared Persianate cultural world, and especially of the miniaturists, contextualized in this moment, see Orhan Pamuk, *My Name Is Red*, trans. Erdag Göknar (New York: Vintage International, 2002).

53. Catherine Evtuhov, David Goldfrank, Lindsey Hughes, and Richard Stites, *A History of Russia: People, Legends, Events, Forces* (New York: Houghton Mifflin, 2004), 126-129; Robert O. Crummey, *The Formation of Muscovy, 1304–1613* (New York: Longman, 1987), 151-155.

54. On the Safavids and Portuguese Hormuz, see Amanat, *Iran*, 96-104, and Gil Fernández, *Imperio luso-español*. On the Deccan sultanates, see Navina Najat Haidar and Marika Sardar, *Sultans of Deccan India, 1500–1700: Opulence and Fantasy* (New York: Metropolitan Museum of Art, 2015); Sanjay Subrahmanyam, *Penumbral Visions: Making Polities in Early Modern South India* (Ann Arbor: University of Michigan Press, 2001); Sanjay Subrahmanyam, *The Political Economy of Commerce: Southern India, 1500–1650* (New York: Cambridge University Press, 2002). At the outset of the sixteenth century, the most commercially important of the sultanates of Southeast Asia was undoubtedly Melaka (Malacca), for which see Luis

Filipe Ferreira Reis Thomaz, "The Malay Sultanate of Aceh," in Anthony Reid, ed., *Southeast Asia in the Early Modern Era: Trade, Power, and Belief* (Ithaca, NY: Cornell University Press, 1993), 69–90. On southeast Asia generally in this period, see Reid, *Southeast Asia in the Age of Commerce: 1450–1680*, 2 vols. (New Haven, CT: Yale University Press, 1988). On the Ottomans in Aceh, see Giancarlo Casale, *The Ottoman Age of Exploration* (New York: Oxford University Press, 2010), 57–59, 124–125, 127, 131, 145–147, 180–181, and 200. See also Sanjay Subrahmanyam, *The Portuguese Empire in Asia, 1500–1700: A Political and Economic History* (New York: Longman, 1993).

55. John F. Richards, *The Mughal Empire* (Cambridge: Cambridge University Press, 1993), esp. 9–12; Amanat, *Iran*, 101. See also John F. Richards, "The Seventeenth-Century Crisis in South Asia," *Modern Asian Studies* 24, no. 4 (October 1990): 625–638; Jos Gommans, *Mughal Warfare* (New York: Routledge, 2002); Annemarie Schimmel, *The Empire of the Great Mughals: History, Art and Culture*, trans. Corinne Attwood, ed. Burzine K. Waghmar (London: Reaktion, 2004). For comparative accounts, see Dale, *Muslim Empires*, and Douglas E. Streusand, *Islamic Gunpowder Empires: Ottomans, Safavids, and Mughals* (Boulder, CO: Westview, 2011).

56. Richards, *Mughal Empire*, 51, 110–112; Streusand, *Islamic Gunpowder Empires*, 148, 154, and 172; Amanat, *Iran*, 134.

57. On the three-way struggle among the Ottomans, Safavids, and Mughals at the beginning of the sixteenth century, see Palmira Brummett, *Ottoman Seapower and Levantine Diplomacy in the Age of Discovery* (Albany: State University of New York Press, 1994), and Amanat, *Iran*, 33–59. For general accounts, see also İnalcık, *Ottoman Empire*; Finkel, *Osman's Dream*; Dale, *Muslim Empires*; Streusand, *Islamic Gunpowder Empires*. For a useful chronology, see İnalcık, *Ottoman Empire*, 207–216. For a concise account of these events and the implications of the fall of Basra (and the role of the Red Sea and Persian Gulf trade routes), see Matthee, *Politics of Trade*, 16–18. For the period after Chaldiran, see Amanat, *Iran*, 59–125.

58. Amanat, *Iran*, 74–125 (esp. 74–82); Dale, *Muslim Empires*, 91–96; Streusand, *Islamic Gunpowder Empires*, 150–153.

59. Matthee, *Politics of Trade*; Amanat, *Iran*, 91–95; Dale, *Muslim Empires*, 91–96; Streusand, *Islamic Gunpowder Empires*, 150–153.

60. Amanat, *Iran*, 82–95; Sebouh David Aslanian, *From the Indian Ocean to the Mediterranean: The Global Trade Networks of Armenian Merchants from New Julfa* (Berkeley: University of California Press, 2011), 1–2 and 23–43.

61. Sanjay Subrahmanyam, *Three Ways to Be Alien: Travails and Encounters in the Early Modern World* (Waltham, MA: Brandeis University Press and the Historical Society of Israel, 2011), 86. Subrahmanyam characterizes Vecchietti as a "Florentine savant."

62. Farina, "Nascita della Tipografia Medicea," 48–49.

63. Farina, "Nascita della Tipografia Medicea," 60 and 63.

64. Farina, "Nascita della Tipografia Medicea," 60–63. Farina suggests that he may have died in Goa.

65. Farina, "Nascita della Tipografia Medicea," 63–65; Angelo de Gubernatis, ed., *Storia dei Viaggiatori Italiani nelle Indie Orientali* (Livorno, It.: Franc. Vigo, 1875), 25 and 25n1.

66. Farina, "Nascita della Tipografia Medicea," 43–44.

67. Farina, "Nascita della Tipografia Medicea," 43–56.

68. Edward W. Said, *Orientalism* (New York: Vintage, 2003), 68–72. The press is perhaps appropriately absent, for instance, from Edward Said's polemical *Orientalism*; its activities fit his argument quite poorly. Indeed, his choice to largely ignore Italy—his comments on Dante notwithstanding— a part of Europe that interacted daily with the Islamic world and that has a strong claim to having actually invented orientalism as a scholarly discipline, renders his work largely inapplicable here. On Selden, see Timothy Brook, *Mr. Selden's Map of China: Decoding the Secrets of a Vanished Cartographer* (New York: Bloomsbury, 2013), 40.

69. Farina, "Nascita della Tipografia Medicea," 43–56.

70. See section 4.2, "Il patriarca Na'matallah" and section 4.4, "I fratelli Vecchietti" in Farina, "Nascita della Tipografia Medicea," 57–60 and 63–65.

71. Farina, "Nascita della Tipografia Medicea," 46.

72. Richard Goldthwaite, *The Economy of Renaissance Florence* (Baltimore, MD: Johns Hopkins University Press, 2009), 298–317.

73. These figures are drawn selectively from a table in Sara Fani, "Gli esiti della Tipografia Medicea," in Fani and Farina, eds. *Le vie delle lettere*, 75.

74. Borbone cites Robert Jones—R. Jones, "The Medici Oriental Press (Rome 1584–1614) and the Impacts of its Arabic Publications on Northern Europe," in *The "Arabick" Interest of the Natural Philosophers in Seventeenth-Century England*, ed. G. A. Russel (Leiden, Neth.: Brill, 1994), 88–108—on the quality of the editions (Pier Giorgio Borbone, "Introduzione" in Fani and Farina, eds. *Le vie delle lettere*, 25).

75. MAP Person ID 775, "Vinta, Belisario di Francesco."

76. Belisario di Francesco Vinta in Florence to Giovanni Battista Vecchietti on January 5, 1610, MAP Doc ID 12630, ASF, MdP 302, 57; Cosimo II de' Medici [but the synopsis suggests the letter is from Belisario Vinta] in Florence to Santi Fabbretti in Pisa, February 3, 1610, MAP Doc ID 12696, ASF, MdP 302, 66.

77. Belisario di Francesco Vinta in Florence to Jacopo di Tommaso de' Medici in Florence, July 15, 1610, MAP Doc ID 12839, ASF, MdP 302, 142.

78. Fani, "Gli esiti della Tipografia Medicea," 73–84, in particular 79–81; MAP Person ID 775, "Vinta, Belisario di Francesco."

79. Subrahmanyam, *Three Ways to Be Alien*, 86.

80. Peter H. Wilson, *Heart of Europe: A History of the Holy Roman Empire* (Cambridge, MA: Harvard University Press, 2016), 150.

81. For Vecchietti's letter, see Giovanni Battista Vecchietti in Madrid to Ferdinando I de' Medici in Florence, December 10, 1588, ASF, MdP 4919, P. II, 602r–603v; MAP Doc ID 16228. Vecchietti mentions that the Tuscan delegation informed Philip II of the progress of the business of Ethiopia as well as that of Persia (p. 602). For Alamanni's letter, see Vicenzo di Andrea Alamanni in Madrid to Ferdinando I de' Medici in Florence, December 10, 1588, ASF, MdP 4919, P. II, 612r–615v; MAP Doc ID 8446.

82. Giovanni Battista Vecchietti in Madrid to Ferdinando I in Florence on November 12, 1588, MAP Doc ID 2718, ASF MdP 4919, 568.

83. Ambassador Vicenzo di Andrea Alamanni in Madrid on May 27, 1589, to Pietro di Francesco Usimbardi in Florence, MAP Doc ID 949, ASF, MdP 4920, 23. For all my references to this letter, see ASF, MdP 4920, 23r–25v. I have inferred from the contents of the letter that Usimbardi was already principal secretary of state to Ferdinando I, but MAP Person ID 469, "Usimbardi, Pietro di Francesco," does not give specific dates for Usimbardi's tenure as principal secretary of state.

84. On the perilous strategic position of Hormuz and its essential outlying affiliate territories, see E. K. Faridany, "Signal Defeat: The Portuguese Loss of Comorão in 1614 and Its Political and Commercial Consequences," in *Acta Iranica: Portugal, the Persian Gulf and Safavid Persia*, ed. Rudi Matthee and Jorge Flores (Leuven, Belg.: Peeters, 2011), 119–141.

85. Richard Raiswell, "Sherley [Shirley], Anthony [*known as* Sir Anthony Sherley], Count Sherley in the nobility of the Holy Roman empire (1565–1636?)," *Oxford Dictionary of National Biography*; Richard Raiswell, "Shirley, Sir Robert, Count Shirley in the papal nobility (c. 1581–1628)," *Oxford Dictionary of National Biography*.

86. Raiswell, "Sherley, Anthony."

87. Raiswell, "Shirley, Sir Robert."

88. Raiswell, "Sherley, Anthony." Raiswell, "Shirley, Sir Robert."

89. Raiswell, "Sherley, Anthony"; Raiswell, "Shirley, Sir Robert"; Subrahmanyam, *Three Ways to Be Alien*, 73–132; Faridany, "Signal Defeat"; Federico M. Federici, "A Servant of Two Masters: The Translator Michel Angelo Corai as a Tuscan Diplomat (1599–1609)," in *Translators, Interpreters, and Cultural Negotiators: Mediating and Communicating Power from the Middle Ages to the Modern Era*, ed. Federico Federici and Dario Tessicini (New York: Palgrave Macmillan, 2014), 81–104.

90. Raiswell, "Sherley, Anthony"; Subrahmanyam, *Three Ways to Be Alien*, 88–99; Simon Adams, "Dudley, Robert, earl of Leicester (1532/3–1588)," *Oxford Dictionary of National Biography*; Paul E. J. Hammer, "Devereux, Robert, second earl of Essex (1565–1601)," *Oxford Dictionary of National Biography*.

91. LPL, MS 656, [222]/[325r-v].

92. Raiswell, "Sherley, Anthony"; Subrahmanyam, *Three Ways to Be Alien*, 91–95. In Paul E. J. Hammer, "Reynoldes, Edward (d. 1623)," *Oxford Dictionary of National Biography*, Anthony Bacon is characterized as "Essex's friend and chief intelligence co-ordinator." See also Alan Stewart, "Bacon, Anthony (1558-1601)," *Oxford Dictionary of National Biography*, which begins with the simple appositive characterization "spy."

93. "Right Honorable Since the writing of my lre I have made a revew both of my shippe men & victuals all w^ch I find so out of order for the performing of my intent presently: that I am constrayned to take new found land in my way where I shall not only refresh my selfe from my present necèssities but also gett so much fish as will royally furnish all my wants by the sales w^ch I shall make of it by passing the straights into Turquie : which because it will aske some tyme & I am not willing to spend that time idlyI will trie if it be possible for me to worke the Turk· to send his Gallies· w^ch ly idle in the redde Sea to make warre upon the east indias so that fortified with the courses w^ch they will make there & my own strenght I shall be able to worke Some very good effect: if the King of Spaine troble us so much at home as wee heare he doth by reperte where . I am I doe not see any reasons why her Ma^tie should not be contented to use him with y^e haeby as many meanes as she may & no way in this world doth promise so greate a liklyhood to dompte all his pretenses as the marrine of his mony trad w^ch is y^e only spirit by w^ch he troubleth y^ewholl world : this cometh to him but two ways: by the west & east indias : for y^e west I have found so trew a means to deprive him or att the least to mambe him so much that his profit shalbe eyther be nothing or at y^e least so unfix that it will be as good as nothing; & that I doe not think but y^r L /̄ will w^n you have well iudged of it be contented to second by y^r best ··· furtherance & favor [262v:] for the east Indias I have so throughly examined his weaknes by a Portingall Prisonner w^ch I have & y^e fittnes of y^e Turck to invade him by y^e redde Sea y^t if he cann be wrought to take it in hand I do not see but eyther he may be utterly disposest of his places or at y^e least deprived of his great marchandinge : to this effect have I taken with me my Sea men of best knowledge to shew them by demonstra̅on i̅o̅ ̔ they may most easily effect if they will because I will the more then I will sett downe a iust tyme of y^e yeare w^n I will meete them ther w^th my shippe But by y^e knowledge w^ch I have how little my industry or any mans can discerne of o^e state I protest before hand that ~~yet~~ it is nothing that hath drawen me into y^e least of any of these thoughts but y^e honor w^ch I beare to y^r L / ̄[Lordship] who I desire Should be advãced to the heith of all honor & therfore I Shalbe ready to receave & to effect any thing w^ch y^u Shall commaund me by any post to venice w^r I will leave continuall notice of my abiding place I have a man of myn owne Ane stokwell w^m if y^r L /̄ will

send unto me will easily & diligently finde me do but y$^r$ L / ‾[Lordship] consider w $^{rin}$ I may do y$^u$ Service eyther w$^{th}$ my lif or purse & it shalbe done if I be compelled to buy his counsell generally or any own of them I will be so furnished of meanes that I will do it as I shall heere y$^r$ L / plea- sure: in y$^e$ meane tyme I will make my acquaintance such : that I will no sooner receave y$^r$ letter but that I wilbe readie to effect it & So I rest y$^r$ Lordships Most humble & faithfull S[er]vant A Sherley," LPL, MS 661 (174, 262r–v).

94. Casale, *Ottoman Age of Exploration*.

95. Raiswell, "Shirley, Sir Robert"; Raiswell, "Sherley, Anthony."

96. Raiswell, "Sherley, Anthony"; Raiswell, "Shirley, Sir Robert"; Subrah- manyam, *Three Ways to Be Alien*, 91 and 94–96; Federici, "Servant of Two Masters," 85–87.

97. Subrahmanyam, *Three Ways to Be Alien*, 90–92 and 96–98.

98. Subrahmanyam, *Three Ways to Be Alien*, 96–97.

99. Subrahmanyam, *Three Ways to Be Alien*, 98–99.

100. Richards, *Mughal Empire*, 19–25 and 60.

101. Richards, *Mughal Empire*, 19–24.

102. "Scapitato quì ùn Dragomanno Soriano, che hà servito d'Interpetre ad ˙un segnor Don Antonio, Gentilh[manuscript damaged at this point] Christiano, ma non dire di qual Provincia di Christianita egli sia per l'appunto , in Persia mentre che ha'$_\wedge$$^{servito\ et}$ trattato con quel Rè, et hora afferma divenire suo Precursire, et che detto signor Don Antonio $_\wedge$ $^{mandato}$ $^{dal\ Persiano}$ porterà lettere d[??]$^{di\ quel\ Principe}$ $_\wedge$P̶e̶r̶s̶i̶a̶n̶o̶ al Papa, all' Impera- tore, al Re di Spagna, al Re di Francia al Doge di Venetia, et al Gran Duca di Toscana; Et che detto signor Don Antonio faccia la strada per Moscovia, perche il Turco, havendo saputa la sua venuta, haveva messe guardie à i passi, per ritenerlo," ASF, MdP 4275, 3r–5r.

103. Matthee, *Politics of Trade*, 54–55 and 79; Raiswell, "Shirley, Sir Robert"; Raiswell, "Sherley, Anthony"; Subrahmanyam, *Three Ways to Be Alien*, 98– 104 (104 for the fall of Essex).

104. Raiswell, "Shirley, Sir Robert"; Faridany, "Signal Defeat," 125.

105. Asdrubale Barbolani di Montauto in Venice to Belisario di Francesco Vinta in Florence on June 14, 1608, MAP Doc ID 15025, ASF, MdP 3000, 398; Giovanni (o Armenio) Persiano in Venice to Belisario di Francesco Vinta in Florence on June 14, 1608, MAP Doc ID 15034, ASF, MdP 3000, 399.

106. Asdrubale Barbolani di Montauto in Venice to Belisario di Francesco Vinta in Florence on March 8, 1609, MAP Doc ID 14777, ASF, MdP 3000, 316. MAP notes that the date as written was March 8, 1608. On agents operating in this region, see Noel Malcolm, *Agents of Empire: Knights, Cor- sairs, Jesuits, and Spies in the Sixteenth Century Mediterranean World* (New York: Oxford University Press, 2015).

107. Asdrubale Barbolani di Montauto in Venice to Belisario di Francesco Vinta in Florence on March 29, 1609, MAP Doc ID 14798, ASF MdP 3000, 333. MAP notes that the date as written was March 29, 1608.

108. Gregory Hanlon, *The Twilight of a Military Tradition: Italian Aristocrats and European Conflicts, 1560–1800* (New York: Holmes and Meyer, 1998), 40-41.

109. Letter to Ferdinando I de' Medici, perhaps in 1608, MAP Doc ID 21099, ASF, MdP 4275, 412.

110. On Cyprus: Letter to Cosimo II de' Medici, perhaps in 1609, MAP Doc ID 21108, ASF, MdP 4275, 435. On Rhodes: MAP Doc ID 21104, ASF, MdP 4275, 419r. Perhaps 1609. On Macedonia: Letter perhaps from Damiano Dinucci, perhaps in 1609, MAP Doc ID 21097, ASF, MdP 4275, 403.

111. From Florence to Cosimo II de' Medici in Florence, perhaps 1611, MAP Doc ID 21131, ASF, MdP 4275, 565.

112. Anonymous note of September 20, 1609, MAP Doc ID 21049, ASF, MdP 4275, 189.

113. Raiswell, "Shirley, Sir Robert." On Robert Sherley's embassy up to his departure for Rome, see Gil Fernández, *Imperio luso-español*, 2: 121-123.

114. Vincenzo di Francesco Giugni in Florence to Curzio di Lorenzo da Picchena in Florence on July 7, 1622, MAP Doc ID 21077, ASF, MdP 4275, 321. The speculation about Anthony Sherley's visit as the trigger for the gift is my own and is based on the point in the MAP transcription that the necklaces were given on March 27, 1601. Anthony Sherley was in Florence in March 1601, as we have seen (Subrahmanyam, *Three Ways to Be Alien*, 104). It seems likely that the embassy of which he was a part received the necklaces as parting gifts. It is not entirely clear what distinction should be drawn between gifts to the ambassadors and those to the shah. See also Raiswell, "Shirley, Anthony."

115. Belisario di Francesco Vinta in Florence to Giovanni Battista Vecchietti on January 5, 1610, MAP Doc ID 12630, ASF MdP 302, 57. MAP notes that the date as written was January 5, 1609. MAP transcription (the bracketed text is MAP's): "È arrivato qui un Armeno, che si professa Christiano, et và alla Messa, et con havere portata l'allegata lettera nell'allegato sacchetto di drappo nel modo appunto, che ella stà senza nè quella cera nè quel coperchietto d'oro, che haveva l'altra portata dal Conte Don Roberto Serley [Robert Shirley], che afferma detta lettera essere del Re di Persia."

116. MAP Person ID 242, "Bartoli, Giovanni." The profile states that he was the legation secretary at the Medici embassy in Venice starting in 1599 and the main Medici ambassador in Venice from 1609 to 1610. See Belisario di Francesco Vinta in Florence to Giovanni Bartoli in Venice on

January 16, 1610, MAP Doc ID 12647, ASF, MdP 302, 59. My summary follows the synopsis closely.

117. Farina, "Nascita della Tipografia Medicea," 64–65.

118. I rely here on Faridany "Signal Defeat" and Gil Fernández, *Imperio luso-español*.

119. Gil Fernández, *Imperio luso-español*, Documentary Appendix, doc. #2, 2: 470. The transcription of the English letter appears as "Doc. n° 2: *Carta de Roberto Sherley a su hermano: Desde Roma, 2 de octubre de 1609:* Original inglés: (ms AL fondo Lerma IX f 429)."

120. This embassy appears frequently throughout Gil Fernández, *Imperio luso-español*, vol. 2; see in particular vol. 2: 152–159 and vol. 2, chapter 3, "La Embajada de Danguis Beg y Fray Antonio de Gouvea." On Dengiz Beg's mission, see Faridany, "Signal Defeat," 125–127. Apparently, his status as ambassador was a matter of disagreement. Faridany, "Signal Defeat," 126n21. I rely here on Faridany, "Signal Defeat," and in particular his insight that Shah 'Abbas's habit of sending second embassies created confusion over who was the real representative (Faridany, "Signal Defeat," 125–126).

121. Faridany, "Signal Defeat," 125–126.

122. Gil Fernández, *Imperio luso-español*, 2: 158–160.

123. Faridany, "Signal Defeat," 125–128.

124. "Al Re di Persia. 25. Gennaio. 1607 Don Ferdinando Medici, per grazia dell' Onnipotente Iddio Gran Duca di Toscana, Duca 4°. dello stato di Firenze, 3°. dello stato di Siena, Principe assoluto della Repubblica di Pisa ^Principe di Capostrano, Gran Maestro de Cavalieri et della Religione di Santo Stefano, Signore del Mar Tirreno et di molte Isole di esso . ~~et Principe dello stato de Capostrano~~ All'altissimo, ^Serenissimo potentissimo. et invittissimo Signore Saa Abbaz, Re di Persia, di Tartaria, di Arabia, e di Turchia, di Stirpe antichissima di Rè, patrone del Mare et della Terra, persecutore et dimatore della Casa Ottomanna, amicissimi de Christiani, che Iddio conservi felicissimo, insieme con tuttala Sua Reale progonie per molti secoli. [22v:] È cosi glorioso trai Principi christiani il nome di Vostra Maestà perli suoi felici progressi contro alla tirannide del Turco, che tutti celebrando le imprese et azzioni sue, stimano ch['ella sia nata al mundo per un flagello della Casa Ottomanna, et percio le desiderano continuate vittorie, con la intera distruzzione del suo nimico. Io tra tutti gli altri ho doppia cagione di rallegrarmene, si per l'affezzione et stima ch['io porto al supremo valere di Vostra Maestà come per la mia propria et antica osservanza verso di lei, cominciata fino altempo della gloriosa memoria della Maestra paterna; et accresciuto per il gran favore ch['alcuni anni sino mi fece Vostra Maestà col mandarme cosi nobile Ambasceria . Percio . [23r:] essendo stato qui ^il Cavaliere Michelagnolo Corai, che già fu Interprete ^di Vostra Maesta con li de suoi Ambasciatori et haven-

domi detto, che di Soria pensa di venire à cotesta Real corte, ho voluto con tale occasione ricordare alla Maestà Vostra con questa lettera la pronta volontà ch['Jio havrò sempre di servirla, se alle volte ella noi favorirà con li suoi comandamenti. et havendo io dato al medesimo <sub>∧</sub><sup>cavaliere</sup> Michelag<sup>lo</sup>. alcune commessioni di trattare con Vostra Maestà per servizio publico, mi rimetterò à lui; il quale la potrà anche ragguagliare in voce, di quello ch['Jio penso et faccio per danneggiare continuamente i Turchi con quelle poche forze marittime che Dio mi ha dato. et per fine bacio alla Maestà Vostra affettuosamente la mano. Di Vostra Maestà affettionissimo Servitore," ASF, MdP 4275 22r–23r.

125. "Copia da Carta que sua Mag.ª escreve ao Rey de persia de[]que faz menca⌐l a carta que sua mag· escreve ao Visorey," Historical Archives of Goa (HAG), Archive Number 12, Livros das Monções do Reino, 9, 10, and 11, 127r.

126. "Serenissimo e Potentissimo Xá Abbá Rej da Persia Nosso muj Charo e amado amigo: Eu dom Phelippe pergraça de Deos Rej da Espanhas e[] das Indias Orientaes e[]Occidentaes . e[]das Ilhas e[]Províncias do[]Mar Occeano, Rej de Napoles e Secilia, de[]Hierusalem, e[]dos Algarves dá quem e dàlem Mar en Africa, Achiduque d'Austria, Ḍuque de Milam Et[] ls.ª," HAG, Archive Number 12, Livros das Monções do Reino, 9, 10, and 11, 127r.

127. The manuscript is faded at this point. It is followed by: "Edina" at the beginning of the next line; I take this latter to be a fragment.

128. "Vỹ a Carta q̇ vossa Serenidade me[]escreveo cò q̇ Reçebir muj grande Contentamento pella boa Correspondençia e[]amisade q̇ me offereçe , eaq̇ escreveo ao Meu Visorej da India queria ter comigo ecò todos meus estados. E na mesma Conformidade a[]tenho eu offereçida a V. Ser.<sup>de</sup> pello seu embaixador Cusen Alibeẏ, ao qual mandei fazer o[]bom tratamento egasalhado q̇ v Ser.<sup>de</sup> delle teḿ entendido ; e[]o[]mesmo mandej hora fazer ao Secretario de Outro seu´ Embaixador q̇ vinha enviado ao nosso Muj santo Padre Cleme[n]te Octavo q̇ faleçeo no Maz. E pera conservaçam e[]augmento desta Conformidade lhe[]envieij o[]Meu Embaixador Luis pereira de[]laçerda fidalgo de[]minha casa e do[]meu Conselho, q̇ espero seja chegado a essa Corte de v. Ser.<sup>de</sup> e[]que por este meo fossa eu ter mui particulares novas de v. Ser.<sup>de</sup> è de[]seus prosperos sucçessos pera[]Com elles me alegrar, como agora fiz cò as novas q̇ o[] meu visorej da India me[]escreveo das grandes victorias q.<sup>e</sup> v.ser.<sup>de</sup> ovve contra seus imigos ; e[]com todas as desta qualidade me alegrarei sempre muito , as quaes folgara saber mais particularmente do seu Embaixador, q̇ o[]dito meu visorej me[]escreve vinha a[]mi enviado de v. Ser:<sup>de</sup> e por[] occasioens q̇ para isso leve se[]ficou em Goa ; e[]lhe[]escrevo q̇ se[]não for vindo lhe dee embarcaçam e[]todo o[]necessario pera sua passagem. cò o[]bom tratamento q̇ desejo se[]faça a[]todos os seus enviados : E[]doq̇ V

ser.<sup>de</sup> Mandou fazer en sua Corte aos Religiosos Frej Antonio de Gouvea, Frej Christovão o Frej Hieronȳmo , recebi muito Contentamento ; e fico por isso ,e[]pella casa q[ue] lhe Mandou dar pera se[]Recolherem e[]fazerem [127v:] os officios divinos da Christandade, Muj obrigado ; e[]terei sempre desta [missing word] Edina da[]grandeza de v Ser<sup>de</sup> o[]Reconhecimento devido , e[]lhe pesso muj affeisuosam.<sup>te</sup> os queira conserver e Sua graca , Que por serem pessoas q[] por[]serviço de nostro senhor e[] da[]sua Religiam deixaraȯ os beṅs do[]Mundo ese[]offereçeram aos trabalhos , Serão mereçedores de. V. ser.<sup>de</sup> os ter en[]sua procteiçam," HAG, Archive Number 12, Livros das Monções do Reino, 9, 10, and 11, 127r–v.

129. The binding or fading obscures at least some of the final word of many lines of this text; I have marked this by inserting "[?]." "E porq̇ o anno passado escrevi a V. Ser.<sup>de</sup> como tinha entendido por Cartas do [?] visorej da India e[]do Capitão de Ormûz q̇ oSoltȧo do Siraz por[]trato[]toman [?] a[]lha de Bârem a El Rej de Ormûz meu vassalo cȯ morte do[]Guazil q̇a tinh [?]em seu nome : e[]signiffiquej a.V.Ser.<sup>de</sup> a[]obrigaçḍo q̇ tinha de[]acodir ao dito Rej como meu vassalo , prinçipalmente na[]Restituiçam desta Ilha q<sup>e</sup> pertence ao Meu estado da India , por se[]aver tomado ao Turco imigo Comum_ cȯ as forç [?] delle, e[]conservado ate o[]presente sė Contradiçam alguȧ Confiando de V. Ser.<sup>de</sup> q̇ folgará q̇ entre nossos vassalos haja a[]mesma boa Correspondėçia e amisade q̇ entre nos há . Pedi a v. ser.<sup>de</sup> per outra Carta minha mandasse dar ordem cȯ q̇ a[]dita Ilha de Bárem fosse Restitum[]da livrem<sup>te</sup> ao[]dito Rej de Ormûz pera q̇ elle a[]tenha e[]possua Comodantes ; e[]os q̇ neste caso forem culpados sedee o Castigo q̇ mereçem, ao[]q<sup>e</sup>Confio tera v ser.<sup>de</sup> Madado satisfazer como herazam, Para q̇ se[]entenda he[]vontade de.V· Ser.<sup>de</sup> Conservar a[]paz e amisade q̂ me tem offereçida, q̇ eu[]desejo vaa cada[]dia em maẏor augmento : E porq̇ sobre[]esta materia fallara ma [?]particularm<sup>te</sup> a. v.ser.<sup>de</sup> o[]meu embaixador luis pr<sup>a</sup> de laçerda ou quem esta Carte lhe der , Pessoa v.Ser.<sup>de</sup> doe inteiro Credito ao q̇ de[]minha parte disser . Serenissimo e Potentissimo Principe Xâ Abbá Rej da Persia, Nosso[]senhor [?] alumie a V.Ser.<sup>de</sup> cȯ sua graça ecȯ ella haja em sua guarda. Sua [?]e Real estado," HAG, Archive Number 12, Livros das Monções do Reino, 9, 10, and 11, 127v.

130. Gil Fernández, *Imperio luso-español*, 2: 247, mentions "la embajada de Luis Pereira de Lacerda en 1602"; pp. 288–295 cover the Lacerda embassy; delays and transit times meant that the embassy actually arrived in Persia in 1604 (289). For a discussion of the specific diplomatic maneuvers that appear to pertain most closely to this letter and that would imply a date closer to 1605–1606, see 291–292.

131. Gil Fernández, *Imperio luso-español*, 1: 291.

132. The Tsar's titles (2r): "Perla Idio gratia Borisso Fedroṿizo: Grande Imperatore, et Gran Dȗca di tutta la Rȗssia: signore et Herede di Valadi-

miria, di Moscov̇ia di : Nov̇oguardia Imperatore di Cassania Imperator
Astracania, Imperator di Siberia Gran' Dùca di Plecov̇ia Gran' Duca di
Smolensco, di Sev̇eria, di Ugaria, di Peresslav̇ia, di viascho di Bùlgaria e
altro Imperatore, é Gran' Dùca di . Casteluovo, é del Paese più basso, di
Viatria di Rosclav̇ia di Polotia, di Rostov̇ia, di Jaroslav̇ia, di laco bi-
ancho, di liflandia, di Udorsia, di Obdorsia, di Codigna et delle altre
parti del Paese basso dell'Alba Rùssia, et di altri Gran Dùchi é principi
delle terre Grùsinense, et Cabardinense, di Circassia di Igoria, et di molti
altri gov̇vernj Gran' Dùca et Imperatore"; the title accorded Ferdinando
I: "Al Ser^{mo}: Gran' Dùca di Toscana et Dùca di firenza Fernando ,
Allissandrov̇[i]zzo di medices," ASF, Misc. Med. 102, ins. 9, 2r-3.

133. This is my general impression from going through the Livros das Monções do Reino. See, for instance, HAG, Archive Number 4, Livro das
Monções do Reino, 3A, 188, and following.

134. Matthee, *Politics of Trade*, 79.

135. Gil Fernández, *Imperio luso-español*. See, for instance, Graça Almeida
Borges, "El Consejo de Estado y la cuestión de Ormuz, 1600-1625:
Políticas transnacionales e impactos locales," *Revista de Historia Jerónimo
Zurita* no. 90 (2015): 21-54, http://hdl.handle.net/10174/21722.

136. Filippo Sassetti, *Lettere dall'India (1583-1588),* ed. Adele Dei (Rome:
Salerno, 1995), Letter 4, 46-47. See also ASF, MdP 4275, 178r-181v; Corai's complaints cover all of 178r. On 181v, Corai gives "142126304925,"
which the cipher secretary renders as "Aspan," but the cipher actually
gives "Aspaan." Neither corresponds to "Isfahan," but phonetically the
latter seems close enough to the Persian rendering, which Google translate gives as "اصفهان" "Esfahan." This is consistent with the MAP entry,
Michelagnolo Corai in Isfahan to Curzio di Lorenzo da Picchena in Florence on June 26, 1608, MAP Doc ID 21047, ASF, MdP 4275, 178. For this
letter from Corai in Iran, I have relied on the manuscript. As ever, the
MAP entries remain valuable points of reference.

137. ASF, MdP 4275, 178r.

138. ASF, MdP 4275, 178v.

139. ASF, MdP 4275, 178v.

140. ASF, MdP 4275, 178v-179r.

141. "hanno 71·[*questo*] anno pass:^{to} dua volta dannegg^e molto 121574 [*il Regno
di Cipri*] la p.^a volta sono sbarco a 181420302224212749 [*Famagosta*] fatto
molti 79· e 162917123219 [*schiavi e rovine*] la 2:^{da} volta alle 211415123334
[*Saline*] dove hanno butate a ter[manuscipt damaged; perhaps: "ra"]
181422·[[la *fortezza*] e con 1518 [*l'Emir*] che hanno 66·[*presso*] fatto molti
altri 79· [*schiavi*] e vanno predando per quel 48·[*mare*] felicem^{te}," ASF,
MdP 4275, 179r.

142. ASF, MdP 4275, 179r. The expression used is "più d'un milione e mezo
d'oro" which is followed by "e pe" before the damage to the MS cuts off

the line. The amount intended is probably 1,500,000 *scudi*, though it was likely meant as a valuation of the goods, not a literal count of gold coins.

143. "30·1014253312201533·[*grandissimi danni al Turco*]," ASF, MdP 4275, 179r.

144. "242920:333420 [*commune nimico* [com:nem]]," ASF, MdP 4275, 179r.

145. "121573· [*il Re*] m'ascolto con somma attentione," ASF, MdP 4275, 179r.

146. "da una villa all'altra," ASF, MdP 4275, 179r.

147. ASF, MdP 4275, 179v.

148. ASF, MdP 4275, 180r. "4014162023151227302532212449151351 [*Carmel-itano* [Carmelitani] *scalzi* mandati dal 62· [*Papa*]."

149. "Che in circa 10 anni pass:$^{ti}$ sono che il d,° 102925165314$^{to}$ [*Don Ruberto*] sen è stato [manuscript damaged] 63 [*Persia*] per 2921271422411253 [*os-taggio*] del suo fr[at]e'llo, Un servit$^{re}$ di 102925143327.° [*Don Antonio* [Don Ant]] hà fatto stampare in 42·[*Italia*] un certo Trattato [the end of this line is damaged, but appears to be "101263·" which means "Di Persia"] cioe della 35·di 72 [*guerra di qua*] sotto il nome di 1029202325122453212 7292639343351 [*Domenico Stoppeni*] nello quale si dice di gran cose da lui com'eg [manuscript damaged; perhaps "li"] ha stato 2234252316144352 [*Generale*] del 73101263·[*Re di Persia*] come per mero suo il 73 [*Re*] habbia acquistato tante 97· [*vittorie*] e faccese gran 1220263·42?[*im* [manuscript damaged, but "imp Persia r"]] ilche fu fatto più al favore suo e del suo fr[at]e'llo, che conforme alla verità. Perche se ben egli s'è trovato alle volte fra 1519· [*l'eserciti*] del[?] che per obligo suo lo seguitava come Cor-tiggiano non per 71· [*questo*] hà havuto mai uffiziali nè di 2223253416141534 [*Generale*], né di altro," ASF, MdP 4275, 180r.

150. ASF, MdP 4275, 180r–v.

151. "li Padri". "Prin'pi Chr'ni per domandare 172512293323 e 44· [*unione e lega*] frà loro e inanimarle di nuovo contra 121533· [*il Turco*]," ASF, MdP 4275, 180v.

152. ASF, MdP 4275, 180v.

153. ASF, MdP 4275, 180v–181r.

154. ASF, MdP 4275, 181v.

155. Michelagnolo Corai in Isfahan to Curzio di Lorenzo da Picchena in Flor-ence on August 10, 1609, MAP Doc ID 21064, ASF, MdP 4275, 245. The claim about the number of copies comes from the synopsis. In addition to the one cited for this entry, according to the synopsis, they are ASF, MdP 4275, 230–235, 237–242, and 252–257.

156. Michelagnolo Corai in Isfahan to Belisario di Francesco Vinta on Oc-tober 29, 1611, MAP Doc ID 21071, ASF MdP 4275, 291.

157. Michelagnolo Corai in Isfahan to an unknown recipient in Florence on July 9, 1612, MAP Doc ID 21074, ASF MdP 4275, 301. Georg Krieger to Cosimo II de' Medici in Florence, perhaps in 1612 (MAP concludes it must be before July 1612), MAP Doc ID 21073, ASF MdP 4275, 298.

158. Faridany "Signal Defeat."
159. Faridany, "Signal Defeat," 128.
160. Faridany, "Signal Defeat," 128.
161. Faridany, "Signal Defeat," 128–129 and 131.

# ACKNOWLEDGMENTS

This book began in January 2007 in Stanford's Special Collections when I encountered MSS M462, *Cose Diverse del Toscana*. This miscellaneous collection of manuscripts pertaining to Tuscany contains a copy of one of Filippo Sassetti's letters from India. Who was this Filippo Sassetti? This specific question proved straightforward to answer, for I quickly found Adele Dei's edition of Sassetti's letters from India, yet Sassetti's correspondence with the Medici raised proliferating new questions about the Grand Duchy of Tuscany's relationship with the wider world. In one form or another these questions have been with me for the last dozen years, which saw my transformation from a co-terminal MA student at Stanford into an Assistant Professor at Syracuse University. I have, therefore, accumulated a formidable list of debts along the way. It is a pleasure take this opportunity to offer some thanks here.

The Stanford dissertation, out of which this book has grown, received extensive support. The archival foundation of this project was laid in Florence on a Fulbright Italy Fellowship (2010–2011). At Stanford, a Graduate Fellowship (2007–2012) and a Weter Dissertation Completion Grant (2012–2013) not only financed time on campus but also provided support for research trips to Italy, England, Spain, and India. A Mellon Foundation Dissertation Fellowship (2013–2014) supported the dissertation's completion. Thanks to Paula Findlen for arranging for me to teach classes in Stanford's Department of History from 2014 to 2016. Thanks to the committee that awarded the dissertation the Ezio Cappadocia Prize for Best Unpublished Manuscript of the Society for Italian Historical Studies (2016).

In summer 2016, a Sixteenth Century Society Fellowship at the James Ford Bell Library at the University of Minnesota introduced me to the jewel of a collection held by the Bell Library; particular thanks are due to Marguerite Ragnow for her advice and support. From Minnesota,

I went to Indiana to take up a Mendel Fellowship at the Lilly Library of Indiana University, whose manuscripts gave insight into the imperial Spanish reaction to the Japanese ambassadors in 1614–1615. The summer ended with my taking up a three-year Visiting Assistant Professor | Postdoctoral Fellow position at Boston College responsible for teaching the history of globalization. In 2017, an Ahmanson Research Fellowship for the Study of Medieval and Renaissance Books and Manuscripts at UCLA enabled a remarkably pleasant two months commuting between a tiny bungalow in Santa Monica and UCLA's Special Collections, where I immersed myself in the large fraction of the Orsini family's paper held there. Thanks are particularly due to the Department of History at Syracuse University, which has proved unfailingly supportive during the final research for and writing of this manuscript. Happily, I have had the opportunity to complete the edits for this book in Florence thanks to a yearlong fellowship from Villa I Tatti: The Harvard University Center for Italian Renaissance Studies.

At Stanford, Paula Findlen is a model of generosity, kindness, and excellence. She has been there for me since before the beginning of this project, when I wandered in one day as a curious sophomore excited to go to Florence. From an undergraduate thesis on the walls of Ferrara through the discovery of the Sassetti document in her seminar, through my long and winding path to develop the dissertation, she has been the patient, wise, and seemingly infinitely knowledgeable guide. She knew when to encourage me to head to India, and when it was time for me to come back from Madrid and write. In the years since graduation, she has not only continued to provide invaluable advice and support but has also continued to actively include me in the remarkable community of current and former students she has built.

Particular thanks are due to my dissertation committee—Paula Findlen, Jessica Riskin, and David Como—whose comments on the dissertation guided further research and the shape of this book. Their questions and those of Brad Bouley led me to make the radical break with the dissertation and rewrite with a new structure from the ground up. Thanks go to Laura Stokes, who has been that most helpful combination of friend and perceptive critic. Thanks also go to the cheerful and knowledgeable John Mustain at Stanford's Special Collections. For help with Russian and Ottoman history, thanks to Nancy and Jack

Kollmann and Ali Yaycioglu. For the advice and support at the very beginning, thanks to Keith Baker, Philippe Buc, Kathryn Miller, Priya Satia, and Londa Schiebinger. I have benefitted greatly from conversations with Marcelo Aranda, Hannah Marcus, Rachel Midura, Noah Millstone, Jeff Miner, Suzanne Sutherland, Corey Tazzara, and Duygu Yildirim. Alex Statman combined good fellowship with wide knowledge, ready insight, and searching questions.

In Italy, thanks go to the staffs of the Archivio di Stato di Venezia, the Biblioteca Angelica, and, above all, the Archivio di Stato di Firenze. In the course of my research, Florence has become a second home thanks to Fosca d'Acierno and Ermelinda Campani at the Stanford Center in Florence, Charles Ellis, Erin Ciulla at Il Torchio, and Alessio at Caffè Amerini. Thanks also to Brett Auerbach-Lynn, Beth Coggeshall, Michael Martoccio, and Giovanni and Gemma Spinicchia. Friendship has sustained this book in good times and especially in difficult ones. Thanks to friends outside academia for their companionship and long conversations about the early modern world and the Grand Duchy of Tuscany.

In doing research in Goa, I was fortunate to enjoy the help and support of Warren DeSouza and Lucindo Faria, who organized my stay with Deric Rebelo at his Vivenda Rebelo. Deric was a marvelous host, solving problems great and small and generously introducing me to his extended family network and the world to which it gives exceptional access. Thanks also go to the staff of the Historical Archives of Goa. Meeting Graça Almeida Borges and Stephanie Hassell in the archives, I had the pleasure of long conversations and mutual advice, support, and introductions in Goa's scholarly community.

This study advances research developed in four essays of mine. I am grateful to the editors of the following volumes for their assurances concerning the presentation of those discussions here. These include: "Renaissance Florentines in the Tropics: Brazil, the Grand Duchy of Tuscany, and the Limits of Empire," in *The New World in Early Modern Italy, 1492–1750*, ed. Elizabeth Horodowich and Lia Markey (Cambridge: Cambridge University Press, 2017), 206–222; "A Florentine Humanist in India: Filippo Sassetti, Medici Agent by Annual Letter," in *The Renaissance of Letters: Knowledge and Community in Italy, 1300–1600*, ed. Paula Findlen and Suzanne Sutherland (New York: Routledge, 2019), 208–226;

"The Advantages of Stability: Medici Tuscany's Ambitions in the Eastern Mediterranean," in *Florence in the Early Modern World: New Perspectives*, ed. Nicholas Scott Baker and Brian Jeffrey Maxson (New York: Routledge, 2019), 142–155; and "Making a New Prince: Tuscany, the Pasha of Aleppo, and the Dream of a New Levant," in *Art, Mobility, and Exchange in Early Modern Tuscany and Eurasia*, ed. Francesco Freddolini and Marco Musillo (New York: Routledge, 2020), 19–32.

Earlier versions of parts of this book were presented at the Renaissance Society of America Conferences in San Diego (2013), New York (2014), and Boston (2016); the Stanford Center in Florence (2011); Scientiae held at the University of Warwick, UK (2013); Stanford University's Center for Medieval and Early Modern Studies workshop (CMEMS, 2016); the Renaissance of Letters conference at the Stanford Humanities Center (2016); the Center for Early Modern Studies at the Pennsylvania State University (2017); the American Academy in Rome (2018); and the University of Verona (2019). This book has benefitted greatly from questions from members of the audience, fellow panelists, and respondents both in formal session and especially in conversations afterwards. Particular thanks are due to Cécile Fromont who, as respondent to the American Academy paper, proposed the phrase "shadow capital."

Arriving in Boston at the end of summer 2016, I met Sarah Ross, who not only welcomed me to Boston College's impressive History Department but also gave invaluable advice. Sarah's support has been too extensive to relate in detail but is well encompassed by her opening mantra repeated throughout the year: "Book, book, book." In the History Department, I would like to thank in particular Kevin Kenny, Zack Matus, Prasannan Parthasarathi, and Virginia Reinburg.

At Syracuse University, Albrecht Diem, Samantha Herrick, Chris Kyle, and Junko Takeda in the Department of History; Sally Cornelison in the Department of Art and Music Histories; Sebastian Modrow and William La Moy in the Special Collections Research Center; and Matteo Duni, Sean Nelson, Jonathan Nelson, and Molly Bourne at SU Florence have welcomed me to a vibrant medieval and early modern community. I have also benefitted from conversations with Amy Kallander, Radha Kumar, Betsy Lasch-Quinn, Tessa Murphy, and Martin Shanguhyia. At Syracuse, this book has benefitted from comments on papers given to the Medieval and Renaissance Studies faculty (2017); at the Joy of Close

Reading in Classical, Medieval, and Renaissance Studies conference (2018); and to the Program for the Advancement of Research on Conflict and Collaboration (PARCC, 2017). Particular thanks are due to Timur Hammond for his invaluable advice, especially on Ottoman bibliography. Norman Kutcher and Susan Branson have been remarkably supportive chairs who have actively aided this project, not least by securing funding that facilitated research at the Biblioteca Angelica in Rome. Conventional as it is to say, it remains absolutely true that I have learned a great deal from my students, their papers and research projects, and especially their questions. This is especially true of graduate students, who have not only introduced me to new approaches and historiography, especially from art history, but also productively questioned long-held assumptions. Thank you to the family and friends who have welcomed me to Syracuse. Thanks to Thomas Anderson for the index and to Kathleen Czerwiak for help with the page proofs.

The editorial review process for this book coincided with the year I spent as a research fellow at Villa I Tatti (2019–2020), an extraordinary opportunity for which I am deeply grateful. Alina Payne and Thomas Gruber provided invaluable support in bringing the project to fruition. Thanks also are due for stimulating conversations with many Tattiani, including Giulia Accornero, Reuven Amitai, Alessandro Benassi, Stefano de Bosio, James Coleman, Mary Doyno, Angela Dressen, Patricia Falguières, Peter Fane-Saunders, Francesca Fantappiè, Ludovica Galeazzo, Christine Göttler, Ingrid Greenfield, Byron Hamann, Nicholas Herman, Cecilie Hollberg, Etienne Jollet, David Kim, Marco Lamanna, César Manrique, Stephen McCormick, Pauline Lafille, Ivan Lupić, Lavinia Maddaluno, Scott Nethersole, Fabio Pagani, Maryam Patton, John-Mark Philo, Katalin Prajda, Michael Rocke, Carlo Taviani, Sezen Unluonen, Joseph Vignone, and Juliane von Fircks. Likewise, thanks to Richard Goldthwaite for productively challenging engagement with my research. Thanks also to Giorgio Tosco for our long-running conversation about our shared research interests, and to Carlo Taviani for insights into archives and academic structures. Thanks are due especially to Francesca Fantappiè and Sergio Tognetti for welcoming me so warmly and for our memorable hike on the last weekend before lockdown. Becoming friends while working together with Giorgio Riello on the Carletti project was a highlight of the year. Spring 2020 was a difficult time for Italy and special thanks are due to the I Tatti community, from the staff to the fellows confined in and around Ponte a Mensola, who formed such a bastion of solidarity. Particular thanks are due to my companions in lockdown in San Martino—Byron Hamman, David Kim, and Nelda Cantarella— who showed friendship of the very best sort in the face of the pandemic. Thanks also to Chloé at Melaleuca for bringing the delicious treats for our quarantine meals.

Over the course of this project's long evolution, my family has been unfailingly supportive, both when it was fun and easy and when things were difficult and uncertain. My brother, Kevin Brege, and I have explored the world together on six continents, where he has shown unfailing interest in and patience with many conversations about Tuscans and global history. My parents, Laura and Bruce Brege, have truly made this book possible, supporting it in every way. Their love of travel and deep knowledge of global business have been tremendously valuable in thinking about the globe-trotting politically connected Tuscan merchants and adventurers who populate these pages. Whether in Delhi or London, Buenos Aires or Zanzibar, Tokyo or Florence, my mother has been ever ready to work through the problem of the moment, notebook and pencil in hand, laying out decision trees and essential points.

Mackenzie Cooley and I met in my final stages of writing the dissertation and we immediately grew to love long intense conversations and working on projects together. Her critical judgment, deep knowledge, endless curiosity, clear advice, and sharp awareness of my blind spots made her a phenomenal editor and demanding interlocutor willing to challenge all assumptions. Over the past six years, she and I have engaged productively, both intensely and immensely, with each other's research and writing; the remaining weaknesses are all my own. This we have done while spanning continents and falling in love during the process. As to the rest, she knows well from our endless conversations that no thanks can begin to capture what she means to me.

# INDEX